Wardley Mapping
The Knowledge

Part One
Typographical Intelligence in Business

GCATI

This work by GCATI is a derivative of
Wardley maps, topographical intelligence in business
and is licensed by GCATI under
Creative Commons Attribution-ShareAlike-4.0-International licence.

ISBN: 978-1-913805-18-0

Table of Contents

Preface — 10
   Licence — 10

Chapter 1 – On being lost — 11
   Serendipity — 13
   The importance of maps in military history — 19
   A game of chess — 22
   Categorising situational awareness — 25
   Climate, Doctrine and Leadership — 27
   The Strategy Cycle — 29

Chapter 2 – Finding a path — 31
   The first map — 34
   Step 1 – Needs — 40
   Step 2 – Value Chain — 41
   Step 3 – Map — 46
   The next step — 52

Chapter 3 – Exploring the map — 53
   Learning climatic patterns — 54
      Climatic pattern: Everything evolves — 54
      Climatic pattern: Characteristics change — 55
      Climatic pattern: No one size fits all — 58
      Climatic pattern: Efficiency enables innovation — 60
      Climatic pattern: Higher order systems create new sources of worth — 62
      Climatic pattern: No choice on evolution — 65
      Climatic pattern: Past success breeds inertia — 66
   Categorising climatic patterns — 67
   Using climatic patterns — 69
   An exercise for the reader — 71

Chapter 4 – Doctrine — 72
   Learning doctrine — 73
      Doctrine: Focus on user need — 74
      Doctrine: Use a common language — 76

Doctrine: Be transparent	76
Doctrine: Challenge assumptions	77
Doctrine: Remove duplication and bias	77
Doctrine: Use appropriate methods	83
Doctrine: Think small	90
Doctrine: Think aptitude and attitude	91
Doctrine: Design for constant evolution	94
Categorising Doctrine	97
Using doctrine with our first map	100
An exercise for the reader	101
Chapter 5 – The play and a decision to act	**102**
Identifying opportunity	103
The dangers of past success	105
The near, the far and the crazy	111
Learning context specific gameplay	114
Context specific play: Accelerators, decelerators and constraints	114
Context specific play: Innovate, Leverage and Commoditise	116
Using context specific gameplay: the play	119
Impacts on purpose	123
What happened next?	123
What went wrong?	125
Categorising Gameplay	127
An exercise for the reader	129
Chapter 6 – Getting started	**130**
Tips for mapping	133
How to implement mapping	135
Continuous learning	139
The anti-pattern organisation	140
Books to read	145
An exercise for the reader	146
Chapter 7 – Finding a new purpose	**147**
The new purpose	150
The Hypothetical Gun company	155
The trouble with maps	158
That first question	162
Uncertainty is the key	164
Comments on and the limits of evolution	174
Before we move on	177
Purpose, Scope and Imperative	177

    Landscape   178
    Climate: Evolution   178

Chapter 8 – Keeping the wolves at bay   180
    The dangers of making it simple   180
    The simple trap   181
    Finding my mojo   182
        Worth based development   183
        Pricing granularity   185
    Flow   186
    Efficiency vs effectiveness   191
    Before we move on   197
        Landscape   197
        Doctrine   200
    An exercise for the reader   200

Chapter 9 – Charting the future   201
    Not all parts of the map are equally predictable   202
        Cheating the system   203
        Conditions, signals and climatic patterns   204
    Climatic Pattern: Coevolution   207
        Complicating the picture a bit more – the rise of Serverless   212
    Climatic pattern: Peace, War and Wonder   217
    Before we move on   223
        Predictability and Climatic Patterns   223
        Re-examining the past   225
        Categorising Predictability   227
        A few takeaways   228
        Climatic patterns   229
    An exercise for the reader   231

Chapter 10 – I wasn't expecting that   232
    An unexpected discovery   236
        Climatic Pattern: Punctuated Equilibrium   238
    Finding the future organisation   243
        Development   249
        Operations   249
        Structure   249
        Learning   249
        Leading   250
    Notes on Peace, War and Wonder   253
        Climatic Pattern: Evolution of a communication mechanism   253

Climatic Pattern: Inertia increases with past success	255
Climatic Pattern: Inertia kills	261
The different forms of disruption	262
Dealing with disruption	265
Some final thoughts	267
An exercise for the reader	271

Chapter 11 – A smorgasbord of the slightly useful 272

Opportunity of change	272
Alternatives in Cloud Computing	273
The Kodak moment of cloud	275
The trouble with contracts	279
FIRE	282
It's all too difficult	285
Disposing of liability	288
Sweat and dump	289
Pig in a poke	289
It'll save me money and other lies we tell ourselves	290
Efficiency will reduce our budgets	290
Cloud will be green	292
We can deal with it later	293
Execution matters more than strategy	295
How common is corporate blindness	301
We're not blind, we have principles!	303
Focus on core!	306
Mastering strategy as simply as I can	309
Step 1 – the cycle	309
Step 2 – Learn the landscape	310
Step 3 – Learn and use climatic patterns	311
Climatic patterns	311
Step 4 – Learn and use doctrine	318
Wardley's Doctrine	318
Step 5 – Learn and use gameplay	326
Gameplay	326
A few things to remember	328
On biology	328
On maps	330

Chapter 12 – The scenario 331

The Company	331
What is Phoenix?	331
Operation of Phoenix	332

Marketing & Business Development	332
Sales	334
Digital and Product Development	335
Cloud Service	335
Technology Changes	336
Strategy	338
Finance	339
Task	340
A note to the reader	341

Chapter 13 – Something wicked this way comes — 343

A map of the scenario	343
Examining doctrine	356
Amber warning	359
Red Alert!	360
By the pricking of my thumbs	361
The Task	361
A note to the reader	362

Chapter 14 – To thine own self be true — 364

My play	365
The grey play – Pig in a Poke	370
The orange play – the Future	371
Feeling guilty and the executives	372

Chapter 15 – One the practice of scenario planning — 374

The "generalised" scenario	375
Play it again	380
The Hedge Fund Manager	383
The grand mistake	385
Phew, that was close	387
Will the maps help me?	398
Common failures of sensible executives	389
The "LFP" Scenario	392
Who are you?	392
The service	392
Sales and Marketing	392
Project Management	393
Finance & Legal	393
Engineering	395
The board	396
Your choice	396

Chapter 16 – Super Looper — 398
- To begin — 398
  - Getting messy with numbers — 407
  - Getting probability probably sort of right — 409
- Managing inertia — 410
- Where are we? — 415
  - Getting primitive — 416
  - Looping around and common problems — 421
- Opportunities multiply as they are seized — 423
  - Something to remember — 427

Chapter 17 – To infinity and beyond — 428
- The Three Horizons — 429
- The issue of legacy — 435
- On Porter — 439
- Examining Canonical — 441
- On the question of timing — 445

Chapter 18 – Better for Less — 455
- All change please — 455
  - A little too much of what you wanted — 460
  - An Opportunity — 461
  - Assumptions and bias — 464
    - Confirmation bias — 464
    - Loss aversion bias — 465
    - Outcome bias — 465
    - Hindsight bias — 465
    - Cascade bias — 465
    - Instrumentation bias — 465
    - Disposition bias — 465
    - Dunning-Kruger effect — 466
    - Courtesy bias — 466
- Applying doctrine — 466
  - On the question of failure — 470
  - Doctrine: Be Humble — 470
- You need to apply thought — 472
  - A question of healthcare — 472
  - A question of planning – OODA and the PDCA — 476
  - A question of privilege — 477
- An exercise for the reader — 481

Chapter 19 – On playing chess — **482**
    Stepping stones — 482
Policy or technology? — 487
Scenario – first pass — 487
Scenario – second pass — 489
Scenario – my answer — 491
The nature of capital and purchasing it — 493
Finding a balance — 497

Preface

Thank you for purchasing this book. As a non-profit, all proceeds from this book will go into developing new training courses and certifications.

This book will form part of the body of knowledge for Wardley Mapping and all of our training and certifications will refer to this series of books.

This book is sourced from Simon's medium.com posts on Wardley Maps and the excellent work from Andrew Harmel-Law.

Please take a look at our latest strategy and technology training courses including Wardley Mapping at gcati.org. This book is included in the Wardley Mapping subscription.

This body of knowledge and other material is available to all trainers and training providers listed on our Wardley Mapping marketplace.

Chapter 1 - On being lost

This is the story of my journey, from a bumbling and confused CEO, lost in the headlights of change, to having a vague idea of what I was doing. I say vague because I'm not going to make grand claims to the techniques that I discuss in this book. It is enough to say that I have found them useful over the last decade, whether in finding opportunity, removing waste, helping to organise a team of people or determining the strategy for a company. Will they help you? That depends upon the context that you're operating in, but since the techniques don't take long to learn then I'll leave it up to the reader to discover whether they are helpful to them or not. Remember, all models are wrong but some are useful.

In the first part of this book, I'm going to talk about my journey in order to introduce the techniques. In later chapters, we will switch gear and dive into a more formal examination of the practice. One thing I am mindful of is we rarely learn from past experience, especially when it belongs to others or when it conflicts with our perception of how things are. However, if you are like I once was, lost at sea, then this might just help you find your path. For me, this journey began two decades ago in the lift of the Hotel Arts in Barcelona. It started when a senior executive handed me a short document and asked, "Does this strategy make sense?"

To be honest, I hadn't a clue whether it did or not. I had no idea what a real strategy was, let alone any concept of how to evaluate the document. I leafed through the pages; it all seemed to make sense, the diagrams looked good, and I didn't know what I was looking for anyway. So I responded, "Seems fine to me." However, the reason why I had chosen those words was more to do with the strategy looking familiar than anything else. I had seen the same words used in other documents, some of the same diagrams in other presentations, and I had been to a conference where an industry thought leader had told me about the stuff that mattered. That stuff — "innovation", "efficiency", "alignment" and "culture" — had all been highlighted in the strategy document.

It was the comfort of familiar words and images that had given me the confidence to proclaim it was fine. My internal logic was a sort of herd mentality, a "backward causality" that since it had been right there then it must be right here. I was also young and had convinced myself that the senior executive was bound to know the answer and they were only asking me to test my abilities. I didn't want to show my inexperience. This moment however continued to irritate me over the years because I knew I had been false and I was just covering up my tracks, hiding from my own inability.

A decade later, I had risen through the ranks to become the CEO of another company. I was the most senior of executives. The company would live or die by the strategic choices I made, or so I thought. I wrote the strategy, or at least variations were presented to me and I would decide. But something had gone terribly wrong in my journey. Somehow, along the path to becoming a CEO, I had missed those all-important lessons that told me how to evaluate a strategy. I still had no means to understand what a good strategy was and it was no longer enough for me to think it "seems fine". I needed more than that as I was the experienced executive that the less experienced took guidance from.

I asked one of my juniors what they thought of our strategy. They responded, "Seems fine to me." My heart sank. Unlike that confident executive in the lift of the Hotel Arts who was testing some junior, I still hadn't a clue. I was an imposter CEO! I needed to learn fast before anyone found out. But how?

In 2004, I sat down in my boardroom with our strategy documents and started to dissect them. There were lots of familiar and comfortable terms. We had to be innovative, efficient, customer centric, web 2.0 and all that this entailed. Alas, I suspected these common "memes" were repeated in the strategy documents of other companies because I was pretty sure I had copied them. I had heard the thought leaders at various conferences and read analyst reports that proclaimed these same lines over and over as the new truth. Well, at least we were following the herd, I thought. However, someone must have started these memes and how did they know if these memes were right? How did I become like that confident executive that I remembered?

Frustrated with my own natural inability, I started to trawl through books on strategy. I was looking for some way of understanding, a framework or a reference point to compare against. More brutally, I was lost at sea and looking for something to grab hold of an executive lifeboat. I found little that gave me comfort and after talking with my peers, I became convinced that our strategy was almost identical to competitors in our industry. I was beginning to feel as though the entire field of strategy was either a cosmic joke played by management consultants or that there was some secret tome everyone was hiding from me. I was getting a bit desperate, despondent even. Someone would rumble that I was faking it.

I started using 2x2s, SWOTS, Porter's forces and all manner of instruments. Everything felt lacking, nothing satisfied. I knew the company to the outside world was doing well but internally, we had communication issues and frustration over direction and organisation. To improve matters, I had arranged for one of those management courses that bring the entire team together. I had been seduced by a simple idea that with better communication, then a strategy would become clear, as if by magic. We just needed to talk more.

I rapidly discovered that despite all of our talking, daily status meetings and our weekly Town Hall that beyond the very senior management, no-one really understood our strategy. I also doubted whether the senior management did. I certainly was unsure of it. I turned inward; the problem was me! There would come a reckoning when everyone would realise that behind the success, the profits, the bold pronouncements and confident exterior lurked a mass of doubt. They would rumble that I was making it up. I shouldn't be the CEO. At that point in time, in mid 2004, I was drowning in uncertainty and an easy mark for any would-be consultant peddling snake oil. I would have gladly bought it. An entire crate of the stuff.

Serendipity

By chance, I had picked up a copy of "The Art of War" by Sun Tzu. Truth be told, I picked up several different translations as the bookseller had advised that none of them were quite the same. That was serendipity and I owe that bookseller a debt of thanks because it was whilst reading through my second translation that I noticed something that I had been missing in my understanding of strategy. Sun Tzu had described five factors that matter in competition between two opponents. Loosely speaking, these are: purpose, landscape, climate, doctrine and leadership. I've drawn them as a circle in Figure 1.

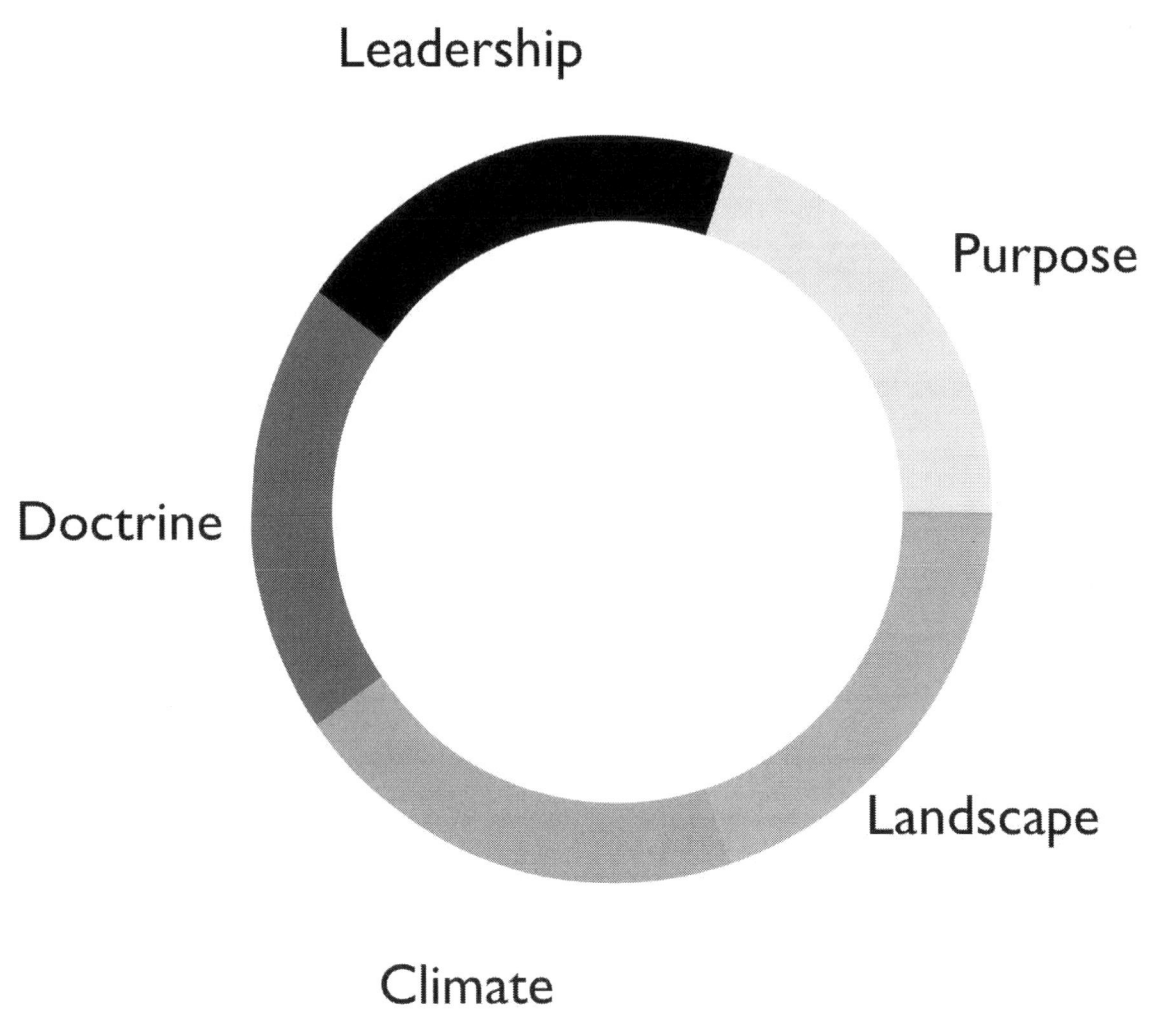

Figure 1: The five factors

When I looked at my strategy document, I could see a purpose and then a huge jump into leadership and the strategic choices we had made. But where was landscape, climate and doctrine? I started to think back to every business book that I had read. Everything seemed to do this jump from purpose to leadership.

For reference, Sun Tzu's five factors are:-

Purpose is your moral imperative; it is the scope of what you are doing and why you are doing it. It is the reason why others follow you.

Landscape is a description of the environment that you're competing in. It includes the position of troops, the features of the landscape and any obstacles in your way.

Climate describes the forces that act upon the environment. It is the patterns of the seasons and the rules of the game. These impact the landscape and you don't get to choose them but you can discover them. It includes your competitors' actions.

Doctrine is the training of your forces, the standard ways of operating and the techniques that you almost always apply. These are the universal principles, the set of beliefs that appear to work, regardless of the landscape that is faced.

Leadership is about the strategy that you choose, considering your purpose, the landscape, the climate and your capabilities. It is to "the battle at hand". It is context specific, i.e. these techniques are known to depend upon the landscape and your purpose.

I started to consider strategy in terms of these five factors. I understood our purpose, or at least I thought I did, but what about landscape? Normally, in military conflicts or even in games like chess, we have some means of visualising the landscape through a map, whether it's the more geographical kind that we are familiar with or an image of the board. These maps are not only visual but context specific, i.e. to the game or battle at hand. A map allows me to see the position of pieces and where they can move to.

This last point struck a chord with me. When playing a game of chess, there were usually multiple moves that I could make and I would determine and adjust my strategy from this. A mistake by the opponent could allow me to switch from a defensive to an attacking play or to consolidate control over part of the board. I would determine one course of action over another because of experience, of context and my understanding of the opponent. Why did this strike me? Well, it's all to do with the question of "Why?"
There are not one but two questions of why in chess. I have the why of purpose, such as the desire to win the game, but I also have the why of movement, as in "why this move over that?"

Strategy in chess is all about the why of movement, i.e. why you should move here over there. This was different from all the business strategy books that I had read. They tend to focus on the goal or the why of purpose as the all-important factor in business. But the purpose of winning the game was not the same as the strategic choices I made during the game. I started to think more on this topic. Though I was quite a reasonable chess player, this had come from experience and obviously I had started as a novice a long time beforehand. In those youthful days, I spent a lot of time losing, especially to my father. But how did I learn? How did I get better at the game? I would see the board, I would move a piece and I would learn that sometimes, a particular move was more beneficial than another. I would refine my craft based upon my gameplay on the board.

It was through understanding the landscape, the rules of the game and context specific play that I had started to master chess. But this was not what I was doing in business. I had no way to visualise the environment, no means to determine why here over there, and no obvious mechanism of learning from one game to another. I've added these two types of "why" into Figure 2, building upon Sun Tzu's five factors.

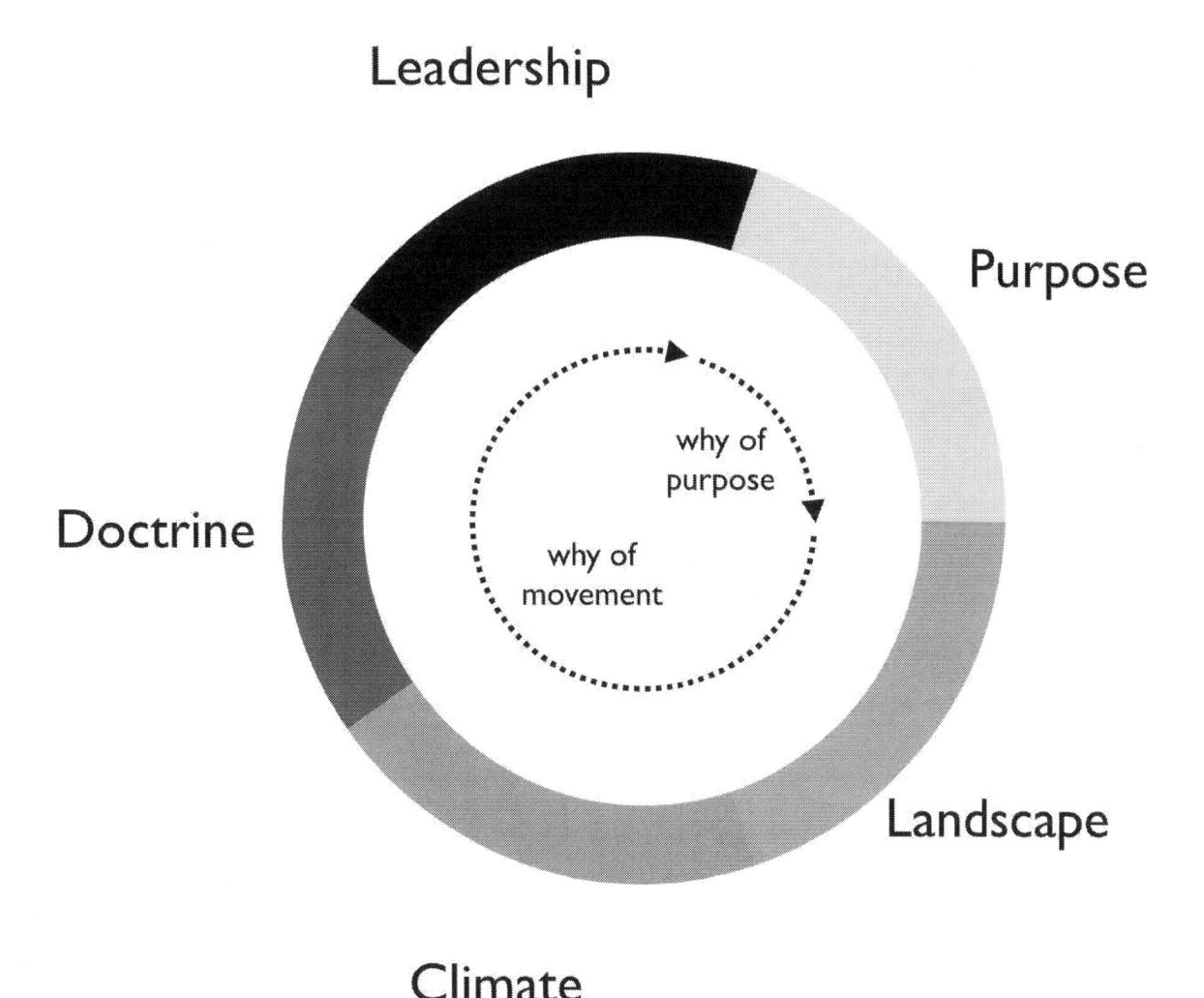

Figure 2: The two types of why

My company had a "why of purpose", which was to be the best "creative solutions group in the world". It sucked. It was actually a botch job because we had multiple lines of business that didn't quite fit together. We were an online photo service, a consultancy, a European CRM, an identity web service, a fulfilment engine, and an assortment of special projects around 3D printing and the use of mobiles phones as cameras. I had no real way of determining which we should focus on and hence, the purpose was a compromise of doing everything.

When I had taken over the company a few years earlier, we were losing money hand over fist. We had to borrow significant sums to stay afloat because we were on our way out. In reality, our purpose had been simply "to survive". In the next few years, we had turned this around; we had become highly profitable, we had paid back the loans and had a million or so in the bank and we were growing. But we had done so not through any deliberate focus on the landscape but instead by just grabbing opportunities and cost cutting where we could. The team was already exhausted.

We weren't heading in a particular direction; we were just opportunists. Deng Xiaoping once said that managing the economy was like "Crossing the river by feeling the stones". Well, we were feeling the stones and being adaptive but beyond simple metrics such as being more profitable than the last quarter, we had no real direction. We lacked this whole "why of movement" that I had seen in chess.

But I kept on coming back to whether it really mattered. I felt instinctively as though I needed to pick one or two areas for the company to focus on, but since we were doing well in all and in the past, we had failed with just one focus then I was unsure whether it made sense. So, how do I choose? Should I choose? Why here over there? I was still lost.

I started to think about how we had made past decisions. In our board meetings, the way we decided upon action was to look at different proposals, the financial state of the company, and decide whether a set of actions fitted in with our purpose, one that admittedly was a compromise of past decisions. The chess equivalent of "my purpose is we're here" and "will this move bring immediate benefits?" Unlike the game, we had no chessboard for business, nor any long-term play. The more I examined this, the more I realised that our choice was often based upon gut feel and opinion, though we had created arcane language to justify our haphazard actions — this project was "core" and another lacked a reasonable ROI (return on investment). This didn't feel right and there was no pattern of learning that I could distinguish.

I became convinced that whilst we had a purpose of sorts, we had no real direction nor any mechanism of learning nor any means to determine the why of movement, which is at the heart of strategy. We were successful in that we stumbled from one opportunity to another but we could just as easily be walking further out to sea as much as crossing the river. I started to think that maybe it didn't matter, but I continued to pursue this line of enquiry. Since Sun Tzu had principally written about military combat, I started diving into military history in the hope of finding other lessons. I became obsessively fascinated by the extensive use of maps in battle and for learning throughout history. Topographical intelligence became a hugely important and decisive factor in numerous battles of the American Civil War. I could think of no equivalent tool in business. I had no equivalent lessons to learn, such as flanking moves, pinning a piece or standard plays such as fool's mate. All I had were endless books giving secrets of other people's success and extolling the virtues of copying great companies such as Fannie Mae, Nokia and Blockbuster. I questioned how did anyone know if any of this was right?

I met up with a few of my peers from other companies and floated this idea of topographical intelligence and the use of mapping in business. How did they learn from one battle to another? To say I was disheartened by the response would be an underestimation. Beyond the blank stares, I was royally lectured on the importance of culture, of purpose, of technology, of building the right team and of execution. However, I had built a great team from around the world. We were agile, we used and wrote open source technology, we had the modern equivalent of a private cloud, we were API driven and had developed advanced techniques for continuous deployment of technology. This was 2004.

In the technology desert that was Old Street in London, we dominated the computing language of Perl. We had remarkable rates of execution, outstanding technology, an exceptional team and a strong development culture. This stuff was fine. The problem was the CEO, i.e. me. I sucked at strategy or at best, I was making it up and we weren't learning. I reasoned that none of my peers were going to tell me how they did this, it probably wasn't in their interests to do so. But I believed that this was somehow important and so I kept on digging.

The importance of maps in military history

It was about this time that I read the story of Ball's Bluff. It is not commonly cited as one of the major engagements of the American Civil War but not only was it one of the largest in 1861, it involved the utter rout of Union forces. Most saliently, Ball's Bluff is an abject lesson in the importance of maps and situational awareness. Through misinformation and miscalculation, 1,700 Union troops were caught in disadvantageous terrain and in effect slaughtered (with an 8 to 1 kill ratio) by Confederates. A thousand men were lost because the Union Generals had no awareness of the landscape and marched soldiers blindly to their deaths on vague ideas of "because the Confederates are somewhere over there".
The more I read into history, the clearer it became that understanding and exploiting the landscape had been vital in battle. Probably the most famously cited example is the ancient battle of the pass of Thermopylae. In 480 BC, the Athenian general Themistocles faced a significant foe in Xerxes and the Persian

army. He had choices; he could defend around Thebes or Athens itself. However, Themistocles understood the environment and decided to block off the straits of Artemisium, forcing the Persian army along the coastal road into the narrow pass of Thermopylae, known as the "Hot Gates". In this terrain, 4,000 odd Greeks would be able to hold back a Persian army of 170,000 for many days, enabling time for the rest of the Greek city states to prepare. You've probably heard part of this story before in the tale of King Leonidas and the "three-hundred" Spartans.

In this singular example, the why of movement and purpose was crystal clear to me. Certainly, Themistocles had a purpose in saving the Greek states, but he also had choices of where to defend. He must have decided why to defend using the "Hot Gates" over defending around Athens. There was a why of movement as in why defend here over there, in much the same way in a game of chess that I will decide to move this chess piece over that. Themistocles had chosen a deliberate set of actions that exploited the terrain to his advantage. Situational awareness, use of terrain and maps appeared to be vital techniques in the outcome of any conflict.

But I wasn't doing any of this in our company strategy. I didn't have any form of maps or understanding of the landscape. I was instead using tools like SWOT diagrams. For those uninitiated in the arcane language of modern business "strategy", a SWOT diagram — strengths, weaknesses, opportunities and threats — is a tool to assess whether some course of action makes sense.

Now, imagine for a second that you were part of that Greek army on the eve of battle, preparing to face overwhelming odds. Imagine that Themistocles is standing before you rallying the troops. He is inspiring you with purpose, to defend the Greek states against a mighty foe. You're all highly trained, excellent soldiers and have outstanding technology for that time. But imagine that just before the blood of battle, you hear him declare that he has no understanding of the environment, no map and no strategy based upon the terrain. However, he shouts, "Have no fear for I have created a SWOT diagram!"

I'd flee in panic.

In Figure 3, I've placed side-by-side a map of the battle of Thermopylae and a SWOT diagram for the same battle.

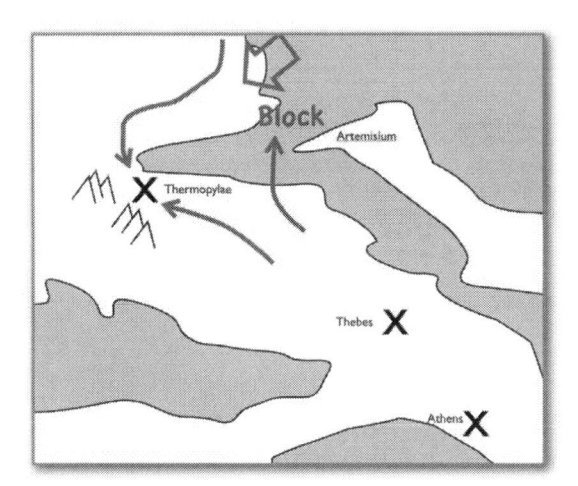

Figure 3: Themistocles SWOT

Now, ask yourself, what do you think would be more effective in combat — a strategy built upon an understanding of the landscape or a SWOT diagram? What do you think would be more useful in determining where to defend against the horde of Xerxes army? Which would help you communicate your plan? Would Themistocles ever be able to exploit the landscape from a SWOT? Which was I using in running my business — a map or a SWOT?

The wrong one.

We had five factors from purpose to landscape to climate to doctrine to leadership, and somehow, I had been jumping from purpose to leadership and missing three of them. Despite what I had read, there existed two very different forms of why that mattered — purpose and movement — and we weren't even considering movement. We had no maps of the environment, no visual means of describing the battle at hand and hence, no understanding of our context. Without maps, I didn't seem to have any effective mechanism of learning from one encounter to the next or even a mechanism of effective communication. The tools that I was using were woefully inadequate in all regards. Whilst situational awareness might be critical in combat, for some reason, it seemed absent in almost all business literature that I had read.

I knew we had been making decisions in a vacuum. I knew a lot was gut feel. I knew we had communication issues and finally, I knew our learning was haphazard at best. But did situational awareness really matter in business? We were doing well, and maybe just copying lessons from those greats would suffice? I'd also heard others talk about how execution was more important than strategy and execution was something we were good at. Maybe strategy just wasn't important? Maybe I was worrying about nothing? Our results were positive, we were growing and we were making a profit.

I started to imagine what it would be like if there was a landscape but somehow, I was unaware of it. I decided to use the analogy of chess to make this comparison, since the common perception of CEOs in business publications is one of grand masters playing a complex game. At least I had some experience of both of those things, though not necessarily at the same time.

A game of chess

I'm going to take you through the same thought experiment that I went through. Remember, back in 2004, I had nothing to support my idea that situational awareness and topographical intelligence might be important in business. I was out on a limb with nothing to back me up.

I want you to now imagine you live in a world where everyone plays chess and how well you play the game determines your success and your ranking in this world. However, in this world, no one has ever seen a chessboard. In fact, all you've ever seen are the following characters on a screen and you play the game by simply pressing a character, your opponent counters and then your counter and so forth. The list of moves being recorded underneath the characters.

Pawn (w), Pawn (b), Pawn (w), Queen (b)

Pawn (w), Pawn (b), Pawn (w), Queen (b)

Figure 4: Chess World

Now both players can see what the other has pressed; white started with Pawn (w), black countered with Pawn (b) and so on. The game will continue until a draw is determined or someone has won. Neither player is aware of the concept of a board or that each of the characters may represent one of many pieces (i.e. there are eight Pawns). However, this lack of awareness won't stop people playing and others collecting numerous sequences from different games. With enough games, people will start to discover "magic sequences" of success. If you press Knight, I should counter with Pawn, Pawn, and Bishop!

Gurus will write books on the "Secrets of the Queen" and people will copy the moves of successful players. People will convince themselves that they know what they're doing and the importance of action — you can't win without pressing a character! All sorts of superstition will develop.

Now imagine you're playing against someone who can see something truly remarkable — the board. In this game, you will move Pawn (w), the opponent will counter Pawn (b), you will move Pawn (w) again, they will counter Queen (b) and you will have lost. I've shown this in the figure below.

Pawn (w), Pawn (b), Pawn (w), Queen (b) ... LOST.

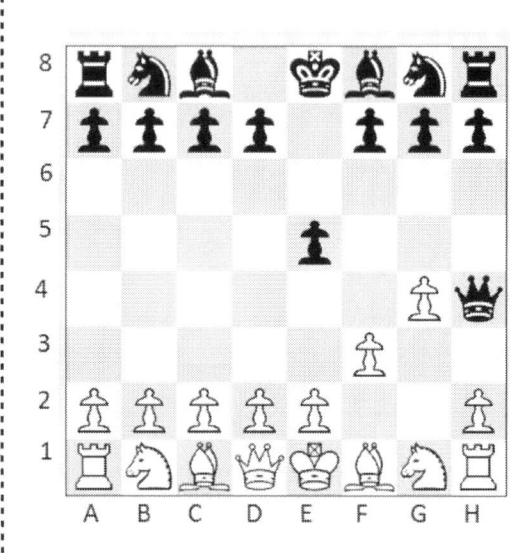

Figure 5: Chess World vs The Board

Remember, you have no idea that the board exists and you can only see what is on the left hand side i.e. the characters you press and the sequence. You will almost certainly be shocked by the speed at which you have lost the game. You'll probably scribble down their sequence as some sort of magic sequence for you to re-use. However, every time you play this opponent, no matter what you do, no matter how you copy them, you will lose and lose quickly.

You'll probably start to question whether there is some other factor to success. Maybe it's the speed at which they press the characters? Maybe they are a happy person and somehow culture and disposition impacts the game? Maybe it's what they had for lunch? To make things worse, the board provides the opponent with a learning mechanism to discover repeatable forms of gameplay, i.e. fool's mate. Against such a player, you are doomed to lose in the absence of lucky breaks for yourself and some sort of calamity for the opponent.

For a young CEO, this started to feel rather disturbing. I had the sneaking suspicion that I was the player pressing the buttons without seeing the board. We were doing fine for now but what happened if we came up against such a competitor? If they could see the board then I was toast. I needed some way to determine just how bad my situational awareness was.

Categorising situational awareness

The problem I faced was trying to determine whether I understood the landscape of business or not? I knew that learning in both chess and military campaigns was different from what I was doing in business, but how? I put a map and a picture of a chessboard side by side and started to look at them. What is it that made these maps useful?

The first, and most obvious thing, is that they are visual. If I was going to move a piece on a map then I could point to where it was and where it needed to go. Navigation was visual but that was normal. Except, I realised it wasn't. When people stopped me in their cars to find their way to the nearest petrol station — this was 2004 and GPS was still not everywhere — if they had no maps then I would give them directions. This invariably took the form of a story — "drive up the road, turn left, turn right, take the second turning at the roundabout" — along with equal amounts of guilt later on that I had sent them the wrong way. This use of storytelling has a long history and was the norm for navigation by Vikings. At some point, at various different times, cultures had found maps to be more effective. When I looked at our strategy documents, all I could see was a story.

The second thing to note with a map is it is context specific, i.e. the battle at hand. You learn from that context and how pieces move in it, in much the same way you learn from games in chess. However, in order to do this, you need to know the position of pieces on the map and where they can move to. But position is relative to something. In the case of a geographical map, it is relative to the compass, i.e. this piece is north of that. The compass acts as an anchor for the map. In the case of a chessboard, the board itself is the anchor as in this piece is at position C1 or B3. This gave me six absolute basic elements for any map, which are visual representation, context specific, position of components relative to some form of anchor, and movement of those components. I've summarised this in Figure 6.

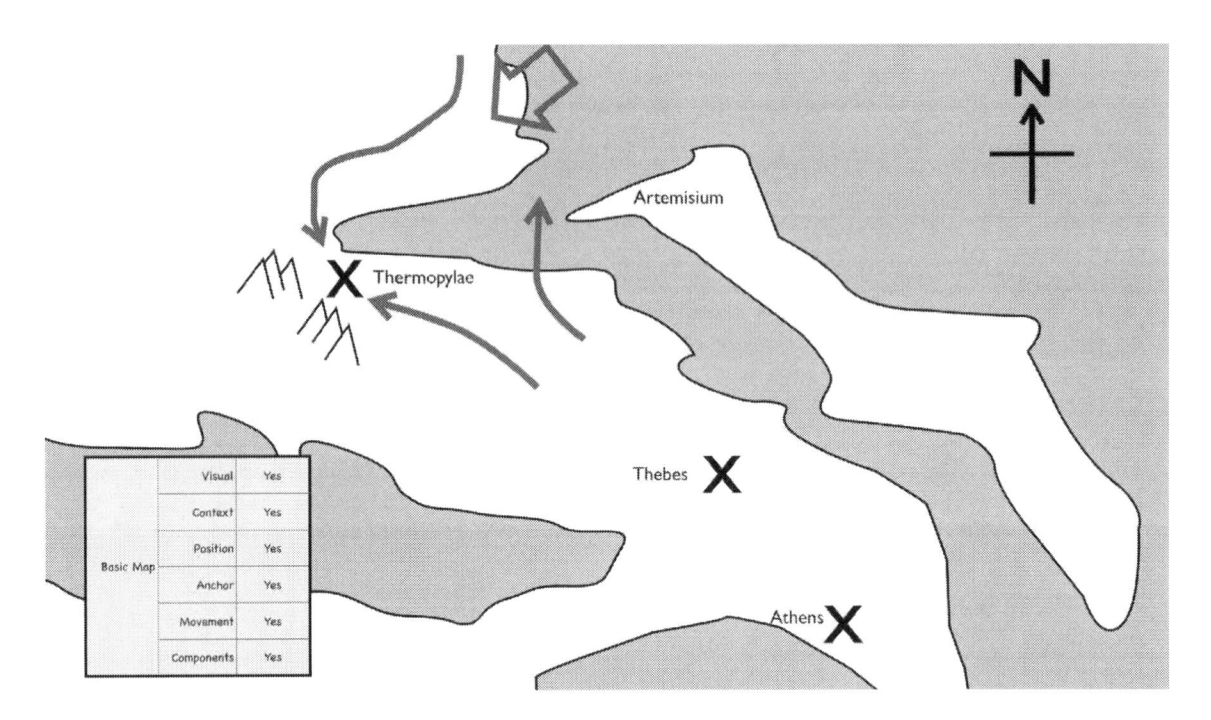

Figure 6: Basic elements of a map

Unfortunately, every single diagram I was using to determine strategy in business lacked one or more of those basic elements. I had business process maps, which were visual, context specific and had position but failed to show any form of movement, i.e. how things could change. Everything from trend maps to competitor analysis maps to strategy maps was lacking and worse than this, we were using different diagrams to explain the same problem in different parts of the business whether IT, marketing or finance. This seemed like an obvious cause of our alignment issues. I was forced to concede that I genuinely had no maps and no common means of understanding.

In a high situational awareness environment such as using a chessboard, then navigation tends to be visual, learning is from context specific play, and strategy is based upon position and movement. However, in my business then navigation was storytelling, learning was from copying others, i.e. secrets of success, and strategy was based upon magic frameworks, e.g. SWOTs. This was the antithesis of high situational awareness and I concluded that my business had more in common with alchemy than chess. We were simply fighting in the dark, occasionally sending our business resources to fight battles they might never win and every now and then, getting lucky.

I knew I needed some form of map to understand the landscape, to learn and determine strategy. However, landscape was only one factor that was missing. What about the other factors that Sun Tzu had talked about?

Climate, Doctrine and Leadership

You can think of climate as the rules of the game. For example, you don't send the Navy into a storm any more than you would send troops walking over a cliff. I had heard Richard Feynman talk about how you could learn the rules of chess simply by observing the board over time. Maybe there were rules of business that I could discover if I could map the environment? Maybe everything wasn't quite so random? But climate is more than just the rules of the game; it's also the opponent's actions and how well you can anticipate the change. Unfortunately, without a map, I was stuck.

Hence, I turned to the next factor, which was doctrine or the standard ways of operating. This I thought would be easy as it's just the good practice of business. I started looking into operational strategy and it was during that time that another one of those blindingly obvious questions hit me. I was reading up on the great and good of business, those wise men and women who ran corporations along with their secrets of success, when a thought popped into my mind — how did I know if they were wise? How do I know this practice is good? What if a lot of it was luck and just outcome bias? The last point is worth exploring more.

Imagine a normal six-sided dice. Imagine you have two possible bets; either 1 to 5 or the number 6. Now, basic probability would tell you to choose 1 to 5. Let us suppose you choose this; we roll the dice and it turns out to be 6. Were you wrong in your choice? Was the person who bet on 6 making the right strategic choice? If you didn't understand basic probability, then on an outcome basis alone, you'd argue they were right but it's clearly the wrong strategic choice. Roll the dice a hundred times and you will overwhelmingly win if you stick to betting on 1 to 5. When we choose to copy another, is it the right strategic choice or because of outcome bias? Am I copying ExxonMobile, Fannie Mae, Nokia and Blockbuster because of some deep strategic insight or because of past success? Am I copying the wrong thing?

So how did I know that what I was copying would be right? Furthermore, even if it was right then how did I know it would be right for my business? When you think about military history, there are many moves that have been learned over time from one battle to another, e.g. flanking an opponent to suppressing fire. These are context specific as in relevant to the battle at hand. In other words, you don't flank an opponent when an opponent isn't at the point you're flanking. But there are also many approaches that are not context specific but more universally useful. For example, training your soldiers to fire a rifle is universal. You never hear a General shout, "Ok, we're going to use suppressing fire, which means you all need to start learning how to fire a rifle." They already know.

These universal approaches are my standard ways of operating, the doctrine that we follow. But if I cannot see the landscape then how do I know whether an approach is universal or context specific?

In one battle, just because a General may have won by flanking an opponent then it doesn't mean that ordering my troops to flank the opponent is going to work every time. This may be completely the wrong thing to do. I can't just simply copy others even if they are successful because I don't know if that success was due to them being wise or just plain luck, nor whether our context is the same. Unfortunately, copying the wise men and women of business who had been successful was all that I had done. I had even heard other people talk about how they had tried to copy this or that approach and it had failed, and I had heard others say that it was their "execution that had failed". Well, what if it wasn't? What if they had copied one context specific approach and applied it to the wrong context? What if it was just the wrong thing to do like betting on 6? How would they know? How would I know?

At this point, my gut was having collywobbles. I clearly had no clue about anything and I was leading the company. Where was I leading them? I had no idea, it could be over a cliff. Even the manner in which I was telling them to act could be completely wrong. I was like a General ordering his troops to walk over the cliff in a flanking movement whilst practicing shooting rifles. Not exactly the future I had hoped for. But still, we were successful. I couldn't figure that bit out and I kept thinking I was worrying about nothing. But we had no maps and without maps, we had no mechanism to learn about common patterns that affect our landscape nor anticipate possible change nor determine the why of movement. We had no real idea whether a change in the market was caused by us or some other force. If we can't see the environment in which we are competing then how do we determine whether a successful approach is universal or specific to that environment? If I can't separate out what is context specific then how do I determine what is doctrine, i.e. universally applicable from that which is leadership — context specific? Everything was a mess.

The Strategy Cycle

I was clearly clueless but at least I had found five factors that I wanted to use to fix our strategy, though I had no idea how to do this. But that presented another problem. What order matters? Is climate more important than landscape? Maybe leadership is more important than purpose? Is there a strict order in which we move through these things? At least we had our purpose, even though it was a bit sucky. That crumb of comfort didn't last long.

The best way I've found to think about this problem is with the game of paintball. You start off with a purpose; maybe it's to capture the flag in a building. The next step is to understand the landscape and the obstacles in your path. Naturally, a bunch of newbies will tend to charge out onto the field of battle without understanding their landscape. The consequences are usually a very quick game. Assuming you understand the landscape then you might determine a strategy of covering fire with a ground assault against the target. You will apply some form of doctrine, i.e. breaking into two small teams. Then you will act. Chances are that during the course of the game, the climate will change — you will come under fire. At this point, doctrine kicks in again. The group leading the ground assault might dive for cover whilst the other group returns fire. Your purpose at this point will change. It might become to take out the sniper in the building that is firing at you. You will update your map, even if it's a mental one, noting where the sniper is. A new strategy is formed. For example, one group might provide suppressing fire whilst the other group flanks the opponent. And so you will act.

The point of this example is to demonstrate three things. First, the process of strategy is not a linear process but an iterative cycle. The climate may affect your purpose, the environment may affect your strategy, and your actions may affect all. Second, acting is essential to learning. Lastly, your purpose isn't fixed; it changes as your landscape changes and as you act. There is no "core", it's all transitional. Nokia's purpose today is not the same as when the company was a paper mill. I could see my last atom of business sanity disappear in a puff. I started to think about all those projects we had dismissed as not being core. What if they were instead our future?

The best way I've found to cope with this cycle is through the work of the mad major himself — the exceptional John Boyd. In order to understand the process of air combat, John Boyd developed the OODA loop. This is a cycle of observe the environment, orient around it, decide and then act. In Figure 7 below, I've married together both Sun Tzu and John Boyd to create a strategy cycle.

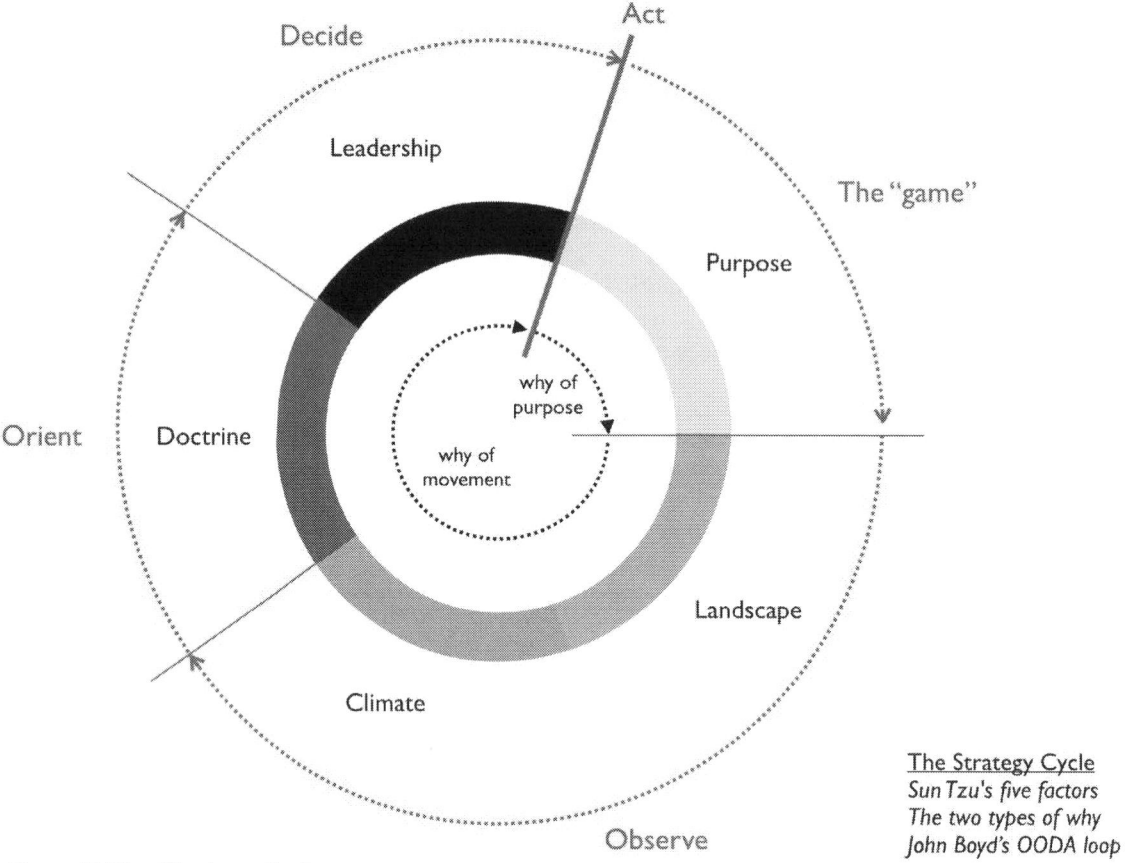

Figure 7: The Strategy Cycle

Now, it's worth remembering where I was back in 2004. I had a purpose that wasn't static, despite my belief it was. I was jumping to strategy whilst ignoring landscape, climate and doctrine. I was using storytelling to communicate with the entire group. I had no mechanism of learning. I was simply copying secrets of success from others, combined with magic frameworks such as SWOTs, and then I was acting upon it. Our strategy was a tyranny of action statements without any inkling about position and movement but instead built upon gut feel and "core". If there was a way to get things more wrong, I haven't found it since and I was the CEO. However, we were doing well and the one thing I had in my favour was that I understood how little I knew about strategy.

I set out to fix this and the first thing I needed was a map.

Chapter 2 - Finding a path

The problem I had was how do I map a business? Unlike a board game such as chess with its turn-based moves, when you consider a business, it is a living thing. It consists of a network of people, a mass of different activities, and reserves of capital including financial, physical, human and social. It consumes, it produces, it grows and it dies. Like all organisms, any business exists within a community of others, an ecosystem. It competes and co-operates for resources and it's shaped by and shapes its environment. Even within a business, people come and go. The things we do, the things we build and the things that others desire change over time. All firms are in a constant state of flux and the ecosystem it lives within never stands still. What sort of map can cope with that?

I struggled with these concepts for many months, playing around with different ideas of mapping and how to represent this maelstrom. I knew any map had to have those basic elements of being visual, context specific, the position of components relative to an anchor and some means of describing movement. But I had no idea where to start.

It was at this point that I thought about mapping **what** was core for my business and questioning **how** this changed using some form of mind map. My reasoning was simple. A business, like all organisms, needs to continuously adapt to changes in order to survive, and if we could somehow describe this then maybe that would give us a map. Take, for example, the multinational Finnish company Nokia. Originally founded in 1865 as a paper mill, the company has undergone many transformations through various close calls with bankruptcy. From a paper mill to a rubber manufacturer to consumer electronics to a telecommunications giant, this organism has radically evolved. The problem for me was the core for Nokia today was not its core in 1865 but instead an unimaginable flight of fancy at that time. How could I connect the two? When you focus on what is core for a company then the question becomes whether you mean core today, core yesterday or core tomorrow. They are not necessarily the same. I followed this logic down endless rabbit holes, getting nowhere fast.

In frustration, I started to ask **why** do things change? The responses I was given when talking to my peers varied from "progress" to "innovation" to "disruption". Examples across history were normally cited including the appearance of random innovations that impact the way we operate — from the telephone to electricity to computing. But given the upheaval they cause, the close calls with bankruptcy, the death of former great companies and the need to continuously learn new skills then why would anyone want this? Surely a more sedate, slower rate of change would be more comfortable? So why are things changing?

Alas, it seems that we don't get a choice. In any industrial ecosystem, novel and new things constantly appear as a consequence of the desire for companies and individuals to gain an advantage over others. Those things that are useful will be copied. They will spread until the once novel and new becomes commonplace. Yesterday's wonders are destined to become today's discounted special offers. The magic of the first electric light bulb, the first computer and the first telephone are now an expected norm. We no longer marvel at such things but instead, we would reel in utter shock if presented with a workplace that did not provide them. Competition and the desire to gain an advantage not only creates change; it spreads it and forces companies to adopt it. Somehow, I had to map this competition itself, including the journey from novel to commonplace. But what is that journey and what are the components that I'm going to map?

The more I looked into this, the more complex it became because that journey from novel to commonplace is not the end of the story. These extremes are connected as one enables the other. A historical demonstration of this would be Maudslay's screw-cutting lathe in 1800. The invention of the first screw thread is often cited as 400 BC by Archytas of Tarentum (428 BC – 350 BC). Early versions of this and the subsequent nut and bolt designs were custom made by skilled artisans with each nut fitting one bolt and no other. The introduction of Maudslay's lathe enabled repeated production of uniform nuts and bolts with standard threads. One nut now fitted many bolts. The artisan skill of building the perfect nut and bolt was replaced by more mass produced and interchangeable components. The novel had become commonplace. Whilst those artisans might have lamented the loss of their industry, those humble components also enabled the rapid creation of more complex machinery. Uniform mechanical components enabled the faster building of ships, guns and other devices.

It also allowed for the introduction of manufacturing systems that took advantage of these components. In 1803, collaboration between Marc Isambard Brunel and Maudslay led to the principles of modern mass production being introduced at Portsmouth dockyard. The use of block-making machinery replaced the craft of custom-made pulley blocks, an essential component in the rigging of Naval ships. A total of 45 machines enabled a magnitude of order increase in productivity with highly standardised outputs. This system of manufacture helped change ship making itself. The practices subsequently spread throughout industries, leading to what became known as the Armory Method and later the American system of manufacturing.

Things not only evolved from novel to commonplace, enabling new things to appear, but they also allowed for new forms of practice and organisation. Throughout our history, it has always been standardisation of components that has enabled creations of greater complexity. We are always standing on the shoulders of past giants, of past innovations, of past wonders that have become commonplace units. Without such well-defined mechanical or electrical components then our world would be a less technologically rich place — no internet, no generators, no TV, no computers, no light bulbs and no toasters.

Why toasters?

In 2009, the designer Thomas Thwaites exhibited his attempt to build a common household toaster from scratch at the Royal College of Art. Beginning with mining the raw materials, he aimed to create a product that is usually built with common components and sold for a few pounds in the local supermarket. This ambitious project required "copper, to make the pins of the electric plug, the cord, and internal wires. Iron to make the steel grilling apparatus, and the spring to pop up the toast. Nickel to make the heating element. Mica (a mineral a bit like slate) around which the heating element is wound, and of course plastic for the plug and cord insulation, and for the all-important sleek-looking casing".

After nine months and at a cost of over a thousand pounds, Thomas finally managed to create a sort of toaster. It lasted 5 seconds, the heating element bursting into flames. However, along his journey, Thomas had been forced to resort to using all sorts of other complex devices built from similar standard components that he could have used to make his toaster. Everything from microwaves to leaf blowers was involved in achieving his goal. Our society and the wondrous technologies that we can create not only consume but are dependent upon provision of these standard components. Remove this and the wheel of progress grinds very slowly and very expensively.

Back in 2004, Thomas hadn't attempted this experiment but I was acutely aware that we lived in a world where there's a constant flow of change, where the novel becomes commonplace and where the commonplace enables the novel. This is the environment that businesses live within. This entire process is driven by competition; the desire to differentiate creates the novel, the desire to keep up with others makes it commonplace. If we define economic progress as the movement of our society to ever more complex technological marvels, then progress is simply a manifestation of this competition. This impacts all organisations. This is what we have to map.

But in all this complexity, there was also comfort. I knew my world was built of components and hence it had its own chess pieces. Those pieces changed but there might be a way of describing evolution and the movement from novel to the commonplace. But movement is not enough for a map; I also needed to find the position of these components and that required some form of anchor. Alas, I had no anchor and without it, I was still lost.

The first map

In later chapters, I'm going to dive into the details of how this first map was created, how I discovered that anchor and ultimately described the movement of evolution. However, for our purposes, I'm going to simply show you a map, explain what bits matter and then use it to navigate the strategy cycle. I would dearly love to claim that this map was the result of some towering intellectual might, but in reality, as you will later discover, it was more trial and error combined with endless accidents. Figure 8 is what a map of a single line of business should look like. I created my first map in 2005 and it was for an online photo service that I ran. Take a few minutes to read it carefully.

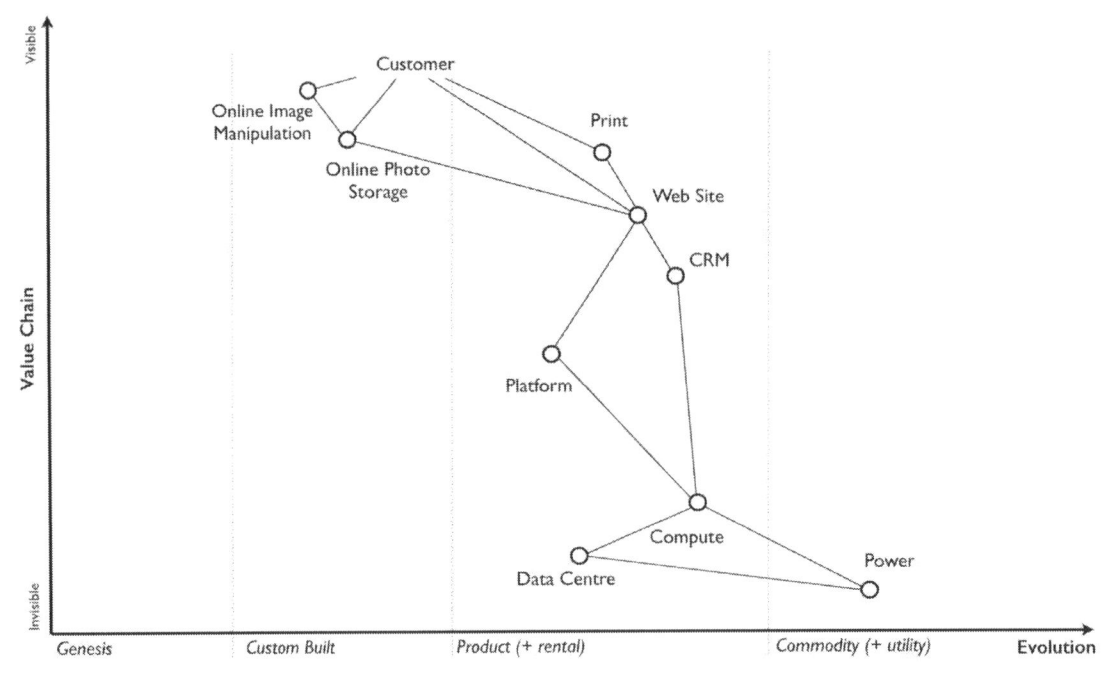

Figure 8: A Map

The map is **visual** and **context specific**, i.e. it is unique to that line of business containing the components that influence it at that moment in time. This is not a map of an automotive industry in 2016 or a pharmaceutical company in 2010, but instead an online photo service in 2005. The map has an anchor, which is the user (in this case, a public customer, though other types of users exist) and their needs. The **position** of **components** in the map are shown relative to that user on a value chain, represented by the y-axis. Each component needs the component below it, however, the higher up the map a component is then the more visible it becomes to the user. The lower it is then the less visible it becomes. For example, in that first map, the user cares about online photo storage but whilst this needs the provision of underlying components such as compute and power, those components are positioned far from the user and hence are less visible.

I could have described this as a chain of needs but I wanted to emphasise what the user valued. They cared about what was provided to them and not who provided my electricity. Of course, as the provider of the service, I cared about everything — my users' needs, what compute we used and even what electricity provider we employed. In much the same way, the user cares about the toaster and what it does and not that you lovingly created nickel heating elements by hand rather than using standard components. Though, they will probably care if you try and charge them a thousand pounds for a toaster that bursts into flames at first use.

The components of the map also have a stage of evolution. These are:-

Genesis. This represents the unique, the very rare, the uncertain, the constantly changing and the newly discovered. Our focus is on exploration.

Custom built. This represents the very uncommon and that which we are still learning about. It is individually made and tailored for a specific environment. It is bespoke. It frequently changes. It is an artisan skill. You wouldn't expect to see two of these that are the same. Our focus is on learning and our craft.

Product (including rental). This represents the increasingly common, the manufactured through a repeatable process, the more defined, the better understood. Change becomes slower here. Whilst there exists differentiation, particularly in the early stages, there is increasing stability and sameness. You will often see many of the same products. Our focus is on refining and improving.

Commodity (including utility). This represents scale and volume operations of production; the highly standardised, the defined, the fixed, the undifferentiated, the fit for a specific known purpose and repetition, repetition and more repetition. Our focus is on ruthless removal of deviation, on industrialisation, and operational efficiency. With time, we become habituated to the act; it is increasingly less visible and we often forget it's even there.

This evolution is shown as the x-axis and all the components on the map are moving from left to right driven by supply and demand competition. In other words, the map is not static but fluid, and as components evolve, they become more commodity-like.

In Figure 9, I've taken the original map above and explicitly highlighted the elements that matter. This map has all the basic elements of any map — **visual,** context specific, **position** of **components** (based upon an **anchor**) and **movement**. In later chapters, as appropriate, we will explore each in more detail.

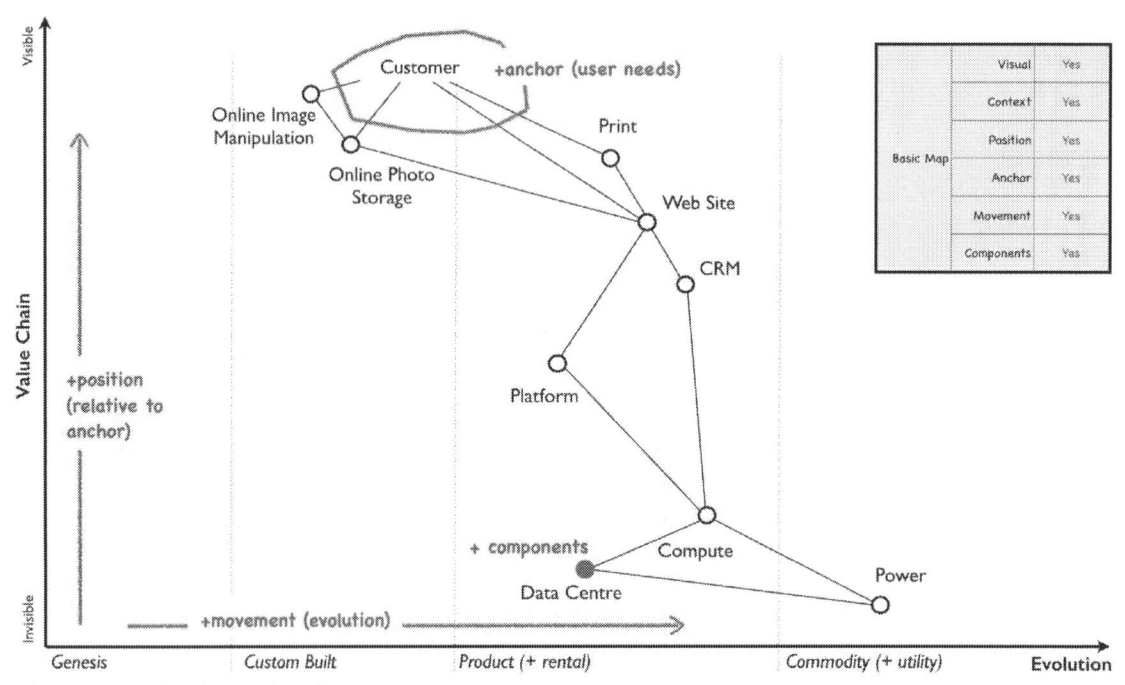

Figure 9: Basic elements of a map

However, the map also has some advanced features that are not so immediately obvious. There is a **flow** of risk, information and money between components. The best way to think of this is by use of a military example. You have components such as troops, which might occupy different positions on the map, but along with movement, you also have communication between the troops. That communication is flow. It's important not to mix those ideas together because it's easy to have troops effectively communicating together but at the same time being ineffective by moving in the wrong direction. There can be several reasons for this, including the wrong orders are given or there is no common understanding of purpose.

The components can also represent different **types** of things, the military equivalent of different troops — infantry, tanks and artillery. In these Wardley Maps, the common name now given to them due to my inability to find something useful to call them, then these types represent **activities, practices, data** and **knowledge**. All of these types of components can move, and in our case, this means evolve from left to right driven by competition. However, the terms we use to describe the separate stages of evolution are different for each type. In order to keep the map simple, the x-axis of evolution shows the terms for

activities alone. The terms that I use today for other types of things are provided in Figure 10.

Type \ Stage of Evolution	I	II	III	IV
Activities	Genesis	Custom	Product + Rental Services	Commodity + Utility Services
Practices	Novel	Emerging	Good	Best
Data	Unmodelled	Divergent	Convergent	Modelled
Knowledge	Concept	Hypothesis	Theory	Accepted

Figure 10: Types and stages of evolution

Lastly, climatic patterns can be shown on the map. I've highlighted these more advanced elements onto Figure 11.

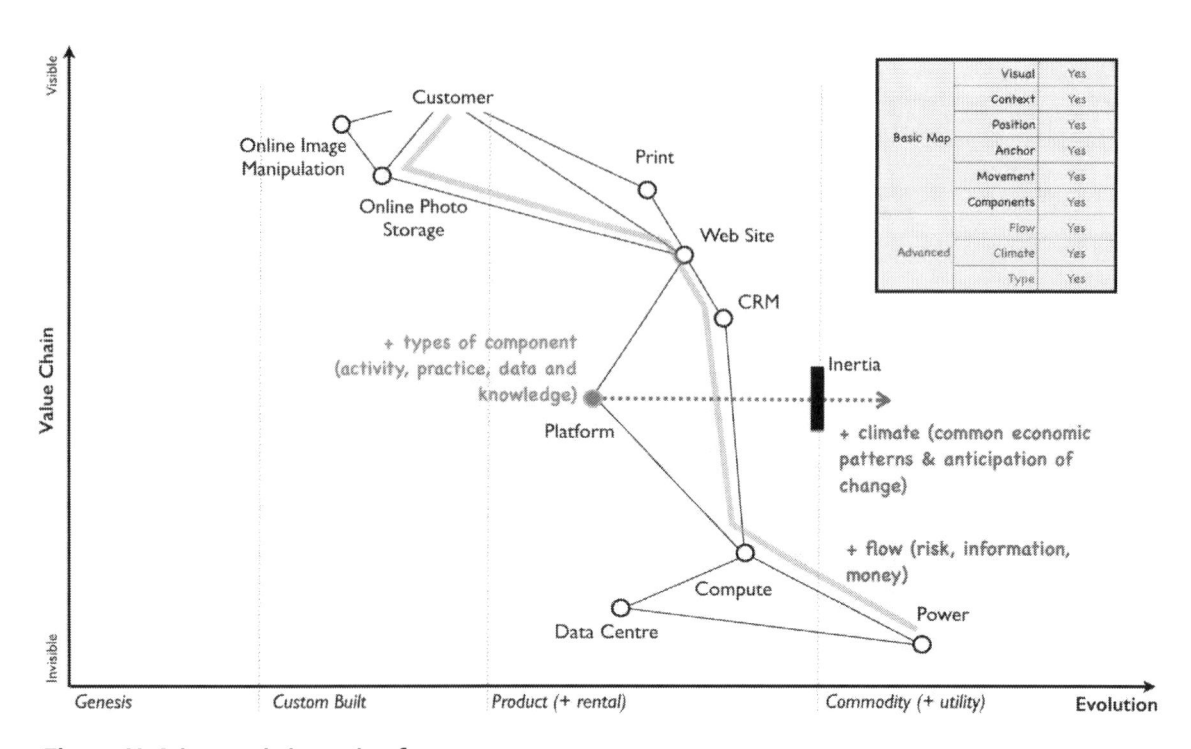

Figure 11: Advanced elements of a map

In the above map, platform is considered to be evolving to a more utility form and inertia exists to the change. Normally, we don't mark up all of these basic and advanced elements in this way. We simply accept that they are there. However, it's worth knowing that they exist. The normal way to represent the above map is provided in Figure 12.

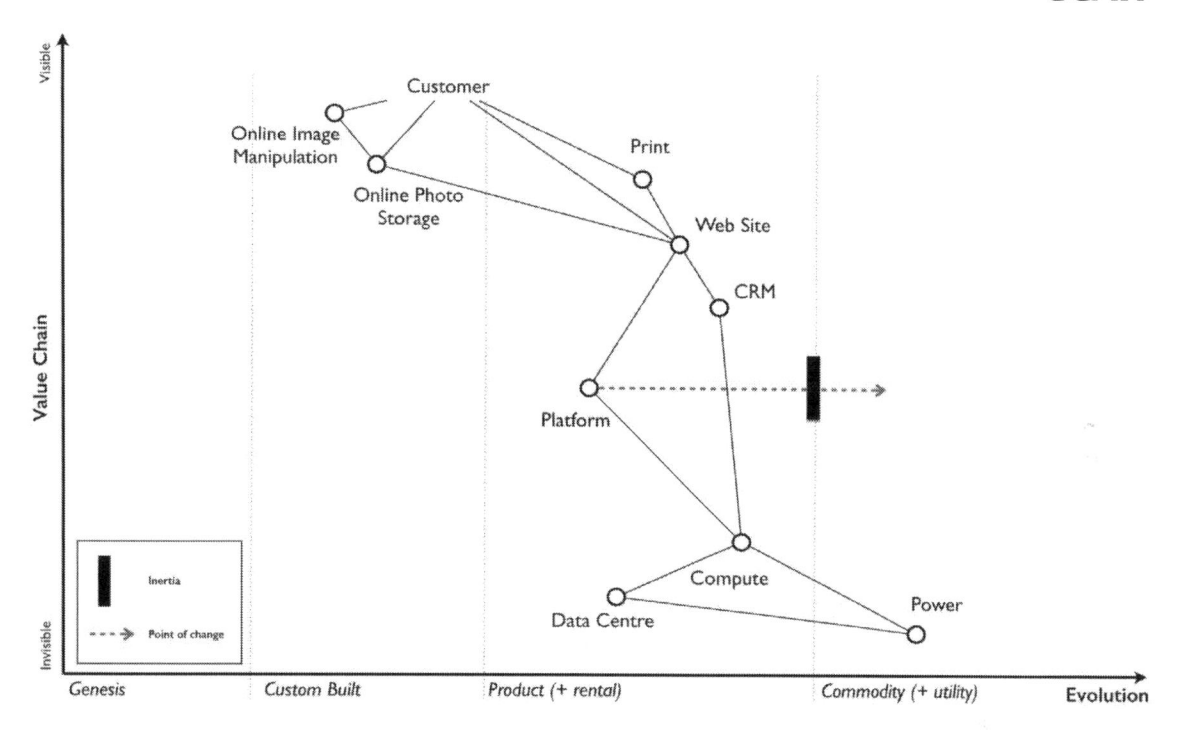

Figure 12: A standard representation

Now with a simple map such as Figure 12, we can start to discuss the landscape. For example, have we represented the user need reasonably and are we taking steps to meet that user need? Maybe we're missing something such as an unmet need that we haven't included? Are we treating components in the right way? Are we using a utility for power or are we somehow building our own power station as though it's a core differentiator visible to the user? If so, why? Have we included all the relevant components on the map or are we missing key critical items? We can also start to discuss our anticipations of change. What happens when a platform becomes more of a utility? How does this affect us? What sort of inertia will we face?

Maps are fundamentally a communication and learning tool. In the next chapter, we're going to loop through the strategy cycle in order for me to teach you some of the basic lessons that I learned. However, before we do this, I just want to describe a few steps to help you create your own maps.

Step 1 – Needs

Critical to mapping is the anchor and hence you must first focus on the user need. This requires you to define the scope of what you're looking at — are we a tea shop, an automotive company, a nation state or a specific system? The trick is to start somewhere. You will often find that in the process of mapping, you need to expand or reduce your scope and there is nothing wrong with this. A map for a particular company is part of a wider map for the ecosystem that the company operates within. A map of a particular system within a company is part of the map for the entire company. You can expand and reduce as necessary. It's worth noting that the user needs of one map are components in another. For example, the user needs for a company producing nuts and bolts become the components used (i.e. nuts and bolts) for a company producing automobiles or bridges.

In our first map, the user needs for an electricity provider are simply drawn as a single component far down the value chain of our map and described as power. As a user, we could describe our needs for power as being reliable, utility like, provided in standard forms and accessible. From the perspective of examining an online photo service then a single component is enough. However, that single component will break into an entire map for an electricity provider, including different forms of transmission, generation and even spot markets. A single node on one map can be an entire map from another person's perspective. Equally, the entire map of your business might be a single component for someone else.

Hence, start with a scope and define the user needs for that scope. Be careful though because a common trap is not to think of your user's needs but instead to start to describe your own needs, i.e. your desire to make a profit, to sell a product or be successful. Yes, your business is a user with its own needs but this is different from say your public customers. To keep things simple for now, focus on them.

You need to think precisely about what your user needs. If you're a tea shop then your users may have needs such as a refreshing drink, a convenient location, a comfortable environment, a quick service and a tasty treat like a piece of lemon drizzle cake. This in turn requires you to have the capability to satisfy those needs. If you don't then your plan for world domination of the tea shop industry might be abruptly halted. At the same time, you should distinguish between the many things that your users want but do not necessarily need. So start with questions such as what does this thing need to do, how will its consumers interact with it and what do they expect from it? There are various techniques to help elucidate this but I've found nothing more effective than talking directly to your own users. Creating a user journey for how they interact with what you provide is always a good start.

As you discuss with users, along with the usual list of wants (i.e. I want my cup of tea to make me fabulously witty, slim and handsome) then you might find they have genuine unmet needs or novel needs that they find difficult in describing. These are important. Don't ignore them just because you don't provide them at this time. Back in 2005, our user needs for the online photo service included such things as sharing photos online with other users. This required us to have a capability such as the storage of digital photos and a web site to upload and share them with others. These capabilities are your highest level components and the manifestation of your user needs. For us, that included the storage of digital photos, manipulation of images (removal of red-eye, cropping), sharing of images via the website and printing to physical products, from photos to mouse mats. This is shown in Figure 13.

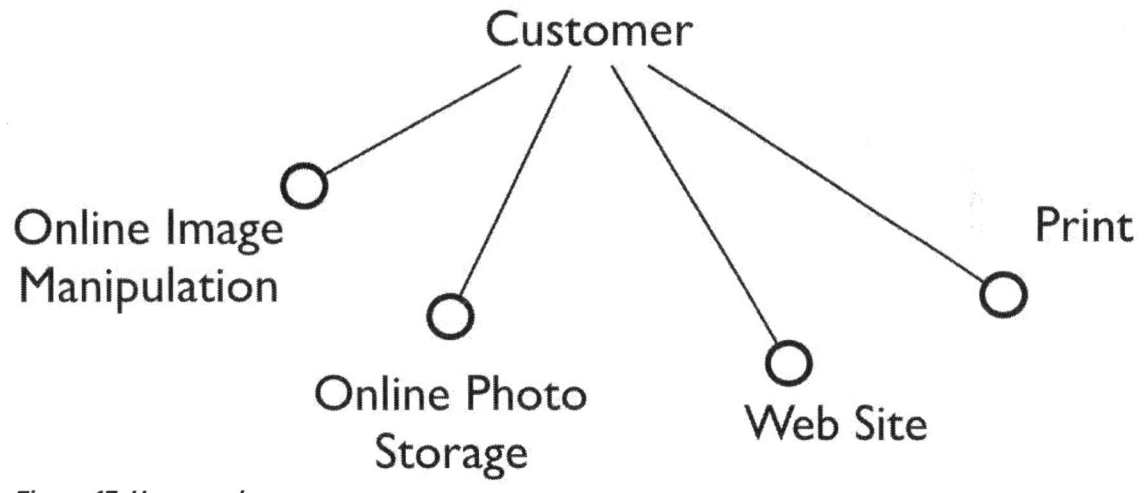

Figure 13: User needs

Step 2 — Value Chain

Whilst having user needs is a great start, just knowing the needs doesn't mean the stuff will now build itself. There are other things involved and this is what we call a value chain. It can be simply determined by first asking the question of "what is the user need?" and then by asking further questions of "what components do we need in order to build this capability?"

For example, in the case of our online photo service, once the basic user needs were known then we could describe our top level capabilities, our top level components. We could then describe the subcomponents that these visible components themselves would need. The best way I've found of doing this, from practice, is to gather a group of people familiar with the business and huddle in some room with lots of Post-it Notes and a huge whiteboard. On the Post-it Notes, write down the user needs and the top level capabilities required to meet them. Place these on the wall in a fairly random order. Then for each capability, using more Post-it Notes, the group should start to write down any subcomponents that these top-level components will use. This can include any activity, data, practice or set of knowledge.

For each subcomponent, further subcomponents should then be identified until a point is reached that the subcomponents are now outside of the scope of what you're mapping. Power doesn't need to be broken down any further if the company consumes it from a utility provider. By way of example, manipulating online digital photos needs some sort of online digital photo storage component. This in turn needs a website, which in turn needs a platform that in turn needs compute resources, storage resources, an operating system, network, power and so forth. These components will become part of your value chain and any component should only be written once. When the group is satisfied that a reasonable set of components for all the needs have been written then draw a single vertical line and mark it as the value chain, as shown in Figure 14.

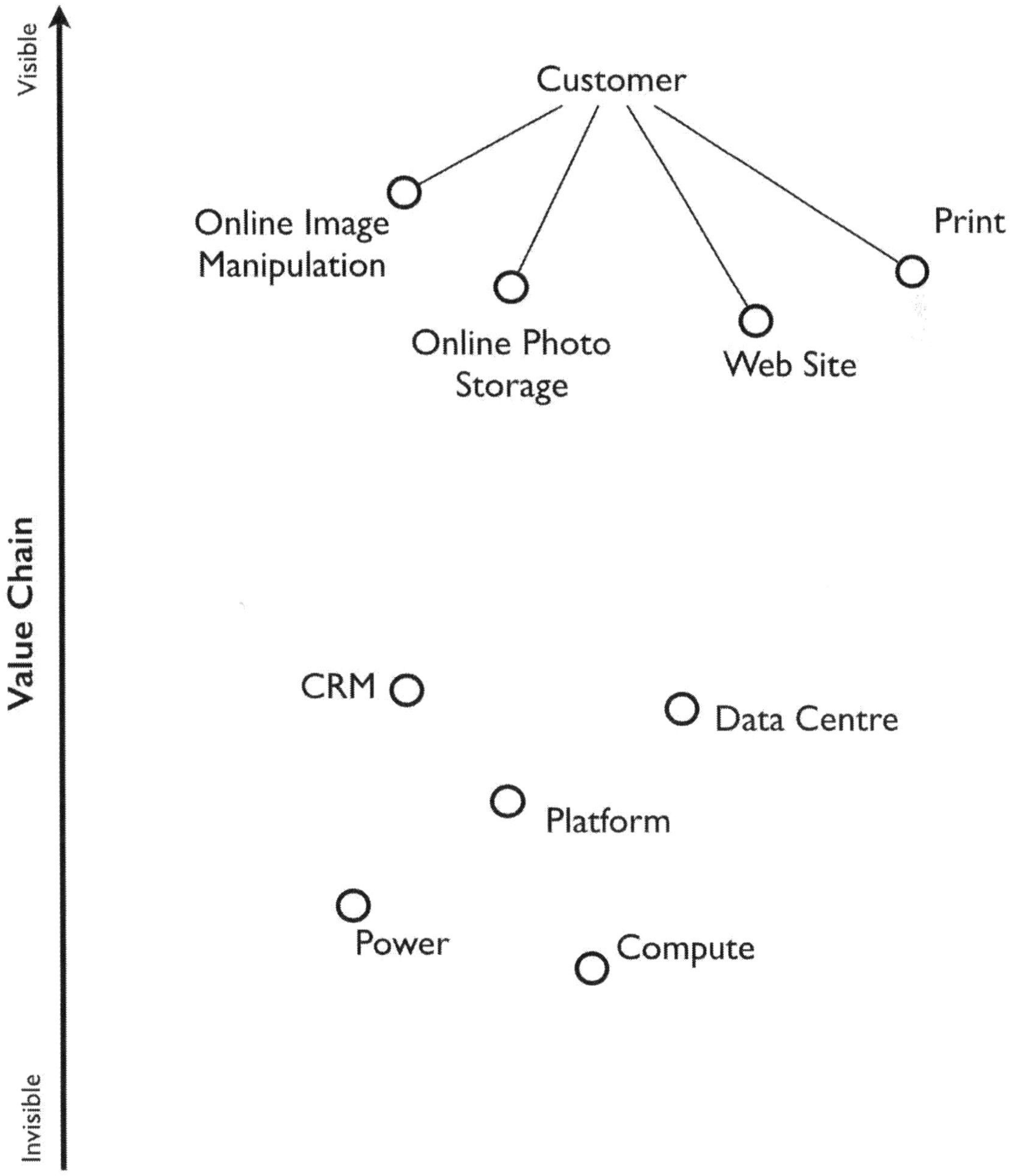

Figure 14: A framework for the value chain

The top-level components (i.e. your capabilities, what you produce, what is most visible to the user) should be placed near the top of the value chain.

Subcomponents should be placed underneath with lines drawn between components to show how they are related, e.g. this component needs that component. As you go through this process, you may wish to add or discard components, depending upon how relevant you feel they are to drawing a useful picture of the landscape. They can always be added or removed later.

In Figure 15, I've provided a value chain for our online photo service, adding in the superfluous term "needs" to emphasise that this is a chain of needs. Obviously, for simplicity, not everything is included, e.g. payment. Before you ask, most users do have a need for not being accused of theft, so providing a payment capability is quite useful to both them and your business, assuming that you're not giving everything away freely.

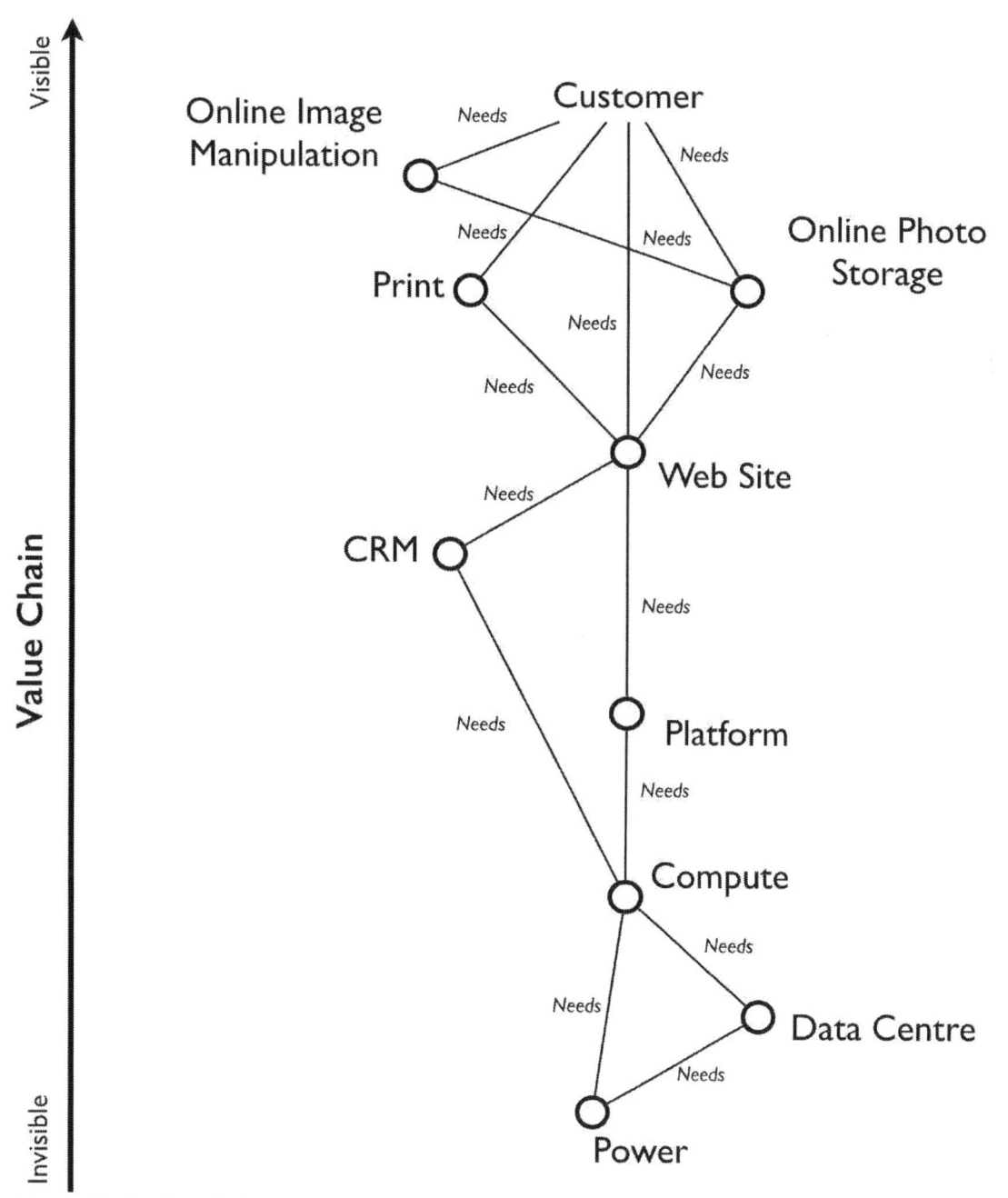

Figure 15: A value chain

To reiterate, things near the top are more visible and have more value to the user. For example, online image manipulation was placed slightly higher than online photo storage because it was seen as a differentiator with other services that

existed in 2005 and hence valued by users. Online photo storage was also a subcomponent of image manipulation and was placed lower. The website, a necessity for sharing, was placed slightly further down because though it was essential, many websites existed and it was also a subcomponent of online photo storage. Now this last point we could easily argue over, but the purpose of doing this in a group is you'll often get challenges and debates over what components exist and how important they are. This is exactly what you want to happen. In the same way that a military commander welcomes challenge on the ground from troops on the position of forces and key features, don't ignore the challenge but celebrate it, as this will become key to making a better map.

But also, don't waste time trying to make a perfect value chain in order to build a perfect map. It's not only impossible, it's unnecessary. All maps, including geographical maps, are imperfect representations of what exists. To draw a perfect geographical map, you would have to use a 1:1 scale, at which point the map being the size of the landscape it covers is anything but useful. A map of France that is the size of France helps no-one.

Step 3 — Map

As I quickly discovered, value chains on their own are reasonably useless for understanding strategic play in an environment. This is because they lack any form of context on how it is changing, i.e. they lack movement. If you think back to the example of Nokia, then its value chains have radically altered over time from a paper mill to telecommunications company. In order to understand the environment, we therefore need to capture this aspect of change and combine it with our value chain.

The largest problem with creating an understanding of the context in which something operates is that this process of change and how things evolve cannot be measured over time. As uncomfortable as it is, you have to simply accept that you don't have a crystal ball and hence you have to embrace the uncertainty of future change. Fortunately, there's a neat trick, because whilst evolution cannot be measured over time, the different stages of evolution can be described. So, this is exactly what you need to do. Take your value chain and turn it into a map with an evolution axis. On the wall or in whatever tool you've used to create your value chain, now add a horizontal line for evolution. Mark on sections for genesis, custom built, product and commodity, as shown in Figure 16.

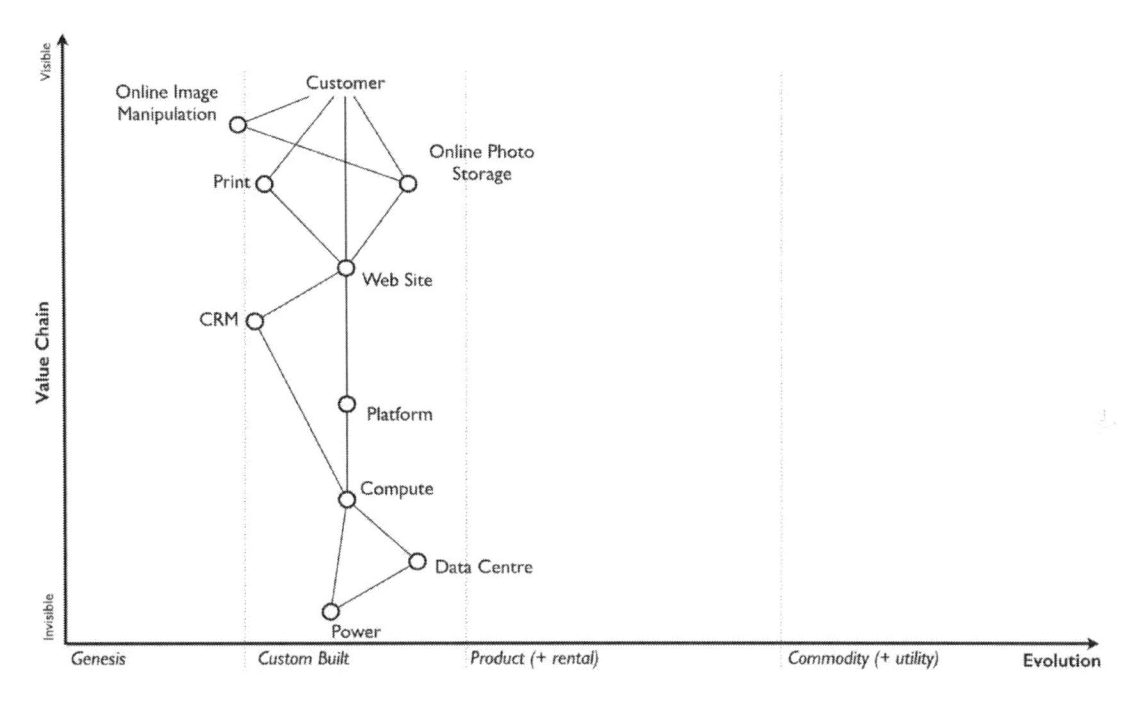

Figure 16: Adding evolution to your value chain

Unless you're extremely lucky then all the components are likely to be in the wrong stages of evolution. Hence start to move the components of the value chain to their relevant stage. For each component, the group should question how evolved it is. In practice, the best way to do this is to examine its characteristics and ask:-

- How ubiquitous and well defined is the component?
- Do all my competitors use such a component?
- Is the component available as a product or a utility service?
- Is this something new?

Be warned, this step is often the main cause of arguments in the group. You will regularly come across components that parts of the group feel passionate about. They will declare it as unique, despite the fact that all your competitors will have this. There is also the danger that you will describe the component by how you treat it rather than how it should be treated. Even today, in 2016, there are companies that custom build their own CRM (customer relationship management) system, despite its near ubiquity and essential use in most industries.

There are many causes for this, some of which are due to inertia and the component being a pet project, and in other cases, it is because the component is actually multiple subcomponents. In the latter case, you'll often find that most of the subcomponents are commodities, with maybe one or two that are genuinely novel. Break it down into these subcomponents. It is essential for you to challenge the assumptions and that is part of what mapping is all about, exposing the assumptions we make and providing a means to challenge. This is also why working in a group matters because it's far too easy for an individual to apply their own biases to a map.

If we think of mapping a tea shop then we might argue that our lemon drizzle cake is home-made and therefore custom built. But in reality, is the provision of a cake in a tea shop something that is rare and hence relatively novel? Or is the reality that a user expects a tea shop to provide cake and it is commonplace? You might market the cake as home-made but don't confuse what you market something as with what it is. The tea shop up the road could just as easily buy mass produced cake, add some finishing flourishes to it and describe it as home-made. If it's cheaper, just as tasty, more consistent and to the user an expected norm for a tea shop, then you'll be at a disadvantage. The same is true of building your own Thomas Thwaites toaster, rather than buying a commodity version to provide toast. To help you in the process of challenge, I've added a cheat sheet in Figure 17 for the characteristics of activities. How this was created will be discussed in later chapters but for now, simply use this as a guide. Where arguments continue to rage then look to see if the component is in fact multiple subcomponents.

Stage (of activity)	Genesis	Custom	Product (+rental)	Commodity (+utility)
Characteristics				
Ubiquity	Rare	Slowly increasing consumption	Rapidly increasing consumption	Widespread and stabilising
Certainty	Poorly understood	Rapid increases in learning	Rapid increases in use / fit for purpose	Commonly understood (in terms of use)
Publication Types	Normally describe the wonder of the thing	Build / construct / awareness and learning	Maintenance / operations / installation / feature	Focused on use
General Properties				
Market	Undefined market	Forming market	Growing market	Mature market
Knowledge management	Uncertain	Learning on use	Learning on operation	known / accepted
Market Perception	Chaotic (non linear)	Domain of experts	Increasing expectation of use	Ordered (appearance of being linear) / trivial
User perception	Different / confusing / exciting / surprising	Leading edge / emerging	Common / disappointed if not used or available	Standard / expected
Perception in Industry	Competitive advantage / unpredictable / unknown	Comptitive advantage / ROI / case examples	Advantage through implementation / features	Cost of doing business / accepted
Focus of value	High future worth	Seeking profit / ROI?	High profitability	High volume / reducing margin
Understanding	Poorly understood / unpredictable	Increasing understanding / development of measures	Increasing education / constant refinement of needs / measures	Believed to be well defined / stable / measurable
Comparison	Constantly changing / a differential / unstable	Learning from others / testing the water / some evidential support	Feature difference	Essential / operational advantage
Failure	High / tolerated / assumed	Moderate / unsurprising but disappointed	Not tolerated, focus on constant improvement	Operational efficiency and surprised by failure
Market action	Gambling / driven by gut	Exploring a "found" value	Market analysis / listening to customers	Metric driven / build what is needed
Efficiency	Reducing the cost of change (experimentation)	Reducing cost of waste (Learning)	Reducing cost of waste (Learning)	Reducing cost of deviation (Volume)
Decision Drivers	Heritage / culture	Analysis & synthesis	Analysis & synthesis	Previous experience

Figure 17: The cheat sheet

Don't worry if some of the terms are confusing in the cheat sheet; just use what you can. Like chess, mapping is a craft and you will get better with practice. Today, topographical intelligence in business is more about a Babylonian clay tablet than Ordnance Survey maps for industries. The art is very much in the custom-built stage of evolution (see the cheat sheet above).

You should aim to complete an entire map of a line of business in a matter of hours, though there is nothing wrong with spending longer in your first attempts in order to get used to the process. I'm afraid there is a big downside here. Mapping, like learning to play chess, is something that only you and your team can do. You will have to follow the path that I took when I was a CEO and learn to map. You can't outsource mapping to someone else any more than you can outsource learning to play chess to a consultancy. Well, technically you can but you won't be learning and you'll just become dependent upon them, constantly asking for your next move. Which, to be honest, is what many of us have done, but then if you're happy with that, stop reading this book and just ask a consultancy for your strategy. If you're not happy with that then be warned that the amount of value that you will get from mapping increases with the amount of work you put into repeatedly using it.

It's also worth noting that when adding practices, data and knowledge to your map then you can use the same cheat sheet for each stage of evolution, i.e. data that is modelled (see Figure 10) should be widespread, commonly understood, essential and believed to be well defined. It shares the same characteristics as commodity activities. Once you have placed the components in their relevant stage to the best of your ability, you now have a map, as per Figure 18. Remember that this map was for an online photo service in 2005 and so the composition of components and their position will not be the same as they are today. We expect an awful lot more from an online photo service in 2016. The map is hence fluid and constantly evolving.

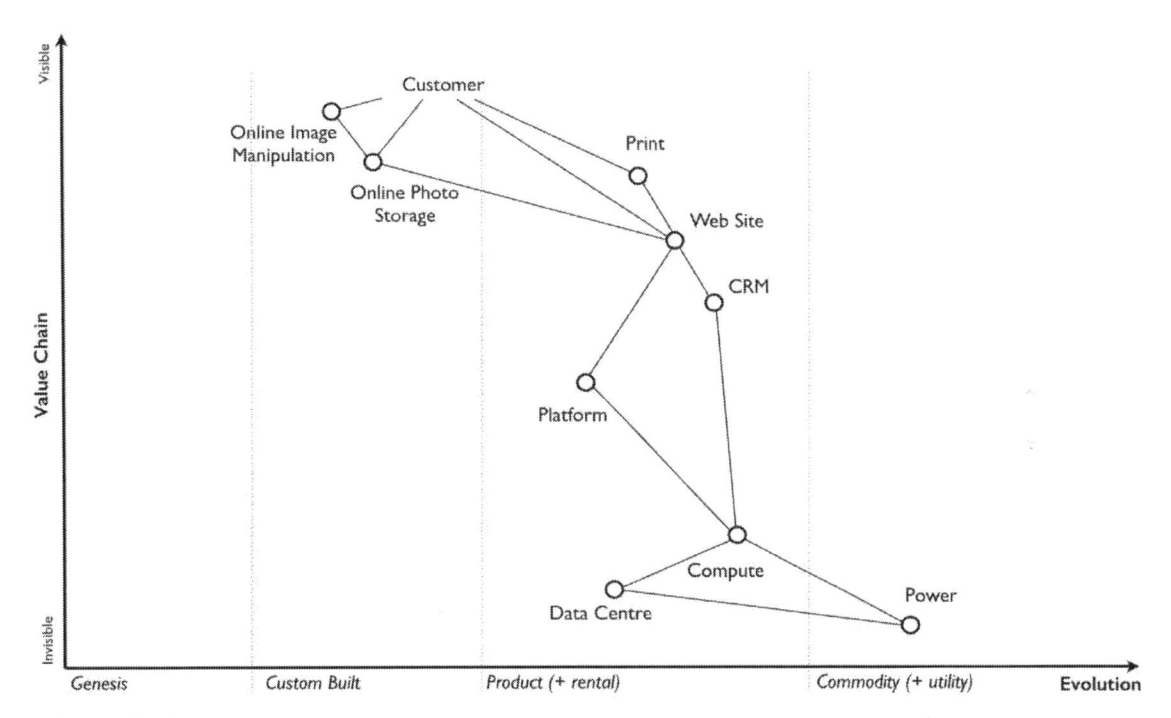

Figure 18: The map

The next thing to do is to share your map with others in your organisation and allow them to challenge you and ideally your group. This is exactly what I did with my colleague, James Duncan (who was CIO of the company at the time). With help from James, I refined both the map and the concept, something that I owe him a great deal of thanks for. If there is a co-inventor of mapping, then it would be James. Our robust debates in the boardroom showed me that business and IT are not separate but we could discuss strategic gameplay together around a map. It's a bit like the Army and the Air Force. They might have different capabilities and strengths but if we use a map to communicate then we can make all of this work together.

I have found subsequently that this process of sharing not only refines the map but spreads ownership of it. You should also use this time to consider any unmet needs, any missing components and ask questions on whether you're treating things in the right way. It's often surprising to find how many companies are spending vast resources on building their own metaphorical Thomas Thwaites toasters when a commodity version is readily available.

The next step

With a map in hand, we're now ready to start exploring the strategy cycle and hopefully start learning some useful lessons. Well, at least that's what I hoped for in 2005. In the next chapter, I intend to show you what I discovered. But before I do, I have a request to make of you.

Take a break, read this chapter again, pick a part of your business and have a go at mapping it. Simply follow the steps and use the cheat sheet. Ideally, grab a couple of other people that are deeply familiar with that business to help you, and don't spend too long on it. Keep it to a couple of hours, three to four at most.

If, within that time, you don't feel you're learning more about that business and the mapping isn't raising questions on user needs and what's involved then stop. You can recover your lost time by simply not reading any more chapters. Pick this book up, aim for the refuse bin and with a shout of "that was a complete waste" then let it fly. If instead you found the exercise interesting, then let us continue this journey together.

Chapter 3 - Exploring the map

Hurray, we've got a map! What now? The purpose of producing a map is to help us to learn and then apply basic climatic patterns, doctrine and context specific forms of gameplay. Maps are our learning and communication tool for discovering these things and enabling us to make better decisions before acting. However, the strategy cycle is iterative and we're not going to learn all the patterns the first time we use a map any more than learning everything about chess in our first game. Instead, like a game of chess then play by play, move by move, we're going to get a little bit better.

This is what happened to me starting in 2005, and even today in 2016, I'm still learning. In this chapter, I'm going to start looping through a single pass of the strategy cycle (see Figure 19).

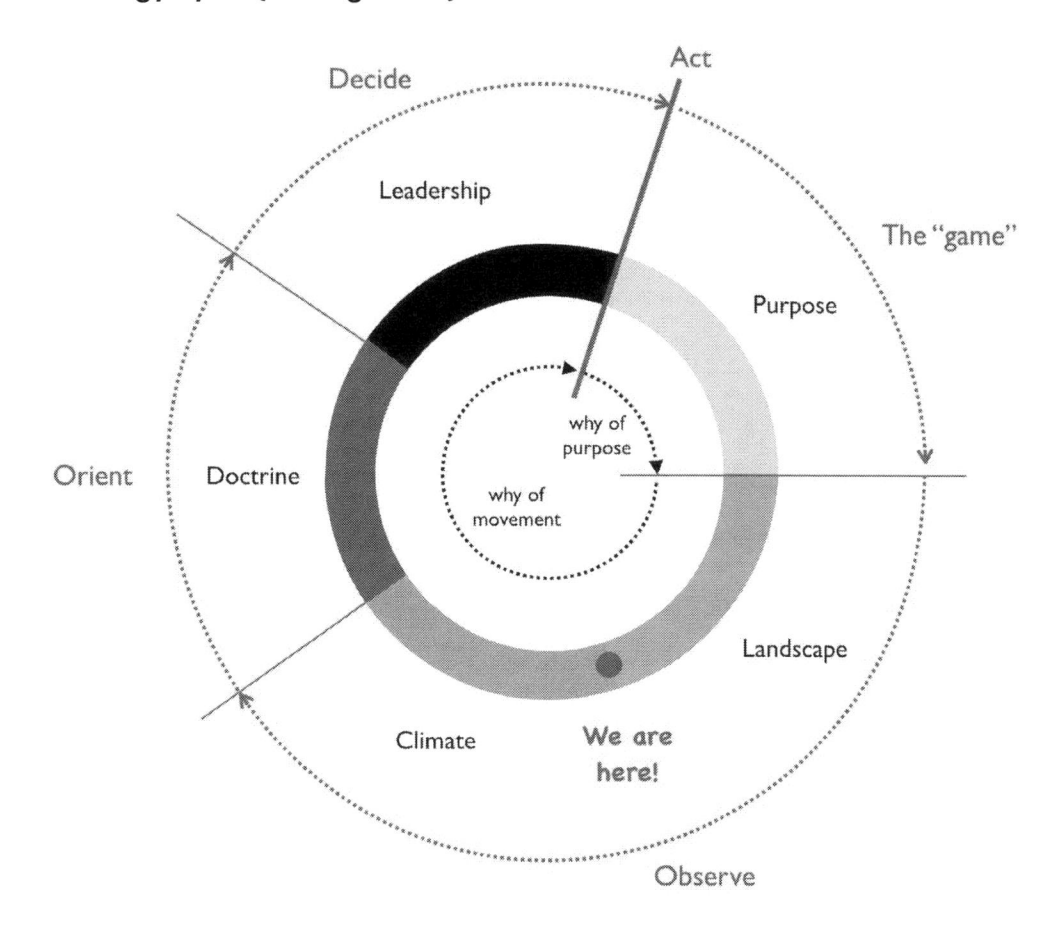

Figure 19: Looping through the strategy cycle

Learning climatic patterns

Climatic patterns are those things that change the map, regardless of your actions. This can include common economic patterns or competitor actions. Understanding climatic patterns are important when anticipating change. In much the same way, chess has patterns that impact the game. This includes rules that limit the potential movement of a piece to the likely moves that your opponent will make. You cannot stop climatic patterns from happening, though, as you'll discover, you can influence, use and exploit them. In this section, I'll go through a number of climatic patterns relevant to business and then we will apply them to our first map.

Climatic pattern: Everything evolves

All components on your map are moving from left to right under the influence of supply and demand competition. This includes every activity (what we do), every practice (how we do something) and every mental model (how we make sense of it). This means that everything has a past and a future. For example, in Figure 20, the component described as platform was considered to be a product, and in 2005, for an online photo service, this was provided by the LAMP (Linux, Apache, MySQL and Perl) stack. There were other competing product sets out there with different features, but few of us would entertain the idea of custom building the lot, i.e. with an online photo service, you wouldn't start by going "we need to build our own novel operating system, our own computing language and our own web server software". However, roll the clock back further in time and that's exactly what you would have needed to do.

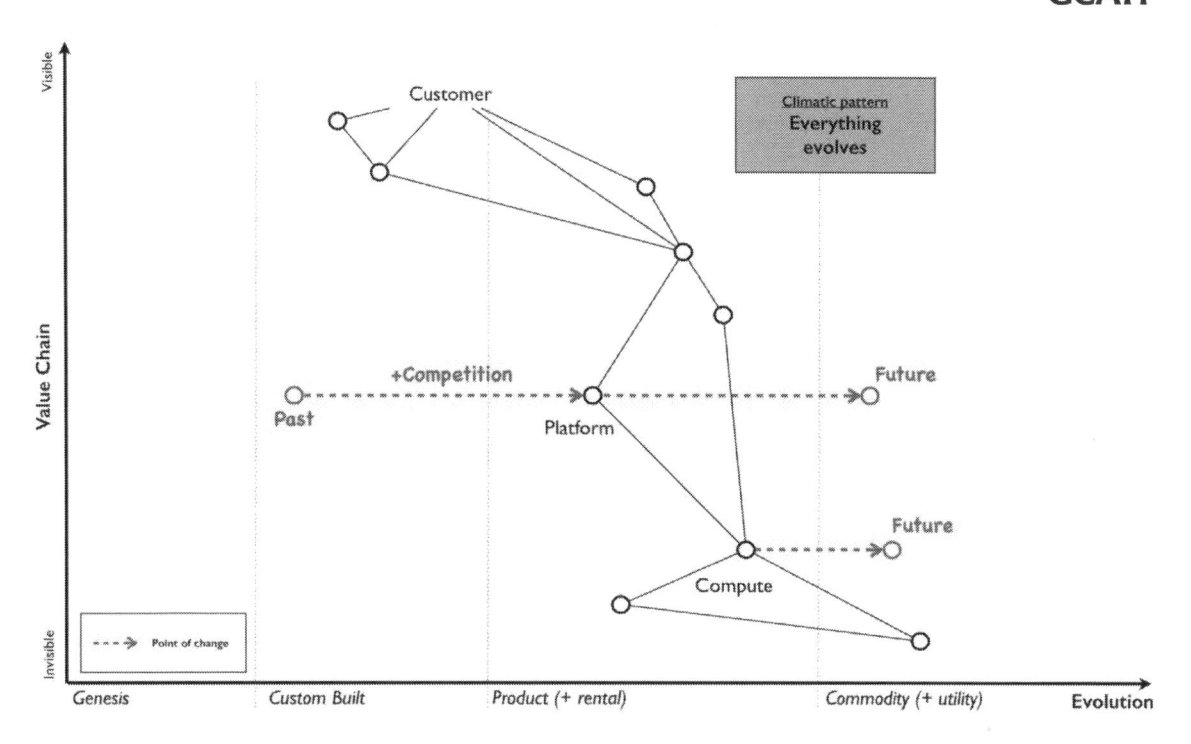

Figure 20: Everything evolves

Even with this product stack, there was still a lot of stitching required. We were far from the highly standardised world of electricity supply where you simply insert a plug and switch it on. We had installation, configuration, setup, networks and many underlying components that had to fit together to provide a working stack. I would have dearly loved to just walk into the office, metaphorically flip a switch and start coding on some form of utility platform, but that wasn't our world in mid 2005. However, platform was evolving and at some point in the future, it would become more of a commodity, even a utility. In much the same way that compute would at some point become a utility. This was a subject that we had discussed at Euro Foo in 2004, and within our own company, we had already created a system known as the Borg, which provided virtual machines on demand. It would only take a small leap from that to the compute utilities described by Douglas Parkhill in his 1966 book, "The Challenge of the Computer Utility".

Climatic pattern: Characteristics change

Organisations consist of value chains that are comprised of components that are evolving from genesis to more of a commodity. It sounds fairly basic stuff but it has profound effects because that journey of evolution involves changing characteristics. For example, let us take the genesis of computer infrastructure and wind the clock back to 1943 and the Z3, the first digital computer. The activity was scarce, it was poorly understood and we were still in the process of discovering what a digital computer could do. The act was uncertain as we had little idea of what it could lead to and, as such, it was unpredictable and rapidly changing. But this activity had the potential to make a difference; it was a source of differential value and competitive advantage. There was however no firm market to speak of; any customers were on as much of a journey of exploration as the suppliers.

Computing infrastructure did turn out to be useful and it started to spread. Custom-built systems such as LEO (Lyons Electronic Office) were built and eventually products released (such as the IBM 650) with diffusion of ever more functionally complete systems. By 2005, computing infrastructure was starting to become treated as a commodity, with racks of fairly standardised servers. It was increasingly commonplace and its purpose and use was well understood by a large number of people. We were already starting to think less about what a digital computer could do and instead on what we could do with vast numbers of fairly standardised units. In our Borg system, we had even abstracted away the concept of the physical machine to virtual ones, which we created and discarded with abandon.

This change of relationship was not unfamiliar to me as I ran an online photo service and could clearly see the same impacts happening with images. As the industry evolved from photo film to digital images then the behaviour of the user was slowly altering in front of us. In the past, every single photo taken was precious and it required some effort, including a trip to a photo processing lab. Accidentally taking a shot with the camera lens cap on was met with sighs of disappointment due to the waste of film, the effort of trying to set up that good shot, and the inevitable wasted print from the lab. However, the format had become a more digital commodity and so users increasingly took many shots and discarded unwanted ones regularly. The idea of taking and throwing away images with abandon was no longer waste but an expected consequence of taking thousands of them. Ditto virtual machines.

The use of computing infrastructure was also not seen as a differential between companies but instead more of a cost of doing business. Whilst in the very early days, you might have had a press announcement with a CEO that this or that company had bought their first computer; those days were long gone. Even the days where our system admins would take care in picking names for our servers, such as famous sci-fi characters or places, were disappearing. These servers were no longer pets; they were becoming cattle.

The market itself was becoming more predictable; customer demands for large volumes of more economically efficient units. This single activity had evolved from rare to commonplace, from poorly understood to well defined, from competitive advantage to cost of doing business, from rapidly changing to standardised. Everything evolves from that more uncharted and unexplored space of being rare, constantly changing and poorly understood to eventually industrialised forms that are commonplace, standardised and a cost of doing business. What happened with computers and images had happened with electricity, the nut and bolt and Penicillin — the once marvel drug that became a generic. However, this assumes survival and though everything evolves, not everything survives. Given a presumption of survival then the progression and change of characteristics is shown in Figure 21, on which I've also marked the domains of the uncharted and the industrialised.

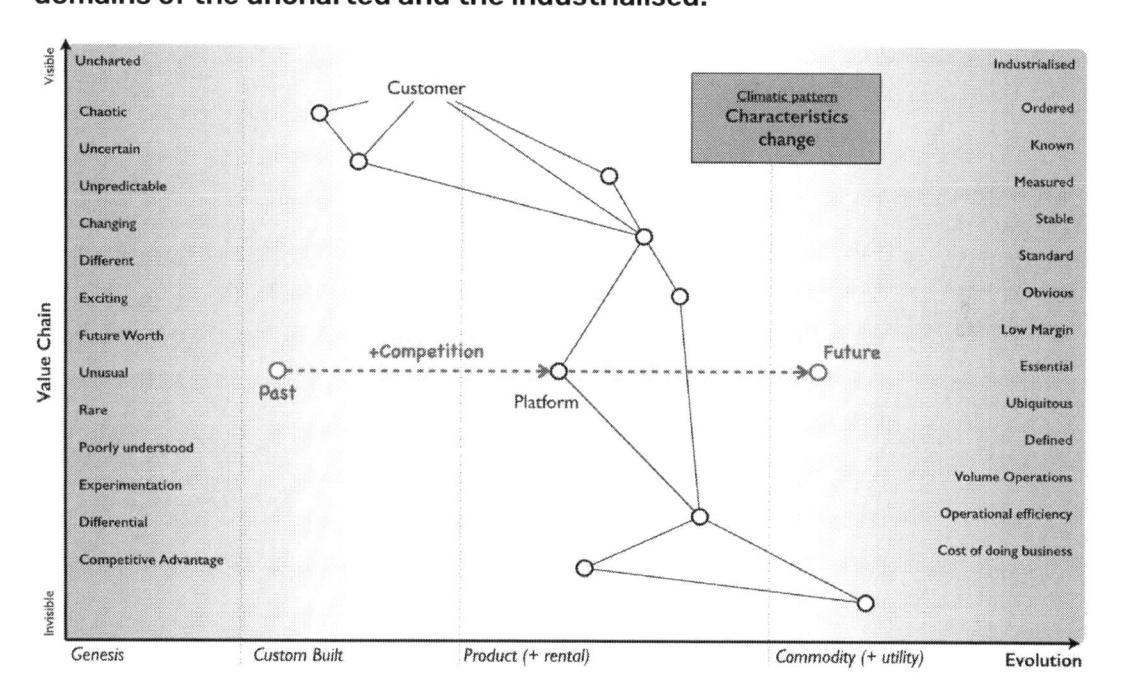

Figure 21: Characteristics change

Since this change is common for all components then I was able to collect a list of characteristics in order to produce the cheat sheet previously shown in Figure 17 (Chapter 2). Now, you might argue that this is circular because I'm stating the extremes are different using a map that is built with a cheat sheet that assumes that the extremes are different. This is a perfectly reasonable challenge and one that requires me to explain how that evolution axis was created. That subject is an entire chapter of this book, and if you wish, you should skip ahead to read it (Chapter 7 — Finding a new purpose). For the time being, it is enough to know that all your components evolve due to competition and as they do so, their characteristics change from the uncharted to the industrialised. You cannot stop them evolving if competition exists around them.

Climatic pattern: No one size fits all

Every large system, whether a line of business, a nation state or a specific IT project, contains multiple components. Those components have a relationship with each other but they're also evolving. As they evolve, their characteristics change from one extreme to another, from the uncharted to the industrialised domain. In order to survive and compete against others, you need to manage both of these extremes. You cannot afford to be building your own Thomas Thwaites toaster when a commodity form exists. You cannot hope to compete against Uber by focusing on a range of custom-built tyres for your taxis to use.

With any business, you need to encourage coherence, coordination, efficiency and stability when dealing with the industrialised domain. However, the exploration and discovery of new capabilities in the uncharted domain requires you to abandon these erstwhile virtues for experimentation. Any structure, whether a company or a team, needs to manage both of these polar opposites. This is known as the Innovation Paradox of Salaman & Storey, 2002. Alas, as I discovered in 2005, the story is even more complex than this because you also have components that are evolving between the extremes and these transitional components have a different set of characteristics and require a third mechanism of management.

The uncharted space is where no-one knows what is wanted, which forces us to explore and experiment. Change is the norm here and any method that you use must enable and reduce the cost of change. In this part of the map, I tend to use an Agile approach that has been cut right back to the core principles; a very lightweight version of XP or SCRUM.

Of course, as a component evolves and we start to understand it more, then our focus changes. Sometime during the stage of custom built, we switch and start to think about creating a product. Whilst we may continue to use underlying techniques such as XP or SCRUM, our focus is now on reducing waste, improving measurements, learning and creating that first minimal viable product. We start to add artefacts to our methodology and the activity has more permanence about it as it undergoes this transition. We've stopped exploring the uncharted space and started concentrating on what we've found. Today, Lean tends to rule the waves here, though back in 2005, we were struggling to find something appropriate. The component however will continue to evolve, becoming more widespread and defined as it approaches the domain of industrialised volume operations. Our focus again switches, but this time to mass production of good enough, which means reducing deviation. At this point, Six Sigma, along with formalised frameworks such as ITIL, then start to rule the waves. Any significant system will have components at different stages of evolution. At any one moment in time, there is no single method that will fit all.

Unfortunately, most companies have no map of their environment. They are unaware of these climatic patterns other than in a vague sense, and so they tend to plummet for a one size fits all method. The arguments are usually supported by some sort of outcome bias, i.e. this method worked well for this particular project and hence, it is assumed that it works well for every project. All of these project methods have their devotees and so regular arguments of agile vs lean, lean vs Six Sigma or agile vs Six Sigma break out, along with finger wagging at failed examples of the "other approach". This is usually defended against with counter accusations and claims that the approach was not used in the right way.

Invariably, there are endless attempts to create a new magic one size fits all method by trying to make a single approach all-encompassing or marrying together different stages, e.g. lean Six Sigma or agile lean or prince agile. This has been going on in one guise or another for a considerable amount of time, and I have little doubt it will continue until people come to terms with the simple issue that there's no one size fits all. For reference, I've shown the suitability of project methodologies with evolution in Figure 22.

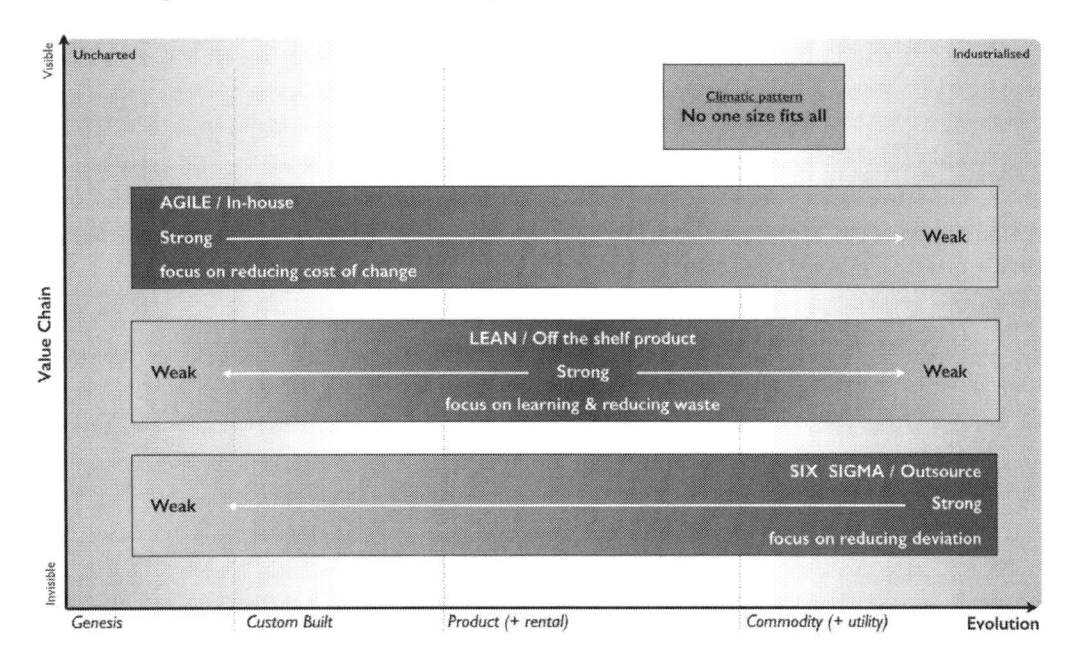

Figure 22: No one size fits all

But this is not just a project methodology issue; it applies to other fields. Purchasing requires a use of a VC (venture capital) based approach in genesis, switching to more outcome and COTS based approach during transition and then more unit based approaches during the industrialised domain. Hence, any large system, whether a company or even a government, needs to use multiple purchasing methods as appropriate. Equally, genesis is more suited to in-house development, whereas the industrialised can be safely outsourced. Even the approaches to budgeting are vastly different from investment accounting to product P&Ls to activity based cost control. Whether it's finance or IT or marketing, there is no single magic method.

Climatic pattern: Efficiency enables innovation

The story of evolution is complicated by the issue that components not only evolve but enable new higher order systems to appear. Standardised electricity supply paved the way for all manner of things, from televisions to computing. These things in turn have evolved. Genesis begets evolution begets genesis.

In the Theory of Hierarchy, Herbert Simon showed how the creation of a system is dependent upon the organisation of its subsystems. As an activity becomes industrialised and provided as ever more standardised and commodity components, it not only allows for increasing speed of implementation but also rapid change, diversity and agility of systems that are built upon it. In other words, it's faster to build a house with commodity components such as bricks, wooden planks and plastic pipes than it is to start from first principles with a clay pit, a clump of trees and an oil well. The same phenomenon occurs in biology, i.e. the rapid growth in higher organisms and the diversity of life is a function of the underlying components. The simplicity of standard building blocks allows higher orders of complexity. But those standard building blocks didn't appear out of nowhere; they started as something novel and they evolved. Genesis begets evolution begets genesis.

This doesn't mean that change stops with the standard components. Take, for example, brick making or electricity provision or the manufacture of windows; there is still a significant amount of improvement hidden behind the "standard" interface. However, the "standard" acts as an abstraction layer to this change. Just because my electricity supplier has introduced new sources of power generation (wind turbine, geothermal), doesn't mean I wake up one morning to find that we're moving from 240V 50Hz to something else and I have to rewire the house. If that constant operational improvement in electricity generation was not abstracted then all the consumer electronics built upon this would need to continuously change — the entire system would either collapse in a mess or at the very least, technological progress would be hampered. It's no different again with biology. If there weren't underlying components from DNA to RNA messaging to transcription to translation to even basic cell structures within more complex organisms, then you and I would never have appeared in the time frame.

Now, as a component evolves to a more standard, good enough commodity then to a consumer, any improvement becomes increasingly hidden behind the interface. Any changes are ultimately reflected as more efficiency or a better price or quality of service, but the activity itself for all sense of purpose will remain as is, e.g. a standard but cheaper brick or power supply or wooden plank. There are exceptions to this but it usually involves significant upheaval due to all the higher order systems that need to change and hence, government involvement is often required, e.g. changing electricity standards, changing currency or even simply switching from analogue to digital transmission of TV.

Hence, activities evolve to become more industrialised and those commodities (or utilities) enable higher order systems that consume them and any operational improvement to the component is increasingly hidden behind its interface. Change can happen but it's costly and ultimately, we aim to reduce all forms of deviation.

For example, electricity generation appeared in the past and then evolved through competition becoming more industrialised. This in turn through componentisation effects enabled higher order systems such as computing, which enabled new industries serving new user needs. Computing in turn evolved through competition, enabling the creation of novel higher order systems such as databases, which enabled new industries. And so the process continues until the modern day where we have intelligent machine agents. I've summarised this in Figure 23, adding a line of the present (i.e. where we are today), but also highlighting the past (where we were) and adding the fairly obvious anticipation that intelligent agents will themselves become commodity like (where we will be). Without a long history of more industrialised forms offering highly efficient components for once magical wonders, then I would never have had the ability nor the capital to write this story on a digital computer in a word processor.

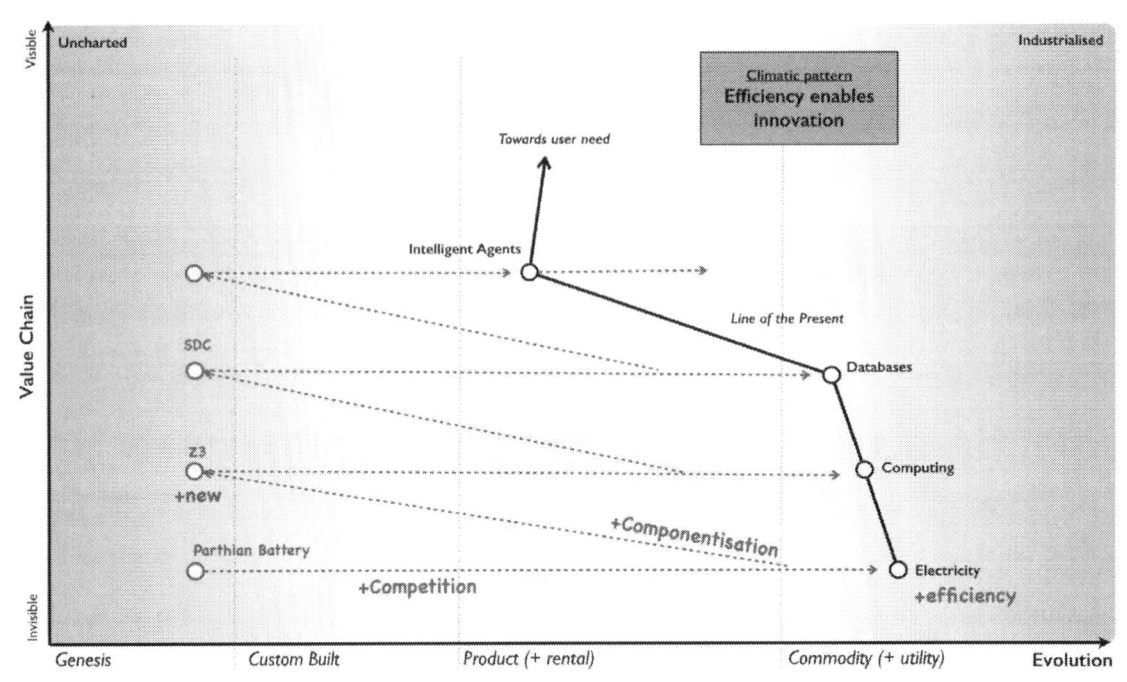

Figure 23: Efficiency enables innovation

In the above map, I've reduced the actual number of the components for the reason of simplicity. Obviously, not everything becomes a component of something else, but mechanical, electrical and even IT systems commonly do. IT is no exception to the effects of evolution and componentisation. The modern day phenomenon of cloud computing represents the evolution of many IT activities, from product to utility services and the provision of good enough, standard components is causing a rapid rate of development of higher order systems and activities. Many services we consume, from Netflix to DropBox, are unlikely to have been practical without commodity and utility computing infrastructure. However, the story of evolution doesn't simply stop at efficiency and the consequential enablement in building higher order systems. It also has an impact on value.

Climatic pattern: Higher order systems create new sources of worth

An idea is something with social value and it is the implementation of that idea as a new act, which can create economic value when that act is useful. This process of transformation from social to economic value is known as commodification. It describes a modification of relationships, formerly untainted by commerce, into commercial relationships.

As that activity evolves, various iterations of it will diffuse throughout society and the activity will become more common in its market. Eventually, these goods or services that have economic value become indistinguishable in terms of attributes (uniqueness or brand) in the eyes of the market. This evolution is the movement of a market from differentiated to undifferentiated price competition and from monopolistic to perfect competition, where the differential benefit of the act reduces towards zero. This is the process of commoditisation.

I specifically use two different terms — commodification and commoditisation — to describe these two very different changes. They are not the same; try not to confuse them.

At the same time that the differential benefit of a component declines, it also becomes more of a necessity and a cost of doing business. For example, the once wonder and differential of telephony has become a necessity for most. This creates a situation where the unit value of something may be declining but the total revenue generated is increasing due to volume. Alongside this, we also see the cost of production of each unit change as it evolves. For example, the cost of production per unit for a standard phone is vastly less today than the cost of production of the first ever phones. As a result, the transitional domain (i.e. the time of products) between the extremes of the uncharted and the industrialised also tends to be associated with the most profitable in an industry. This wealth generation is due to a combination of high unit value, increasing volume and declining production costs. As a rule of thumb:-

The **uncharted** domain is associated with high production costs, high levels of uncertainty but potentially very high future opportunity. Being first is not always the best option, due to the burden and risks of research and development.

The **transitional** domain is associated with reducing uncertainty, declining production costs, increasing volumes and highest profitability. However, whilst the environment has become more predictable, the future opportunity is also in decline as the act is becoming more widespread, well understood and well defined. So at the same time we reach the zenith of wealth creation, the future is looking decidedly less rosy for the industry itself.

The industrialised domain is associated with high certainty, high levels of predictability, high volumes, low production costs and low unit margin. The activity is not seen as a differential but an expected norm; it has become commonplace. Those activities that have evolved to this state (e.g. nuts and bolts) are seen as having a minimal differential effect. They are not associated with high future opportunity, except in early stage replacement of any existing product industry. Their future is seen as one of stable and increasingly low margin revenues that may nevertheless be significant due to volume.

However, along with this change of value, the more industrialised components enable new higher order systems. These systems are themselves future sources of worth and wealth generation. Hence, as electricity became more of a utility, it enabled new sources of future worth such as television, computing and radio, which then evolved to become significant. The downside is those higher order systems are uncertain, and without a crystal ball then you do not know which will be successful. Standard electricity supply enabled all manner of novel things, which took a one-way trip to the dustbin, from Thomas Edison's electric pen to Gaugler's refrigerating blanket. Before you laugh, the idea of people sitting in front of a box to watch moving pictures probably sounded more ridiculous than a blanket that keeps you cool on a warm night. We have the benefit of hindsight.

Though we cannot say what new higher orders systems will become sources of significant wealth generation, we can say that higher order systems create new sources of worth — Figure 24.

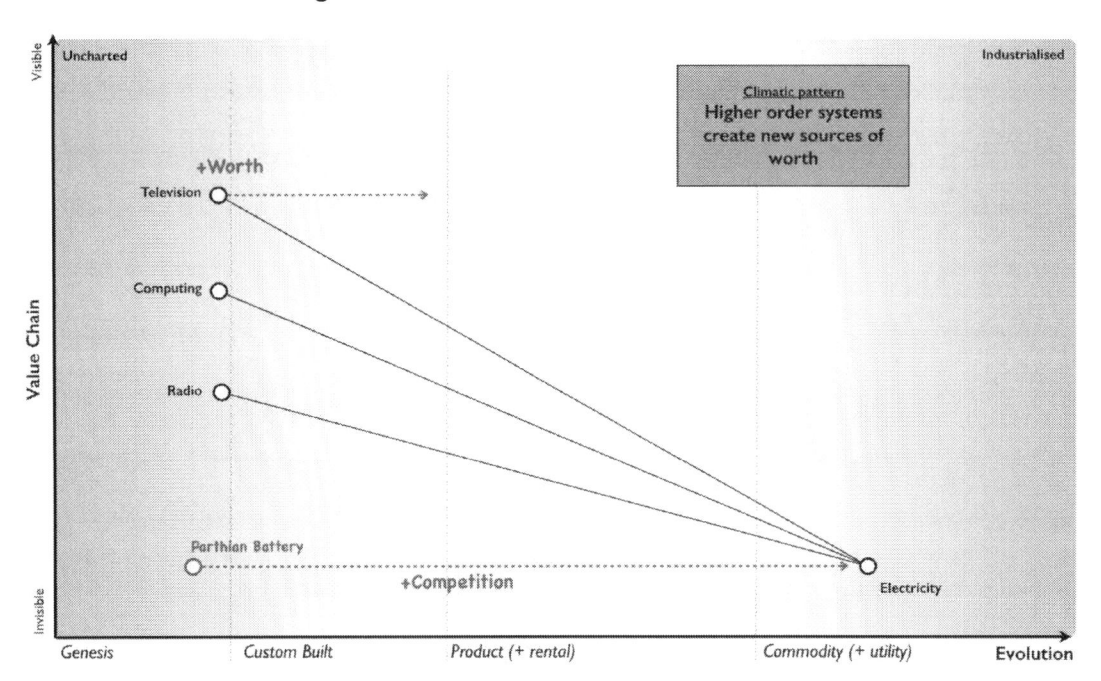

Figure 24: Higher order systems create new sources of worth

Climatic pattern: No choice on evolution

As components within your value chain evolve then unless you can form some sort of cartel and prevent any new entrants, some competitors will adapt to use it, whether utility computing, standard mechanical components, bricks or electricity. The benefits of efficiency, faster creation of higher order systems, along with new potential sources of worth will create pressure on others to adapt. As more adopt the evolved components then the pressure on those who remain in the "old world" increases until it is overwhelming. In Figure 25, a company (in grey) adapts creating pressure on all the others to adapt. As more adapt, the pressure on the remaining companies increases.

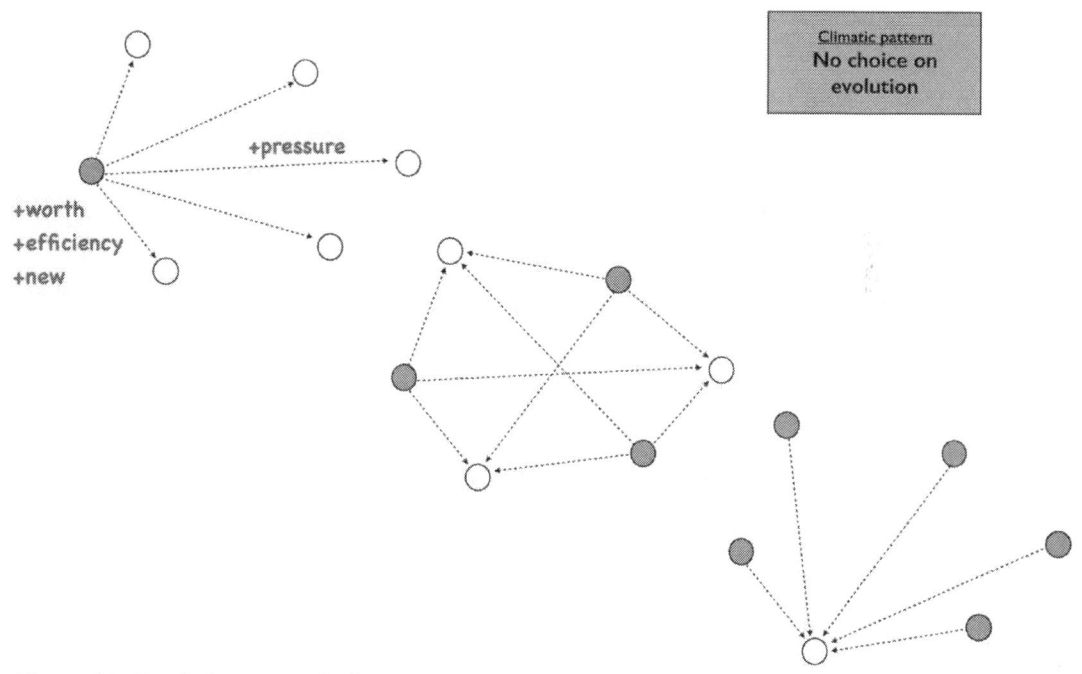

Figure 25: No choice on evolution

This effect is known as Van Valen's "Red Queen Hypothesis" and it is the reason why we don't see your average company building its own generators from scratch to supply their own electricity. There exists a secondary impact of the Red Queen, which is it limits one organisation (or in biology, one organism) from taking over the entire environment in a runaway process. If, for example, only Ford had ever introduced mass production with every other good being entirely hand-made then not only would every car be a Ford today but so would every TV, every radio and every computer. However, those practices spread and other industries adapted, hence the advantage that Ford created was diminished.

Climatic pattern: Past success breeds inertia

The Red Queen might force organisations to adapt, but this process is rarely smooth — the problem is past success. For example, let us take a component evolving from product to more of a utility and let us assume that you are a supplier of that product. As mentioned in the above section on worth, the transitional domain (i.e. the time of products) is associated with the highest profitability for an industry. Despite any pressure to adapt, you and your industry are likely to resist its industrialisation and your enjoyment of such wealth creation. You want to stay exactly where you are. This resistance to movement is known as inertia — see Figure 26. Both consumers and suppliers exhibit various forms of inertia due to past success in either supplying or using a product.

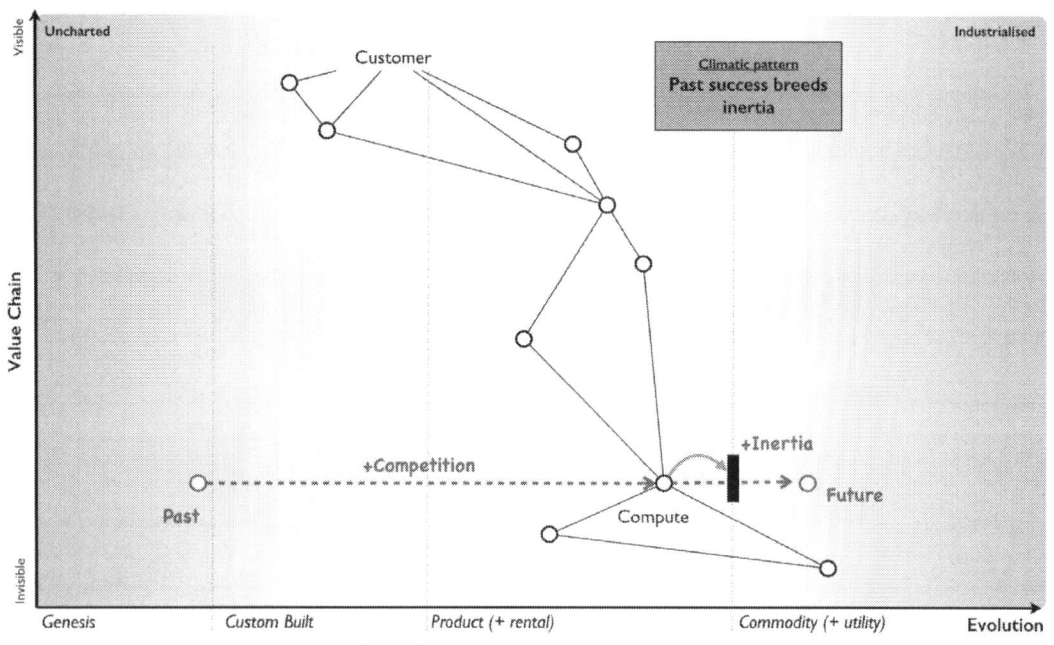

Figure 26: Past success breeds inertia

It is almost always new entrants who are not encumbered by past success that initiate the change. Whilst VMware CEO Pat Gelsinger might state that Amazon as a "company that sells books" shouldn't beat VMware and its partners in infrastructure provision, it is precisely because Amazon was not encumbered by an existing business model that it could so easily industrialise the computing infrastructure space.

Naturally, the initial reaction to the change is sceptical, despite any latent frustrations of consumers with the costs associated with past models. However, some consumers — usually new entrants themselves entering into other industries — start to adopt the more evolved components because of the benefits of efficiency, agility and ability to build higher order systems of value. The Red Queen kicks in, pressure mounts for others to adopt, and what started with a trickle suddenly becomes a raging flood. The resistance to change of existing suppliers will still continue until it has become abundantly clear that the past model is going to decline. Unfortunately for those suppliers, by the time this happens, it is often too late as the new entrants have dominated the future market. Many past giants don't survive. This process of new entrants, a trickle of adoption becoming a flood, and slow moving past giants due to inertia is common in history.

Categorising climatic patterns

We've now covered in a very superficial way some basic climatic patterns. As we journey through this book, we will iterate around the strategy cycle and revisit them, refining as we go along and adding new patterns. It's worth knowing that there are many economic patterns, but I wanted to provide enough for now that we could start to explore our first map.

In Figure 27, I've provided a list of the common economic patterns that we will cover in this book. Those marked in grey, we've just skimmed over. I've also categorised these patterns into whether they mainly influence:-

- how we deal with components
- financial aspects of the company
- the speed of change
- resistance to change (inertia)
- the impact of competitors
- our ability to predict

Components	Everything evolves through supply and demand competition	Rates of evolution can vary by ecosystem *(e.g. consumer vs industrial)*	Characteristics change as components evolve *(Salaman & Storey)*	No choice over evolution *(Red Queen)*
	No single method fits all *(e.g. in development or purchasing)*	Components can co-evolve *(e.g. practice with activity)*	Evolution consists of multiple waves of diffusion with many chasms.	
Financial	Higher order systems create new sources of value	Efficiency does not mean a reduced spend *(Jevon's Paradox)*	Capital flows to new areas of value	Creative Destruction *(Joseph Schumpeter)*
	Future value is inversely proportional to the certainty we have over it.	Evolution to higher order systems results in increasing local order and energy consumption		
Speed	Efficiency enables innovation	Evolution of communication mechanisms can increase the speed of evolution overall and the diffusion of a single example of change	Increased stability of lower order systems increases agility & speed of re-combination	Change is not always linear (discontinuous & exponential change exists)
	Shifts from product to utility tend to demonstrate a punctuated equilibrium			
Inertia	Success breeds inertia	Inertia can kill an organisation	Inertia increases the more successful the past model is	
Competitors	Competitors actions will change the game	Most competitors have poor situational awareness		
Prediction	Not everything is random *(p[what] vs p[when])*	Economy has cycles *(peace, war and wonder)*	Two different forms of disruption *(predictable vs non-predictable)*	A "war" (point of industrialisation) causes organisations to evolve
	You cannot measure evolution over time or adoption, you need to embrace uncertainty.	Evolution consists of multiple diffusion curves	The less evolved something is then the more uncertain it becomes	

Figure 27: Climatic patterns

Using climatic patterns

Now let us take the same step that I did back in 2005 and apply some of these basic patterns to my first map, which I've highlighted in red — see Figure 28.

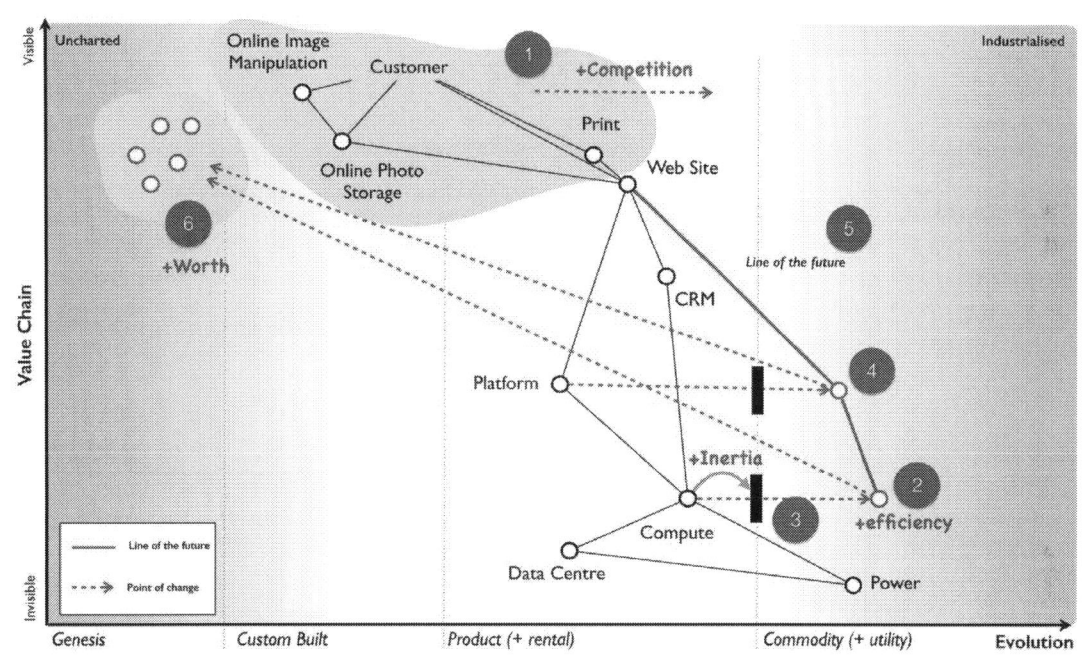

Figure 28: First map with patterns

So back in 2005, I was able to anticipate that:-

Point 1 — Our online photo service was moving more into the product stage of wealth generation. What this meant was it was going to become much easier for others to create a competing service around online photos and there were likely to be some big players in the space. This was already happening and our diversified focus might have enabled us to "survive" but we were rapidly falling behind competitors. We were doing well because everyone was doing well, but on a relative basis, we were small fry, and unless we refocused here, it wasn't going to get better. We needed to either invest or find some new angle and some new differentiator. However, I had to be mindful of the fact that we lacked the financial muscle of others and any investment in something novel would be a gamble.

Point 2 — Compute was likely to become more of a utility. I didn't know quite when but I had signals that this transformation was going to happen soon, especially given a company like ours could create our own internal private utility (or what is now called a private Cloud). Compute was a massive industry with huge profitability and revenues. Someone was likely to attack it. That someone would not be encumbered by an existing product or rental model. I honestly expected it was going to be Google, but it was Amazon that moved quickly.

Point 3 — There would be resistance to the change (i.e. inertia) of compute becoming a utility. That inertia would exist in both suppliers of hardware and rental services, along with their customers. Regardless, that component was going to evolve and companies would be under pressure to adopt. The first movers would likely consist of unencumbered companies, e.g. startups.

Point 4 — What was going to happen to compute was going to happen to coding platforms. This was another area that there was considerable revenue and profitability to attack. All those "yak shaving" tasks (a term used to describe an unpleasant and unnecessarily repeated activity) such as configuration, setup and installation would disappear. We were going to enter a future world where I could just code and deploy.

Point 5 — These utility coding platforms would eventually run on utility compute environments. We could anticipate a "line of the future" where the relationships between components remained the same but the manner in which they were provided differed.

Point 6 — The transition from product to utility for both compute and platform was going to enable all sorts of novel higher order systems to be created rapidly. I have no idea what these would be, but within them, there would exist many new sources of worth, along with many more failed efforts. Everything novel is a gamble.

I sat in the boardroom looking at the huge map that I had created with James' help. It was far more complex than the simplified version above and used slightly different terms for evolution. What was noticeable was for the first time in my business life then, I was able to have a conversation about what we thought was going to change, without resorting to popular memes and hand waving. Had you been in that room, you might have disagreed with how we had positioned the pieces or the patterns we saw, but at least we could have had a good discussion about this. Our assumptions were visibly on the map not locked away in our minds. We had a common language through which we could use to discuss the future and collaborate over.

It felt exciting but also nerve-wracking. We were talking about fundamental changes to the computing industry staring us in the face with what seemed like blinding obviousness. I had a visual means of demonstrating what Nicholas Carr had described in his exceptional 2003 paper on "Does IT Matter?". As it happens, I was a huge fan of that paper and his subsequent prophetic book and had gotten into many an argument over it in those years. Most of my peers when I mentioned what I thought were amazing ideas had roundly ridiculed them. Compute, it seemed, was considered a relationship business; it was all about trust and I didn't know what I was talking about. I disagreed. One part of this confusion was that people had taken Carr's book to mean all IT at the same time would industrialise. It was obvious from the map that parts would, at different times, and this would enable new things to be built.

Of course, what I now know is that I was only at the beginning of my journey. The rabbit hole gets much deeper. However, climatic patterns were a start, and though I could apparently anticipate certain changes, I had no idea if any of this was actually right. I could easily be deluding myself and it certainly felt that I was going against popular opinion. But at the very least, I could discuss it and have those conversations. Undaunted, I decided to carry on. My attention now turned to that next factor, which is doctrine.

An exercise for the reader

In Chapter 2, I asked you to have a go at mapping something. Well, take that map, look at the common climatic patterns described in Figure 27 and have a go at applying them to your map. See what you can anticipate. It helps to get others involved as mapping is fundamentally a communication and learning tool and the best results come from collaborating with others. If you're mapping an aspect of your company then try and find someone with a different skill-set to yourself, i.e. if you're in finance, go grab someone from IT or operations or marketing.

Chapter 4 – Doctrine

I had created my first map and applied an understanding of some basic climatic patterns that might influence it. These patterns were the ones that I could not stop but I could anticipate. Whether I liked it or not, the components on my map would evolve through the actions of the market. However, whilst I had no choice over the market, that didn't mean I had no choice over my actions. I might be able to influence the landscape through action; I could decide how I organised myself, the principles that I emphasised within the company, and our manner of operating.

Some of my choices might be context specific, i.e. a decision to flank an opponent requires an opponent to be in a known position. This doesn't mean that everything is context specific. There could exist in business generally useful principles that everyone should apply. These principles are doctrine and in this chapter, we're going to examine that part of my journey — see Figure 29 on the next page.

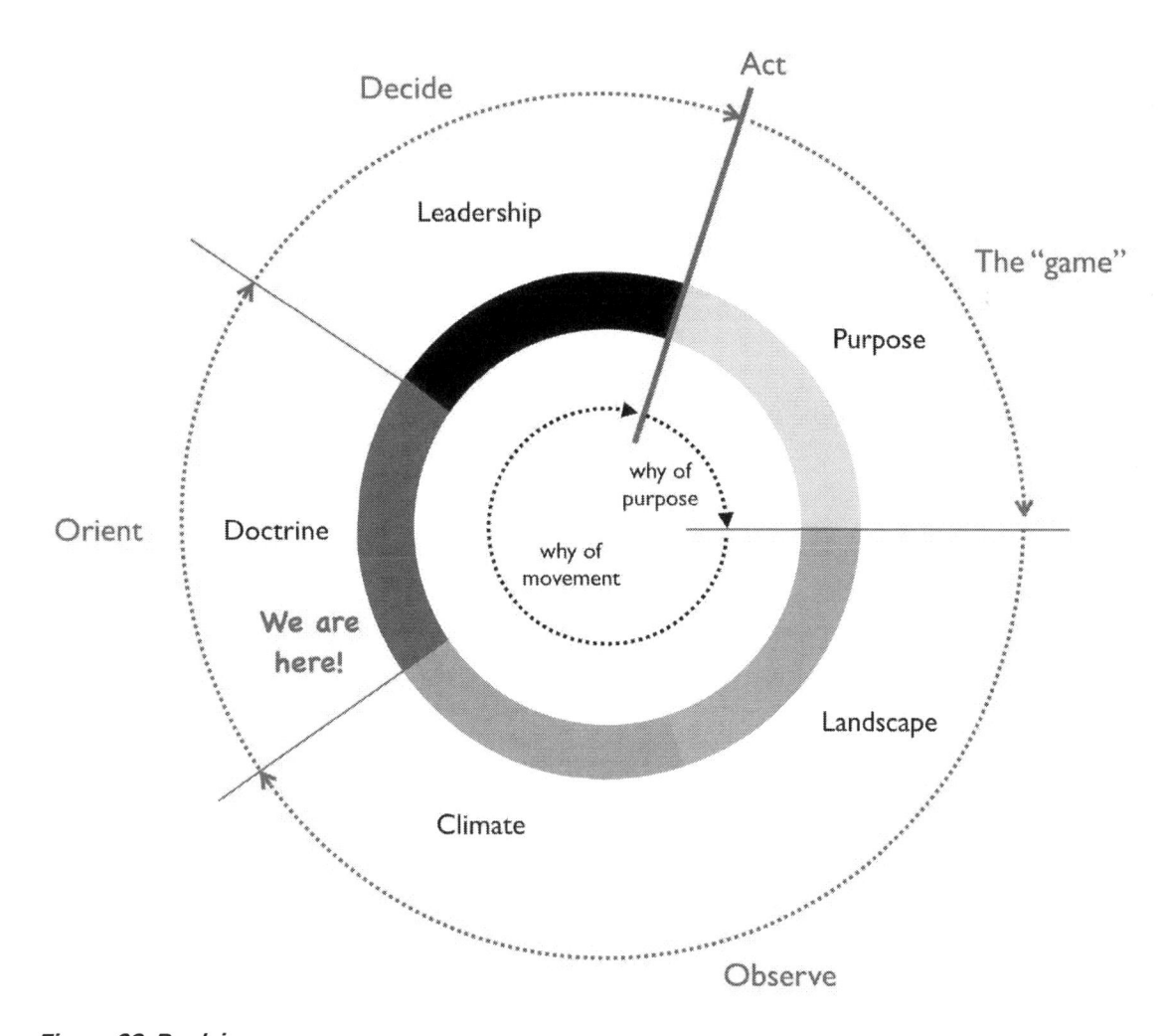

Figure 29: Doctrine

Learning doctrine

Doctrine are the basic universal principles that are applicable to all industries, regardless of the landscape and its context. This doesn't mean that the doctrine is right but instead, that it appears to be consistently useful for the time being. There will always exist better doctrine in the future. As with climatic patterns, we will go through some basic forms and refine in future passes through the strategy cycle.

Doctrine: Focus on user need

Any value we create is through meeting the needs of others. Even our ability to understand our environment by creating a map requires us to first define the user need, as it is the anchor for the entire map — see Figure 30. Alas, a mantra of "not sucking as much as the competitors", whilst rarely explicitly stated, is surprisingly common. An alternative mantra is "we must be the best we can", but to do that, we must understand what it is we need to be. Despite this, the usual response I receive when asking a company or a specific project to explain its user needs is a blank stare. I have seen many large projects in excess of $100M with endless specification documents where the scale of spending and paperwork is only matched by the inability of the group to explain what the user actually needs.

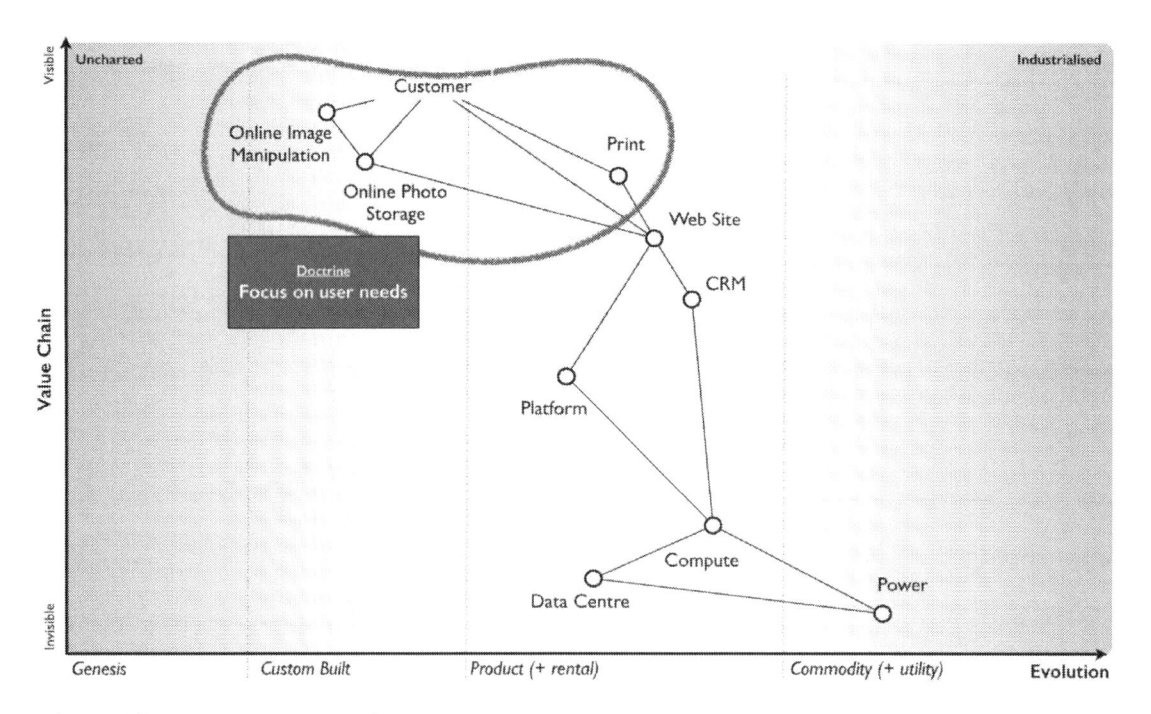

Figure 30: Focus on user needs

It should be obvious that failing to meet the needs of your users, especially when competitors do manage to achieve this, is a bad idea. There is a conceit here in the assumption that your competitors will try to achieve this. If you're operating in a market where everyone ignores user needs or better still, tells users what they want (regardless of needs) then no-one gains an advantage.

But how do we work out those user needs? This is extremely tricky because we bring our own biases to the table. The first thing to do is to understand what users are we talking about — your customers, the regulators of your industry, your shareholders, your employees, or even your own business? If you're talking about customers then you need to focus on their needs, not your business needs, i.e. you might need to make revenue and profit but that is NOT your customers' need. By meeting the needs of your customers then you should aim to satisfy your business needs to make revenue and profit, not the other way around.

But surely I should focus on my business first! This is a topic known as flow, which we will cover later. When you look at a map, each component represents a store of capital (whether physical, financial or otherwise). The lines between components represent capital flows from one component to another. If you think about a business then you want a flow of capital (in this case, revenue) from customers to yourself. To do this, you're going to have to meet their needs because they're unlikely to give you money for nothing. Unless you're operating in a bizarre market where everyone ignores the customer or you tell the customer what they want.

Due to this flow then the best way I've found for determining user needs is to start by looking at the transactions that an organisation makes with them. This will tend to give you an idea of what it provides and what is important. The next step is to examine the customer journey when interacting with those transactions. By questioning this journey and talking with customers, you will often find pointless steps or unmet needs or unnecessary needs being catered for. Another mechanism I've also found to be exceptionally useful, especially when your users are in fact other corporations, is to go and map out their landscape. In most cases, I find these users have a poor idea of what they actually need. If you're a supplier to such a company then discussions tend to degenerate to things they want and things they think are necessary, rather than things they need. By mapping out their landscape, you can often clarify what is really needed, along with finding entire new opportunities for business.

Discussion and data collection are a key part of determining user needs, and so talk with them and talk with experts in the field. However, there is a gotcha. In many cases, they turn out to be both wrong! Gasp! What do you mean they're wrong? There are two important areas where the users and the experts are usually wrong in describing their own needs. By happenstance, both are crucial for strategic gameplay.

The first area is when a component is moving between stages of evolution, e.g. when something shifts from custom built to product or, more importantly, from product to commodity (+utility). The problem is that the pre-existing installed base causes inertia to the change. Invariably, users will be fixated on a legacy world and hence, they will have a bias towards it. This is the equivalent to a user saying to Henry Ford, "we don't want a car; we want a faster horse!" The bias is caused by a climatic pattern known as coevolution, but for the time being, you simply need to be wary of the legacy mindset.

The second area to note is that of the uncharted domain. These needs are both rare and highly uncertain, and this means you're going to have to gamble. There is no consistent way of determining what the user actually needs with something novel because they don't know themselves. Hence, be prepared to pivot. You might think you're building a machine that will stop all wars (the Wright Brothers' original concept for the airplane), but others will find alternative uses — the fighter plane, the bomber.

When it comes to dealing with needs then there are three different approaches according to the domains of uncharted, transitional and industrialised. In the uncharted domain, you have to gamble. Users and experts don't actually know what is needed beyond vague hand waving. In the transitional domain, you have to listen. Users and experts can guide you to what they need. In the early days of the industrialised domain then you have to be mindful of users and experts' bias caused by the inertia of past success. You already know what is needed but it has to be provided on a volume operations and good enough basis.

Doctrine: Use a common language

Instead of using multiple different ways of explaining the same thing between different functions of the company, then try to use one, e.g. a map. If you're using business process diagrams on one side and IT systems diagrams on another, you'll end up with translation errors, misalignment and confusion. Collaboration is important but it's very difficult to achieve if one group is speaking Klingon and the other Elvish, and let's face it, Finance is Klingon to IT and IT is generally Elvish to Finance. This is why companies often value people skilled in multiple areas who act as translators. But a soldier doesn't need to know how to operate a boat to work with someone from the Navy, nor does a sailor need to know how to operate a mortar to work with the Army. They use maps to collaborate and coordinate. The problem in business is the lack of a common language, i.e. the lack of any form of mapping. If you can't map what you are doing then I recommend you hold back from acting and spend a few hours mapping it.

Doctrine: Be transparent

Sharing a map will enable others to challenge and question your assumptions. This is essential because it helps us to learn and refine our maps. The downside of sharing is it allows others to challenge and question your assumptions. Many people find this uncomfortable. As the CEO of the company, did I really want one of my juniors ripping apart my strategy using the map that I had created? Yes. I'd rather someone point out to me that our strategy involved walking an army through a minefield than let me discover this for myself. However, don't underestimate how difficult this transparency is within an organisation.

Doctrine: Challenge assumptions

There is little point in focusing on user needs, creating a common language through the use of a map and sharing it transparently in the organisation, if no-one is willing to challenge it. This act should be a duty for everyone in the company. I didn't care if it was my pet project, I needed people to openly and honestly tell me where they thought I was going wrong. This requires not only transparency but also trust. Any form of retribution or bias against someone for challenging is a deadly sin that will harm your company. As the CEO, I made my CFO the XO back in 2004. One of his duties was to challenge my choices and to encourage this sort of questioning.

Doctrine: Remove duplication and bias

You should not only share maps; you should collate them in an effort to remove duplication and bias, i.e. rebuilding the same thing or custom building that which is already a commodity. Mapping is itself an iterative process, and you've probably been making decisions for a long time without understanding the landscape. So you don't need to map the entire landscape to start making decisions, but rather think of maps as a guide that tells us more the more we use it.

With your first map, you can probably challenge whether we've adequately met user needs or maybe how we're treating components. As you collect more maps of different systems or lines of business then you start to discover the same component is on multiple maps. I've marked some examples in Figure 31 in green.

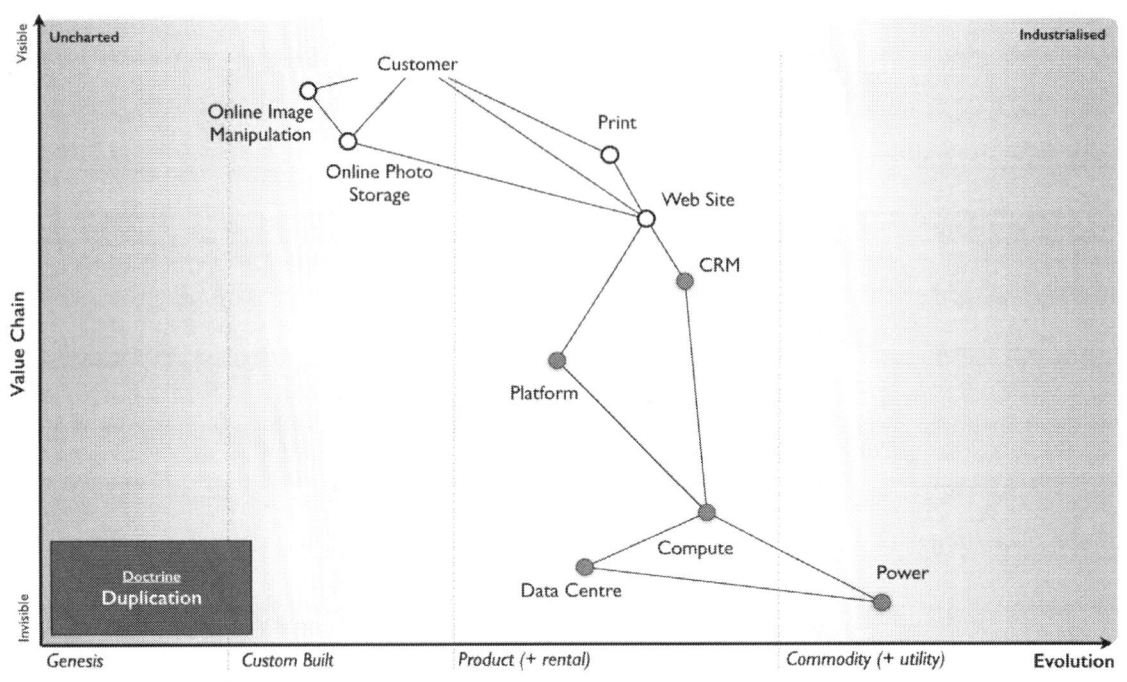

Figure 31: Duplication

Now, the same component being on different maps is fine except for when we're saying it's a different instance of that component. For example, if you have ten maps all with a database or call centre or print facility as a component then that's not necessarily a problem, but it might be if you're actually saying we have 10x different databases running on 10x different systems. There can be legitimate reasons for duplication, such as locality, but even then, you'd hope there would be 10x fairly standardised print facilities and not 10x highly customised.

In large organisations such as petrochemical or banking companies with committees of architects then you don't normally see duplication on a scale of tenfold. Instead, from experience, what I commonly find in a single global organisation built by acquisition with a federation of business units is more on the scale of a hundred fold. There is nothing quite like discovering 380x isolated teams custom-building 380x ERP systems to meet the same user needs with 380x different systems (a chemical company). The worst case example I have is an energy company that has a duplication in excess of 740x. That said, I'm now aware of a bank that might have even exceeded this with over 1,000 risk management systems. These days, I'm positively elated by meeting a large global organisation that has duplication down at the scale of tens or even units. Of course, be aware that most companies might claim this but in practice, they have no idea of what their duplication levels really are and significantly underestimate the problem.

One technique I find useful in helping to highlight this problem is to create a profile diagram. I simply collate maps together, identifying commonly described components, and then place them onto the profile. This gives me an idea of both duplication and bias. From the profile diagram below in Figure 32, the following points are noted:-

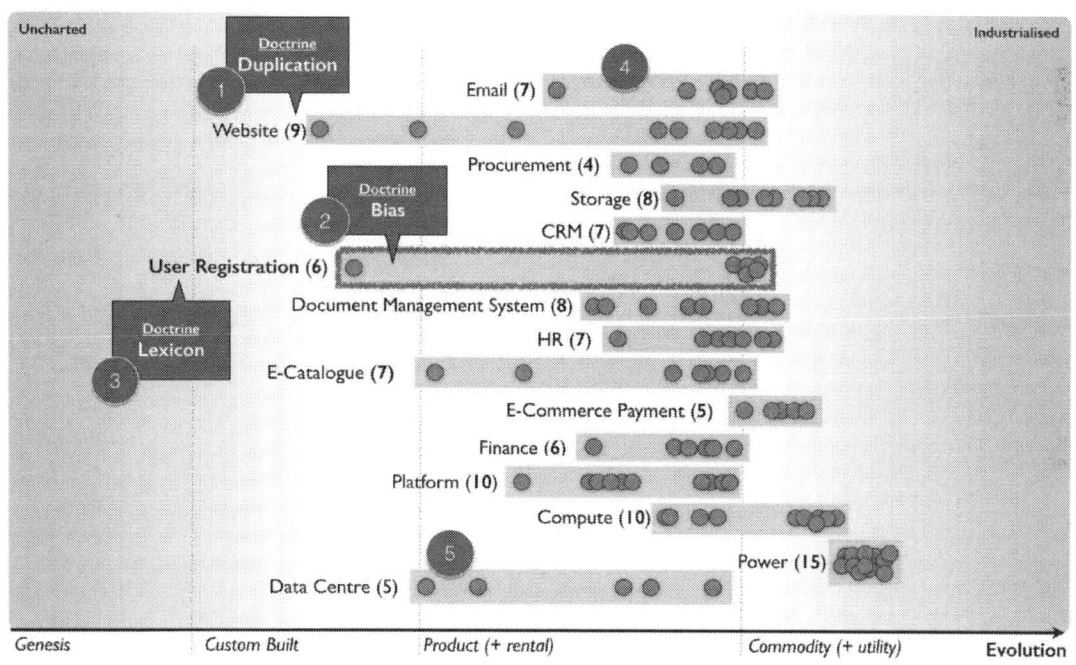

Figure 32: Profile

Point 1 — For each common component, you record how many times it is repeated. High numbers of repetition is not necessarily a problem as there may be a legitimate reason, or it could be the same component in different maps. In this case, our maps show seven references to websites.

Point 2 — Recording how evolved a component is can provide you with an idea of bias within the organisation. From above, there are six examples of user registration in the maps. One of which is distanced from the others. This could be because one group simply thought in their map that user registration was a unique activity (it isn't) or alternatively, you might have five groups using a common service and one group custom-building their own. In this case, they might have a legitimate reason, but it's worth the challenge.

Point 3 — Collating maps often helps in creating a common lexicon. The same thing is often described with different terms in a single organisation.

Point 4 — There are seven references to email within the maps. Hopefully (though alas not always the case) this refers to one email system used in different places. There is also some bias with most groups considering email to be more commodity but one group thinking it's an evolving product. This should probably set alarm bells ringing.

Point 5 — There are five references to data centres. Again, hopefully this refers to a couple built for specific geographical reasons. Alas, a popular sport in many large enterprises seems to be building data centres as though they're the first ones ever built. In the worst cases, I have been shown around a lovingly created data centre and then gone to the shop floor to find a sad, solitary rack standing in the middle of a large, empty hall. The rack invariably contains servers given loving names such as Seven, Janeway, Paris, Chakotay (all characters from Star Trek's Voyager series).

The maps and the profile are simply guides to help you remove duplication and bias. This is a necessity for efficient operations. However, duplication should not be solely considered as a financial cost because it impacts our ability to develop more complex capabilities. In the case of the bank with 1,000 risk management systems, then one of the problems it is facing is its ability to get anything released.

Another technique I find useful in a dispersed structure is to determine what capabilities we need as a group. For example, in Figure 33, a map is provided that explicitly highlights both the customer journey and the associated capabilities. I've derived this map from a real world example used by the Methods Group. In this map, the customer journey (described as service patterns) is more clearly highlighted and we're focusing not only on the technology required to meet higher order system needs but also those higher order systems, e.g. manage call, determine sponsorship. For reasons of confidentiality, I've changed and removed many of the terms.

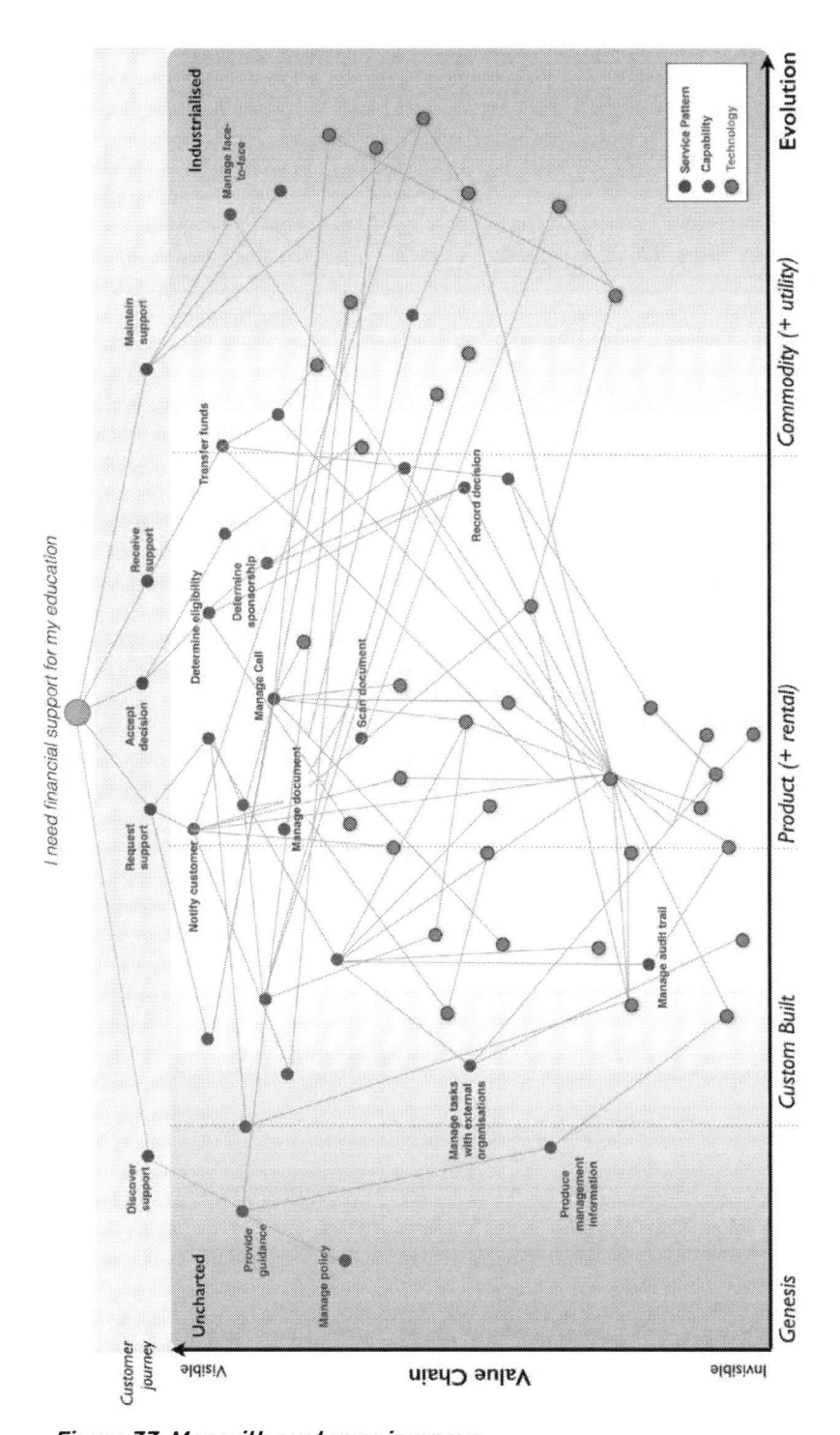

Figure 33: Map with customer journeys

By aggregating many of these maps together, you can develop a picture of what the company actually does and what its existing capabilities are through a capability profile — see Figure 34.

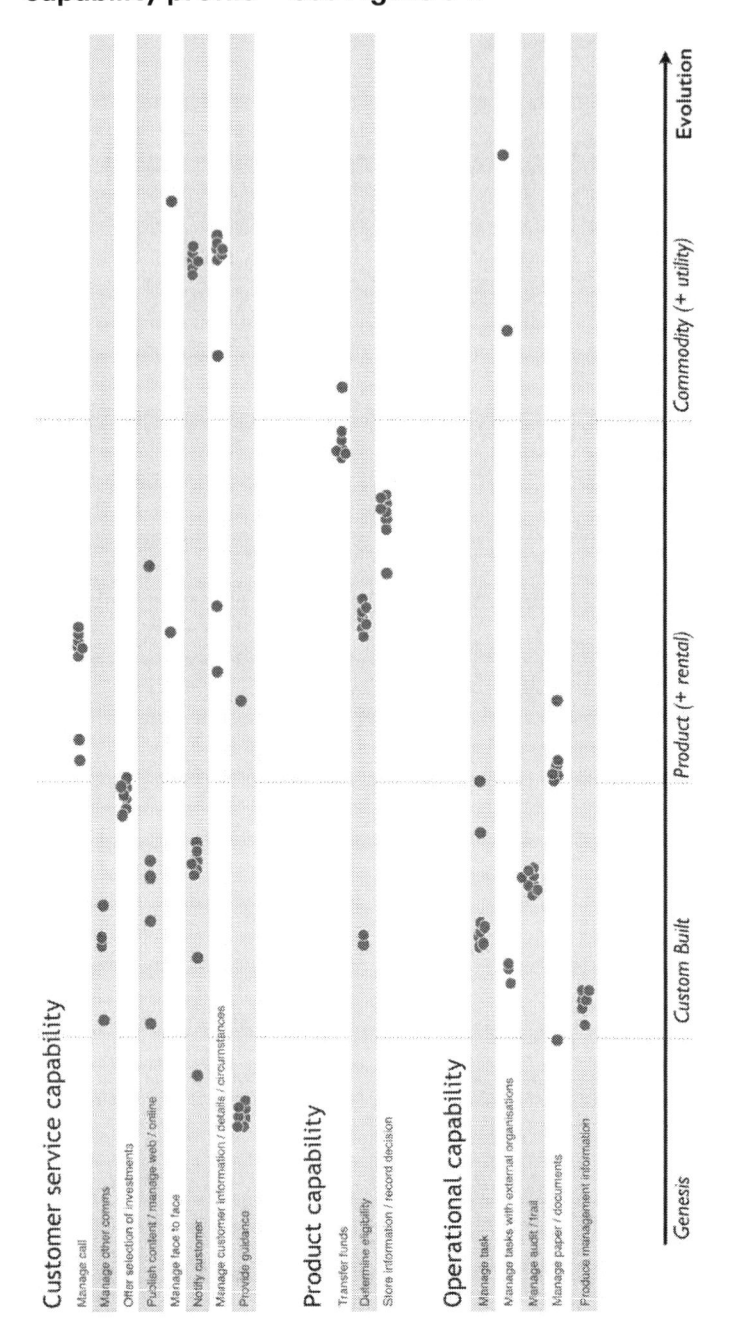

Figure 34: Capability profile

You may find that common capabilities are often assumed to be custom (e.g. offer a selection of investments), when in reality, they should be far more defined. You may also find that you have a plethora of duplicated and custom-built technology providing a single capability that should be streamlined. It never fails to surprise me how a simple business with limited capabilities is made incredibly complex and slow by a smorgasbord of duplicated custom-built solutions underneath.

Doctrine: Use appropriate methods

One of the climatic patterns we examined in figure 22 (Chapter 3) was how no one size fits all method exists. Assuming you are removing bias in your maps, either by challenging directly or with the aid of a profile built from multiple maps, then the next question becomes what methods are suitable? The most common mistake that I find is with outsourcing. The issue with outsourcing isn't that the concept is wrong but instead, that we have a tendency to outsource entire systems for which we do not understand the landscape. This is often done in the hope that someone else will effectively take care of it.

Let us imagine a system with multiple components spread across the evolution axis but we have no map. Let us now apply a single highly-structured process to the system, often through a contract detailing what should be delivered. Unfortunately, unbeknownst to us, some of those components will be in the uncharted domain and hence, are uncertain by nature. They will change and hence, we will incur some form of change control cost. These costs can be significant in any complex system that contains many uncharted components. As a result, arguments tend to break out between the buyer and the supplier. Unfortunately, the supplier has the upper hand because they can point to the contract and show that the components that did not change were efficiently delivered and the cost is associated with the components that changed. The old lines of "if you had specified it correctly in the first place" to "you kept on changing your mind" get trotted out and the buyer normally feels some form of guilt. It was their fault and if only they had specified it more! This is a lie and a trap.

The problem was not that a highly-structured process with detailed specification was correctly applied to industrialised components but that the same technique was also incorrectly applied to components that were, by their very nature, uncertain and changing. The buyer could never specify those changing components with any degree of certainty. Excessive change control costs caused by a structured process applied to changing components are inevitable. The fault is with the supplier who should have the experience to know that one size fits all cannot work. Unfortunately, and there is no polite way of saying this, it's a lucrative scam.

Even better, if the scam works — especially if the supplier waives some cost as a gesture of goodwill — then the next time, the buyer will try even harder to specify the next system in more detail. They'll often pay the supplier or a friendly consultancy to help them do this. Unfortunately, once again, it will contain uncharted components that will change and thus, costs will be incurred. The only way to avoid this is to break the system down into components and treat them with appropriate methods, e.g. Figure 35.

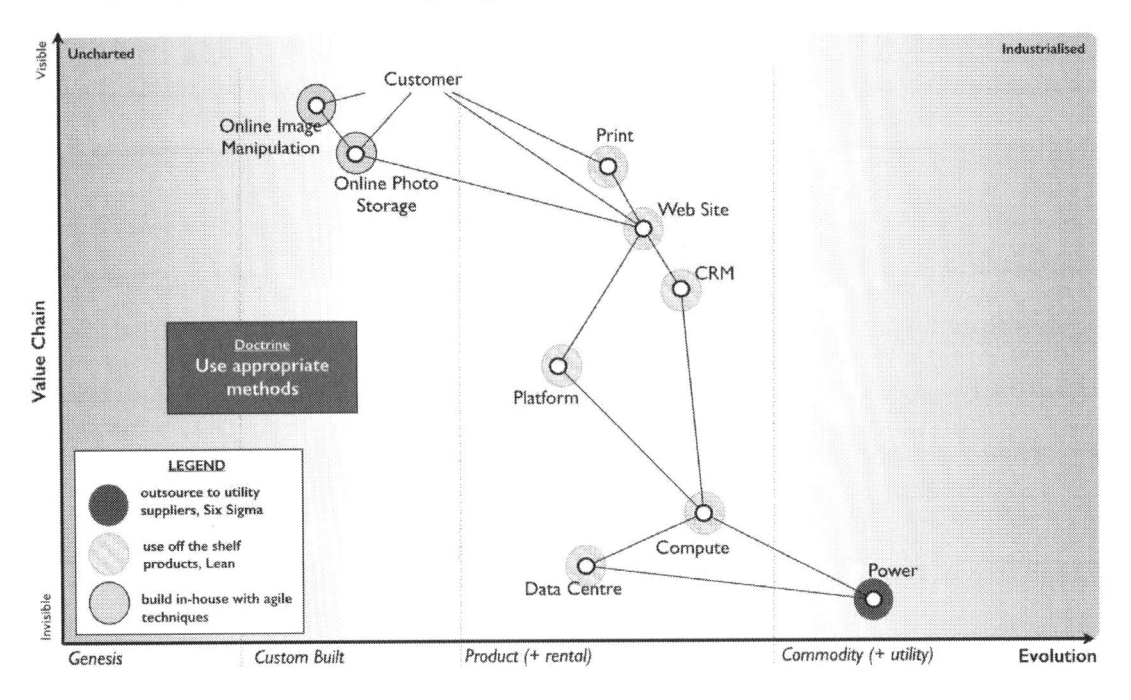

Figure 35: Use appropriate methods

In the above example from 2005, power should be outsourced to a utility provider, whereas CRM, platform, data centre and compute should use off the shelf products or rental solutions (e.g. hosting) with minimal change where possible. The online photo storage and image manipulation components that are going to rapidly change should ideally be built in-house with our own engineers and using an agile approach. Whilst we might use more detailed and specific contracts for items such as data centre (hosting), we are also mindful that we cannot fully specify image manipulation at this time. If, in 2005, we had outsourced the entire system in the figure above to a single highly-structured approach using a detailed specification, then I could almost guarantee that we would have ended up with excessive change costs around image manipulation and photo storage.

The problem of inappropriate outsourcing is so rife that it's worth doing a simple example to reinforce this point. In Figure 36, I've provided a box and wire diagram (commonly used in IT systems) for a self-driving car. However, I've translated the description of the components into Elvish because, as I've said, most IT is elvish to people in business. I'd like you to look at the diagram and answer the questions labelled as **1** and **2**.

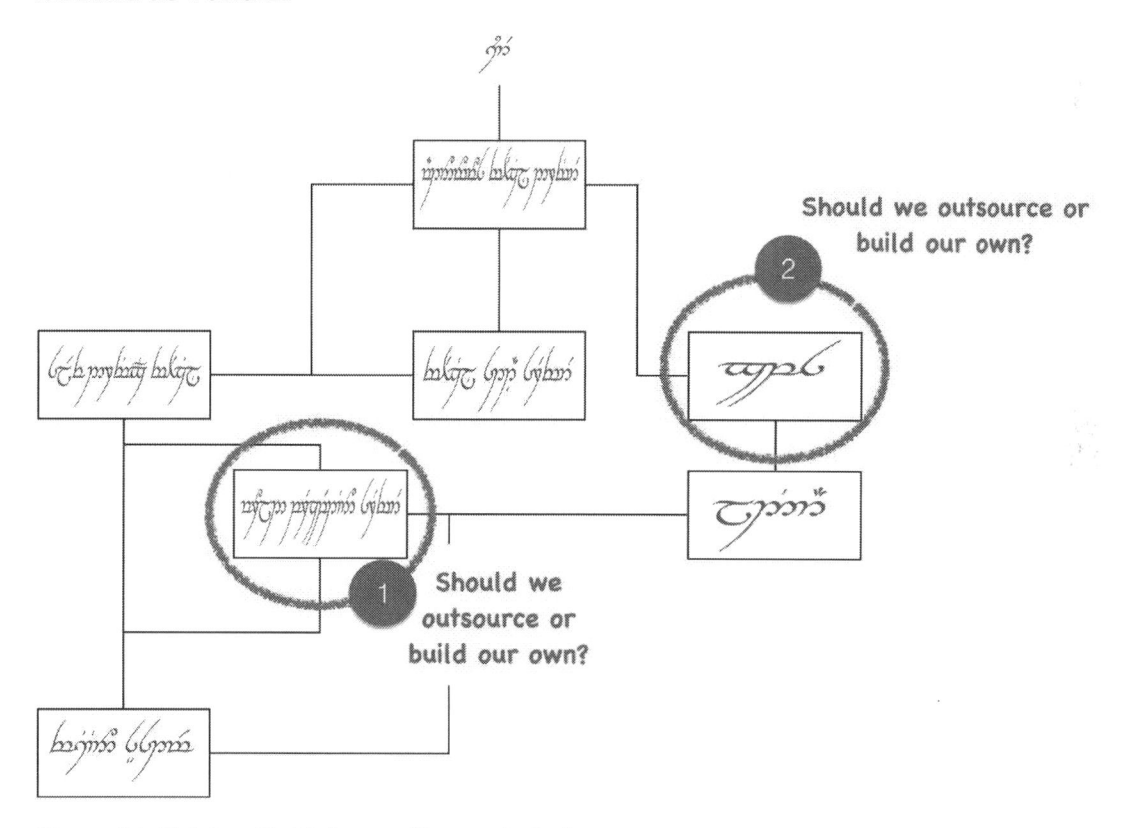

Figure 36: Elvish self-driving car (box and wire)

Now, in Figure 37, I've provided exactly the same diagram in a mapping format. It's still in Elvish. See if you can answer questions 1 and 2.

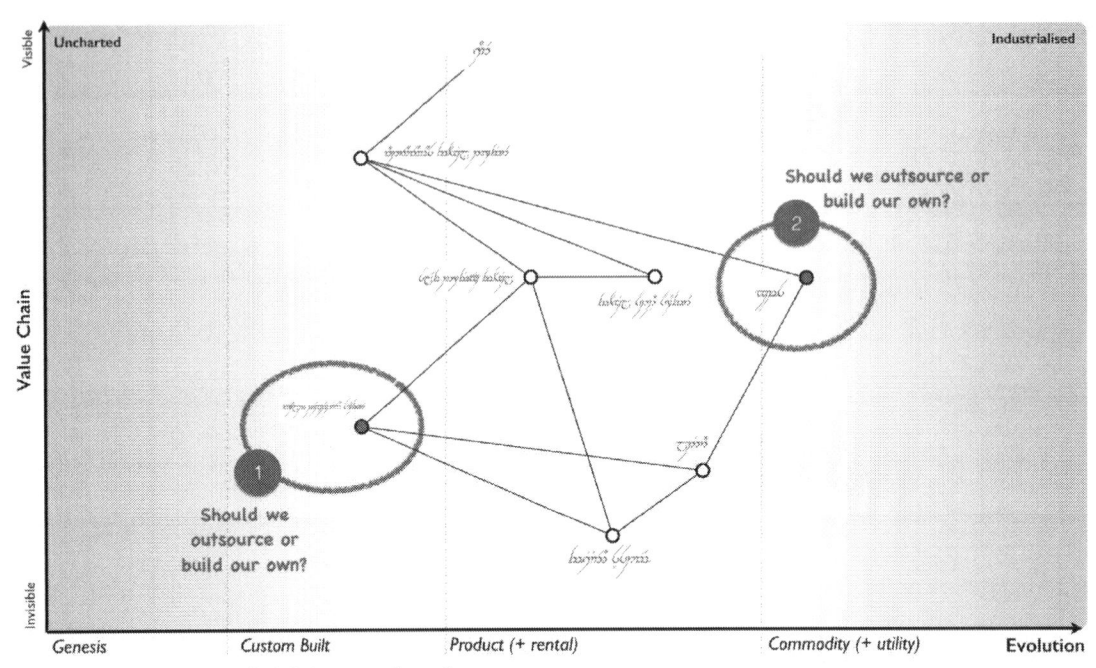

Figure 37: Elvish self-driving car (map)

You should find you can say something reasonable about how you treat questions 1 and 2. If you're struggling, look at Figure 22 (Chapter 3).

For reference, question 1 should probably be built in-house with our own engineers in an agile fashion, whereas question 2 should be either outsourced with a structured and well-defined process or some sort of commodity consumed. In Figure 38, I've provided the same diagram without the Elvish so you can check your thinking.

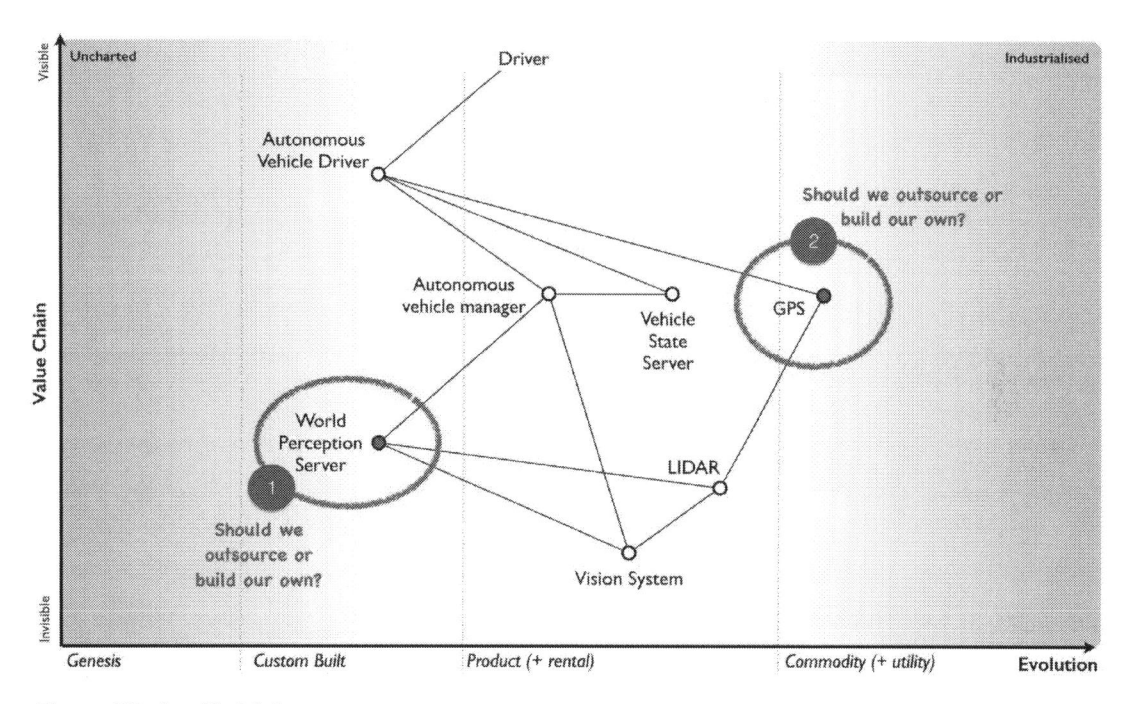

Figure 38: A self-driving car

What enables you to do this feat of Elvish sensibility is the movement axis of evolution. Unfortunately, in most outsourcing arrangements that I've seen, diagrams such as box and wires or business process maps (see Figure 39) tend to dominate. Alas, these lack that all-important movement characteristic. Box and wires and business process maps are not actually maps; you are relying solely on contextual information from the words (i.e. knowing that process payment is a commodity). The diagrams themselves will not provide you with a guide as to what you should or should not outsource.

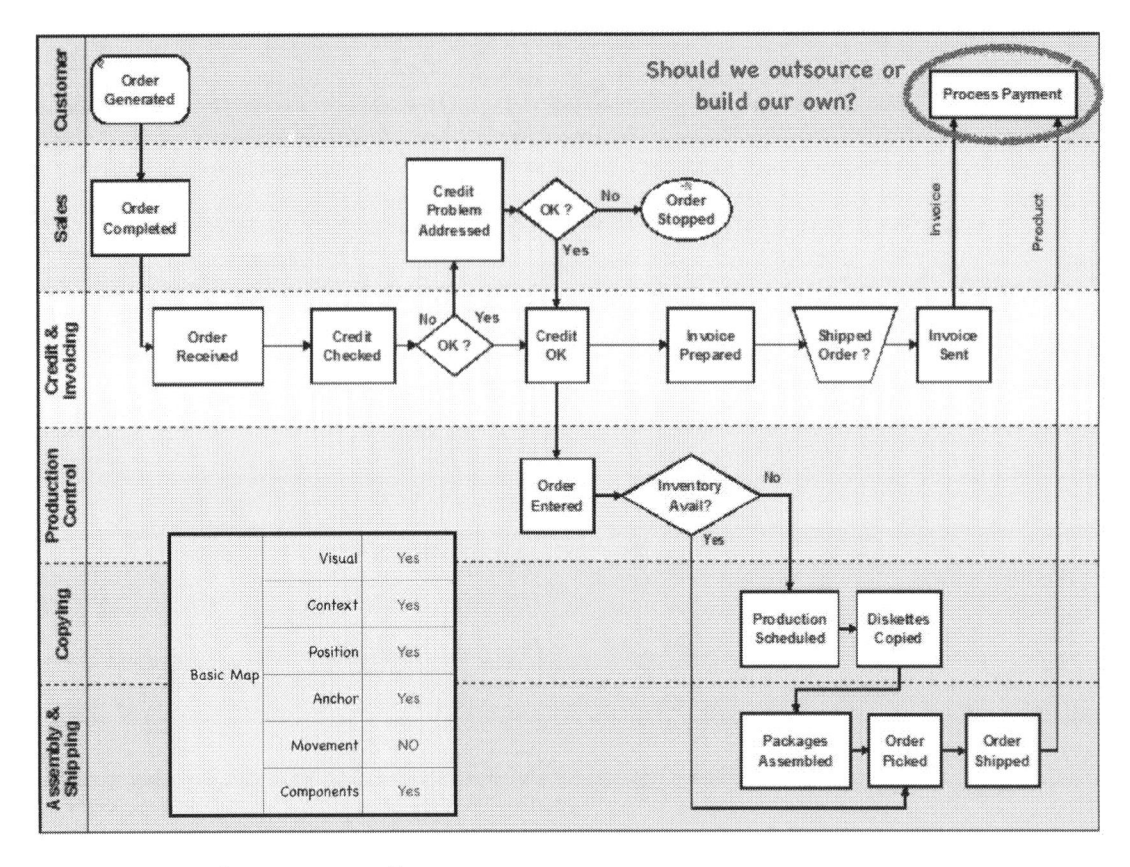

Figure 39: A business process diagram

Before you go and ask your friendly consultancy or vendor to make a map for you, remember that their interests are not necessarily your own. Equally, it's important to challenge any bias your company may have in your maps. A team building our own homegrown electricity supply may well argue that electricity is not a commodity but instead, we need to custom build our own supply. Along with common sense, the cheat sheet (Figure 17, Chapter 2) and those profile diagrams built from aggregated maps (Figure 32) should give you ample evidence to challenge this.

At this point, someone normally tells me "that's obvious, we wouldn't do that", however, ask yourself how many enterprise content management (ECM) systems you have. If you're of any scale and a typical global company built by acquisition, then experience would dictate that you'll probably say 5–8x. In practice, it is often more likely to be 40–250x customised versions with probably 3–5x separate groups building a global ECM, whilst being unaware that the other groups exist. The problem is, most of you won't know how much duplication or bias you have. Of course, there are a wide range of excuses that are deployed for not breaking up entire systems into components and then applying more appropriate methods. My favourite ones include:-

"We need better experts and specification" — that's called not dealing with the problem. It's like saying our Death Star project to clean up the mess of failed Death Star projects has failed; we need a new Death Star! There's a famous quote about repeating the same thing and expecting different results, which is relevant here.

"It's too complex; splitting into parts will make it unmanageable" — the age old effort to pretend that a system containing 100 different moving parts doesn't actually contain 100 different moving parts. We don't build cars by pretending they are one thing; in fact, we often have complex supply chains meeting the different needs of different components with appropriate measurement and contracts deployed based upon the component. Yes, it does make for a bit more work to understand what is being built but then, if you're spending significant sums, it is generally a good idea to know this.

"It will cause chaos" — cue the old "riots on the street" line. Given construction, automotive and many other industries have no problem with componentisation then I can't see how anyone ever jumps to this notion of chaos. The truth is usually more of a desire to have "one throat to choke", though there is nothing stopping a company from using one supplier to build all the components with appropriate methods.

"You'll end up with hundreds of experimental startups" — at this point, we're getting into the surreal. If you break a complex system into components then some of the uncharted components are going to be experimental. This is not a bad thing; this is just what they are. For those components then you're likely to do this in-house with agile techniques or use a specialist company focused on more agile processes. But you won't give that company all the components because the majority of components tend to be highly industrialised and hence, you'll use established utility providers such as Amazon for computing infrastructure. I'm not sure how people make the jump from componentisation to giving it all to "hundreds of experimental startups". In general, this tends to be caused by a desire to keep the current status quo.

"Complexity in managing interfaces" — this is my favourite excuse, which takes surreal to a whole new level. Pretending that a complex 100 component system with uncharted and industrialised components that have interfaces between them is in fact one system with a one size fits all method and non-existent interfaces is the very definition of fantasy. Those components are there, those interfaces are there — the complexity doesn't go away simply by "outsourcing".

All you've done is try and pretend that the complex thing you're building is somehow simple because then it's easier to manage. It would be like BMW or Apple outsourcing their entire product lines to someone else and trying to have no involvement because it makes management simple.

Doctrine: Think small

In order to apply appropriate methods then you need to think small. You can't treat the entire system as one thing, but you need to break it into components. I will often extend this to using small contracts localised around specific components. Knowing the details helps you manage a landscape. But you can take this further and even use small teams such as cell-based structures. Probably the best known approaches to using small teams are Amazon's Two Pizza model and Haier's cell-based structure.

Such teams should be given autonomy in their space and this can be achieved by the team providing well-defined interfaces for others to consume, along with defined boundaries often described through some form of fitness function, i.e. the team has a goal around a specific area with defined metrics for delivery. Maps themselves can be useful in helping you identify not only the teams you should build but also the interfaces they need to create — see Figure 40.

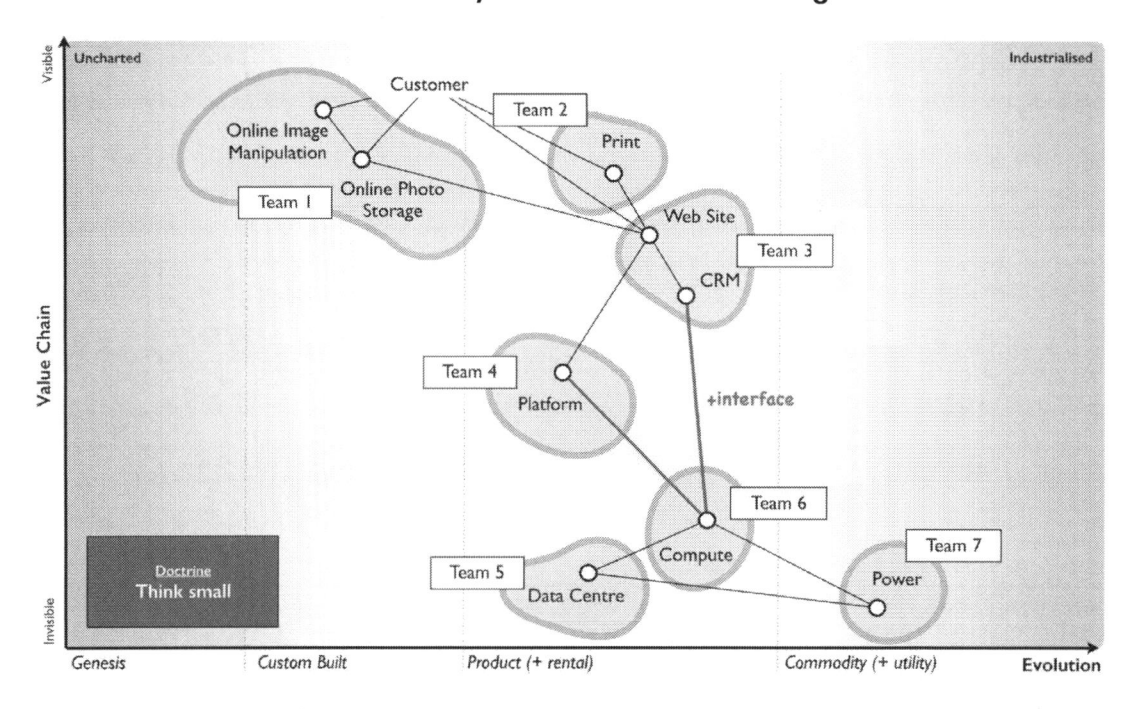

Figure 40: Think small (as in teams)

Doctrine: Think aptitude and attitude

Now let us suppose that you embark on a cell-based structure and you're thinking small. Then each cell is going to require different skills, i.e. aptitudes. However, there's another

factor at play here — attitude. When we look at a map, we know that activities evolve from the uncharted to industrialised domain and the methods and techniques we need are different. The genesis of something requires experimentation, and whilst you might need the aptitude of engineering, you need a specific form, i.e. agile engineering. Conversely, the type of engineering you need to build a highly industrialised act requires a focus on volume operations and removing deviation such as Six Sigma. Hence, we have one aptitude of engineering that requires different attitudes. It doesn't matter what aptitude we examine — finance, engineering, network or marketing — the attitude also matters. There isn't such a thing as IT or finance or marketing but instead, multiples of.

To resolve this problem, you need to populate the cells with different types of people — **pioneers, settlers** and **town planners**. It's not realistic to think that everyone has the same attitude; some are much more capable of living in a world of chaos, experimentation and failure, whilst others are much more capable of dealing with intensive modelling, the rigours of volume operations and measurement. You need brilliant people with the right aptitudes (e.g. engineering, finance) and different attitudes (e.g. pioneers, settlers).

Pioneers are brilliant people. They are able to explore the never before discovered concepts, the uncharted land. They show you wonder but they fail a lot. Half the time, the thing doesn't work properly. You wouldn't trust what they build. They create 'crazy' ideas. Their type of innovation is what we describe as core research. They make future success possible. Most of the time, we look at them and go "what?", "I don't understand?" or "is that magic?" They built the first ever electric source (the Parthian Battery, 400 AD) and the first ever digital computer (Z3, 1943). In the past, we often burnt them at the stake or they usually died from malaria in some newly discovered swamp.

Settlers are brilliant people. They can turn the half-baked thing into something useful for a larger audience. They build trust. They build understanding. They make the possible future actually happen. They turn the prototype into a product, make it possible to manufacture it, listen to customers and turn it profitable. Their innovation is what we tend to think of as applied research and differentiation. They built the first ever computer products (e.g. IBM 650 and onwards), the first generators (Hippolyte Pixii to Siemens generators). They drain the swamp and create some form of settlement.

Town Planners are brilliant people. They are able to take something and industrialise it, taking advantage of economies of scale. This requires immense skill. You trust what they build. They find ways to make things faster, better, smaller, more efficient, more economic and good enough. They create the components that pioneers build upon. Their type of innovation is industrial research. They take something that exists and turn it into a commodity or a utility (e.g. with electricity, then Edison, Tesla and Westinghouse). They are the industrial giants we depend upon. They build Rome.

In 2005, we knew that one culture didn't seem to work, and enabling people to gain mastery in one of these three attitudes seemed to make people happier and more focused. Taking one attitude and placing them in a field that requires another attitude is never a good idea. Try it for yourself. Find a pioneer software engineer in your company, someone used to a world of experimentation and agile development, and send them on a three-week ITIL course. See how miserable they come back. Try the same with a town planner and send them on a three-week course of hack days and experimentation with completely uncertain areas and lots of failure. Watch the smile drop from their face.

When using a map, you should not only break into components and build small cells around this, you should also consider attitude — see Figure 41.

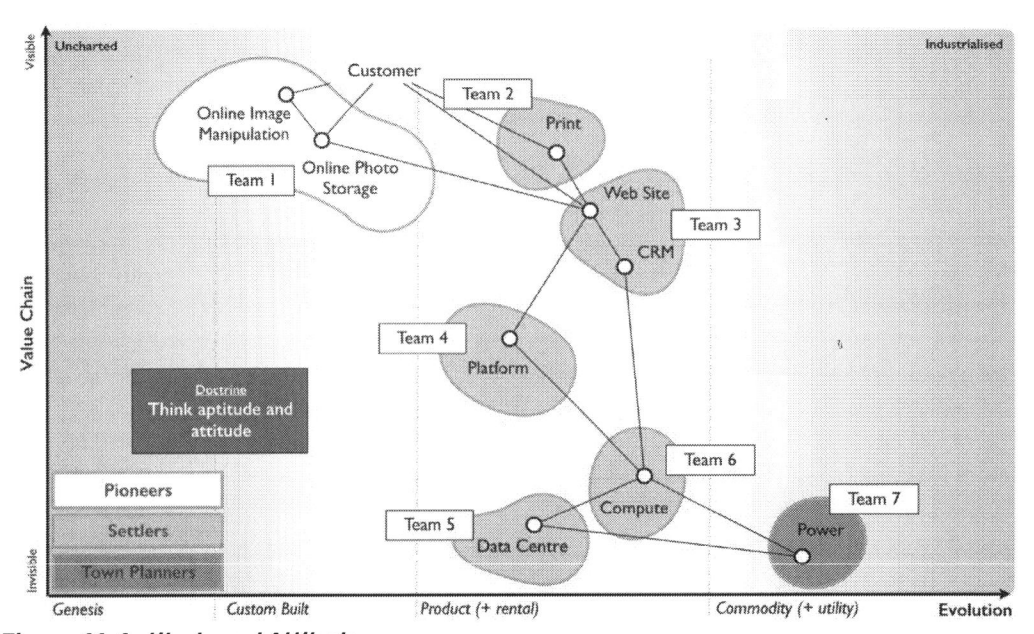

Figure 41: Aptitude and Attitude

It's really important to understand that pioneers build and operate the novel. Pioneers are responsible for their pioneering and that means everything. They tend to do this by consuming components built by settlers (e.g. product or libraries) and town planners (e.g. industrialised services). Town planners, on the other hand, build and operate the industrialised components of huge scale. Don't fall into the trap that pioneers build new stuff and hand it off to someone else to run or operate. That's not how this works.

This three-party idea is also not new. A bit of digging will bring you to Robert X. Cringely's book, Accidental Empires, 1993. Cringely described how there were three different types of companies known as infantry, commando and police. The PST (pioneer, settler and town planner) structure is a direct descendant of that idea, but applied to a single company and put into practice in 2005. To quote from his book, which I strongly recommend you read:-

"Whether invading countries or markets, the first wave of troops to see battle are the commandos. Commandos parachute behind enemy lines or quietly crawl ashore at night. Speed is what commandos live for. They work hard, fast, and cheap, though often with a low level of professionalism, which is okay, too, because professionalism is expensive. Their job is to do lots of damage with surprise and teamwork, establishing a beachhead before the enemy is even aware they exist. They make creativity a destructive art.

[Referring to software business] But what they build, while it may look like a product and work like a product, usually isn't a product because it still has bugs and major failings that are beneath the notice of commando types. Or maybe it works fine but can't be produced profitably without extensive redesign. Commandos are useless for this type of work. They get bored.

It's easy to dismiss the commandos. After all, most of business and warfare is conventional. But without commandos, you'd never get on the beach at all. Grouping offshore as the commandos do their work is the second wave of soldiers, the infantry. These are the people who hit the beach enmasse and slog out the early victory, building the start given by the commandos. The second wave troops take the prototype, test it, refine it, make it manufacturable, write the manuals, market it, and ideally produce a profit. Because there are so many more of these soldiers and their duties are so varied, they require an infrastructure of rules and procedures for getting things done — all the stuff that commandos hate. For just this reason, soldiers of the second wave, while they can work with the first wave, generally don't trust them, though the commandos don't even notice this fact, since by this time, they are bored and already looking for the door. While the commandos make success possible, it's the infantry that makes success happen.

What happens then is that the commandos and the infantry advance into new territories, performing their same jobs again. There is still a need for a military presence in the territory. These third wave troops hate change. They aren't troops at all but police. They want to fuel growth, not by planning more invasions and landing on more beaches, but by adding people and building economies and empires of scale."

Doctrine: Design for constant evolution

Everything is evolving due to competition. The effects of this on business can be seen in their continual restructuring to cope with new outside paradigms. Recent presidents of cloud and social media are no different from the former presidents of electricity and telephony that most companies employed. Today's bolt-on includes Chief Digital Officers. This new stuff is tomorrow's legacy, and this creates a problem. We might introduce a cell-based structure with consideration for not only aptitude but attitude, however, the map isn't static. We need to somehow mimic that constant state of evolution in the outside world but within a company. The solution is to introduce a mechanism of theft, which means new teams need to form and steal the work of earlier teams, i.e. the settlers steal from the pioneers and productise the work. This forces the pioneers to move on. Equally, the town planners steal from the settlers and industrialise it, forcing the settlers to move on but also providing component service to enable the pioneers. This results in a cycle shown in Figure 42.

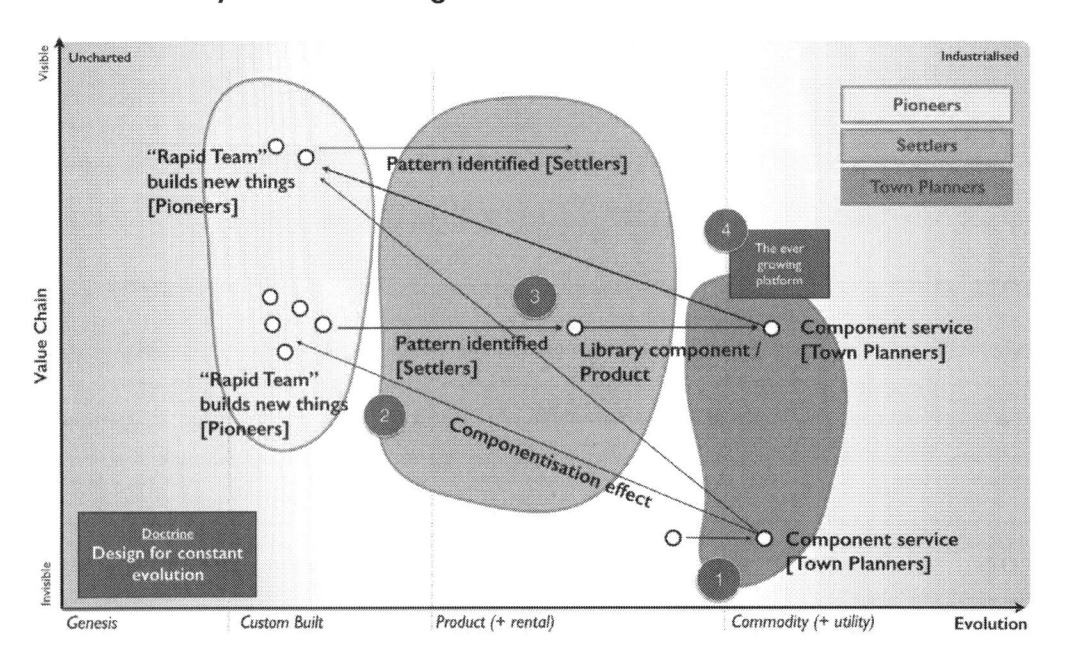

Figure 42: Design for constant evolution

Point 1 – The town planners create some form of industrialised component that previously existed as a product. This is provided as a utility service.

Point 2 – The pioneers can now rapidly build higher order systems that consume that component.

Point 3 – As the new higher order systems evolve, the settlers identify new patterns within them and create a product or some form of library component for re-use.

Point 4 – As the product or library component evolves, the town planners complete the cycle by creating an industrialised form (as per Point 1). This results in creating an ever-expanding platform of discrete industrialised components for which the pioneers can build on.

Maps are a useful way to kick-start this process. They also give **purpose** to each cell as they know how their work fits into the overall picture. The cell-based structure is an essential element of the structure and it need to have *autonomy* in their space; they must be self-organising. The interfaces between the cells are therefore used to help define the fitness functions, but if a cell sees something they can take tactical advantage of in their space (remember, they have an overview of the entire business through the map,) then they should exploit it. The cells are populated with not only the right aptitude but attitude (pioneers, settlers and town planners). This enables people to develop **mastery** in their area and allows them to focus on what they're good at. You should let people self-select their type and change at will until they find something they're truly comfortable with. Reward them for being really good at that. Purpose, mastery and autonomy are the subjects of the book Drive by Daniel H. Pink.

As new things appear in the outside world, they should flow through this system. This structure doesn't require a bolt-on that you need to replace later. No chief digital, chief telephony, chief electricity, chief cloud officer required. The cells can grow in size but ultimately, you should aim to subdivide into smaller cells, and maps can help achieve this. Be aware of the Hackman problem that communication channels increase exponentially as the team grows. The US Navy Seals learned long ago that 4 "is the optimal size for a combat team".

You will however increasingly have to structure the monitoring and communication between cells using a hierarchy, and yes, that means you need a hierarchy on top of a cell-based structure. I've found that an executive structure that mimics the organisation to be of use, i.e. a CEO, a chief pioneer, a chief settler and a chief town planner can be applied. However, you'll probably use more traditional sounding names such as Chief Operating Officer, Chief Scientist etc. We did. I'm not sure why we did and these days, I wouldn't bother; I'd just make it clear. You will also need separate support structures to reinforce the culture and provide training with some form of pool of resource (for forming new cells).

Contrary to popular concepts of culture, the structure causes three separate cultures to flourish. This is somewhat counter to general thinking because the culture results from the structure and not the other way around. It also means that you don't have a single company culture but multiple that you need to maintain. I've described the basic elements of this within Figure 43.

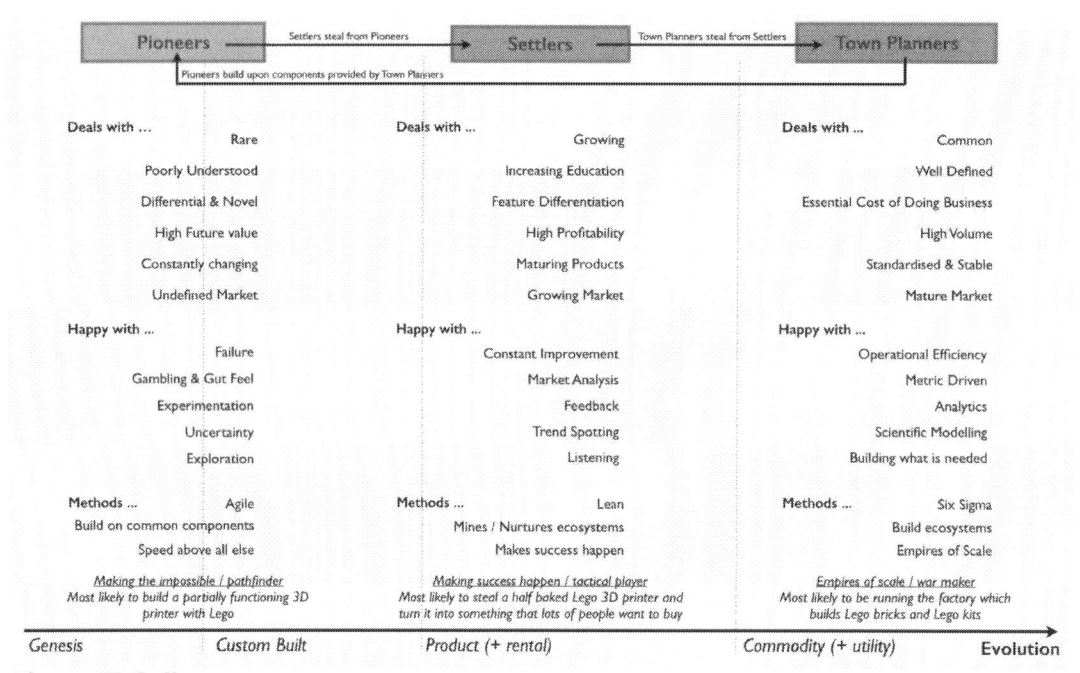

	Pioneers	Settlers	Town Planners
	Settlers steal from Pioneers →	Town Planners steal from Settlers →	
	← Pioneers build upon components provided by Town Planners		
Deals with ...	Rare	Growing	Common
	Poorly Understood	Increasing Education	Well Defined
	Differential & Novel	Feature Differentiation	Essential Cost of Doing Business
	High Future value	High Profitability	High Volume
	Constantly changing	Maturing Products	Standardised & Stable
	Undefined Market	Growing Market	Mature Market
Happy with ...	Failure	Constant Improvement	Operational Efficiency
	Gambling & Gut Feel	Market Analysis	Metric Driven
	Experimentation	Feedback	Analytics
	Uncertainty	Trend Spotting	Scientific Modelling
	Exploration	Listening	Building what is needed
Methods ...	Agile	Lean	Six Sigma
	Build on common components	Mines / Nurtures ecosystems	Build ecosystems
	Speed above all else	Makes success happen	Empires of Scale
	Making the impossible / pathfinder Most likely to build a partially functioning 3D printer with Lego	*Making success happen / tactical player* Most likely to steal a half baked Lego 3D printer and turn it into something that lots of people want to buy	*Empires of scale / war maker* Most likely to be running the factory which builds Lego bricks and Lego kits
Genesis	Custom Built	Product (+ rental)	Commodity (+ utility) → Evolution

Figure 43: Culture

Lastly, PST is a structure that I've used to remarkable effect in a very small number of cases. That's code for "it might just be a fluke". However, in the last decade, I've seen nothing that comes close and instead, I've seen endless matrix or dual systems that create problems. Will something better come along? Of course it will. However, to invoke Conway's law, if you don't mimic evolution in your communication mechanisms (e.g. through a mechanism of theft) then you'll never be able to cope with evolution outside the organisation.

So how common is a PST structure? Outside certain circles, it's extremely rare. At best, I see companies dabbling with cell-based structures that, to be honest, are pretty good anyway and are probably where you should go. Telling a company that they need three types of culture, three types of attitude, a system of theft, a map of their environment and high levels of situational awareness is usually enough to get managers running away. It doesn't fit into a simple 2 x 2. It also doesn't matter for many organisations because you only need high levels of situational awareness and adaptive structures if you're competing against organisations that have the same or you're at the very sharp end of ferocious competition. Personally, for most companies, I'd recommend using a cell-based structure and reading "boiling frogs" from GCHQ, which is an outstanding piece of work. It will give you more than enough ideas and contains a very similar structure.

I will note that in recent years, I've heard plenty of people talk about dual structures. I have to say that from my perspective and experience, these are fundamentally flawed and you're being led up the garden path. It's not enough to deal with the extremes; you must manage the transition in between. Fail to do this and you will not create an organisation that copes with evolution. If you focus on the extremes then you will diminish the all-important middle; you will tend to create war between factions and because the components of the pioneers never evolve (the town planners will describe these systems as "flaky"), then you create a never growing platform and on top of this, an increasing spaghetti junction of new built upon new. I've experienced this myself back in 2003, along with the inevitable slow grinding halt of development and the calls for a Death Star project of immense scale to build the "new platform for the future". I've never seen that work.

Categorising Doctrine

Doctrine are universal and applicable to all landscapes, though many require you to use a map in order to fully exploit them. It's worth making a distinction here (courtesy of Trent Hone). Whilst doctrine consists of basic principles, the application of those principles will be different in different contexts. For example, "Focus on user needs" does not mean we all focus on the same user needs but instead, the exact user needs will vary with landscape and purpose. The user needs of an automotive company are not the same as a tea shop. Equally, the user needs of "the best tea shop in Kent" are not the same as the user needs of "the most convenient tea shop in Kent". Hence, doctrine can be subdivided into the principles of doctrine (i.e. "focus on user needs") and the implementation of doctrine (i.e. "the user needs for the most convenient tea shop in Kent").

Furthermore, doctrine are a set of beliefs over which you have choice. They are something that you apply to an organisation, unlike climatic patterns, which will apply to you regardless of your choice. They also represent our belief as to what works everywhere. I've listed the basic forms of doctrine (the principles) that we will cover in this book in Figure 44, marking those we've just skimmed over in grey. This is not an exhaustive list but enough for now. In later chapters, we will loop back around this section, refining both the concepts and different aspects of doctrine as we go. For reference, the categories I use for doctrine depend upon whether it mainly impacts:-

- methods of communication
- the mechanics of development or building things
- the operation of an organisation
- how we structure ourselves
- the manner by which we learn
- how we lead

	Communication: Be transparent	Focus on high situational awareness (understand what is being considered)	Use a common language (necessary for collaboration)	Challenge assumptions (speak up and question)
Communication				
Development	Know your users (e.g. customers, shareholders, regulators, staff)	Focus on user needs	Think fast, inexpensive, simple and tiny	Remove bias and duplication
	Use appropriate methods (e.g. agile vs lean vs six sigma)	Focus on the outcome not a contract (e.g. worth based development)	Be pragmatic (it doesn't matter if the cat is black or white as long as it catches mice)	Use standards where appropriate
	Use appropriate tools (e.g. mapping, financial models)			
Operation	Manage inertia (e.g. existing practice, political capital, previous investment)	Optimise flow (remove bottlenecks)		Effectiveness over efficiency
	Do better with less (continual improvement)	Set exceptional standards (great is just not good enough)	Think small (as in know the details)	
Structure	Provide purpose, mastery & autonomy	Think small (as in teams)	Distribute power and decision making	Think aptitude and attitude
	Design for constant evolution	There is no one culture (e.g. pioneers, settlers and town planners)	Seek the best	
Learning	Use a systematic mechanism of learning	Learn by playing the game (a bias towards action)	Be curious and take appropriate risks (a bias towards the new)	Listen to your ecosystems (acts as future sensing engines)
Leading	Be the owner (take responsibility)	Move fast (an imperfect plan executed today is better than a perfect plan executed tomorrow)	Think big (inspire others, provide direction)	Strategy is iterative not linear (fast reactive cycles)
	Strategy is complex (there will be uncertainty)	Commit to the direction, be adaptive along the path (crossing the river by feeling the stones)	There is no core (everything is transient)	Be humble (listen, be selfless, have fortitude)

Figure 44: Doctrine

Using doctrine with our first map

When you read the list of doctrine, it mainly sounds like common sense. Most of them are but then again, they're very difficult to achieve. You really have to work hard at them. In the case of "remove duplication and bias", you can't effectively apply it to your first map because it requires multiple maps. However, even with a simple map, you can apply some of these doctrines. In Figure 45, I've taken our first map, which we applied common economic patterns to Figure 28 (Chapter 3) and shown where doctrine is relevant.

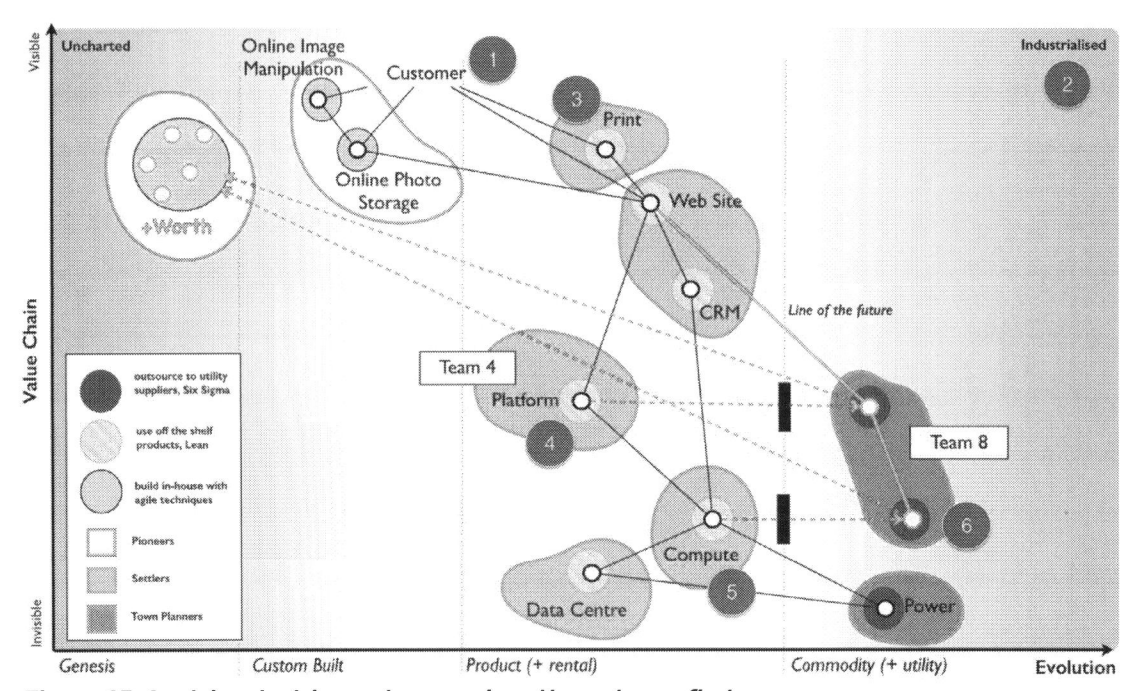

Figure 45: Applying doctrine and economic patterns to our first map

Point 1 — Focus on user needs. The anchor of the map is the user; in this case, a customer.

Point 2 — The map provides a common language. It provides a mechanism to visually challenge assumptions.

Point 3 — Use appropriate methods (agile, lean and Six Sigma or in-house vs outsource) and don't try to apply a single method across the entire landscape.

Point 4 — Treat the map as small components and use small teams (e.g. team 4).

Point 5 — Consider not only aptitude but attitude (pioneers, settlers and town planners).

Point 6 — Design for constant evolution. The components will evolve and this might require the formation of new teams (e.g. team 8) with new attitudes.

It's worth taking a bit of time to reflect on Figure 45. What we have is not only the user needs, the components meeting those needs and the common economic patterns impacting this, but also an anticipation of change, the organisational structure that we will need, and even the types of methods and culture that are suitable. All of this is in one single diagram. In practice, we normally only show the structures on the map that are relevant to the task at hand, i.e. if we're anticipating change then we might not show cell structure, attitude and hence, cultural aspects. However, it's worth noting that they can all be shown and, with practice, you will learn when to include them or not. After a few years, you will find that much of this becomes automatic and the challenge is to remember to include structures for those who are not initiated in this way of thinking.

We are now in a position of understanding our landscape, being able to anticipate some forms of change due to climatic patterns, and we have an understanding of basic universal doctrine to help us structure ourselves. We're finally at a point where we can start to learn the context specific forms of gameplay, which are at the heart of strategy. With a few basic lessons about gameplay, then we will be ready to act.

An exercise for the reader

In Chapter 3, I asked you to apply some basic economic patterns to a map you created in Chapter 2. If you've been skipping these exercises then now is the time to go back and complete them. Mapping isn't something you can just read and become an expert in; it's something you have to apply and learn.

I want you to now take your map and look at the various forms of doctrine highlighted in Figure 44. Try and work with others and apply them to your map. Are you thinking about user needs? Are you challenging your assumptions? How would you organise yourself? Do you know the details?

Chapter 5 - The play and a decision to act

In Chapters 1-4, I've covered the basics of mapping, common economic patterns and doctrine. However, these Wardley Maps of business don't tell you what to do any more than a geographical map tells an Admiral how to win a battle. The maps are simply a guide and you have to decide what move you're going to make, where you're going to attack and how you navigate your ship through the choppy waters of commercial competition. In other words, you have to apply thought, decide to act and then act. In this chapter, we're going to cover my journey through this part of the strategy cycle — see Figure 46.

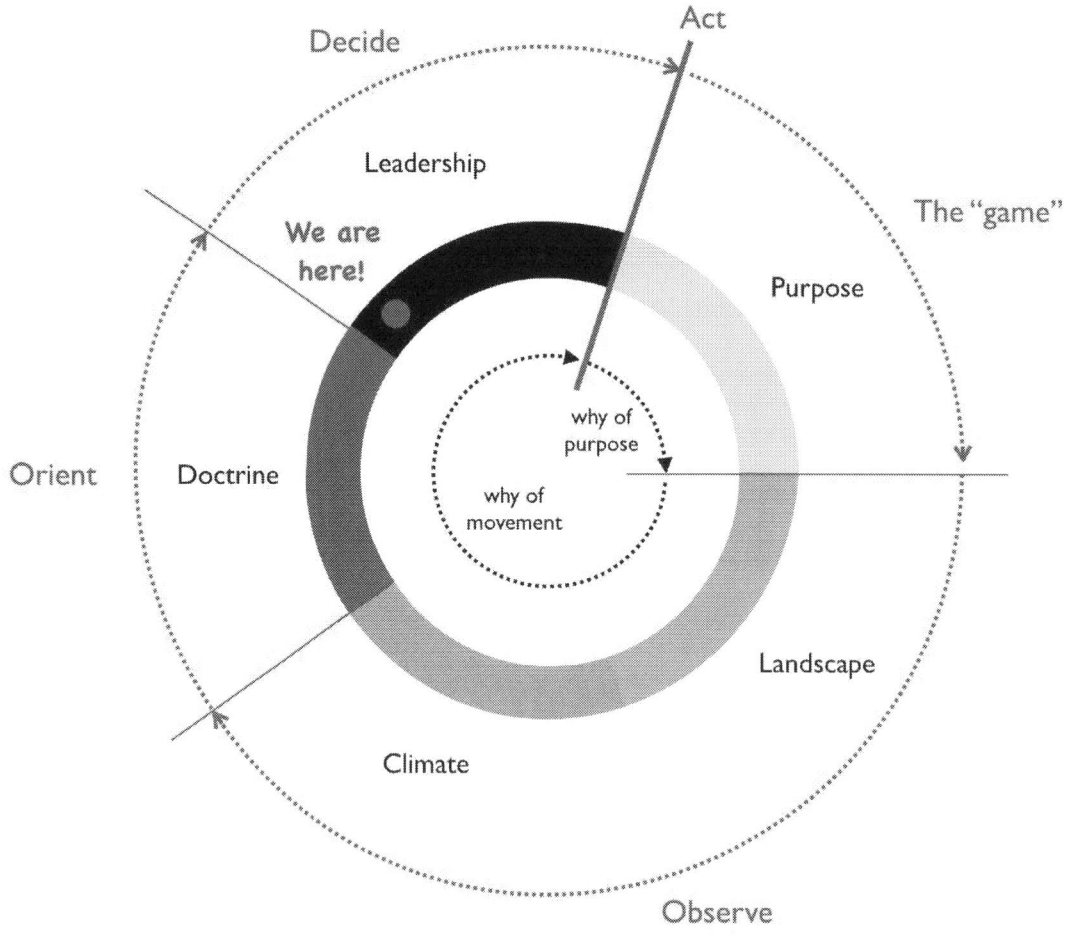

Figure 46: The play and a decision to act

Identifying opportunity

There exists **two different forms of why** in business — the why of purpose (i.e. win the game) and the why of movement (i.e. move this piece over that). The why of movement is what I'm going to concentrate on here, but in order to examine this then we must first understand the landscape, orientate ourselves around this and then we can determine **where** to attack.

Prior to 2005, I had sat in many meetings where options were presented to myself and my executive team and then we made a choice based upon financial arguments, gut feel and concepts of core. We had never used a landscape to help determine where we could attack. This was a first for us and very much a learning exercise. I've taken that earliest map from 2005 and highlighted on it the four areas that we considered had potential. There were many others, but for the sake of introduction, I thought I'd keep it simple. These four **wheres** are shown in Figure 47.

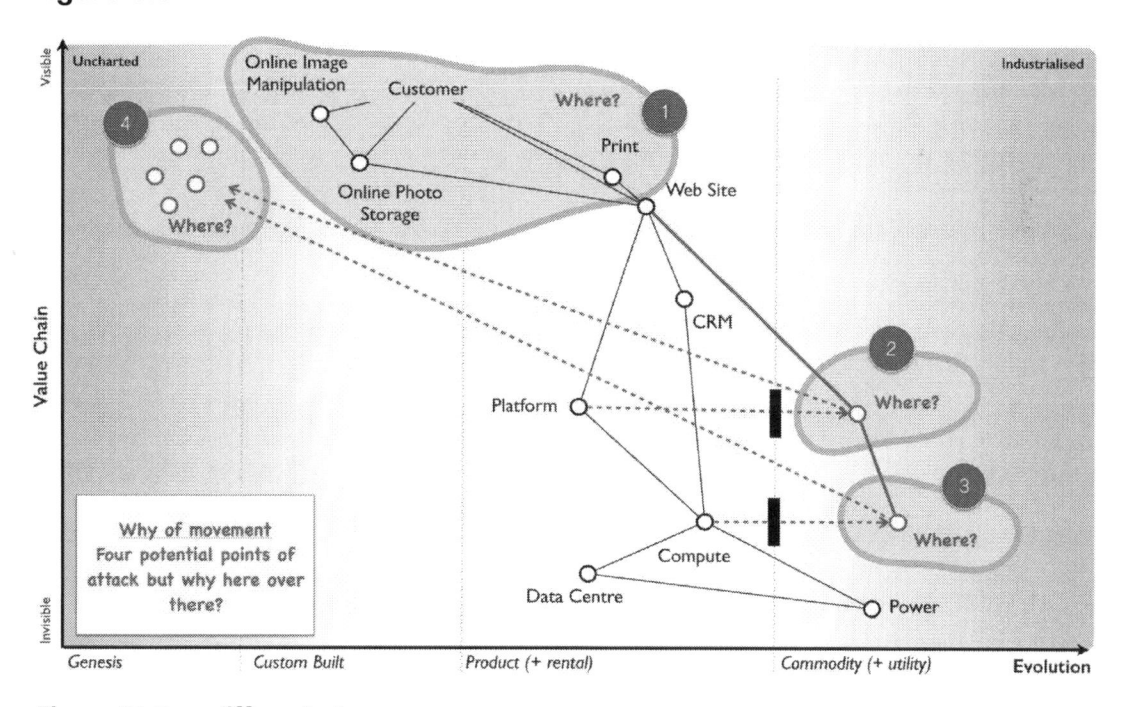

Figure 47: Four different wheres

Where 1 — We had an existing online photo service that was in decline but that we could concentrate on. There existed many other competitors in this space, many of which were either well financed (e.g. Ofoto) or ahead of us in terms of offering (e.g. Flickr). There were also unmet needs that we had found. As a company, we had acquired many capabilities and skills, not necessarily in the online photo business, as the group developed many different types of systems. We also had an internal conflict with our parent company's online photo service, which we built and operated. Whilst our photo service was open to the public, the parent company's service was focused on its camera owners and we had to tread a careful game here as our own service was sometimes considered a competitor. We had two external users (our public customers and our parent company), and though not explored in the map above, they had conflicting needs. By meeting the needs of our public consumers in the public site, we could diminish the value seen by our parent company in their own version. For example, making it easier for public consumers to upload images from mobile phones did not sit well with a parent company trying to sell cameras.

Where 2 — We had anticipated that a code execution platform would become a utility (what today is called serverless). Remember, this was 2005 and long before systems such as AWS Lambda had appeared. We had ample skills in developing coding platforms but most importantly, we had also learned what not to do through various painful all-encompassing Death Star projects. There would be inertia to this change among product vendors that would benefit us in our land grab. To complicate matters, many existing product customers would also have inertia and hence, we would have to focus on startups, though this required marketing to reach them. There was also a potential trade-off here as any platform would ultimately be built on some form of utility infrastructure similar to our own Borg system (a private utility compute environment that we operated providing virtual machines on-demand, based on Xen), and this would reduce our capital investment. Our company had mandates from the parent to remain profitable each and every month and to keep headcount fixed, hence, I had no room to expand and any investment made would have to come out of existing monthly profit, despite the reserves built up in the bank. A platform play offered the potential to reduce the cost of our other systems and increase the speed of development of our other revenue-generating projects, hence freeing up more valuable time until a point where the platform itself was self-sustaining.

Where 3 — We had anticipated that a utility infrastructure would appear. We had experience of doing this but we lacked any significant investment capability. I was also mindful that in some circles of the parent company, we were considered a development shop on the end of a demand pipeline and the parent was heavily engaged with an external hosting company. In this case, the parental company needs (many of which could be described as political) were potentially in conflict with our business needs. Unfortunately, I had painted ourselves into this corner with my previous efforts to simply "survive". If we made this move then, in essence, many of these problems were no different from the platform space, except the agility benefits of platform were considered to be higher. The biggest potential challenge to us would not be from existing product (e.g. server manufacturers) or rental vendors (e.g. hosting companies), but the likes of Google entering the space. This we expected to happen in the near future and we certainly lacked the financial muscle to compete if it did. It seemed more prudent to prepare to exploit any future move they made. However, that said, it was an attractive option and worth considering. One fly in the ointment was concerns that had been raised by various members of the team on issues of security and potential misuse of our systems by others. It seemed we would have our own inertia to combat due to our own past success with using products (i.e. servers), and despite the existence of Borg. Fighting multiple forms of inertia and the parent company whilst competing against a likely service from Google seemed a bad deal.

Where 4 — We could instead build something novel and new based upon any utility environments (either infrastructure or platform) that appeared. We understood that using utility systems would reduce our cost of investment, i.e. the gamble in the space. However, any novel thing would still be a gamble and we'd be up against many other companies. Fortunately, we were very adept at agile development and we had many crazy ideas we could pursue, generated by the regular hack days we ran. It might be a gamble in the dark but not one we should dismiss out of hand. It had the benefit of "just wait and see"; we could continue building and wait for the market to launch services we could exploit. Alas, I'm not the sort of person who wants to sit back and watch others create the field before I exploit it.

Looking at the map, we had four clear "wheres" we could attack. We could discuss the map, the pros and cons of each move in a manner, which wasn't just "does this have an ROI and is it core?" Instead, we were using the landscape to help us anticipate opportunity and points of attack. I suddenly felt our strategy was becoming more meaningful than just gut feel and copying memes from others. We were thinking about position and movement. I was starting to feel a bit like that wise executive I had met in the lift in the Hotel Arts in Barcelona when he was testing that junior (i.e. me) all those years ago. It felt good but I wanted more. How do I decide?

The dangers of past success

One significant problem around making a choice usually stems from past success and the comfort it brings. We had an existing photo service, along with other lines of business that generated a decent revenue. We were comfortably profitable and life was pretty easy. Would it not be better for me to just continue doing what we were doing? Why rock the boat? I'd be taking a risk changing the course we were on. However, I had recently watched another company fail to manage change and was acutely aware of the dangers of not taking a risk. That company was Kodak.

Being an online photo service, I had a ringside seat to the fundamental shift happening in the image market between 2000 to 2005. The photo had been seen as something with value to customers due to its costs in terms of time and money to produce — the visit to the photo lab, the cost of processing and the wait for it to be delivered via the post. Film was at the centre of this and the only thing more annoying than waiting for it to be processed was not having enough film to take that next shot on holiday. Many times in the past, I had to make choices over which picture I took due to a limited number of shots left. However, the image and the film were really just components to delivering my overall need, which was sharing my experiences. The image was also evolving from analog film to a new digital world in which I could take pictures and delete the ones I didn't like. I might have a limit in terms of memory card but I could always download to a computer and share with others. There was no film processing required.

I've created a map for that changing landscape in Figure 48, and as I go through more of my experience with the Kodak story, I'll make references to that map. The old world was one of analog film (**Point 1 below**). Sharing a moment was about sitting on the sofa with friends and family and passing the photo album. The film itself needing some mechanism of fulfilment such as the photo lab. However, the camera industry was rapidly becoming commodity with good enough disposable cameras. The analog world of images was also changing to one that was more digital (**Point 2**). Digital still cameras (DSC) had developed from cameras (**Point 3**) and were becoming more common. I could share an image by simply emailing it to others. Kodak had led the charge into this brave new world with early research in the mid 1970s, but somehow, it also seemed to be losing ground to others such as Sony and Canon.

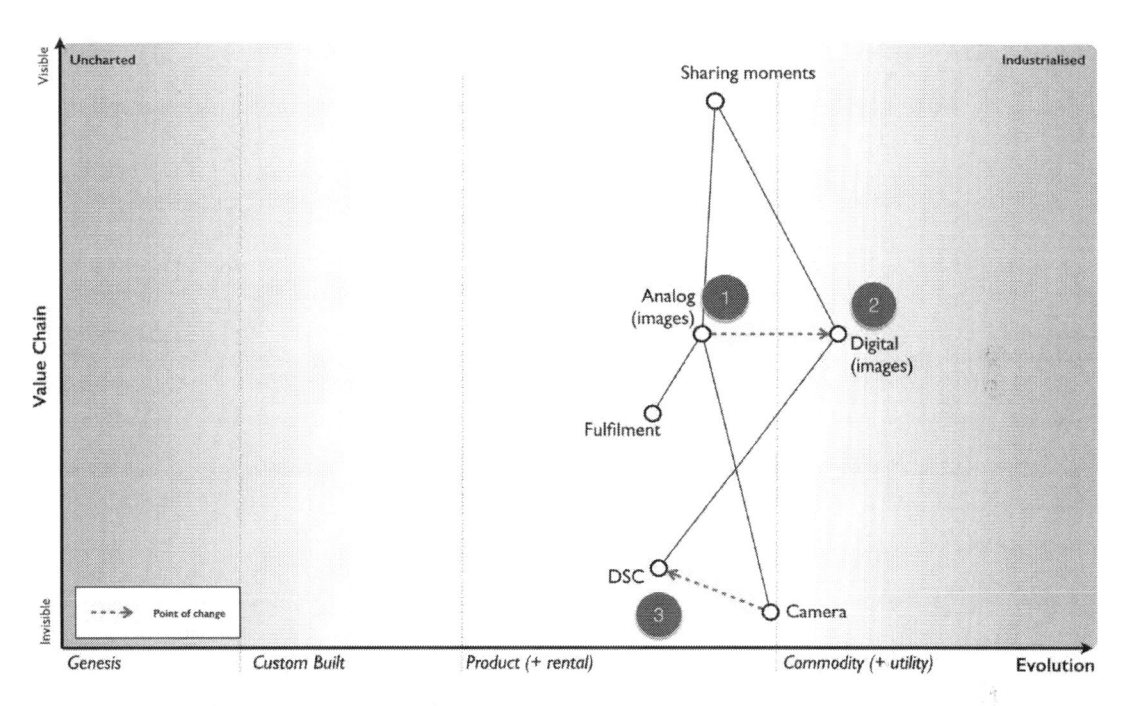

Figure 48: How images were changing

The growth of digital images and the spread of the internet had enabled the formation of online photo services. These provided simple ways of printing out your images, along with easier means for sharing with others. There was a very noticeable shift occurring from printing to sharing. You could create social networks to share images about hobbies or instead share with a close circle of friends. One of the early pioneers in this space was Ofoto, which had been acquired by Kodak in 2001. The messaging of Kodak had also changed around that time; it became more about sharing experiences and moments. However, Kodak wasn't the only competitor in the space and unlike many others, Kodak seemed to have a problem in that it made significant revenue from film processing. I've shown this problem in Figure 49 with the rise of online photo services (**Point 4**) and the inertia created by fulfilment (**Point 5**).

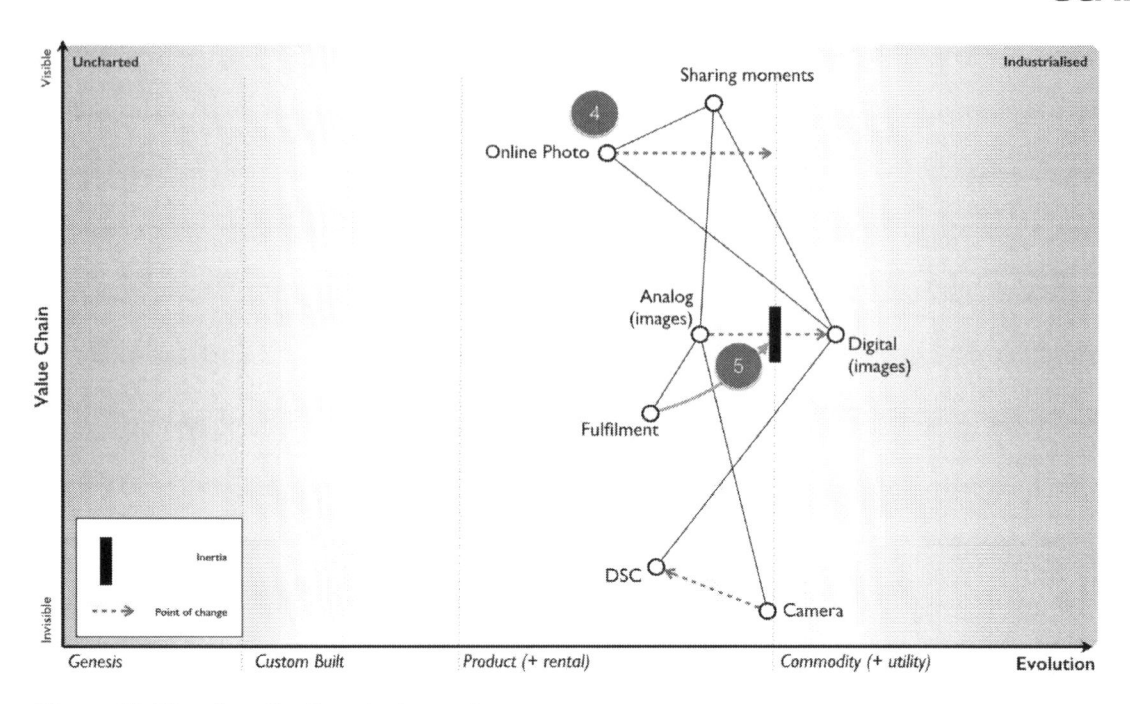

Figure 49: The rise of online photo services

Whilst it had a strong position in digital still cameras and online photo services, Kodak didn't seem to be maximising this. Others were quickly catching up and overtaking. I can only assume that the inertia created by its past success with film was significant. I suspect there was opposition to the change within the organisation. I'll guess the usual sort of lines of "digital is just small fry", "photos are the real business", "this will cannibalise our business" were trotted out. To an outside observer, it certainly seemed that Kodak was in conflict with itself. The first signs of this were already apparent in the late '90s with the release of the Advantix camera system; a curious blend of digital camera that produced film for processing. A somewhat odd attempt to have the digital world but still keep the analog — "It's the new but just like the old!"

There were also conflicting messages coming out of Kodak, despite its messaging. Whilst one part of the organisation seemed to be pushing digital, another part seemed to be resisting. Finally, in 2003, Kodak had introduced the Easyshare Printer Dock 6000, which enabled consumers to produce Kodak photo prints at home from digital images. When I first heard of this, it felt as though Kodak had finally overcome its inertia through a compromise between the fulfilment and the digital business (Point 6 in Figure 50 below). The future was one of a self-contained Kodak system from digital still camera to online service to photo printer. But there was a problem here. "Camera phones" had emerged, combining the two value chains of the mobile phone and the digital still camera.

Already, on our online site, we had witnessed the rapid growth of images taken with camera phones (**Point 7**).

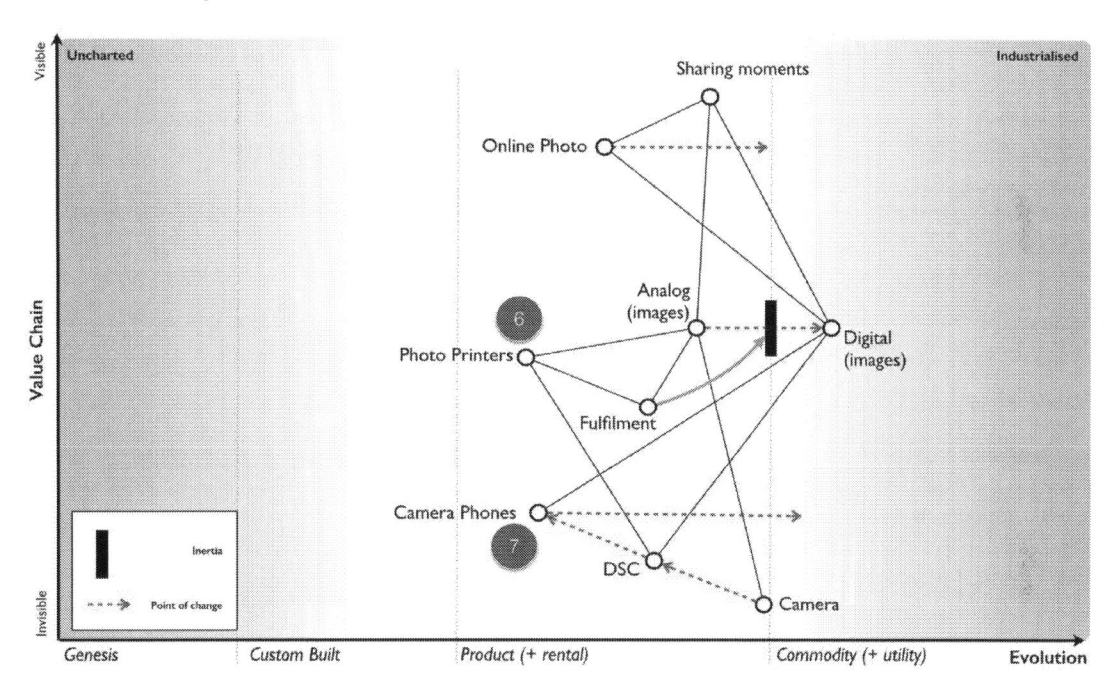

Figure 50: The solution and its doom

These "camera phones" were still uncommon but they seemed to herald a future where people would take pictures with their phones and share online. Today, few people call them camera phones; we just call them mobile phones. It's assumed that every mobile phone is a camera.

Back then however, it was clear there was no mass market future for print; only a niche compared to an enormous market of shared digital images. It seemed as though Kodak had overcome its inertia through a compromise, which meant investing in exactly where the future market wasn't going to be. By early 2005, from our perspective, the future of the entire industry from fulfilment to photo printers to cameras to film to digital still cameras (**Point 8**) was starting to look grim.

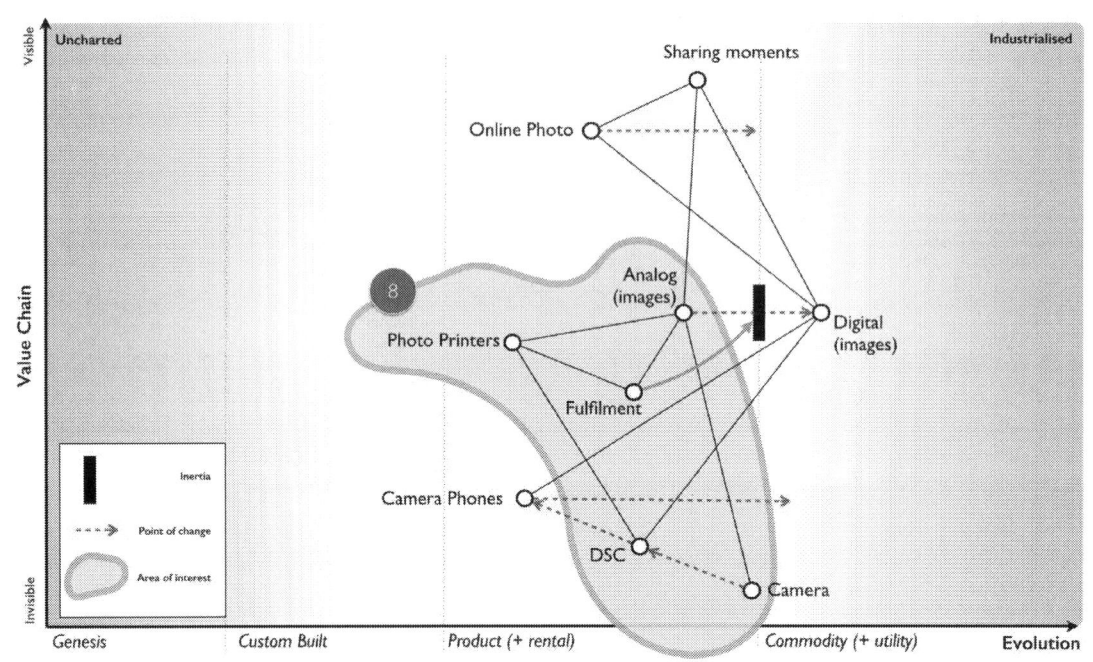

Figure 51: The end of the analogue world

For us, the future of pictures looked more like Figure 52 and printed photos were barely worth mentioning, unless you intended to specialise in a profitable niche.

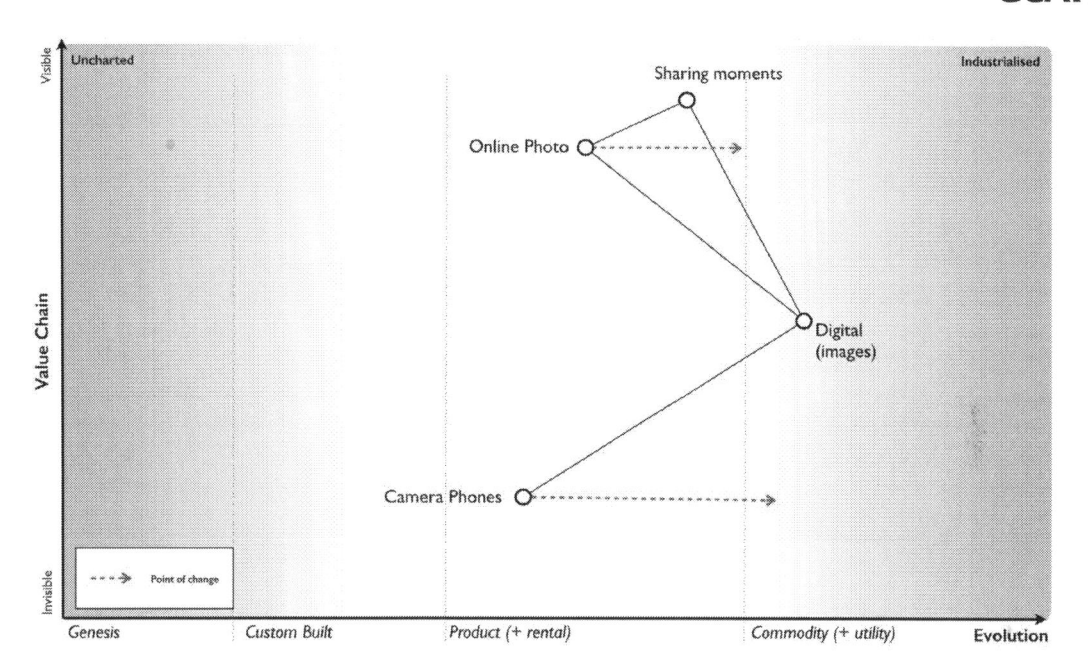

Figure 52: A future picture

In any choice I was going to make, I had to be careful of inertia and past success. Simply standing where we were might be the comfortable option but it didn't mean we would have a rosy future. Our fraught issues around our parent's photo service could grow if we embraced a camera phone future, as this would put us in direct conflict with its core DSC business. However, Kodak was a clear example of what could go wrong if you didn't move fast enough into the future, allowed inertia to slow you down, or compromised by placing the bets in the wrong place. But maybe there was another future we could find, but how far into the future should we peek?

The near, the far and the crazy

Back in the late '90s, I had taken a deep interest in 3D printing. It was the main reason why I had originally joined the near bankrupt online photo service in early 2000, because I envisaged a future where images of physical things would be shared. I wanted to learn about the space of sharing images. When we were acquired by one of the world's largest printer manufacturers, I was overjoyed. I assumed that they too would share my passion. I gave numerous presentations on the topic both externally and internally within the parent company on this subject, and to my disappointment, it was always the external crowd that got more excited. In 2004, I gave a presentation at Euro Foo on the future of 3D printers. The subject was a pretty hot topic at the time and one of the audience that I was fortunate enough to meet was Bre Pettis, who was demonstrating his felt-tip pen printer, the DrawBot. Why fortunate? Bre founded MakerBot and subsequently rocked the world of 3D printing.

Whilst 3D printing was a passion, I also had an interest in printed electronics, especially the work of Sirringhaus and Kate Stone. I started to use these concepts to describe a future world of how manufacturing would change. The basics are provided in Figure 53 but we will go through each step of this map. I'm going to assume you're becoming more familiar with maps and so we will just dive in.

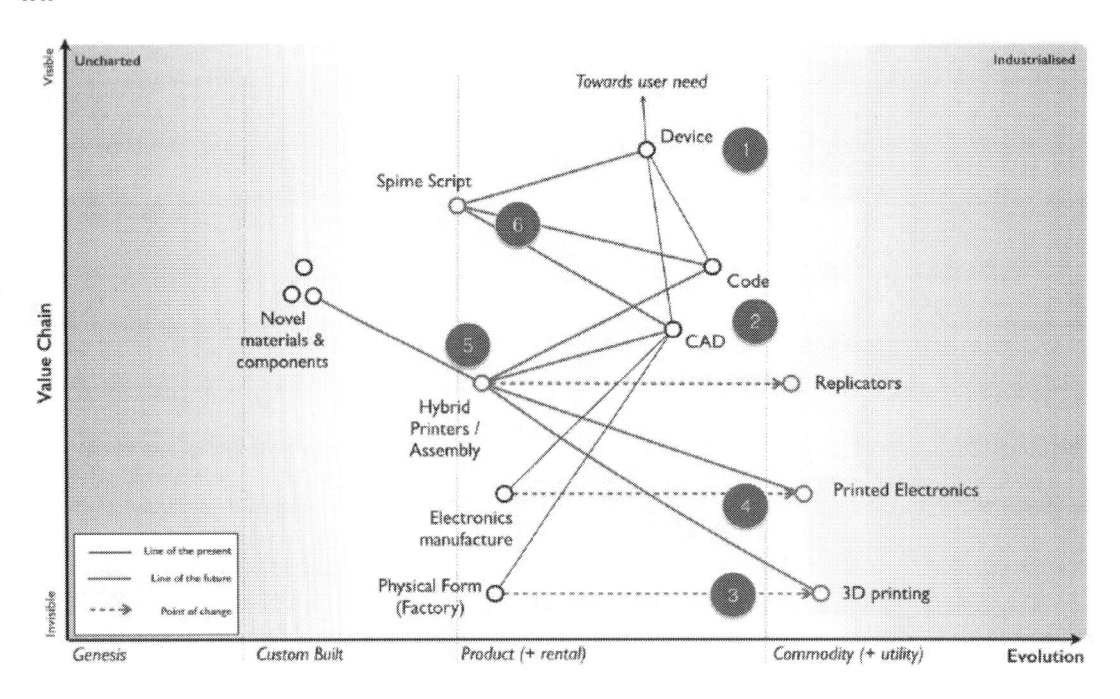

Figure 53: The near, the far and the crazy

First, let us start with the user need for some device (Point 1). I'll leave it as generic because I want to cover manufacturing itself and not the specific use of one device over another. Our device would have physical elements, including electronics, along with any software that would interact with it. The physical and electronic elements are commonly described through some form of computer-aided design (CAD) diagram, which provides instructions on what to build, and this is combined with our software, which is simply our code (Point 2).

The physical form would normally be manufactured by a factory that generally used common machinery involved in significant custom processes. However, this was starting to change with concepts such as digital factories and even 3D printers, which were becoming less magical and more common (Point 3). This promised a future world of highly industrialised factories without extensive re-tooling for each product run. Also, since those first inkjet-printed transistors of Sirringhaus in 2001, a new field of plastic and printed electronics was rapidly growing (Point 4). Electronics manufacture was on the path to becoming industrialised and I would just print the electronics I needed rather than combine a mix of commodity and non-commodity components on my own circuit board, created on some assembly line that changed with every product run.

For me, the interesting aspect of this was the combination of both physical and electronic forms. In 2005, I had become aware of several university-led efforts to create hybrid objects, including junction boxes where both the physical form and electrical components were printed (Point 5). This too would become industrialised to a world in which I printed my entire device rather than used factories which assembled. Now, along with potential for creating novel materials and components, this also had the opportunity to fundamentally change the concept of design.

The function of a device is a combination of its physical form, its electronics and any software that interacts with this. As hybrid printers industrialise then this function is described by purely digital means — the CAD (an instruction set), which is then printed, and the code (an instruction set), which is run. When we wish to change the function of a device then we need to change one of those two instruction sets, along with considering the interaction between the two. Normally, we try to make changes in software because it's less costly, but as hardware becomes more malleable then that equation changes. It also means we are now in a position to simply describe the function of the device that we want and allow a compiler to determine how that should be instantiated in the instruction sets.

My desire to add a sundial to my phone could be achieved through software or electronic or physical means, or a combination of all — a compiler could work out that decision tree for me. This opens up a possibility for an entire new form of programming language that compiles down to physical, electronic and coding forms, and where designers concentrate on describing the function of the thing and even object inheritance in the physical world. I called this theoretical programming language SpimeScript (Point 6), in honour of the marvellous book by Bruce Sterling on Shaping Things. This topic was my central theme of a talk I gave at Euro OSCON in 2006.

However, I had previously raised these discussions within the parent company and had become aware that whilst we might be able to make far future anticipations of change, they were increasingly built on layers of uncertainty and were increasingly unfamiliar and uncomfortable to others. The further we went, the crazier the ideas sounded and the more concerned people became. This itself creates a problem if you intend to motivate a team towards a goal. Hence, if I was going to choose a course of action, it needed to push the boundary, but not too far that it seemed like science fiction.

I was starting to feel uncomfortable with:-

Where 1 — Focus on the online photo service, for reasons of inertia and conflict.

Where 4 — Build something novel and new based upon future industrialised services, for being too far reaching.

The question now became, given our choices, could we influence the market in any way to benefit us? Could that help us decide why here over there?

Learning context specific gameplay

Context specific play: Accelerators, decelerators and constraints

I understood that everything evolved due to competition and had plenty of evidence to show past examples from electricity to nuts and bolts. The question was, could I somehow influence this? By coincidence, from the very early days of 2001, we had not only been users of open source but also contributors to it. We supported the Perl language and many other open source projects.

I had purposefully used these as fertile hunting grounds to recruit my amazing team during 2002–2005. But I had also observed how open source efforts through collaboration with others had produced stunning technology that out-surpassed proprietary efforts in many fields. In many cases, open source technology was becoming the de facto standard, and even the commodity in a field. It seemed that the very act of open sourcing, if a strong enough community could be created, would drive a once magical wonder to becoming a commodity. Open source seemed to accelerate competition for whatever activity it was applied to.

I had also witnessed how counter forces existed, such as fear, uncertainty and doubt. This was often applied by vendors to open source projects to dissuade others by reinforcing any inertia they had to change. Open source projects were invariably accused of being not secure, open to hackers (as though that's some form of insult), of dubious pedigree and of being a risk. However, to us, and the millions of users who consumed our services, then they were an essential piece of the jigsaw puzzle. By chance, the various battles around open source had increased my awareness of intellectual property. I became acutely conscious of how patents were regularly used for ring-fencing to prevent a competitor developing a product. This was the antithesis of competition and it was stifling. I started to form an opinion that certain actions would accelerate competition and drive a component towards a commodity, whilst others could be used to slow its evolution. The landscape could be manipulated.

At the same time, I had noticed that as certain activities became more industrialised and therefore more widespread, then it often became difficult to find people with the right skills or there were shortages of underlying components. The evolution of a component could therefore be constrained by a component it depended upon, such as knowledge. I've summarised these points in Figure 54 by applying them to our first map.

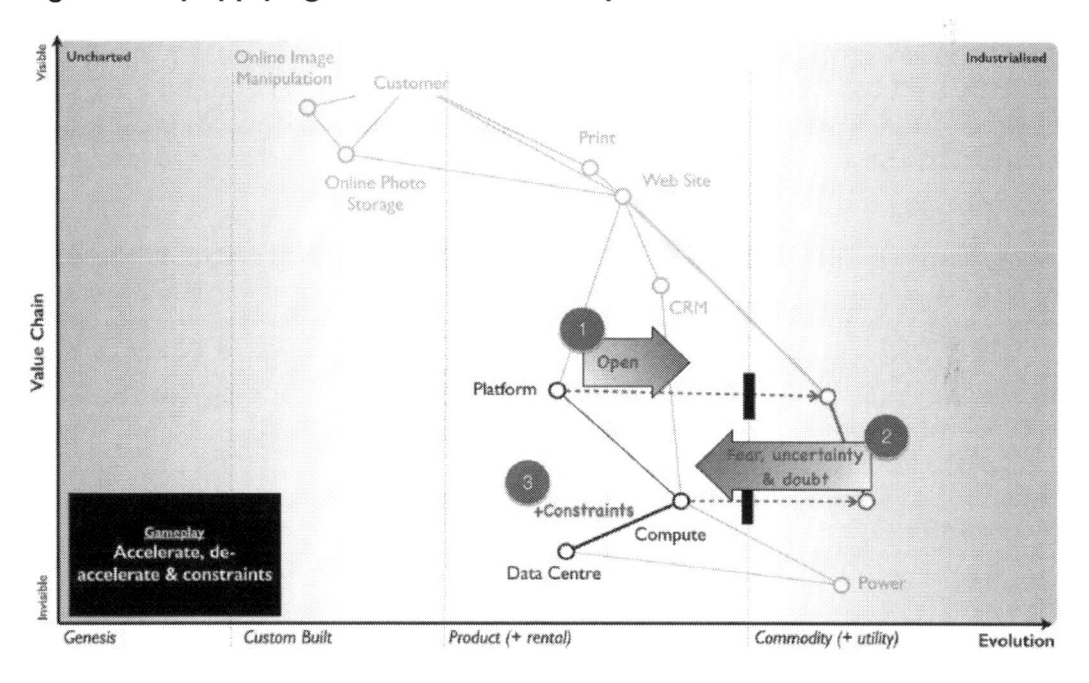

Figure 54: Accelerators, decelerators and constraints

Point 1 — The evolution of a component can be accelerated by an open approach, whether open source or open data.

Point 2 — The evolution of a component can be slowed down through the use of fear, uncertainty and doubt when crossing an inertia barrier or through the use of patents to ring-fence a technology.

Point 3 — The evolution of a component can be affected by constraints in underlying components, e.g. converting compute to a utility would potentially cause a rapid increase in demand (due to new uncharted components that are built upon it or the long tail of unmet business needs), but this requires building data centres. Whilst the provision of virtual machines could be rapid, the building of data centres are not.

I started to explore the map further, looking for other ways we could exploit.

Context specific play: Innovate, Leverage and Commoditise

I have frequently been told that it is better to be a fast follower than a first mover. But is that true? Using the map told me a slightly more complex story. Certainly, when exploring an uncharted space, there was lots of uncertainty and huge costs of R&D. It certainly seemed better to let others incur that risk and then somehow acquire that capability. But researchers and companies were constantly creating new things and so there was also a cost of discovering that new, successful thing in all the noise. We wouldn't be the only company trying to play that game, and any acquisition cost would reflect this. If we wanted to play that game then somehow, we needed to be able to identify future success more effectively than others.

By comparison, when taking a product to a utility then the component was already quite well known. It was defined, there was an existing market, but yes, there would be inertia. I realised there was a connection between the two and we were sitting on the answer. Our pioneer — settler — town planner structure had enabled us to cope with evolution and connect the two extremes. The settler's role was simply to identify future successful patterns and learn about them by refining a product or library component. In 2005, we actually referred to our settlers as the framework team and their success came from understanding the patterns within what the pioneers — our development team — had built. The pioneers were our gamblers.

However, what if our pioneers weren't us but instead other companies? Could our settlers discover successful patterns in all that noise? The problem of course was where would we look? Like any product vendor, we could perform some marketing survey to find out how people were using our components, but this seemed slow and cumbersome. Fortunately, our online photo service gave us the answer.

Between 2003 to 2005, we had exposed parts of the photo service through URL requests and APIs to others. It wasn't much of a leap to realise that if we monitored consumption of our APIs then we could use this to identify in real-time what other companies were being successful at without resorting to slow and expensive marketing surveys. This led to the **innovate — leverage — commoditse** (ILC) model. Originally, I called this innovate — transition — commoditise, and I owe Mark Thompson a thank you for persuading me to change transition to something more meaningful. The ILC model is described in Figure 55 and we will go through its operation.

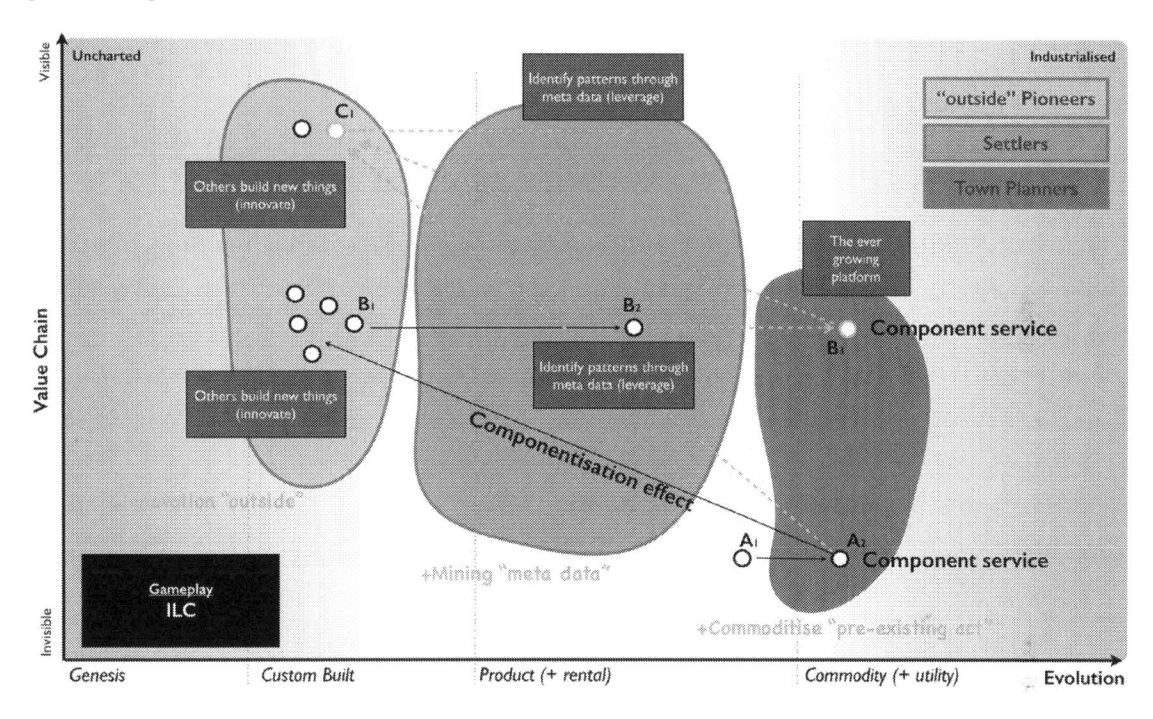

Figure 55: ILC (innovate, leverage and commoditise)

Take an existing product that is relatively well defined and commonplace and turn it into an industrialised utility (Point A1 to A2). This utility should be exposed as an easy to use API. Then encourage and enable other companies to innovate by building on top of your utility (Point B1). You can do this by increasing their agility and reducing their cost of failure, both of which a utility will provide. These companies building on top of your utility are your "outside" pioneers, or what we commonly call an "ecosystem".

The more companies you have building on top of your utility (i.e. the larger your ecosystem) then the more things your "outside" pioneers will be building, and the wider the scope of new innovations. Your "outside" ecosystem is in fact your future-sensing engine. By monitoring metadata such as the consumption of your utility services then you can determine what is becoming successful. It's important to note that you don't need to examine the data of those "outside" companies, but purely the metadata; hence, you can balance security concerns with future sensing. You should use this metadata to identify new patterns that are suitable for provision as industrialised components (B1 to B2). Once you've identified a future pattern then you should industrialise it to a discrete component service (B3), provided as utility and exposed through an API. You're now providing multiple components (A2, B3) in an ever-growing platform of component services for others to build upon (C1). You then repeat this virtuous circle.

Obviously, companies in any space that you've just industrialised (B2 to B3) might grumble "they've eaten our business model", so, you'll have to carefully balance acquisition with implementation. On the upside, the more component services you provide in your platform then the more attractive it becomes to others. You'll need to manage this ecosystem as a gardener encouraging new crops ("outside companies") to grow, and being careful not to harvest too much.

Do note, this creates an ever-expanding platform in the sense of a loose gathering of discrete component services (e.g. storage, compute, database), which is distinct from a code execution platform (i.e. a framework in which you write code).

There is some subtle beauty in the ILC model. If we take our ecosystem to be the companies building on top of our discrete component services, then the larger the ecosystem is:-

- the greater the economies of scale in our underlying components
- the more metadata exists to identify future patterns
- the broader the scope of innovative components built on top and hence, the wider the future environment that we can scan

This translates to an increasing appearance of being highly efficient as we industrialise components to **commodity** forms with economies of scale, but also highly customer focused due to **leveraging** metadata to find patterns others want. Finally, others will come to view us as highly innovative through the **innovation** of others. All of these desirable qualities will increase with the size of the ecosystem, as long as we mine the metadata and act as an effective gardener.

Being constantly the first mover to industrialise a component provides a huge benefit in enabling us to effectively be a fast follower to future success and wealth generation. The larger the ecosystem we build, the more powerful the benefits become. There is a network effect here and this model stood in stark contrast to what I had been told — that you should be a fast follower and that you could be one of highly innovative, efficient or customer focused. Looking at the map, I knew that with a bit of sleight of hand then I could build the impression that I was achieving all three by being a first mover to industrialise and a fast follower to the uncharted. I normally represent this particular form of ecosystem model (there are many different forms) with a set of concentric circles. I've transposed Figure 55 above into such a circular form and added some notes (see Figure 56). In this world, you push your "pioneers" outside of the organisation by allowing other companies to be your pioneers.

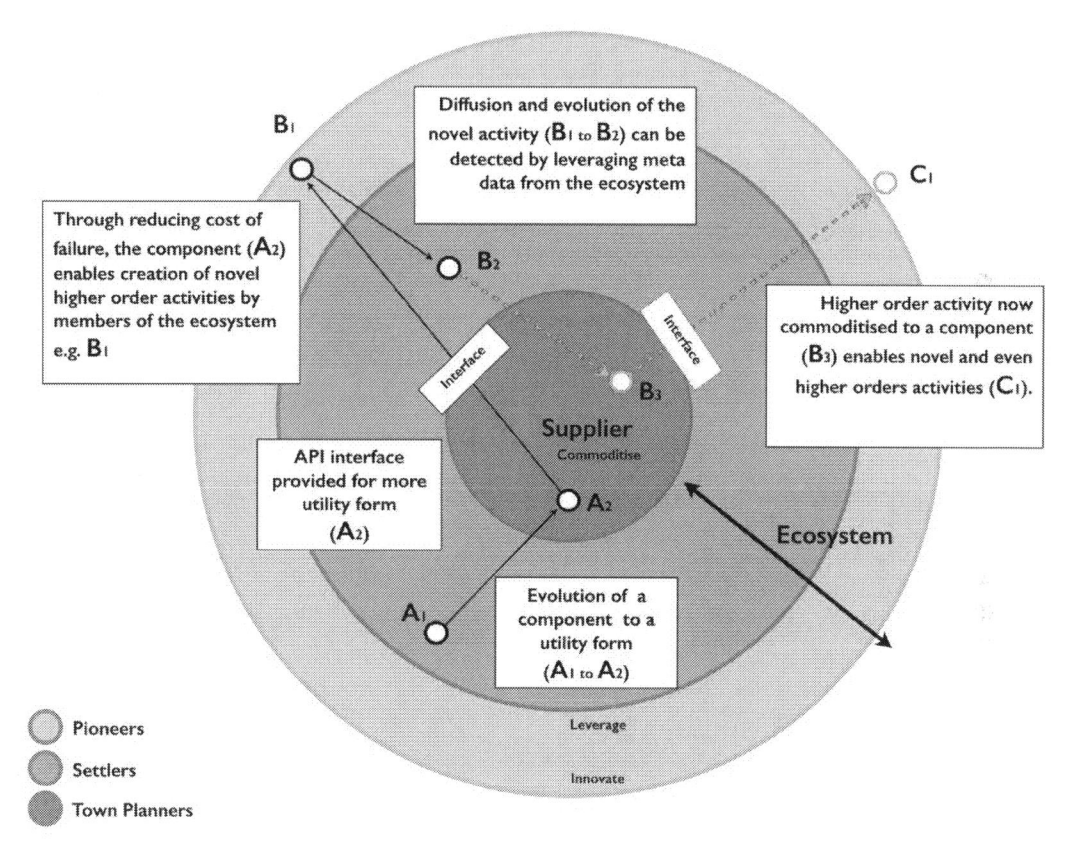

Figure 56: Circular view of ILC

Using context specific gameplay: the play

It was at this point, with some context-specific gameplay in hand, that I started to run through a few scenarios with James, my XO and my Chief Scientist, in our boardroom. Our plan started to coalesce and was enhanced by various experiments that the company had conducted. Not least of which was the head of my frameworks team walking in to tell me that they had just demonstrated we could develop entire applications (front end and back end) in Javascript.

At the same time as refining our play, I had encouraged the group to develop component services under the moniker of LibApi, as in liberation API, i.e. our freedom from endlessly repeated tasks and our existing business model. To say I was rapturous by this experiment would underestimate my pure delight. This fortuitous event helped cement the plan, which is summarised in Figure 57. I'll break it down and go through each point in detail.

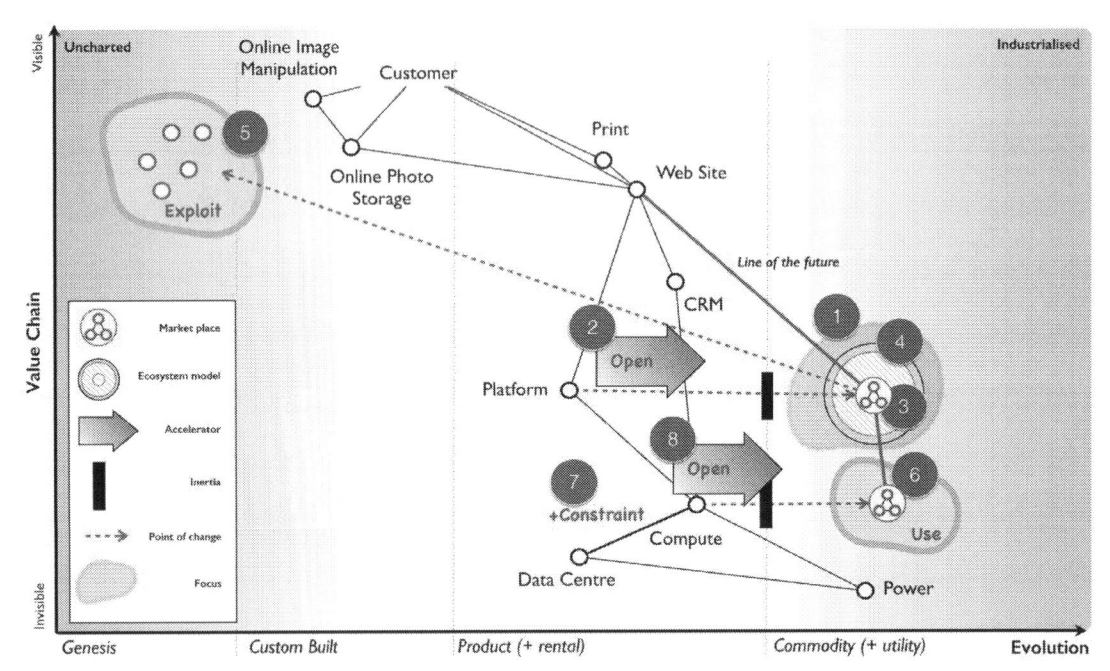

Figure 57: The Plan

Point 1 — The focus of the company would be on providing a code execution platform as a utility service, alongside an expanding range of industrialised component services for common tasks such as billing, messaging, an object store (a key-object store API), email, etc. All components would be exposed through public APIs and the service would provide the ability to develop entire applications in a single language — JavaScript. The choice of JavaScript was because of its common use, the security of the JS engine, and the removal of translation errors with both the front and back end code built in the same language. The entire environment would be charged on the basis of JavaScript operations, network usage and storage. There would be no concept of a physical or virtual machine.

Point 2 — To accelerate the development of the platform, the entire service would be open sourced. This would also enable other companies to set up competing services, but this was planned for and desirable.

Point 3 — The goal was not to create one Zimki service (the name given to our platform) but instead, a competitive marketplace of providers. We were aiming to grab a small but lucrative piece of a very large pie by seeding the market with our own utility service and then open sourcing the technology. To prevent companies from creating different product versions, the entire system needed to be open sourced under a licence, which enabled competition on an operational level but minimised feature differentiation of a product set — GPL seemed to fit the bill.

We still had a problem that service providers could differentiate and undermine the market. However, we also had a solution as our development process used test-driven development and the entire platform was exposed through APIs. In the process of developing, we had created an extensive testing suite. This testing suite would be used to distinguish between community platform providers (those who have taken the code but modified it in a significant way) and certified Zimki providers (those who complied with the testing suite). Through the use of a trademarked image for Zimki providers, we could enforce some level of portability between the providers.

By creating this marketplace, backed by an Open Zimki Foundation, we could overcome one source of inertia (reliance on a single provider) whilst enabling companies to try their own platform in- house first and developing new opportunities for ourselves from an application store, market reporting, switching services, brokerage capability, training, support and pre-built stand-alone Zimki clusters. Such an approach would also reduce our capital exposure, given the constraints we existed under.

Point 4 — We needed to build an ecosystem to allow us to identify the future services we should create and hence, we had to build an ILC model. Obviously, we could only directly observe the consumption data for those who built on our service, but what about other Zimki providers?

By providing common services such as GUBE (generic utility billing engine), along with an application store, a component library (a CPAN equivalent) and ultimately, some form of brokerage capability, then we intended to create multiple sources of metadata. We had a lot of discussion here over whether we could go it alone, but I felt we didn't have the brand name. We needed to create that marketplace and the potential was huge. I had estimated that the entire utility computing market (i.e. cloud computing) would be worth $200bn a decade later in 2016, and we would grab a small piece.

Our longer term prize was to be the market enabler and ultimately, build some form of financial exchange. We would require outside help to make this happen, given our constraints, but we decided not to promote that message as it was "too far in the future and too crazy" for most.

Point 5 — We needed to make it easy, quick and cheap for people to build entire applications on our platform. We had to ruthlessly cut away all the yak shaving (pointless, unpleasant and repeated tasks) that were involved in developing. When one of the development team built an entirely new form of wiki with client side preview and went from idea to launching live on the web in under an hour, then I knew we had something with potential. Pre-shaved Yaks became the catch-phrase to describe the service, and something we plastered across our T-shirts in 2005 and 2006.

Point 6 — We anticipated that someone would provide a utility infrastructure service. We needed to exploit this by building on top of them. We had become pretty handy at building worth based services (i.e. ones we charged for on a percentage of the value they created) over the years, and I knew we could balance our charging of the platform against any variable operational cost caused by a utility infrastructure provider.

By building on top of any utility infrastructure service, we would also have the advantage of cutting that supplier off from any metadata other than our platform was growing. If I played the game well enough then maybe that would be an exit play for us through acquisition. If we were truly going to be successful, then I would need to break the anchor of the parent company at some point in the future.

Point 7 — We knew that building data centres would be a constraint in utility infrastructure and that compute demand was elastic. This gave options for counter play, such as creating a price war to force up the demand beyond the ability of one supplier to provide. But in order to play one provider off against another, we needed to give competitors a route into the market. Fortunately, we had our Borg system, and though we had talked with one large well-known hardware provider (who had been resistant to the idea of utility compute), we could open source (Point 8) this space to encourage that market to form. I had counter plays I could use if I needed them, and it was to our advantage if a fragmented market of utility infrastructure providers existed. We should aim for no one company to gain overall control of this space.

The option looked good based upon our capabilities. It was within the realm of possibilities and mindful of the constraints we had. This seemed to provide the best path forward. It would mean refocusing the company, removing services like our online photo site, and putting other revenue services into some form of minimal state until the platform business grew enough that we could dispose of them. I was ready to pull the trigger but there was one last thing I needed.

Impacts on purpose

The decision to act can impact the very purpose of your company — the strategy cycle is not only iterative, it's a cycle. In this case, our purpose was going from a "creative solutions group", a meaningless juxtaposition of words, to a "provider of utility platforms". Just stating that purpose was not enough, it never is. If I wanted to win this battle then I needed to bring everyone onboard and make the purpose meaningful. I had to create a moral imperative, a reason for doing this, a vision of the future, a rallying cry, a flag we could wave and our very own crusade.

For us, this became embodied in the words "Pre-shaved Yaks". We intended to rid the world of the endless tasks that got in the way of coding. We would build that world where you just switched on your computer, opened up a browser and started coding. Everything from worrying about capacity planning, configuring packages to installing machines would be gone. Every function you wrote could be exposed as a web service. Libraries of routines written by others could be added with ease through a shared commons, and you could write the entire application in hours, not days or weeks or months. This was our purpose. It was my purpose. And it felt good.

What happened next?

We built it.

I refocused the company, we cut away that which didn't matter and we developed our platform. By 18th February 2006, we had the platform, core API services, billing system, portal and three basic applications for others to copy. We officially beta launched in March 2006 (our alpha had been many months earlier); this was a full two years before Google appeared on the scene with AppEngine. The public launch was at dConstruct in September 2006.

By 18th April 2006, we had 30 customers, 7 basic applications and a monthly rate of 600K API calls. By 19th June 2006, we were clocking a run rate of 2.8M API calls. We were growing at a phenomenal rate, and by the first quarter of 2007, we had passed the 1,000 developer mark, i.e. others building systems for their own users. After a slow start, our growth was now exceeding even my optimistic forecasts, given the huge educational barriers I expected — see Figure 58.

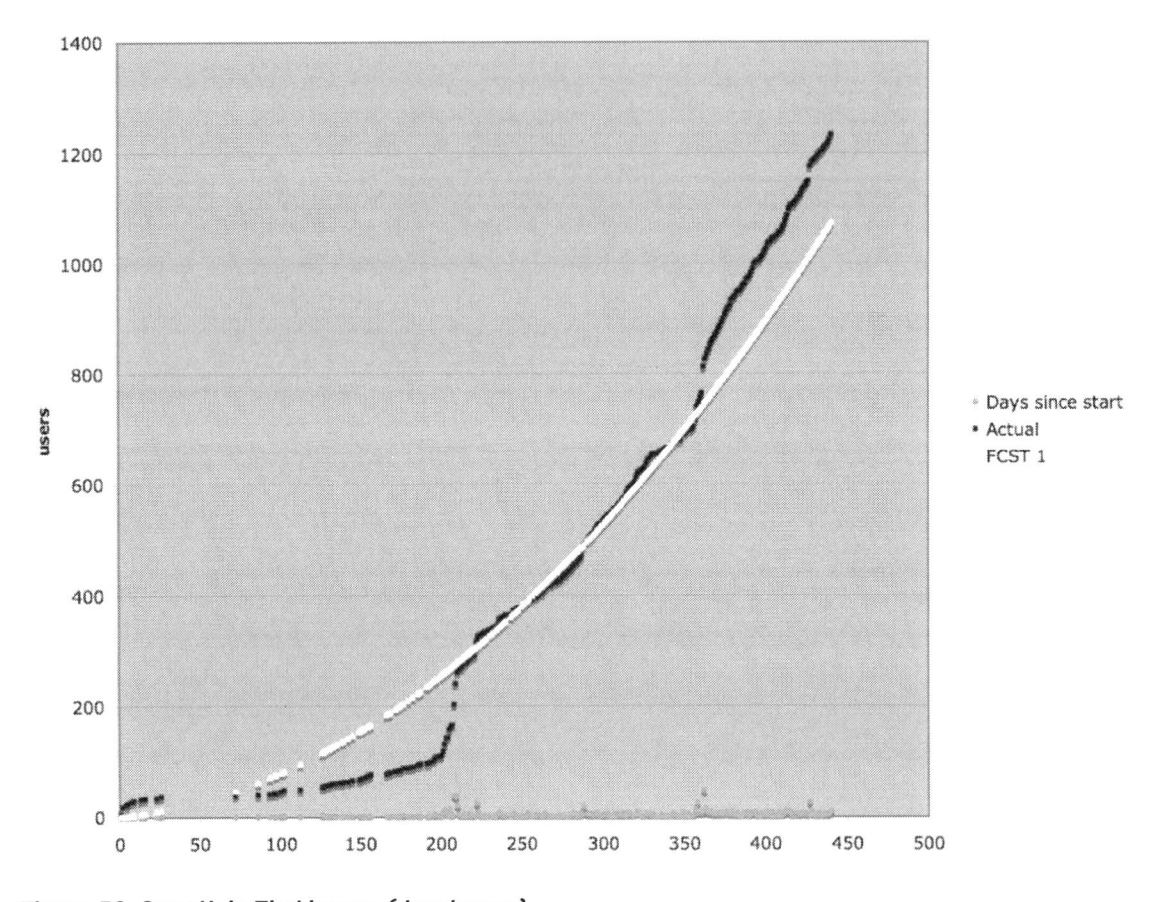

Figure 58: Growth in Zimki users (developers)

But during that time, something exceptional had also happened. On 25th August 2006, it wasn't Google but Amazon that launched with EC2. I was rapturous once again. Amazon was a big player; they had provided instant credibility to the idea of utility computing and in response, we immediately set about moving our platform onto EC2. Every time we presented at events, our booths tended to be flooded with interest, with crowds of people often four, five or six layers deep. The company had embraced the new direction (there were still a few stragglers) and there was a growing buzz. We were still very small and had a huge mountain to climb, but we had taken our first steps, announced the open sourcing, secured a top billing at OSCON in 2007, and the pumps were primed. But Houston, we had a problem.

What went wrong?

The problem was me. I had massively underestimated the intentions of the parent company. I should have known better, given that I had spent over three years (2002–2005) trying to persuade the parent company that 3D printing would have a big future, or my more recent attempts that mobile phones would dominate the camera market. The parent company had become preoccupied with SED televisions and focusing on its core market (cameras and printers). Despite the potential that I saw, we were becoming less core to them and they had already begun removing R&D efforts in a focus on efficiency. They had brought in an outside consultancy to look at our platform and concluded that utility computing wasn't the future and the potential for cloud computing (as it became known) was unrealistic. Remember, this was 2006. Amazon had barely launched. Even in 2009, big name consultancies were still telling companies that public cloud wasn't the future, or at least, it was a long way away.

The parent company's future involved outsourcing our lines of business to a systems integrator (SI), and as I was told "the whole vision of Zimki was way beyond their scope".

I had several problems here. First, they wouldn't invest in our service because apparently, a decision had been made higher up within the parent company on what was core. What they were concerned with was the smooth movement of our lines of business to the SI. That supported their core aims and their needs. When I raised the idea of external investment then the problem became that they couldn't keep a stake in something that they said was not core.

When I raised the idea of a management buy-out, they would always go to what they had described as an "unrealistic" $200bn market figure for 2016. Surely I would be willing to pay a hefty sum based upon this future market as a given for a fledgling startup in a fledgling market? No venture capital firm would take such an outrageous one-sided gamble. In any case, I was told the discussion could always be left until after the core revenue services were transferred to the SI. This was just shorthand for "go away".

The nail in the coffin was when I was told by one of the board that the members had decided to postpone the open sourcing of our platform and that they wanted me to immediately sign contracts cancelling our revenue-generating services at an unspecified date to be filled in later. As the person who normally chaired the board meeting then, I was annoyed at being blindsided, the choice and myself. Somehow, in my zeal to create a future focused on user needs and a meaningful direction, I had forgotten to gain the political capital I needed to pull it off. I might have created a strong purpose and built a company capable of achieving it but I had messed up big time with the board. It wasn't their fault; they were focusing on what was core to the parent company and their needs.

The members were all senior executives of the parent company and it should have been obvious that they were bound to take this position. I realised that I had never truly involved them in our journey and had become preoccupied with building a future for others. I had not even fully explained to them our maps, relying instead on stories, but this was because I still hadn't realised how useful maps really were. In my mind, maps were nothing more than my way of explaining strategy because I hadn't yet found that magic tome that every other executive learnt at business school. This was a powerful group of users — my board and the parent company — that had needs that I had not considered. Talk about a rookie mistake. I had finally been rumbled as that imposter CEO.

There was no coming back from this; they were adamant on their position and had all the power to enforce it. I was about to go on stage at OSCON (O'Reilly open source conference) in 2007 and rather than my carefully crafted message, I had to somehow announce the non-open sourcing of our platform and the non-creation of a future competitive utility market. I was expected to break a promise I had made to our customers and I was pretty clear that postpone was a quaint way of saying "never". I couldn't agree with the direction they had chosen and we were at loggerheads. My position was untenable and I resigned.

The company's services were quickly placed on the path to being outsourced to the SI and the employees were put through a redundancy program, which all started a few days after I resigned. The platform was disbanded and closed by the end of the year. The concepts however weren't lost, as a few of these types of ideas made their way through James Duncan into ReasonablySmart (acquired by Joyent) and another good friend of mine, James Watters, into Cloud Foundry. I note that Pivotal and its platform play is now valued at over $2.5bn and serverless is a rapidly-growing concept in 2016. As for SED televisions? Well, some you win, some you lose.

As for the consultancy, any frustration I might have is misdirected because I was the one who failed here. It was my job to lead the company and that didn't just mean those who worked for me but also the board.

In these first chapters, I've hopefully shown you how to understand the landscape you're competing in, anticipate the future, learn to apply doctrine, develop context specific gameplay, build the future and then finally blow it by ignoring one set of users. Would Zimki have realised its potential and become a huge success? We will never know, but it had a chance. This was my first run through of the strategy cycle and at least I felt as though I had a vague idea as to what I was doing rather than that naïve youth of "seems fine to me". I was still far from the exalted position of that confident executive that I had met and I was determined to get better next time. Fortunately for me, there was a next time, but that's another part of the story.

Categorising Gameplay

Gameplay is context specific. You need to understand the landscape before you use it. The purpose of gameplay is once you determine the possible "wheres" that you could attack (which requires you to understand landscape and anticipate change from common economic patterns), then you look at what actions you can take to create the most advantageous situation. As we go through this book, we will cover all sorts of gameplay and refine the concepts discussed above. To give you an idea of what we need to cover, I've put some basic forms in Figure 59, marking off in grey some that we've already mentioned.

User Perception	Education	Fear, uncertainty and doubt	Creating artificial needs	Confusion of choice
	Brand and marketing	Bundling	Artificial competition	Lobbying / counterplay
Accelerators	Market enablement	Open approaches	Exploiting network effects	Co-operation
	Industrial policy			
De-accelerators	Exploiting constraint	IPR	Creating constraints	Limitation of competition
Dealing with toxicity	Pig in a poke	Disposal of liability	Sweat and dump	Refactoring
Market	Differentiation	Pricing policy	Buyer / supplier power	Harvesting
	Standards game	Last man standing	Signal distortion	Trading
Defensive	Threat acquisition	Raising barriers to entry	Procrastination	Defensive regulation
	Limitation of competition	Managing inertia		
Attacking	Directed investment	Experimentation	Centre of gravity	Undermining barriers to entry
	Fool's mate	Press release process		
Ecosystem	Alliances	Co-creation	Sensing Engines (ILC)	Tower and moat
	Two factor markets	Co-opting and intercession	Embrace and extend	Channel conflicts & disintermediation
Competitor	Ambush	Fragmentation play	Reinforcing competitor inertia	Sapping
	Misdirection	Restriction of movement	Talent raid	
Positional	Land grab	First mover	Fast follower	Weak signal / horizon
Poison	Licensing play	Insertion	Designed to fail	

Figure 59: Gameplay

I've categorised the above forms of gameplay depending upon their main impact:-

- Alteration of user perception
- Accelerators to evolution
- De-accelerators to evolution
- Means of dealing with toxicity (i.e. legacy)
- Market plays
- Defensive plays
- Attacking plays
- Ecosystem models
- Positional plays
- Poison mechanisms (prevents a competitor using the space)

I have to reiterate that every time that I've gone around the cycle, I've got better at playing the game. As we travel along the same path, I'll be adding in more economic patterns, more doctrine and more context specific gameplay, along with deep diving on some of the parts I've glossed over or were merely general concepts in those early days. But as with all journeys, let us stick to the path and no short-cutting. Every step is valuable; every landscape is an opportunity to learn from.

An exercise for the reader

Hopefully by now, you may have created a map or two. Using the concepts in this chapter, examine your map and first try to identify where you might attack. Now, using the gameplay in Figure 59, have a go and try to see where you might use gameplay and whether one route or another stands out. It really does help to work with others on this. Fortunately, maps provide you with a mechanism to communicate, collaborate and learn.

Chapter 6 - Getting started

I often talk about that wise executive that I met in the Hotel Arts in Barcelona. I'll jump ahead in the story and let you into a little secret. He didn't have a clue either and I wasn't the only person faking at being an executive. However, I didn't find this out until six years after I had started mapping when someone pointed it out to me. I had always assumed that there was some secret tome out there and mapping was just my poor man's way of emulating what everyone else was already doing. It turned out that most of the industry was instead fighting battles with little to no understanding of the landscape. It's like generals fighting without maps. It boils everything down to luck and individual heroism.

When I discovered this, and it was an almighty shock, I started to question the trove of business strategy books in my small library. I had an onerous task of going through it all and categorising individual pieces as doctrine, climatic pattern, context specific or just plain luck. These days, when someone tells me they know strategy then I ask them for a map of their business. If they can't show me it, then regardless of their claims, I take a sceptical position. They probably don't know as much as they hope they do. They might even be more dangerous than this as it's rarely the unknown that gets you but what we think we know but don't.

This doesn't mean I think people are daft but instead, that understanding your landscape, the context that you're competing in and having a modicum of situational awareness is not a luxury for strategy; it is at the very core of it. Inspiring vision statements, well-trained forces, a strong culture and good technology will not save you if you fail to understand the landscape, the position of forces and their size and capabilities. Colonel Custer is a worthy lesson here and even he had maps that were better than most corporates today. I've seen billions wasted by companies that have charged into battles that they have no hope of winning. I've seen endless SWOT diagrams, stories and other magic thinking used to justify such actions. I've also seen others tear apart industries with ease.

Unfortunately, for those who lack some form of military background then situational awareness is rarely a topic of discussion. It's often a struggle to make executives appreciate that it might matter, that the secrets of success they've recently read about might not work everywhere and you have to apply thought to the landscape. It's the same with chess. I can show you the board (a map) and then teach you the rules of the game (climatic patterns), universally useful principles like supporting or pinning pieces (doctrine), and then specific moves like Fool's mate (context-specific gameplay). However, even with all this then you still have to apply thought and decide where you're going to move or use some form of computer to work through billions of permutations. There is no magic guide or 2x2 solution. Games can teach us a lot about management.

In more recent years, I've even started to recommend that executives spend a month or two in some form of coaching that involves playing a massive multiplayer online role-playing game (MMORPG) such as World of Warcraft (WoW). You might think that this sounds like goofing off from the real work of business but for those who are uninitiated then there are some basic practices that an MMORPG will teach you. These include:-

The importance of situational awareness. Before launching your team of elves and dwarves into the midst of a battle then the first thing you do is scout out the landscape and improve your situational awareness. Understanding the landscape is critical to strategic play, to learning, to using force multipliers and to not getting spanked, i.e. beaten soundly by the opponent. Play the game long enough and you'll know this by instinct, along with moaning at players who haven't bothered to look at the map, hence wasting both their and your time with constant questions of "Where is this?" or "How do we get there?"

The importance of aptitude. The biggest battles require a multitude of aptitudes from damage (those who do our spanking usually from range) to tanking (defensive protection) to healing (those tanks get spanked a lot and need healing) to crowd control (those mage sleep spells aren't there for just looking at). The way you play and how the roles are deployed depends upon the scenario. Of course, without situational awareness then you're at a huge disadvantage as you can often turn up with precisely the wrong sort of forces.

The importance of collaboration. A multitude of roles requires team play, which means communication, coordination and acting in the interests of the team. It also helps if everyone uses a common language such as a map.

The importance of preparation. There's no point turning up to the fight with an assortment of weapons if you don't know how to use them. The largest guilds in some of these MMORPGs have many hundreds to thousands of players supported with extensive wikis, communication mechanisms, training and development, tactical game plays, UI engineering, structure, leadership, specialist cells and information systems. These provide a systematic mechanism of learning.

So, how does an MMORPG compare to business? In general, we don't have maps in business. Most companies suffer from poor situational awareness, being caught out by predictable changes. The most telling factor here is that business strategy is normally a tyranny of action — how, what and when — as opposed to awareness — where and why. On the whole, we do a bit better at recognising that multiple aptitudes are needed. However, we often fall down by not considering attitude, the context and then compound this with isolation (operation in silos). We certainly try when it comes to team play, often having team-building exercises, which can be a bit hit or miss.

We also tend to complain about communication, despite the plethora of tools available. This can usually be traced back again to poor situational awareness — if we don't know the landscape and fail to create a plan of attack based upon this, replacing instead with vague notions of vision or a story, then it becomes difficult to communicate how things are actually going. It's far better that the question "Where are you" receives a response of a coordinate on a map than a response of "I've just walked along a path, I'm by a tree and I can see lots of orcs. The sun is shining."

In fact, abundant communication mechanisms rather than efficient communication can itself become a problem without good situational awareness, as new players constantly ask "where should we go?" as they run around in a daze. This can take up valuable time from other team members and weaken your overall strength. Preparation itself is almost non-existent in corporates. In some areas, we might attempt scenario planning and a few exec games about imagining you're a startup trying to disrupt your business, but on the whole, we're often so busy with immediate work such as firefighting and keeping up with competitors that we create little time to prepare.

There's an awful lot to be said for learning about these aspects from online games. Anyone under the illusion that business is some bastion of strategic play should spend a few minutes watching an experienced group run an organised raid. Those people tend to use levels of strategic play and doctrine that most businesses can only dream of. Fortunately, in business, we're often up against other organisations that equally lack situational awareness, suffer from isolation, have weak team play, ineffective but abundant communication and lack preparation.

The effect is somewhat remarkably similar to a group of inexperienced World of Warcraft players just charging at each other with cries of "Attack" followed by "Will someone heal me?" An exciting brawl of chaos with often single participants — hero players, the Steve Jobs of your Elven army — making the difference. Of course, face either team or in fact both teams against an experienced and well-rehearsed group then it stops becoming a brawl and starts becoming a massacre. The healers get wiped first, followed by crowd control, tanks and then poor and undefended damage dealers.

In the world of business, there are some really dangerous groups out there. Don't expect to go up against them with the usual "Here's the vision, we've got great people... now charge!" approach. It's far more sensible to find a profitable exit in order to fight another day. That's a hint to those gaming companies starting to be concerned about Amazon's encroachment into their space with Lumberyard. Either start learning from your own online players or find a new industry to bunker down in. Finally, don't expect to just read a few chapters on mapping or play a couple of games and instantly transform into a master of strategy; there is a long journey ahead of you.

Tips for mapping

There are a couple of general tips, common terms and diagrammatic forms that I apply to mapping itself. My tips include:-

All models are wrong; some are merely useful.

Mapping is not the answer; it's simply a guide. Hence, don't try to create the perfect map; the key is to produce good enough that you can collaborate around, and this requires you to share and open yourself up to challenge. Also, you'll likely use other tools alongside mapping when scenario planning and examining the viability of different points of attack. This can include financial models to my current favourite of business model canvas.

Where before why

When thinking about strategy, the first thing you need to do is identify **where *you can attack before *why** here over there? It's all about position (y-axis) and movement (x-axis).

Iterative and continuous learning

The entire strategy cycle is iterative and you're going to have to follow the same path. Which means mapping is not going to be a one-off exercise but something that happens all the time. Again, the temptation is to map the entire landscape in some sort of Death Star — large scale, all-encompassing, doomed to fail — effort in order to create that perfect answer. You should instead embrace the uncertainty, think small and start somewhere (have a bias towards action). If you're using mapping and it's either taking a long time or doesn't seem to help answer any of your questions, then stop. Don't be afraid to find a better way of doing this. No model is perfect.

Learn yourself

If you are responsible for strategy then you need to learn to play the game yourself and take responsibility for it. I often give strategy consultants a hard time, but this doesn't mean they don't have a use. Don't however rely on third parties to give you an answer; instead, use them to help you challenge your strategy and to learn new forms of gameplay.

Terms

There are numerous terms associated with mapping. I'm often guilty of using them without clearly explaining to others, so in order to rectify this, I've provided the most common in Figure 60.

Context	Our purpose and the landscape
Environment	The context and how it is changing
Situational awareness	Our level of understanding of the environment
Actual	The map in use
Domain	Uncharted vs Transitional vs Industrialised
Stage	Of evolution e.g. Genesis, Custom, Product, Commodity
Type	Activity, Practice, Data or Knowledge
Component	A single entity in a map
Anchor	The user need
Position	Position of a component relative to the anchor in a chain of needs
Need	Something a higher level system requires
Capability	High level needs you provide to others
Movement	How evolved a component is
Interface	Connection between components
Flow	Transfer of money, risk & information between components
Climate	Rules of the game, patterns that are applied across contexts
Doctrine	Approaches which can be applied regardless of context
Strategy	A context specific approach

Figure 60: Terms

Symbols

Maps are obviously visual, and whilst they are far from the Ordnance Survey maps of geography, it's useful to have a common lexicon of symbols. In Figure 61, I've provided the ones I use.

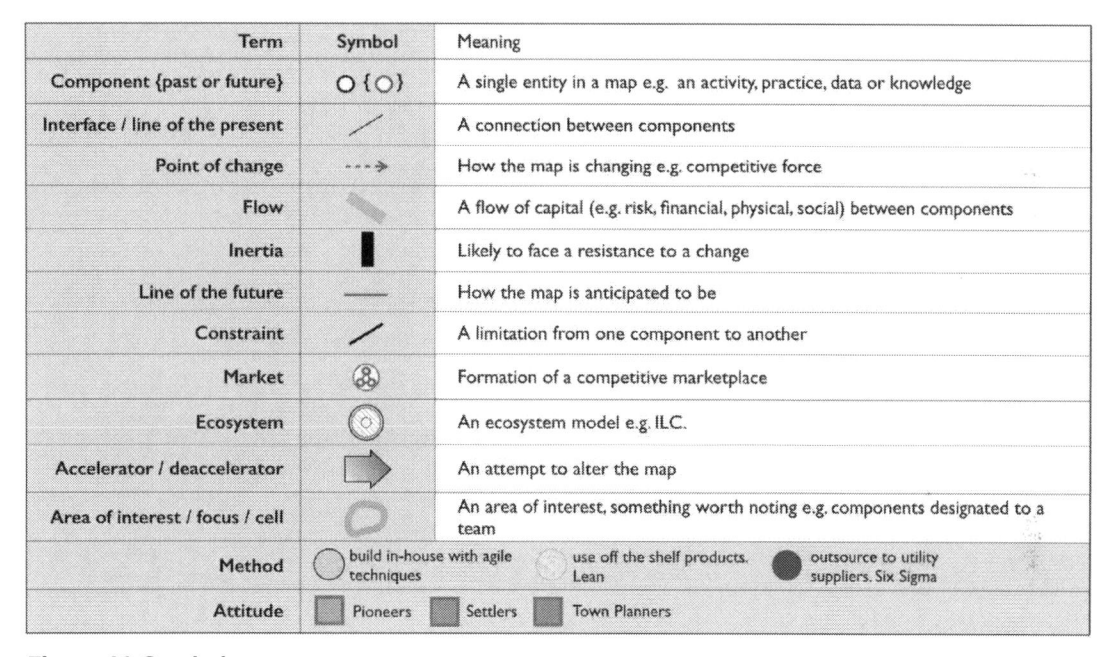

Term	Symbol	Meaning
Component {past or future}	O {O}	A single entity in a map e.g. an activity, practice, data or knowledge
Interface / line of the present	/	A connection between components
Point of change	--→	How the map is changing e.g. competitive force
Flow		A flow of capital (e.g. risk, financial, physical, social) between components
Inertia	▮	Likely to face a resistance to a change
Line of the future	—	How the map is anticipated to be
Constraint	/	A limitation from one component to another
Market		Formation of a competitive marketplace
Ecosystem		An ecosystem model e.g. ILC.
Accelerator / deaccelerator	⇒	An attempt to alter the map
Area of interest / focus / cell		An area of interest, something worth noting e.g. components designated to a team
Method	○ build in-house with agile techniques	○ use off the shelf products. Lean	● outsource to utility suppliers. Six Sigma
Attitude	Pioneers	Settlers	Town Planners

Figure 61: Symbols

A nod to early terms

Mapping itself has evolved over time, hence the terms I used in the past are slightly different to the terms I use today. These cosmetic changes are purely to help refine the craft; the underlying meaning has remained constant.

How to implement mapping

Most organisations have structures in place that can be used to embed mapping, whether it's an architectural group or an office of the CEO or a business relationship function or some other home. Typically, in a distributed organisation, you normally have the business units that are responsible for delivery, some form of executive function that covers policy, approval and accountability, and a common or shared services supply group that provides some element of commonality, as per Figure 62.

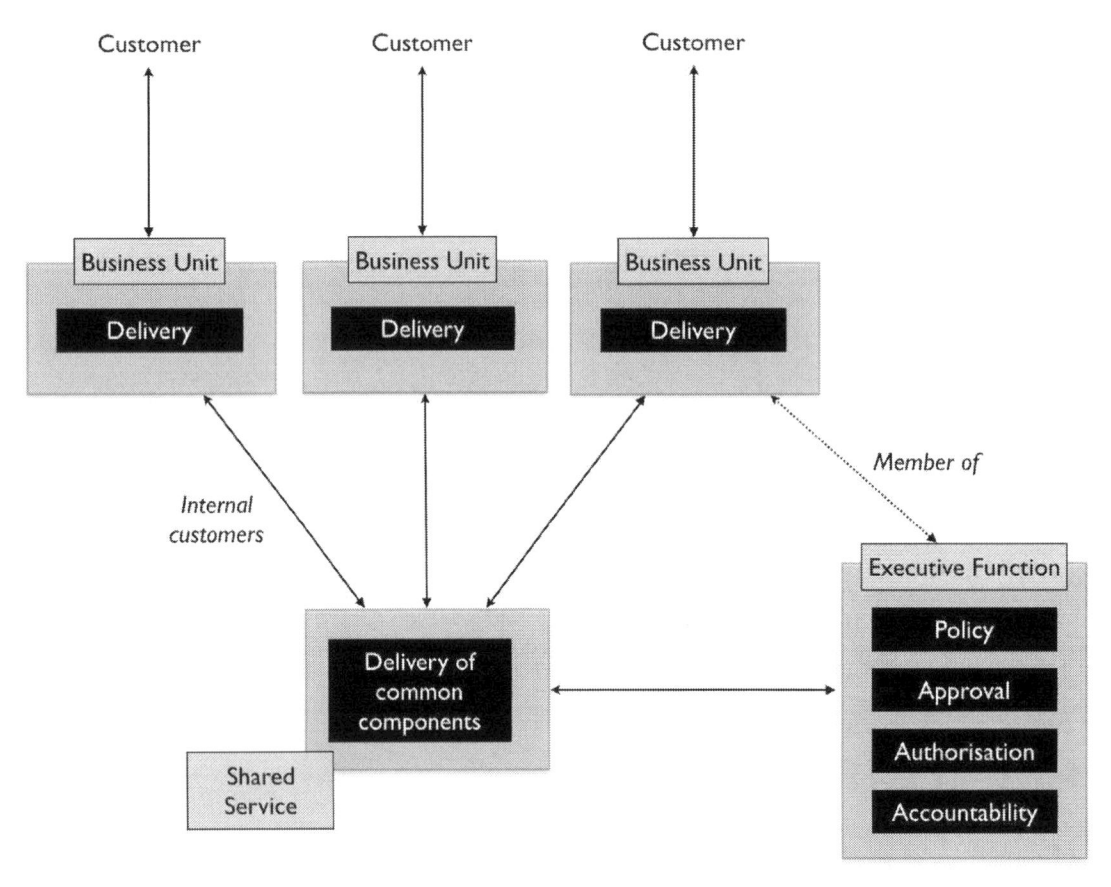

Figure 62: Common structure

However, the common components provided are often a bit hit or miss. Without a form of mapping then it's difficult to find what is duplicated and how it should be provided between the different business units. It will often degenerate into plucking things from the air. There also tends to be an element of political conflict between the business units and the shared services, and in the worst cases, the shared services function can be viewed as a hindrance.

To resolve this, we need to separate out the delivery of shared services from the identification of what is common. I've found the best way to achieve this is not to remove budget from the business units (often a political bone of contention) but instead to introduce a coordination function. The role of the coordination function is to encourage compliance to policy (doctrine), often via a spend control mechanism, and to enable sharing between the business units through the use of maps. This doesn't require some big bang overhaul but usually the formalisation of an existing structure, e.g. office of an executive function or an architectural board can be converted into this role. When spend control is used then a policy limit (e.g. £100K) should be set above which any project must be mapped and the map sent to the coordination function. The function can then analyse the map, make recommendations and introduce elements of transparency and challenge within the organisation. As more maps are gathered then the function can also identify patterns for common services. This should become a relatively quick process, lasting a few hours from initiation to recommendation.

It's through such a function that other forms of doctrine such as cell-based structure, use of pioneer-settler-town planner, along with more context-specific gameplay, can be introduced into the business units. I've summarised this in Figure 63, adding in the coordination function (Point 1). I've also noted that your shared service (Point 2) should be elevated to a business unit and not just limit itself to provision of common components within an organisation, but look to public provision, particularly if you intend to run an ecosystem model such as ILC. If it's important enough for you to create a shared and common service, then there either exists an outside market opportunity or you're just rebuilding what already exists in the market.

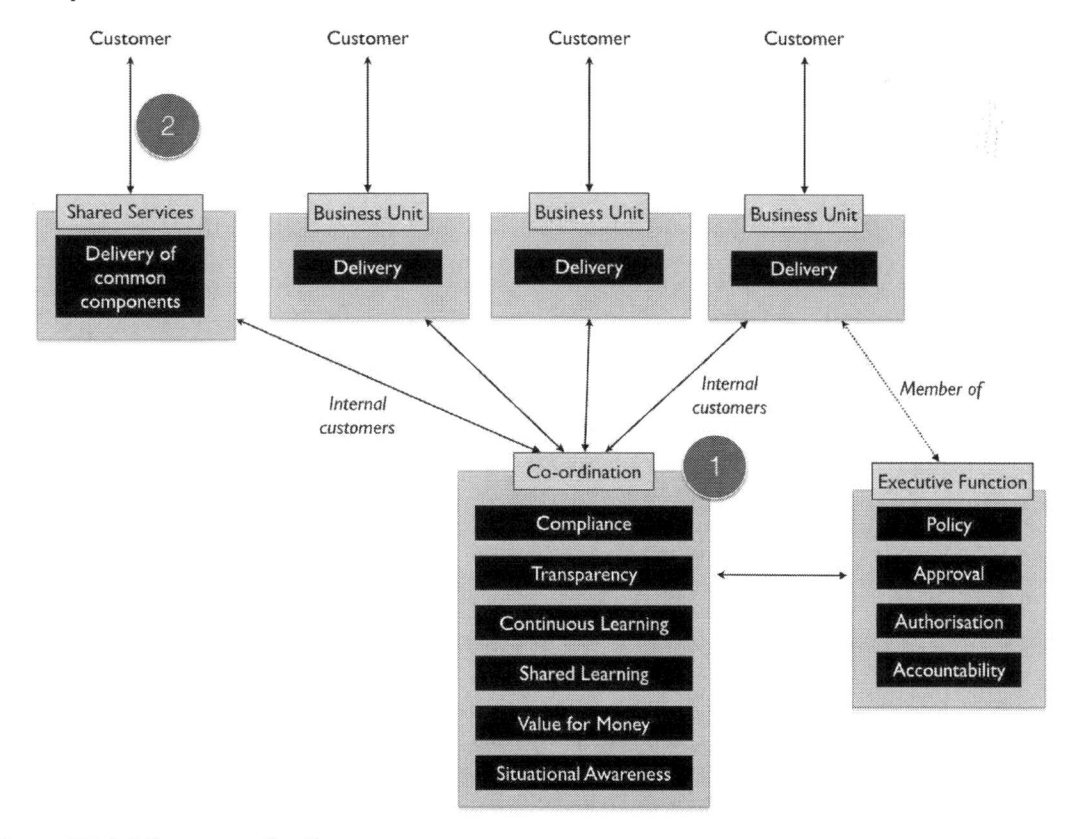

Figure 63: Adding co-ordination

With your shared services group, you should aim to populate it with small cells of town planners providing industrialised components. Your business units will tend to become dominated by cells of pioneers and settlers providing custom to product and rental services. Your co- ordination function will mainly become settlers focused on ensuring transparency and learning within the organisation itself. However, this is over time.

It's really important that if this is your first coordination function (in UK Government, this was called Spend Control), it is staffed by people with experience of "future" ways of operating, i.e. you want them to challenge the organisation, and pioneers can be useful here. In 2016, I still see companies creating a digital team and pointing the way by giving an example of good but without any mechanism to deal with the existing organisation. This invariably creates a them versus us situation, and without any mechanism to force challenge, you're likely to revert back to the past. The corporate antibodies will overwhelm you.

Hence, start with a small coordination team of highly-skilled people helping other business units create, share maps and learn from them. You will probably find that some business units start to offer their own homegrown capabilities as common components to other business units. Don't discourage these emergent behaviours. Whilst there may be an element of opportunistic "empire building" involved, if units are sharing and learning from maps then this is supportive. You can always migrate those components to a shared services group at a later date. The one thing to be careful of is business units trying to subvert the process, e.g. trying to find exclusions to sharing or spend control.

Often, some will claim they are "too busy to write a map" or "it's too complex". For me, the idea that someone could be willing to spend £100K on something they can't map sets alarm bells ringing. For such an expense, we should know what the user needs are and what is involved. Mapping provides us the means to reflect on this, to challenge the assumptions, to question what is being considered, and to demonstrate we have thought about it. Be warned however; these excuses are often code for resistance to sharing due to concerns that it will reduce their power base within an organisation. Knowledge is power often translates to shared knowledge is less power for me! If you ever want to stop the self-harm that occurs in corporations, from the endless duplication and bias to the poor gameplay, then you need to counter this. Expect a few battles and a few bruises.

You'll also have lots of people claim that "we have architecture groups" or "good communication". Most federated organisations have hundreds of duplicated examples of the same thing being built, and communication is anything but effective. Ask yourself, how many pet IoT or AI projects doing roughly the same thing are actually going on in your organisation right now? If you're of any size and the answer is "don't know" or "not sure", then from experience, it's going to be vastly more than whatever number you might guess at. Without a communication tool such as mapping and some form of coordination function, you will be unlikely to find out. Hence, use this issue of duplication to help introduce a common language and the sharing of information.

Be warned though; resistance to this sharing will clamour for exclusions and protection of silos. Fall for this and any emergent sharing will be lost. Also, keep an eye on communication mechanism, from chat to wikis, because they can be used to consolidate resistance as much as enable change. You'll have to be firm.

To the question, shouldn't the coordination function be part of the executive function, then I'd answer yes. In my company, the coordination function was the executive team. In a larger company, you will want to create a specialised unit. Remember, you are unlikely to have any maps of your landscape and your SVPs & VPs won't be able to magic them out of hand. They'll need support and help, as much of this will be as unfamiliar to them as it was for me.

Continuous learning

This entire book is dedicated to a process of continuous learning, however it's more important for me to demonstrate how to achieve this (the strategy cycle) rather than the specifics of particular patterns. Once you have the basics, you will learn the patterns for yourself. However, it's also worth me recapping as we go along this journey. In Figure 64, I provided the basic patterns so far examined.

Climatic (rules of the game)	Doctrine (universal actions you should take)	Gameplay (context specific actions you could take)
Everything evolves	Focus on user need	Accelerator (open source)
Characteristics change	Use a common language	De-accelerator (ringfencing with patents)
No one size fits all	Be transparent	Exploiting constraint
Efficiency enables innovation	Challenge assumptions	ILC (ecosystem model)
Higher order systems create new sources of worth	Remove duplication and bias	
No choice on evolution	Use appropriate methods	
Past success breeds inertia	Think small	
	Think aptitude and attitude	
	Design for constant evolution	
	Enable purpose, autonomy and mastery	

Figure 64: Patterns covered

The anti-pattern organisation

I'm a great believer in using anti-patterns to examine the effect of not doing something. In this case, what are the anti-patterns for mapping? In general, they will be the reverse of the doctrine that is developed from mapping, along with a failure to cope with climatic patterns and incorrect use of context-specific play. We can use this to describe what an organisation that doesn't understand its landscape should look like. I often use this as a way of analysing competitors but be careful; there's a whole topic of misdirection that we haven't touched upon yet. The anti-pattern organisation will look something like this.

Fails to focus on user needs

Has an inability to describe its user needs and often confuses its own needs — profitability, revenue, data acquisition — with those of its customers.

Fails to use a common language

Uses multiple different ways of describing the same problem space, e.g. box and wire diagrams, business process diagrams and stories. Often suffers from confusion and misalignment. None of the tools used will meet those basic characteristics of any map — visual, context specific, position (relative to an anchor), movement and components.

Fails to be transparent

Has difficulty in answering basic questions such as "How many IoT projects are we building?"

Information tends to be guarded in silos.

Fails to challenge assumptions

Action is often taken based upon memes or Hippo (highest paid person's opinion) or popular articles in the HBR (Harvard Business Review). Often, parts of the organisation will admit to building things they know won't work.

Fails to remove duplication and bias

The scale of duplication is excessive and exceeds in practice what people expect. Any investigation will discover groups custom building what exists at a commodity in the outside world — their very own Thomas Thwaite toaster. Often, resistance is given to changing this because it is somehow unique, despite any inability of the group to explain user needs.

Fails to use appropriate methods

Tends towards single size methods across the organisation, e.g. "outsource all of IT" or "use Agile everywhere". This can often be accompanied with a yo-yo between one method (the old emperor) and a new naked emperor, based upon its success in a specific example (outcome bias). Expect to hear statements of the form, "Six Sigma worked on this project; it'll work on every project."

Fails to think small

Tends toward big scale efforts (e.g. Death Star projects) and big departments. This can include frequent major platform re-engineering efforts or major re-organisations.

Fails to think aptitude and attitude

Tends to consider all of a specific aptitude (e.g. finance, operations or IT) as though it's one thing. Promotes a mantra of there is only "IT", rather than a nuanced message of multiple types. Tends to create general training courses covering the entire subject, e.g. "Let's send everyone on agile training."

Fails to design for constant evolution

Tends to bolt on new organisational structures as new memes appear. A cloud department, a digital department, a Big Data group, etc. There is another example of what can go wrong here, which is best explained by the examination of dual, bimodal and twin speed IT concepts that have become all the rage. The basic premise is that we have two groups, one of which is focused on the new (often the digital) and one is focused on the core operational aspects of the company. It sounds sensible but as I discovered long ago, it creates a headache, best explained through mapping (see Figure 65).

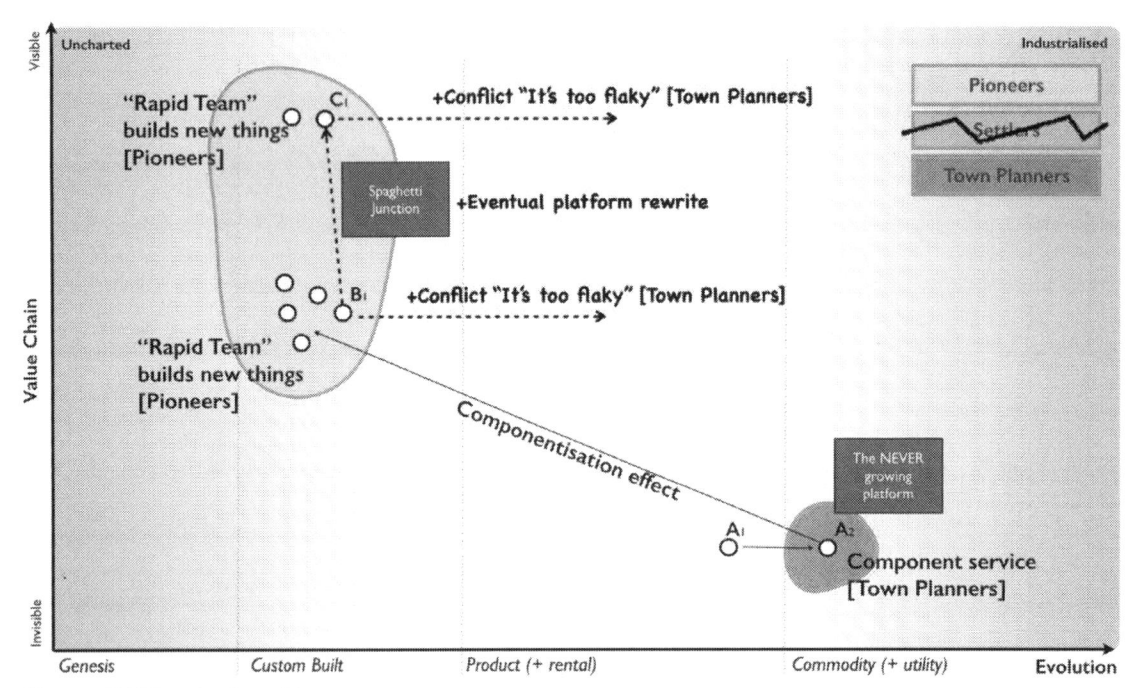

Figure 65: The dual problem

This figure is derived from Figure 42 (Chapter 4) and I've simply cut out the middle "settler" group. What happens is your town planner builds a new component service (A1 to A2), which your pioneers build upon (B1). All is working well so far until the pioneers ask the town planners to take over the new activity.

The response will generally be negative, as in "it's too flaky" because it hasn't become a well formed product yet; it's unstable and it lacks documentation as there is no-one managing its evolution. The pioneers also want to move on and so arguments ensue. Eventually, the pioneers start building on top of their own component (B1 to C1). The net result is a never growing platform and an increasingly unreliable spaghetti junction of new built upon new. This will negatively impact performance until someone suggests a Death Star like grand platform reengineering effort.

Unfortunately, the new platform will suffer from the same problems when we start building upon it because the structural problem (the "missing" settlers) hasn't been fixed. Unbeknownst to most, these dual structures might give a short-term win but they will lead you down a path of never growing platforms, spaghetti junctions and costly platform rewrites. Great for consultants in re-organisation and flogging new memes but terrible if you're actually a business trying to get something done in a sustainable manner.

Fails to enable purpose, mastery and autonomy

There is often confusion within the organisation over its purpose, combined with feelings of lacking control and inability to influence.

Fails to understand basic economic patterns

Often conducts efficiency or innovation programmes without realising the connection between the two. Assumes it has choice on change (e.g. cloud), where none exists. Fails to recognise and cope with its own inertia caused by past success.

Fails to understand context-specific play

Has no existing language that enables it to understand context-specific play. Often uses terms as memes, e.g. open source, ecosystem, innovation, but with no clear understanding of where they are appropriate.

Fails to understand the landscape

Tends to not fully grasp the components and complexity within its own organisation. Often cannot describe its own basic capabilities.

Fails to understand strategy

Tends to be dominated by statements that strategy is all about the why but cannot distinguish between the why of purpose and the why of movement. Has little discussion on position and movement, combined with an inability to describe where it should attack or even the importance of understanding where before why. Often, strategy is little more than a tyranny of action statements based upon meme copying and external advice.

Hence, if you're unsure of where your organisation currently stands, use the above to help you reflect on the state of situational awareness within the company. I've provided this also as a comparison in Figure 66, but do remember that this is solely a guide for you to discuss and reflect upon your own organisation's state.

Higher levels of situational awareness	Indicator of ...	Lower levels of situational awareness
Visual (maps)	Navigation	Verbal (story telling)
Action & reflection	Learning	Secrets of success
Position and movement	Strategy	Magic thinking (SWOTs, 2x2s)
Where before why	Order	Tyranny of action (how, what and when)
Detailed	Landscape	Vague
Context specific & universal	Patterns	Universal memes
Aptitude and attitude	Organisation	Functional or business silos
Thinks small	Granularity	Thinks big
Mixed (agile + lean + six sigma)	Methods	Single (all agile etc)
Known	Duplication and bias	Unable to quantify
Embraced	Challenge	Defended against
Essential	Transparency	Resisted
Common	Language	Tribal factions
User needs	Anchor	Own needs

Figure 66: Signals of

Books to read

Alas, I haven't found any books that deal with topographical intelligence in business (i.e. the use of maps and situational awareness), which is why, after almost eight years of badgering, I'm finally getting around to writing one. I'm a very reluctant writer and hopefully, someone will take this and write a better book. That said, there are lots of other books that I'd recommend reading because of the general concepts they provide. I don't necessarily agree with everything they state, but these are definitely worth exploring. I find all of these books are worth spending time with.

The Art of Warfare by Sun Tzu (Robert Ames translation)

Science, Strategy and War by Frans P. B. Osinga

Atlas of Military Strategy 1618–1878 by David Chandler

The Simplicity Cycle by Dan Ward

Accidental Empires by Robert X. Cringely

Hierarchy Theory, The Challenge of Complex Systems by Howard H. Pattee

The Evolution of Technology by George Basalla

Thinking in Promises by Mark Burgess

Diffusion of Innovations by Everett Rogers

Customer-Driven IT by David Moschella

Digitizing Government by Alan Brown, Jerry Fishenden and Mark Thompson

Learn or Die by Edward D. Hess

The Oxford Handbook of Innovation by Jan Fagerberg, David Mowery and Richard Nelson

The Starfish and the Spider by Ori Brafman and Rod Beckstrom

Does IT Matter? by Nicholas Carr

Technological Revolutions and Financial Capital by Carlota Perez

The Entrepreneurial State by Marriana Mazzucato

Topographical Intelligence and the American Civil War by Daniel D. Nettesheim

The Intelligent Investor by Benjamin Graham

Cybernetics by Norbert Wiener

Systems Thinking by Jamshid Gharajedahi

The Age of Discontinuity by Peter F. Drucker The Red Queen by William P. Barnett

An exercise for the reader

There's a lot of things I could recommend here. Obviously, top of my list is practice mapping within your organisation. I'd also spend some time with the books above.

However, can I also strongly recommend that you go and play World of Warcraft if you have any doubts over the importance of situational awareness? I understand that Fernando Flores (former Finance Minister and Senator for the Chilean Government) runs an executive training course on this. I know it sounds daft but where better to learn how to play games than in a game?

In the next section of six chapters, I'm going to cover my wilderness years and the formalisation of mapping as we loop around the strategy cycle again.

Chapter 7 - Finding a new purpose

It was 2007, I was at home and I was unemployed. I twiddled my thumbs for a couple of days, did some DIY and then set about thinking about my future. This is code for watching my bank balance plummet whilst not doing anything useful. I was exhausted; running a company, inspiring a future and being broadsided had taken its toll. However, whilst I wasn't ready to immerse myself into a new role, I couldn't just sit idle. So, I undertook a few paid speaking gigs, did some advisory work, wrote a few articles, ghost wrote a few more, and researched. At least, it would keep the wolves at bay for a bit.

I was convinced that there was some mileage in the mapping concept but I had two major problems. First, I had failed to create that bright future with it. Second, I had no real evidence to support it. I had collected data that hinted that components evolved but the evolution axis was no more than a pattern that I had observed and talked about at Euro Foo in 2004. Maybe it was completely wrong? Maybe that's why I failed? Maybe that's why no-one else seemed to be talking about these concepts? I decided my library wasn't big enough to answer these questions and became a reader at the British Library. I collected, collated and trawled through a huge volume of written work in pursuit of my answers. At the very least, I was keeping myself busy and providing time to recoup.

As I read more into the subject of strategy then I noticed that disquiet over the field was palpable. Phil Rosenzweig, in the Halo Effect (2007), pointed to the cause being a marriage of convenience: "Managers are busy people, under enormous pressure to deliver higher revenues, greater profits and ever larger returns for shareholders. They naturally search for ready-made answers, for tidy plug-and-play solutions that might give them a leg up on their rivals. And the people who write business books — consultants and business school professors and strategy gurus — are happy to oblige."

I wanted to change this, to somehow give people the tools they needed to learn themselves by exposing that secret tome of strategy to everyone. I wanted to be free of this marriage of convenience. I still believed there was a secret tome back in 2007 and that it was probably guarded in the halls of business schools. I started to think about doing an MBA, shuddered at the expense and borrowed copious notes and books from friends who had. However, I was disappointed. Beyond basic concepts in financial, marketing and operational "strategy", there was no discussion of landscape or context. Maybe the tomb was guarded in the halls of strategy consultancies themselves.

I applied for a job with one of the more prestigious consultancy firms and was invited to a competitive interview process with dozens of other candidates. We would be put through our paces in a number of rounds in a Darwinian battle, a survival of the fittest. In my first round, I was asked a question — "A news media company is looking at divesting itself of its print and distribution business. What things should it consider?"

I immediately started mapping out the landscape, pointing to opportunities and impacts from loss of control through disposal of such physical capital to provision of distribution as a public utility to redirecting print capabilities into printed electronics — "Those large-scale printers have the potential to be tomorrow's Intel," I declared! There was a wealth of opportunity, but before making a choice, we needed to understand the landscape more. I started to dig, asking questions about the user, their needs and what did we understand about the landscape. I met a wall of silence, followed by the line that "it's not relevant". The company had already decided to take this action. It was part of its strategy. My role was to give some input into how to achieve this. I asked what was this strategy based upon and an argument ensued. Needless to say, I didn't make it past round one and was the very first to leave the competition. Mapping had failed on its second outing. So I carried on researching.

It was at this time that I was also becoming quite well known in certain technology circles as a speaker on open source, web 2.0 and cloud computing. I kept being invited to more and more conferences and to present and discuss technology changes within companies. I was flattered but quickly discovered that I needed to keep things simple. I was told the mapping concepts were just "too confusing" and so I restricted myself to talking about the impacts in more general terms. However, here, I hit a snag. General concepts such as the world moving towards more utility provision of IT were often brushed aside for lacking any understanding of "real business", and the maps I needed to demonstrate on why this would happen were considered "too confusing". I felt increasingly trapped in a Paul Valéry paradox of "Everything simple is false. Everything which is complex is unusable." I found myself sitting in rooms listening to conversations of the form:-

CTO: "All the new servers are installed; systems are running fine."

CIO: "Excellent. Apparently, the latest thing is cloud, hence I've asked Simon to come along. According to this business magazine then numerous successful companies are considering future pilots that might use it. We should look into it and whether it's worth considering as part of our long-term strategy."

CTO: "We've already examined the subject. Cloud just means virtualisation of the data centre. The latest research I have says that virtualisation has entered the plateau of performance and provides an extremely efficient mechanism of infrastructure provision over our existing data centre technology. Our technology partners have virtualisation based products in this space that we should consider buying."

CIO: "Excellent work. Well let's look at getting this up and running. There's some business interest and I'd like to tell the CEO we've been using cloud if it comes up in conversation. We don't want to be left behind in this technology war. Any thoughts, Simon?"

It sounded so simple but it was so wrong; my heart always sank. To explain why, I'm going to perform a mental translation that I started to do by converting IT speak into military speak. For some reason, I just find it becomes easier for people to understand.

Captain: "All the new cannons arrived. We installed them and fired them this morning."

Colonel: "Excellent. Apparently, the latest thing is bombing hills, hence I've asked Simon to come along. According to General's weekly then numerous successful military leaders are considering future campaigns that might use it. We should look into it and whether it's worth considering as part of our long-term strategy."

Captain: "We've already examined the subject. Bombing hills just means using mortars. The latest research I have says that mortars have entered the plateau of performance and provide an extremely efficient mechanism of killing, compared to our existing technology. Our technology partners have mortar based products in this space that we should consider buying."

Colonel: "Excellent work. Well let's look at getting this up and running. There's some military interest and I'd like to tell the General that we've been bombing hills if it comes up in conversation. We don't want to be left behind in this technology war. Any thoughts, Simon?"

There seemed to be an overwhelming predilection towards copying others, technology faddism and buying pieces of kit, rather than dealing with the problems at hand. There was no discussion of the users, the landscape or how it was changing. When I would raise how the cloud was simply an evolution of an existing act from product to more industrialised utility models and as such, it was more of a change of business model rather than buying some tech… well, it was almost like I had spoken heresy in gobbledygook.

Business and IT both seemed to be operating in an environment that they did not understand and often with an assumption that buying more high tech wins the day. But this is flawed. Low tech can be used to overcome a high tech opponent that has poor situational awareness. The U.S. Seventh Cavalry, with access to gatling guns and "hi-tech" weaponry suffered a severe defeat at the Battle of the Little Bighorn against bows, arrows and stone clubs. Occasionally, I would let my guard down and deep dive into the topic, thereby hitting the other side of Valéry's paradox. Nearly every time I did this, I was dismissed by the simple question, "What evidence do you have that evolution works in this way?"

The new purpose

Unbeknownst to me, I had just been given a new purpose by others. I had my own crusade, to explain topographical intelligence to the world of business and to provide an "uncommon sense to the common world of strategy". It wasn't quite as catchy as "Pre-shaved Yaks" but it became the title of my first failed attempt to write a book on mapping in 2007.

I needed to demonstrate or disprove the concept of evolution in technology and mapping itself. I had no clue on how to do this but that didn't stop me becoming a bit obsessed. My beard grew longer and I'm pretty sure I was mumbling mapping in my sleep. The reason why my purpose became all-consuming was it had two other things that mattered. First, it had a defined scope that was tangible and could be understood, i.e. I was looking at the validity of this mapping technique. Second, it also had a moral imperative. I was rebelling against the hordes of management consultants that enslaved us with 2x2s in this marriage of convenience! It felt good. I had:-

Purpose: Explain topographical intelligence to the world of business.

Scope: Demonstrate or disprove the concept of evolution and mapping.

Imperative: Rebel against the hordes of management consultants that enslave us by enabling ordinary people to learn.

Being mindful of this purpose, I could now start thinking about the potential users of mapping and try to define what their needs might be. The users would need some way of exploiting mapping, some way of learning how to map given the complexity of the topic, and also some sort of confirmation or validation that mapping was based upon something sensible. There was a chain of needs from purpose to user need (the very anchor of mapping), which I've drawn in Figure 67.

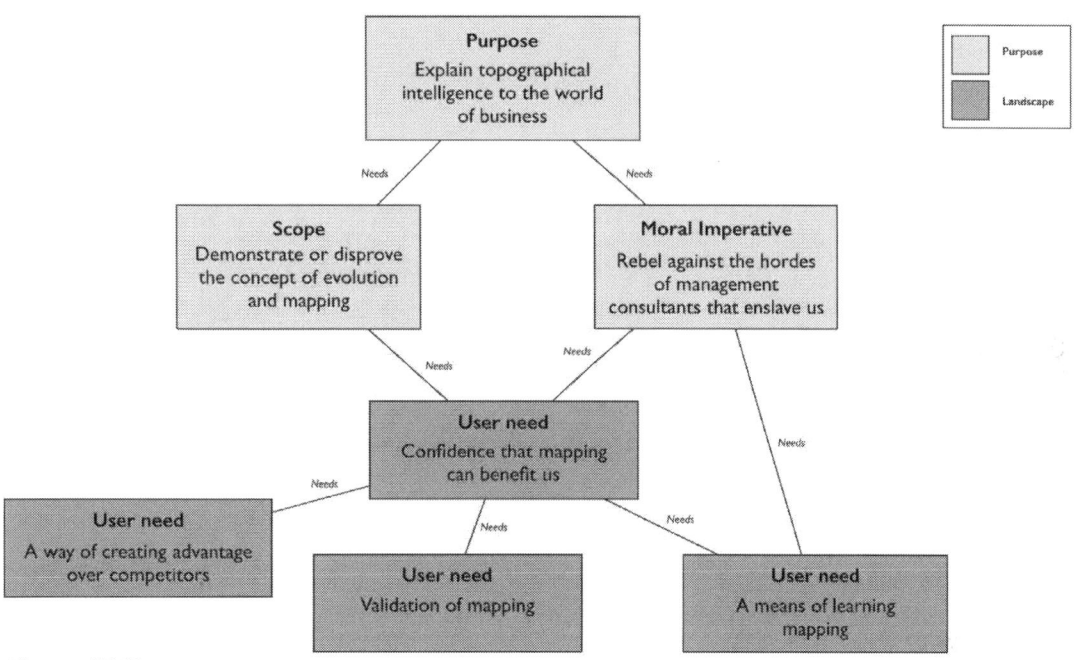

Figure 67: Purpose

Given I had user needs then the very least I could do was map out that environment. Taking the user need of "Confidence that mapping can benefit us" from above, I've created a map of what is involved in Figure 68. I'll use this to describe some particular points on mapping itself. One thing you will notice is the x-axis that I'm using here is slightly different. Whilst I normally just use the descriptions for activities (genesis to commodity), in this case, because we're talking about knowledge, then I'll add those descriptions for the different stages of evolution. For more on the terms used when describing evolution, see Figure 10 (Chapter 2).

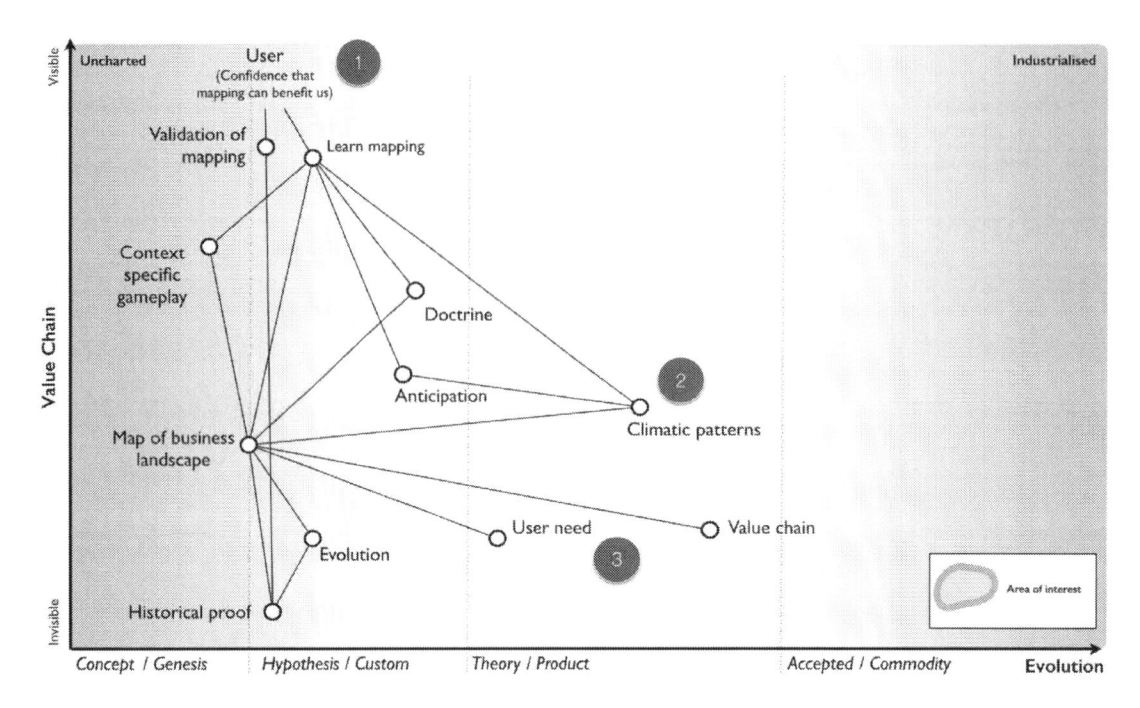

Figure 68: A map of mapping

From the map above:

Point 1 – From "confidence that mapping can benefit us" then we had two high level user needs, which were a means to learn mapping and some form of validation.

Point 2 – Learning mapping requires not only the ability to create a map of the landscape but to understand common economic patterns, doctrine and even context-specific gameplay. Whilst common economic patterns are often discussed in a multitude of economic sources, the issue of context-specific gameplay is fairly unique and rarely covered.

Point 3 – The map itself is based upon user needs (anchor), which is reasonably well discussed, a value chain (position), which itself is a common topic in business books, but also evolution (movement). This last topic was rarely discussed back in 2007, other than in vague and hand-waving notions. There were certainly concepts and competing hypotheses on how things evolved, but no clear definitive path.

One of the first things that struck me was that there existed a chain of needs above my users. When I am a supplier of a component to others (e.g. providing nuts and bolts to a car manufacturer) then my map extends into their map.

However, my map also extends into my own purpose and my own needs. In other words, any map is part of a wider chain of needs.

In Figure 69, I've drawn an extended map from my purpose and my needs through to my user and their needs. I've reverted back to the more typical x-axis because you should be familiar that multiple types (activities, practices, data and knowledge) can be used on a map, and it makes it less busy just to show evolution terms for activities rather than all.

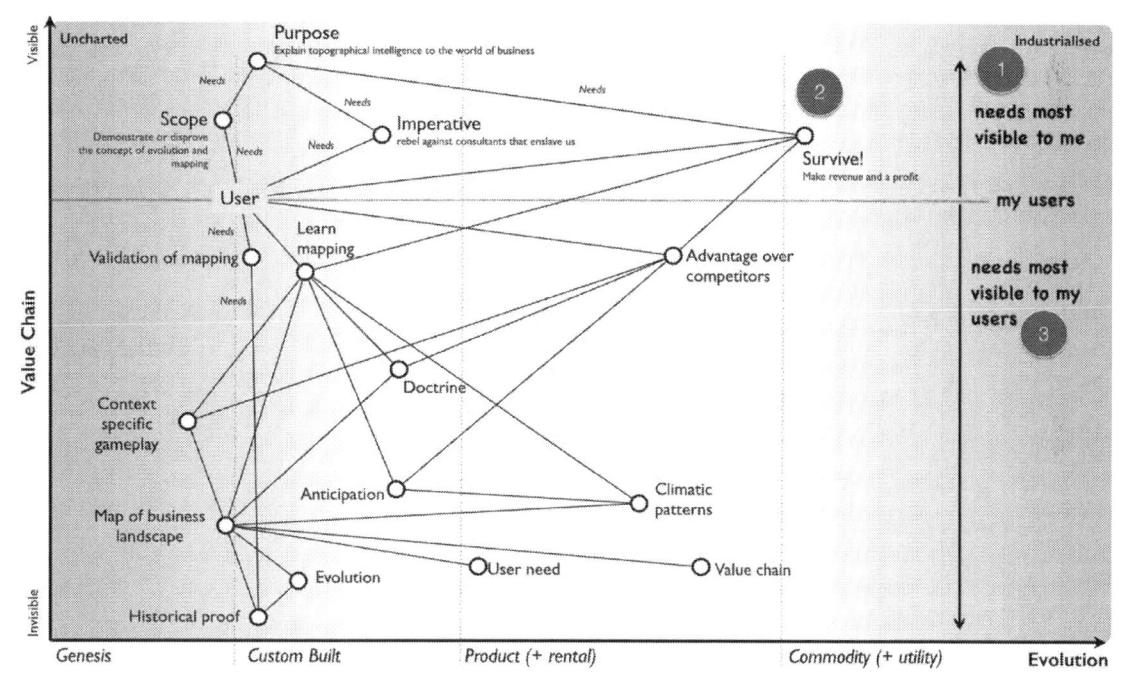

Figure 69: The chain

From the map above:

Point 1 — We have my needs, i.e. my purpose, my scope and my moral imperative. This is my why of purpose expressed as a chain of needs, e.g. be the world's best tea shop or teach everyone to map. Naturally, I'd hope that my purpose would lead to others doing something and hence, there would be users. In 2007, my scope was relatively novel as few seemed to be talking about mapping. However, my imperative wasn't quite so unique. There were many rallying against the imposed consultancy industry.

Point 2 — Whilst I hadn't expressed this before, I had an unwritten need to survive, to make revenue and a profit. This is a very common and well understood need. In my case, I hoped that I could achieve this by meeting my users' needs of either teaching them how to map or helping them create advantage over others.

Point 3 — My users had needs themselves. If my needs (i.e. purpose) didn't fit in some way with the needs of my users, then this mismatch was likely to cause problems. For example, if my highest purpose was to make profit rather than explain topographical intelligence, then I would be focusing on extracting money from my users (this is not one of their core needs,) rather than providing a means of learning mapping and creating advantage (which is a core user need). You should always strive to generate revenue and profit as a direct consequence of meeting users' needs and providing value to them.

There are few other subtler things worth noting about the map above. First, my purpose is part of a chain of needs and as such, it is influenced by the underlying components as they evolve. Over time, if mapping and the related activities become more industrialised, then a scope of "demonstrate the concepts of evolution and mapping" ceases to be relevant. Even my moral imperative might disappear if the world becomes one where everyone maps, learns about their environment and has rebelled against management consultants with their 2x2s. If you think back to the strategy cycle, this is simply a reflection of the issue that as you act, as your landscape changes, then your purpose, scope, moral imperative and even how you survive have to adapt. Nothing is permanent.

The second thing to note is that everything is evolving. At some point in the future, I will need to adapt my scope, not only because the underlying components have evolved, but also that my scope has become industrialised. There would be a point that you will be able to read endless free guides on how to map and even Wikipedia articles. If at that point, my scope isn't something else designed to meet users' needs and provide value to them, then I'll be attempting to survive against free.

The final issue is the balancing act between different user needs. I thought I had learned that lesson in my past doomed attempt to build a platform future by ignoring one set of very powerful users (the board), but I repeated the same mistake in my strategy consultancy interview. I was trying to engage in a discussion on the environment, whereas they needed a financial and HR analysis of impacts caused by a disposal. Whether it was the right or wrong decision wasn't something they cared about, and I wasn't thinking about their needs. Any play I created may have been right, but without support of these users then it didn't matter.

The Hypothetical Gun company

This concept of conflict between user needs is worth exploring a bit more. Let us take a trawl back through time and imagine you're the boss of a hypothetical gun company, just when the market is learning how to industrialise mechanical components. We're moving away from the world of highly customised mechanical components built by a cottage industry to having things like more uniform pipes and bolts. Let us imagine that you've taken a bold move and started to buy more standard bolts and pipes (for barrels). You then use these components in the manufacture of your guns by combining them with your skills and practice as gunsmiths. I've highlighted this in a map in Figure 70. Remember, it's a hypothetical and I've no idea how to actually make a gun.

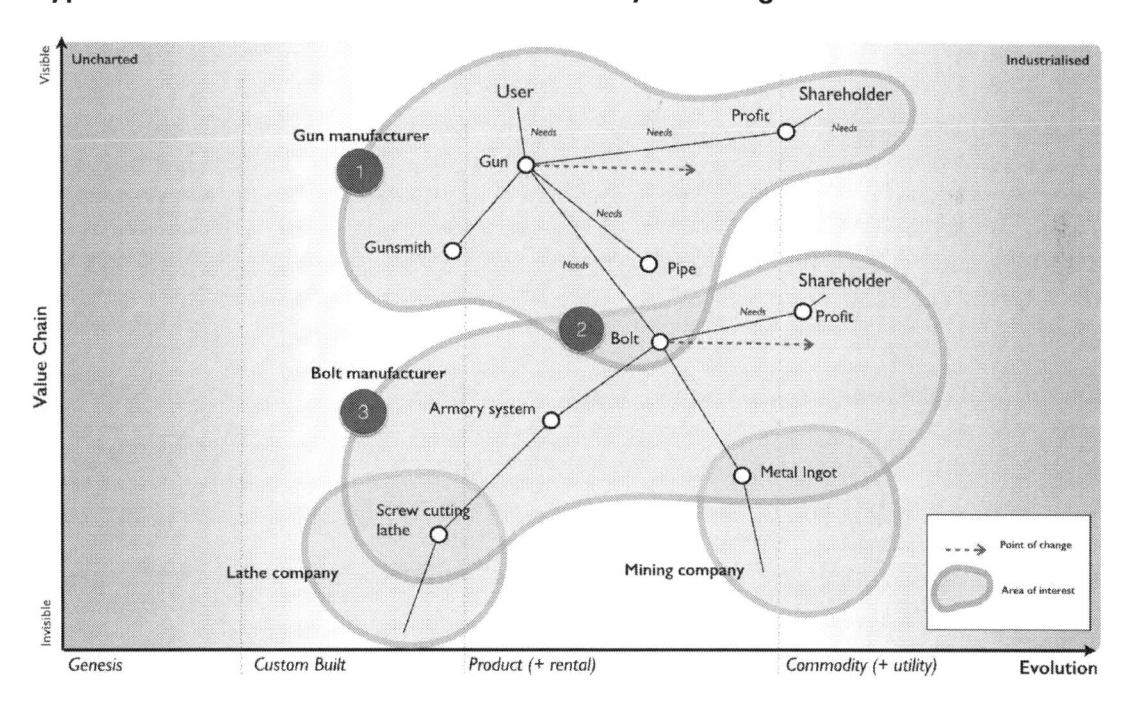

Figure 70: The hypothetical gun company

You are the gun company (Point 1) and you're reliant upon bolts (Point 2) from a company that manufactures them (Point 3). The first thing to note is that a map can cover many different organisations if you wish. Each of those organisations could be expanded into, providing more detail. When you map an environment then you're only ever looking at a fraction of a vast chain of needs. Hence the importance of defining a scope that is tangible rather than attempting to create a perfect map of an entire industry right down to every knob and whistle. You will learn over time how to simplify maps but to begin with, keep your ambitions small. Think small! As in know the details (see Chapter 4, Doctrine).

In the above, I've highlighted that guns are evolving and heading towards more of a commodity. This can create conflict with your own desire to survive and your shareholders' desire for profit as the revenue per unit decreases. Such change can be compensated by volume but the desire is always to keep the same margin but increase units. We almost want the thing to become ubiquitous but seen as unique. There are ways of achieving this through branding and persuading others that your "commodity" is somehow special. It's not a rock, it's a "pet rock", as Gary Dahl might say. Alternatively, you can bundle new features or characteristics onto it. It's not just a gun, it's a special gun that makes you popular, or it's a vacuum that doesn't lose suction!

At the same time your gun is becoming a commodity (something you may not want) then you do want the components that you consume in manufacturing your gun to become more commodity-like. This will obviously reduce your cost. However, the shareholders of the bolt company would like to have volume operations but maintain the margin per unit. They'll be hoping their management use branding to try and persuade you that their "commodity" is somehow special. It's not just a bolt, it's a special bolt that makes you popular with others or doesn't lose suction! There will inherently be conflict between different types of users (whether customers, the business, shareholders or regulators) throughout the landscape.

But that conflict doesn't even require another person. Your own purpose can create its own conflict when faced with an evolving landscape. Take for example my map of mapping above (Figure 69). My moral imperative was to rebel against the hordes of consultants that enslave us. By definition, I wanted mapping to spread far and wide. But as mapping spreads then my ability to make revenue from teaching others how to map will ultimately diminish, especially as basic guides on mapping become free. I could either pursue a path of "it's not just a map, it's a special map that makes you popular with others" or I would have to find another way of surviving, e.g. selling context-specific forms of gameplay rather than just teaching people how to map.

Fortunately, context-specific forms of gameplay aren't just one thing. If I taught people how to exploit ecosystems with an ILC model (see Chapter 5), then I should expect that model to become industrialised over time. However, mapping is itself a means of exploring and learning about new forms of context-specific gameplay, i.e. there should be a constant pipeline of new forms of gameplay, as long as we are willing to learn.

I've drawn this map up in Figure 71 below. Whilst teaching mapping will ultimately industrialise (Point 1), there is also a constant pipeline of gameplay (Point 2) with new forms of gameplay emerging. I could create a business with a strong purpose, and though it would have to adapt as components changed, there would be other opportunities for me to exploit. Even if I open sourced the mapping method to encourage it to spread (which I did by making it all creative commons), then I knew that I could create a future as an "arms dealer" of gameplay.

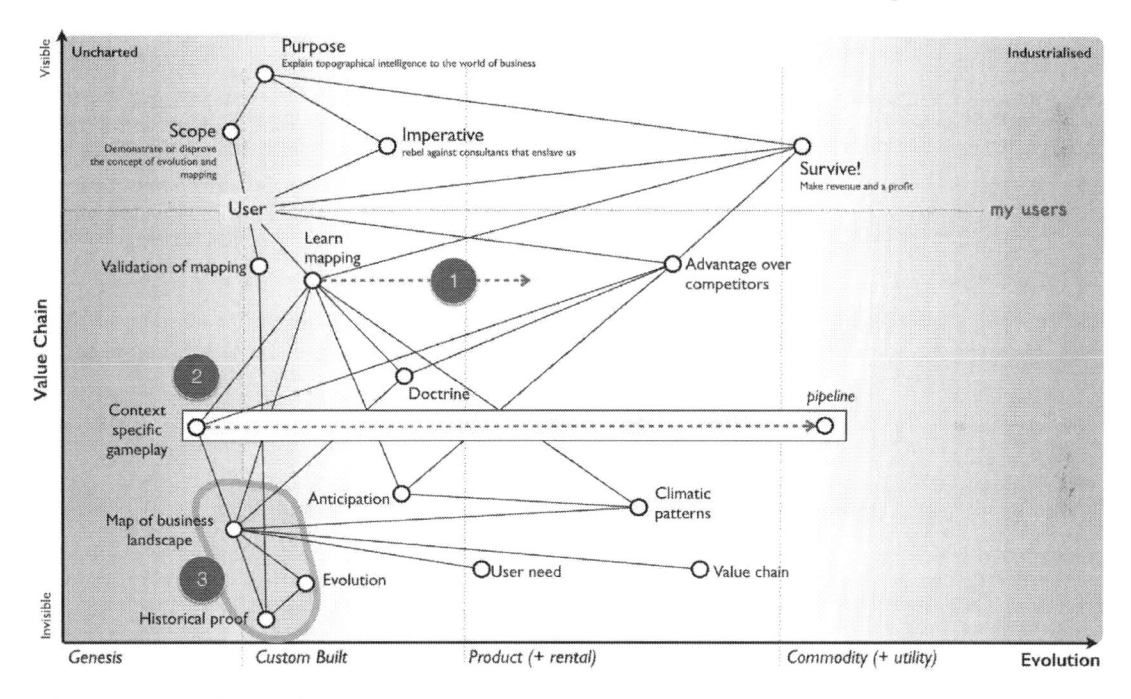

Figure 71: Mapping the landscape

There was a weakness however to this plan, caused by Point 3. The whole play would depend upon some sort of validation of mapping and, at that time, I had nothing to back up my evolution axis, no success stories and no volume of users. I also needed users with success stories to entice other users because, like it or not, the mantra of "67% of other generals bomb hills, I should learn to bomb a hill" dominates our industry. It was a chicken and egg moment (P.S. the answer is egg) and I had nothing to encourage someone to try.

The trouble with maps

I had to find some way of either showing the evolution scale had merit or disprove it and hence, get on with my life. I thought this was going to be easy. I couldn't have been more wrong.

In his 1962 book on the Diffusion of Innovation, Everett Rogers explained a theory of how new technology spreads through cultures. These innovations are communicated over time through various social structures, from early adopters to late adopters (or laggards), and are consequently either spread through adoption or rejected in a society. This spread is measured using adoption versus time through what are known as diffusion curves. As Rogers noted, not all innovation spreads: even where an innovation has apparent usefulness, a number of factors can influence its adoption. In 1991, Geoffrey Moore refined these concepts and noted that there was a chasm between the early adopters of an innovation and the early majority. Many innovations failed to cross this chasm. Numerous effects would impact the probability that the chasm would be crossed from positioning of the product to its target market to distribution channels to product pricing and even to marketing.

Before we continue, there's often some confusion between diffusion curves and Moore's presentation of this. I don't know why; one is purely the sum of the other.

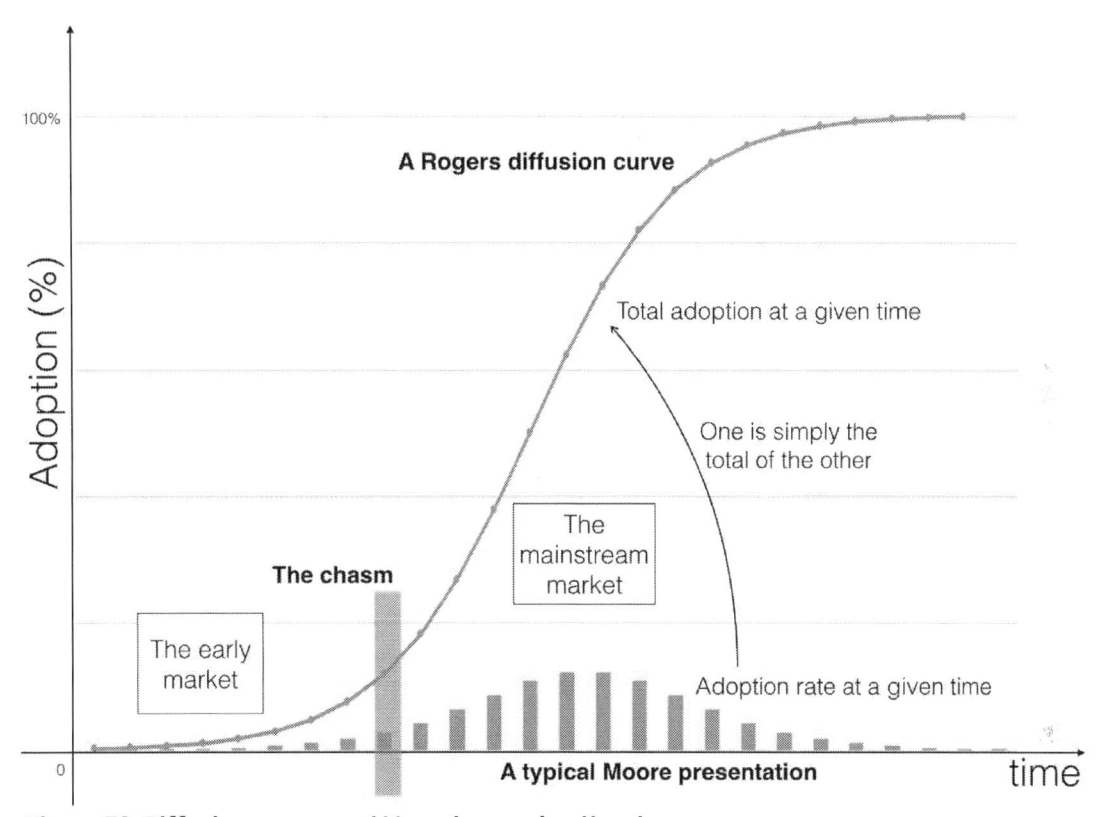

Figure 72: Diffusion curves and Moore's crossing the chasm

It seemed self-obvious to me at that time that if something diffused, crossing the chasm on the way to the mass majority, then it would become more of a commodity. All I had to do was find what percentage of adoption did things on a diffusion curve start to evolve, i.e. at what percentage did it become a product or a commodity (see Figure 73)?

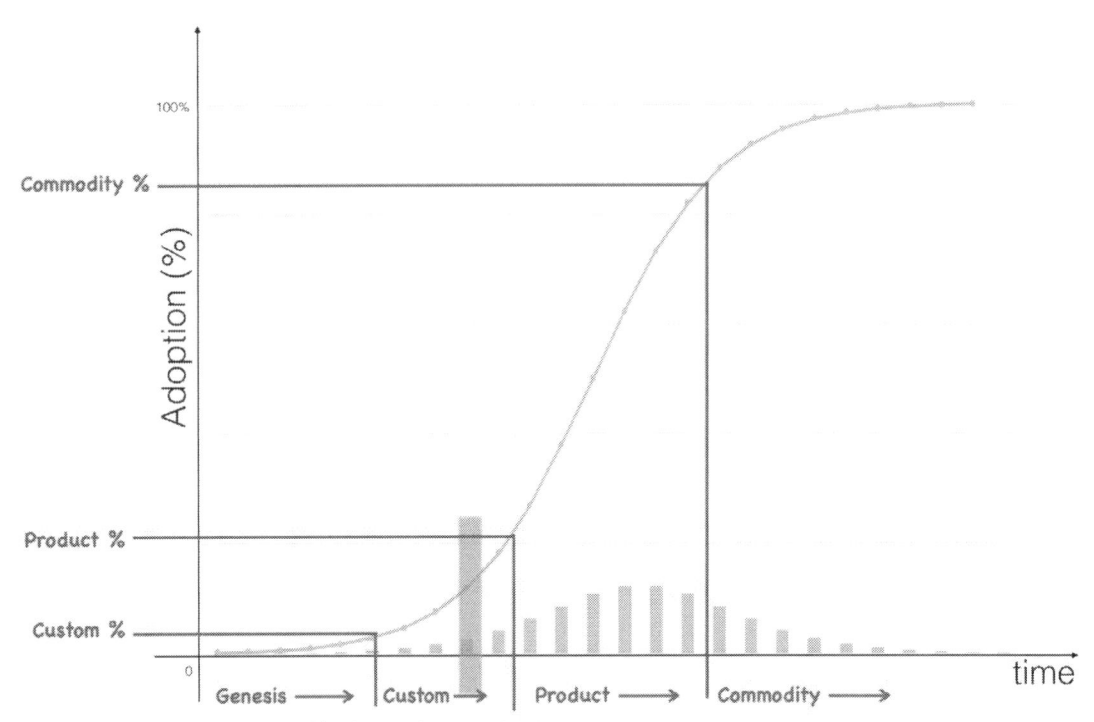

Figure 73: When does a diffusing thing evolve?

Unfortunately, as simple as it sounded, any analysis of data shows that Figure 73 is just plain wrong. You cannot take a diffusion curve and slap on evolution. If you take something like a smartphone and ask people whether it's a product or more of a commodity, then today, you'll probably get a range of answers and some disagreement. However, there are more smartphones in the US than people, so we can say it's widely diffused, despite a lack of clarity over whether it's a product or a commodity. But, if I ask people whether a gold bar is a commodity then they'll say yes. This is bizarre because only a tiny fraction of the population actually own gold bars. On one hand, you have a thing that is diffused but not a commodity, whilst on the other hand, you have something that is uncommon but is a commodity.

I spent months collecting diffusion curves for different activities and found there was no clear correlation between a percentage of adoption and when something evolved. I was unable to make statements such as "when 10% of the population have this, it'll become a product". Hence, I looked at the time axis. Surely, if it wasn't adoption then we must be able to measure this evolution over time? I took the diffusion curves and hypothesised that we could measure over time when the transition between stages would occur, e.g. the first five years would be genesis and in the next three years, we would see custom-built examples. However, when looking at the data then it turned out not to be constant, and comparisons over time demonstrate a wide variety of different timescales for how things evolved. I was stuck. I couldn't seem to use time or adoption to measure evolution.

To make matters worse, I was in the middle of a very visible evolution of computing infrastructure from products (e.g. servers) to more utility forms (cloud). The very companies that could be described as early adopters of computing when it was a product were often the laggards in this shift to a utility world. The act of computing was the same, though it was now provided in a more evolved form and the social groups leading this change were different from the past. The simplistic association of diffusion and evolution was clearly failing to explain what was happening right in front of me.

Even today, in 2016, some nine years later, I still see "business gurus" take diffusion curves and start slapping on evolution characteristics. Here it's "innovation" and here it's a "commodity". I tend to ask them to demonstrate this and I get the usual reply of "well, it's obvious". Alas, it's not and the "it's obvious" turns out to be unsubstantiated. If you're feeling evil then you can test this yourself. Just ask "How many years from innovation to commodity?" and they'll normally reply "it's variable". Then ask, "At what percentage adoption does something become a commodity?" and they'll normally reply "it's variable". Then ask "well, if it's variable in terms of time and adoption, then how have you put a marker on a graph of time and adoption?" This should make a suitably uncomfortable moment. It's not that these gurus are daft but instead, it's incredibly easy to fall into that "well, it's obvious" state of mind.

Back in 2007, my problem was that I had also been lulled into the same confident belief that we somehow understood the process of change and it was "obvious". The popular view tends to be that innovations appear somewhat randomly, either through the efforts of a group of people or often by happenstance, e.g. a fortuitous accident such as the discovery of inkjets through the placing of a hot syringe in a well of ink. These innovations then diffuse as above, some succeeding and crossing the chasm, whilst others fail. We often have competing examples — AC vs. DC electricity or BetaMax vs. VHS — until one becomes more established and dominant. Over time, the same innovation becomes a commodity. It feels simple and logical.

However, the rate of diffusion is not constant and we cannot measure the change of evolution over adoption or time. Furthermore, whatever process was occurring was not always continuous. As highlighted by Christensen's work on disruptive innovation, an existing industry can be disrupted by the introduction of a new technology that offers different performance attributes from those established. In other words, the diffusion of one thing can be substituted for another. For example, hydraulic excavators disrupted cable excavators and its associated suppliers. However, the same process could also be continuous. These innovations could be improving and sustaining, e.g. a better car, a better phone, a better computer or a more efficient means of steel manufacturing such as the Bessemer converter.

It seemed that organisations were competing in an ecosystem with others and the desire to differentiate was driving the creation of innovations that diffuse, forcing all companies to adapt (the Red Queen effect, Chapter 3). The innovations themselves appear somewhat randomly, often by fortuitous accident, and whilst some innovations disrupt, others will sustain. Furthermore, the innovations themselves might be novel or represent an incremental improvement to some past innovation, e.g. a better car rather than the first car. The process of diffusion itself is complex, changing in terms of the rate of diffusion, and has pitfalls such as the chasm. Given this complexity, how could I hope to describe a process of evolution?

With such an environment, how could any CEO be anything but bewildered and lost by the apparent randomness of competition? Where will the next great innovation appear? Will it be sustaining or a disruptive change? How quickly will it spread? Will it not spread? Will it jump the chasm? Will it impact me? Should we be early adopters or not? Is it any wonder that our ability to predict the future is often lamentable? Is it any surprise that given the fluid nature of our environment, we are reduced to hoping to keep afloat by catching the latest wave of change? Is it really that shocking that in practice, we're forced to copy what others are doing, to go with the market as we all swarm around new concepts?

All of these thoughts were swirling through my mind as I looked at that evolution axis of genesis, custom, product and commodity on map. It seemed so simple. I had obviously been seduced by this. But it seemed to work! I could find no evidence to support this pattern. I had probably wasted months trying to solve an impossible problem. Help!!!

That first question

The standard model I've outlined contains the random appearance of innovation, different rates of diffusion, and both sustaining and disruptive change. Whilst it sounds simple, it is hopelessly complex in practice. It was probably a day or two after I had decided that this was probably a lost cause that I thought of the first question that I needed to ask. What actually constitutes an innovation?

Whether something is an innovation or not partially depends upon the perspective of the observer. Hence, the Bessemer converter was a process improvement to iron and steel manufacturers, but a product innovation to suppliers of equipment for those industries. Equally, the modern day provision of computing resources through large utility suppliers (such as Amazon's EC2 service) is certainly a new business model for those suppliers, but for its consumers then the use of computing resources in business is hardly new.

Jan Fagerberg defined innovation as the "first attempt to put an idea into practice". Unfortunately, this equally applies to something novel or a feature improvement or a new business model for an existing activity. However, is a feature improvement to a phone really the same as the creation of the first phone? Is this equivalent to the introduction of rental service for phones? They are all called innovations but are they really the same or are we using one word to describe many different types of change? Maybe this was the confusion? I was looking at the diffusion of innovations but maybe we were talking about diffusion of different types of innovation?

Somehow, in a mad frenzy of writing on whiteboards, I connected three pieces of information to challenge my view of random and equivalent innovation impacting across society. Rogers and Kincaid in "Towards a new Paradigm of Research" published the first piece of the puzzle in 1981. When examining continuous and sustaining technological innovation, they noted that the rate of improvement tends to be slow and then accelerates until reaching a plateau of a more mature and slow, improving stage. Each improved version increasingly adds definition, eventually providing something that can be considered feature complete, mature and generally well understood. The insight here is that the maturing of a technology requires multiple improved versions, with each reducing uncertainty about the technology.

The second piece of the puzzle was published in 1996 by Paul Strassmann, a great and often under-acknowledged economist. In "The value of computers, information & knowledge", Strassmann showed that within business, there was no correlation between IT spending and the value it created for the business. The work demonstrated that IT wasn't one thing but instead, consisted of many activities. The insight here is that organisations consist of multiple components, some of which create value whilst others did not.

The third piece was a Harvard Business Review paper, "Does IT Matter?", published by Nicholas Carr in 2003. This paper discussed the IT industry and demonstrated that as certain aspects of IT became widespread and common, they had diminishing differential value and became more of a cost of doing business.

In isolation, the three pieces were interesting to note, but in combination, they implied something remarkable but obvious in hindsight about how activities (i.e. the things we do) change.

- **Activities evolved** through multiple improving versions.
- **Activities were not uniform**; any system could contain multiple components that were at different stages of evolution, i.e. there was no "IT" but a mass of components that made "IT".
- **The characteristics of activities changed as they evolved**; as they became more commonplace, they had diminishing differential value, became more of a cost of doing business and more certain. The improving versions of the same activity would have different characteristics. These seemed to imply that climatic patterns I had noticed were occurring but somehow, I just couldn't get evolution to fit with diffusion. I felt that I must be wrong. Then, I started to realise that maybe these two processes are related but separate.

Maybe I had just got stuck on trying to tie diffusion of innovation to evolution? What if instead, evolution consisted of multiple waves of diffusion, e.g. the diffusion of the first innovation of the act followed by waves of diffusions of improving innovations? Maybe those waves were different? An examination of historical records clearly showed that technological change tends to mature through multiple waves of diffusion of ever-improved versions. The pattern of evolution was there and I had collected a wealth of data over the years, which suggested it. I just had to break out of the shackles of diffusion.

Uncertainty is the key

I started to think in terms of multiple diffusion curves. Let us take an activity; we shall call it A — it could be television or the telephone, it doesn't matter. Now let us assume this activity will evolve through several versions — A1, A2, A3, A4 and A5. Each version might be disruptive or sustaining to the previous and each will diffuse on its own diffusion curve — see Figure 74.

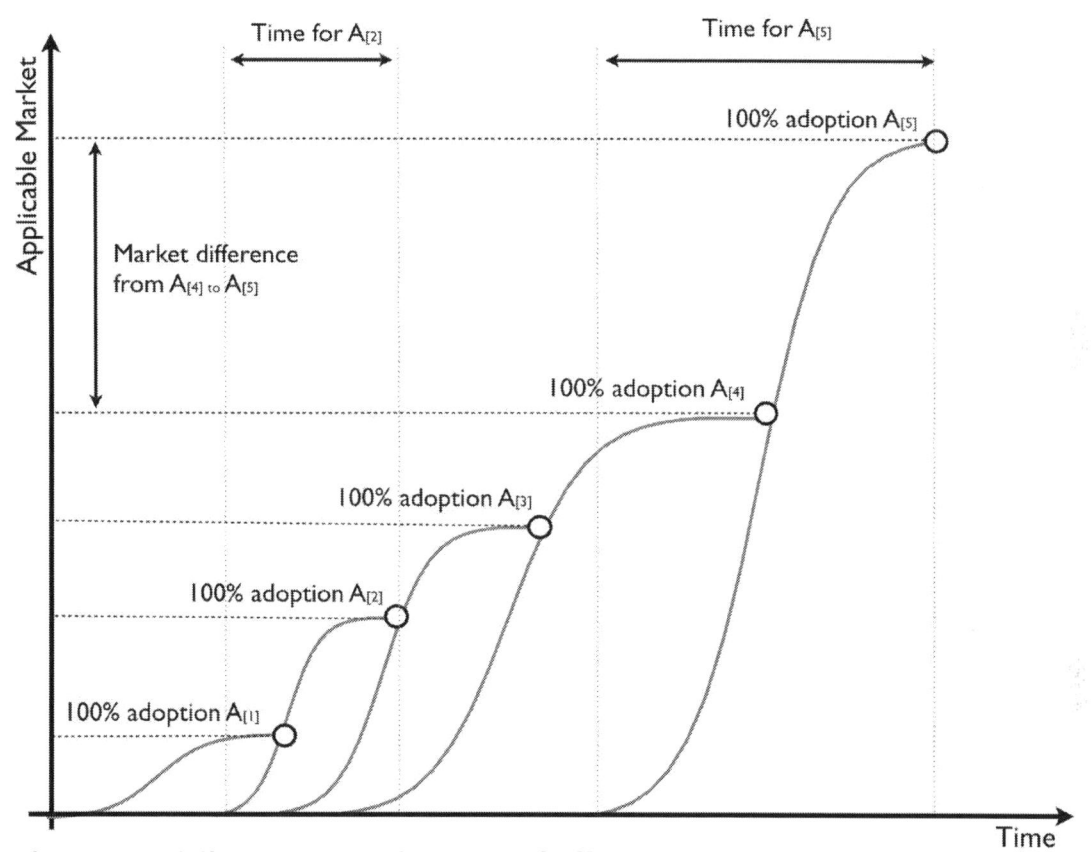

Figure 74: Evolution through multiple waves of diffusion

Whilst each version of the act diffuses to 100% adoption of its market, those applicable markets could be different sizes for different versions. Hence, the market for the first phones might not be the same market for later, more evolved phones. The time for diffusion of each version could also be different.

I had been assuming that by looking at adoption in a population then we could determine how evolved something was because of how "ubiquitous" it had become. This idea had come from concepts that commodity was commonplace. But what if the applicable markets were fundamentally different? Maybe ubiquity for gold bars meant 2% of the total population owning them, whereas ubiquity of smartphones meant everyone owns three of them? I couldn't just measure adoption because there could be a bigger market just around the corner. What I needed to do was measure adoption in its "ubiquitous" market. But was it that? How do I calculate it?

By pure serendipity, it was just at this time that I stumbled upon the Stacey Matrix. This is a mechanism for classifying types of agreements between groups. At one extreme, you had groups that were far from agreement with high levels of uncertainty; this was the domain of chaos and anarchy. At the other extreme, you had groups that were close to agreement with high degrees of certainty, the domain of simple. What struck me with the Stacey Matrix (see Figure 75) was the polar opposite nature of the domains and how the language was not dissimilar to the apparent process of evolution.

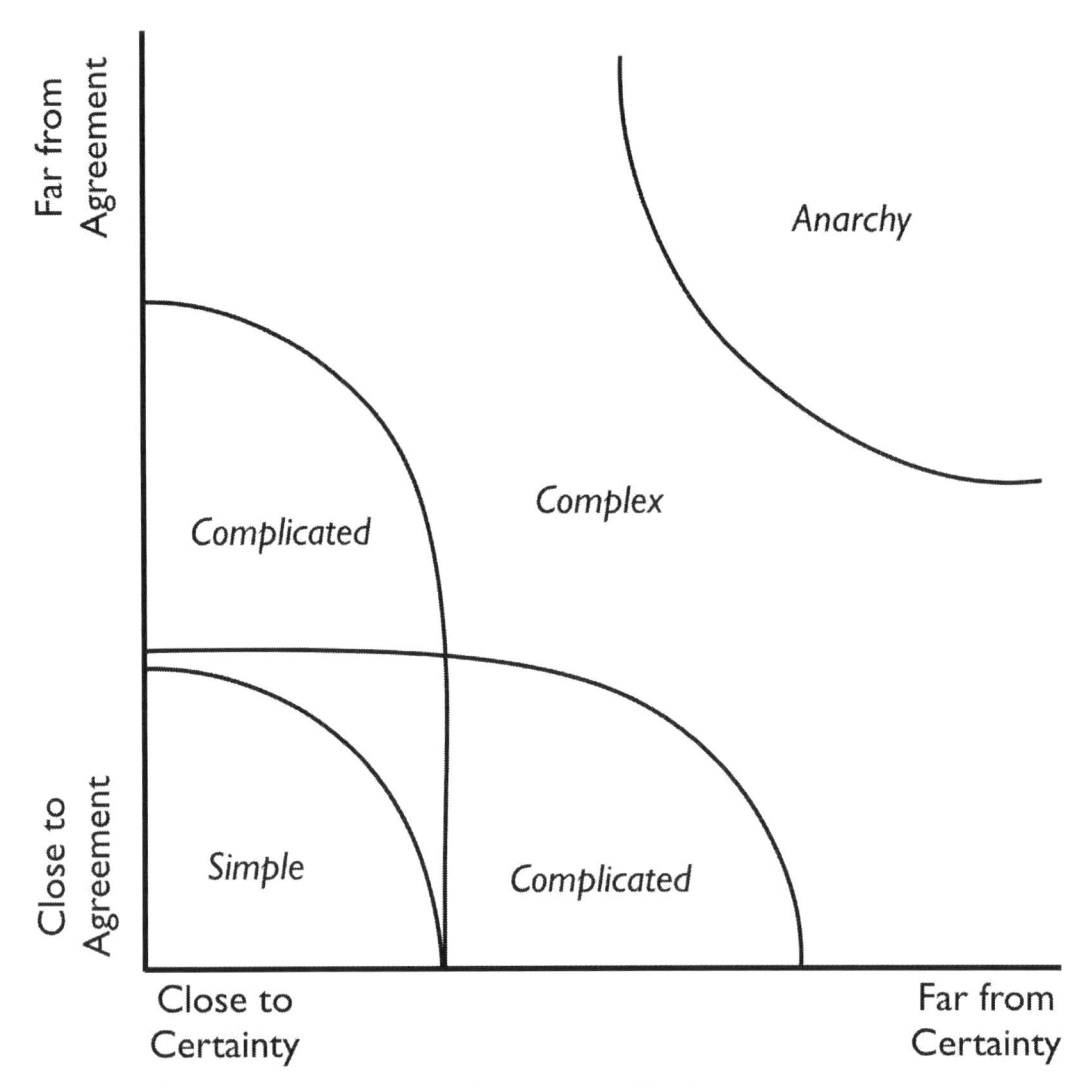

Figure 75: Brenda Zimmerman's simplified version of The Stacey Matrix

With evolution, we had the more chaotic world of the novel and new, with high degrees of uncertainty at one extreme whilst at the other were more well understood activities. The matrix mimicked the same sort of conversations that I was having where people could agree that a commodity was a commodity but disagreed vehemently on what stage of evolution a less evolved component was in. It occurred to me that maybe these sorts of discussion and arguments would be occurring in journals and that somehow, I might be able to use this to get an idea on how evolved something was. To be honest, I was just guessing by this point and was hoping to find some book where the answer would be magically written.

I headed back to the Library. I spent many months reading and trying to determine a measure for the certainty for an act. I was collecting all sorts of journals and categorising them when suddenly, I noticed something odd. To be a bit more specific, I suddenly woke up one morning with this idea.

It was by looking into the detail of journals and papers on various activities that I noticed how the words they used had started to change. They always started talking about the "wonder" of some new thing such as the "wonder of television", but over time, it became more about "use". I then took 9,221 articles related to various activities and categorised those articles into four main stages based upon the words they used. I then plotted the frequency of publications — see Figure 76.

Stage	I	II (key)	III (key)	IV
Publication Type	Wonder	building, construction and awareness	operation, maintenance and feature differences	use

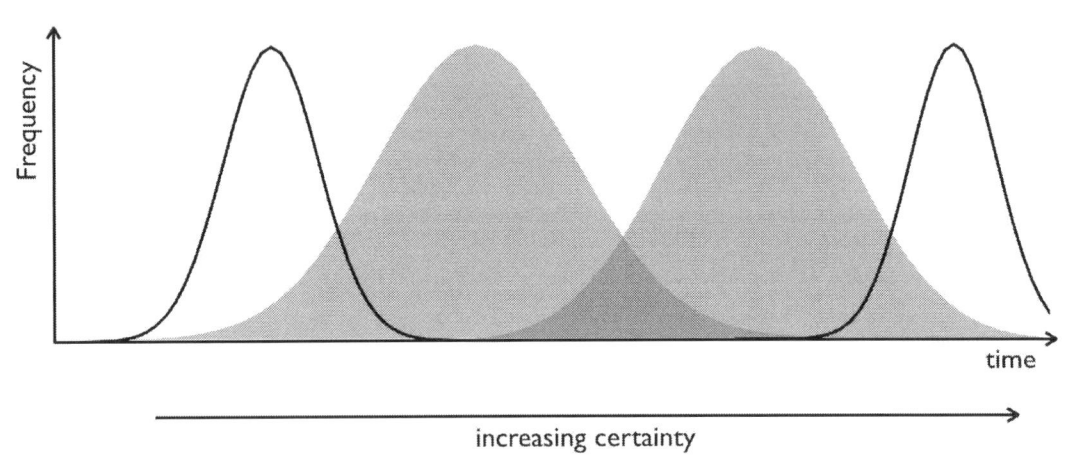

Figure 76: Changing nature of publications

To begin with, articles would discuss the wonder of the thing, e.g. the wonder of radio. This would then be replaced with articles discussing building, construction and awareness, e.g. how to build your own radio. These would then be replaced by articles discussing operation, maintenance and feature differentiation, e.g. which radio is best. Finally, it would become dominated by use, e.g. the Radio Times and what programmes to listen to. Using stage II and III publications, I developed a certainty scale.

I felt I was getting close to something but I still couldn't quite describe how evolution works or why. I'm not sure what possessed me to do this, it was another one of those sleepless nights, but I started to question if I could connect certainty to the applicable market and somehow work out the ubiquitous market. Obviously, I could only do that for things that had already become a commodity. So, for various activities, I marked a point of stability (I described this as 100% certain), the moment when publications changed from being dominated by operations, maintenance and feature differentiation to being dominated by use — see Figure 77.

Stage	I	II (key)	III (key)	IV
Publication Type	Wonder	building, construction and awareness	operation, maintenance and feature differences	use

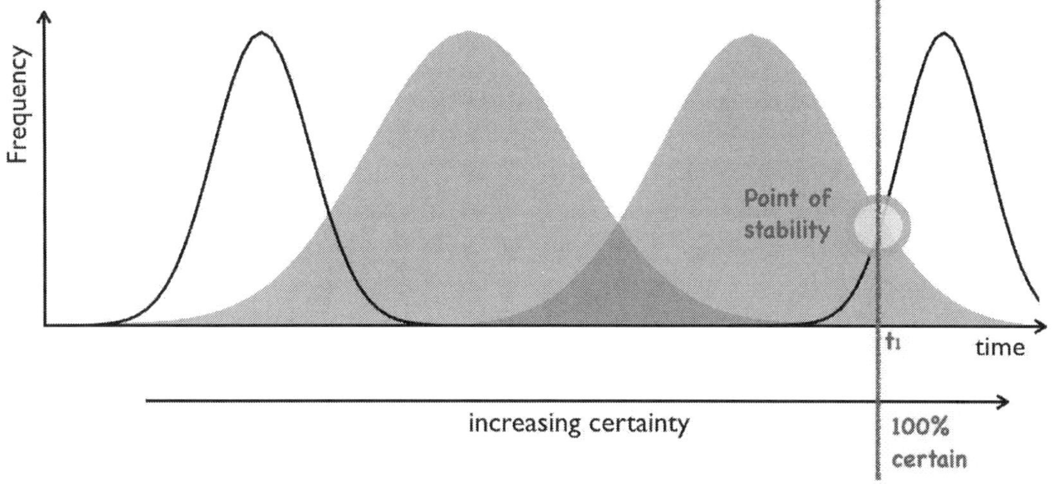

Figure 77: The point of stability

Then, I would take the time that this occurred (T1) and look up the applicable market for that activity at that time. I defined that applicable market as the point of ubiquity (i.e. 100% ubiquitous) – see Figure 78. I did this for radios, for TVs and all sorts of other common appliances.

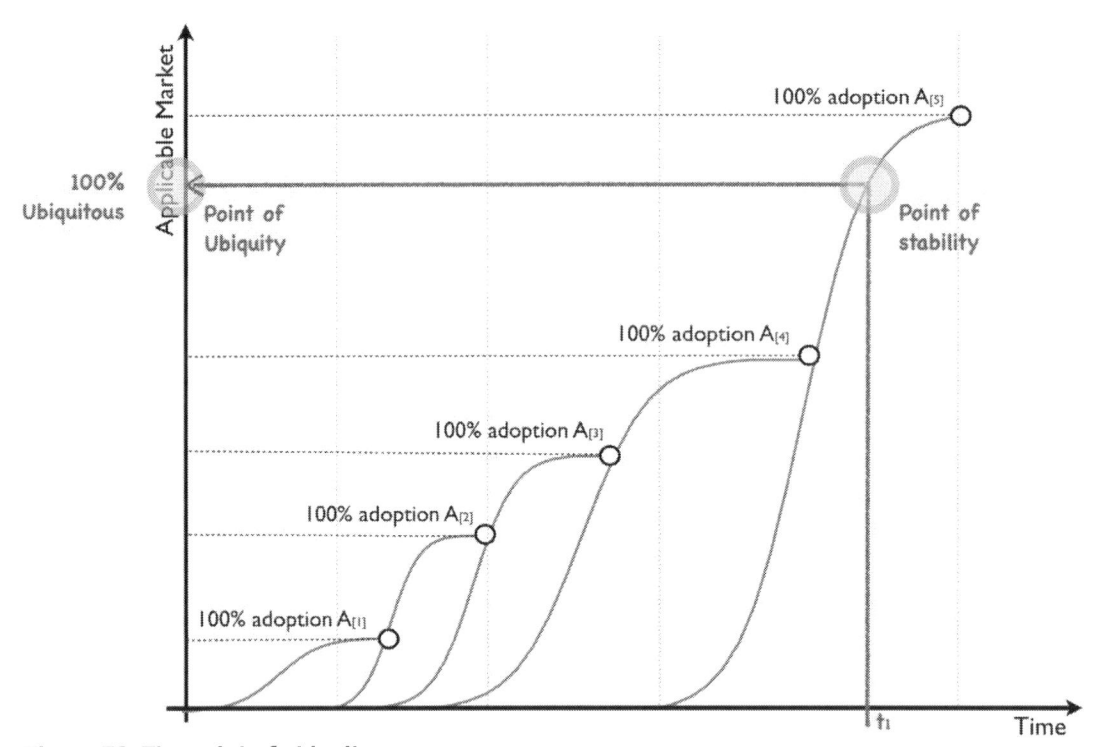

Figure 78: The point of ubiquity

All of these markets were different sizes and different percentages of adoption, and there was no obvious connection. At first, I was disappointed but then, I was just stumbling in the dark and didn't know what I was looking for. By pure chance, whilst experimenting around with this, I took a wild stab and decided to plot ubiquity versus certainty for a range of activities. I had defined a point as 100% certain on my certainty scale and I had a corresponding point of ubiquity. I could now trace back through history to determine how certain and ubiquitous an act was. This is what I did for a range of activities and finally plotted a graph of ubiquity versus certainty. The result is provided in Figure 79.

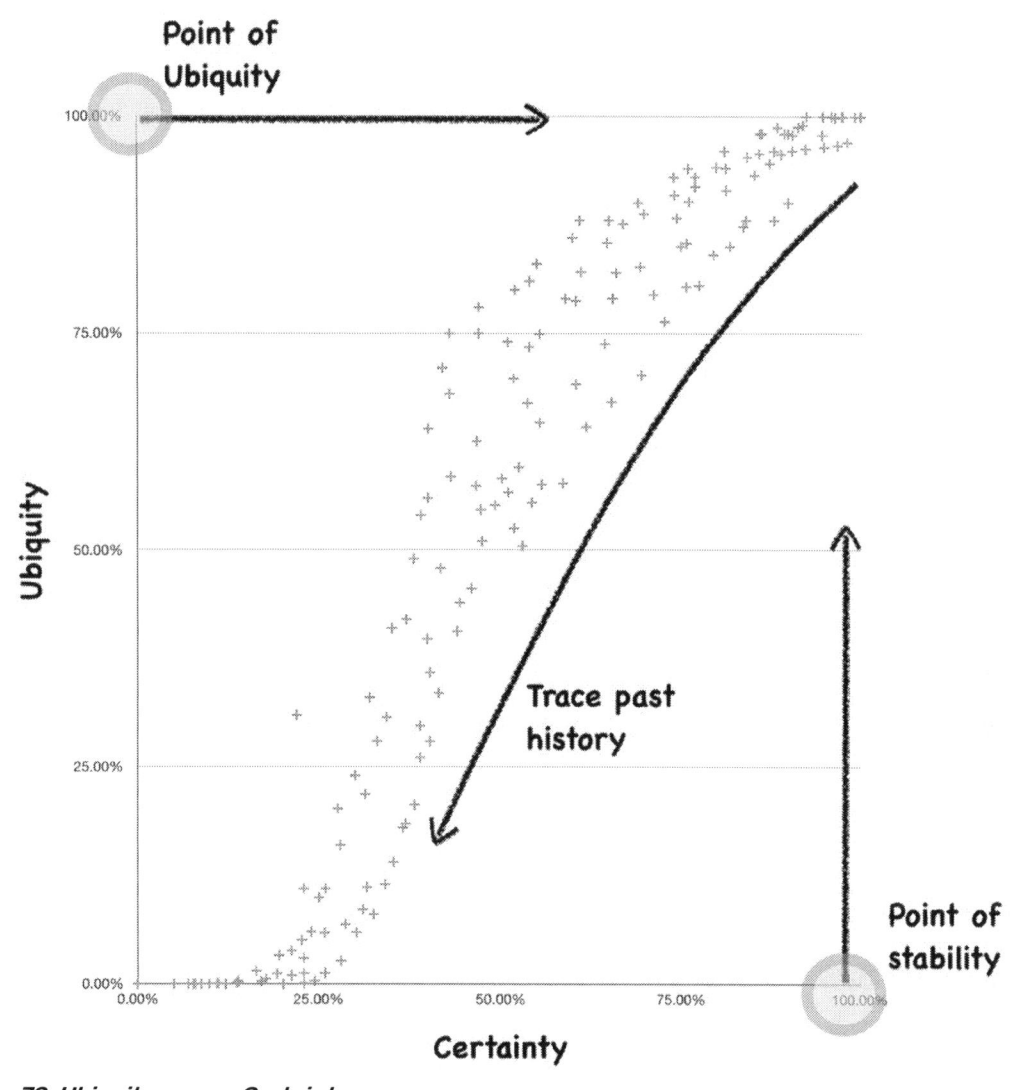

Figure 79: Ubiquity versus Certainty

I spent several hours staring at the result, trying to understand what it meant. It suddenly dawned on me that every activity seemed to be following the same path. There was a strong correlation here. I then went back and overlaid those different stages of publication onto the graph and extended both ends as activities emerge before people start writing about them and continue well after becoming a commodity. I also gave each stage a generic term, e.g. product for stage III and commodity for stage IV. The result was the evolution curve in Figure 80 that I published in various guises (e.g. Butler Group Review, March 2008, Why

Nothing is Simple in Management) and spoke enthusiastically about it at numerous conferences.

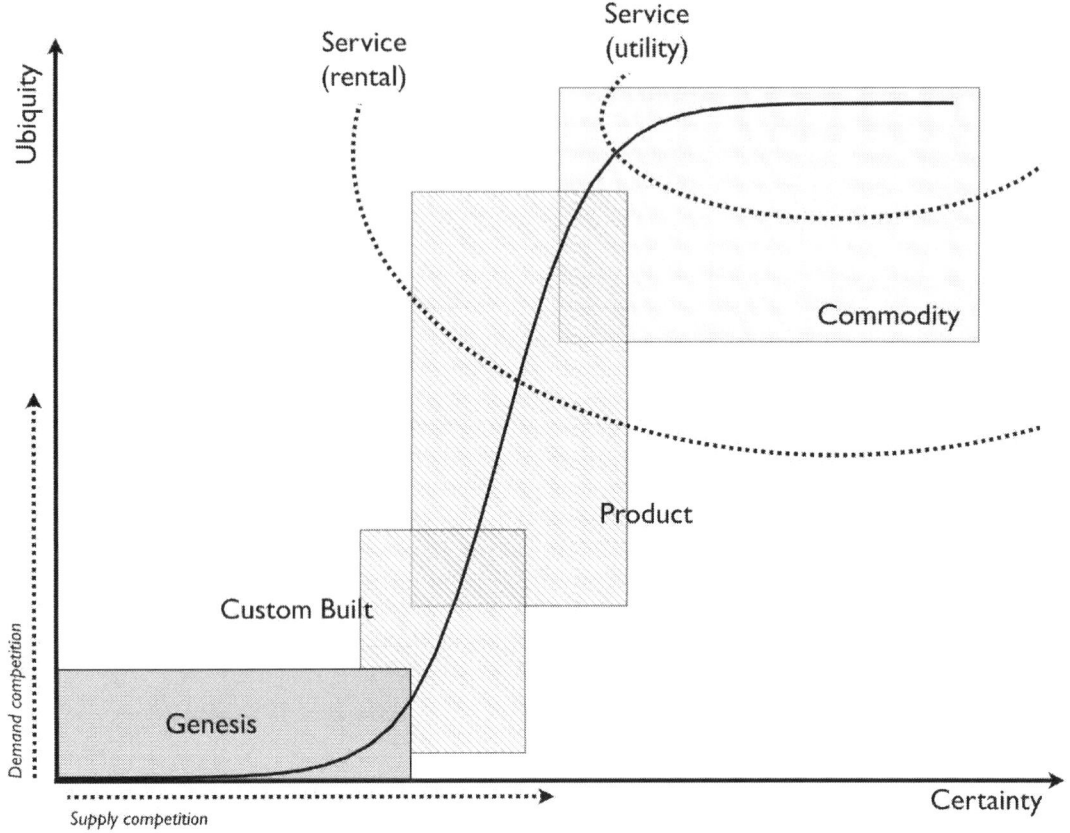

Figure 80: The evolution curve

Evolution begins with the genesis of an activity, e.g. the first battery, the first phone, the first television or the first digital computer, such as the Z3 in 1943. If it is successful then it will diffuse in its applicable market. If it is useful then others will copy, and custom-built examples of that activity will appear (e.g. systems such LEO – Lyons Electronic Office). They will also diffuse in what tends to be a larger applicable market. As the activity spreads through custom-built systems then pressure mounts for adoption and products are produced. These products themselves diffuse through an even wider market, often with constant improvements or disruptive changes, with each diffusing in turn and growing the market. As the act becomes more widespread and well understood, alternative models of provision appear, such as rental services. Eventually, the act becomes so widespread and well defined that it becomes "ubiquitous", well understood and more of a commodity. It will tend to be standardised with little feature differentiation between offerings. At this stage of volume operations then utility services are likely to have appeared, especially if the act is suitable for delivery by such a mechanism.

There is no time or adoption axis on the evolution curve, only ubiquity (to its ubiquitous market) versus certainty. It may take ten years or a hundred for something to make its journey from genesis to commodity. It may become a commodity when 2% of the population own it or everyone has three. However, regardless of this, I know the path it will take. What causes things to take that journey turns out to be simple competition represented in two forms:-

Demand competition and the consumer desire for anything that is useful or makes a difference or creates an advantage is the driver for ubiquity, i.e. anything useful spreads.

Supply competition and the desire of providers to supply an activity to consumers is the driver for feature completeness and improvement of an activity. For example, an average car today includes, as standard, numerous things that were once novel feature differentiations, such as electric windows, air bags, alarm systems, a stereo, seat belts, roll bars and windscreen wipers. It's the desire to differentiate and to make things better combined with competition and copying that drives things to become more uniform, more complete and more certain.

It is important not to confuse evolution with diffusion, though both patterns have an S-curve shape. The pattern of diffusion is one of adoption of a specific change over time, whether that change is something novel or a feature differentiation or a particular business model. The first telephone diffused, a better method of producing glass known as the Pilkington float glass method diffused, new and improved washing powder diffuses, and a utility model for provision of electricity diffused.

The pattern of evolution deals with the changing nature of something. It does not concern itself with adoption of a specific change (i.e. a better computer) but instead, it shows how that activity itself has evolved from custom built to more of a product.

Diffusion and evolution are of course connected. The evolution of an act can consist of thousands of diffusion curves of improving versions of that act, each with their own chasms. As an activity evolves, each more evolved version will diffuse from early adopters to laggards through its own applicable market. That market can and does grow as the act becomes more accessible to a larger audience. For example, with the first computing products, you had early adopters and laggards within a relatively small market. As the products improved through constant incremental changes, the applicable market grew significantly and later versions diffused through a much broader public market. Today, computing infrastructure is "ubiquitous", which is why we have utility services like Amazon EC2.

Comments on and the limits of evolution

It's important to note that unlike diffusion, evolution cannot be determined over time. It can only be measured over the ubiquity of the act versus its certainty, i.e. how complete, well understood and fit for purpose it is. Whilst we can use the evolution curve to say that a specific component will evolve over an undetermined amount of time to become more of a commodity, we cannot say precisely when this will happen but only what will happen if it survives. It is less prediction (in the formal sense of change over time) and more anticipation of change.

Furthermore, the evolution curve can only be precisely determined for the past, i.e. the act needs to become stable and reach the point of certainty for us to determine its point of ubiquity and therefore calculate the path it has taken. This means we cannot accurately determine where something is on the evolution curve until it has become a commodity, at which point we can determine where it was in the past. Hence, we are forced to rely on a cheat sheet based upon changing characteristics (Chapter 2), along with weak signal analysis to estimate where something is.

There is, unfortunately, no crystal ball to the future, and we have to embrace a degree of uncertainty until it reaches the point of stability and becomes certain. Since we must rely on changing characteristics and weak signals (if available) to determine where something is on a map then a current map is developed from the consensus of those involved. This can be manipulated or influenced by existing bias, hence it is important to not only be transparent with the maps but allow for challenge to them. The maps are imperfect representations of what exists and the axes do constrain a view of the world based upon the anchor (user need), the value chain (position) and evolution (movement). The mapper must accept that the maps are not real any more than a geographical map is real. The question however is not whether it is real but whether it is useful.

As evolution deals with the change to the act itself, it does not care whether some specific change is incremental or disruptive to the past. A company may produce a better product (e.g. a better cable excavator) or instead, a product may be substituted by another (e.g. cable vs. hydraulic excavators), but the act of "digging holes" doesn't change. Instead, we simply have a more evolved way of doing this. Today, the evolution of computing infrastructure from product to utility is disruptive for the past product industry, but the act of consuming computing infrastructure isn't new, it is simply more evolved.

Every activity I have examined throughout history follows this path.

- The genesis of the humble screw can be traced back to Archytas of Tarentum (400 BC). The principle was later refined by Archimedes and also used to construct devices to raise water. Over the next two-thousand years, most screws (and any associated bolts) were cut by hand, however, demand for screw threads and fasteners created increasing pressure for a more industrialised process. J. and W. Wyatt had patented such a concept in 1760 and Jesse Ramsden in 1770 introduced the first form of screw-cutting lathe. However, without a practical means of achieving industrialisation and with no standards then the industry continued primarily as was. Maudslay then introduced the first industrially practical screw-cutting lathe in 1800, which combined elements such as the slide rest, change gears and lead-screw to achieve the effect. However, whilst screws and bolts could be manufactured with interchangeable components, the lack of any standards thwarted general interchangeability. In 1841, James Whitworth collected a large number of samples from British manufacturers and proposed a set of standards, including the angle of thread and threads per inch. The proposals became standard practice in 1860 and a highly standardised and industrialised sector developed that we recognise today.
- The history of electrical power generation can be traced from its genesis with the Parthian battery (around 200 AD) to custom-built examples of generators such as the Hippolyte Pixii (1832) to the first products such as Siemens Generators (1866) to Westinghouse's utility provision of AC electricity (1886) and the subsequent standardisation of electricity provision from the introduction of the first standard plugs and sockets to standards for transmission and the formation of national grids (UK National Grid, 1926).
- The history of modern computing infrastructure can be traced from its genesis with the Z3 computer (1943) to custom-built examples such as LEO or Lyons Electronic Office (1949) to the first products such as IBM 650 (1953) to rental services such as Tymshare (1964) to commodity provision of computing infrastructure, and more recently, utility provision with Amazon EC2 (2006). It's also worth noting the hockey stick effect of the graph. When a novel activity appears, it first evolves mainly through understanding rather than rapidly spreading. As our understanding of the activity increases, we reach a tipping point that the act now rapidly spreads through multiple waves of custom-built examples and then products. As the act becomes widespread, our understanding of it

increases until this becomes embedded in our social systems and in many cases, almost invisible. We no longer consider how it is constructed; it is almost a given and can in many cases be buried in higher order systems as a component, e.g. the once wonder of the nut and bolt is now hidden inside the machine or the car or the toaster.

For interest, this hockey stick pattern is similar to that found by Boiset, Canals and Macmillan in their simulation of I-Space using an agent-based approach to modelling knowledge flows. Their work looked at how knowledge spreads through economic and social systems by examining the interactions of agents (i.e. individuals). One of the things they demonstrated confirmed a previous expectation that knowledge is first abstracted and codified before it rapidly diffuses (see Figure 81). This is the same pattern within my data where first, our understanding and certainty over an activity increases (i.e. it is abstracted and codified) before it rapidly becomes widespread.

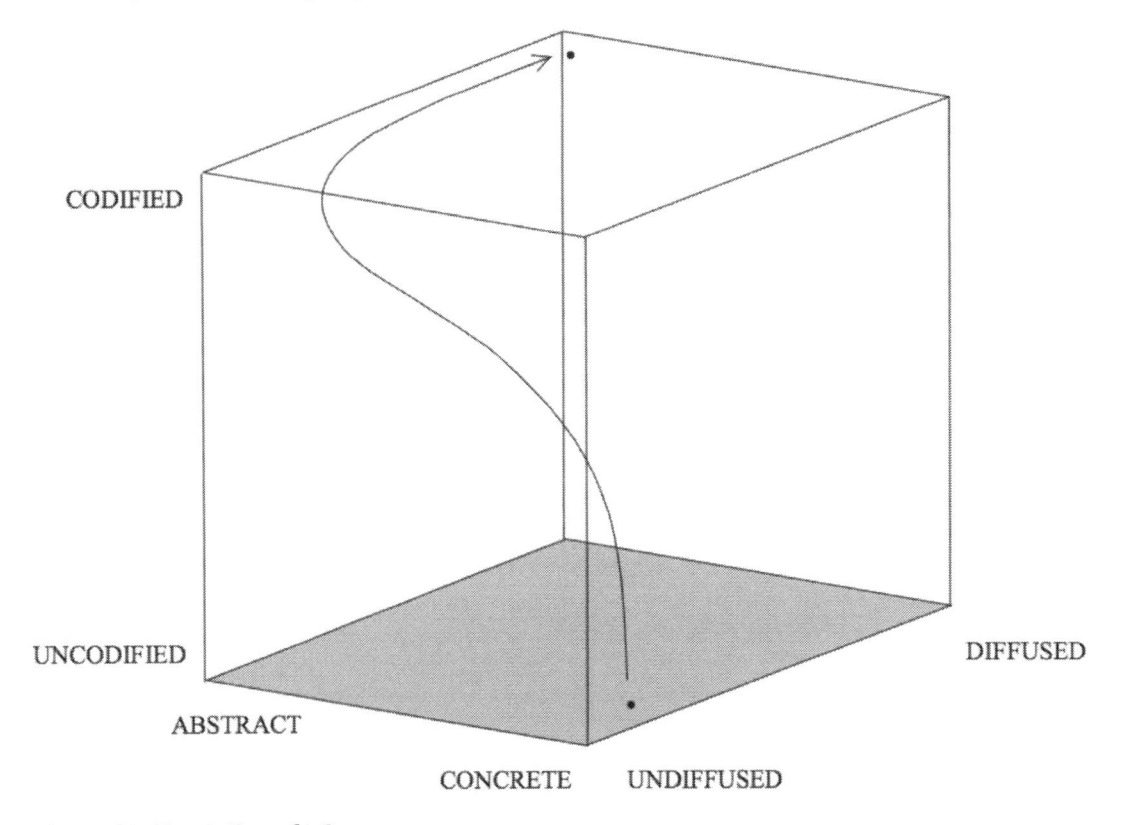

Figure 81: Simulation of I-Space

The pattern of evolution that I used as the x-axis of my map had some sense of validity in history. I could, with some confidence, describe how things would evolve, even though I couldn't say precisely when.

Looking back, I could now see that the term "innovation" does appear to be currently used to describe changes in different states of evolution. Some things described as "innovations" are genuinely novel, new and hence, uncertain activities (i.e. genesis). By virtue of being uncertain then the appearance of these is almost impossible to predict and you cannot know with certainty what will appear. However, many things described as "innovations" are simply improvements to an existing activity and part of a visible process of evolution that is driven by competition. Whilst you cannot predict when these changes will occur, as evolution cannot be plotted over time, you can predict what will happen. This notion is contrary to the more random perception of "innovation". Amazon EC2, a utility computing infrastructure service (commonly known as cloud computing), wasn't a random accident but instead, it was inevitable that some company would provide utility computing infrastructure.

Far from being like navigators in a storm, constantly coping with the maelstrom around us, it appears that the sea has structure. Mapping seemed to have merit and I had a purpose, to teach everyone who would listen. Alas, it was 2008 and I was fast running out of cash. I would have to turn mapping to a profit one way or another.

Before we move on

I've covered quite a few concepts and hypotheses in this chapter, and to be honest, I could probably write an entire book on this one topic alone. However, we've got a lot more to cover and so I think it's probably worth highlighting some lessons and moving on.

Purpose, Scope and Imperative

- Purpose, scope, moral imperative, survival and user needs can be connected in a chain of needs.
- All will evolve and be affected by the chain they exist within. Nothing is permanent.
- Scope should be tangible and easy to understand, but you also need a moral imperative to enthuse people.
- Aim to create revenue and profit — your need to survive — by meeting your users' needs.
- There is often a balancing act between different conflicting user needs.

Landscape

- Your map is always part of a wider chain of needs; it is no more than a window on an industry. A perfect map covering an entire industry and all its components is probably as unusable (Valéry's paradox), as a perfect map of France (i.e. 1 to 1 scale). You have to accept some compromise.
- You can draw many organisations onto a single map. The value chain is only a guide, and higher up the value chain simply means more visible to that user. You can always draw chains of users, e.g. the user needs for a gun company break down into the user needs for a bolt company.
- Maps are a communication tool. Don't be afraid to modify or clarify the terms on the axis if it helps in the discussion. The key is to keep within the bounds of what is a map, particularly position (e.g. value chain) and movement (e.g. evolution).
- The map of mapping (Figure 69) contains components that are also the axes of the map, i.e. the idea of evolution is itself evolving along the evolution scale. Mapping can be applied to itself. It also means that these current maps are little more than Babylonian Clay Tablets. Someone will make a better map.
- There are many different things that we call innovation – this includes genesis of an act, feature differentiation of a product, and a shifting business model from product to utility. They are very different, despite our use of a single term to describe them.

Climate: Evolution

- You cannot measure evolution over time or adoption.
- Evolution is measured over ubiquity versus certainty. The "ubiquitous" market for one activity (e.g. smartphones) is not necessarily the same as the "ubiquitous" market for another (e.g. gold bars).
- Evolution consists of multiple diffusion curves. Evolution and diffusion are connected but separate concepts. Don't confuse the two.
- Evolution is driven by supply and demand competition.
- Whilst we cannot say when things will happen (we can cheat with weak signal analysis), we can describe what will happen, i.e. this will evolve to more of a commodity. Evolution shows you a path but there is no crystal ball to predicting the future. We have to embrace uncertainty. The less evolved something is (i.e. the less certain we are about it – Figure 71), then by definition, the more uncertain it becomes.
- The idea of evolution is itself evolving and is therefore uncertain. All models are wrong; some are merely useful. I've marked off the list of climatic patterns that we've covered so far in grey in Figure 82. Before long, we will be anticipating change like a professional.

Components	Everything evolves through supply and demand competition	Rates of evolution can vary by ecosystem *(e.g. consumer vs industrial)*	Characteristics change as components evolve *(Salaman & Storey)*	No choice over evolution *(Red Queen)*
	No single method fits all *(e.g. in development or purchasing)*	Components can co-evolve *(e.g. practice with activity)*	Evolution consists of multiple waves of diffusion with many chasms.	
Financial	Higher order systems create new sources of value	Efficiency does not mean a reduced spend *(Jevon's Paradox)*	Capital flows to new areas of value	Creative Destruction *(Joseph Schumpeter)*
	Future value is inversely proportional to the certainty we have over it.	Evolution to higher order systems results in increasing local order and energy consumption		
Speed	Efficiency enables innovation	Evolution of communication mechanisms can increase the speed of evolution overall and the diffusion of a single example of change	Increased stability of lower order systems increases agility & speed of re-combination	Change is not always linear (discontinuous & exponential change exists)
	Shifts from product to utility tend to demonstrate a punctuated equilibrium			
Inertia	Success breeds inertia	Inertia can kill an organisation	Inertia increases the more successful the past model is	
Competitors	Competitors actions will change the game	Most competitors have poor situational awareness		
Prediction	Not everything is random *(p[what] vs p[when])*	Economy has cycles *(peace, war and wonder)*	Two different forms of disruption *(predictable vs non-predictable)*	A "war" (point of industrialisation) causes organisations to evolve
	You cannot measure evolution over time or adoption, you need to embrace uncertainty.	Evolution consists of multiple diffusion curves	The less evolved something is then the more uncertain it becomes	

Figure 82: Climatic patterns

Chapter 8 - Keeping the wolves at bay

To keep funding my research, I took a few more paid gigs, which basically meant becoming a gun for hire. Cloud computing was colliding with the technology scene and there was lots of confusion about it. Hence, I had a constant stream of conferences — including some that actually paid — along with plenty of opportunity for piecemeal work. It was a wild west in computing with unfortunately, some fairly shady practices and exploitation in the industry. I tried not to cause harm but I had an Achilles heel in simplicity.

The danger of making it simple

One of the obstacles with mapping was that some people found it complex. This is not really surprising because you're exposing people to a world that the majority are unfamiliar with. Few in business have practical experience with situational awareness or the use of maps. Many don't understand why it might be important. It also takes time and effort to become comfortable with creating a map. A common response tends to be "can you create the map for us?", based upon an idea that they will then apply their general-like strategy to it. This always degenerates into "can you show us what moves we can make?" to which they'll apply their general-like intellect to. In the end, it becomes "which move should we make?" and then general-like nodding of their approval.

However, confusion over cloud computing had created an opportunity for a new way of thinking and hopefully learning. Alas, piling on the complexity of mapping onto a bewildered person who has no connection to situational awareness can cause more confusion. Most people just wanted answers they could agree to, such as how to solve their need of being in the cloud without rocking the boat too much. I'm guessing that's why there has been an awful lot of questionable efforts in the private cloud.

Hence, I looked for ways to simplify mapping, to make it more palatable and more familiar. I started with spot painting. I'd take a business process diagram or a box and wire for an existing system, such as our Elvish self-driving car in Figure 36 (Chapter 4), and then colour different parts according to whether they were more genesis or commodity. I'd produce something like Figure 83.

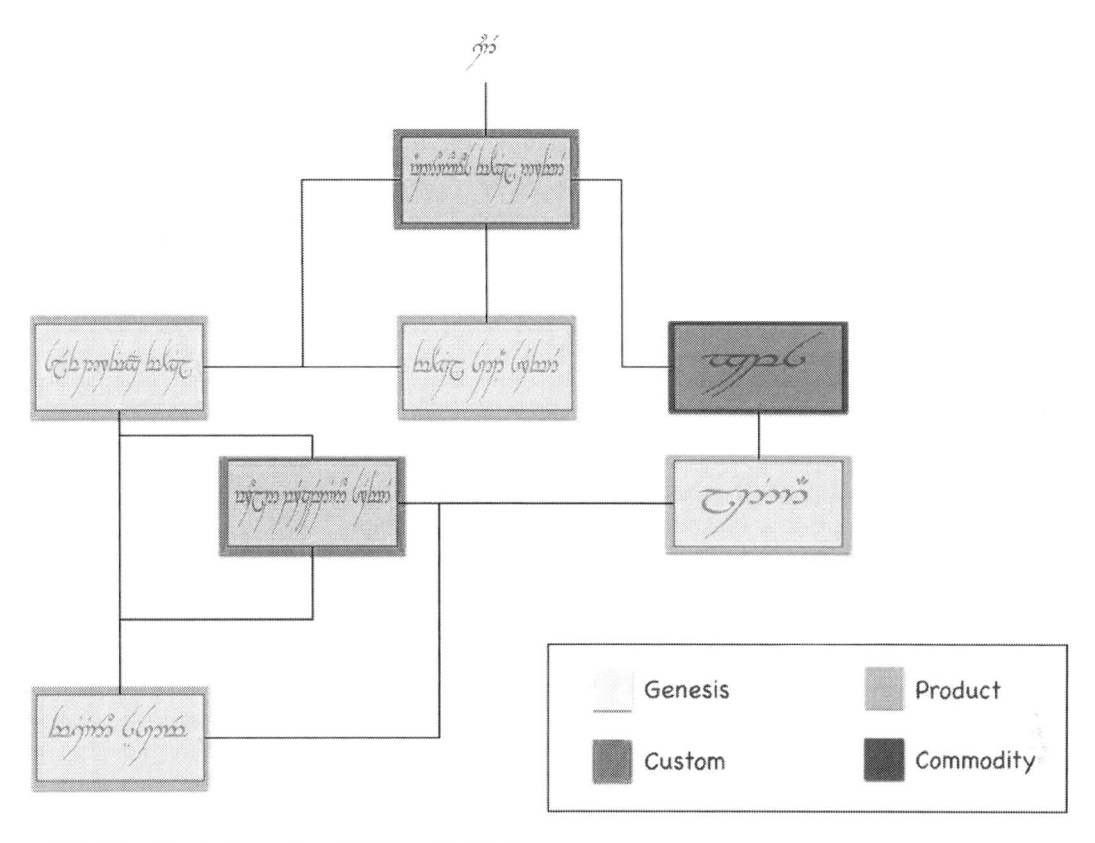

Figure 83: "Spot" painting of an Elvish self-driving car

Such annotated diagrams along with being colourful were more familiar and less threatening to the people who had written the originals. They enabled me to fairly easily introduce the concepts of evolution into an organisation and hence, we could have a discussion about what methods to use. But without position and movement then these diagrams were unhelpful for effective challenge and continuous learning of economic patterns or forms of gameplay. There was a trade-off between simplicity and usefulness.

The simple trap

Ashby's law of requisite variety describes how the controlling mechanism of a system must be capable of representing what is being controlled. Organisations are both complicated and complex things. They are generally complicated because they have a large scope, contain many components that require specialisation, and are difficult to grasp and manage. They are also complex because there are many emergent behaviours. For example, they have many components in the uncharted space for which there is uncertainty, and you cannot predict this. The best you can do here is to feel your way. Whilst mapping provides you with a window into this, you need to have a management capability able to cope with it.

There is unfortunately another solution to Ashby's law. Instead of coping with a complicated environment that contains complexity, you make the choice to pretend that what is being managed is simple. In business, we like things such as 2x2 diagrams; not because they represent reality but because they obscure it and hence, are easy to understand. We trade off our ability to continuously learn about the environment for an illusion of simplicity and easy management.

It's important to make a distinction here. The act of taking something complicated (like a machine) and breaking it down into small but manageable components or using a mechanism to sense uncertain change in a complex environment is not the same as trying to manage such a system by pretending it's a 2x2 matrix. As Einstein would say, "Everything should be made as simple as possible, but no simpler."

Eventually, I was faced with a choice. Do I keep using these "spot" diagrams, thereby making the concepts of evolution more accessible and just accept the flaws (and the cash), or do I take a slower path and try to push organisations towards a higher understanding of position and movement? If they struggled then I could compromise and do the heavy lifting for them by just providing a map and the results. However, I already knew that this would make them dependent upon me, which was the consultant path that I was trying to fight. My purpose was to free people from the shackles of consultants and not to chain them up even more. This compromise was out of the question. I had to take the slower path. I like to think that I stood my ground here, but with very few companies mapping, bills mounting, and clients taking an interest in the simplified concepts, then it's fair to say that I was starting to wobble.

Finding my mojo

My salvation was a piece of paid work that I'm particularly fond of. It concerned a question of efficiency versus effectiveness, and to have any hope of explaining it then we first need to introduce three concepts— worth based development, pricing granularity and flow. After which, we can connect them all together to examine this question. I'm going to have to jump around in history in order to do this but hopefully, I can keep it all together.

Worth based development

In 2003, the company that I ran built and operated small-sized systems for others. There were no big systems; these were more of the £100k – £2M scale, covering a few million users. Our clients usually wanted to write a detailed specification of exactly what they needed to ensure we delivered. That doesn't sound too bad, but even at this small scale then some of the components in these projects would be in the uncharted space and hence, no-one knew exactly what was wanted. Unfortunately, back then, I didn't have the language to explain this. Hence, we built and operated the systems and inevitably, we had some tension over change control and arguments over what feature was in or out of a particular contract.

During one of these discussions, I pointed out to the client that we were sitting around a table arguing over a piece of paper but not one of us was talking about what the users needed. The contract wasn't really the customer here; the client's end users were. We needed to change this discussion and focus on the end user. I suggested that we should create a metric of value based upon the end user – something we could both work towards. The idea fell on deaf ears as the client was preoccupied with the contract, but at least the seed was planted. It wasn't long after this that another project provided an opportunity to test this idea. The client gave me a specification and asked how much it would cost to build. I replied, "How does free sound?" They were a bit shocked but then I added, "However, we will have to be paid to operate the system. We need to determine a measure of value or worth and I'll get paid on that." There was a bit of um and ah but eventually, we agreed to try out a method of worth based development.

In this case, the goal of the system was to provide leads for an expensive range of large format printers (LFPs). The client wanted more leads. Their potential end users wanted a way of finding out more on these printers, along with a way of testing them. I would build something that would marry the two different sets of needs. But rather than the client paying upfront and taking all the risk, I would build it for free and take a fee on every new lead created.

We (as in the client and my company) were no longer focused on what was in or out of a contract, but on a single task of creating more leads. We both had an incentive for this. I also had a new incentive for cost effectiveness because the more efficient I made the system then the more profit I retained. We agreed and so I built and operated a system that enabled consumers to upload an image, test it on a large format printer and get delivery of their print, plus information on the kit's performance, plus a sales call. The system soared.

In three months, we had generated more leads than the client normally had in a year and this was accelerating. It was stunning. The client's revenue was rocketing but so was my revenue, as the system was based upon a metric of leads. The more success they had, the more success I had. It was a win-win situation, or so I thought. Alas, this actually created two problems and one headache.

The problems were caused by the client being unprepared for this level of interest and internal budgeting systems that weren't designed to cope with such variable success. What has budgeting got to do with this? Well, for the client then success was more leads, which translated into more revenue. This was good from a budgeting point of view. But the more success the client had then the more my fee increased as it was also based on leads. This was bad from a budgeting point of view. The system became so successful that it exceeded an internal budget figure the client had set for costs, and this caused an internal conflict with demands to switch off the system until a new budget was allocated (a very lengthy process). Switch off a revenue-generating system because it's doing better than expected and passed some arbitrary budget figure? This is what happens when an inflexible one size fits all approach of budgeting hits reality.

Before you go "this is daft", actually, it's not. Over time, companies tend to build up a body of work and processes — the corporate corpus — designed to stop past failure. It's all done with reasonable intentions. The desire to spend money effectively and the desire to know resources are being well used. That mass of good intentions is often the cause of many problems when you try to change the system. That corpus can become a corpse; a zombie killing off innovation whenever it is found. I had attempted to change the system by introducing a worth based approach and I should have known that this would cause tensions with the corpus; in this case, the budgeting system. I learned that lesson quickly.

I've used worth based approaches (often called "outcome") many times over the last decade. In fact, I prefer them. Whilst they tend to solve the issue of an excessive focus on contracts, they have invariably hit other roadblocks such as a client not being able to describe a metric of value or the purpose of the system or even conflict and politics within internal processes. You need to be aware of this and to mitigate against it.

Along with problems such as lack of preparation for the surge in demand or the corporate corpus, there was also the headache that this worth based approach caused. This was my migraine. There was some financial risk associated with this project and some investment needed. I had to be concerned with not only the development but operations. This included lots of capital investment, along with costs that weren't either truly variable or ones that I could only guess at. To minimise the risk, we shared common components with other projects but in a large, heterogeneous application environment then this just complicates allocation of costs. How much would a user visiting our application cost us in terms of compute, power and data centre usage was an incredibly tough question.

In my risk models, I also had no clear way of determining operational costs as it scaled. I had to make lots of estimates on stepwise changes and how much compute resources would be used by an application that hadn't been built. The financial model was more akin to art than any form of science. Some of that uncertainty ending up as "padding" in the metric, e.g. the price per lead that I would charge. Fortunately, other areas had better cost models. In the LFP example above then distribution systems and even printing were more variable (i.e. price per print or price per package) because we had experience of running an online photo and printing service. This brings me to the next topic of pricing granularity.

Pricing granularity

With a worth based approach then I have a strong incentive to:-

- reduce the operational cost of the project because the cheaper it is then the more profit I make.
- provide reliability because if the system went down, I wasn't making any money.
- ensure the system maximises the value metric. In the case of LFP then this metric was "generating leads".

But I also had questions on where to invest. In the case of LFP, it was doing very well (this was prior to the budget shenanigans) and so I decided to look at investing an additional $100K. But where do I best put the money? Improving the site reliability? Reducing the operational cost of the application through better code? Maximising the number of users through marketing? Improving conversion of users to leads? Which choice brings me the better return? This is a particularly tough question to answer if you can't effectively determine the operational cost of an application beyond hand waving or if other data is also guessed at.

One of the huge benefits of Zimki (our platform as a service play in 2006) was not only its serverless nature and how you could simply write code through an online IDE but also its pricing granularity was down to the function. This was no accident as I had a genuine need to know this. Any application is nothing more than a high level function that calls other functions. If I developed a function in Zimki, whenever that function was called then I could see exactly how much it had cost me. I was charged on the network, storage and compute resources used by that function. This was quite a revelation. It changed behaviour significantly because suddenly, in the sea of code that is my application, I could find individual functions that disproportionately cost me more.

As far as I know, this pricing per function was unparalleled in the world of IT in 2006, and we didn't see an equivalent pricing granularity until AWS Lambda was launched in 2014. Now, obviously, I was also the provider of Zimki and behind the scenes, there was a complex array of basket of goods concepts and all manner of financial instruments to be able to provide those cost figures. But this was abstracted from the developer. All they saw was a cost every time their function ran, no matter how much it scaled. There was no capital investment and this turned the operational cost of an application into a manageable variable.

Flow

I'm now going to combine the ideas of worth based (outcome) development and pricing granularity to introduce an idea known as flow. To do this, we're going to revisit the LFP project but this time, with a map and the knowledge of what a utility platform can bring. Back when we were actually working on the LFP project, I hadn't developed the mapping concept fully and Zimki wasn't released. Hence, this is a post event analysis and more of what could have happened rather than what did.

So, let us go back to 2008. We know how to map (we knew this in 2005). Let us imagine that Zimki (launched in 2005) had survived or some other equivalent platform as a service has arisen. Let us now imagine a scenario where the client has turned up with the LFP project and is willing to build this using worth based development (as happened in 2003).

In Figure 84, I've created a map of the worth based LFP project. I won't mark up points on this map; hopefully, you've enough experience now to start reading them.

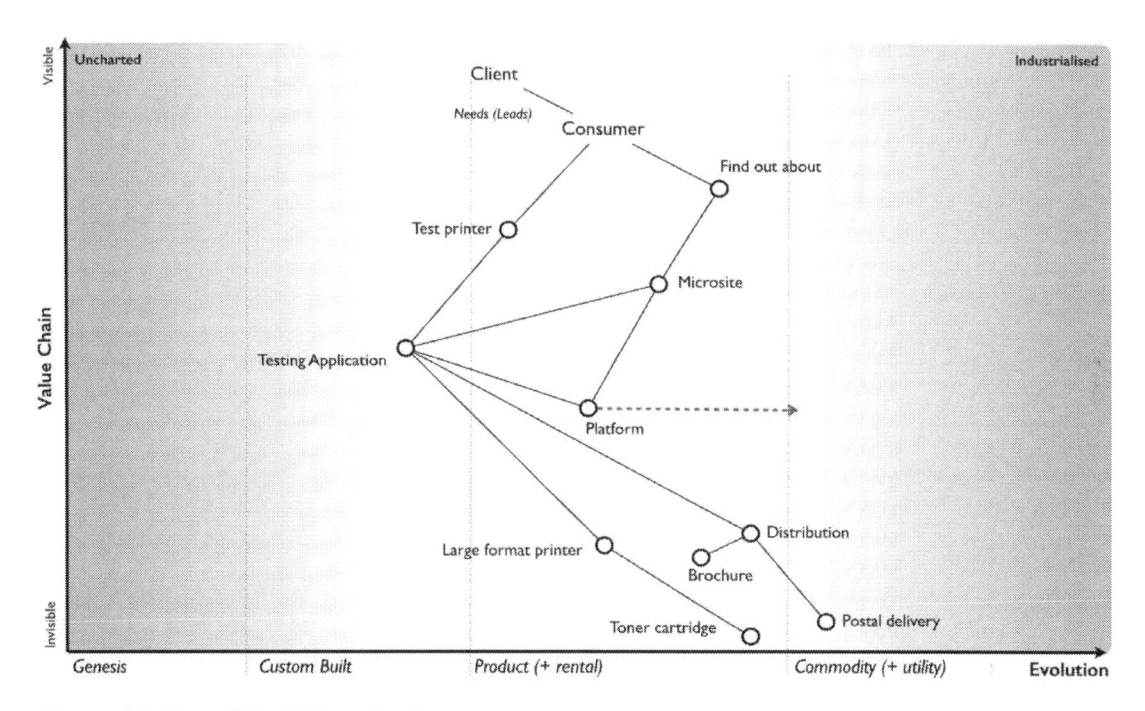

Figure 84: Map of the LFP project

The map begins with our client, who has a need for more leads and ultimately, consumers buying their product. The conversion from lead to actually purchasing a printer is beyond the scope of this project as that was within the client's sales organisation. We're focused solely on generating leads. The other type of user in this map is the consumer, who hopefully will buy one of these expensive printers. They have different needs; they want to find out about the right sort of printer for their commercial operations and to test it before buying something they will use. In this project, we're aiming to provide an online mechanism for the consumer to find out about the printer (a microsite), along with a method to test it (the testing application).

The test is a high resolution image that the user uploads and which is then printed out using the printer of their choice. Their poster (this is large format) would then be distributed to the user, along with a standard graphical poster (showing the full capabilities), relevant marketing brochures and a sales call arranged. The platform space — which was the source of my original headaches due to my inability to provide a variable operational cost for application use — is evolving towards more of a utility service.

So, let us assume that we decide to use a utility platform. I'm now going to add some financial indicators onto this map. See Figure 85.

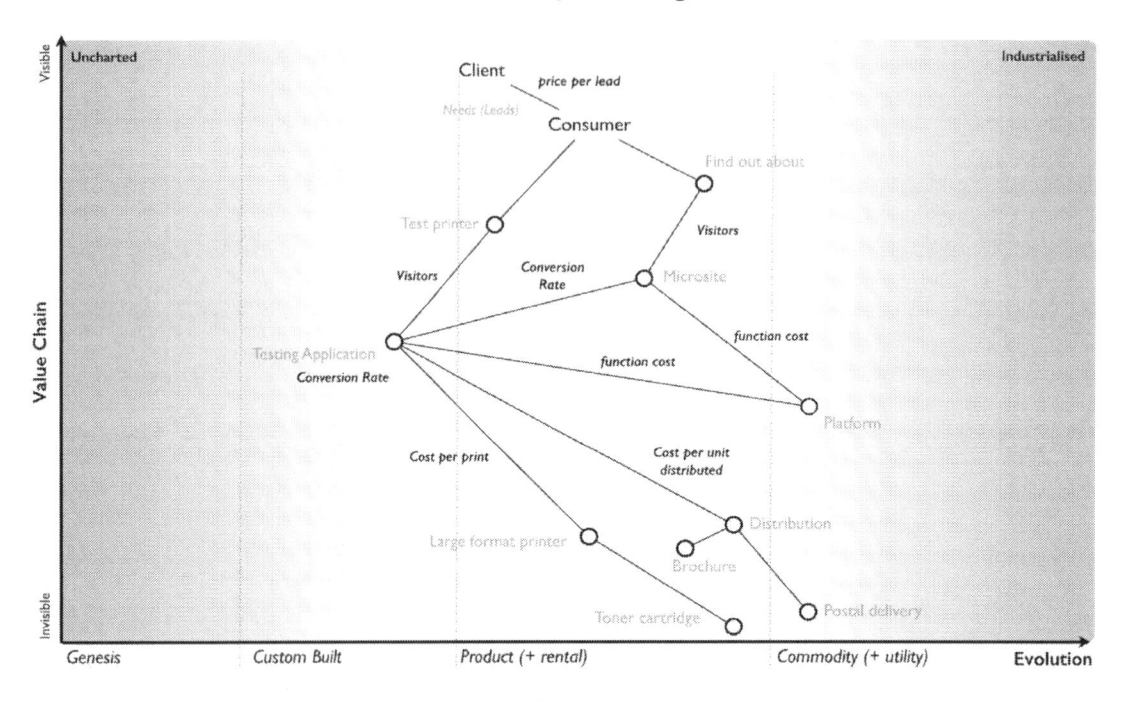

Figure 85: Financial indicators in the LFP project

From the map, we hope to have users visit our microsite, which would extol the benefits of owning a large format printer. This hopefully persuades some of these visitors to go and test it out. The act of turning a visitor into an actual lead requires the user to test a printer. So we have multiple conversion rates, e.g. from microsite to testing application and from visitor to lead. At the start, these will be unknown, but we can guess.

Normally, operating a microsite requires all those hard to calculate costs, but in a utility platform world, your application is simply a function running on the platform and I'm charged for use. The operational cost of my microsite is basically the number of visitors x the average cost of the microsite function. Remember, an application consists of many functions and users can navigate around it, which means some "wandering" users turn out to be more expensive than others. But we can cope with that by taking an average for our microsite.

The same will apply to my "test the printer" (testing) application, but in this case, the users will include converted visitors from the microsite, along with those who directly visit. Every use of the testing application (a function) will incur a cost. But as with the microsite, this is a variable. Of course, the actual functional cost of the testing application could be wildly different from the microsite, depending upon what the applications did and how well the code was written, but at least we would have a granular price for every call. Finally, every visitor who tests a printer will create a distribution and printing cost for me but also revenue, as they have become a lead.

This isn't the only path by which someone can print out a poster. The visitor might not come from the microsite but instead go directly to the testing application through word of mouth, or if we expose the testing application as an API. There are a number of potential flows through the map.

When you look at any map, there can be many forms of flow within it, whether financial or otherwise. It could be flows of revenue or flows of risk. For example, if the utility platform dies due to some catastrophic event then it'll impact my microsite and my testing application, which will impact the consumer needs and stop any lead generation. This would incur a financial penalty for me in terms of lost revenue. Whereas, if I run out of brochures then this impacts distribution and I have a choice on whether to send out the prints now or delay until the brochures are available. In Figure 86, I've given an example of a flow within a map from a potential consumer through their need to microsite to testing application to distribution.

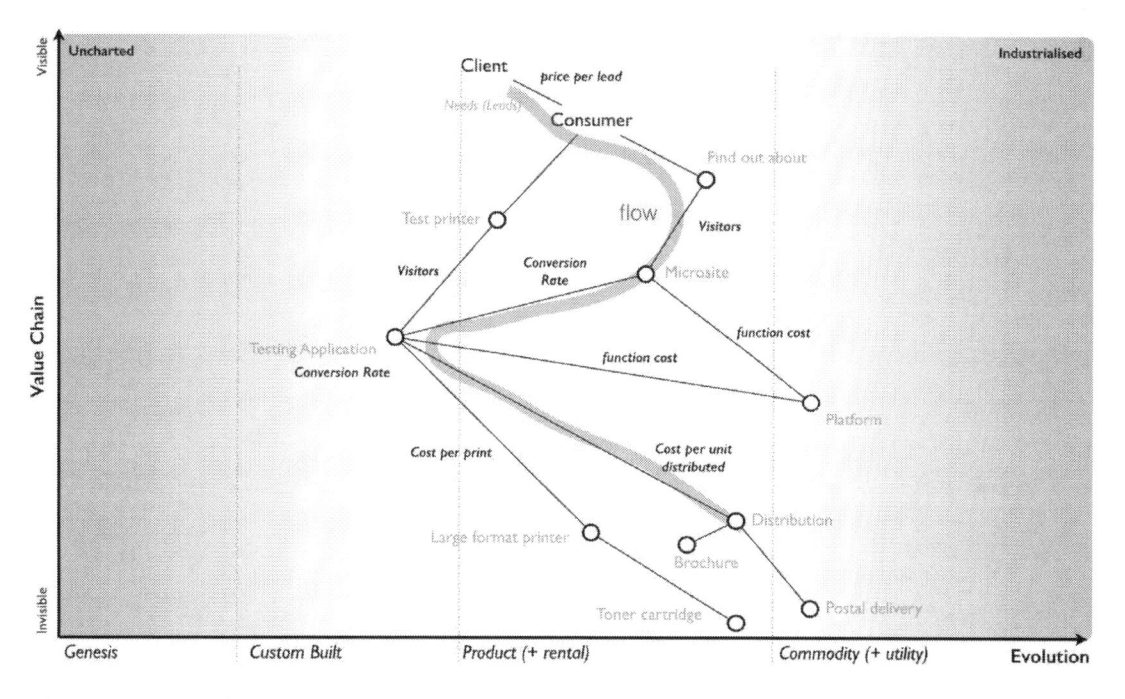

Figure 86: Flow of the LFP project

It's important to note that the interfaces between components in a map represent these flows of capital, whether physical, financial, information, knowledge, risk, time or social. It could be anything that we trade. Things are rarely free. Whenever you use a service then you're trading something, whether it's information or social capital (e.g. loyalty to a scheme) or even just your time (e.g. to create new entries, to edit the content).

By using the concept of flow, it is relatively simple to build a financial model for the system. In Figure 87, I've created the skeleton of such a model for the map above.

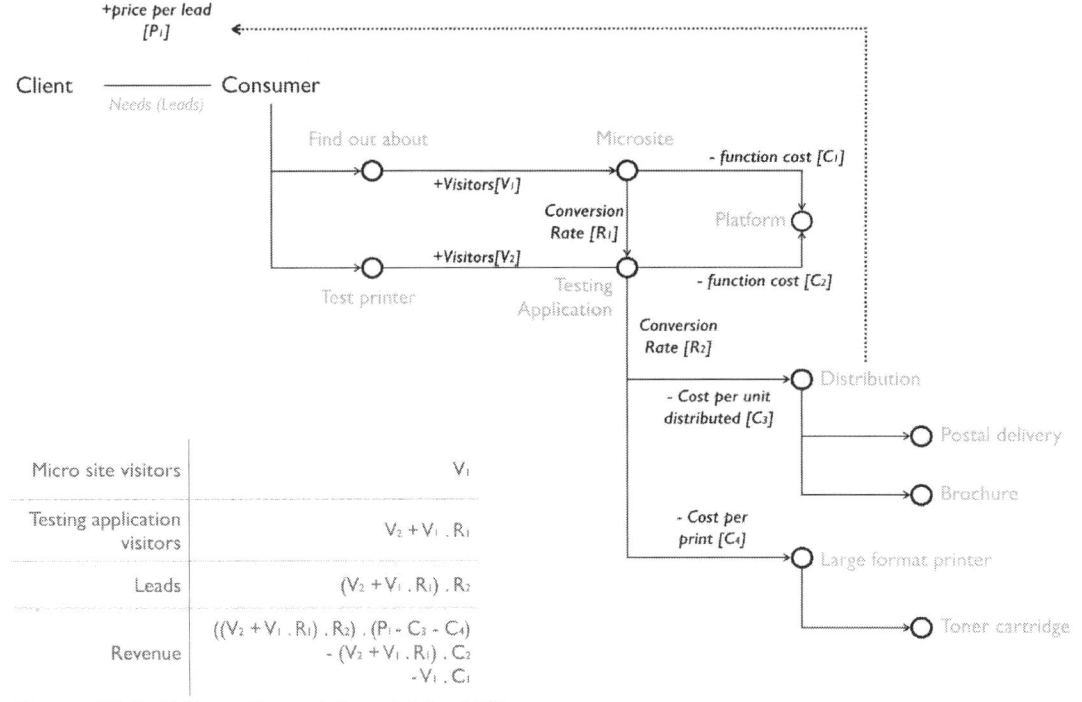

Micro site visitors	V_1
Testing application visitors	$V_2 + V_1 \cdot R_1$
Leads	$(V_2 + V_1 \cdot R_1) \cdot R_2$
Revenue	$((V_2 + V_1 \cdot R_1) \cdot R_2) \cdot (P_1 - C_3 - C_4)$ $- (V_2 + V_1 \cdot R_1) \cdot C_2$ $- V_1 \cdot C_1$

Figure 87: Building a financial model for LFP

This is like manna from heaven for someone trying to build a business. Certainly, I have the investment in developing the code, but with the application being a variable operational cost then I can make a money-printing machine that grows with users. It also changes my focus on investment — do I want to invest in increasing marketing for more users, or the conversion rate, or maybe the testing application is so badly written (or a function within it) that investing in coding improvement will bring me better returns? Suddenly, the whole way I build a business and invest is changed.

Now back to when we originally built LFP in 2003. There wasn't a utility platform, I didn't have maps and I didn't have the concept of flow. Instead, myself and my CFO had a mass of spreadsheets, trying to calculate what the above did and cope with all the stepwise investments and capital costs needed. What was a nightmare in 2003 is child's play in 2016.

Whenever you're building something novel then the game is to use operational expense over capital as much as possible in order to reduce risk, either due to the system not being used or growing rapidly. You want to tie the cost as close to the path of revenue generation, especially within any worth based system when you're gambling on an uncertain outcome. However, there will always be some investment, e.g. writing the application, marketing the microsite. This sort of modelling can help you identify which options improve the equation and hence, where you should invest for the future.

Efficiency vs effectiveness

Having introduced the concepts of worth based development, pricing granularity and flow, let us now get back to our main story.

So there I was in 2008 with an understanding of the importance of maps and of the flow of capital within them. This helped me explain a question of efficiency versus effectiveness in one of my client's projects. I was quite proud of this. There is unfortunately a problem.

Hopefully, you're discovering that maps can be a quite useful strategic tool. The information they contain can be very sensitive. I'm certainly not going to break the trust of a client by exposing their dirty laundry. This is why many of the maps that I use in this book are slightly distorted and don't identify the original owner, unless I was the one running the show. I don't mind you knowing all the mistakes and failings that I've made, but not everyone is like that. If you're uncomfortable with this and you need the reassurance of being told that "big company X did Y" then you'll need to find someone else to help you.

To overcome this issue of confidentiality, the next section covers a hypothetical that blends a story related to a modern company to help tell a past story, which I've set into a technology context. Yes, maps are part of storytelling, but as J. R. R Tolkien said on writing The Lord of the Rings, "I wisely started with a map."

Our story begins, as many do, with a challenge and unfortunately, no maps. The company was expanding and needed to increase its compute resources. It had created a process flow diagram for this (Figure 88), which involved a request for more compute to the actions needed to meet that demand.

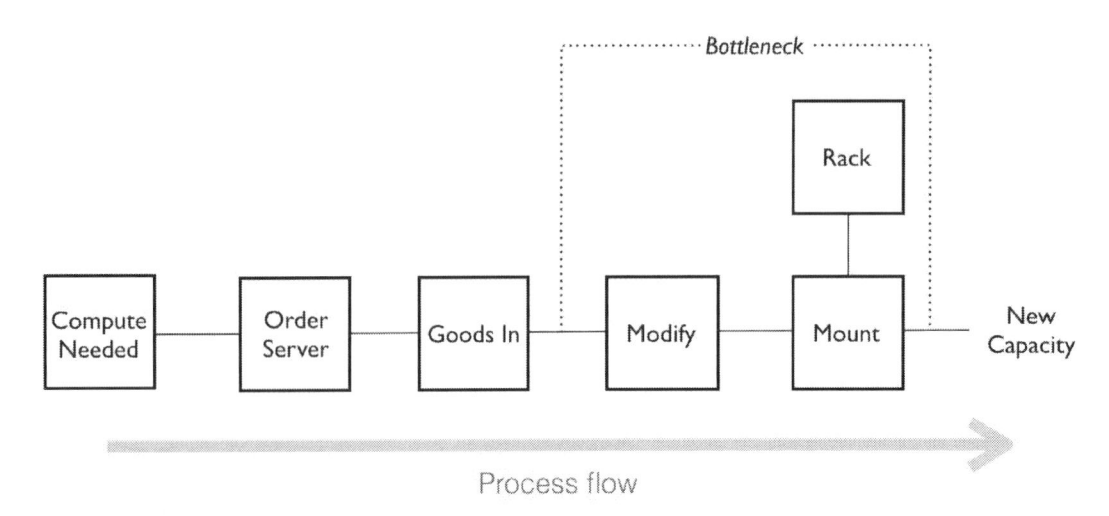

Figure 88: The process flow

The process however had a bottleneck. Once servers were delivered at "goods in" they needed to be modified before being racked. This was time-consuming and sometimes prone to failure. They were focused on improving the efficiency of the process flow as it was important for their future revenue generation. A proposal was on the table to invest in robotics to automate the process of modifying the servers. Whilst the proposal was expensive, the benefits were considerable, especially given the significant future revenue that was at risk. A strongly positive ROI had been calculated.

I want you to consider the above for a moment and decide whether a proposal to invest in improving the efficiency of an inefficient process makes sense, particularly when the benefits of the proposal vastly outweigh the costs and your future revenue stream is at risk.

I had met the company, talked about the concept of evolution, and it would be fair to say they had no interest in mapping. I had mentioned the "spot" diagram and we agreed to take a look at the proposal through this lens. I've taken those first same steps (see Figure 89) and "spotted" the process. Whilst the ordering and goods-in process were quite industrialised, the modify part of the process was very custom.

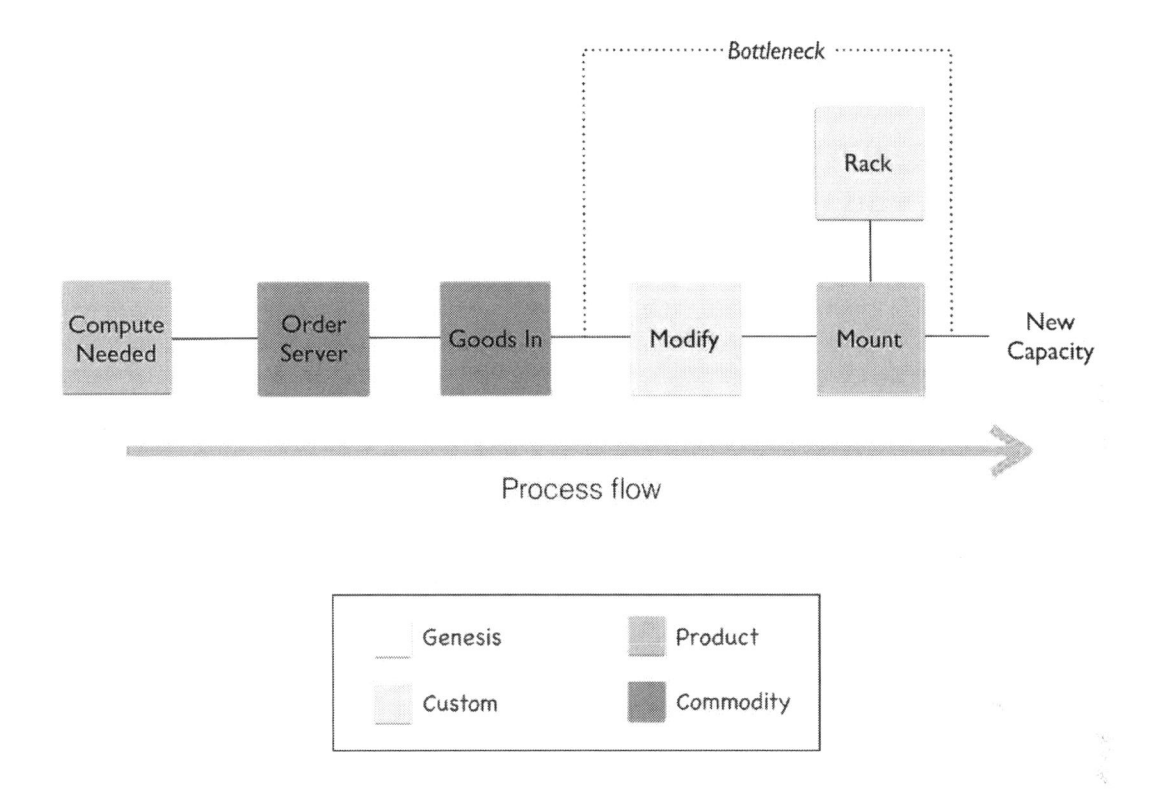

Figure 89: Spot diagram of the process

It's important to take a break for a minute here and have a good look at the diagram above. Try and see if you notice anything interesting or odd before continuing with this story.

I'm now going to turn the diagram above into a map and hopefully, the problem will become clearer. Let us start from the user need of more compute. This actually has two needs; the ordering of a server and the racking of the server once it has been delivered. Apparently, mounting the equipment (i.e. racking, adding power and cabling) needs modifications to be made to the server, hence the company's interest in automation with robotics. Both of these chains are connected at the point of the "server" and "goods in". I've drawn this in Figure 90 with both flows.

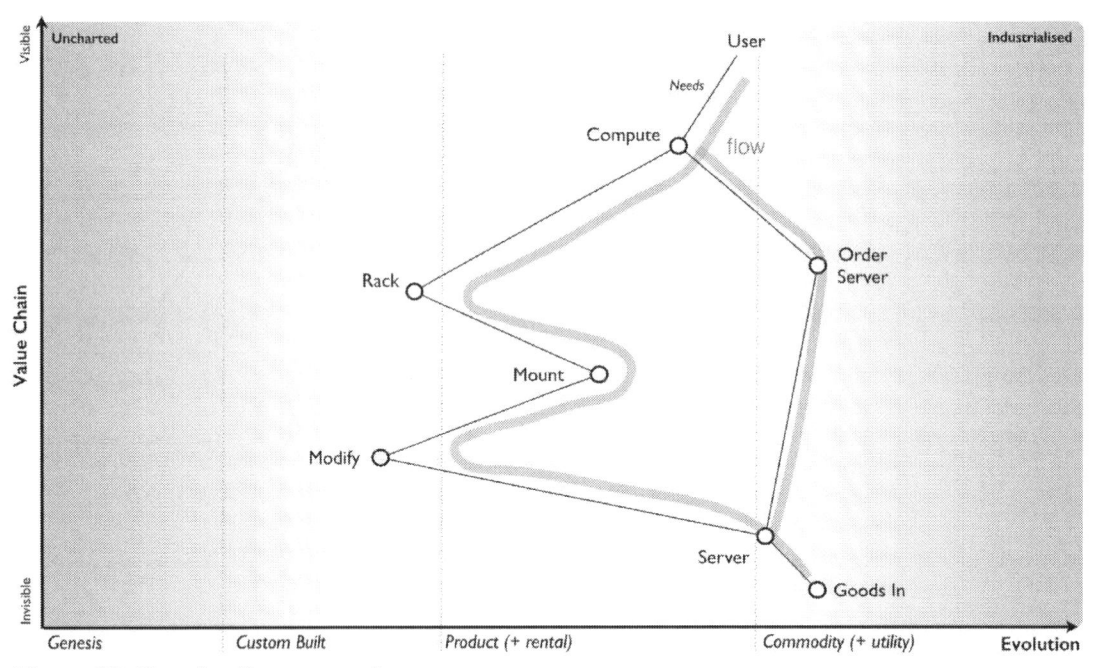

Figure 90: Mapping the proposal

Take another break for a minute here and have a good look at the diagram above. Try and see if you notice anything interesting or odd this time before continuing with this story.

What is worth noting is that the racks were considered custom. On investigation, the company had always used custom-built racks and it even had a friendly company that made them for it. This was just part of its corporate corpus; a ghost from a long gone past that still haunted the place. If you asked the company why they were using custom-built racks, they'd tell you that this is what they've always done, it was how they worked, and the racks were designed for them. They'd also tell you that racks were irrelevant to the project at hand, which was all about automation.

However, dig a little bit more and we come to reason why the servers needed modification. It turns out that standard servers are designed to fit standard racks. They didn't fit the custom-built racks that the company had so lovingly built. Hence, additional plates needed to be added, holes drilled into the servers — this was the modification that was required. Let us be clear. On the table was a proposal to invest in robotics in order to customise standard servers in order that they fit into custom-built racks that the company was buying. Does the proposal still make sense? Is it a good investment? Are there alternatives? Do I hear you shout "use standard racks"?

Now, the question is whether we should just use standard racks. This obviously moves racks towards the commodity (which is where they should be) and the modification part disappears, though we still have mounting, cabling and power. It seems a lot better though (see Figure 91).

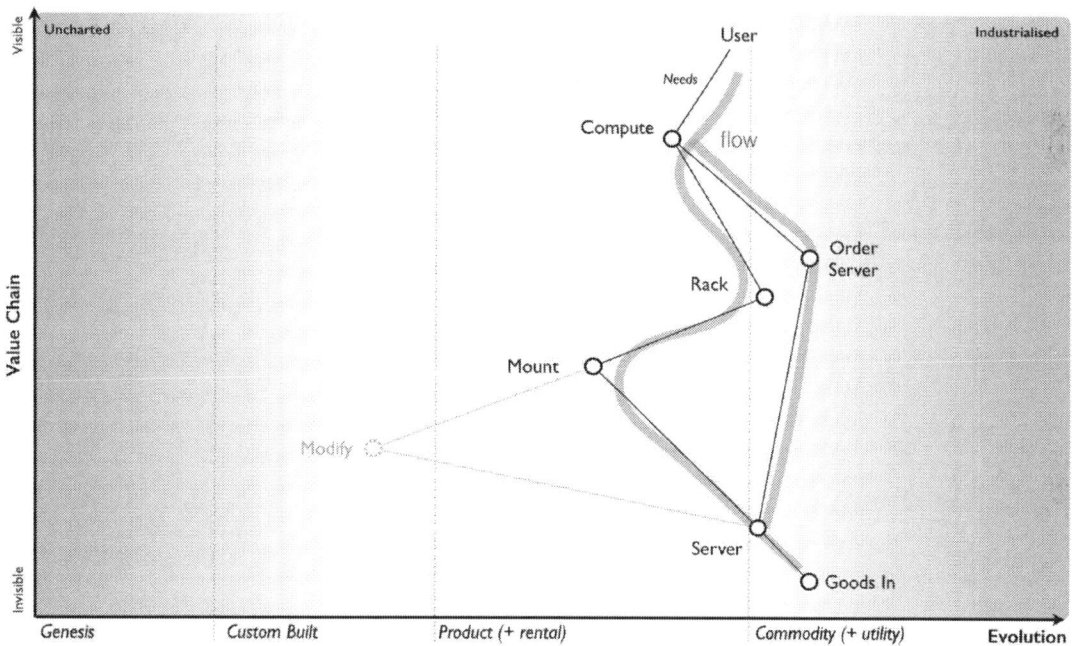

Figure 91: Using standard racks

However, you still have a problem, which is the legacy estate. Are you going to migrate all the racks? What about our sunk costs? How are we going to maintain our existing systems? There will be a long list of reasons to counter the proposed change. Before you go "this is daft, we should just change", remember the budget example, the corporate corpus, and don't expect to change a system without some resistance.

In this case, despite resistance, we should go a step further. Computing was becoming a commodity provided by utility services. We can simplify this whole flow by just adopting utility services for any new work. We don't need to think about robotic investment or even converting to using standard racks (itself a cost that might be prohibitive). This entire chunk of the value chain should disappear over time, along with any additional costs it might be hiding (see Figure 92).

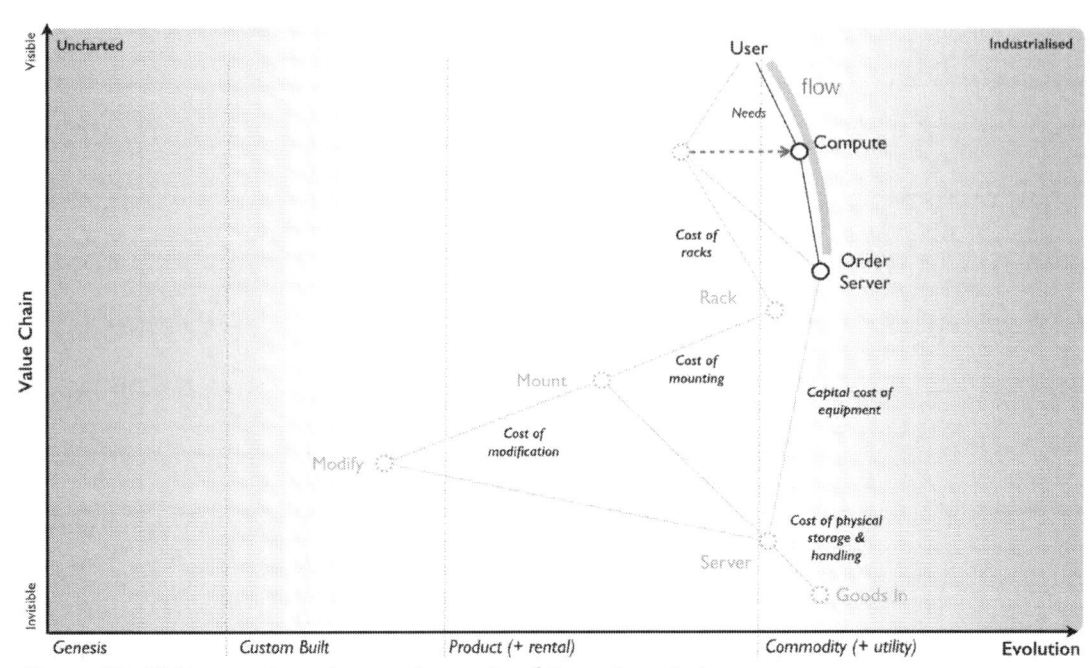

Figure 92: Hidden costs and removing parts of the value chain

In this story, we started with a proposal of investment into robotics, based upon improving the efficiency of an existing process. It sounded reasonable on the surface, but if they had taken that route then they would have invested more in maintaining a highly ineffective process. In all likelihood, it would have exacerbated the problem later because the corporate corpus would have expanded to include this robotic investment. If some future person had said "we should get rid of these custom racks" then the response would be "but we've always done this and we've invested millions in robotics".

I used the "spotted" process flow to get us part of the way, i.e. identifying the custom-built rack as the problem. However, to really understand this space then we needed a map and the flows within it. The "efficient" thing to do might be investing in robotics, but the "effective" thing to do was to get rid of this entire part of the value chain. It's a bit like the utility platform question. I can either invest in making my infrastructure and platform components more efficient by automation or I could just plan to get rid of that entire part of the value chain by using a utility platform. Often, the "efficient" thing to do is not the "effective" thing.

However, a word to the wise. This was 2008 and the idea of getting rid of custom-built racks and adopting a move towards using infrastructure from a utility provider was not welcomed. It's easy in 2016 to say "this is obvious", but that's because most people now have the benefit of hindsight. In 2008, such ideas were seen as radical and even dangerous. The changes necessary were far from welcomed within the organisation, and it was fought every step of the way, from executives to the ground floor. Without the courage and conviction of the CEO and a few "rebels", the company would have happily spent millions on robotics and would be still building custom racks today.

From experience, you should be careful with both your use of simplification when viewing a landscape and the inertia that exists. You should be very careful of process improvements focused solely on efficiency. You should be extremely careful when dealing with the corporate corpus.

The company in question was a manufacturing company, the real scenario had nothing to do with computing and yes, they were about to spend many millions making a highly ineffective process more efficient. They didn't, they are alive and doing well. I also kept the wolves at bay. That's what I call a "win-win", except obviously for the vendors who lost out.

Before we move on

In the last few chapters, we've been sneaking around the strategy cycle, covering mainly purpose and then landscape. You should be familiar enough with the strategy cycle that I don't need to repeat it. We will keep on looping around this, sometimes diving into interconnections as we go. Anyway, this will be the last time that I'll mention that. We should recap on some of the ideas from this chapter.

Landscape

- **Be careful of simplicity**. There's a balancing act here caused by Ashby's law. Be aware that you're often trading your ability to learn for easier management. In some cases, you can simplify so far that it becomes harmful, e.g. one size fits all and group-wide KPIs. Often, people talk about the KISS principle (Keep it simple, stupid). Just remember that by keeping it too simple, you can make some pretty daft choices.
- The map contains **flows of capital**, which are represented by the interfaces. There are usually multiple flows in a single map. Such capital can be physical, financial, information, knowledge, risk, time or social. It could be anything that we trade and is traded between the components.
- **Maps are a means of storytelling**. Despite my dour attitude to storytelling (especially the hand-waving kind of verbiage often found in strategy), maps are a form of visual storytelling.

Doctrine

- **Focus on the outcome, not the contract.** Worth (outcome) based tools can be useful here, but be warned, they can also expose flaws in the understanding of value and become stymied by the corporate corpus, e.g. a budgeting process and its inability to cope with variable charging.
- **Use appropriate tools.** When using maps, if I'm looking at financial flows, then I'll often dive into financial modelling when considering multiple investment paths, e.g. focus on increasing visitors through marketing or the conversion rate from a microsite. Equally, if I've identified multiple "wheres" that I can attack, then I'll often dive into business model canvas to compare them. Don't be afraid to use multiple tools. Maps are simply a guide and learning tool.
- **Optimise flow.** Often when you examine flows then you'll find bottlenecks, inefficiencies and profitless flows. There will be things that you're doing that you just don't need to.
- Be very careful to consider **not only efficiency but effectiveness**. Try to avoid investing in making an ineffective process more efficient when you need to be questioning why you're doing something and uncovering hidden costs. Also, don't assume that an "obvious" change will be welcomed. Beware the corporate corpus.
- When it comes to managing flow then granularity is your friend. Be prepared though; most companies don't have anywhere near the level of granularity that you'll need and you may even encounter politics when trying to find out. Think small, as in know the details.
- Any map can contain multiple **different users** and often, the needs of those users can be in conflict, though you should try to bring them all together.

We've covered quite a bit of doctrine so far. I've highlighted this (in grey) in Figure 93. Though we've skated over several other areas of doctrine, I do want to come back to them later in the book with a more formal examination.

Category				
Communication	Be transparent	Focus on high situational awareness *(understand what is being considered)*		Challenge assumptions *(speak up and question)*
Development	Know your users *(e.g. customers, shareholders, regulators, staff)*	Focus on user needs	Think fast, inexpensive, simple and tiny	Remove bias and duplication
Development	Use appropriate methods *(e.g. agile vs lean vs six sigma)*	Focus on the outcome not a contract *(e.g. worth based development)*	Be pragmatic *(it doesn't matter if the cat is black or white as long as it catches mice)*	Use standards where appropriate
Development	Use appropriate tools *(e.g. mapping, financial models)*			
Operation	Manage inertia *(e.g. existing practice, political capital, previous investment)*	Optimise flow *(remove bottlenecks)*	Think small *(as in know the details)*	Effectiveness over efficiency
Operation	Do better with less *(continual improvement)*	Set exceptional standards *(great is just not good enough)*		
Structure	Provide purpose, mastery & autonomy	Think small *(as in teams)*	Distribute power and decision making	Think aptitude and attitude
Structure	Design for constant evolution	There is no one culture *(e.g. pioneers, settlers and town planners)*	Seek the best	
Learning	Use a systematic mechanism of learning	Learn by playing the game *(a bias towards action)*	Be curious and take appropriate risks *(a bias towards the new)*	Listen to your ecosystems *(acts as future sensing engines)*
Leading	Be the owner *(take responsibility)*	Move fast *(an imperfect plan executed today is better than a perfect plan executed tomorrow)*	Think big *(inspire others, provide direction)*	Strategy is iterative not linear *(fast reactive cycles)*
Leading	Strategy is complex *(there will be uncertainty)*	Commit to the direction, be adaptive along the path *(crossing the river by feeling the stones)*	There is no core *(everything is transient)*	Be humble *(listen, be selfless, have fortitude)*

Figure 93: Doctrine

We've also mentioned an aspect of gameplay — trading. Maps are a form of knowledge capital and they tend to have value. Don't expect people to just share them with you. You'll need to trade or create your own.

In the next section, we will focus on climate, including common economic patterns and anticipation.

An exercise for the reader

I'd like you to take some time and look at Figure 93 — doctrine. Go through each of the sections marked in grey, re-read any chapters in this book that you need to, and make sure you're familiar with them. Then ask yourself, does your company have these forms of doctrine? How do you implement them? If not, why not? What is stopping you?

Chapter 9 - Charting the future

Most people don't have a desire to learn mapping for the sake of it. Instead, what people are looking for is a way to create advantage, either through learning of context-specific play (i.e. outsmarting others), the application of doctrine (i.e. being more effectively organised than others), or anticipation of change (i.e. seeing change before others). Back in early 2008, I had become quite a dab hand at using maps and common economic changes (i.e. climatic patterns) to anticipate change in business. I was regularly invited to speak at huge events and published articles in which I would declare that over the next decade, we would see:-

- Rapid increases in the rate of innovation on the web
- New entrants dominating IT
- High rates of disruption in the IT markets
- Radical changes in IT practices
- Higher levels of efficiency within IT
- Widespread adoption of cloud services
- Increasing organisational strain, especially focused on IT, creating a necessity for organisational change

I was often greeted with a few gasps of wonder and a cacophony of derision and dismissal. I think I've been tagged with every label, from "idiot" to "rubbish" to "gibberish" to "unrealistic". The most vociferous insults came from the world of established vendors, enterprises, analysts and strategy consultants who had oodles of inertia to such changes. Fortunately, the gasps of wonder were enough to pick up some advisory work and keep booking a few gigs.

I need to be clear. I don't have mystical powers of anticipation, a time machine, some great intellect or a crystal ball. In fact, I'm a lousy prognosticator and a very normal sort of person. My "predictions" were all sleight of hand. What I'm good at is taking pre-existing patterns that are in the wild and repeating them back to everyone. It's more of the "I predict that the ball you've thrown in the air will fall to the ground" or the "I predict the General currently ordering troops to 'walk off the cliff' will lose the battle" kind. A basic understanding of the landscape and climatic patterns can be used to remarkable effect with an audience of executives that lacks this. To begin our journey into anticipation, we're going to have to start with areas of predictability.

Not all parts of the map are equally predictable

When we talk about the uncharted space, we're discussing things that we really don't understand. I'm often tempted to write "Ere be Dragons". This area is inherently uncertain and risky, but at the same time, it contains sources of future value and difference. As any component evolves over an unspecified amount of time (evolution can't be measured over time directly), it becomes more defined, more certain and less risky. We increasingly know what we need. It also becomes less of a differential. The future value of something is inversely related to the certainty we have over it. When it comes to the predictability of something then there are three aspects we need to consider — the "what", the "when" and the "who".

The predictability of what is not uniform. It varies from genesis, where the "what" is undefined, to commodity, where the "what" is defined. In the early days of electricity provision with the Parthian battery, then we were discovering what it could do. Could electricity give us eternal life? Could it provide light? Would it create monsters? We had no idea where it would take us. Today, it's taken for granted and considered a well-defined known. The questions are more about the provision of defined frequencies (50Hz), defined voltages (240V), defined interfaces (3 pin plug) and the cost per kWh.

In Figure 94, I've taken a single activity A from its early appearance (A[1]) to some future version (A[1+n]) that has evolved through n iterations, each including their own chasms and diffusion curves. It's the same activity throughout but with more evolved characteristics. You could pick electricity or computing or penicillin or money — they all followed this path

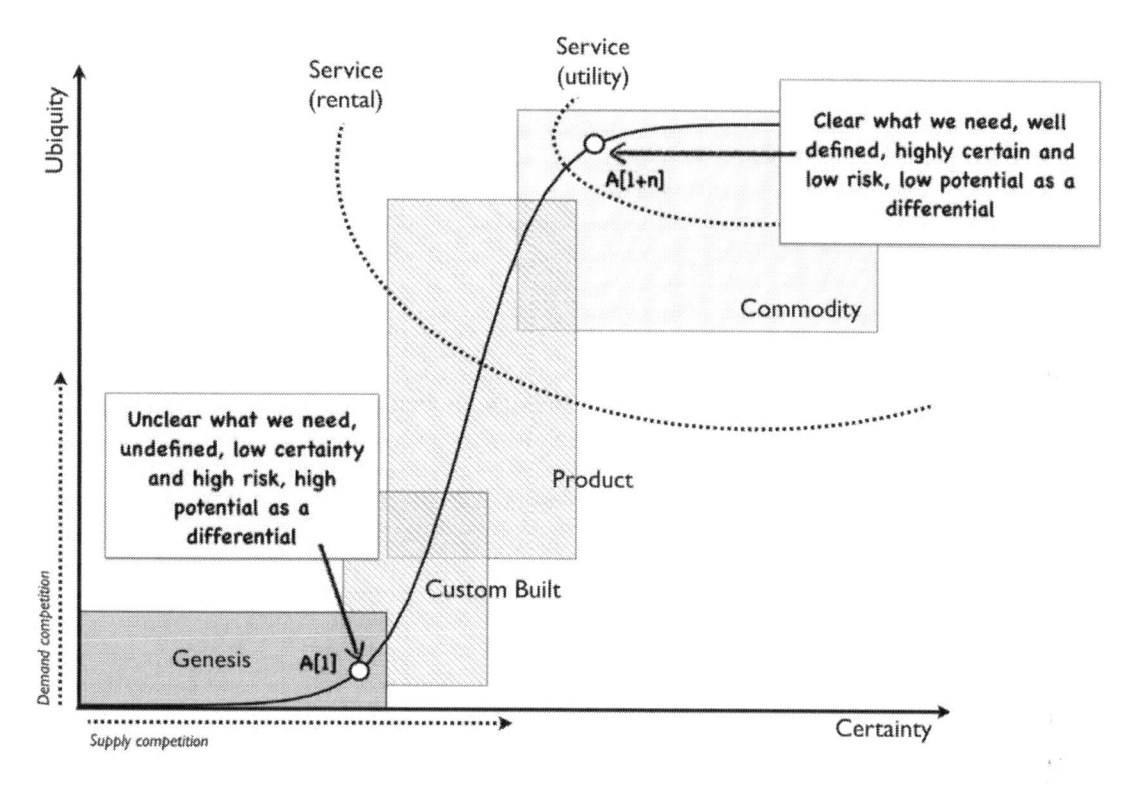

Figure 94: Predictability of what

Since evolution is one of the axes on our map, we know the predictability of what is not constant across our map. How about "who" and "when"? Individual actors' actions are notoriously difficult to predict. There are however ways to cheat the system, but this uses weak signals.

Cheating the system

I was asked by a client whether the growing field of social media could be used to identify which companies were interested in acquiring others. The idea was very simple. If there were lots of increasing connections between two companies on a service such as LinkedIn, does that mean the companies are talking to each other? The problem is that such connections could be a signal of people wanting to jump ship or some conference that company employees met up at. What we really wanted to know is whether the executives were talking to each other, and unfortunately, in those days, few executives were using social media and tools like LinkedIn. They certainly weren't linking up with competitor CEOs prior to an acquisition.

Fortunately, executives like private jets. The tailplane numbers of private jets and company ownership were easily accessible, and so were the flight plans. By monitoring the movement of private jets and looking for disturbances in the data, i.e. the repeated landing of the jet of one company in the same area at roughly the same time as the jet of another company, ideally in a location where neither had headquarters (i.e. "off-site" and away from prying eyes), then it would indicate that executives were meeting. This is an example of a weak signal and such tools can be surprisingly effective. Companies tend to spend an awful lot of time and money trying to secure corporate M&A information and then leak the same information like a sieve through some form of weak signal.

Weak signals can be used to anticipate an actor's action, e.g. before the common use of tumble dryers, Russian sailors hanging out clothes on a drying line would be a signal that the Russian fleet was about to set sail. Unfortunately, it's often time-consuming and demanding work to collect and analyse weak signals. You usually need to examine a single or small sample of actors rather than an entire market. In general, you have to accept that the predictability of who is going to take a specific action is low. However, though you cannot easily predict individual actors' actions, we do know that there are aggregated effects caused by all actors. Evolution itself is a consequence of demand and supply competition by all actors, and the Red Queen forcing us to adapt. We do know that if there is competition then components will evolve. We might not be able to say who will produce the more evolved form but we can say what will happen — it will evolve! This leads to the final aspect — when?

Unfortunately, evolution cannot be anticipated over time or adoption. Hence, at first glance, the predictability of when things will happen would seem to be low. Fortunately, there are conditions, signals and patterns that can help us cheat this a bit.

Conditions, signals and climatic patterns

Let us consider the evolution of an act, from a product to a commodity. In order to achieve this, a number of conditions need to be met. The **concept** of providing the act as a commodity must exist. The **technology** to achieve this must be available. The act must be **suitably** well defined and widespread. Finally, you need a willingness or **attitude** amongst consumers to adopt a new model. This latter part is normally represented by dissatisfaction with existing arrangements, e.g the constant consumer complaint that "this product is costly".

These four conditions — **concept, suitability, technology and attitude** — are essential for any change of state, whether custom-built to product or product to commodity. In 2008, the idea of utility compute had been around since the

1960s. The technology to achieve utility compute was clearly available; I had been running my own private version years earlier. Compute itself was suitable for such a change being widespread and well-defined. Finally, there was the right sort of attitude with clear concerns and dissatisfaction with the expense of existing systems. The four conditions clearly indicated a change was possible.

Along with the four conditions, there are also weak signals that can help. In Chapter 7, I talked about the use of publication types to help elucidate the evolution curve. Those publication types form the basis of a weak signal. By examining the change of wording in publications then you can estimate whether we're likely to be approaching a state change or not. For example, a rapid increase in publications focused on use (Point 1 in Figure 95 below) and a decline in publications on operation, maintenance and feature differentiation (Point 2) implies that we're approaching stability and a crossover into the more commodity world.

Stage	I	II	III	IV
Publication Type	Wonder	building, construction and awareness	operation, maintenance and feature differences	use

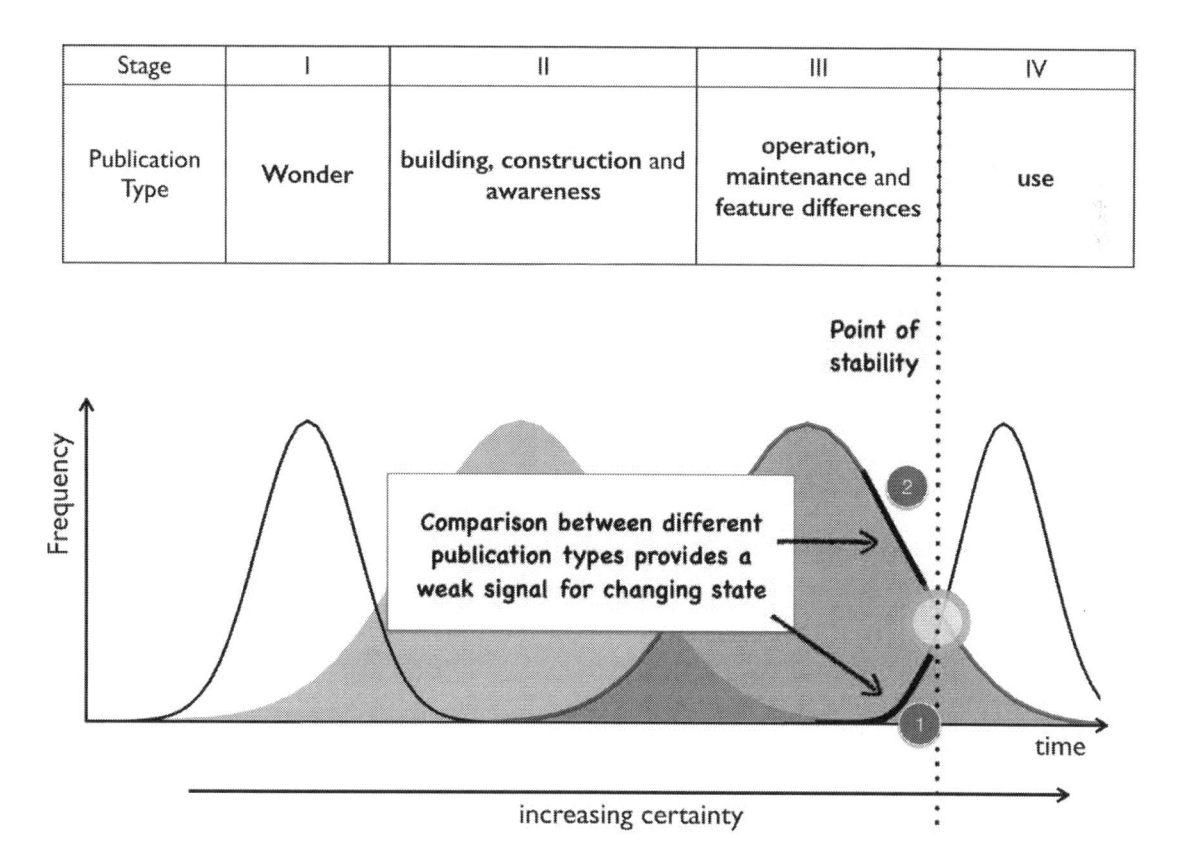

Figure 95: Weak signals and evolution

Lastly, there are certain climatic patterns that can help us to predict when things will change. For example, in Chapter 3, we discussed how efficiency enables innovation through componentisation effects. When a component evolves to more of a commodity (or a utility service), we can anticipate that this will cause a rapid rise in novel things built upon it, i.e. the genesis of new acts. We won't be able to say what those novel things are, but we can say (in conjunction with the weak signal above) when we're likely to see a rapid increase in this genesis. So, let us put these lessons on anticipation onto a map containing a single activity that is evolving. Starting with Figure 96 then:-

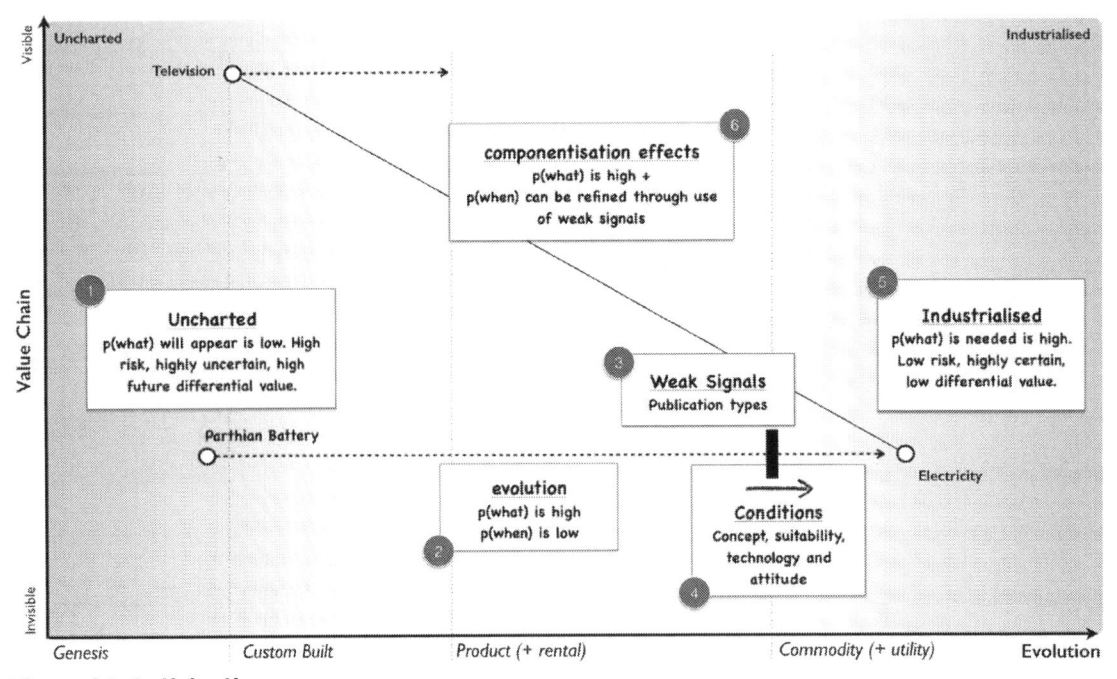

Figure 96: Anticipation on a map

Point 1 — Activities in the uncharted space are highly uncertain in terms of what is needed — "Ere be Dragons!" They have a low predictability of what — a low p(what). Despite the risk due to their uncertainty, they also have the highest future potential value. It's a space you have to gamble and experiment in, but it provides future opportunity.

Point 2 — Activities will evolve. The path of evolution can be described, hence predictability of what will happen is high. We know that custom-built systems combined with supply and demand competition will lead to products. However, the predictability of when this will happen is low, as it depends upon individual actors' actions. Furthermore, the predictability of specific change, e.g. this product will substitute that product is low because we're still learning. Hence, we know that smartphones will eventually evolve to a commodity but we don't know whose smartphone will win the race at any point during that evolution.

Point 3 — There are weak signals we can use, such as publication types. Whilst the signals won't give us a definitive answer (the two executives travelling to the same location in their corporate jets might just be friends going on holiday), it can give us an indication.

Point 4 — There are conditions that need to be met before something can evolve to the next stage — concept, suitability, technology and attitude.

Point 5 — Activities in the industrialised state are well-defined in terms of our interface to them, such as the plug and the socket for electricity. They give the appearance of being well-known, highly predictable, low risk and have little differential value. Continued evolution will be about more efficient provision.

Point 6 — The introduction of industrialised forms will encourage new activities to be built upon them — genesis begets evolution begets genesis. The predictability of what will happen — the appearance of new things — is high. However, just because we can anticipate the growth of new things, don't assume we can specify what those new things are. As noted in Point 1, the predictability of what those new things will be is low. Don't confuse the two. We can anticipate what will happen (growth of new things) but we can't anticipate what those new things will be (genesis). We can also refine our estimate of when this will happen through weak signals.

The point of the above is to show that not everything that occurs is quite as random as some would make out. There are things we can anticipate. I use the terms p(what) and p(when) when discussing our ability to predict something. A high p(what) means we can accurately anticipate what a change will be. A low p(what) means we can't but we still might get lucky. We're now going to build on this by introducing two more climatic patterns — coevolution and the cycle of peace, war and wonder.

Climatic Pattern: Coevolution

In 2016, the rage is all about "serverless" computing. I'm going to exploit this fortuitous circumstance to explain the concept of coevolution, but to begin with, we need to take a hike back through time to the '80s/'90s. Back in those days, computers were very much a product, and the applications we built used architectural practices that were based upon the characteristics of a product; in particular **mean time to recovery** (MTTR).

When a computer failed, we had to replace or fix it, and this would take time. The MTTR was high and architectural practices had emerged to cope with this. We built machines using N+1 (i.e. redundant components such as multiple power supplies). We ran disaster recovery tests to try and ensure our resilience worked. We cared a lot about capacity planning and scaling of single machines (scale up). We cared an awful lot about things that could introduce errors and we had change control procedures designed to prevent this. We usually built test environments to try things out before we were tempted to alter the all-important production environment.

But these practices didn't just magically appear overnight; they evolved through trial and error. They started as novel practices, then more dominant but divergent forms emerged until we finally started to get some form of consensus. The techniques converged and good practice was born. The same has happened with accounting, with manufacturing, with HR, and every other practice of business that you can think of. Ultimately, these architectural practices were refined and best architectural practice developed. In such confident days, you'd be mocked for not having done proper capacity planning, as this was an expected norm.

Our applications needed architectural practices that were based upon (needed) compute, which was provided as a product. The architectural norms that became "best practice" were N+1, scale up, disaster recovery, change control and testing environments, and these were ultimately derived from the high MTTR of a product. I've shown this evolution of practice in the map below.

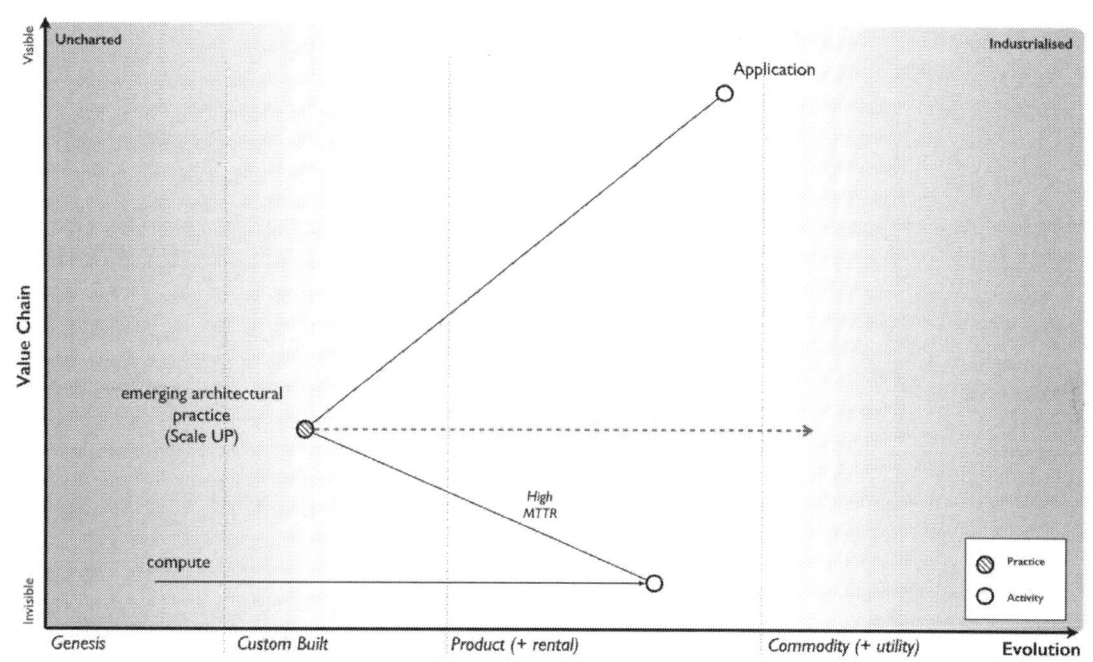

Figure 97: Evolution of Architectural Practice

Normally with maps, I just use the description of evolution for activities. This evolution is exactly the same with practice but with slightly different terms, e.g. novel, emerging, good and best rather than genesis, custom, product and commodity. For background on this, see Figure 10 (Chapter 2).

The thing is, compute evolved. As an activity then compute had started back in the 1940s in that uncharted space (the genesis of the act) where everything is uncertain. We then had custom-built examples (divergent forms) and then products (convergence around certain characteristics with some differentiation between them). However, compute by the early 2000s had started to transform and become more commodity-like, with differentiation becoming far more constrained, the activity itself becoming far more defined. In this world, a server was really about processor speed, memory, hard disk size, power consumption and how many you could cram in a rack. In this world, we built banks of compute and created virtual machines as we needed them. Then we got public utility forms with the arrival of AWS EC2 in 2006.

The more industrialised forms of any activity have different characteristics to early evolving versions. With computing infrastructure then utility forms had similar processing, memory and storage capabilities, but they had very low MTTR. When a virtual server went bang, we didn't bother to try and fix it, we didn't order another, we just called an API and within minutes or seconds, we had a new one.

Long gone were the days that we lovingly named our servers; these were cattle, not pets.

This change of characteristics enabled the emergence of a new set of architectural principles based upon a low MTTR. We no longer cared about N+1 and resilience of single machines, as we could recreate them quickly if failure was discovered. We instead designed for failure. We solved scaling by distributing the workload, calling up more machines as we needed them — we had moved from scale up to scale out. We even reserved that knowing chortle for those who did "capacity planning" in this world of abundance.

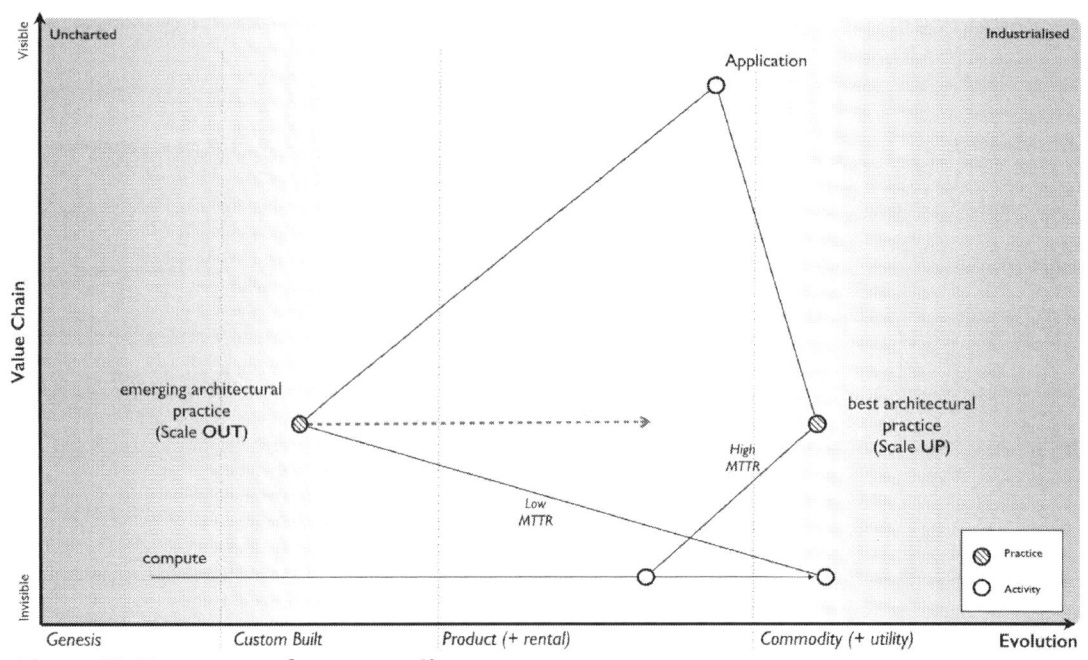

Figure 98: Emergence of a new practice

We started testing failure by the constant introduction of error — we created various forms of chaos monkeys or masters of disasters that introduced random failure into our environments. One-off disaster recovery tests were for the weak; we constantly adapted to failure. With a much more flexible environment, we learned to roll back changes more quickly. We became more confident in our approaches and started to use continuous deployment. We frowned at those that held on to the sacred production and less hallowed testing environments. We started to mock them.

These novel practices — scale out, design for failure, chaos engines and continuous deployment amongst others — were derived from an increasingly low MTTR environment, and such practices were simply accelerated by utility compute environments. Our applications were built with this in mind. The novel practices spread, becoming emergent (different forms of the same principles), and have slowly started to converge with a consensus around good practice. We even gave it a name – DevOps. It is still evolving and it will in turn become best architectural practice.

What happened is known as coevolution, i.e. a practice co-evolves with the activity itself. This is perfectly normal and happens throughout history. Though steel-making itself industrialised, we can still produce swords (if we wish) but we have lost the early practice of forging swords. One set of practices has been replaced with another. I've shown the current state of coevolution in compute in the map below. The former best architectural practice we now call "legacy," whilst the good (and still evolving) architectural practice is called "DevOps".

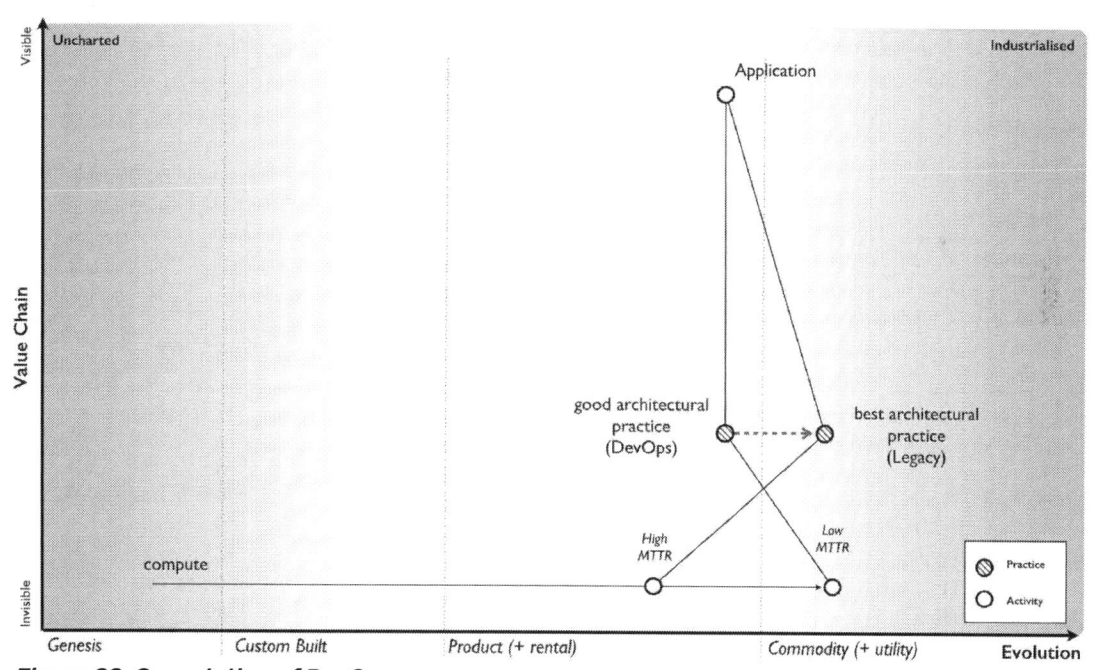

Figure 99: Coevolution of DevOps

This transformation of practice is also associated with inertia, i.e. we become used to the "old" and trusted best practice (which is based upon one set of characteristics) and the "new" practice (based upon a more evolved underlying activity) is less certain, requires learning and investment. Hence, we often have inertia to the underlying change due to governance. This was one of the principle causes of inertia to cloud computing.

Furthermore, any application we had that was based upon the "old" best practice lacks the benefits of this new more evolved world. These benefits of industrialisation always include efficiency, speed of agility and speed of development in building new things. Our existing applications became our legacy to our past way of doing things; part of the corporate corpus. They needed re-architecting, but that involves cost and so, we try to magic up ways of having the new world but just like the past. We want all the benefits of volume operations and commodity components but using customised hardware, designed just for us! It doesn't work; the Red Queen eventually forces us to adapt. We often fight it for too long though.

This sort of coevolution and the inevitable dominance of a more evolved practice is highly predictable. We can use it to anticipate new forms of organisations that emerge, as well as anticipate the changes in practice before they hit us. It's how in Canonical in 2008, we knew we had to focus on the emerging DevOps world and to make sure everyone (or as many as possible) that were building in that space were working on Ubuntu — but that's a later chapter. It's enough to know that we exploited this change for our own benefits. As one CIO recently told me, one day everyone was talking about Red Hat and the next, it was all Cloud plus Ubuntu. That didn't happen by accident.

Complicating the picture a bit more — the rise of Serverless

Of course, the map itself doesn't show you the whole picture because I've deliberately simplified it to explain coevolution. Between the application and the architectural practice we used for computing infrastructure layer is another layer — the platform. Now, platform itself is evolving. At some point in the past, there was the genesis of the first platforms. These then evolved to various divergent but still uncommon custom-built forms. Then we had convergence to more product forms. We had things like the LAMP stack (Linux, Apache, MySql and Perl or Python or PHP — pick your poison).

Along with architectural practice around computing infrastructure, there were also architectural practices around the platform. These were based upon the characteristics of the platform itself. From coding standards (i.e. nomenclature) to testing suites to performance testing to object orientated design within monolithic program structures. The key characteristic of the platform was how it provided a common environment to code in and abstracted away many of the underpinnings. But it did so at a cost — that same shared platform.

As I've mentioned before, a program is nothing more than a high level function that often calls many other functions. However, in general, we encoded these functions altogether as some monolithic structure. We might separate out a few layers in some form of n-layer design — a web layer, a back end, a storage system — but each of these layers tended to have relatively large programs. To cope with load, we often replicated the monoliths across several physical machines. Within these large programs, we would break them into smaller functions for manageability, but we would less frequently separate these functions onto a different platform stack because of the overhead of all those different platform stacks. You wouldn't want to have a machine sitting there with an entire platform stack to run one function that was rarely called. It was a waste! In the map below, I've added the platform and the best practice above the platform layer.

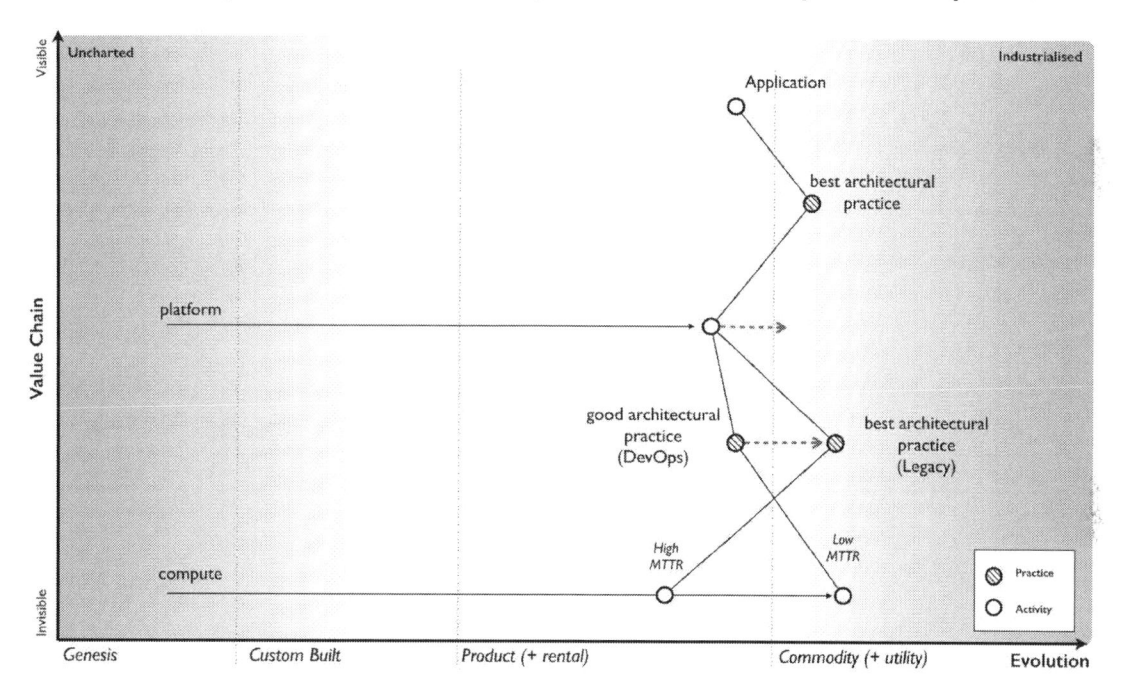

Figure 100: Evolution of Architectural Practice (platform)

In 2005, the company I ran was already using utility-like infrastructure. We had evolved early DevOps practices — distributed systems, continuous deployment, design for failure — and this was just the norm for us. However, we had also produced the utility coding platform known as Zimki, which happened to allow developers to write entire applications, front and back end in a single language — JavaScript. As a developer, you just wrote code, you were abstracted away from the platform itself, and you certainly had no concept of servers. That every function you wrote within your program could be running in a different platform stack was something you didn't need to know. From a developer point of view, you just wrote and ran your program and it called other functions. However, this environment enabled some remarkable new capabilities, from distribution of functions to billing by function. The change of platform from product to utility created new characteristics that enabled new architectural practices to emerge at this level. This is coevolution. This is normal. These new practices I've nicknamed FinDev for the time. The "old" best architectural practices; well, that's legacy. I've drawn a map to show this change.

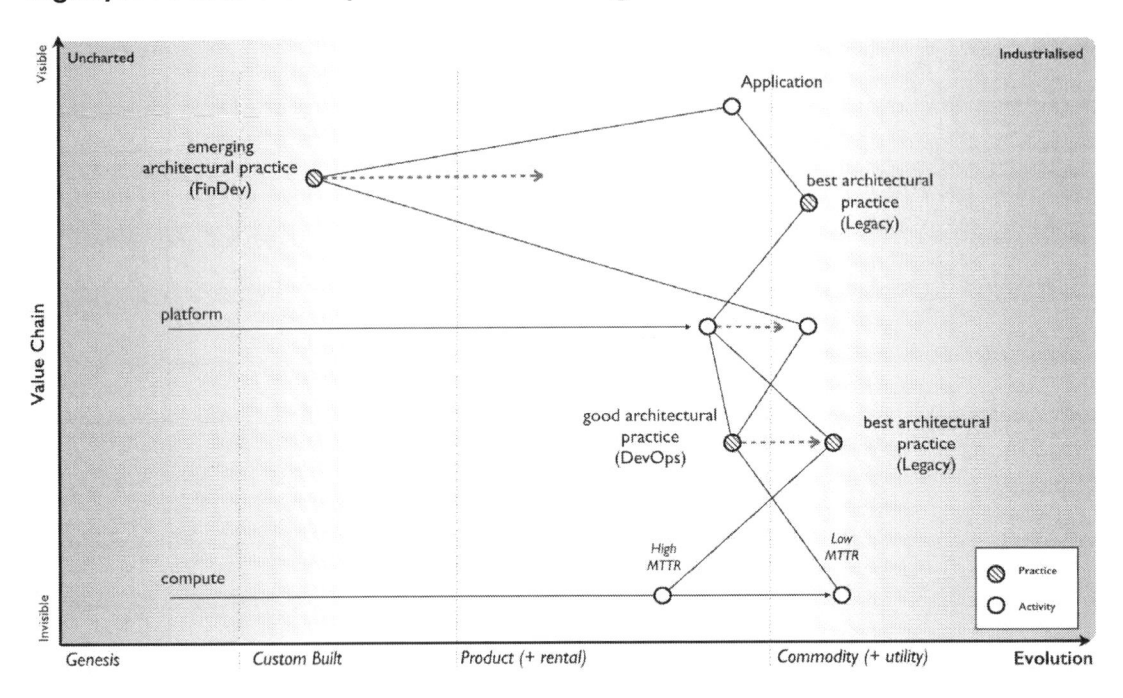

Figure 101: Coevolution of Architectural Practice (platform)

The more mundane of these architectural changes is it encourages componentisation; the breaking down of complex systems into reusable discrete components provided as services to others. In Zimki, every function could be exposed as a web service through a simple "publish" parameter added to the function. Today, we use the term micro services to describe this separation of functions and provision as web services. We're moving away from the monolith program containing all the functions to a world of separated and discrete functions. A utility platform just enables this and abstracts the whole underlying process from the developer.

The next mundane point is it encourages far greater levels of re-use. One of the problems with the old object orientated world was there was no effective communication mechanism to expose what had been built. You'd often find duplication of objects and functions within a single company, let alone between companies. Again, exposing as web services encourages this to change. That assumes someone has the sense to build a discovery mechanism such as a service register.

Another, again, rather trivial point is it abstracts the developer further away from the issues of underlying infrastructure. It's not really "serverless" but more "I don't care what a server is". As with any process of industrialisation (a shift from product to commodity and utility forms), the benefits are not only efficiency in the underlying components but acceleration in the speed at which I can develop new things. As with any other industrialisation, there will be endless rounds of inertia caused by past practice. Expect lots of gnashing of teeth over the benefits of customising your infrastructure to your platform and... just roll the clock back to infrastructure as a service in 2007 and you'll hear the same arguments in a slightly different context.

Anyway, back to Old Street (where the company was) and the days of 2005. Using Zimki, I built a small trading platform in a day or so because I was able to re-use so many functions created by others. I didn't have to worry about building a platform and the concept of a server, capacity planning, and all that "yak shaving" was far from my mind. The efficiency, speed of agility and speed of development are just a given. However, these changes are not really the exciting parts. The killer, the gotcha, is the billing by the function. This fundamentally changes how you do monitoring and enables concepts such as worth based development (see Chapter 8). Monitoring by cost of function changes the way we work — well, it changed me, and I'm pretty sure this will impact all of you.

"Serverless" will fundamentally change how we build business around technology and how you code. It will create an entire new set of practices, and your future in 2016 looks more like Figure 102 (simply take the Coevolution of Architectural Practice map from above and remove the legacy lines). Of course, this hasn't happened yet, but by the simple re-application of a common pattern of coevolution, I can make a fairly reasonable case for the future. I can use coevolution to anticipate a change.

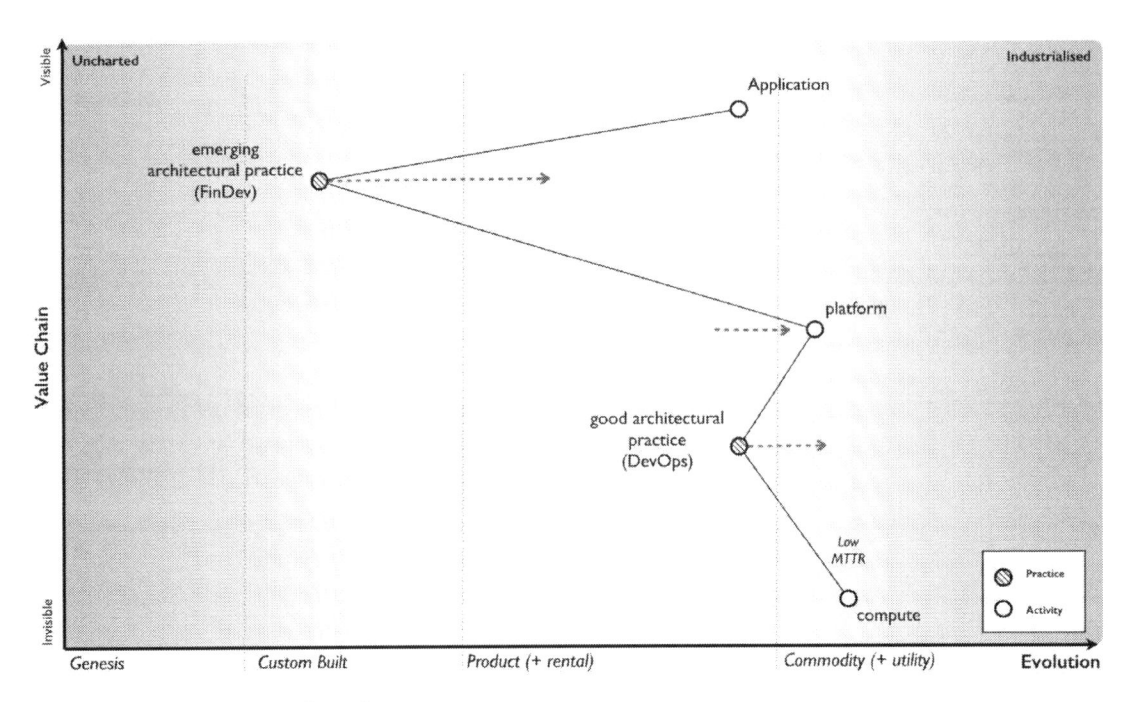

Figure 102: The future of platform

So given our knowledge of this climatic pattern, let us add coevolution onto our map of anticipation — see Figure 103 — adding in Point 7 for coevolution. I've generalised the map for any activity A, starting from an early version (A[1]) to some later more evolved act (A[1+n]) after n iterations, each with their own diffusion curve. This leads to both co-evolved practice B and new forms of activities C.

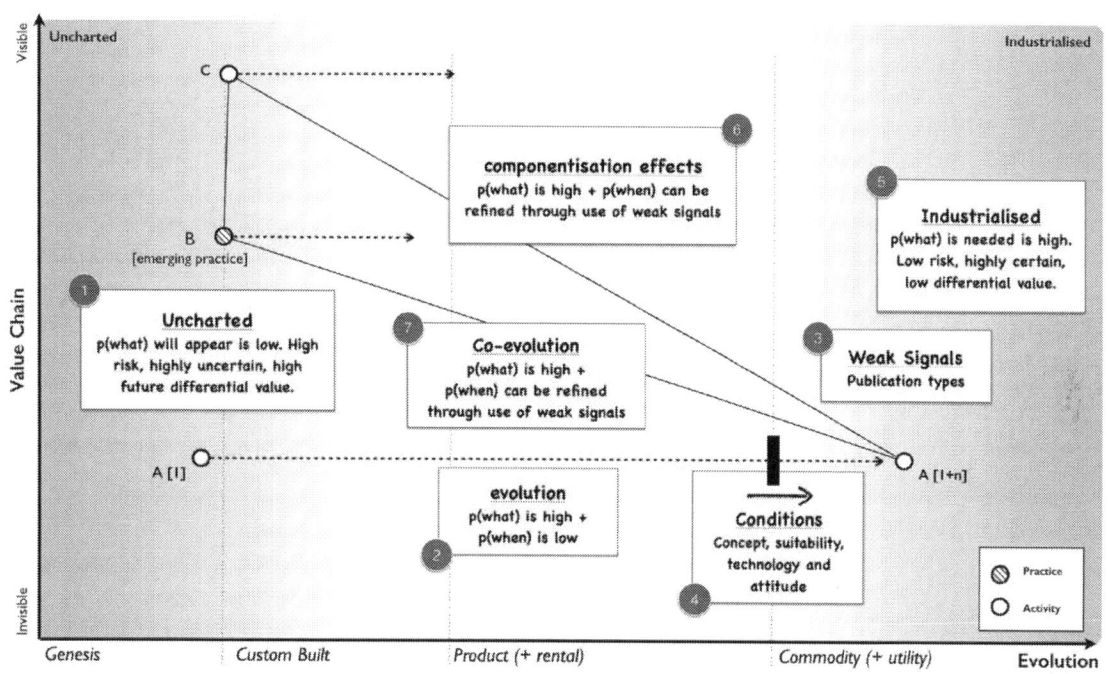

Figure 103: Expanding anticipation with coevolution

The above is remarkably powerful and allows us to introduce our first economic cycle, a climatic pattern known as peace, war and wonder.

Climatic Pattern: Peace, War and Wonder

Let us consider the path by which something evolves. We first start with the appearance of this novel thing; its genesis. The component is highly uncertain, of potential future value and risky. We don't know who will introduce it, whether it will go anywhere or what it will transform into. But, it's a potential source of **Wonder**. It may well disappear into the bin of history, along with refrigeration blankets, or become a soaring success. We just don't know. If it does find a use then supply and demand competition will start to cause its evolution. We will see custom-built examples in other companies and eventually, products introduced when the act becomes ubiquitous enough and well-defined enough to support this.

The nature of competition will now shift to suppliers of products with constant feature improvement. It's no longer about exploration of the uncharted space but about defining, refining and learning about the act. It's about settling the space. This evolution will continue, with constant release of ever more improved versions of the act — a better phone, a better television. It is a time of high margin, increasing understanding of customer needs, the introduction of rental services and relative competition, i.e. a jostle for position between giant competitors. Disruptive change caused by new entrants will occur, but such product versus product substitution is in the minority, as most change is gradual and sustaining of those competing companies. Because of their success, inertia to change builds up within those giants, whilst the activity itself continues to evolve, becoming more widespread, better understood and declining in differential value. In the latter stages, customers can even start to question whether they are getting a fair benefit for what they are paying, but overall, this is a time of Peace in that industrial ecosystem. Whilst we cannot say who will win or when things will evolve from one version to another, we can say that evolution will continue if there is competition. We have a high predictability of "what" will happen with evolution… it will evolve from product to commodity!

The successful activity has now become ubiquitous and "well understood". It is now **suitable** for more commodity or utility provision. Assuming that the concept and technology exists to achieve this then the likelihood of more industrialised forms increases. However, the existing giants have inertia to this change and so it is new entrants that are not encumbered by pre-existing business models that introduce the more commodity form. These new entrants may include former consumers who have gained enough experience to know that this activity should be provided in a different way, along with the skills to do it. In this case of computing infrastructure, it was an online bookseller that heavily used computing.

These more commodity forms (especially utility services) are often dismissed by existing customers and suppliers of products who have their own inertia to change. Customers see it as lacking what they need and not fitting in with their norms of operating, i.e. their existing practice. However, new customers appear and take advantage of the new benefits of high rates of agility, speed of genesis of new higher order activities and efficiency. Novel practices and norms of operating also co-evolve and start to spread.

Customers who were once dismissive start to trial out the services; pressure mounts for adoption due to the Red Queen. A trickle rapidly becomes a flood. Past giants who have been lulled into a sense of gradual change by the previous peaceful stage of competition see an exodus. Those same customers who were only recently telling these past giants that they wouldn't adopt these services because it didn't fit their needs and that they needed more tailored offerings have adapted to the new world. They are leaving the giants in droves. The old world of products and associated practices are literally crumbling away. The new entrants are rapidly becoming the new titans. The former giants have old models that are dying and little stake in this future world. There is little time left to act.

The cost to build equivalent services at scale to compete against the new titans is rapidly becoming prohibitive. Many past giants now face disruption and failure. Unable to invest, they often seek to reduce costs in order to return profitability to the former levels they experienced in the peace stage of competition. Their decline accelerates. This stage of competition is where disruptive change exceeds sustaining, it has become a fight for survival and it is a time of **War**, with many corporate casualties. This period of rapid change is known as a punctuated equilibrium.

The activity that is now provided by commodity components has enabled new higher order activities. Things that were once economically unfeasible now spread rapidly. Nuts and bolts beget machines. Electricity begets television. These new activities are, by definition, novel and uncertain — "Ere be Dragons!" Whilst they are a gamble and we can't predict what will happen, they are also potential sources of future wealth. Capital rapidly flows into these new activities. An explosion of growth in new activities and new sources of data occurs. The rate of genesis appears breathtaking. For an average gas lamp lighter, there are suddenly electric lights, radio, television, tele-typing, telephones, fridges, and all manner of wondrous devices in a short time span. We are back in the stage of **Wonder**.

There's also disruption, as past ways of operating are substituted — gas lamps to electric lights. These changes are often indirect and difficult to predict. For example, those that are caused by reduced barriers to entry. The fear that the changes in the previous stage of war (where past giants fail) will cause mass unemployment often lessens because the new industries built upon the new activities we could not have predicted will form. That doesn't stop authors writing books prophesying calamity, whether Nehemiah Hawkin's "New Catechism of Electricity" (1896) or Donald Michael's "Cybernation: The Silent Conquest" (1962), or the endless stream of books on machine intelligence. "This time it's different" is one of those phrases I frequently hear, shortly before we discover it isn't.

Despite the maelstrom, it is a time of marvel and of amazement at new technological progress. Within this smorgasbord of technological delights, the new future giants are being established. They will take these new activities and start to productise them. We're entering into the peace phase of competition again. Many are oblivious to the future war. The pattern of peace, war and wonder continues relentlessly. I've marked this onto Figure 104. At this point, you might go "but that's like the pioneer, settler and town planner diagram" — yes, it is. There's a reason I use those terms and call the town planners the "war makers".

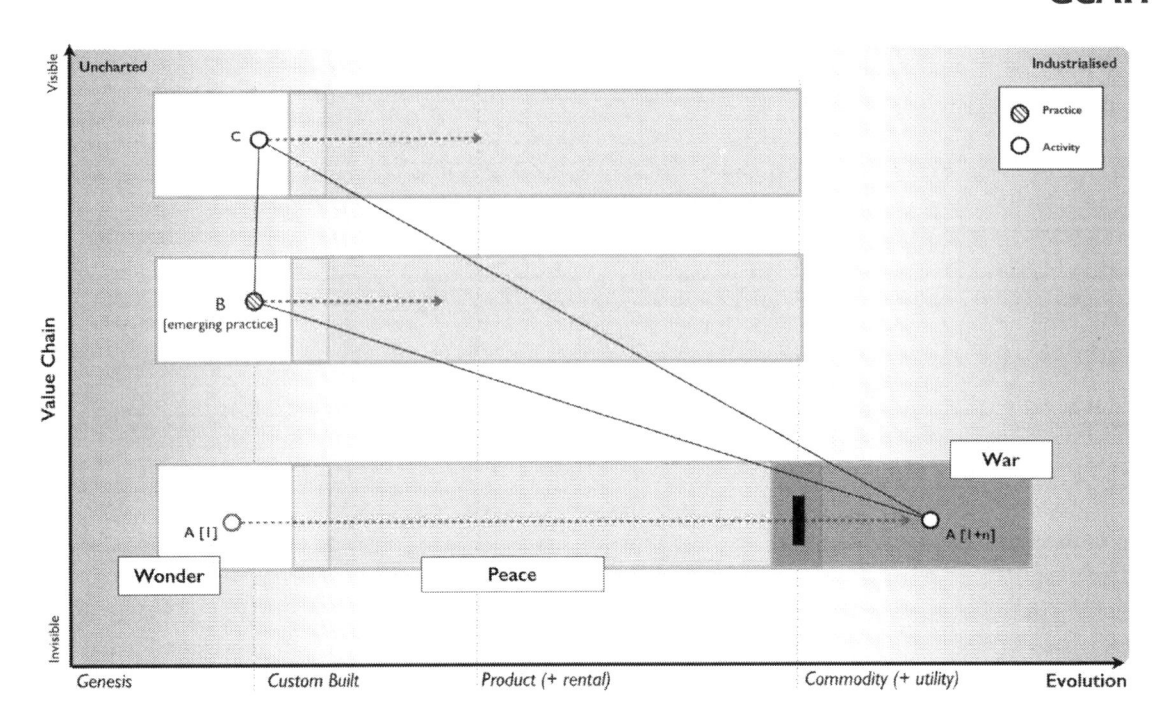

Figure 104: Peace, War and Wonder

Now, in this cycle, the **War** part is the most interesting because we can say an awful lot about it; it has a very high **predictability of what**. We know we're likely to see:-

- Rapid explosion of higher order systems and the genesis of new acts

    e.g. an increase at the rate at which innovative services and products are released to the web

- New entrants building these commodity services as past giants are stuck behind inertia barriers caused by past success

    e.g. new entrants dominating IT

- Disruption of past giants

    e.g. high rates of disruption in the IT markets

- Coevolution of practice

    e.g. radical changes in IT practices

- Higher levels of efficiency in provision of underlying components e.g. higher levels of efficiency within IT

- Widespread shifts to the new model driven by the Red Queen effect

  e.g. widespread adoption of cloud services

Wait, aren't those the predictions I was giving at conferences? Yes, I told you I was cheating and giving cowardly custard predictions of the kind "the ball that was thrown will fall to the ground". However, not only do we have a high predictability of "what", but we can also use weak signals from publication types and conditions to give us a pretty decent probability of "when". This is what makes the "War" state of change so remarkable. We can anticipate what's going to happen and have a reasonable stab at "when" well in advance.

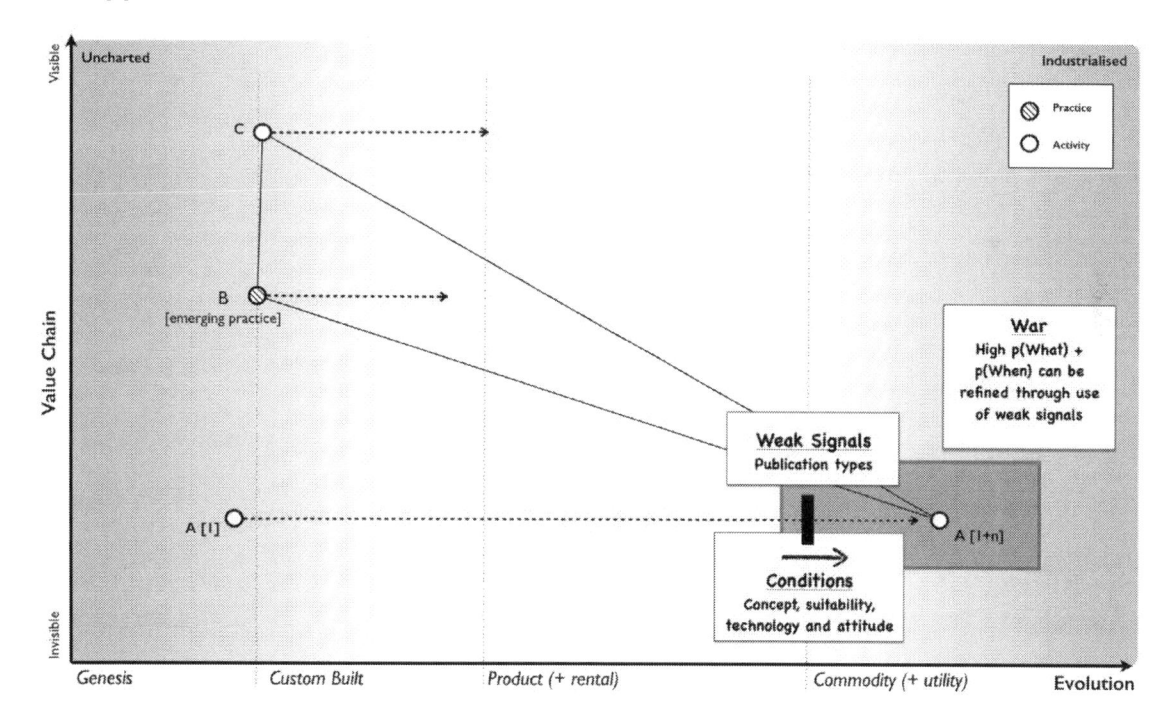

Figure 105: The war state of economic competition

I've been using this peace, war and wonder cycle in anger for about eight years. There's many things it helps explain, from how organisations evolve to the different types of disruption. However, we will cover that in the next chapter. For now, I just want to share the last time I ran the cycle. This was more recently in a piece of work for the Leading Edge Forum in 2014. The points of war are the points that the signals indicate that these particular activities will become more industrialised. Of course, there's a world of product competition beforehand, but at least we have an idea of when the changes will hit.

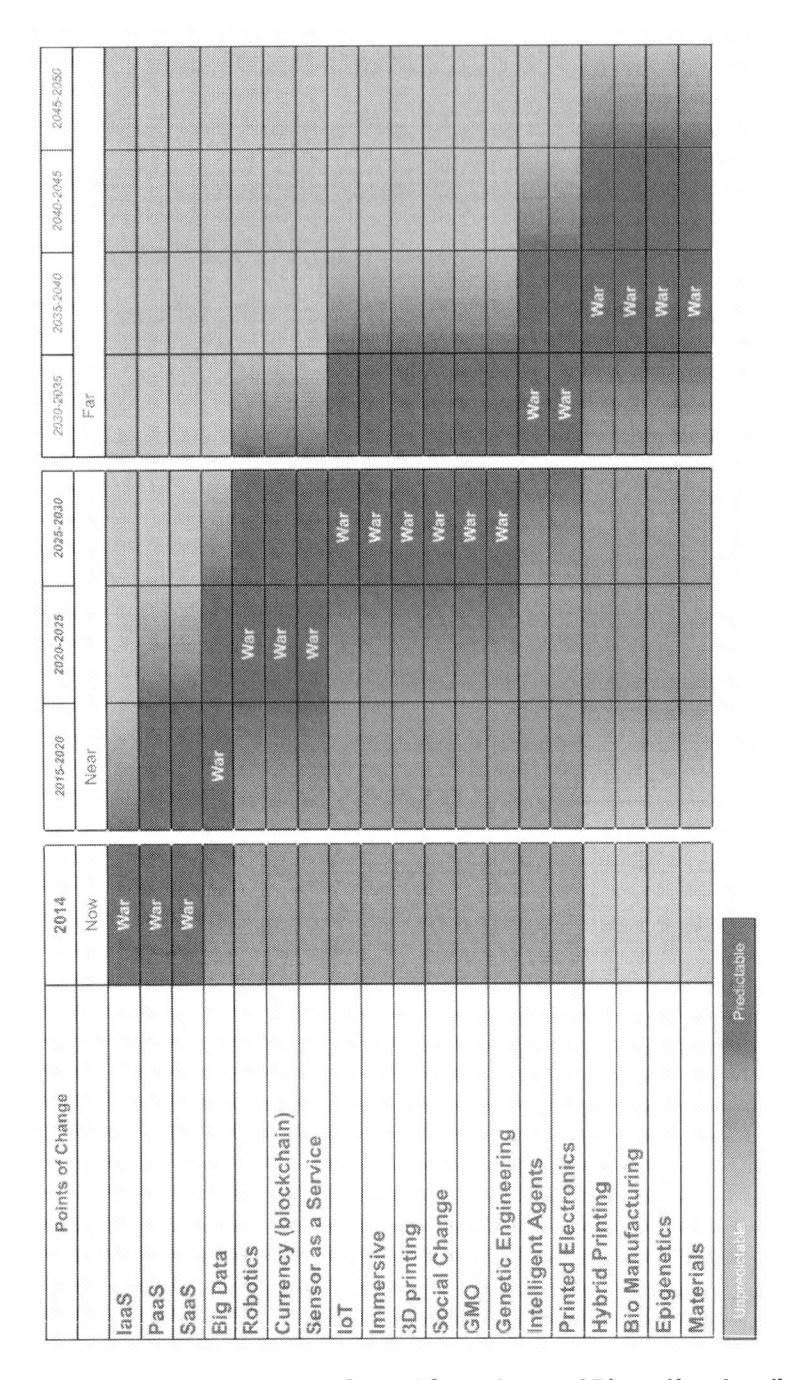

Figure 106: Future points of war. Of Wonders and Disruption, Leading Edge Forum, 2014

From the above, we can take an example such as intelligent software agents and see the weak signals indicate a world of developing products, but quite a long period until the formation of industrialised forms, sometime around 2025–2030. However, there will be a future when intelligent software agents will become industrialised, and the intelligent agent driving your car will become the same one that powers your future mobile device or your home entertainment system. This will cause all forms of disruption to past giants, along with changing practices. Closer to home, we can see that Big Data systems have already entered the war phase and sure enough, we have growing utility services in this space. That means product vendors that have dominated that space are in real trouble but probably don't realise it. They will have plenty of inertia and past success to deny that the change will happen.

Before we move on

In this last section, I'd like to first reflect on a few finer points of anticipation and then summarise the section.

Predictability and Climatic Patterns

There can be many climatic patterns involved in anticipation. I've taken the map from Figure 105 and highlighted in grey those you will be familiar with, and added in a few others to demonstrate the point. Whilst there are many areas of uncertainty in a map, there's an awful lot of things we can say about change.

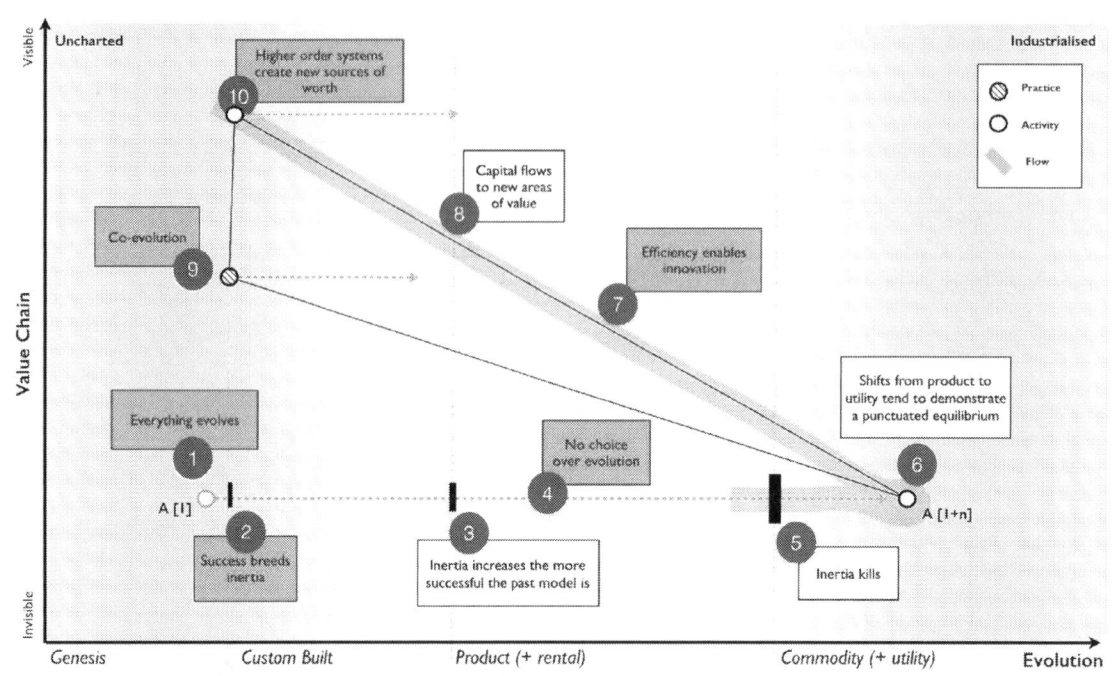

Figure 107: Climatic patterns and predictability

From Figure 107, then:-

Point 1 — Everything evolves. Any novel and therefore uncertain act will evolve due to supply and demand competition if it creates some form of advantage.

Point 2 — Success breeds inertia. It doesn't matter what stage of evolution we're at; along with past success comes inertia to change.

Point 3 — Inertia increases the more successful the past model is. As things evolve then our inertia to changing them also increases.

Point 4 — No choice over evolution. The Red Queen effect will ultimately force a company to adapt, unless you can somehow remove competition or create an artificial barrier to change.

Point 5 — Inertia kills. Despite popular claims, it's rarely lack of innovation that causes companies to fail but inertia caused by pre-existing business models. Blockbuster out-innovated most of its competitors through the provision of a website, video ordering online and video streaming. Its problem was not lack of innovation but past success caused by a "late fees" model.

Point 6 — Shifts from product to utility tend to demonstrate a punctuated equilibrium. The speed of change across different stages tend to be exponential.

Point 7 — Efficiency enables innovation. A standard componentisation effect.

Point 8 — Capital flows to new areas of value. A shift from product to more industrialised forms will see a flow of capital (marked as a light blue line) from past product companies to utility forms, along with investment in those building on top of these services.

Point 9 — Coevolution. The shift from product to more industrialised forms is accompanied with a change of practice.

Point 10 — Higher order systems create new sources of worth. The higher order systems created through being uncertain are also the largest sources of future differential value.

As you develop skill in understanding the landscape and climatic patterns involved, you will find yourself being able to increasingly anticipate common forms of change.

Re-examining the past

With our new understanding of anticipation then we can go back and look at those original maps of Fotango. I have taken one from Figure 28 (Chapter 3) and simply marked on points of war (purple) and wonder (light blue).

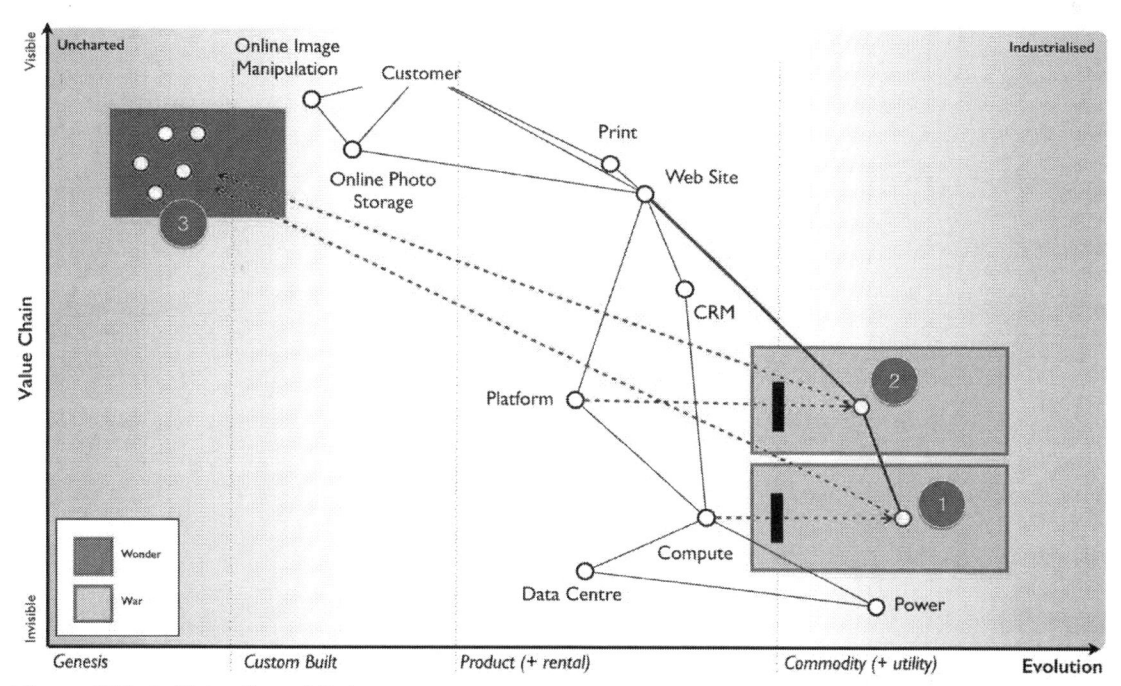

Figure 108: Anticipation at Fotango

From the above, in 2005, we had anticipated that compute was moving towards a utility (Point 1, a state of war). This was a reasonable assumption to make. Such a change is highly predictable and we could have said a lot more about it — the change of practice, for example, or the rapid speed of adoption. We had also anticipated that the platform (Point 2) would move to a utility and there would be inertia to the change. Again, this is a perfectly reasonable anticipation to have made. It was a highly predictable change. Finally, we had anticipated a rapid growth in new activities (Point 3), but we didn't know what they would be. This also was a reasonable anticipation.

In contrast, the parent company had decided the future was going to be SED television. This was a product to product substitution and it turns out that such changes are highly unpredictable. They were simply making a gamble in the dark. We threw away the highly predictable changes, which we had first mover advantage in (e.g. cloud), in order to gamble on an unpredictable area where we were behind the game (TV).

The same issue occurs with the Kodak example from Chapter 5. Kodak had three areas (Points 1 to 3 in Figure 109), which it could anticipate and therefore comfortably attack — the dominance of digital images, the rise of camera phones, and the industrialisation of online photo services. There was plenty of room for Kodak to play and plenty of opportunity. It should have easily anticipated the change of market and exploited this.

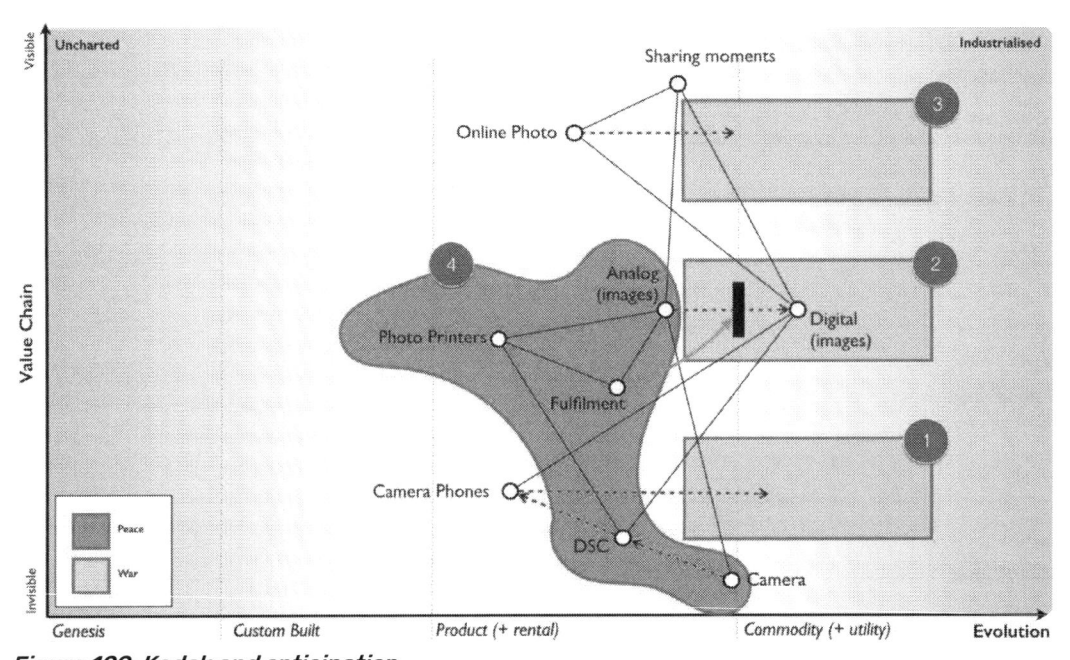

Figure 109: Kodak and anticipation

Unfortunately for Kodak, it bet its future in areas (Point 4) that were highly unpredictable in the short term (e.g. product substitution for printers) and where it was behind the game. To make matters worse, the long term was even more dire. The entire reason for the existence of fulfilment mechanisms and photo printers was to enable physical images (analog) to be shared, whether they came from processing of film from a camera or printing a digital image from a digital still camera. As we moved to sharing digital images then the whole reason for this part of the value chain to exist had started to disappear. Just to add salt into the wounds, cameras had evolved to higher order systems in digital still cameras, which have evolved (and become part of) higher order systems such as smartphones. Every smartphone would become a good enough digital still camera. The future of digital still cameras was in high-end photography, which is a niche. Everything inside Point 4 was in trouble. This was easily anticipatable at the time and not somewhere you should be relying upon for a future, unless you planned to carve out a high-end niche.

Maps are powerful tools when it comes to anticipation and avoiding betting your future on stuff that doesn't matter or giving the order to "walk off the cliff".

Categorising Predictability

Now I've introduced the basics of anticipation, I'd like to refine the concept. When I'm talking about predictability, I am talking about how accurately we can predict a change. If we assign a 10% probability to something then a high level of predictability means our 10% assignment is roughly right. A low level of predictability means we just don't have a clue. It could be 10%, 0.1% or 99%. We literally have no idea. You can still assign a precise probability to the change but it's likely to be wildly inaccurate. You're in the land of crystal balls and Mystic Megs. Predictability is the degree to which we anticipate something.

When it comes to anticipating change then at a market level, it's extremely difficult to identify who is going to make a change. In general, the predictability of who is always low. That doesn't stop you from preparing for changes, especially points of war, i.e. the industrialisation of a component. Cloud computing was highly anticipatable and could have been prepared for well in advance, despite us not knowing who was going to lead the charge. There is a broad spectrum of change that I've categorised in Figure 110, using predictability of What and When as the axis. The categories are:-

- **known** : trivial and obvious existing trends, i.e. diffusion of an existing act. There is little advantage to be found here as almost everyone else knows it, e.g. diffusion of cloud computing in 2016.

- **unknown**: trends that you cannot effectively determine beforehand, such as product to product substitution. There is little advantage to be found here in terms of anticipation because you cannot anticipate. It's a gamble.
- **knowable**: trends that can be determined to some degree prior to occurrence but are considered unknown by the majority. These trends are where you can take advantage of others' poor situational awareness.

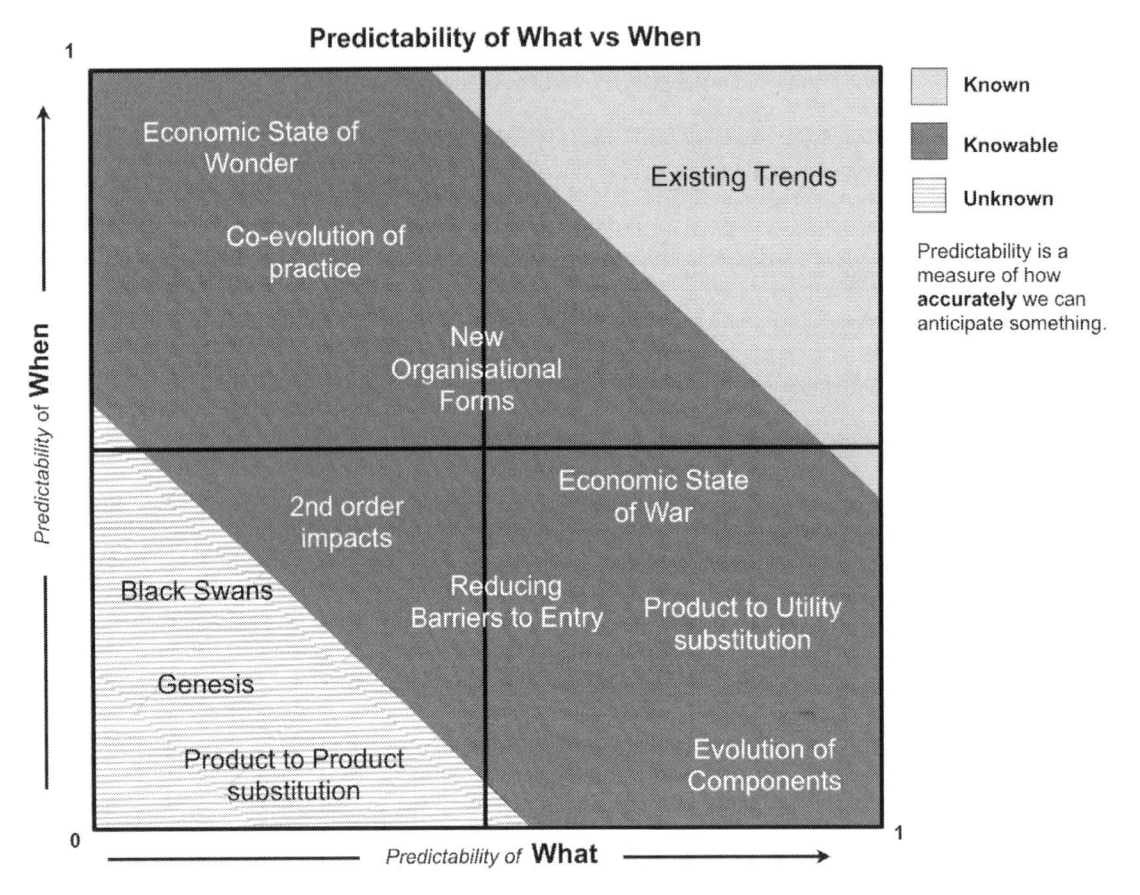

Figure 110: Categories of change. Of Wonders and Disruption, Leading Edge Forum, 2014

A few takeaways

By now, I've hopefully given you a basic introduction into anticipation. This is a topic that is worthy of its own book and there are many methods and techniques to be used here. However, as with the whole cycle of strategy, this is an area that you will refine with practice, learning of climatic patterns and understanding of the landscape. Using a map enables you to discuss your anticipation of change with others and allow for that all-important challenge. There are still lots of areas of uncertainty but with practice, you'll find yourself embracing that uncertainty and using mechanisms that exploit it. I've covered quite a bit in this chapter, but there are some key points I'd like you to remember.

Climatic patterns

- **Not everything is random.** Some things are predictable over when or what or both.
- **The future value of something is inversely proportional to the certainty we have over it.** As the predictability of a component increases with evolution, so does its ubiquity and hence, there is a corresponding decline in differential value.
- **Components can co-evolve**, e.g. practice with activities.
- **The economy has cycles**, e.g. peace, war and wonder. We're now halfway through our list of climatic patterns. I've marked them off in Figure 111 in grey. (P.S. I like orange. My car is an orange Mini. I told you I was a fairly normal person.) Anyway, read through the list and make sure you're comfortable with them. We're going to be relying on these later.

Components	Everything evolves through supply and demand competition	Rates of evolution can vary by ecosystem (e.g. consumer vs industrial)	Characteristics change as components evolve (Salomon & Storey)	No choice over evolution (Red Queen)
Financial	No single method fits all (e.g. in development or purchasing)	Components can co-evolve (e.g. practice with activity)	Evolution consists of multiple waves of diffusion with many chasms	
Financial	Higher order systems create new sources of value	Efficiency does not mean a reduced spend (Jevon's Paradox)	Capital flows to new areas of value	Creative Destruction (Joseph Schumpeter)
Financial	Future value is inversely proportional to the certainty we have over it.	Evolution to higher order systems results in increasing local order and energy consumption		
Speed	Efficiency enables innovation	Evolution of communication mechanisms can increase the speed of evolution overall and the diffusion of a single example of change	Increased stability of lower order systems increases agility & speed of re-combination	Change is not always linear (discontinuous & exponential change exists)
Speed	Shifts from product to utility tend to demonstrate a punctuated equilibrium			
Inertia	Success breeds inertia	Inertia can kill an organisation	Inertia increases the more successful the past model is	
Competitors	Competitors actions will change the game	Most competitors have poor situational awareness		A "war" (point of industrialisation) causes organisations to evolve
Prediction	Not everything is random (p[what] vs p[when])	Economy has cycles (peace, war and wonder)	Two different forms of disruption (predictable vs non-predictable)	
Prediction	You cannot measure evolution over time or adoption, you need to embrace uncertainty.	Evolution consists of multiple diffusion curves	The less evolved something is then the more uncertain it becomes	

Figure 111: Climatic patterns

We've also added in a type of gameplay in the use of weak signals, which can help refine anticipation.

An exercise for the reader

I'd like you to take some of your maps and try to anticipate change. Look for shifts from product to commodity. Think about the coevolution of practice that may occur and whether it will expose new worlds of wonder. Try applying the climatic patterns list above to your map and see what you come up with. Preferably, do this in a group.

Chapter 10 - I wasn't expecting that

I was in a quandary. Having described the three states of war, wonder and peace, I then found myself in the unusual position of finding them everywhere. All activities seemed to show these three competitive states. However, I had no real way of testing the existence of these states, and my ability to perceive them might be caused by some sort of bias. It's a bit like owning a Mini Cooper; once you have one then you suddenly notice how many other cars are Mini Coopers. I started to scout around for some means of testing these concepts. Did the states really exist? How could I test them? Do they just affect individual activities in industries or could they have a wider effect?

At the very least, I had a set of predictions (from weak signals) for when a range of activities would start to industrialise, and so I could just wait. Of course, this could just mean the weak signals were wrong, or I was just lucky? There was also something strangely familiar about those three stages. I'm a geneticist by training. I hold a second masters in environmental management and I also have a background in economics, courtesy of a mother who, as an economist, ignited my interest in the subject. I knew I'd seen these three states elsewhere. It didn't take me long to re-discover that first example — C. S. Holling's Adaptive Renewal cycle.

The adaptive cycle describes the dynamics of a complex ecosystem in response to change. We start with the creation of some form of disturbance — the genesis of a new act, some form of wonder. This is followed by a rapid stage of exploitation and accumulation in a stage of conservation where the change has become more stabilised in the ecosystem — the equivalent to a time of products, a peaceful state of competition. Eventually, the change has been normalised, which releases energy, enabling re-organisation and the genesis of new acts and new disruptions — the time of war. The Holling's cycle is measured over the potential of the system for change and the connectedness of the system. Whilst not an exact corollary, I've overlaid an approximation of the peace, war and wonder cycle onto the Holling's cycle in Figure 112.

Adaptive Renewal Cycle

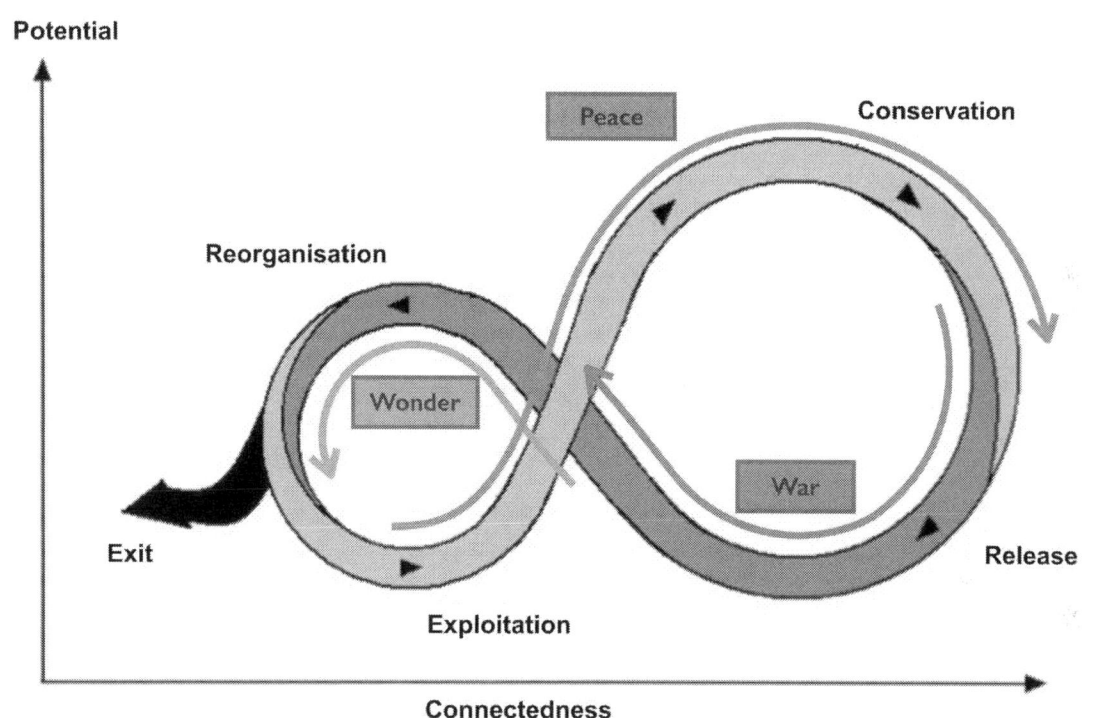

Figure 112: Adaptive renewal cycle. C. S. Holling, Adaptive Renewal Cycle

The importance for me of this was it gave rise to a number of concepts. First, when considering economic systems, we would have to look at them, as we do with biological systems, and consider how an ecosystem reacts to a change and how competition will drive that change throughout the system. Secondly, the size of the ecosystem impacted should reflect the connectedness of the system that is changing, i.e. industrialisation of legal will writing would only impact the legal industry, whereas industrialisation of computing should have a much broader macroeconomic effect. Lastly, there may well be an element of re-organisation involved. I was already aware of coevolution but maybe this enabled broader organisational change?

With this in mind, I started to explore macroeconomic scale effects on an assumption that a suitably connected technology should not only have microeconomic impacts to its industry but wider impacts. I was aware that the economy exhibited cycles known as Kondratiev waves (thanks to my interest in economics), and the largest waves we described as Ages. The first thing I noted was that these ages were not initiated by the genesis of some new activity but always by the industrialisation of a pre-existing activity that enabled higher order systems to develop. For example, the Age of Electricity was not caused by the introduction of electrical power, which occurred with the Parthian Battery (sometime before 400 AD), but instead, utility provision of A/C electricity with Westinghouse and Tesla, almost 1,500 years later. Equally, the Mechanical Age was not caused by the introduction of the screw by Archimedes, but by the industrialisation of standard mechanical components through systems such as Maudslay's screw-cutting lathe. The Age of the Internet did not involve the introduction of the first means of mass communication such as the Town Crier, but instead, industrialisation of the means of mass communication.

Whilst born out of industrialisation, each of these Ages were associated with a major cluster of "innovations" (i.e. genesis of new activities) that are built upon the industrialised components. Each age therefore had a "time of Wonder". The ages were also associated with a change in organisations. I started collecting approximate dates for these different ages, trying to identify the point of technology that may have initiated it and also the type of organisation structure that was dominant. A later version of this is provided in Figure 113.

Point of Change	Date Range (approx.)	Time Span (approx.)	"Age" (common name)	Organisational change (associated with)
Agriculture (Crop rotation) Agriculture (Plough)	1650-1780	130 years	Agricultural Revolution	Commercial Farmer / Markets
Power (Water Mill) Resource (Puddling iron) Manufacture (Screw Cutting Lathe)	1770-1840	70 years	Industrial Revolution	American System of Engineering / Time Management
Power (Steam) Communication (Postage Stamp)	1830-1880	50 years	Age of Steam & Transport	Joint stock company
Resource (Bessemer) Power (Electricity)	1870-1920	50 years	Age of Electricity & Heavy Engineering	Scientific Management / Taylorism / Hierarchy of Offices
Power (Petrochemical) Communication (Telephone)	1910-1970	60 years	Age of oil	Fordism / Mass Production
Information (Microprocessor)	1960-2000	40 years	Age of Information & Telecommunications	JIT / TPS
Communication (TCP/IP) Communication (mobile)	1990–2010	20 years	"Internet / Network" Age	Web / Web 2.0
Information (ubiquitous compute, utility compute)	2005-2025 (??)	20 years (??)	The "people are still coming up with names for it" Age	A "Next" generation (??)

Figure 113: Waves of organisational change

I still had no narrative linking it all together. Instead, it was a loose collection of almost connected concepts. Then, in mid 2008, I came across Carlota Perez's marvellous book – Technological Revolutions and Financial Capital. Perez has characterised these K-Waves around technological and economic paradigm shifts. For example, the Industrial Revolution included factory production, mechanisation, transportation and development of local networks, whereas the Age of Oil and Mass Production included standardisation of products, economies of scale, synthetic materials, centralisation and national power systems. Carlota had talked about the eruption of change, the frenzy of exploitation and later stages involving synergy and maturity (a more peaceful time of competition, of exploitation and conservation). It reminded me of Holling's adaptive renewal cycle. It reminded me of peace, war and wonder.

- The wonder of eruption and frenzy of new ideas, the explosion of the new and the re- organisation of systems around it. A time of exploration and pioneers.
- The exploitation and growth of these concepts, the synergy and the maturity of products in a more peaceful state of change. A time of settlers.
- The eventual release of capital and tumultuous shift from one cycle to another, the loss of the old, the birth of the new, the time of war and creative destruction of the past. A time of industrialisation and town planners. I've taken Carlota's description of K-Waves and added onto it the overlapping stages of peace, war and wonder in Figure 114.

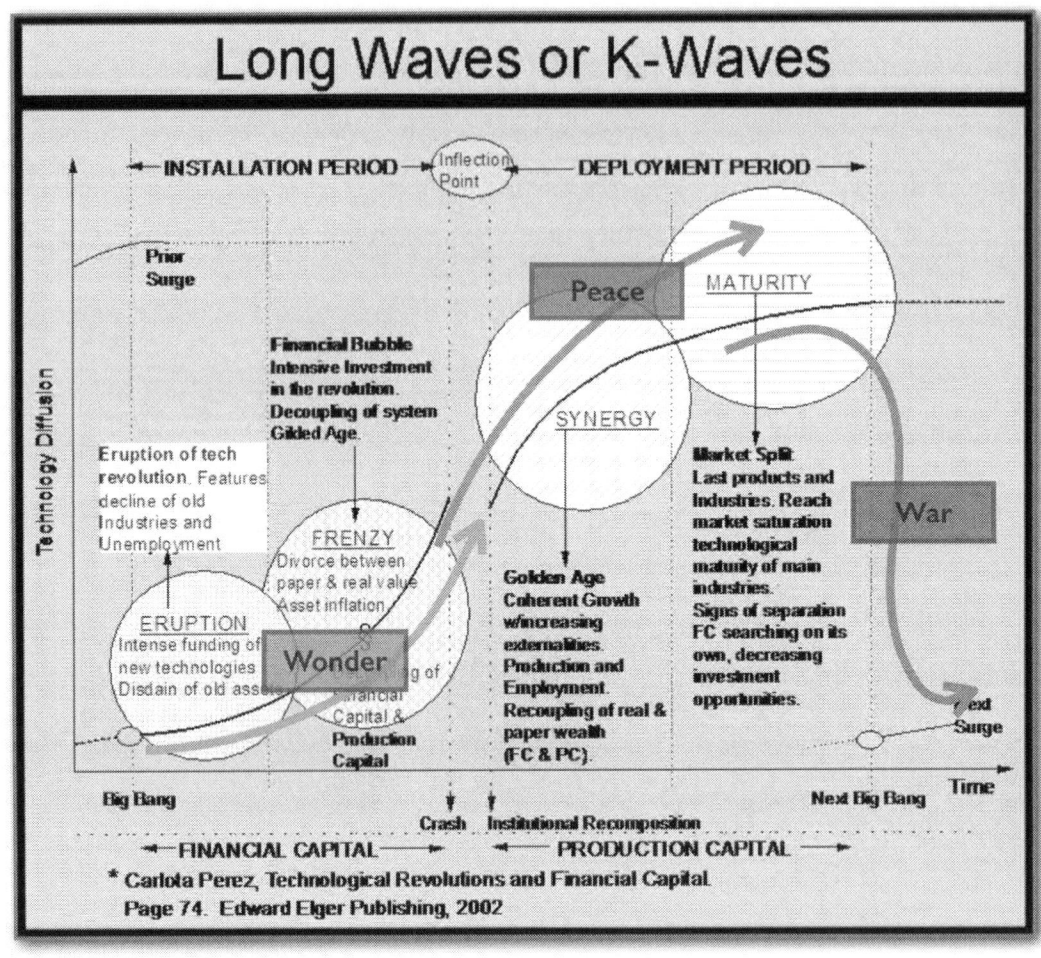

Figure 114: Carlota Perez and Kondratiev waves. Carlota Perez, Technology Revolutions and Financial Capital, 2002

An unexpected discovery

In my pursuit of discovering a way to test the peace, war and wonder cycle then I had accidentally stumbled upon a narrative for describing a system-wide organisational change. How widespread a change would be depended upon how well connected the components that were industrialising are. They could be specific to an ecosystem (e.g. legal will writing) and a small set of value chains, or they could impact many industries (e.g. computing) and many value chains.

The narrative would start with the birth of a new concept A[1], which would undergo a process of evolution through competition, from its first wonder and exploration to convergence around a set of products (Point 1 in Figure 115 below).

These products, after x iterations crossing many chasms and following many diffusion curves, would become more stabilised with well-defined best practice for their use (Point 2 in Figure 115). Large vendors would have established, each with inertia to future change due to past success, but the concept and the activity it represents will continue to evolve.

Eventually, the component would be suitable for industrialisation and new entrants (not suffering from inertia) would make the transition across that inertia barrier, introducing a more commodity form of A[x+1]. This would trigger a state of war, a shift to industrialised forms, a release of capability and capital (Point 3), enabling an explosion of new activities due to componentisation effects and new practices (Point 4) through coevolution. The underlying activity would continue its evolution to ever more industrialised forms until some form of stability is achieved with A [1+n]; a long and arduous journey of n iterations from the first wonder of its first introduction. The past ways, the past forms of the activity, the past practice, would have died off (Point 5) and they would have done so quickly.

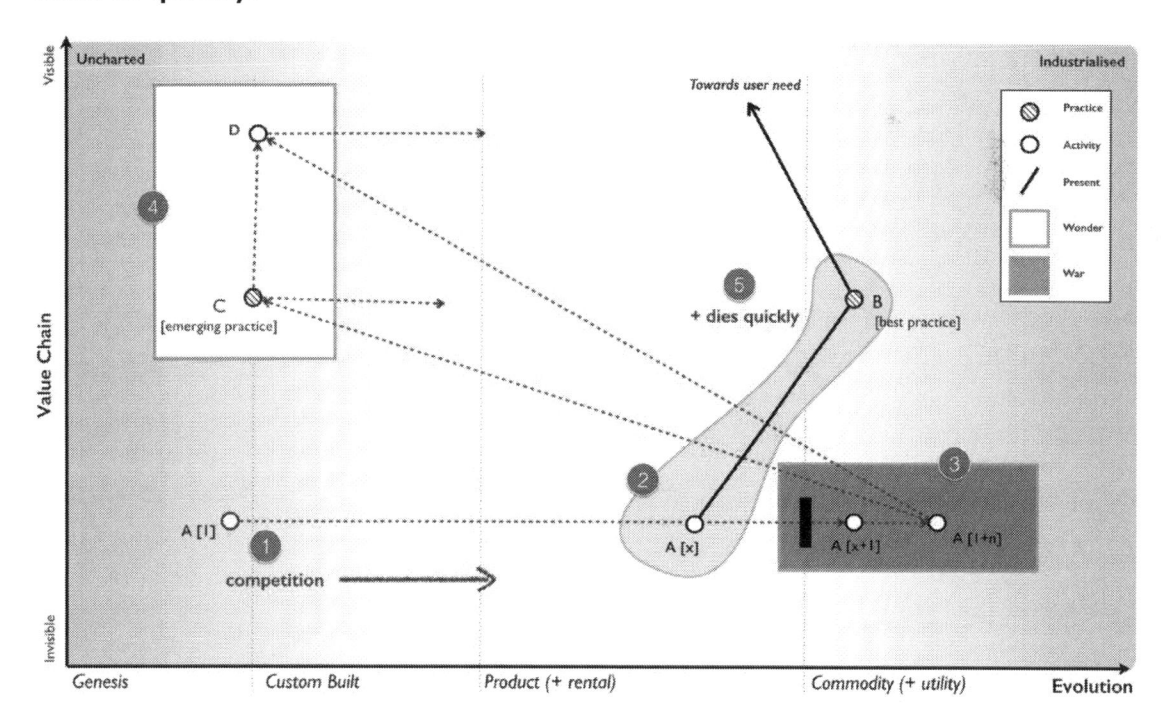

Figure 115: Understanding why

In 2008, this was exactly what was starting to happen around me in cloud computing. But the vast majority of people seemed to be assuring me that the change would take many decades; it would be very slow. Why would this be a slow progression? Why wouldn't the change happen quickly? To understand this, we need to introduce a climatic pattern known as the punctuated equilibrium.

Climatic Pattern: Punctuated Equilibrium

Throughout history, there have been periods of rapid change. The question should be, when is change a slow progression and when is it rapid? Part of this is caused by an illusion, an application of our bias to the concept of change. Let us consider an evolving act — A. From Figure 74 (Chapter 7), we know that the evolution of an act consists of the diffusion of many improving instances of that act. Let us assume that the activity quickly progresses to a product — A[2] — and evolves through a set of feature improvements — A[2] to A[x] — as shown in Figure 116, below. This will be the time a product, a constant jostle for improving features and through individual iterations, will rapidly diffuse (e.g. the 586 processor replaced the 486, which replaced the 386 and the 286 in the x86 family); the characteristics of products (the x86) are broadly the same, and the overall time of products appears to be long. This had happened with servers; a constant improvement and a long product run of 30 to 40 years.

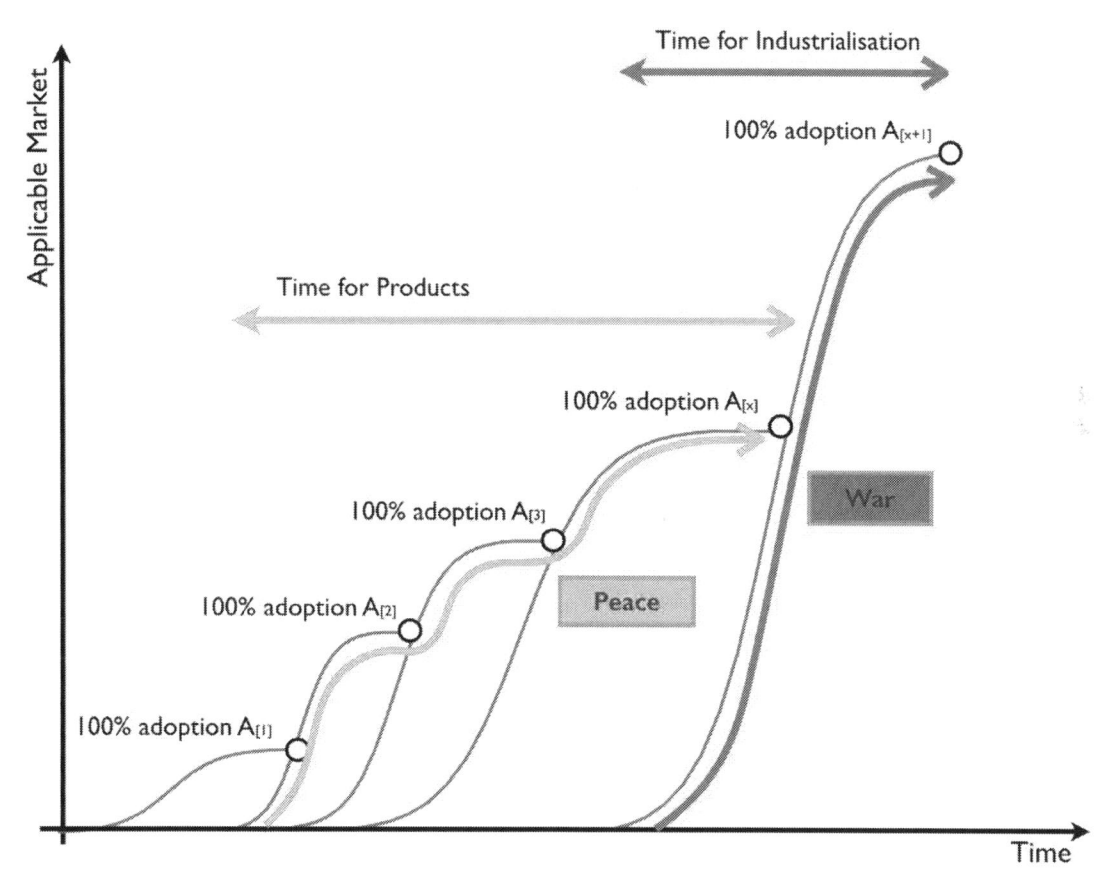

Figure 116: The illusion of speed

With the advent of more utility forms, you gain all the benefits of efficiency and agility; you're under pressure to adopt due to the Red Queen but invariably, people suffer from a bias towards a slow change because this is what they've experienced with products. They forget that we've had successive iterations (286 to 386 to 486 etc.) and label this all as one thing. They expect the progression to more utility forms will take equally long, but the transition is not multiple overlapping diffusion curves and the appearance of slow but steady progress but a single rapid shift (see figure above). Rather than 30 to 40 years, the change can happen in 10 to 15 years. We are caught out by the exponential growth and the speed at which it moves. This form of transition is known as a punctuated equilibrium and invariably, shifts from product to utility forms exhibit it.

It's the exponential nature that really fools us. To explain this, I'll use an analogy from a good friend of mine, Tony Fish. Consider a big hall that can contain a million marbles. If we start with one marble and double the number of marbles each second, then the entire hall will be filled in 20 seconds. At 19 seconds, the hall will be half full. At 15 seconds, only 3% of the hall, a small corner, will be full. Despite 15 seconds having passed, only a small corner of the hall is full, and we could be forgiven for thinking we have plenty more time to go; certainly, vastly more than the fifteen seconds it has taken to fill the small corner. We haven't. We've got five seconds.

Alas, these punctuated equilibriums are often difficult to see because we not only have the illusion of slow progress but confusion over what speed actually is. Let us assume that today, it takes on average 20 to 30 years for an act to develop from genesis to the point of industrialisation, the start of the "war", which changes so much in industry. Organisations consist of many components in their value chains, all of which are evolving. We can often confuse the speed at which something evolves with the simultaneous entrance of many components into the "war" state. For example, in Figure 117, I've provided the weak signal analysis (from Chapter 9) of many points of change. We can see that each component takes roughly 20 to 30 years to evolve (Point 1) to the point of industrialisation, followed by 10 to 15 years to industrialise (the "war"). However, if you examine Point 2 then we have many components, from robotics to immersive technology to IoT, which are embroiled in such a war. This can give us the impression that change is happening vastly more rapidly, as everything around us seems to be changing. It's important to separate out the underlying pace of change from the overlapping coincidence of multiple points of change.

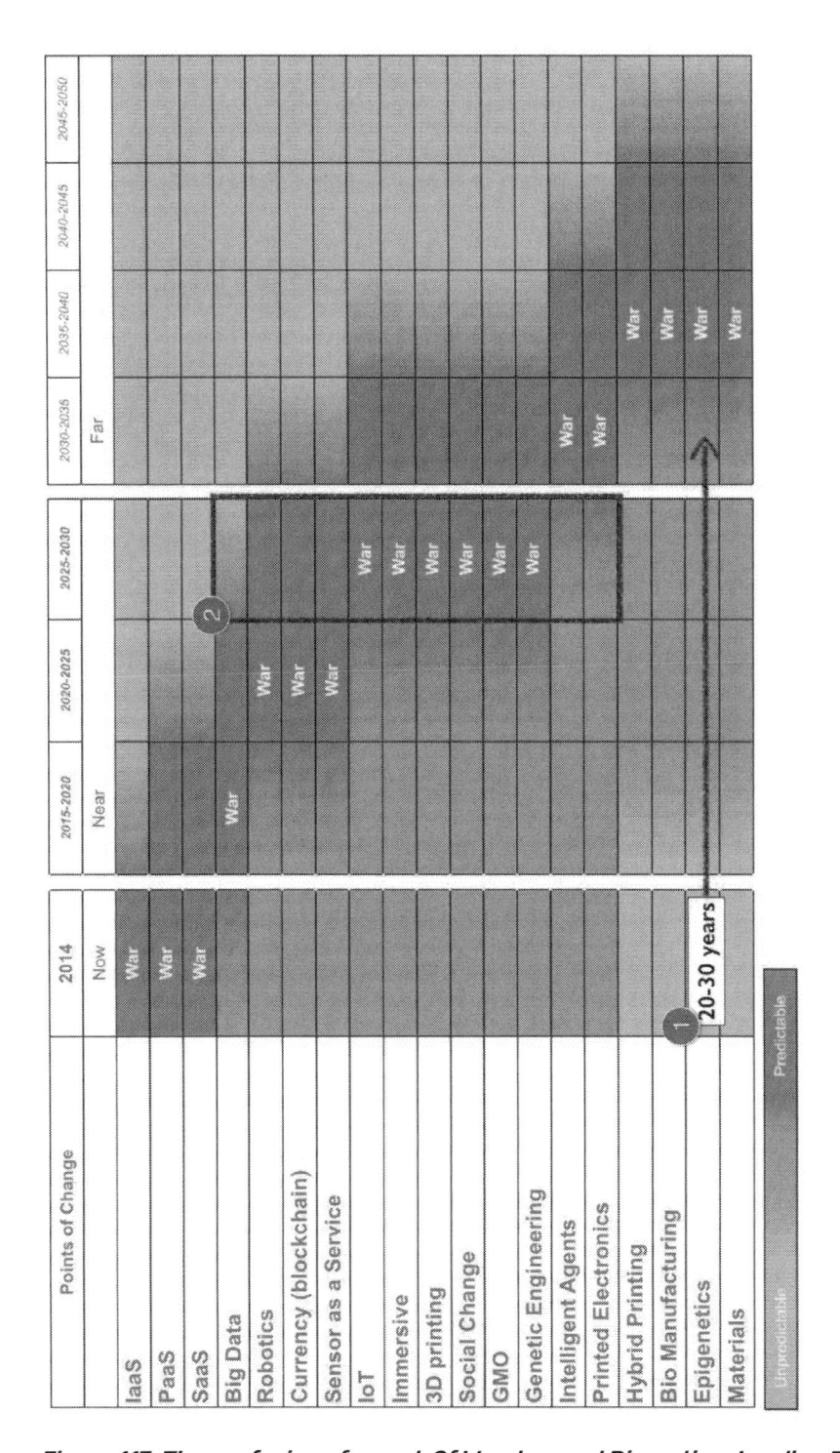

Figure 117: The confusion of speed. Of Wonders and Disruption, Leading Edge Forum, 2014

Given this, it should be possible to test the punctuated equilibrium. By selecting a discrete activity, we should be able to observe its rapid change, along with the denial in the wider industry that such a change would be rapid. Cloud computing gave me a perfect example to test this. In 2010 (when I was at Canonical), I produced a forward revenue chart for Amazon. This estimated the forward revenue at the end of each year for AWS (Amazon Web Services) and was based upon what little data I could extract, given that Amazon wasn't breaking out the figures. I've provided this estimate in Figure 118.

By the end of 2014, I had anticipated that AWS would have a forward revenue rate of $7.5 billion p.a., which means that every year after 2014, it would exceed this figure. In fact, AWS clocked over $7.8 billion in 2015. Now, what's not important is the accuracy of the figures; that's more luck, given the assumptions that I needed to make. Instead, what matters is the growth, its non-linear nature and the general disbelief that it could happen. Back in 2010, telling people that AWS would clock over $7.5 billion in revenue some five years later was almost uniformly met by disbelief.

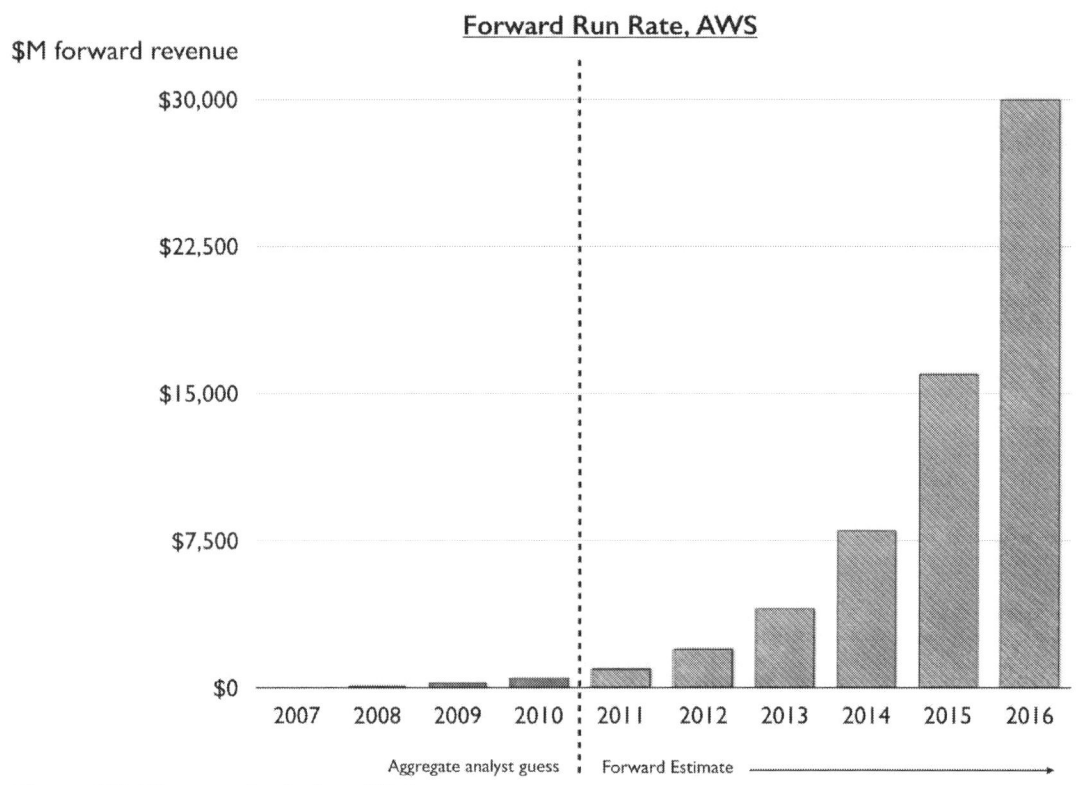

Figure 118: The punctuated equilibrium

Finding the future organisation

In 2008, I had the narrative of how organisations change and though I still had to demonstrate aspects of this (by anticipating a punctuated equilibrium before it happened), it did provide me with a path to test the concepts. I knew that if the concept was right then over the next decade, we would see a rapid change to more industrialised computing, coevolution of practice and a new form of organisation appearing. In the case of the rise of DevOps then this process had already started. Beyond just simply observing the growth of new practices and new activities, along with the death of the past (see Figure 119), I wanted a more formal method to evaluate this change. What I wanted to know is could we catch this next wave? Would the shift of numerous IT based activities to more utility services create a new organisational form? Timing would be critical, and unlike my earlier work in genetics, where populations of new bacteria are grown rapidly, I had to wait. So, wait I did.

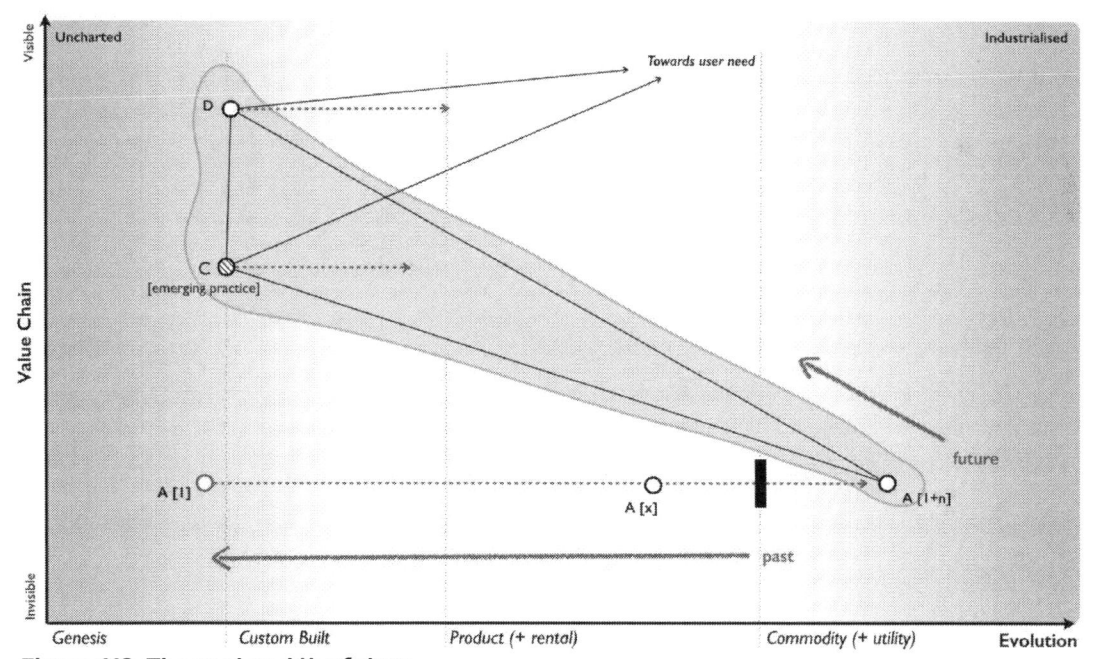

Figure 119: The past and the future

By 2010, the signals were suggesting that this was happening, and in early 2011, I had exactly the opportunity I needed. Being a geneticist, I was quite well versed in population characteristics, and so as part of a Leading Edge Forum project (published in the same year), we decided to use such techniques to examine populations of companies, specifically a hundred companies in Silicon Valley. We were looking for whether a statistically different population of companies had emerged and their characteristics (phenotypes) were starting to diffuse. It was a hit or miss project; we'd either find a budding population or it was back to the drawing board.

We already knew two main categories of company existed in the wild — those that described themselves as traditional enterprise and those using the term "web 2.0". The practices from the web 2.0 were already diffusing throughout the entire environment. Most companies used social media, they thought about network effects, used highly dynamic and interactive web based technology and associated technology practices. The two populations were hence blurring through adoption of practices (i.e. the traditional were becoming more web 2.0 like), but also partially because past companies had died. But was there now a next generation budding? A new Fordism?

I interviewed a dozen companies that I thought would be reasonable examples of traditional and web 2.0, and where I hoped a couple of highly tentative next generation companies might be hiding. I developed a survey from those companies, removed them from the sample population to be examined, and then interviewed over 100 companies divided roughly equally among those that described themselves as web 2.0 and those who called themselves more traditional. The populations all contained a mix of medium and huge companies. I examined over 90 characteristics, giving a reasonable volume of data. From the cycle of change and our earlier interviews, we had guessed that our next generation was likely to be found in the self-describing "web 2.0" group, and in terms of strategic play, they would tend to be focused on disruption (the war phase), rather than profitability (the peace phase). From our earlier interviews, I had developed a tentative method of separating out into candidate populations. So, I divided the population sample out into these categories and looked at population characteristics — means and standard deviations. Were there any significant differences? Were the differences so significant that we could describe them as a different population, i.e. in a sample of mice and elephants then there exist significant characteristics that can be used to separate out the two populations?

I ran our analysis and waited. It was an edgy moment. Had we found something or as per many attempts before, had we found nothing? I tend to assume nothing, and when there is something, I tend to doubt it. Within our data set, we found statistically significant population differences across a wide number of the characteristics but also significant similarities. I re-examined, looked through my work, tested, sought the advice of others and tested again — but the differences and similarities remained. For example, I examined each company's view on open source and whether it was primarily something that means relatively little to them — a mechanism for cost reduction, something they relied upon, something they were engaged in — or whether open source was viewed as a tactical weapon to be used against competitors. The result is provided in Figure 120 with the subdivision by population type.

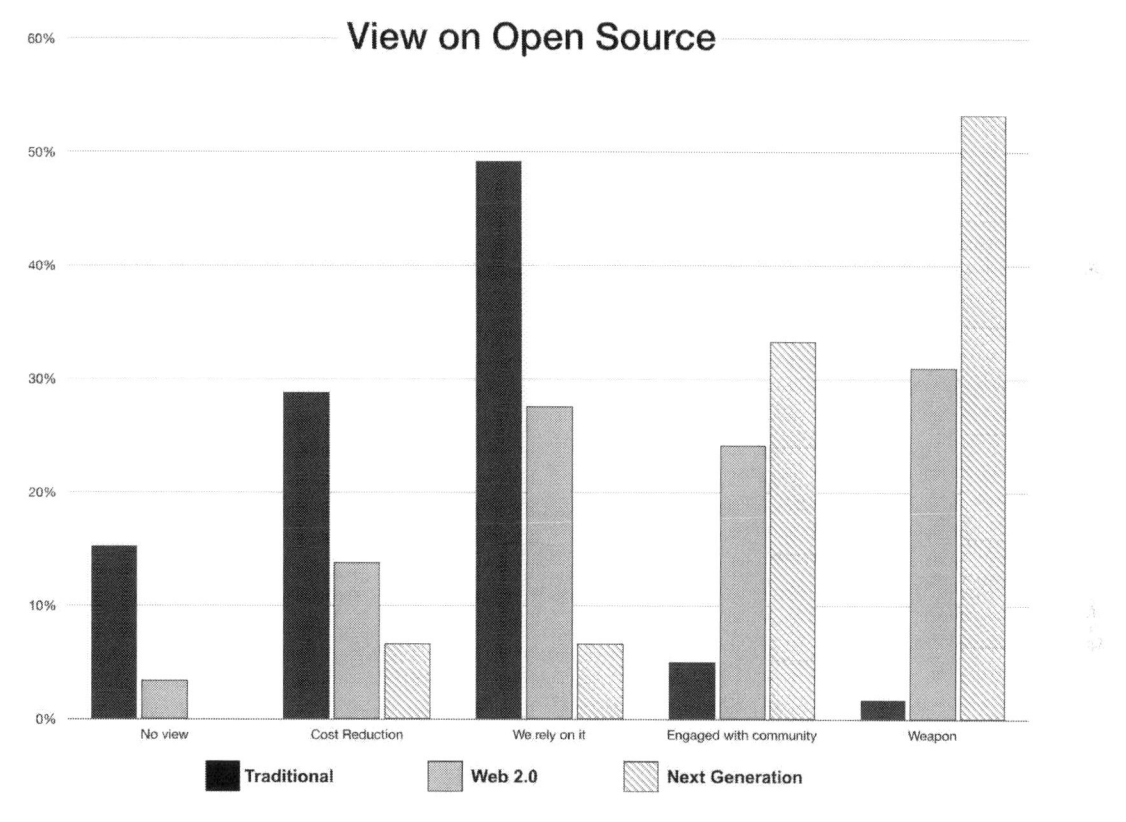

Figure 120: Views on open source. Learning from Web 2.0, Leading Edge Forum, 2011

Whilst the traditional companies mainly viewed open source as a means of cost reduction and something they relied upon, this next generation viewed it as a competitive weapon and something they were heavily engaged in. The web 2.0 group had a broader view, from cost to weapon. This difference in population was repeated throughout many characteristics, spanning strategy, tactics, practice, activities and form. The odds of achieving the same results due to random selection of a single population were exceptionally low. We had found our next generation candidate.

To describe this next generation, it is best to examine them against the more traditional. Some of the characteristics show overlap, as would be expected. For example, in examining the highest priority focus for provision of technology by a company, whether it's profitability, enhancement of existing products and services, innovation of new products and services, enabling other companies to innovate on top of their products and services or creating an engaged ecosystem of consumers, then overlaps exist. In other areas, the differences were starker. For example, in an examination of computing infrastructure then traditional favoured enterprise class servers, whereas the next generation favoured more commodity. A good example of this similarity and yet difference was the attitude towards open source. When asked whether a company open sourced a source of differential advantage on a scale of strongly disagree to strongly agree, then both traditional and next generation gave an almost identical response (see Figure 121).

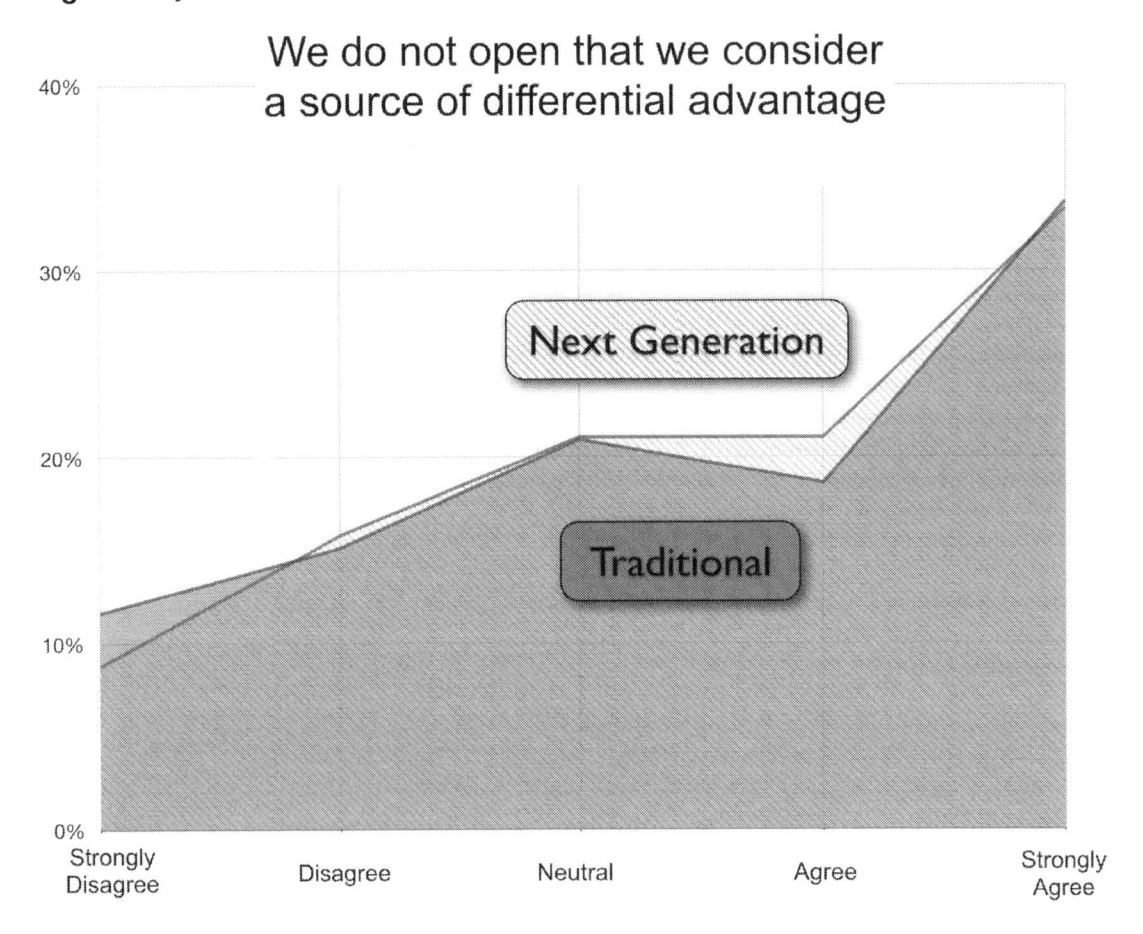

Figure 121: Finding similarity. Learning from Web 2.0, Leading Edge Forum, 2011

However, when asked whether they would open source a technology to deliberately out-manoeuvre a competitor then the answers were almost polar opposites (see Figure 122).

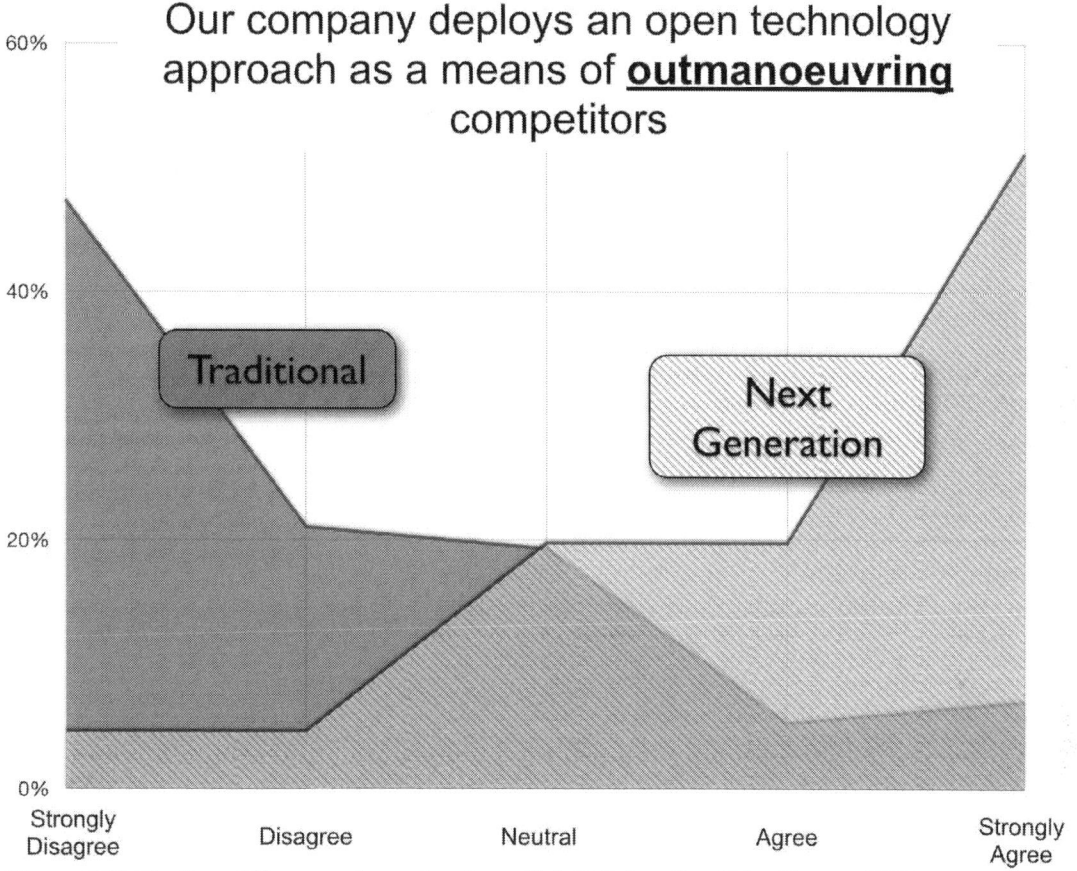

Figure 122: Finding difference. Learning from Web 2.0, Leading Edge Forum, 2011

Using these populations, I then characterised the main differences between traditional and next generation. These are provided in Figure 123 but we will go through each in turn. I've also added some broad categories for the areas of doctrine the changes impact.

Area	Traditional	Next Generation	Category (Doctrine)
Technique	Single methods	Mixed methods	Development
Deployment	Change Control	Continuous	Development
Resilience	N+1	Design For Failure	Development
Infrastructure	Enterprise Class	Commodity	Development
Failure Testing	Disaster Recovery	Chaos Engines	Operations
Capacity	Scale Up	Scale-out	Operations
Structure	Departmental	Service / Cell	Structure
Culture	Inertia	Fluid / Game-able	Structure
Learning	Analysts	Ecosystem	Learning
"Big" Data	Used	Driven By	Learning
Focus	Profit	Disruption	Leading
Open source	Cost reduction	Weapon	Leading

Figure 123: The phenotypic differences. Source data from "Learning from Web 2.0", Leading Edge Forum, 2011

Development

Traditional companies tend to focus towards singular management techniques for development (e.g. Agile or Six Sigma) and often operate on a change control or regular process of updates. The next generation tends towards mixed methods, depending upon what is being done, and combine this with a continuous process of release.

Operations

Traditional organisations tend to use architectural practices such as scale-up (bigger machines) for capacity planning, N+1 (more reliable machines) for resilience and single, and time critical disaster recovery tests for testing of failure modes. These architectural practices tend to determine a choice for enterprise class machinery. The next generation has entirely different architectural practices, from scale-out (or distributed systems) for capacity planning, design for failure for resilience and use of chaos engines (i.e. the deliberate and continuous introduction of failure to test failure modes), rather than single, time critical disaster recovery test. These mechanisms enable highly capable systems to be built using low cost commodity components.

Structure

Traditional organisations used a departmental structure, often by type of activity (IT, Finance, Marketing) or region, with often a silo mentality and a culture that was considered to be inflexible. The next generation used smaller cell based structures (with teams typically of less than twelve), often with each cell providing services to others' cells within the organisation. Each cell operated fairly autonomously, covering a specific activity or set of activities. Interfaces were well-defined between cells and the culture was viewed as more fluid, adaptable and dynamic.

Learning

Traditional organisations tend to use analysts to learn about their environment and changes that are occurring. They tend to also use Big Data systems, which are focused primarily on providing and managing large sets of data. The next generation use ecosystems to more effectively manage, identify and exploit change. They also tend to not only use "Big Data" but to be run by it with extensive use of modelling and algorithms. The focus is not on the data per se but the models.

Leading

In traditional organisations, the use of open systems (whether source, data, APIs or other) is viewed primarily as a means of cost reduction. A major focus of the company tends to be towards profitability. In some cases, technology or data is provided in an open means with an assumption that this will allow others to provide "free" resources and hence, reduce costs. In the next generation, open is viewed as a competitive weapon, a way of manipulating or changing the landscape through numerous tactical plays, from reducing barriers to entry, standardisation, eliminating the opportunity to differentiate, building an ecosystem, and even protecting an existing value chain. Next generation are primarily focused on disruption of pre-existing activities (a war phase mentality) and exhibit higher levels of strategic play.

The LEF published the work in December 2011 and since then, we have observed the diffusion of many of these changes as the traditional become more next generation. In the parlance of "Boiling Frogs" (an outstanding open sourced document on management, provided by GCHQ), then we're seeing "less of" the traditional and "more of" the next generation over time. However, I very much don't want you to read the above list and get the impression that "this is how we create an advantage!" Instead, be realistic. The above characteristics are already diffusing and evolving; tens, if not hundreds of thousands, of people and their companies are well aware of them today. You'll need to adapt simply to survive. Any real advantage has already been taken and any remaining advantage will be over those who are slower to adapt.

I do however what to expand the above Figure 123 and include some specific examples of doctrine (see Figure 124 below). For example, the shift from single to multiple methods is just a refinement of the principle "to use appropriate methods". There was a time when we thought that a single method was appropriate, but as we've become more used to the concepts of evolution and change then we've learned that multiple techniques are needed. This doesn't stop various attempts to create a tyranny of the one, whether agile or Six Sigma or some purchasing method, but for many of us, the way we implement that principle has changed. In other words, the principle of doctrine has remained consistent but our implementation has refined and become more nuanced. Equally, our principle of "manage failure" has simply refined from one time disaster recovery tests to constant introduction of failure through chaos engines. Now, certainly, the implementation has to be mindful of the landscape and purpose; for example, constant failure through chaos engines is not appropriate for the generation components of a nuclear power plant.

Area	Traditional	Next Generation	Principle (Doctrine)	Category (Doctrine)
Technique	Single methods	Mixed methods	Use appropriate methods	Development
Deployment	Change Control	Continuous	Think fast, inexpensive, simple and tiny	Development
Resilience	N+1	Design For Failure		Development
Infrastructure	Enterprise Class	Commodity		Development
Failure Testing	Disaster Recovery	Chaos Engines	Manage failure	Operations
Capacity	Scale Up	Scale-out	Effectiveness over efficiency	Operations
Structure	Departmental	Service / Cell	Think small teams	Structure
Culture	Inertia	Fluid / Game-able	There is no one culture	Structure
Learning	Analysts	Ecosystem	Listen to your ecosystems	Learning
"Big" Data	Used	Driven By	A bias towards data	Learning
Focus	Profit	Disruption	There is no core	Leading
Open source	Cost reduction	Weapon	Exploit the landscape	Leading

Figure 124: The change from traditional to next generation. Source data from "Learning from Web 2.0", Leading Edge Forum, 2011

In other cases, the principle "Think small teams" is relatively young in management terms (i.e. less than forty years). The theory of management tends to move extremely slowly and its practices can take a considerable amount of time to evolve. The point that I want to emphasise is that when we talk about the evolution of organisation, this is normally reflected in terms of a change in doctrine and either evolution or addition of principles. However, not everything changes. There are many practices and concepts that are simply copied to the next generation. It should never be expected that there are no common characteristics or overlap but instead, what you hope to find is significant difference in specific characteristics (i.e. mice have two eyes, the same as elephants, and hence, there are some similarities, along with huge differences). I've provided a small subset of the similarities in Figure 125, but it should be remembered that of the 90 odd characteristics I examined, only twelve showed significant change.

Area	Traditional AND Next Generation	Category (Doctrine)
Focus on product improvements & new features	High Importance	Development
Focus on process improvements	High Importance	Development
Maintaining difference with competitors through brand	High Importance	Development
How long would it take to get a new wiki set up	Hours or less	Operations
Is your company highly efficient	Disagree	Operations
Are your IT systems better than those of your competitors	Agree	Operations
Company has legacy IT	>80%	Operations
Sales is a …	value generator to be invested in	Structure
Marketing is a …	value generator to be invested in	Structure
IT is a …	value generator to be invested in	Structure
Past success inhibits future success	Disagree	Learning
Suffers outsourcing failures	Occasionally	Learning
Suffers business alignment failures	Occasionally	Learning
Innovation is NOT generally a function of the IT group	Strongly Disagree	Learning
Invests in internal IT innovation	Strongly Agree	Leading
Does not open source a differential advantage	Agree	Leading
Does IT provide a competitive advantage	Frequently	Leading
Spends time on strategy and planning future impacts	Frequently	Leading
Shifting focus between innovation and efficiency	Frequently	Leading

Figure 125: Not everything changes. Source data from "Learning from Web 2.0", Leading Edge Forum, 2011

In 2008, I understood the cycle of change (peace, war and wonder), which had evolved from the concept of evolution, and I had a hypothesis for the process of how organisations evolve. By 2011, we had not only anticipated this change but observed a budding next generation. I say "budding" because we had no real idea of whether they would be successful or not. It turns out that they are, but that's a story for a later chapter. For now, there are a couple of refinements that I'd like to make to these models.

Notes on Peace, War and Wonder

There are a number of patterns that are worth highlighting.

Climatic Pattern: Evolution of a communication mechanism can increase the speed of evolution overall

In Figure 117 above, I discussed the confusion of speed and how we often mix concepts about the underlying rate of change with the circumstantial overlapping of multiple points of industrialisation. Does this however mean the underlying rate of change is constant? The answer is no. There is another pattern here that deals with communication mechanisms.

On the 1st May,1840, a revolution in industry was started by the introduction of the Penny Black. This simple postage stamp caused a dramatic explosion in communication, from 76 million letters sent in 1839 to 350 million by 1850. It wasn't a case that postal services didn't exist before, but the Penny Black turned the act of posting a letter into a more standard, well-defined and ultimately ubiquitous activity. The introduction caused a spate of copycat services throughout the world, with the US introducing their first stamps in 1847. The 125 million pieces of post sent through their system in that year mushroomed to 4 billion by 1890. From stamps to street letter boxes (1858) to the pony express, railway deliveries (1862), money orders, and even international money orders by 1869.

The humble stamp changed communication forever. But it wasn't alone. Telegraph lines that later enabled the telephone that later enabled the internet have all led to corresponding explosions of communication. In all cases, it wasn't the invention of the system (the first stamp for example being created by William Dockwra in 1680) but instead, the system becoming more standard, well-defined and more of a commodity that created the explosion. Each time we've experienced one of these communication changes, we've also experienced significant industrial change. The growth in postal services and telegraph lines coincides with the Railway and Steam Engine era, where diffusion of new machine concepts became rampant.

Of course, the origin of industrial steam engines started in the earlier first industrial revolution, which itself arguably started with Maudslay's screw-cutting lathe and the introduction of interchangeable mechanical components. By providing mechanical components as more of a commodity, we saw a growth in new machine industries and new manufacturing processes. From the Plymouth system for manufacturing, which later became the armoury system in the US, an entirely new method of manufacturing was started by the humble nut and bolt.

Whilst this might appear to be nothing more than the peace, war and wonder cycle in action, there is something quite unique here. When we examine how things have evolved over time then nuts and bolts took over 2,000 years to industrialise, electricity took 1,400 years, the telephone merely 60 to 80 years, and computing some 60 to 70 years. What has changed during that time is industrialisation of communication mechanisms. As we move up the value chain (see Figure 126) then the speed at which things evolve across the landscape is impacted by industrialisation of communication mechanisms. The printing press, the postage stage, the telephone and the internet did more than just industrialise a discrete component in a value chain; they accelerated the evolution of all components.

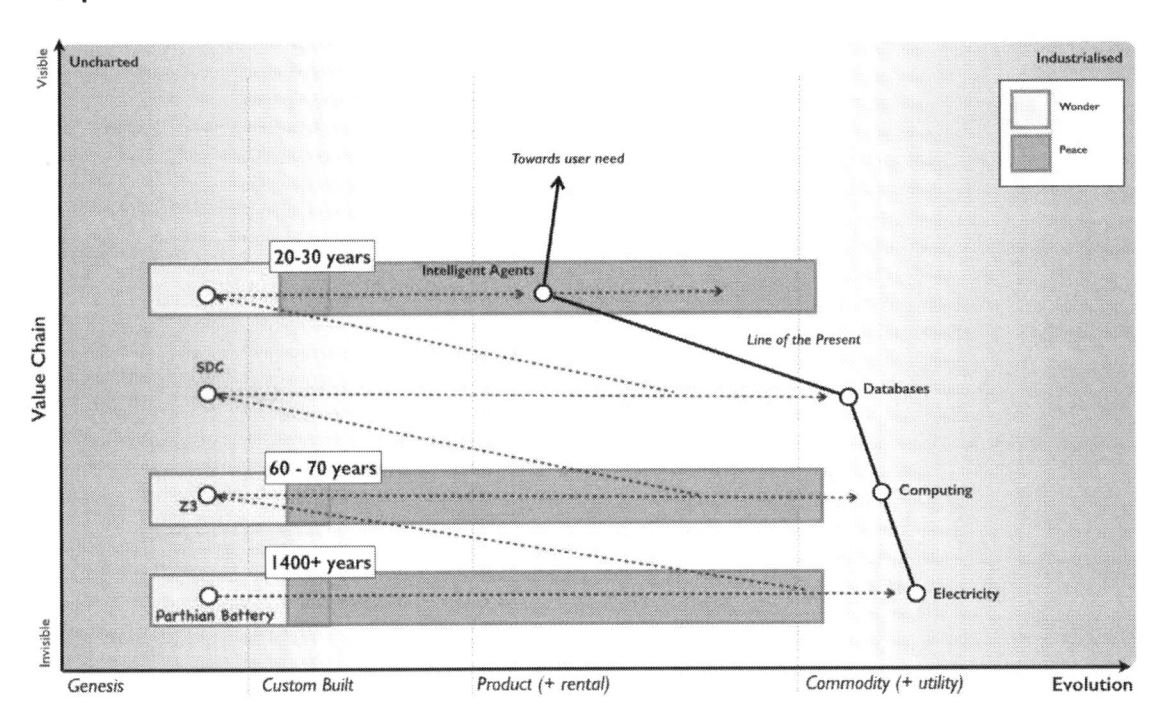

Figure 126: The speed of evolution

Do not however confuse this with how innovative we are as a species. Rather, realise that the speed at which something evolves has accelerated. My best guess is the speed of change today now corresponds to about 20 to 30 years on average, from genesis to the point of industrialisation, and then around 10 to 15 years for the "war" to work through the system and the change to become the dominant form. The jury is out at the moment (i.e. I'm collecting more data) as to whether it really is that fast, and not all industrial ecosystems work at the same speed. Obviously, as per Figure 117, the confusion of speed then during your lifetime, it is likely you will experience multiple overlapping waves or points of industrialisation. However, an increase in the underlying speed means we should experience more of these, and life going forward will probably feel a lot more disruptive.

Climatic Pattern: Inertia increases with past success

One of the subjects I've mentioned is inertia and our resistance to change. With any established value chain, there are existing interfaces to components, along with accompanying practices. There is a significant cost associated with changing these interfaces and practices, due to the upheaval caused to all the higher order systems that are built upon it, e.g. changing standards in electrical supply impacts all the devices that use it. This cost creates resistance to the change. You also find similar effects with data, or more specifically, our models for understanding data. As Bernard Barber once noted, even scientists exhibit varying degrees of resistance to scientific discovery. For example, the cost associated with changing the latest hypothesis on some high level scientific concept is relatively small, and often within the community, we see vibrant debate on such hypotheses. However, changing a fundamental scientific law that is commonplace, well understood and used as a basis for higher level concepts will impact all those things built upon it and hence, the level of resistance is accordingly greater. Such monumental changes in science often require new forms of data, creating a crisis point in the community through unresolved paradoxes, including things that just don't fit our current models of understanding. In some cases, the change is so profound and the higher order impact is so significant that we even coin the phrase "a scientific revolution" to describe it.

The costs of change are always resisted, and past paradigms are rarely surrendered easily — regardless of whether it is a model of understanding, a profitable activity provided as a product or a best practice of business. As Wilfred Totter said, "the mind delights in a static environment". Alas, this is not the world we live in. Life's motto is "situation normal, everything must change", and the only time things stop changing is when they're dead.

The degree of resistance to change will increase, depending upon how well established and connected the past model is. In Figure 127, I've shown this as inertia barriers, which increase in size the more evolved the component becomes.

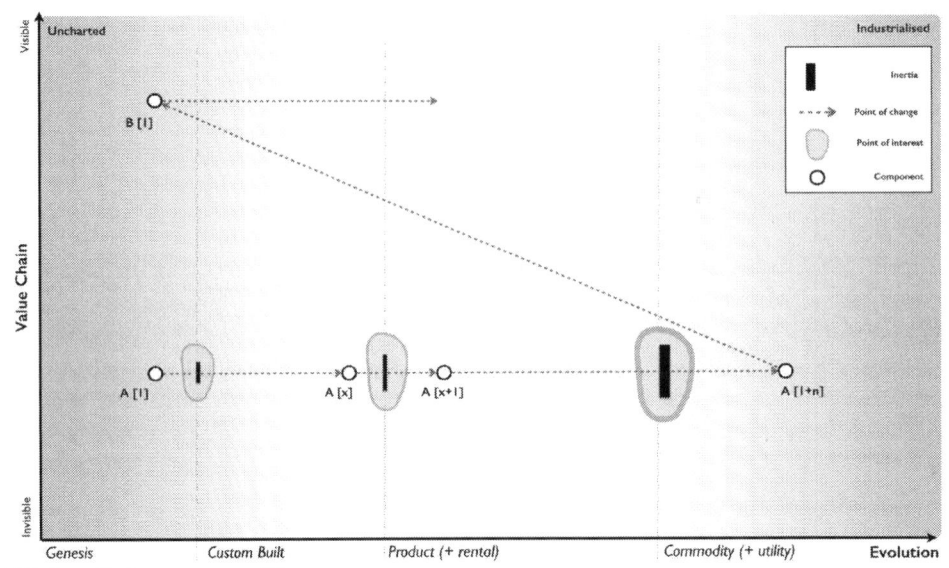

Figure 127: Inertia increases with success

There are also many forms of inertia. In the example of coevolution (provided in Chapter 9), there were two forms of inertia. The first is due to the success of past architectural practice. The second is caused by the co-evolving practice being relatively novel and hence, there existing high degrees of uncertainty over it. Both sources will create resistance due to adopting the change, which in this case is the shift from product to utility of computing (see Figure 128).

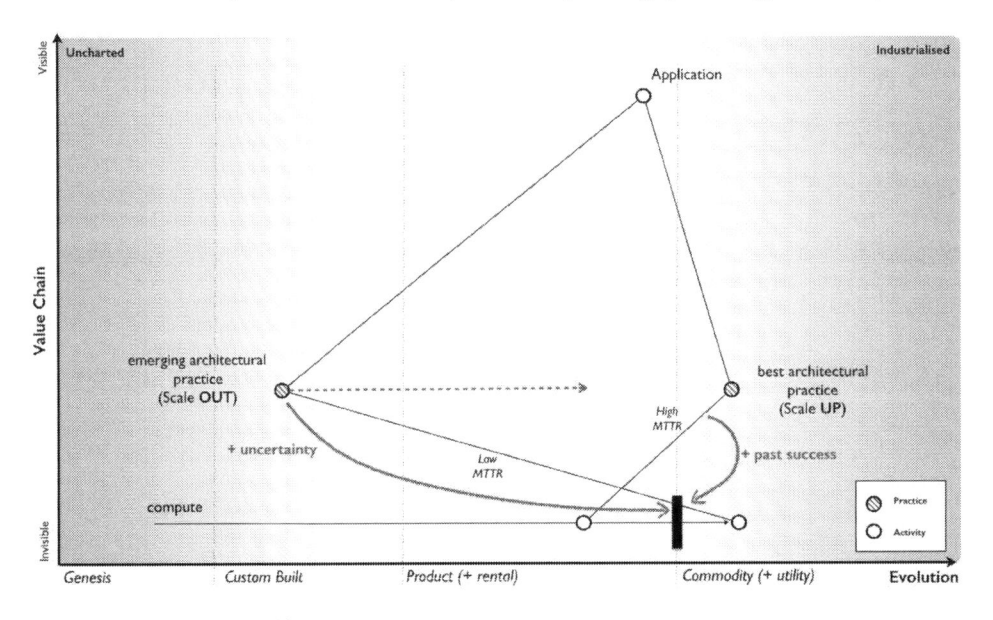

Figure 128: Practices and inertia

So what makes up inertia and this resistance to change exist in business? That depends upon the perspective of the individual and whether they are a consumer or supplier.

The Consumer

From a consumer of an evolving activity, a practice or a model of understanding then inertia tends to manifest itself in three basic forms – disruption to past norms, transition to the new, and the agency of new. I'll explain each using the example of cloud computing.

The typical concerns regarding the **disruption to past norms** include:-

- Changing business relationships from old suppliers to potentially new suppliers.
- A loss of in financial or physical capital through prior purchasing of a product, e.g. the previous investment needs to be written off.
- A loss in political capital through making a prior decision to purchase a product, e.g. "What do you mean I can now rent the billion dollar ERP system I advised the board to buy on a credit card?"
- A loss in human capital as existing skill-sets and practices change, e.g. server huggers.
- A threat that barriers to entry will be reduced, resulting in increased competition in an industry, e.g. even a small business can afford a farm of supercomputers.

The typical concerns regarding the **transition to the new** include:-

- Confusion over the new methods of providing the activity, e.g. isn't this just hosting?
- Concerns over the new suppliers as relationships are reformed, including transparency, trust and security of supply.
- Cost of acquiring new skill-sets as practices co-evolve, e.g. designing for failure and distributed architecture.
- Cost of re-architecting existing estates that consume the activity. For example, the legacy application estates built on past best practices (such as N+1, Scale-Up) and assume past methods of provision (i.e. better hardware) and will now require re-architecting.
- Concerns over changes to governance and management.

The typical concerns regarding the **agency of the new** include:-

- Suitability of the activity for provision in this new form, i.e. is the act really suitable for utility provision and volume operations?

- The lack of second sourcing options. For example, do we have choice and options? Are there multiple providers?
- The existence of pricing competition and switching between alternatives suppliers. For example, are we shifting from a competitive market of products to an environment where we are financially bound to a single supplier?
- The loss of strategic control through increased dependency on a supplier. These risks or concerns were typical of the inertia to change I saw with cloud computing in 2008. However, it wasn't just consumers that had inertia but also suppliers of past norms.

Suppliers of past norms

The inertia to change of suppliers inevitably derives from past financial success. For example, the shift from product to utility services is a shift from high-value model to one of volume operations, and over time, declining unit value. There is a transitional effect here that causes a high volume, high margin business for a period of time, but we will cover that later. In general, existing suppliers need to adapt their existing successful business models to this new world. Such a change is problematic for several reasons:-

- All the data the company has demonstrates the past success of current business models, and concerns would be raised over cannibalisation of the existing business.
- The rewards and culture of the company are likely to be built on the current business model, hence reinforcing internal resistance to change.
- External expectations of the financial markets are likely to reinforce continual improvement of the existing model, i.e. it's difficult to persuade shareholders and financial investors to replace a high margin and successful business with a more utility approach when that market has not yet been established.

For the reasons above, the existing business model tends to resist the change, and the more successful and established it is then the greater the resistance. This is why the change is usually initiated by those not encumbered by past success. The existing suppliers not only have to contend with their own inertia to change but also the inertia their customers will have. Unfortunately, the previous peaceful model of competition (e.g. one product vs another) will lull these suppliers into a false sense of gradual change, in much the same way that our existing experience of climate change lulls us into a belief that climate change is always gradual. This is despite ample evidence that abrupt climate change has occurred repeatedly in the past. For example, at the end of the Younger Dryas period, the climate of Greenland exhibited a sudden warming of +10°C within a few years. We are as much a prisoner of past expectations of change as past norms of operating.

Hence, suppliers with pre-existing business models will tend to view change as gradual and have resistance to the change, which in turn is reinforced by existing customers. This resistance of existing suppliers will continue until it is abundantly clear that the past model is going to decline. However, this has been compounded by the punctuated equilibrium, which combines exponential change with denial. Hence, by the time it has become abundantly clear and a decision is made, it is often too late for those past incumbents to survive. For a hardware manufacturer who has sold computer products and experienced gradual change for thirty years, it is understandable how they might consider this change to utility services would also happen slowly. They will have huge inertia to the change because of past success; they may view it as just an economic blip due to a recession, and their customers will often try to reinforce the past asking for more "enterprise", like services. Worst of all, they will believe they have time to transition, to help customers gradually change, to spend the years building and planning new services, and to migrate the organisation over to the new models. The cold, hard reality was that many existing suppliers didn't comprehend that the battle would be over in three to four years, and for many, the time to act was already passing. In 2008, they were in the last chance saloon and the clock was ticking towards last orders, though they claimed this event was far in the future and they had plenty of time. Like the rapid change in climate temperature in Greenland, our past experience of change does not necessarily represent the future.

In Figure 129, I've classified various forms of inertia, including tactics to be used to counter and various forms of messaging you might wish to consider in your struggle against it. When looking at a map, it's extremely helpful to identify the forms of inertia you will face and how to counter them before charging straight on into the battle. There's little worse than leading the charge into battle, only to discover that the rest of the organisation is still getting dressed for a party and is convinced the war is sometime next decade.

Category	Example	Tactic to counter	Counter points and messaging
Disruption of Past Norms	Change of business relationship (loss of social capital)	Vendor Management	Right for its time / Past has evolved / Point to other departments / Lead the charge
	Loss of existing financial or physical capital	Future Planning	Asset write down / Look to sweat and dump or dispose / Point to savings vs increasing running costs of legacy
	Loss of political capital	Modernisation	Emphasis on future agility & efficiency / Make the business aware / Building for the future
	Threat to barriers to entry	Unavoidable Change	Already happening in the market
Transition to the New	Investment in knowledge capital	Training	Cost of acquiring external skills will be high / motivation of staff
	Cost of acquiring new skillsets	Organisational development	Develop capabilities in-house / use hack days / use conferences / create centres of gravity
	Investment in new business relationships	Vendor Management	Developing relationships with the right suppliers / understanding the market
	Changes to governance, management and practices	Awareness of Co-evolution	Practices have to adapt as activities evolve / Point to other past practices
Agency of the New	Suitability	Weak Signals & prior identification	Examine ubiquity vs certainty
	Lack of second sourcing options	Supply Chain Management	Use and development of standards, open source options, limit feature use to reduce lock-in, use of abstraction layers)
	Lack of pricing competition	Market Analysis	Single or multiple vendors, examine switching costs, use of brokers
	Loss of strategic control	Strategic Planning	Examine buyer / supplier relationship, understand the market is commoditising and is now a volume operations game)
Business Model	Declining unit value	Awareness of Evolution	Avoid death spiral, Look at alternative opportunities e.g. ecosystem use
	Data for Past Success counteracts	Portfolio Management	Risk Mitigation, look at disposal / spin-off
	Resistance from rewards and culture	Human Resources	Higher rewards for adaptation, Education, Promote situational awareness
	External financial markets reinforce existing models	Analyst Relationships	Spinning a future story

Figure 129: Classifying inertia

One of the more dangerous forms of inertia are financial markets. Despite the illusion of the future thinking world of finance, in most cases, stability is prized. There is an expectation set by the market on past results and often significant discounting of the future. If anything, 2008 was a very visible reminder of this as the economy crumbled around us. The problem for a CEO of a hardware company at that time was the market comes to expect a certain level of profit, revenue, growth and return. There is only so much you can do to blame a change on general economic factors (e.g. a downturn), as the market expects you to return to norm and most executives are rewarded on short-term measures based upon this. The result is one of the most peculiar aspects of the "war" stage of competition — the death spiral.

Climatic Pattern: Inertia kills

I mentioned previously in Chapter 5 how Kodak had inertia, which it finally overcame in order to invest in exactly the wrong part of the industry. We often think that companies die due to lack of innovation, but this rarely appears to be the case. Kodak out-innovated most (with digital still cameras, with online photo services and with photo printers), but it was inertia caused by past success in fulfilment and blindness to the environment that caused it to collapse. Equally, Blockbuster out-innovated most competitors with its early entrance into the web space, being first with ordering videos online and the first experiments with video streaming. Alas, it was wedded to a business model based upon late fees. There are many different examples of how inertia, usually amplified by blindness to a change, can cause a company to crumble, but none is as common as the death spiral, and the cause of it is something that, at another time, is perfectly sensible — cutting costs.

If your industry (i.e. the parts of the value chain that you sell) are in a peace era then cutting costs through efficiency to increase profitability can be a good play, assuming you don't reduce barriers to entry into the space. There are many reasons why you would do this and often, you can clear out a lot of waste in the organisation. However, if your industry has moved into the war then cutting costs through staff to restore profitability due to declining revenue is often a terrible move. The problem is your revenue is eroding due to a change in the value chain and the industrialisation of the activity to more commodity forms. You need to respond by adapting and possibly moving up the value chain. However, by layoffs, you're likely to get rid of those people who were seen to be less successful in the previous era. That doesn't sound too bad, but the result is that you end up with a higher density of people successful in the past models (which are now in decline due to evolution) and hence, you'll tend to increase your cultural inertia to change. In all likelihood, you've just removed the very people who might have saved you.

Revenue will continue to drop and you'll start a death spiral. You'll start scrambling around, looking for "emerging markets", i.e. less developed economies for you to sell your currently being industrialised product into. The only result of this however is you're laying the groundwork for those economies to be later industrialised once your competitors have finished chewing up your existing market. What you of course should be doing is adapting and realising that the tactics you play in one era are not the same as another (peace vs war etc.). Now, any large organisations have multiple different value chains in different evolutionary phases, and you have to see this and know how to switch context between them in order to choose the right tactics. Naturally, most people don't manage to achieve this, nor do they effectively anticipate change or cope with industrialisation in the right way. This is why big companies often die, but at least that keeps things interesting.

Of course, if you do embark on the death spiral then, whilst it's appalling for those employed by the company, the executives are often rewarded. Why? Well, it comes back to the financial markets. If a market knows this transition is occurring then one tactic is to invest in the future industry (e.g. Amazon), whilst extracting as much short-term value as possible from the past (e.g. existing hardware players). This requires a high expectation of share buy-backs, dividends and mergers in those past giants. It's not that you're expecting a long-term gain from such investments, but instead, highly profitable short-term wins, which are balanced with your long-term investment in the future. From a financial point of view then the death spiral is exactly what you want to see as you don't care about the long-term survivability of the company (your investment will be gone by then), but you do want maximum extraction of value. If you're a canny executive then running a death spiral can bring big personal financial rewards, as long as you're comfortable with the destruction you'll cause to people and companies alike. However, not all executives are canny. Often, people find themselves in this position by accident. Which leads me to my next topic on the different forms of disruption.

The different forms of disruption

One of the more interesting discussions in recent times has been Professor Jill Lepore's arguments against Clayton Christensen's concept of disruptive innovation. In her now famous New Yorker 2014 article on "the disruption machine", Lepore argued that disruptive innovation doesn't really explain change, but is instead mostly an artefact of history, a way of looking at the past, and is unpredictable. Christensen naturally countered. For me, this really was a non-argument. What I had determined back in 2008 was there are many forms of disruption — some of which are predictable and some of which aren't. When the argument started then from my perspective, both Christensen and Lepore were right and wrong. The problem stems from the issue that they're not arguing over the same thing.

The three main forms of potential disruption that we will discuss are genesis, product to product substitution and product to utility business model substitution. The genesis of new acts are inherently unpredictable. If some novel activity appears that genuinely alters pre-existing value chains then there's little you can do to predict this; you have to simply adapt.

When product to product substitution occurs due to some new capability or feature then the predictability of when and what is low. The when depends upon individual actors' actions, and this is unknown. Equally, the addition of some new capability is also inherently unpredictable. Note, we know that things will evolve and the pathway for evolution (from genesis to commodity), but we don't know nor can we predict the individual steps, such as this product will beat that product. This means a new entrant can at any time create a disruptive product that will substitute an existing market, but a company will have no way of ascertaining when that will occur or what it will be. Though this does happen, in the time of peace, the time of product giants, then such changes are less frequent than the rampage of sustaining changes. There are exceptions, and Apple's iPhone disrupting the BlackBerry is a good example of this type of disruption. I'll note that Christensen quite famously dismissed the iPhone and has subsequently gone on to claim that it's not an example of it; in any case, this sort of substitution is unpredictable. Equally, hydraulic versus cable excavators would fall into this category. They are easy to analyse post event, but next to impossible to determine pre event. In these instances, Lepore seems to be on firm footing.

With product to utility substitution, the what and when can be anticipated. We know we're going to enter a state of war, an explosion of higher order systems, coevolution of practice, disruption of past vendors stuck behind inertia barriers and so forth. Weak signals and the four conditions (suitability, technology, concept and attitude) can give us an idea of when it will happen. In any case, even without the weak signals, the transition to more industrialised forms is inevitable if competition exists. So, we can be prepared. A new entrant can more effectively target this change to disrupt others. However, it also means an existing player can effectively mount a defence, having prior knowledge of the change and time to prepare. Fortunately, for the new entrants, the incredibly low levels of situational awareness that exists in most industries combined with the inertia faced by incumbents in terms of existing business models, developed practices, technological debt, behavioural norms, financial incentives, Wall Street expectations and self-interest are often insurmountable and hence, the startups often win when they shouldn't. Whilst the change is entirely defendable against (with often many decades of prior warning), companies fail to do so. This form of disruption is entirely predictable and it is here where Christensen's theory excels. The more industrialised forms are considered lower quality, not meeting the performance requirements, and usually dismissed by the incumbents.

Hence, let us follow the evolution of an act. We start (in Figure 130) with the appearance of some new activity A[1]. It is found useful and starts to diffuse with custom-built examples. As it evolves, early products start to appear and we jump across one inertial barrier, from custom-built to products (Point 1). Obviously, those companies that have invested in their own custom solution argue that their solution is better, but eventually, pressure mounts and they adopt a product. The act continues to evolve, with a constant stream of more "feature" complete products as we understand the space. Sometimes, the progression is sustaining but sometimes, a product appears that substitutes the previous examples. There's inertia to the change (Point 2) from customers and vendors invested in the existing product line. The thing is, we don't really know if this new product line is going to be successful, any more than Apple knew it could beat BlackBerry or others. This form of disruption is unpredictable. Someone wins. The product giants continue to grow until eventually, the act becomes suitable for industrialised provision.

New entrants jump the barrier first (Point 3) and this barrier is significant. That act has become established in many value chains and it is highly connected with its own practices. There's a lot of dismissal of the industrialised version, claims it will take a long time, but the punctuated equilibrium bites, the past vendors are struggling, practices have co-evolved and the old way is now legacy. Many past vendors start the death spiral in the hope of recapturing their glory days; their demise accelerates. This form of disruption was predictable, but for most, it wasn't. Of course, the world has moved on to inventing novel and new things built upon these industrialised components (Point 4); new forms of organisation appear based upon those co-evolved practices. A next generation of future giants has arisen. Whether we notice them depends upon whether the cycle is localised at a microeconomic scale to a specific industry, or in other cases, the component is so vastly connected that it appears at a macroeconomic scale. In any case, the cycle continues. Ba-da-boom, ba-da-bing.

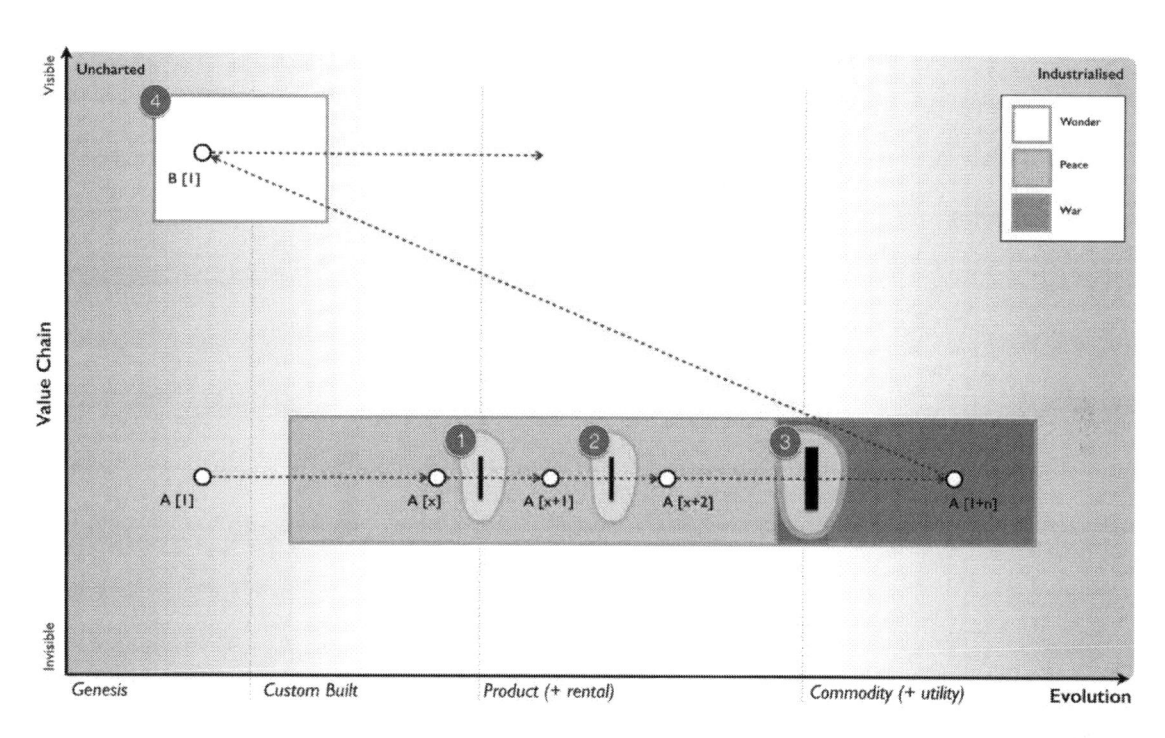

Figure 130: Different types of disruption

Dealing with disruption

The problem is there isn't one form of disruption and hence, there isn't one way to deal with it. The techniques and methods you need to use vary. Unfortunately, if you don't have a map of your landscape and you don't understand the basic climatic patterns then you don't have a great deal of chance in separating this. For most people, it's all the same thing, and they end up facing off against highly predictable disruption without any preparation or planning. In 2008, this was common in the computing industry. I'd end up with many arguments in boards, pointing out that cloud computing (the shift from product to utility) was inevitable and not a question of "if" but "when" and that "when" was starting now. I'd explain the impacts and how they were going to be disrupted and people would retort with product examples. They'd start discussing the current situation with Apple versus BlackBerry and how BlackBerry could counter. These weren't even remotely the same thing. Don't mix the unpredictable world of product versus product substitution with the predictable world of product to utility substitution. In Figure 131, I've provided three main types of disruption and the characteristics associated with each.

Evolutionary Change	Genesis (Uncharted)	Product to Product Substitution	Product to Utility (becoming industrialised)
Competitive State	Wonder	Peace	War
Competition characteristics	uncertain, fight to become established, time of marvels, time of discovery	relative competition, established players, sustaining exceeds disruptive change, time of highest profit, illusion of gradual change, strong inertia to change develops	fight for survival, new entrants, disruptive changes exceeds sustaining, co-evolution of practice, new organisational forms appear, punctuated equilibrium
Example	Powered flight	Apple vs RIM	Cloud Computing (IaaS)
Inertia	Moderate *(due to uncertainty)*	Moderate to High	High
Co-evolution of practice	No, practice has yet to develop	No, practice tends to remain stable	Yes
Prediction	Difficult *(due to uncertainty)*	Difficult on specifics *(due to uncertainty)*	What and when are both predictable many years in advance
Discovery	Horizon scanning	Horizon scanning	Situational awareness
Disruption	Difficult to determine what will be impacted	Difficult to Defend against	Trivial to defend against and anticipate
Doctrine — Focus on high situational awareness *(understand what is being considered)*	Minor role *(due to uncertainty)*	Minor role *(except in user needs)*	Key role
Doctrine — A bias towards action *(learn by playing the game)*	Key role	Key role	Minor role

Figure 131: Dealing with disruption

From the above:-

The genesis of powered flight was with Félix du Temple de la Croix in 1857. What? No Wright Brothers? Well, this came later, but since my American cousins get very sensitive on this topic, we will skip ahead to the much later. I'll just note Elliot Sivowitch's law of First — "Whenever you discover who was first, the harder you look, you'll find someone who was more first" — and hence, the first electric lightbulb was developed by Joseph Wilson Swan; the person who actually flew a kite into the night that was hit by lightning was Thomas-François Dalibard; and when it comes to the telephone, bar shenanigans with patent clerks then we owe a debt to Elisha Gray. Cue endless arguments and gnashing of teeth.

Let us however stick with the Wright Brothers, who invented powered flight to end all wars. The first planes sold to the US Army in 1909 were observation planes, and the common idea of the time was "With the perfect development of the airplane, wars will be only an incident of past ages." There was no existing practice associated with aircraft, there was some inertia to their adoption (similar to British concerns over the machine gun prior to World War I), and it was notoriously difficult to predict what would happen. Rather than airplanes ending all wars because no army could gain an advantage over another (all movements could be observed from the air), a rather different path of development occurred and bombs and machine guns were soon attached. With the genesis of such an act like powered flight, it's difficult to anticipate what might change, and your only defence is to adapt quickly. In such circumstances, a cultural bias towards action, i.e. quickly responding to the change, is essential. With the example of Apple versus RIM (i.e. BlackBerry) then similar characteristics exist. There are existing practices, but a different type of smartphone product does not significantly change this. Again, the main way to react is to spot the change quickly (through horizon scanning) and have developed a culture with a bias towards action. These sorts of change are notoriously difficult to defend against. In the case of cloud computing then there was high levels of inertia and coevolution of practice to tackle. However, the change was highly predictable and trivial to defend against. Despite this, most failed to react.

Some final thoughts

We've covered a lot in this section, from refinement of the peace, war and wonder cycle to the introduction of different climatic patterns, to the manner in which organisations evolve and the different forms of disruption. There are a couple of things I want to call out in particular.

Do the states of peace, war and wonder really exist?

No, it's just a model and all models are wrong. The model appears to predict secondary effects such as organisational change; it is developed from first principles of competition and there seems to be historical precedent. However, it's no more than appearance at the moment until such time as I can confirm future points of industrialisation, and even then I still have the question of whether that was just luck.

Do the states just affect individual activities in industries or could they have a wider effect?

The cycle's effect depends upon how connected the components are. If they're involved in many value chains then this can have a pronounced macroeconomic effect. When considering economic systems, we have to look at them as we do with biological systems and consider how an ecosystem reacts to a change and how competition will drive that change throughout the system.

Can we anticipate organisational change?

We know roughly when such changes should occur (from weak signals), though we cannot detail what the impact will be, as in whether new doctrine will appear or what doctrine will refine. Population dynamics in companies is a non-trivial exercise due to inherent bias in questions and responses. However, we can at least say something reasonable about the process of change and its likelihood.

Is life getting faster?

Certainly, the evolution of acts appears to have accelerated, but don't confuse that with a higher rate of innovation. It's highly questionable whether we have become more innovative as a species, though we certainly can't rely on novel things to create a differential for long. Furthermore, be careful to avoid confusing multiple and coincidental points of industrialisation with a general change of speed.

There are also a number of climatic patterns that I've mentioned, which are worth noting.

- **Evolution of a communication mechanism can increase the speed of evolution overall.** Not only can evolution not be measured over time but the speed of evolution is not constant over time.
- **Inertia increases with past success.** Be careful with inertia; it will grow and tempt you away from change, even when you must.
- **Inertia kills.** It's rarely lack of innovation that gets you, but past success.

- **Change is not always linear.** Not all change is smooth and progressive; some is very rapid, and be wary of being caught out by a slow-moving past.
- **Shifts from product to utility tend to exhibit a punctuated equilibrium.** Probably one of the most dangerous times or the biggest opportunity, depending upon whether you're an incumbent or new entrant.
- **There are many different forms of disruption (two broad classes are predictable versus non-predictable).** Don't get caught into the trap of thinking that all disruption is the same.
- **A point of "war" is associated with organisational change.** It's not just things that evolve but entire organisations.

I've marked off all the patterns we've covered so far in grey in Figure 132.

Components	Everything evolves through supply and demand competition	Rates of evolution can vary by ecosystem (e.g. consumer vs industrial)	Characteristics change as components evolve (Salaman & Storey)	No choice over evolution (Red Queen)
	No single method fits all (e.g. in development or purchasing)	Components can co-evolve (e.g. practice with activity)	Evolution consists of multiple waves of diffusion with many chasms.	Commoditisation <> Centralisation
Financial	Higher order systems create new sources of value	Efficiency does not mean a reduced spend (Jevon's Paradox)	Capital flows to new areas of value	Creative Destruction (Joseph Schumpeter)
	Future value is inversely proportional to the certainty we have over it.	Evolution to higher order systems results in increasing local order and energy consumption		
Speed	Efficiency enables innovation	Evolution of communication mechanisms can increase the speed of evolution overall and the diffusion of a single example of change	Increased stability of lower order systems increases agility & speed of re-combination	Change is not always linear (discontinuous & exponential change exists)
	Shifts from product to utility tend to demonstrate a punctuated equilibrium			
Inertia	Success breeds inertia	Inertia can kill an organisation	Inertia increases the more successful the past model is	
Competitors	Competitors actions will change the game	Most competitors have poor situational awareness		
	Not everything is random (p(what) vs p(when))	Economy has cycles (peace, war and wonder)	Two different forms of disruption (predictable vs non-predictable)	A "war" (point of industrialisation) causes organisations to evolve
Prediction	You cannot measure evolution over time or adoption, you need to embrace uncertainty.	Evolution consists of multiple diffusion curves	The less evolved something is then the more uncertain it becomes	

Figure 132: Climatic patterns

An exercise for the reader

The first thing I'd like you to do is to look at Figure 124 — the change from traditional to next generation — and determine what type your organisation is. Are you adopting those principles or is there some context-specific reason as to why you cannot? Have you challenged this?

The second thing I'd like you to do is look at your maps and start to consider what sort of inertia you might face in changing the landscape. Use Figure 129 — classifying inertia — as a guide.

Lastly, I want you to try and discover components in your value chains that are on the cusp of becoming industrialised and shifting from product forms. Ask yourself, are you prepared for such a rapid change? What planning have you in place? How will you deal with the inertia?

Chapter 11 - A smorgasbord of the slightly useful

"Here's one I made earlier" is the staple diet of TV programmes when faced with the possibility that something might go wrong. Demonstrations are always a risky business. In the case of this book, doubly so. I want to let you loose on a scenario but alas, I'm not even there to correct things if it all goes pear-shaped. To manipulate the odds slightly in my favour of a beneficial result then before we get to the scenario (Chapters 12 and 13), I'm going to cover some aspects of mapping in a little more detail. This is somewhat naughty because these ideas being fresh in your mind are likely to create a bias, which is exactly what I'm hoping for. I'm signposting the answer before we've even got there. It's the closest I could get to "Here's one I made earlier" without writing down the answer first.

However, to make the exercise still challenging then I've taken the liberty of hiding the clues throughout this chapter, which is interspersed with lots of useful but not directly relevant concepts in a smorgasbord of the slightly useful. The concepts we will examine are on the opportunity of change, the trouble with contracts, common lies we tell ourselves and how to master strategy.

Opportunity of change

Activities, practices, data and knowledge all evolve and co-evolve in a process that is not always smooth or continuous. In Chapter 10, we covered the peace, war and wonder cycle, and how previous giants in a peaceful product phase of competition can be overtaken by new entrants in the "war". Those new entrants are likely to settle down to become the titans of that industry. The most interesting aspect of this cycle is in the change (Point 1 in Figure 133) between the two states of peace and war, and it's here we will focus.

Whilst the act (e.g. computing) may be well understood, this transition (e.g. computing shifting from products such as servers to utility services such as cloud) causes a great deal of confusion because the nature of the act is changing — we're moving from a world of constant feature differentiation to a world of volume operations of good enough. This change is compounded by co-evolved practices (such as DevOps), our inertia to it, the surprising speed at which it occurs, and vested interests usually spreading all manner of fear, uncertainty and doubt.

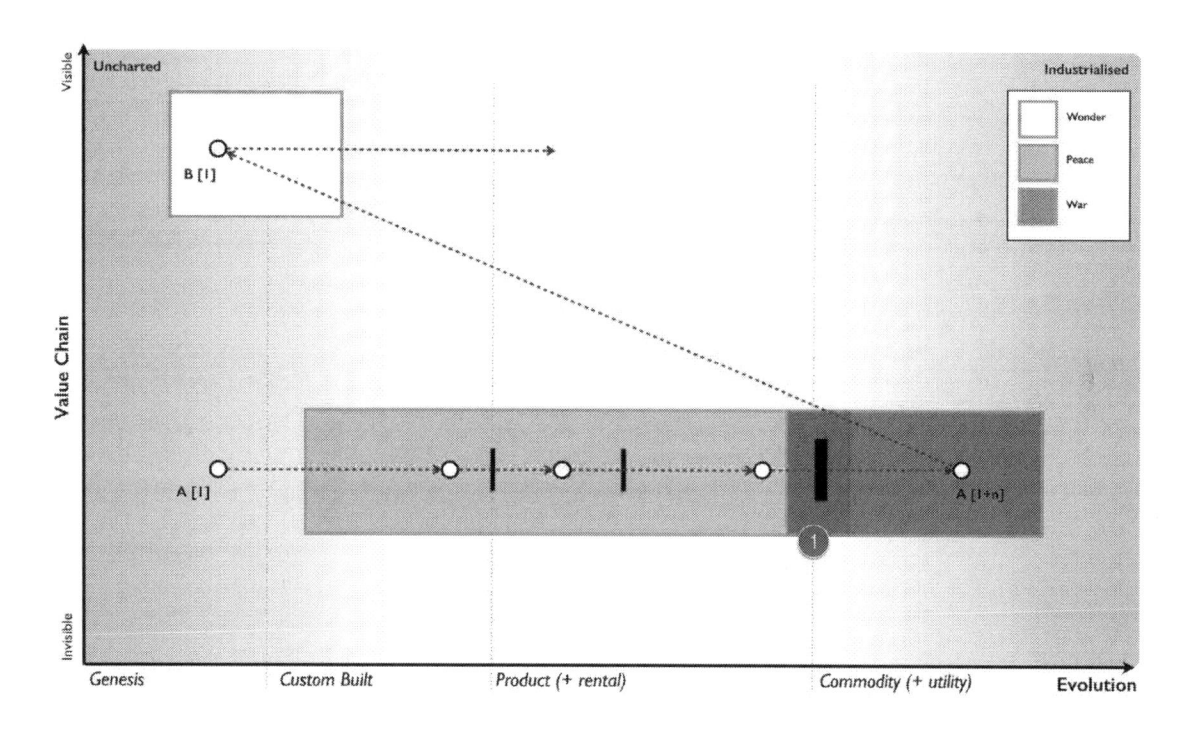

Figure 133: A time of change

Behind the confusion, what is fundamentally occurring is the rise of new standards, the de facto optimisation of a market and a shift towards commodity. This doesn't mean that alternatives aren't available; we often have a battle over standards, e.g. AC versus DC in the "electricity wars" or VHS versus Betamax for video recording standards. It's however marketplace adoption and network effects that will choose the winner and consign others to the niche of history. It's important to understand that in the early stages then everything is up for grabs.

Alternatives in Cloud Computing

When Amazon launched EC2 (its utility compute environment) in 2006, I made a number of calls to executives in traditional hardware companies and offered to help them set up a competing service using our Borg technology — a suite of tools that we had used to provide on-demand virtual machines within my own company. I was confident we could easily emulate the APIs of Amazon, and though we were behind the game in some areas, we were ahead in others. Overwhelmingly, there was no interest, and the couple of meetings I managed to arrange always ended up with the same result — "how will this help us sell more servers?"

I'd like to say that by 2008, the attitude had changed, but it hadn't. In late 2008, in the first of many such trips, I flew to the US, met a number of executives, told them their entire hardware business would be lost, showed them how by creating a market of AWS clones and creating a price war, they could exploit a constraint that Amazon would have in building data centres and use this to fragment the market by pushing demand beyond supply. I explained why they wouldn't do this due to existing inertia and why they would lose the war. The lack of interest was beyond palpable; it was dismissive. Amazon was not considered a threat but a minnow, and only a "madman" would think otherwise. To paraphrase what I was told, these companies would be "doing something in the future in that market, creating their own standards and taking this industry away from Amazon if it ever became serious", which they assured me it wouldn't. In all but actual words, the message was clearly, "go away little boy and let the grown-ups deal with this in a responsible manner". The air was always thick with endless prognostications of their own future greatness, along with the old trope of "how will your stuff sell more servers?"

The truth be told, I did feel like the naughty boy pointing at the Emperor and going, "He's got no clothes on!" It was like staring generals in the face and telling them that ordering troops to continue walking north over a cliff wasn't a good idea and getting a gentle pat on the head or a pinch on the cheeks with the kindly guffaw of "Walking north is what we do!"

The problem with evolution in business is the threat is much larger than most realise due to the punctuated equilibrium and the rapid speed of change. You can either create a large ecosystem fast, which means a very focused effort around creating a marketplace based upon some form of open standards, or you can co-opt and eventually aim to own the standard. What you cannot afford to do is dilly dally, rest on your laurels or try to create another differentiated product solution to compete against evolution. Unfortunately, this is exactly what happened. The companies that have lost the cloud war had all the advantage — they had the finances, the skills, the talent, the reach, the brand and everything you could possibly want to win it. They were like generals in charge of massive modern armies going up against a David armed with a sling and a spud gun. Fortunately for David, the generals all ordered their troops to walk north, over the cliff and to their doom.

The cloud war in infrastructure was lost, not due to some magical engineering capability of Amazon, but instead due to executive failure of past giants. Every single one of them could have won the war with ease. When they finally did act, it was too late, with too little investment and often in the wrong direction because of a preoccupation with what they wanted ("selling servers") and not what their users needed. But users also had inertia to this change, and in a somewhat tragic act of desperation, this was seized upon. Past giants had found their Kodak moment.

The Kodak moment of cloud

When Kodak had finally overcome its own inertia to the shift to digital images, it solved the conflict with its traditional fulfilment business by promoting the idea of the digital photo printer. They would bring fulfilment of photo printing into this digital world! It tanked because users just started sharing images and bypassed the whole point of the traditional photo. In the cloud world, this same tragic mistake has been created with the private cloud. We will bring you all the benefits of volume operations with commodity components through a public provider, but using enterprise-like hardware customised to your needs and running in your own data centre! In other words, they planned to bring "selling servers" into this utility world.

Certainly, private cloud has some merit for dealing with inertia (i.e. often unjustified security concerns), but this is a transitional play at best. It's short-lived and it's not the end game. Alas, even today, in 2017, there are people arguing that the future is a hybrid mix of public and private cloud. It's not, it never has been. The future has always been a hybrid of multiple public clouds. But why multiple public clouds? The first concern is resilience, which is solved through those co-evolved practices such as distributed systems and design for failure. Now, multiple public clouds doesn't necessarily mean multiple public cloud providers. You could use multiple Amazon regions or availability zones, and that is a hybrid model. The decision to use multiple providers is a trade between the risk of a single provider failure, the cost of switching between multiple providers, and any bargaining power it might provide.

Within the Amazon ecosystem then the cost of switching between regions is low, your bargaining power is relatively weak, but you can mitigate risks by designing across many zones. For many, this is more than adequate. When you need to go that extra mile and combine multiple public providers then you're incurring an increased cost of switching, not only through any movement of data but also any change in the syntactic or semantic compatibility of APIs. Syntactic compatibility simply means the APIs have the same structure and form. Semantic means they operate in the same way. Without this compatibility then your management tools that work with one might not work with another, and that incurs a cost of transition.

To reduce this cost then either you want multiple public providers that are interoperable or management tools that cover both. But management tools can only cover both by offering the lowest common denominator, i.e. the common factors between both. Unless you have a way of ensuring interoperability then switching incurs an additional cost beyond the movement of data, through either transition costs or some loss of useful functionality. But switching is still desirable in terms of bargaining power and ensuring competitive pricing in a market. These are the trade-offs that you need to consider. Well, in practice, you don't. There is no interoperable and competitive market between multiple providers. There is instead one continent (Amazon), some substantial islands, and then a lot of small atolls, most of which are sinking fast into the sea. But it didn't have to be this way, nor will it necessarily stay this way.

If I go back to the Zimki plan (Figure 134) then along with creating an ecosystem model around a serverless platform, we also intended to create a marketplace of platform providers, and we hoped for a marketplace of infrastructure providers. It's worth making a distinction here. You have a consumer ecosystem (as in companies or individuals that use your component), a supplier ecosystem (as in companies or individuals that provide components for you to use), and a marketplace (of consumers and suppliers around a component). These are not the same.

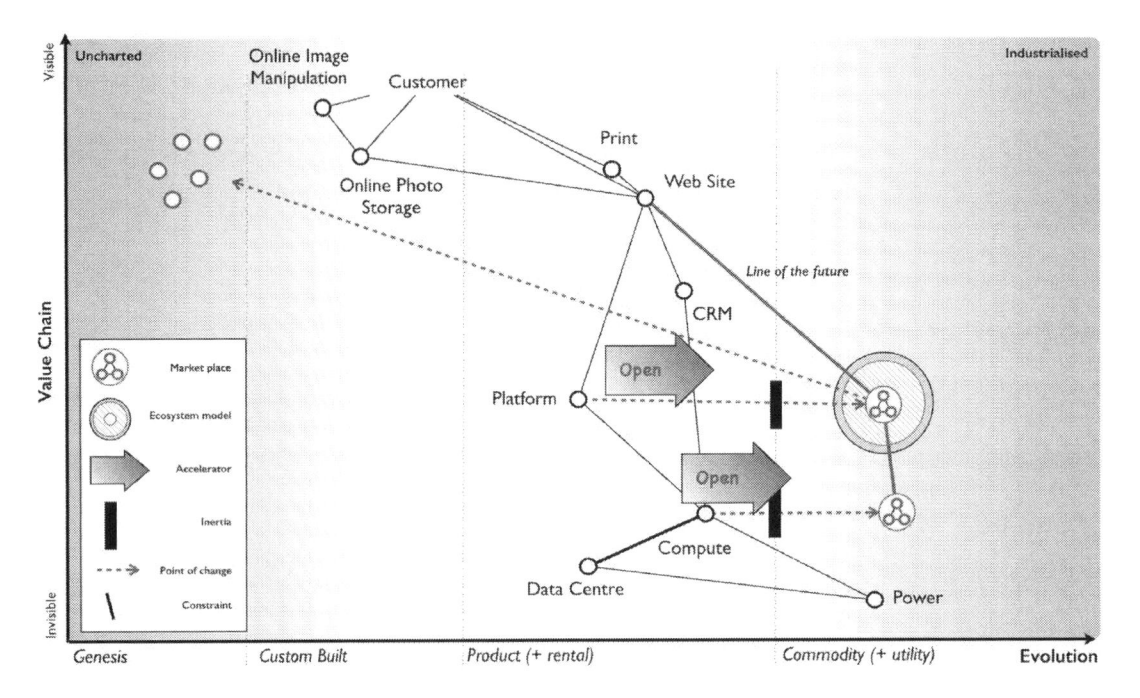

Figure 134: Marketplace or ecosystem or both?

In the case above, we aimed to build a consumer ecosystem around our platform as a service, i.e. we hoped many others would consume our component, enabling us to run that "innovate-leverage-commoditise" model and to sense future change. We also aimed to provide a marketplace of providers (i.e. to enable others to set up as platform players) in order to overcome concerns over lock-in to a single provider. To achieve this, we had announced the open sourcing of Zimki along with testing services to enable others to become Zimki providers.

However, in our value chain, we also consumed components of infrastructure from others and hence, it was advantageous to us (for reasons of pricing competition) that our ecosystem of suppliers consisted of a competitive marketplace with interoperability and easy switching between them. We intended to achieve this by open sourcing Borg (our infrastructure play), which would co- opt the APIs of any major utility provider if it appeared. Hence my early phone calls to those executives offering to provide them with an Amazon competitor.

Open sourcing a technology not only enables that component to evolve quickly but it can help in creating an interoperable marketplace with switching between providers, especially when combined with testing services. The last part is crucial, as there is always the danger that providers will try to differentiate with features in a commodity market, creating what's known as a collective prisoner dilemma — everyone weakening their own position and that of others through self-interest. Unfortunately, whilst this was my plan in 2005, the entire project had been killed off in 2007 for not being "the future". By the time the hardware executives finally woke up and started to play an open source game around OpenStack in 2010, they invested far too little and far too late. They failed to co-opt (arguing for differentiation) and failed to prevent a collective prisoner dilemma forming.

It's water under the bridge but if the competitors had reacted more timely, put in enough investment, focused on co-opting APIs, created a price war to force up demand beyond supply due to Amazon's constraint, then we might have seen a vibrant marketplace of many providers. Instead, we've seen not only industrialisation of computing infrastructure to utilities but also centralisation towards Amazon. This is another point to highlight in this sorry tale. Industrialisation does not necessarily mean centralisation. What it means is standardisation to a de facto. The question of whether something centralises or decentralises is influenced by other factors beyond evolution, including executive gameplay.

The reason why Amazon dominates the market is because it has played the game well, whilst most competitor executives have failed, despite all their advantage. Equally, this is not a permanent state of affairs. A better set of players may emerge (e.g. from China) and cause the market to decentralise. The game however becomes much harder once a standard becomes established and the victors of the war have emerged. The time to change the players and to play the game well is in the overlap between the states of peace and war during the change from product to utility. If you miss this then to change the game again requires a bloody battle of attrition to unseat a titan, a game of last man standing and often political intrigue. It is unlikely that those who so spectacularly lost this battle will have the skill to win such a war of attrition.

For infrastructure, this shift from peace to war has long passed and the victors have emerged. For the "serverless" platform world, we're in the midst of this change at the moment. The war has been raging but it will soon be over. By 2020, we should probably know who the winners and losers will be.

Opportunity on a map can be found in several places. From the genesis of the novel or the provision of unmet needs or differentiation of a product or the time of transition from one state (e.g. peace) to another (e.g. war) — see Figure 135.

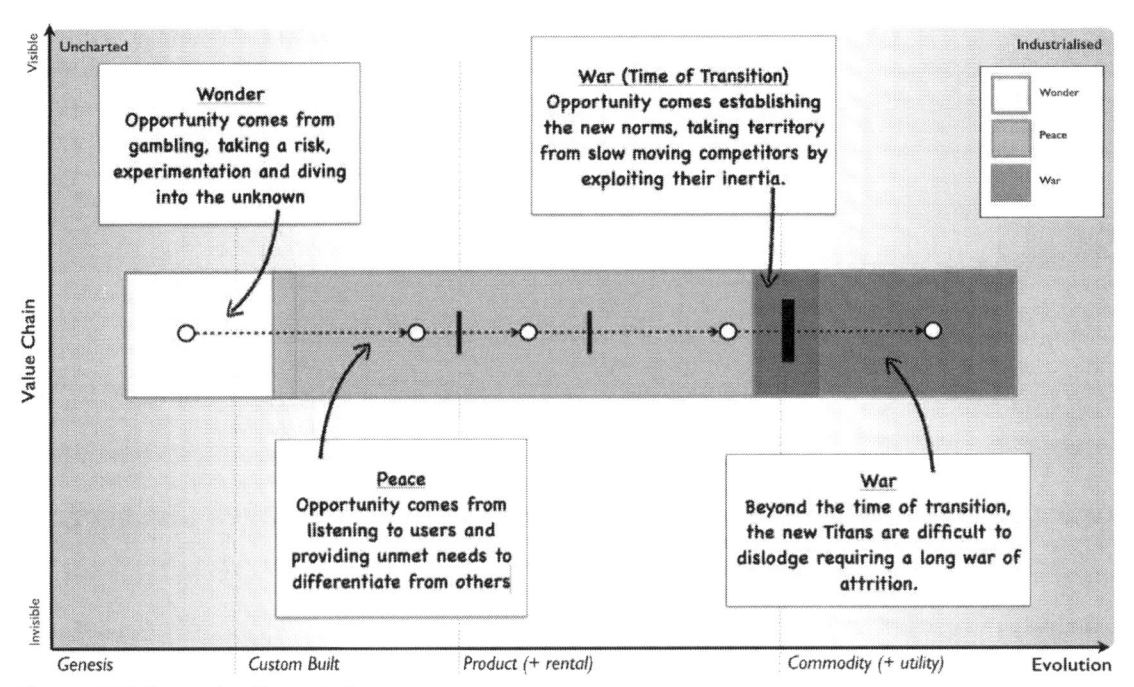

Figure 135: Opportunity and change

The maps won't tell you what path you should take but they are a guide to help you discuss and decide.

The trouble with contracts

Contracts like plans are often the bane of my life. It's not that they don't have a use; they do in terms of setting expectations. Unfortunately, for some reason that I have yet to fathom, people tend to invoke mystical properties around contracts. They tend to believe that the contract or plan represents a reality that is foretold — "If it's in the contract then it must happen as it is written." This is quickly followed by disappointment and disputes when it doesn't. But surely, that's the point of the contract — "We want to know what is being delivered!"

To explain why that principle is the problem then I'm going to use an example for a communication platform for a large organisation with a distributed workforce that often worked on events. This organisation had a detailed plan for the communication platform, an exhaustive specification (hundreds of pages) and a division of the system into lots for contracting. It all seemed very sensible. However, as is my usual style, when I first met the team, I then asked the question — "What is the user need?"

The responses were somewhat elusive and wispy. It was felt that the answers were in the pages of the specification, but they were not to hand. No-one had put them together. So, we spent a few hours and mapped the system out (see Figure 136). The basic user needs were device to device communication (e.g. "I need to tell Joe to pick up a box"), point to multiple points (e.g. "I need to tell all my team to come to Sheffield"), emergency function (e.g. "We need more staff at this event"), scheduling (e.g. "I need to know where to go next") to various applications, video recording and even simple use as a telephone.

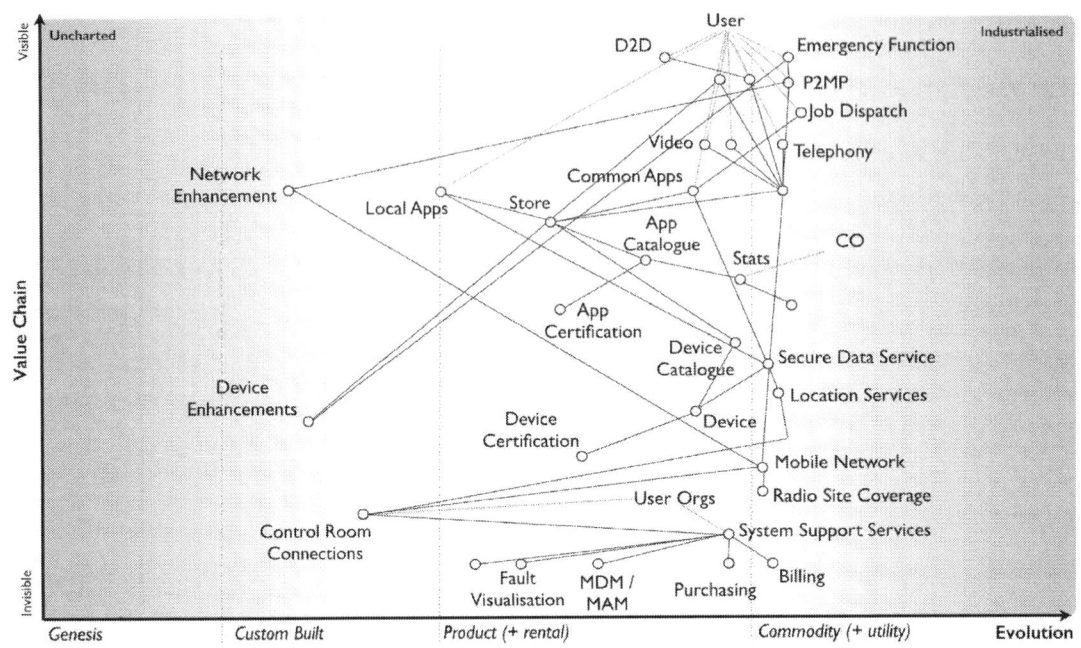

Figure 136: Communication Platform

To make the system manageable, the organisation had broken it down into what it considered to be sensible contracts, based broadly upon financial value and other characteristics. However, when I overlaid those contract "lots" onto the map then there was an obvious problem. One lot, known as "C", was very broad, including items that were industrialised and others that were highly specialised, often custom-made (see Figure 137).

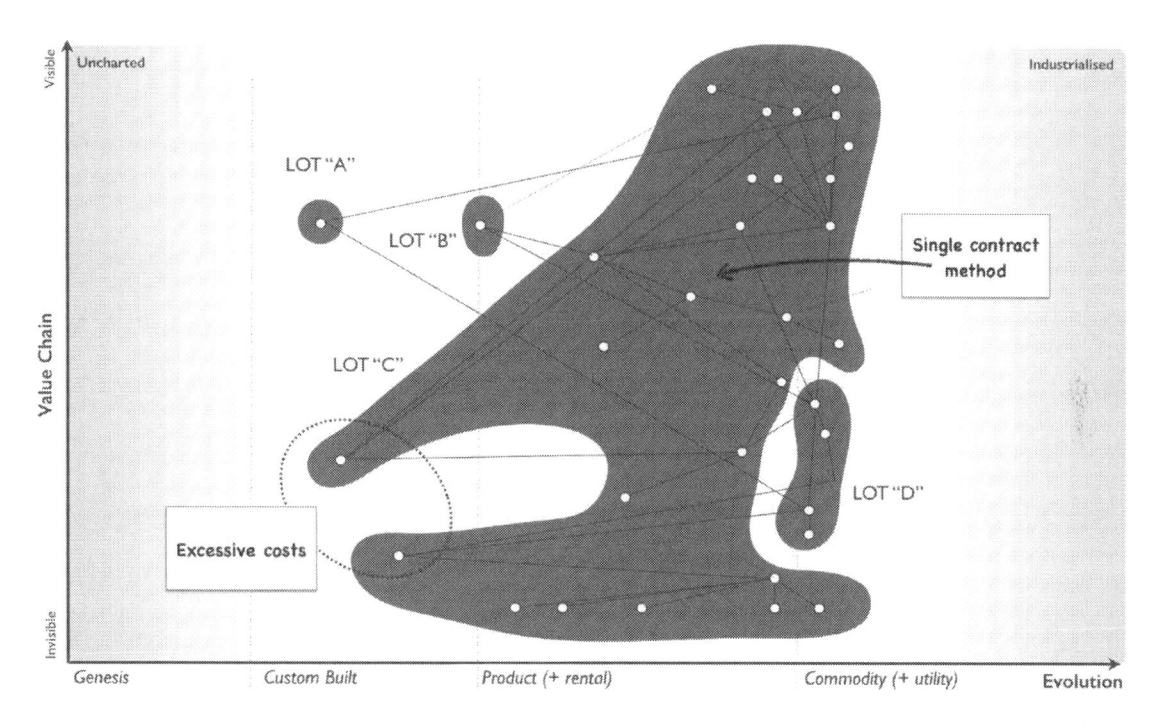

Figure 137: Trouble with outsourcing

Why is this a problem? Let us assume we apply an outsourcing contract to Lot "C" for delivery against some specification. Obviously, we want to know what's being delivered, hence we put effort into writing the specification. We have some form of competitive tender process that many potential suppliers bid for.

We hope the suppliers will naturally try to be competitive in their bids. However, in order to do so then the suppliers need to manage their own risks. One of the risks is the change of specification. For example, if you asked me to bid for providing 10 tons of gold and I won the lot with a competitive price, then it would be for delivering 10 tons of gold and not 10 tons of platinum or 10 tons of diamonds. If you change the specification then I'm going to charge you.

In any system governed by such contracts and specification then there will be a change control process as it's only reasonable that if we change our mind then we incur the cost of this. These change control processes tend to be burdensome and expensive because they're designed for minimising change and for delivering against the specification. Even a simple change can incur rewrites of the specification, analysis of impacts and many other steps that add up to considerable costs.

But look again at the map above and in particular, Lot "C". Some of the components are industrialised, which means they are unlikely to change and are suited to this contract approach. We can specify what we want here. However, some of the components are nearer the uncharted space. We don't know what we want here, no-one does. These components will change and we will incur that change control cost. The problem is that we're applying a principle of "we want to know what is being delivered" to components that we cannot possibly know what is going to be delivered. The one thing we can guarantee with those custom-built activities is they will change. We are doomed to invoke the expensive change control cost process at the point the contract is signed. The cost will spiral and dispute will happen.

Let me be crystal clear. We can anticipate dispute, even though we haven't yet started. I can also tell you that some fool of a Took will decide that the solution to this problem for future projects is "better specification". This will not only increase the costs in trying to describe the unknown but repeats the same mistake of change control costs by trying to define the unknown. Unfortunately, without mapping the environment and overlaying the contract structure then you won't be able to find this problem until you hit it, i.e. after the contracts are signed. Specification documents and business process diagrams don't provide you with the situational awareness you need for sensible contracting.

In 2008, I would commonly see this problem. Outsourcing had already got a bad name, but in truth, the problem isn't outsourcing — it isn't even contracts — it's the way we apply such approaches across very broad systems containing both industrialised and often novel components. There's a far better way to deal with such systems.

FIRE

One case worthy of praise in business is the truly marvellous work of Lieutenant Colonel Dan Ward. If you've never read FIRE or the Simplicity Cycle then stop what you're doing (i.e. reading this) and go read them. I first came across FIRE (fast, inexpensive, restrained and elegant) when it was called FIST (fast, inexpensive, simple and tiny) and was used in military circles. The rename is more about a reboot to make it applicable to the wider marketplace. I happen to prefer the old term (probably my own inertia for having used it) because it's just a bit more punchy.

Fast means build things quickly, i.e. short time scales. It's a constraint on time and reduces the risks of change, which comes with long schedules. Inexpensive is more than a constraint on budget; it's a mindset of thrift and re-use. Simple is a constraint on complexity but also a mindset for the pleasing elegance of simplicity. It's less about adding on more but taking stuff away. Whereas the A10 Warthog is an example of elegant simplicity in ground attack aircraft, the F35 is the polar opposite. Tiny means small, as in constrained or restrained, as in small budgets, short schedules, small documents, small teams and small components. It's again about mindset, a love of the detail and of self-control. It's about saying, "Do we really want to add short take off and vertical landing to our bombing run, ground attack, air-to-air combat and reconnaissance aircraft?"

Fast + Inexpensive + Restrained + Elegant = FIRE

Taking these FIRE principles, I've applied them to our map of a communication platform from above, which I've broken down into small, discrete areas, avoiding any broad systems, i.e. no mixing of industrialised with the uncharted. Each of these areas should be managed using small budgets, short schedules — see Figure 138.

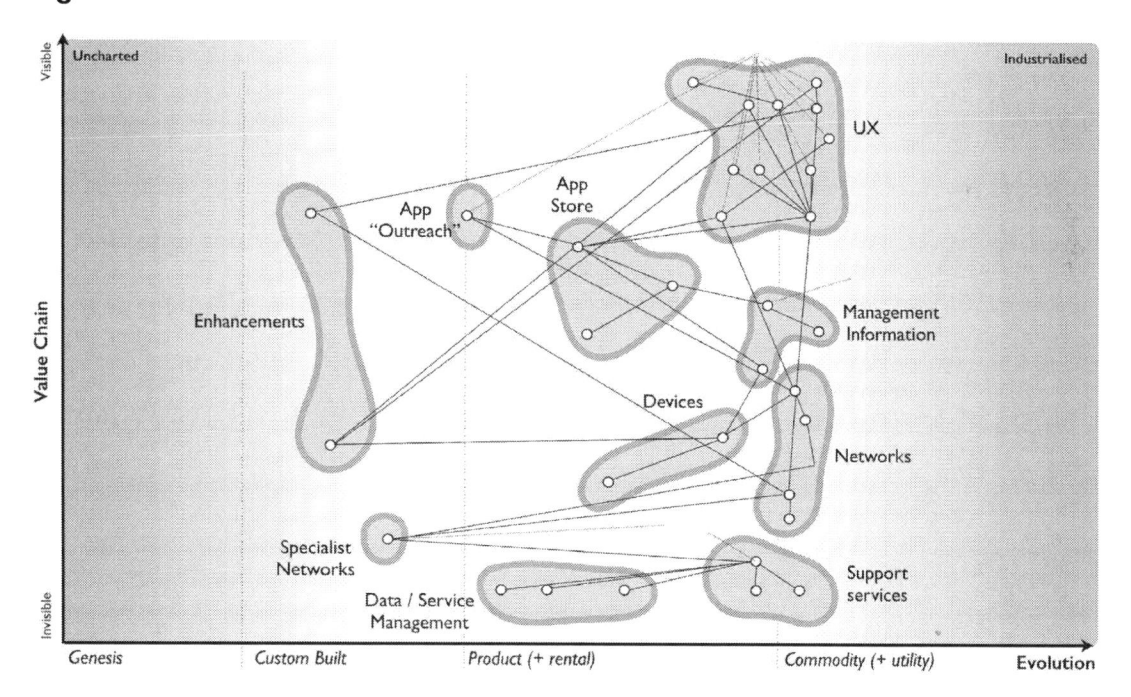

Figure 138: FIRE

With such a map, we can now apply the use of appropriate methods and techniques. For the more industrialised components, we can look to re-use market standards or outsourcing arrangements under detailed specification or even utility providers such as cloud services. For the more novel, we can build in-house or have contracts based upon time and material basis (see Figure 139).

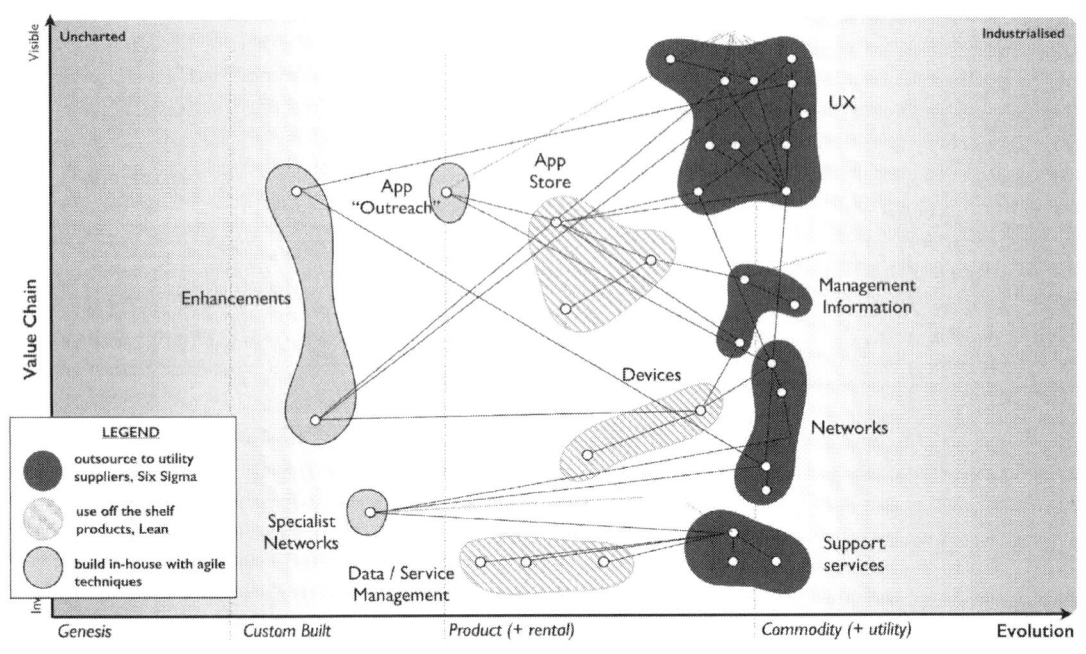

Figure 139: Using standard components and appropriate methods

It's worth noting that with novel items then you will tend to try and build these in-house. There are alternatives. You could outsource them under a time and material basis to a group that specialises in the experimentation required, but this is a different type of arrangement from outsourcing under a specification or volume operations. You might even outsource the novel to the market, i.e. just let the market get on with discovering what is there and take a back seat until the component becomes more evolved. Procrastination can be a useful tool if consciously used as such, and with a good understanding of the landscape.

We can also use the map to organise ourselves with small teams, distributing power away from some central planning office and giving autonomy and control to those on the "ground", at the "coalface", who can make decisions more quickly and with a greater understanding of detail (see Figure 140).

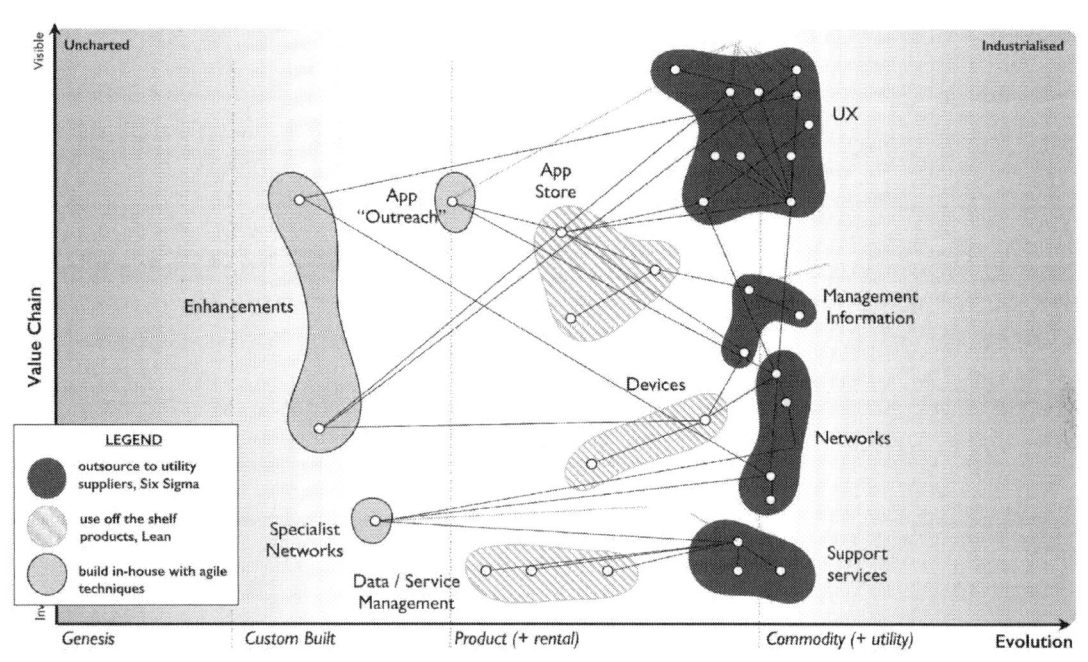

Figure 140: Distribute power

Using appropriate methods, tighter control on schedules and budgets with empowered people — what's not to like? Actually, there's often huge resistance to this.

It's all too difficult

Despite all the horrors caused and the endless stream of disasters, there is one commonly cited advantage of the all-encompassing contract that seems to trump everything. The advantage is that it makes it simple to manage. The unpleasant old phrase of "one throat to choke" comes to mind. In practice, it provides someone else to blame when things go wrong or as change control costs spiral (as they would in the original contract structure).

Of course, the vendor will blame you for not knowing what you wanted, thus leading to the endless calls for better specification, which only exacerbates the problem. We inevitably fall for this in business because of the fear of taking the risk, of managing what we need to manage, of embracing the complexity and uncertainty that exists. We fool ourselves (despite all the evidence) into believing that we can outsource this risk through massive, one size fits all contracts using detailed specification. To compound this, given enough time, we even outsource the skills we need to effectively negotiate "reasonable" terms (if such a thing exists) for these contracts. These problems are acute in business but generally swept under the carpet. They are more visibly exposed in Government contracts with Government IT and "horrendous, costly failure" being synonymous in some quarters.

The normal reaction to breaking down a complicated (and possibly complex) system is that it makes it difficult to manage. It exposes many areas to consider, many teams and many interfaces (see Figure 141). The reality is that those areas and interfaces existed beforehand and the use of large (and broad) contracts is just a way of trying to make it someone else's responsibility to manage. We are often willing participants in a game where to avoid managing the environment then we accept excessive cost overruns, inappropriate methods, loss of strategic control and ultimately greater risk, whilst claiming the approach reduces risk. Outsourcing is a global practice that is often disparaged in the popular press due to these associations.

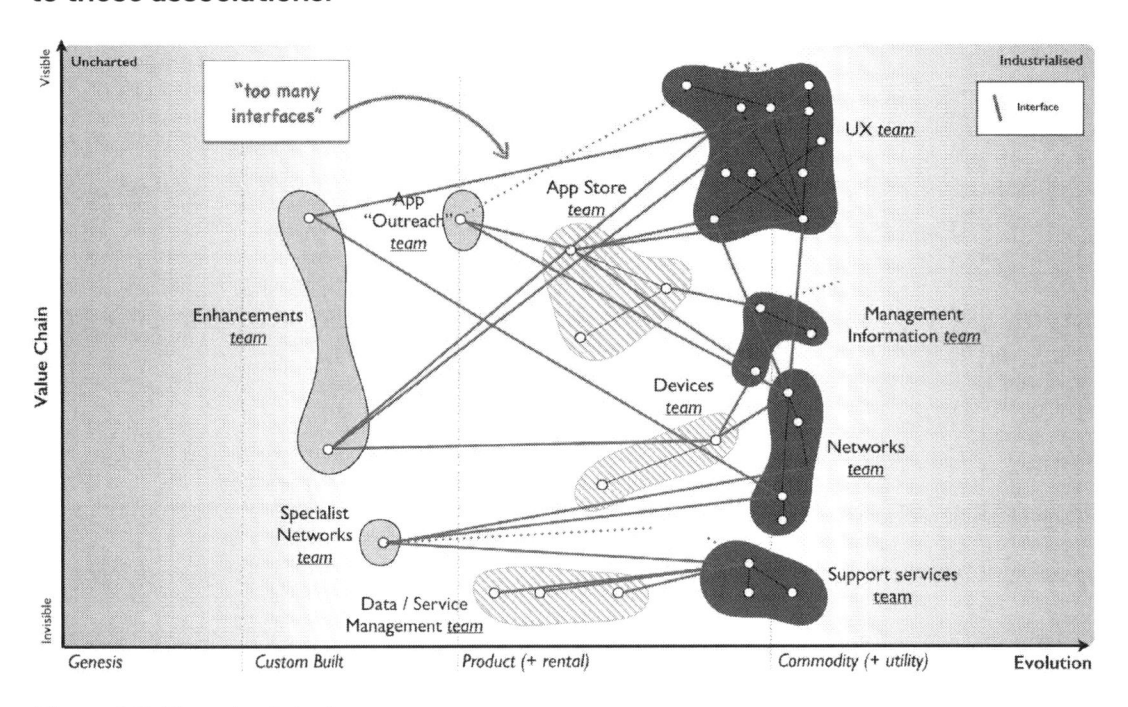

Figure 141: Exposing interfaces

I need to emphasise that the problems are not with outsourcing per se but instead with what is being outsourced. The concept of outsourcing is based upon a premise that no organisation is entirely self-sufficient, nor does any have unlimited resources, and some work can be conducted by others at a lower cost. This is entirely reasonable. The organisational focus should not be on the pursuit of capabilities that third parties have the skills and technology to better deliver and can provide economies of scale. Every tea shop does not need to be a power generator, a tea plantation, a dairy herd and a kettle manufacturer. This practice occurs safely in more mature industries; the machine manufacturer doesn't have to make its own nuts and bolts and can instead buy those from a supplier.

Alas, IT is not such an industry. A recent study that examined 54,000 projects concluded that over 66% of large-sized (in excess of $15M) software projects "massively blow their budgets", and 17% went so bad that they threatened the very existence of the company. The larger the project, the higher the rate of failure. Let us focus on those points. In an attempt to avoid managing what we should manage, then under a banner of reducing risk, we put the existence of entire companies at stake in 1 out of 6 cases and go disastrously wrong in 4 out of 6. If this is management then to quote Inigo Montoya from The Princess Bride, "You keep using that word. I do not think it means what you think it means."

In comparison, the approach of SOCOM (special operations command) in the US Military is towards smaller projects, short acquisition cycles and re-use. As Dan Ward points out, 88% of SOCOM projects fit the FIRE principles, with over 60% of those projects staying within cost and schedule estimates, with the remaining 40% experiencing only "modest" overruns. The problems are not outsourcing as a concept but the size and breadth of the projects under such contracts. It is far more effective to think small — as in small teams, small contracts and small areas of focus.

But there's more to the game than this. It also offers up opportunities. Within the communication platform, there is a requirement for an application store (see Point 1, Figure 142). It's not uncommon, even in 2017, with the abundance of well-established application stores such as Google Play, for companies to still believe that they need to build their own. Often, such actions can be taken over concerns of control or because some pre-existing effort is under way or in production. These are all forms of inertia. But how do you deal with such inertia and any pre-existing systems? How can you turn this into an opportunity?

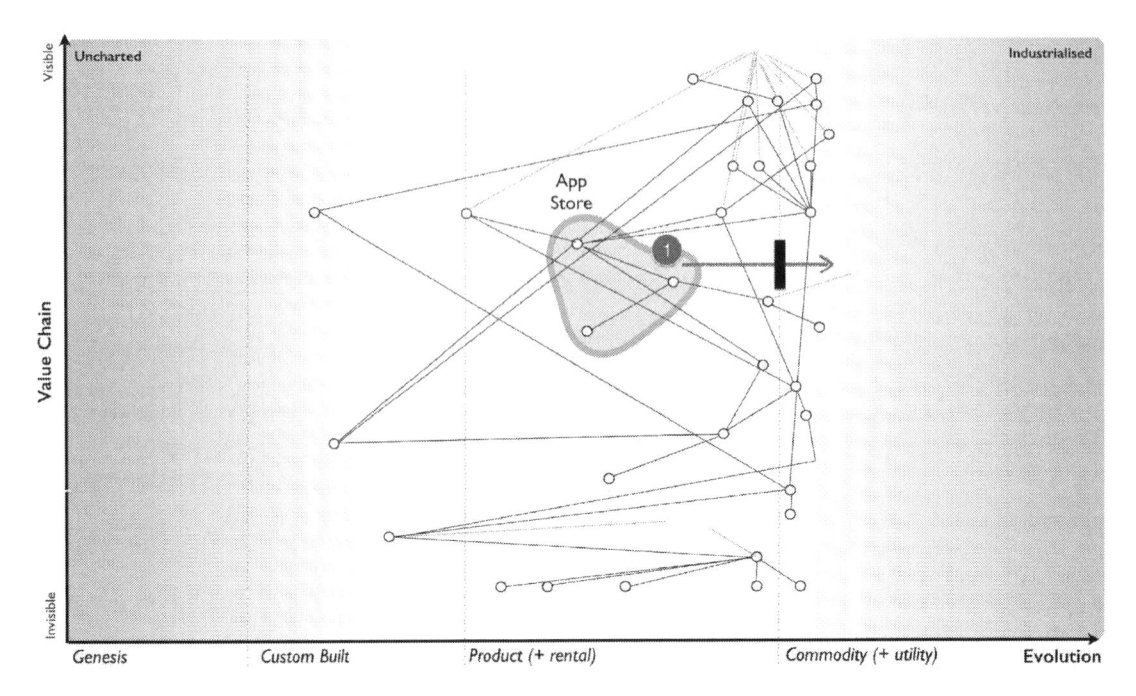

Figure 142: Dealing with legacy

In 2008, one of the big inertia barriers to adopting cloud services was legacy environments. These systems depended upon different architectural principles and were not suited to adoption of cloud infrastructure. Many companies decided that what they needed was a cloud service that acted like their "enterprise" environment. The reality is that such environments are a trade-off between the cost of re-architecting versus the benefit of standardised commodity components. Whilst not a long-term future, the appearance of vendors offering such enterprise clouds does provide an opportunity for exploitation. To explain this, I'll outline three basic ways of dealing with legacy:-

Disposing of liability

The first and most obvious approach is to simply recognise that a change is occurring, that you have inertia caused by past systems and you need to invest in re-architecting for the change. All technology investment is toxic over time and you need to continuously refactor to remove this. In many cases such refactoring is not done on a continual basis, which stores up problems for the future by creating a large (toxic) landscape that then needs to evolve. To avoid huge-scale projects (known in the industry as "Death Stars"), which attempt to resolve this mess (with the usual catastrophic results), then such change is best done in a piecemeal fashion, using small components over time. You dispose of the liability bit by bit, often using techniques such as the strangler pattern. Even a relatively new company such as Netflix took seven years to remove its legacy and become data centre zero (all cloud). Unfortunately, many will wait and fail to continually invest in refactoring. They leave the liability to grow until it becomes obvious that they have to change, at which point they will scramble to build a "Death Star", along with many other companies who have done the same. This creates an inevitable shortage of skills that piles on the misery and cost. So, start early and dispose of it bit by bit.

Sweat and dump

A variation of the approach is to deliberately sweat the legacy (i.e. minimise investment) whilst you build the new world. In the case of cloud, this is where enterprise cloud services might have some benefit. By shifting a legacy environment to an "enterprise cloud" provider with minimal architectural changes, then you move any responsibility for capex investment to the provider. You sweat the legacy whilst preparing a new environment with components that you have built or use from third parties. What you want is for the "enterprise cloud" service to provide utility based charging with no long-term contract. Despite the empty words you might have given the provider regarding long-term future, when you are ready, you unceremoniously start dumping the legacy. By such an approach, you're shifting future capex investment to the provider and reducing this cost for yourself. This method is unlikely to make you friends with the provider, so plan accordingly.

Pig in a poke

By far the best approach is to convince someone to pay you for your legacy. Just because you are aware that the environment is changing, does not mean everyone else is aware. You'll need a bit of misdirection here such as generating a future story for the legacy. In the case of the communication platform above, you might convince another company that enterprise application stores are the future. If you have a pre-existing home-grown application store then you can sell it to them, including some of the underlying environment (from infrastructure to staff) as a "future business", whilst ensuring you have access, ideally on a utility basis, hence providing a revenue stream for the buyer and making the deal seem "sweeter". During this time, you work on your replacement (e.g. shifting to Google Play) before dumping your use of the legacy store. This can be a surprisingly effective way to monetise legacy. This will definitely not win you friends with the people you sell it to, but then caveat emptor!

When you think about contracts then look to break them down into small components; don't be afraid to manage the risk and also think about how you can even turn your legacy into an opportunity with a bit of sleight of hand.

It'll save me money and other lies we tell ourselves

There are many lies we tell ourselves in business: the environment changes slowly, we can predict the uncertain, we can outsource our own risk, management can be made simple, the key to success is implementing this culture or that innovation or this principle or that method. If anything, I hope that mapping is teaching you that there are no single methods or simple answers, but you can still manage this.

These maps help you to describe an environment that consists of multiple evolving components. They contain simple components that have the perception of being well-known, well-defined and common, such as the nut and bolt or the plug. They also contain chaotic components that are uncertain and we do not yet understand, such as the genesis of the new. The environment itself can be complicated with many components, and at the same time, complex in that you have to dynamically respond to changes both caused by climatic patterns and other competitors' actions. These terms of simple, chaotic, complex and complicated have quite precise meanings, and I'd recommend the reader spending some time becoming familiar with the work of Dave Snowden and the Cynefin framework.

Despite all of this, we try to grab for simple truths. In 2008, this was commonplace in the world of cloud computing, mainly due to the confusion that existed. I thought I'd use a few "simple truths" that turn out not to be either simple or true to illustrate some climatic patterns that are worth knowing about.

Efficiency will reduce our budgets

One of the most common ideas was that cloud computing would reduce IT budget expenditure. It's a notion that if cloud computing is more efficient then we will spend less on IT. Sounds simple, sounds obvious, and yet, it is so wrong.

I gave a talk at IT@Cork (in 2008) on how this assumption ignored creation of new industries, componentisation and price elasticity effects. By increasing efficiency and the reducing cost of providing infrastructure then a large number of activities that might have been economically unfeasible become feasible. Furthermore, the self-service nature of cloud not only increases agility by enabling faster provision, but it also enables user innovation through provision of standardised components (the componentisation effect). Building a house is faster with bricks than a clay pit. This in turn can encourage the creation of new industries in the same manner that the commoditisation of electronic switching — from the innovation of the Fleming valve to complex products containing thousands of switches — led to digital calculators and computers. As these industries evolved, they drove further demand for electronic switching.

The effect of these forces is that whilst infrastructure provision may become more efficient, the overall demand for infrastructure will outstrip these gains precisely because infrastructure has become a more efficient and standardised component. We end up using vastly more of a more efficient resource. This effect is not new. It was noted by Willam Stanley Jevons in the 1850s, when he "observed that England's consumption of coal soared after James Watt introduced his coal-fired steam engine, which greatly improved the efficiency of Thomas Newcomen's earlier design".

In Figure 143, I've outlined the main effects. First (Point 1), you have an activity that has evolved from genesis through to product and is finally becoming more industrialised, e.g. a commodity or a utility. This will allow for more efficient provision of the act through volume operations.

However, the more industrialised component can enable greater use of the component, as previously uneconomical acts become viable (Point 2). There can be a long tail of things we'd like to do and unmet needs that are enabled by the efficiency of provision. The final aspect (Point 3) is consumption of the component will increase as new industries that it enabled start to evolve.

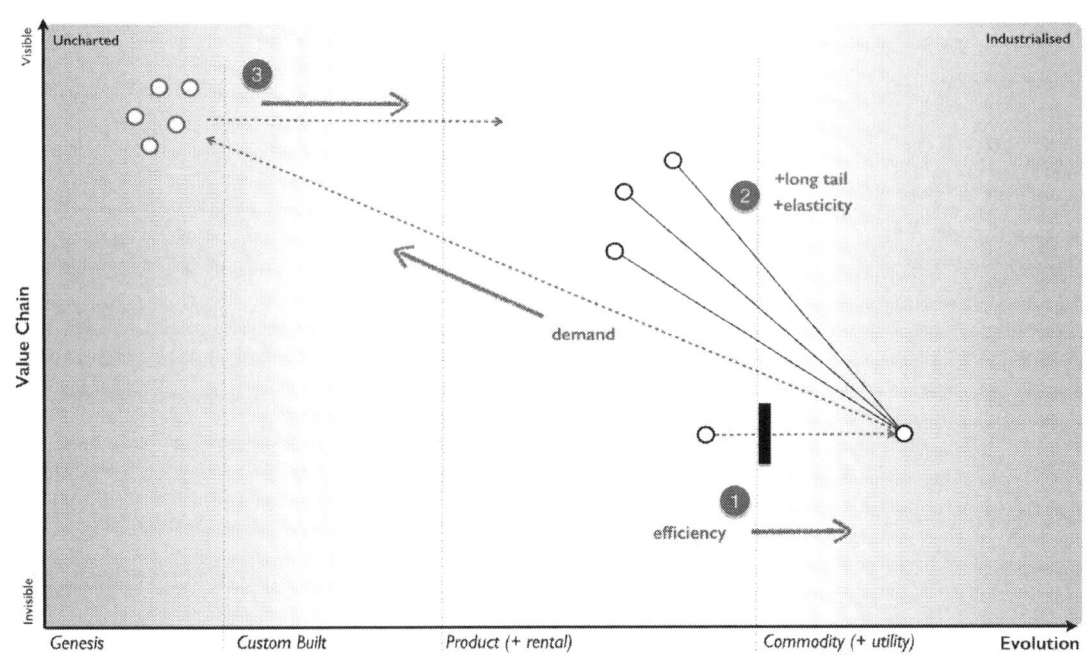

Figure 143: Jevons paradox

But can't I just ignore this? We're talking market effects here. Won't it reduce my budget because all I care about is what I produce and not what new-fangled industry is created or what unmet needs can now be met?

If you look at computing then I can buy a million times more resource for the same money than I could twenty years ago. This doesn't mean that IT budgets have reduced a million fold in that time; instead, we've ended up doing more stuff. Don't confuse efficiency with reduced IT spend.

Cloud will be green

Another common talking point in 2008 was whether cloud computing would be green. There was a lot to this, from the substitution of physical goods for digital to the levels of inefficiency in the existing industry to the material waste in unused capacity to the means of energy provision. There was undoubtedly a lot of waste and potential for improvement, hence an argument could be made for cloud being green. However, there's something more long term to be thought about here.

When we consider a value chain, we're constantly industrialising components and building new systems on top of them. Machinery on top of the nut and bolt.

Intelligent software agents on top of databases on top of computing on top of electricity. We are constantly creating higher order systems built upon more industrialised and ordered components. We are building towers of order out of the chaos. As with other biological systems, we are decreasing local entropy and that requires energy. We might be far from efficiently using energy today but regardless, our underlying demand and consumption of power will increase (see Figure 144). In order for progress to be green then inevitably, we need to turn to the means of energy production.

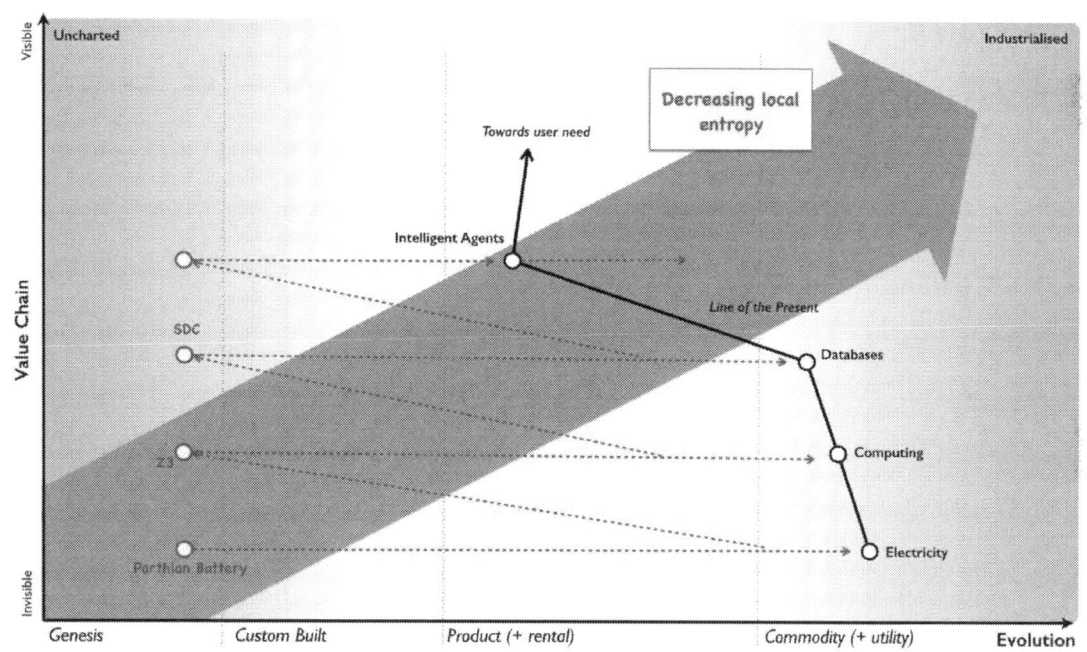

Figure 144: Feel the power

We can deal with it later

Whenever we see a shift from products to more industrialised forms such as utilities, then most large companies (with the exception of the enlightened) will tend to ignore the change. This is due to inertia caused by pre-existing practice, assets and markets. The most telling signs are often overlooked until it is too late. One of these signs is the flow of financial capital. We tend to see a marked movement of capital away from the existing industries (the past) and towards both the more industrialised forms and the new activities built upon it.

If I take Figure 143 from above and overlay onto it this flow of capital, along with the peace, war and wonder cycle, then we can get a sense of what is happening. At the same time that an act is to become more efficiently provided through industrialised forms with its demand increasing due to a long tail of unmet needs and the creation of new industry, then financial capital is flowing away from past product vendors towards the new vendors and new companies serving those new markets. Now add in the coevolution of new practice caused by the evolving act, the new forms of organisation that arise, the speed of change caused by a punctuated equilibrium, the inevitability of change (i.e. the Red Queen), and the inaction of past giants caused by inertia, then what you have is destruction of the past at the same time as the future is being created. The combination of competition with basic climatic patterns such as inertia and coevolution creates this constant pulse of new consumer needs, new vendors, new methods of production, new markets and new forms of organisation. This heart-beat was described by Joseph Schumpeter as "creative destruction" (see Figure 145,) and by the time it becomes obvious, it's usually too late to react.

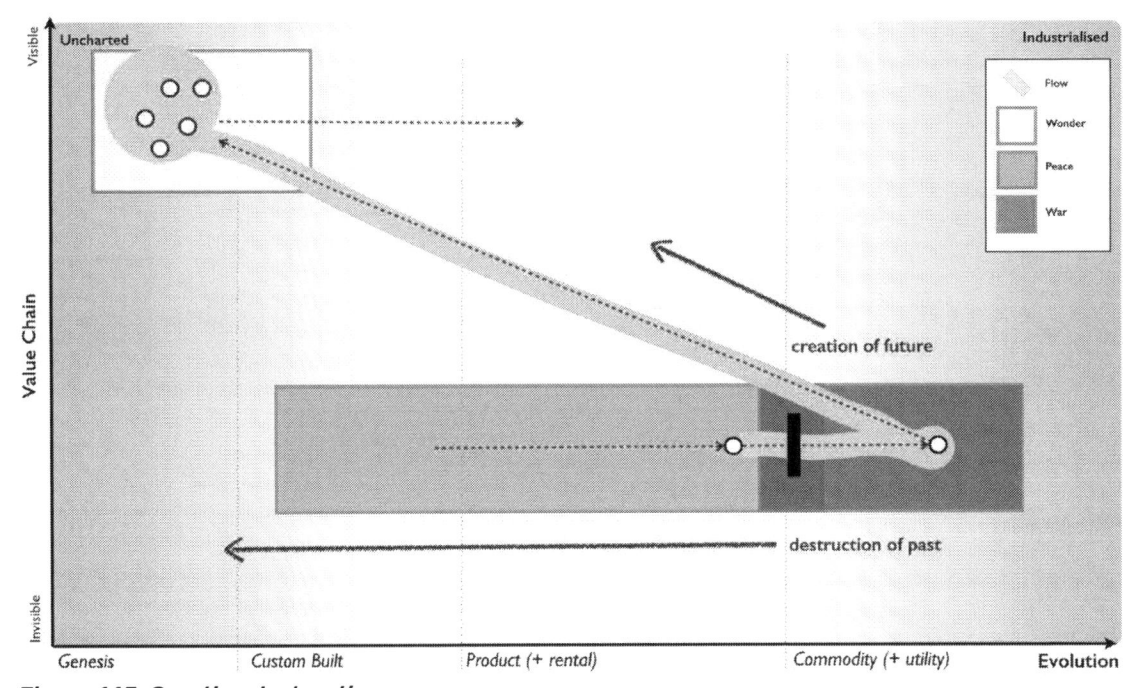

Figure 145: Creative destruction

But hang on! If we know about the cycle, if we can use weak signals to anticipate it, if we understand the different forms of inertia, then surely we can prepare and adapt when it occurs? Why on earth would any company be disadvantaged or eliminated by it? The problem is blindness, and this leads to the next lie we tell ourselves.

Execution matters more than strategy

One thing I had become aware of in my journey around companies was that few seemed to have examples of maps. They had things they called maps but these diagrams lacked those essential characteristics, e.g. visual, context specific, position relative to an anchor and movement. When I pointed this out, I'd often get a lot of pushback, especially on the aspect of movement. This still happens today, so it's worth emphasising.

Movement isn't simply about drawing a line on a picture, it's about the consistency of meaning of such a line. Position, anchor and movement are essential for navigation. Take a look at Figure 146. It's a farm (that's the context), it's visual, it has position of fields relative to an anchor (in this case, the compass), and you can draw movement on it. You'd probably agree that you can give this map to someone else and they could quite happily find the barley field with it.

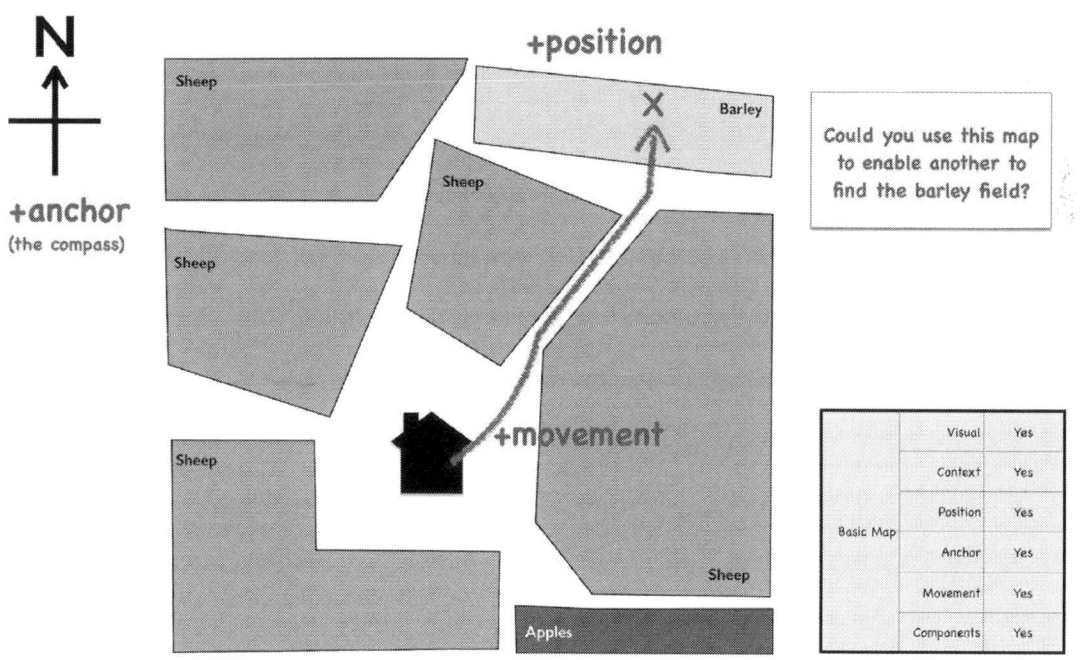

Figure 146: A map of a farm

I've taken the same map, kept the same number of fields, plus their shape and relative areas, but removed any concept of position and the anchor. I've just placed the fields in order of what type they are — fruit, livestock and crop. I've also added a movement line to it. The question is, could you hand this "map" (Figure 147) to someone else and expect them to find the barley field?

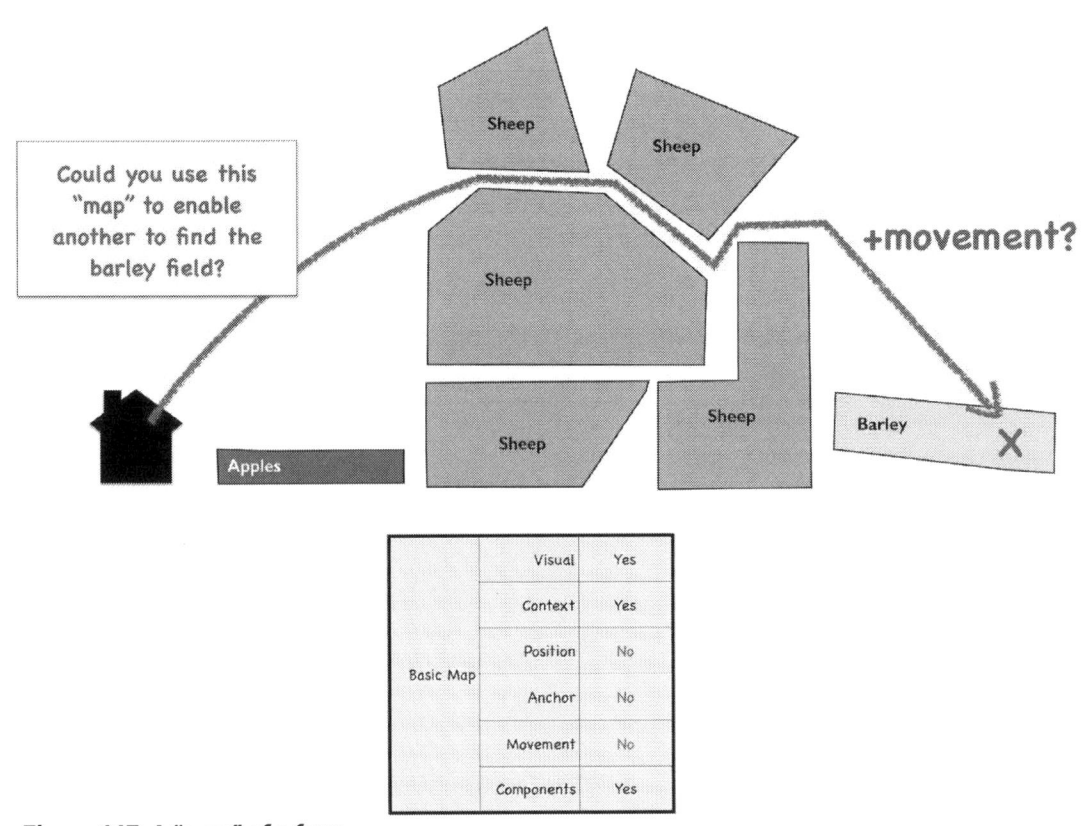

Figure 147: A "map" of a farm

It should be obvious that the answer is no. Movement and its consistency — you can follow this path to go from A to B — are not only essential qualities of a map but they also turn out to be essential for map making. Explorers can't explore by just sitting still; something has to move (whether it's them, a drone or a satellite is immaterial). Action is a necessity for exploration.

These navigational qualities enable us to learn about the environment, whether through a visual form or an equivalent internalised mental model. Take for example the tube map. The stations might not be in exactly the right geographical position but it is nevertheless a useful map. It has the position of stations (anchored by the tube network itself) and consistent movement between them. If I'm at Bond Street, there are multiple routes for me to get to Cannon Street, but there is consistency. If I'm travelling anticlockwise on the Circle Line, then I know I will travel through South Kensington, Sloane Square, Victoria, St James' Park and Westminster on my journey (Point 3, Figure 148). If there was no consistency then the Circle Line might take me via Victoria, St James' Park and Westminster one day and Victoria, Edgeware Road and Mornington Crescent the next. I wouldn't know where I would end up and it would be impossible to navigate.

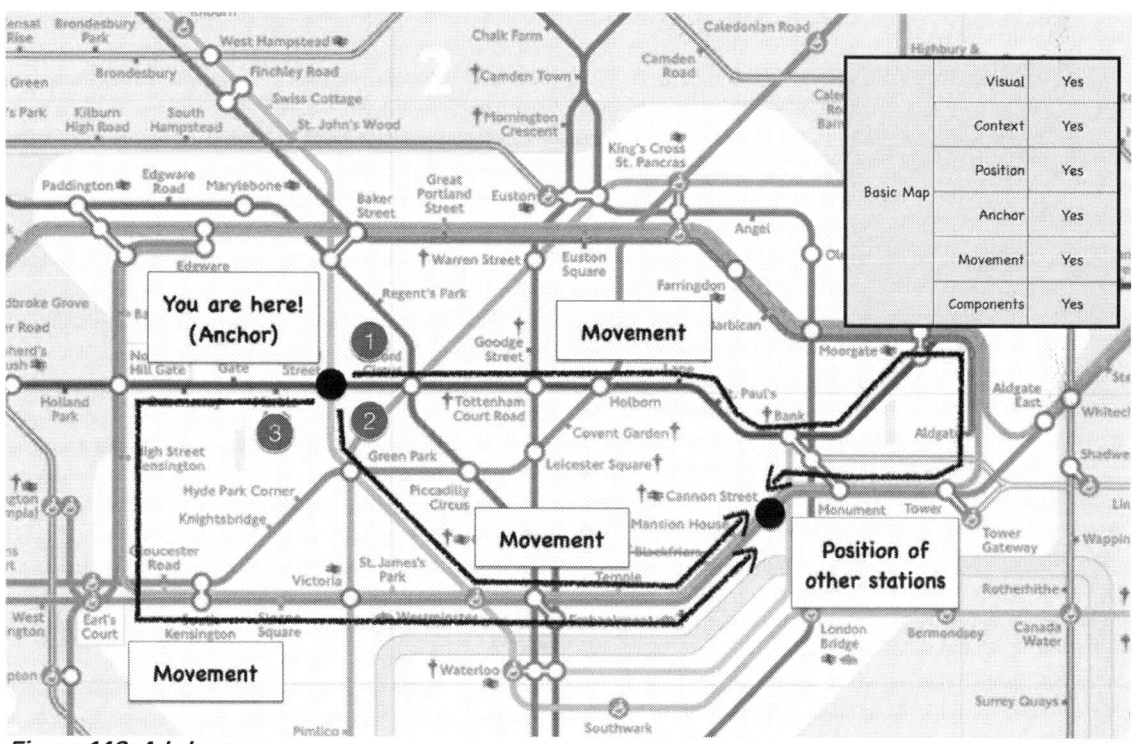

Figure 148: A tube map

Of course, the tube map doesn't have to look like the above. You could build your own variety by simply travelling on the trains and recording the stations, but as long as you can consistently describe movement then it is a map you can share with others. Now, tube maps are currently a vogue in the business world, with various companies creating them to describe complex environments. For example, in Figure 149, we have a "tube map" of the digital world. The map lacks context, being simply a grouping of technology and digital concepts. It has the position of components but it is not clear what anchor is used. Lastly, according to the "map" then to go from Online Ad Networks to Agency Holding Companies, you need to travel through social advertising then email marketing then digital agencies then management consultants then campaign management then media metrics then media agencies to reach the destination. Is this true? On what basis is that movement consistent and justified? I suspect it's not. This is not a map; it's a diagram of loosely-connected concepts and questionable relationships.

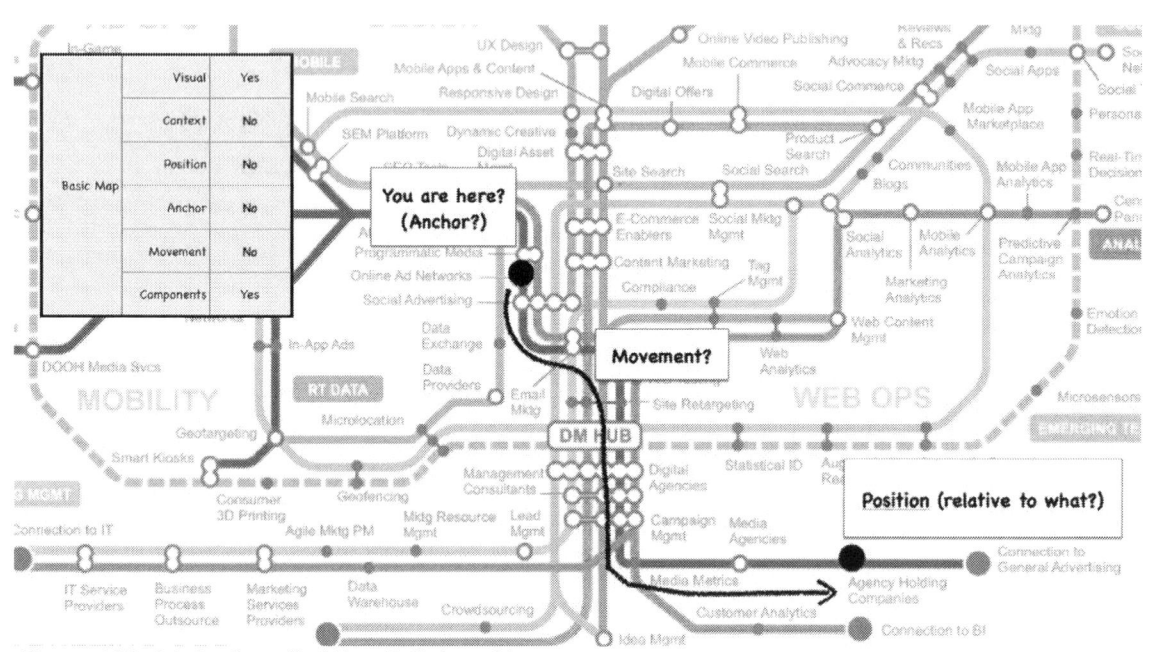

Figure 149: A tube "map" of the digital world

So, why does this matter and what has this got to do with execution? Without maps then situational awareness will be poor. In 2008, I was still firmly under the illusion that people were just keeping their maps secret from me, but doubts were growing. I started to have this notion that some companies might actually be blind to change and if people couldn't see the environment they were operating in then how could they prepare for predictable forms of change? By the time such changes would become obvious, their pace and any inherent inertia would make them unsurmountable and even fatal. However, in discussion with others, I was often told that this didn't matter, that strategy was fairly meaningless compared to the real key, which was execution. I also had doubts about this because firing a gun rapidly doesn't help you if you don't know where to fire it.

In 2010, Professor Roger L. Martin challenged this notion head on in The Execution Trap. If you haven't read it, go do so. Martin's argument was there was no distinction between execution and strategy; they were part of the same thing. By pure chance, in 2012, under an LEF research project, I had the opportunity to test this.

Every company told me they had strategy but I was acutely aware that there existed different levels of situational awareness. I had been interviewing 160+ Silicon Valley companies, looking for examples of open gameplay, whether open source, open data or open standards. I plotted these companies against their level of strategic play based upon situational awareness (i.e. using their understanding of own and competitors' value chains and how they were evolving) versus their propensity to take action (in this case, to use an open approach to change a market). The result is shown in Figure 150.

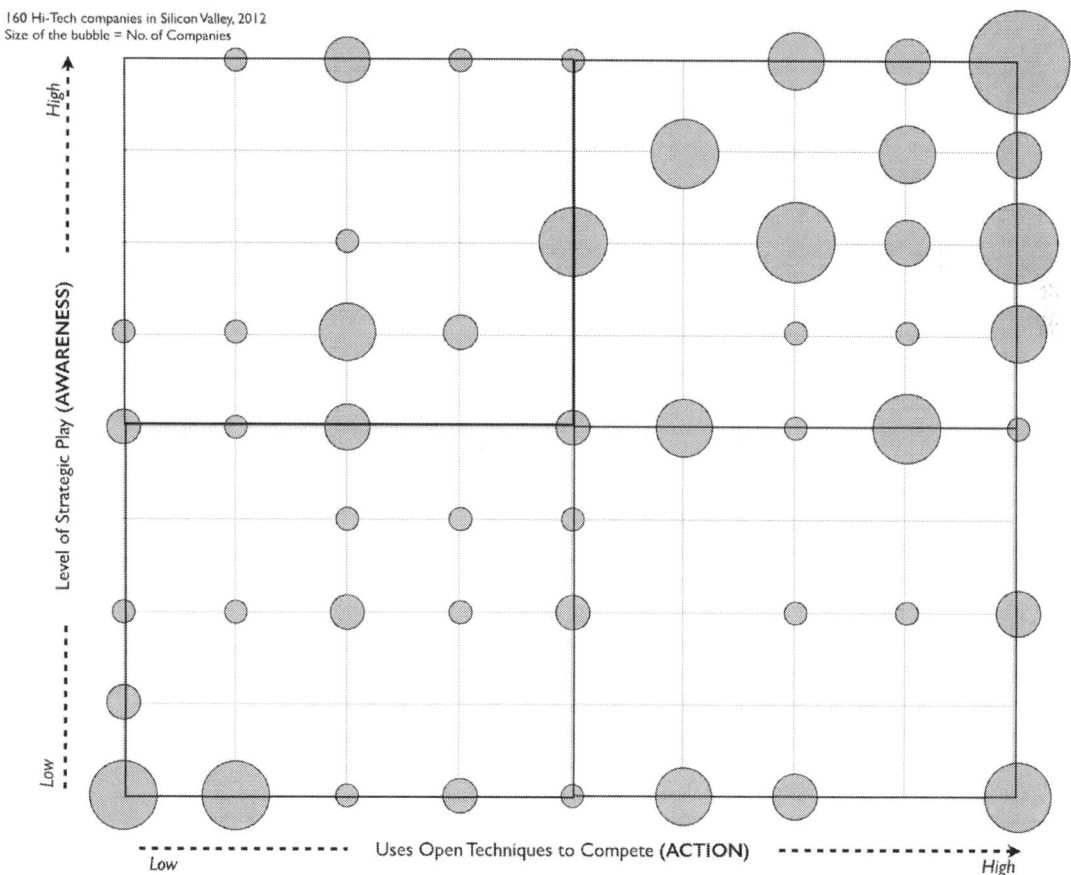

Figure 150: Awareness vs Action. Leading Edge Forum 2012 study on situational awareness versus action

The bigger the bubbles, the more companies at that point. This was Silicon Valley, supposedly the top end of competition, and even here there were companies building strategic play based upon low levels of situational awareness, and in some cases, near blindness to their environment. Quite a few not only didn't understand evolution, they didn't know their value chains or even what their users needed.

Now, if execution rules then the companies on the right hand side of this graph with a high tendency towards taking action should probably on average perform better. Of course, if strategic play based upon situational awareness was important then the companies at the top of the graph should perform better. Out of curiosity, I decided to examine market cap changes of those companies over the last 7 years. The results are shown in Figure 151.

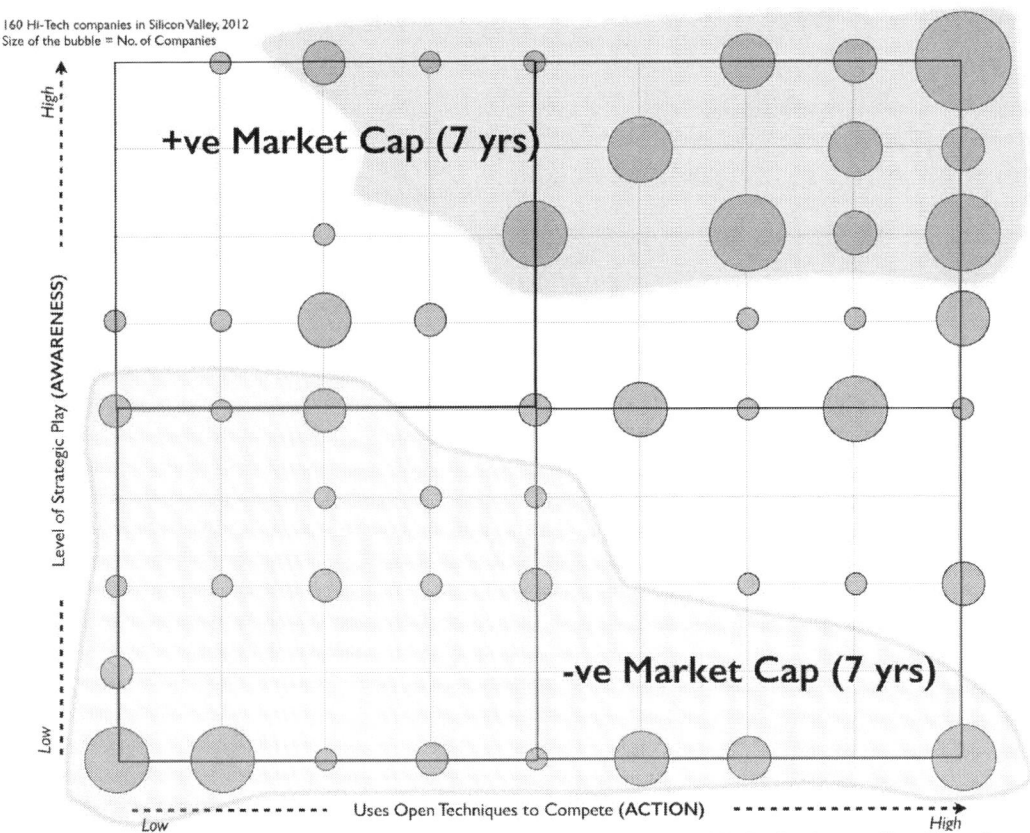

Figure 151: Market Capitalisation impact. Leading Edge Forum 2012 study on situational awareness versus action

I can't repeat what my first response was but let's just say that I was very surprised. What the data strongly suggests is those companies with high levels of strategic play based upon situational awareness and a propensity towards action perform better than those who don't. Just having a focus on action is not enough.

In the case of companies having low levels of situational awareness (i.e. those in the bottom half), then action (and how well you execute on it) does matter. Those with poor situational awareness and low propensity for action performed negatively, whilst those with poor awareness but a high tendency towards action were more neutral. In other words, if you're blind to the environment then it's better to shoot faster and with more

impact, just in case you do actually hit something. Hence, if you're competing against others with poor situational awareness then I can see how an argument that "execution matters more than strategy" can occur.

However, if you have poor situational awareness and are competing against someone with high situational awareness then you might have a much higher propensity towards action and better execution of such, but they will still tend to outperform you. I find myself strongly in agreement with Professor Martin that strategy and execution are part of the same thing but also, I'll add that situational awareness is a key part of this. This study however was in Silicon Valley and the levels of situational awareness tended to deteriorate outside that cauldron of creativity. It had taken me several years to discover some weak evidence to back up my initial suspicions that corporate blindness (i.e. very low levels of situational awareness) was a problem. But how commonplace is this?

How common is corporate blindness?

In 2014, I was messing around with modelling agents in a competitive market and looking at various impacts on company longevity. This was partially out of curiosity, a desire to learn and general play. I wasn't expecting to find anything. I created a simulation with 1,000 agents (companies) competing against each other, with each company having a starting age of 45 years. I added some variables for disruption through product versus product substitution, overlaid a peace, war and wonder cycle, including new entrants and disruption of past players. I then added steps for acceleration of evolution due to industrialisation of communication mechanisms. I ran a multitude of scenarios and noticed patterns starting to emerge. One of the most interesting is shown in Figure 152.

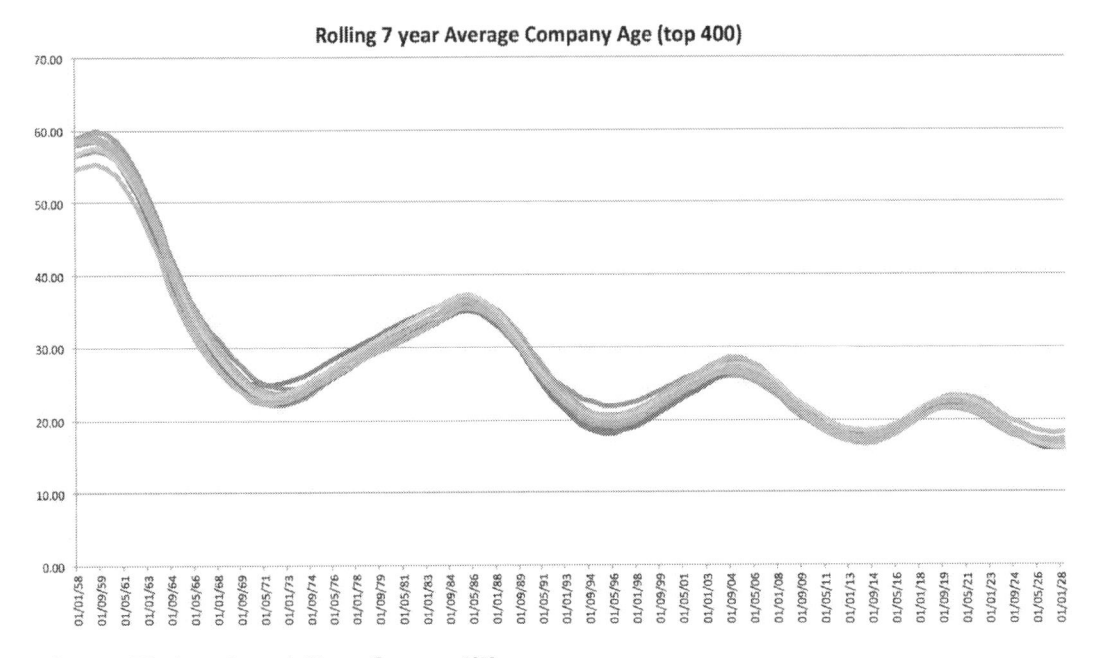

Figure 152: Agent modelling of competition

What's happening in the above is a constant undulation in average company age of the top 400 in the simulation. The system is constantly attempting to return to a higher average age but the constant wars and disruption by new entrants (on top of the normal product to product substitution) keeps this in check. However, the acceleration of evolution (due to industrialisation of the means of communication) is causing a shift downwards to a lower age and a new stable plateau around which age will oscillate. What's interesting about this pattern is it reasonably closely mimics Richard N. Foster's examination of average company age in the S&P 500, despite being a random agent model with set rules and parameters, i.e. automatons in a variation of Conway's Game of Life.

Why is that interesting? Well, the agents are automatons that are blind to the environment. The pattern is highly influenced by the ability of the agents to adapt, i.e. if we assume high levels of situational awareness and the ability of companies to evolve, then this pattern doesn't happen and a completely different pattern of dominance emerges. This, combined with my own experiences of industry and previous experiments on situational awareness versus action, was enough to give me some confidence in what I started to suspect in 2008. Large parts of industry are blind to the environment they are competing in.

We're not blind, we have principles!

A common counter to this idea that companies were playing blind was that it didn't matter. If we could find the ideal algorithms, rules or principles then we could create that sustaining organisation. You can think of this as a variation of Conway's Game of Life but with the conceit that all we need to do is to find the right code, and the problem with my simulation is I just had the wrong principles. To challenge this, I'll use a bit of WoW.

I've often found World of Warcraft (a massive multiplayer online role-playing game known as WoW) to be a useful vehicle for explaining and exploring basic concepts of strategy, and this is no exception. In this example, I want you to imagine two teams of players — the Horde and the Alliance — preparing to fight for the first time in a battleground called Warsong Gulch.

Both teams have a short time to prepare before the battle commences. The winner is the team that captures the opponent's flag three times. Let us assume that neither team has been to Warsong Gulch before or has experience of fighting in battlegrounds. Just for reference, when your character is killed in the battleground, it resurrects a few moments later in your team's graveyard. One team (the Alliance) outlines its strategy for how it's going to win the battle. It consists of what they describe as five principles that they've all agreed upon. These are:-

Focus: Capture the flag and win the game!

Doctrine:

- Do this with great people! We're going to be the best fighters, wizards and healers.
- Be prepared to take risks and fail fast! We're not going to just play it safe.
- A supportive culture! We're going to help each other when asked.
- Open to challenge and asking the hard questions.

The team is enthusiastic and ready to go. Facing off against them is the team of Horde players. They've also spent their time preparing, but the result is somewhat different. This team understands the importance of maps and uses them for strategic play. They have a map of Warsong Gulch and have developed a "strategy", which consists of:-

Focus: Capture the flag and win the game!

Doctrine:

- Perform your role the best you can (develop mastery).
- Act as a single unit (a cell), i.e. fight and move together.

Context specific play:

- To begin with, the team will act as one cell in an initial all-out attack. The group will quickly move through the central tunnel towards the enemy base, taking out opposing players that interfere.
- Always take out opposing healers first, then wizards and then fighters.
- Once their flag is captured by our fighter, the group will work to take out opposing players and set up camp in the opponents' graveyard – see map (Figure 153) – killing off their players as they are resurrected and before they create any form of group. Taunting Alliance players is encouraged.
- Once their graveyard is contained, the cell will split into two cells. A small offensive group consisting of a couple of wizards will take out opposing stragglers and the larger cell (including our flag-carrying fighter) will continue to camp out in the opposing team's graveyard, killing all players that resurrect. Once opposing players are contained in the graveyard, the cell will reform and our fighter will keep running the flag. If the plan fails then the group will reform around our flag carrier.

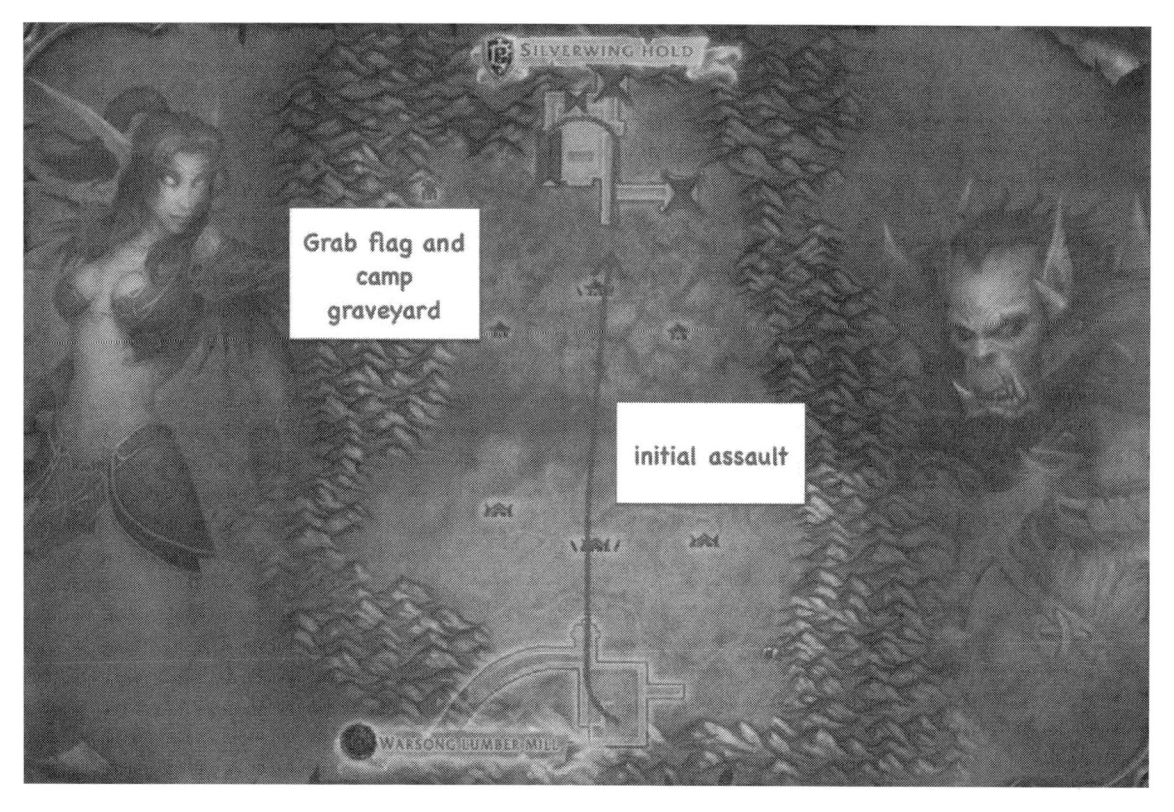

Figure 153: The map of the play. Annotated in game Map of Warsong Gluch, World of Warcraft

Now, the Horde team has focus, principles and some form of context-specific strategy based upon an understanding of the environment. It might not work, but then the Horde players can use their maps to refine their gameplay with time. I can almost guarantee that when the battle kicks off, the first questions from the Alliance players will be "Should we attack or defend?" and "Where do we need to go?"

Arguments within the Alliance team will quickly happen and before they know it, the Horde will be upon them. The next cries you'll hear from the Alliance members will be "Help!" and "Why is no- one helping me, I need help here!" and "Where are you?" followed by endless bickering that this or that player isn't good enough to be part of the team, combined with lots of shouts of "What is going on?" or "Where is everyone?" or "Should I grab their flag?" In all likelihood, the Alliance team will be quickly broken into a panicked rabble. I know, I've been on that team and watched the mayhem.

The point I want to emphasise is that principles are fine and yes, strategy has to adapt to the game, but don't confuse the two. A set of principles does not make a strategy. Though, it's certainly better to have a set of principles than to have no principles and no strategy. This is equally applicable in business.

There is however another aspect to consider. Within World of Warcraft, there are many teams of Horde and Alliance players. Imagine that the Alliance players not only have no map, they're not even aware of the concept of a map. All they can do is try some principles and share them from one team to another as "secrets of success". Imagine the Horde players understand the concept of maps, use them and share between them. Pretty soon, every Horde team will be winning using a wide variety of strategic plays. The Alliance doesn't stand a chance until every player in the Alliance has built some mental model of the world (an internal map). Of course, every new player that joins the Alliance reduces this shared understanding. The best the Alliance can do is to tell the new player to "apply the principles and follow Morgana the Wizard, just do what she does" in the hope the new player will build up some mental map.

Principles aren't going to save you against vastly higher levels of situational awareness. Now ask yourself, what do we do in business? Are we using maps for context-specific gameplay, learning and communication, or is our strategy more akin to copying "secrets of success" and "following others", i.e. should we be like Amazon, Netflix or Airbnb? Are we playing the game like the Alliance or the Horde? As tempting as it is, there is no secret formula and no magic secret to success.

Conway's Game of Life consisted of automaton that did not learn from the environment. We are not that. Awareness of the environment will always create an advantage over others, and yes, I'm afraid the very nature of competition (even cooperative competition) is about creating an advantage. If anything, understanding the landscape better than competitors is the one area of continual sustained advantage because the landscape of business is always shifting.

Focus on core!

Another common counter that was raised was the importance of core, having a goal and clearly defined purpose. At the same time that people were talking about the "goal", Silicon Valley was raving about the "pivot". In short, you should have a goal unless you pivot to another goal. Go figure!

The problem of course is that strategy is not a long, linear path but a constantly iterative process. The actions you or others take can change that game. All you can hope to do is to set a direction and adapt along the way, or as Deng Xiaoping would say, "Cross the river by feeling the stones." Core is at best transitory; it doesn't matter whether you're a software company or a legal firm.

Let us take the example of a legal firm. You only need to travel back to the 1980s to find a world where will writing was a rather bespoke activity and legal firms made not inconsiderable sums from such practices. There was a constraint in terms of lawyers, i.e. you needed a lawyer to write your will. Of course, industrialisation happened, wills became more of a commodity, automated through standard templates and online services. Despite the gnashing of teeth and inertia created by past success (Point 1, Figure 154), the industry had to adapt. I've taken a liberty and simplified the components, such as templates and computing to automation. What I want you to note is that the constraint between lawyers and wills was broken. Fortunately, there was a wide variety of other contract structures that users demanded.

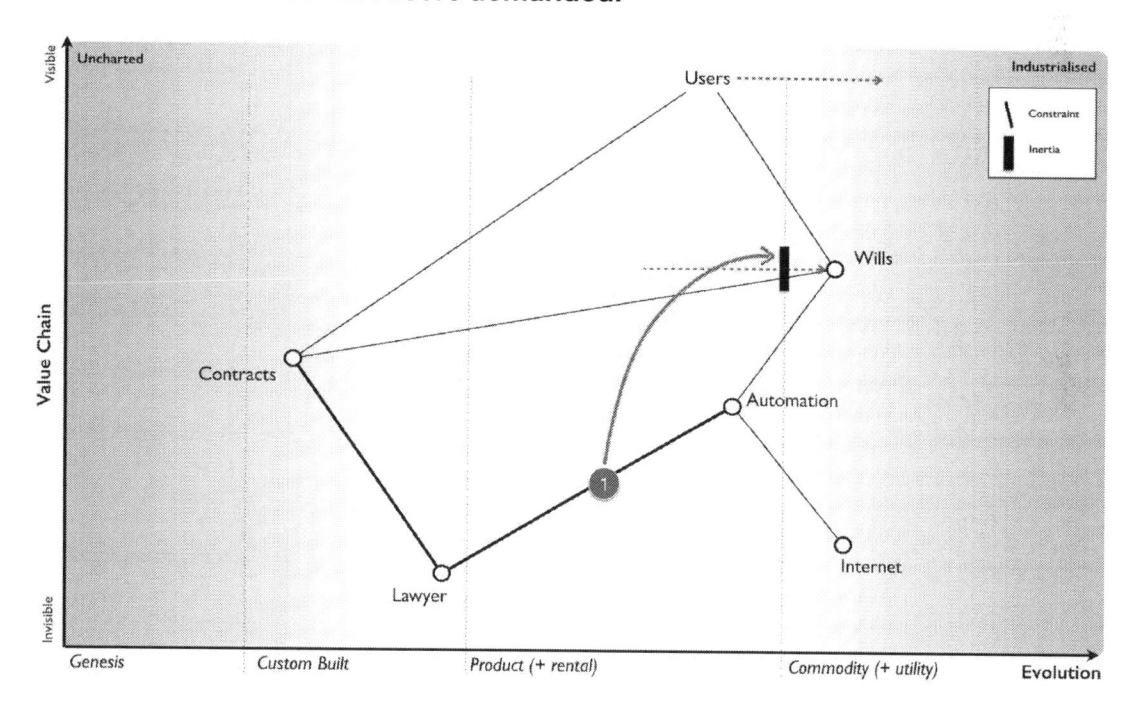

Figure 154: Change to Wills

Alas, despite recent experience of this change, the industry is once again facing industrialisation of general contract writing through the use of AI systems. Naturally, there is the usual inertia to such changes — it's a relationship business, they won't be good enough — but since we've gone through this cycle in that industry within living memory, it's hopeful that more will adapt successfully this time. I suspect not (see Figure 155). Once again, the constraint of lawyers, but this time, contracts will be broken.

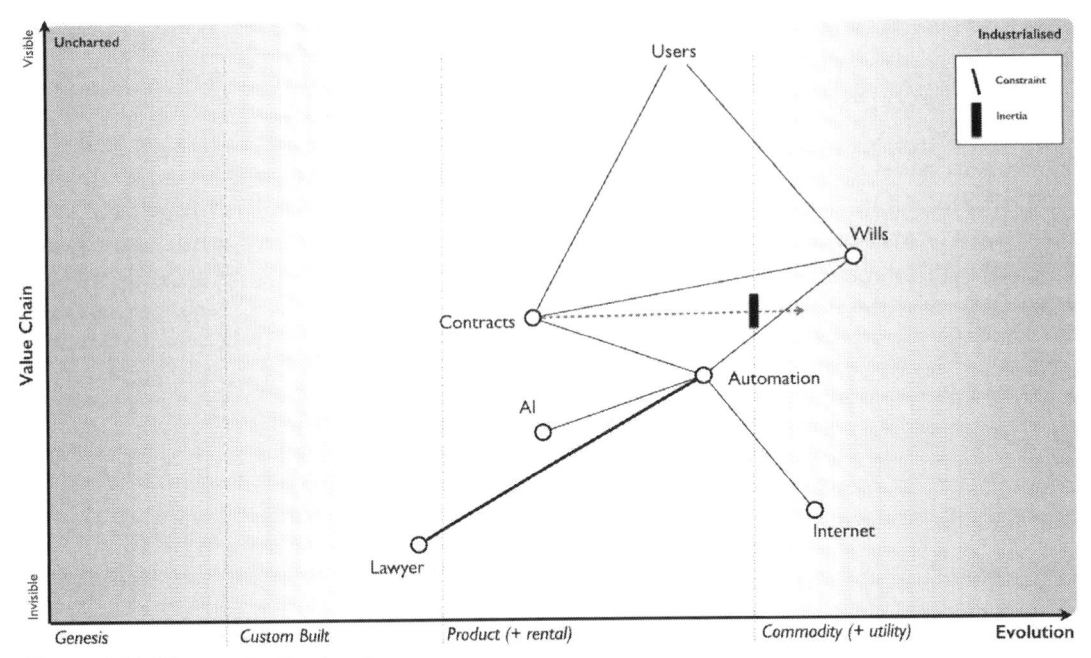

Figure 155: Change to Contracts

The point of this is that if your vision had been to provide personal will and contract writing services based upon access to lawyers, then what worked in the 1980s will by 2030 be mainly irrelevant or at best a niche market. There's nothing you can do about this because you're not solely in control — there are other players in the market — and just because you don't want it to become a commodity, doesn't stop someone else exploiting it as such.

These sorts of changes can also hit you from multiple directions, including from lower down the value chain via reducing barriers to entry into your market. The newspaper industry has suffered a recent example of this with the printing press. Back in the 1980s, if you wanted to be a journalist then you had to work for a newspaper that owned or had access to a distribution network and printing presses. These capital intensive assets were a constraint that acted as a barrier to entry. They were also a mechanism of control over journalists — there was a limited number of newspapers you could work for.

Industrialisation of the means of mass communication through the internet was first considered a potential boon for media industries. However, it broke the constraint, which has meant a flood of new entrants came into the market. Also, any journalist can now set up their own online paper. This liberation changed the main reason of why you'd work for a newspaper. It was no longer because they control the means of distribution but instead because of social capital — its network, brand, reputation — and access to other services. The media industry had to adapt or, in some cases, fail.

But even the act of collecting, curating and writing news is now under pressure from AI with its more widespread use in business and sport reporting. The National Society of Newspaper Columnists, founded in 1977, has a core focus to promote professionalism and camaraderie among columnists and other writers, but how does that mission fit into a world of computer-generated copy? It's the same with automotive industry, where a core focus on the human driving experience might be relevant for the past but irrelevant or niche in a future of self-driving cars. Of all the terms I come across then focus on core is probably the most destructive for the longevity of a company. To overcome it, you simply have to accept the truth that there is no core other than a transient focus.

Mastering strategy as simply as I can

We've covered a lot of ground in these chapters, so I thought in this final section, I'd recap some of the basics on how to master strategy. You'll need this for the scenario. I've italicised master because I don't really have a clue how to do that. I'm still learning and I've been using maps for over a decade. For now, all I can say is that strategy seems to be a journey of constant learning and the more I learn, the more I realise how little I know. If anyone does actually become a master then I'd be pleased to read about how they did it. There may be a faster way to master strategy than a seemingly endless journey of learning. There might even be a 2x2 that'll explain everything, but so far, I haven't found it. Hence, in the absence of some marvellous solution, I'll give you some basic steps.

Step 1 — The cycle

Understand that strategy is a continuous cycle. You don't have all the information you need, you don't know all the patterns, and there are many aspects of life that are uncertain. Fortunately, not all is uncertain. Start with a direction (i.e. a why of purpose, as in "I wish to win this game of chess"), but be prepared to adapt as the game unfolds (i.e. the why of movement, as in "should I move this chess piece or that one?"). Your first step on the journey is to understand the cycle of strategy — Figure 156. Lots of people can help you here, from John Boyd (OODA loops) to Sun Tzu (Art of War).

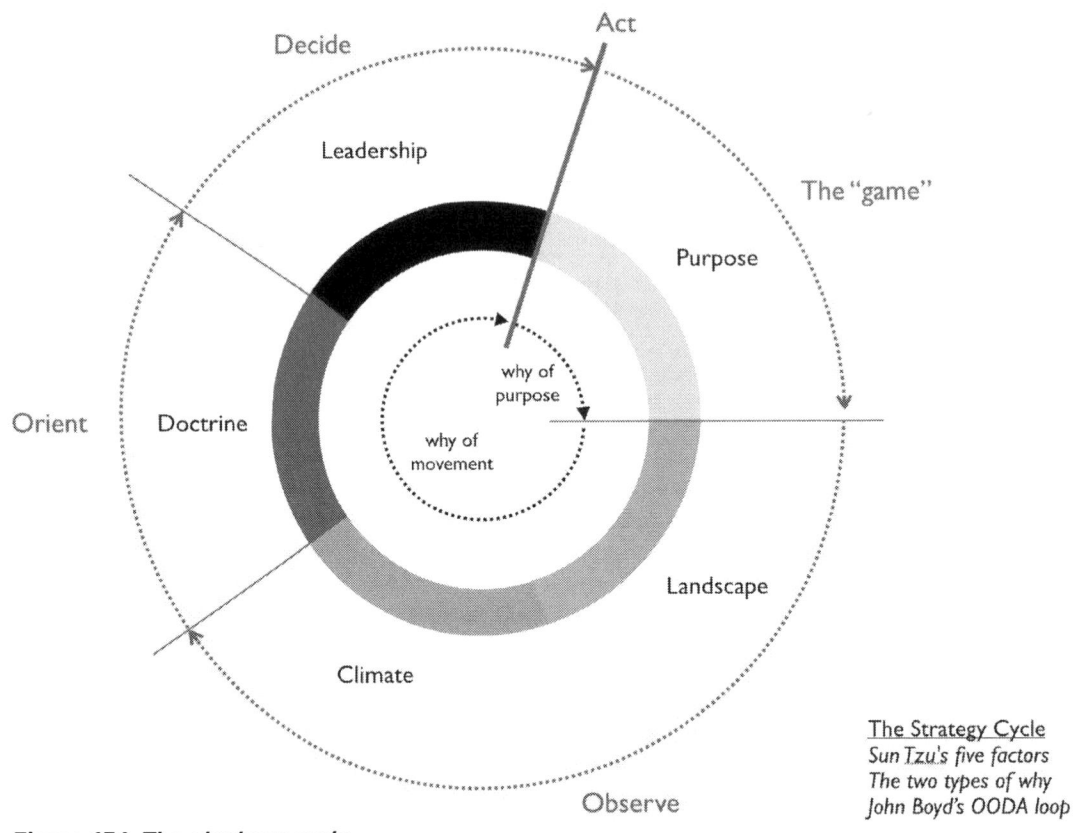

Figure 156: The strategy cycle

Step 2 — Learn the landscape

Your next step is to observe the game, i.e. to look at the landscape — Figure 157. This is essential for you to be able to learn about the game, to communicate with others and to anticipate change. To observe the landscape, you must have a map of its context. Any map must have the basic characteristics of: being visual, context-specific (i.e. to the game at hand, including the pieces involved), position of pieces relative to some anchor (in geographical maps, this is the compass; in chess, it is the board itself), and movement (i.e. how things can change, the constraint of possibilities). In business, extremely few companies have maps, so don't worry too much about where others are going or grand proclamations that they might make.

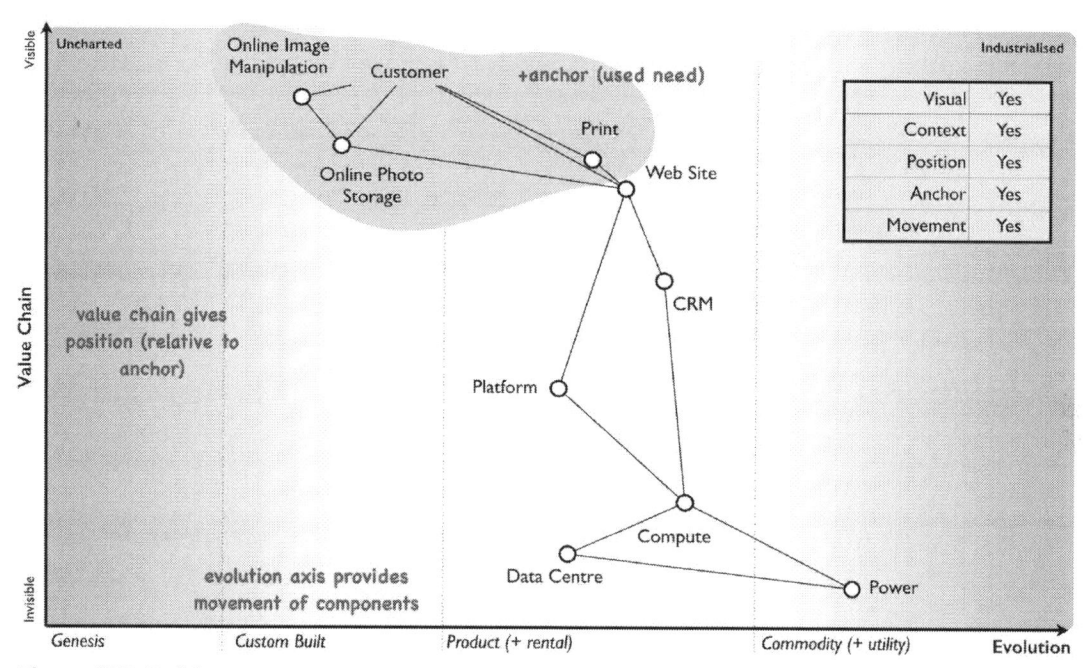

Figure 157: Build a map

Step 3 — Learn and use climatic patterns

Once you have a map, then you can start to learn the next part of the strategy cycle, i.e. climatic patterns. In business maps, these are the common economic patterns that affect all players and can be considered the rules of the game. Use those patterns to try and anticipate where the market is heading. The more you play, the more rules you'll discover. It's really important that before you start trying to organise and structure yourself (i.e. apply doctrine), you look at where the market is going and not where it has been. No-one ever wins by building the perfect structure for the past. We've covered a pretty extensive number of the basic economic patterns, but as a reminder, I'll list them, adding a few more flourishes where needed.

Climatic Patterns

Everything evolves through supply and demand competition

If the conditions exist that a person or groups of people will strive to gain some form of advantage or control over others due to a constraint (i.e. a limitation of a resource or time or money or people), then we have competition. If competition exists then the components affected will evolve until they become industrialised. This impacts everything from activities (what we do), practices (how we do something), data (how we measure something) to knowledge (how we understand something). The map is never static but dynamic. It's also important to understand that if competition exists then you will be in conflict with others. Sometimes, the best way of resolving this is through coopetition (i.e. cooperative competition) and building alliances. In other cases, depending upon the context, then you have to fight, even to the point of a game of last man standing. In any significant landscape then you're likely to find yourself building alliances on one part of the map, whilst at the same time, fighting other companies in another and withdrawing from a third. However, as the components on your map evolve then your former allies can become foes and vice versa. Microsoft and open source used to be mortal enemies; they're now often found to be best buddies. To manage such a dynamic and fluid environment then you're going to need to be able to observe it.

Evolution consists of multiple waves of diffusion with many chasms

Evolution consists of many instances of the same act, e.g. a phone, a better phone and an even better phone. Every instance of an evolving act will diffuse through its applicable market. Those markets will change as the act evolves, i.e. the market for the first custom-built phones is not the same as the market for more industrialised phones. The process of evolution can include sustaining, incremental and discontinuous change, e.g. product to product improvements or product to product substitution. This path is not smooth, it is not linear, it has many branches and dead ends (e.g. phones that failed). Furthermore, the actions of individual players are unpredictable. Hence, you can know the direction (e.g. phones will industrialise over time) but not the steps and the exact path taken (this phone will be more successful than that phone) until you have walked it.

You cannot measure evolution over time or adoption

The only consistent mechanism I've found for measuring evolution is ubiquity and certainty, i.e. how well understood, complete and / or fit something is for the environment.

The less evolved something is then the more uncertain it is

By definition, the novel and new are more uncertain than industrialised components such as commodities and utilities. The uncharted space consists of the unknown, i.e. "Ere be Dragons".

No choice over evolution

In a competing ecosystem then the pressure for adoption of a successful change increases as more adopt the change. This is known as the "Red Queen" effect, i.e. you have to continuously adapt in order to keep still (in terms of relative position to others). The one thing that standing still will guarantee is that you will be overtaken. The Red Queen has a secondary effect, which is by adaptation, then competitors limit the growth of a single company and prevent a runaway process.

Commoditisation does not equal Centralisation

Don't confuse evolution to a commodity with centralisation. They are governed by different factors and an industrialised component can easily yo-yo between centralised and decentralised forms. Competitor gameplay is one of those factors that determine whether we're going to start with a more centralised or decentralised world.

Characteristics change as components evolve

The characteristics of a component in the uncharted space are not the same as the characteristics of the same component when it becomes industrialised. In any large system then you're likely to have components at different ends of the evolution scale. This leads to the Salaman & Storey Innovation paradox of 2002, i.e. the need to innovate requires polar opposite capabilities to the need to be efficient. However, a word to the wise; a company has to manage both the extremes, along with the evolution between them. It's really important to remember that there is a transition from uncharted to industrialised. Don't organise by the extremes alone.

No single method fits all

Because of these changing characteristics, there is no one size fits all methods or technique applicable across an entire landscape. You have to learn to use many approaches and so avoid the tyranny of any single one. However, expect tribes to form and endless pointless debates such as agile versus Six Sigma or outsourcing vs insourcing.

Components can co-evolve

All components can evolve, whether activities, practices, data or knowledge, but they can also co- evolve. This is commonly seen with the coevolution of practice (how we do something), with the evolution of an activity (what we do), especially as we shift from products to more industrialised forms. What causes this is the change of characteristics of the activity. DevOps is one such example of coevolution.

Efficiency enables innovation

Genesis begets evolution begets genesis. The industrialisation of one component enables novel higher order systems to emerge through componentisation effects. But it also enables new features for existing products to appear or even the evolution of other components. The industrialisation of mass communication to a standardised utility such as the internet enabled the industrialisation of computing to a utility. I use the word innovation to describe all those changes from the genesis of a new act, feature differentiation of an existing act or a change of business model (e.g. shift from product to utility). The evolution of one component and its efficient provision enables innovation of others.

Higher order systems create new sources of value

It is the genesis of new components enabling new user needs that creates future sources of differential value. I specifically state "enabling" because in many cases, the users are unaware of the future needs they might have.

Future value is inversely proportional to the certainty we have over it

Genesis of a component is inherently uncertain, but it is also the point at which a component has its highest future value. You have to gamble with the novel but there's also the potential for huge rewards. As the component evolves, its potential for differential value declines as it becomes more ubiquitous in its applicable market. This also means that any component that has not reached ubiquity must retain some uncertainty and some element of risk. The only conditions where a well understood, almost risk-free component exists that is not ubiquitous and is of high value, is when there is some form of restriction on competition, e.g. a constraint through patents or monopoly. Care must also be taken not to confuse the terms common, as in "everyone has one", with ubiquity to its applicable market. Many components have resource constraints (e.g. gold) or the market need is specific (e.g. wigs for barristers and judges).

Efficiency does not mean a reduced spend

Whilst evolution does result in more efficient provision of a component, this should be not be confused with a reduction of spending on it. In many cases, there is a long tail of unmet demand that efficiency will enable, or previously uneconomical acts that become feasible, or even the creation of new industries that result in greater demand. This is known as Jevons paradox.

Evolution to higher order systems results in increasing energy consumption

The constant evolution of components and creation of higher order systems that then evolve means we are always moving to a more ordered environment by reducing local entropy. This requires the constant input of greater amounts of energy, though in some cases, this can be hidden due to efficiency gains from previous wasteful consumption.

Capital flows to new areas of value

The lines on the map represent flows of capital, whether it's between two existing components or a component and its future more evolved self. Financial capital will seek the area of most consistent return. Hence, in the evolution from product to a utility then capital will tend to move away from the pre-existing product forms and towards the more industrialised component and the new industries built upon it

Evolution of communication can increase the speed of evolution overall

Evolution consists of many diffusion curves. If a means of communication evolves to a more industrialised form — whether printing press, postage stamp, telephone, the internet — then the speed of diffusion curves can increase. This in turn can accelerate the rate at which future components evolve. Care should be taken here not to confuse faster evolution with us becoming more innovative as a people. Certainly, we have greater opportunity to build new things, but don't assume we're getting smarter.

Change is not always linear

There can often be a perception that change is gradual because one instance of a component (e.g. a product) is replaced by another in the same stage of evolution (i.e. a more feature complete product). This illusion of smooth and gradual change lulls us into a false sense of security that all change is such.

Shifts from product to utility tend to demonstrate a punctuated equilibrium

The shift across a boundary, e.g. from custom to product or from product to commodity tends to visibly exhibit rapid exponential change and a shift from the past. This is known as a punctuated equilibrium.

Success breeds inertia

Any past success with a component will tend to create resistance to changing that component. There are many different forms of inertia.

Inertia increases the more successful the past model is

The more success we have had with a component then the more resistance and bias we have against it changing.

Inertia can kill an organisation

Contrary to popular belief, it's not a lack of innovation that harmed companies such as Blockbuster and Kodak but instead, inertia to change created by past success. Both these companies helped develop the future industries but suffered at the hands of their past business models.

Creative Destruction

The combination of inertia, a punctuated equilibrium, the Red Queen and coevolution of practice means that as we shift across a boundary, e.g. product to utility, then we tend to get rapid destruction of the past (from business models to practice), along with creation of the new (industry and practices). This was described as creative destruction by Joseph Schumpeter.

Competitors' actions will change the game

Climatic patterns are ones that depend upon aggregated market effects, e.g. evolution through supply and demand competition. This means that you cannot stop them without preventing competition in the market, and the existence of competitors will cause them to happen.

Most competitors have poor situational awareness

Competitor actions are an important part of anticipation. In general however, this is not something that you can directly control or even anticipate beyond aggregated effects. Fortunately, in today's climate then most competitors act as blind players, in which case, you do not need to dwell too much on their actions. When you make a move, they are unlikely to understand why or counter you. In the near future, given the potential interest in business algorithms, they may even become anticipatable blind automatons following coded secrets of success. In much the same way that Dan Mirvish noted that when Anne Hathaway was in the news, Warren Buffett's Berkshire Hathaway's shares went up due to suspected sentiment analysis run by robotic trading platforms. This could make the game even easier.

Not everything is random

Not everything is uncertain within the map. There are various aspects that can be anticipated, though the level of predictability is not uniform. In some cases, you can say what will happen due to aggregated market effects (e.g. this act will evolve), but not precisely when the next iteration of a more evolved product will appear (e.g. it depends upon actors' actions). In other cases, you can anticipate both the what and the when.

Economy has cycles

The economy demonstrates cycles such as the peace, war and wonder cycle. We start with the wonder of a new, uncommon and poorly understood thing. As we learn more then the applicable market grows and products are produced. New giants form and dominate a rather peaceful time of sustaining competition. There is some disruption (i.e. product to product substitution) and the competition is still fierce, but the giants generally weather these storms. Then the act evolves to more industrialised forms, new entrants become the new titans, past giants tend to fall, being stuck behind inertia barriers created from their own success. This is the time of war where competition becomes life-threatening for those past giants. New industries built on the industrialised components form and a new state of wonder is born.

Two different forms of disruption

There is more than one form of disruption, such as the unpredictable product to product substitution to the more predictable product to utility substitution. The latter can be anticipated through weak signals.

A "war" (point of industrialisation) causes organisations to evolve

The industrialisation of an act will tend to cause coevolution of practice and changes to how organisations operate. If the component is significant then this can lead to a new form of organisation.

You need to apply these patterns to your map to start to learn how things could change. You then need to allow others to challenge your assumptions and the scenarios you create — another key part of learning — until you've got a map you all agree with or at least understand, e.g. Figure 158.

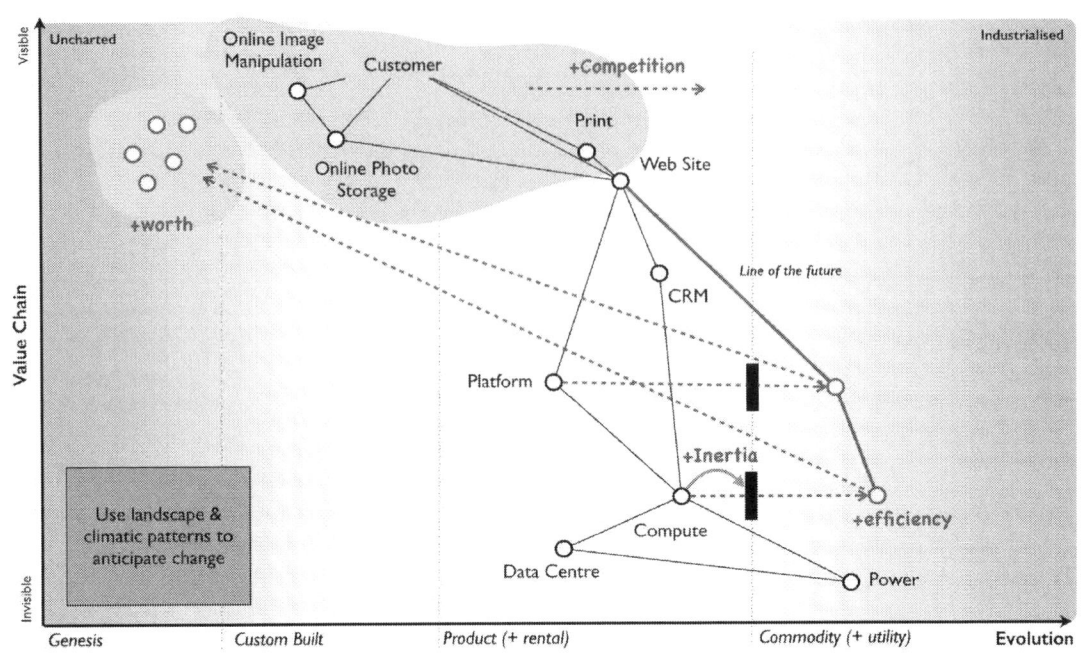

Figure 158: Anticipating change

Step 4 — Learn and use doctrine

Now you have an idea of your landscape and how it can change, you'll want to start doing stuff about it. However, there are two classes of choice; those that are universally applicable and those that are context-specific. The universally applicable choices are a set of principles that we all should apply. These are your doctrine.

At the time of writing, this is my list of basic doctrine — hence Wardley's Doctrine (I really am that unimaginative). This is based upon my observations over many maps with many organisations and contains universal principles that I consider to be reasonably sound. Many of these we have already covered

Wardley's Doctrine

Be transparent

Have a bias towards openness within your organisation. If you want to effectively learn about the landscape then you need to share your maps with others and allow them to add their wisdom and their challenge to the process. Building maps in secret in your organisations is a surefire way of having a future meeting where somebody points out the blindingly obvious thing you have missed.

Focus on high situational awareness

There is a reasonably strong correlation between awareness and performance, so focus on this. Try to understand the landscape that you are competing in and understand any proposals in terms of this. Look before you leap.

Use a common language

A necessity for effective collaboration is a common language. Maps allow many people with different aptitudes (e.g. marketing, operations, finance and IT) to work together in order to create a common understanding. Collaboration without a common language is just noise before failure.

Challenge assumptions

Maps allow for assumptions to be visually exposed. You should encourage challenge to any map, with a focus on creating a better map and a better understanding. Don't be afraid of challenge; there is no place for ego if you want to learn.

Know your users

When mapping a landscape then know who your users are, e.g. customers, shareholders, regulators and staff.

Focus on user needs

An essential part of mapping is the anchor of user needs. Ideally, you want to create an environment where your needs are achieved by meeting the needs of your users. Be mindful that these needs will evolve due to competition, and in the uncharted space, they are uncertain. Also, be aware that users may have different and competing needs, and be prepared to balance the conflict.

Think fast, inexpensive, elegant and restrained (FIRE)

Break large systems down into small components, use and re-use inexpensive components where possible, constrain budgets and time, build as simply and as elegantly as possible.

Be pragmatic

There will always be edge cases or a way to make something more perfect, but if what you're building could use a component that already exists then try to avoid the urge to re-invent it. If you're a taxi company then investing your funds into making that perfect tyre will not help your business. Always challenge when you depart from using something that already exists. The old adage of "It doesn't matter if the cat is black or white, as long as it catches mice" is relevant here.

Remove bias and duplication

Use multiple maps to help you remove duplication and bias within an organisation. You will often find in any large organisation that there are people custom-building what is a commodity or rebuilding something that exists elsewhere. Remember, that they're not doing this because they're daft but because of pre-existing inertia or the lack of any effective communication mechanism, i.e. they simply don't know it exists elsewhere. Be warned, the level of duplication within most organisations vastly exceeds any expectations that they might have, and you're often treading on the toes of someone's pet project. Large distributed companies often talk about duplication in the single digits, e.g. we have six enterprise content management systems. They tend to react in horror when it is "discovered" that they have hundreds or even "thousands". People can get very defensive in this space and want to shut you down.

Use appropriate methods and tools

Try to avoid the tyranny of one. Understand that there is no magic solution and that you have to use multiple methods (e.g. agile or lean or Six Sigma) as appropriate. In any large system, multiple methods may be used at the same time. Be mindful of ego here; tribes can form with almost religious fervour about the righteousness of their method. Have fortitude; you'll often find you're arguing against all these tribes at the same time.

Focus on the outcome, not a contract

Try to focus on the outcome and what you're trying to achieve. Realise that different types of contract will be needed, e.g. outsourced or time and material based or worth based development. Along with a focus on outcomes, try and keep contracts constrained in terms of time and budget.

Use standards where appropriate

If something is industrialised and if standards exist then try to use them. There's always a temptation to build a better standard, but avoid this or building abstraction layers on top of other "standards" unless you have an extremely compelling reason to do so. If you need a toaster, buy a toaster and don't try building one from scratch.

Optimise flow

Within a map, there will be many flows of capital — whether information, risk, social or financial. Try to optimise this and remove bottlenecks.

Effectiveness over efficiency

Whilst optimising flow is important, be careful not to waste valuable time making the ineffective more efficient. Understand the landscape and how it is changing before you attempt to optimise flow.

Manage inertia

At some point, you will face inertia to change, e.g. existing practice, political capital or previous investment. Try and understand the root cause. Ideally, use a map to anticipate this before you encounter it and hence, have prepared solutions and counter arguments. If possible, use the maps to enable people to discover their own inertia.

Manage failure

In any system, there is risk. Use the maps where possible to help you understand failure modes, what can go wrong and what will be impacted if a component fails. Try where possible to mitigate risks by distributing systems, by designing for failure, and by the constant introduction of failure (use of chaos engines such as Netflix's chaos monkey). Avoid known failure modes such as building large scale (Death Star) like efforts.

Think small

Know the details, use small teams and break large landscapes into small contracts. Don't be chased away by fears of complexity of management.

Distribute power and decision-making

Have a bias towards distributing power from the centre, including yourself. Put power in the hands of those who are closest to the choices that need to be made.

Provide purpose, mastery & autonomy

Provide people with purpose (including a moral imperative and a scope) for action. Enable them to build mastery in their chosen area and give them the freedom (and autonomy) to act.

Think aptitude and attitude

Understand that people not only have aptitudes (e.g. finance, engineering, operations and marketing) but different attitudes (pioneer, settler and town planner). The mindsets are different.

There is no one culture

Understand that a company that plans for longevity needs to cope with not only the discovery of uncharted components but the use of the industrialised and the transition between these two extremes. You will need different attitudes. You will therefore create many cultures in your organisation, e.g. pioneers, settlers and town planners have different cultures. This is not a negative and don't try to grind everyone into a single bland culture. It will not make them happy.

Seek the best

Try to find and grow the best people with the best aptitude and attitude for their roles. Invest in keeping them. Don't force them into becoming something they're not. It's perfectly reasonable for a truly gifted systems tester who excels in a town planning world of massively complicated and automated systems to be paid more than the project manager. What you want to avoid is taking exceptional people out of their role and putting them into something they are not suited to, simply because they think that is the only way to progress. Leadership, management and engineering are all aptitudes, they are all valuable and they have to work in concert. If the hierarchy of your organisation uniformly reflects your pay scales then you're likely to be draining talent from where it should be and putting it into roles that it is not suited for. This is often done for arguments of "responsibility" or "managing bigger teams" (which also causes people to try and accumulate empires) or "spreading experience" or "career path", but there are alternative ways of achieving this. Taking a gifted engineer and turning them into a mediocre project manager is not wise. This is probably one of the most difficult areas as ego is quickly encountered.

Design for constant evolution

Create an organisational system that copes with the constant ebb and flow in the landscape. Ideally, changes should flow through your organisation without the need for constant restructuring. A cell based structure using a system of theft with pioneers, settlers and town planners is one such process.

Use a systematic mechanism of learning

The purpose of mapping is not just to create a map and a shared understanding but also to learn climatic patterns, doctrine and context-specific play. Maps provide a systematic way of doing this, as long as you collate, review and learn from them. Have a bias towards such learning and the use of data.

A bias towards action

This is best explained through the words of Rimmer's Study Habit (an episode from Red Dwarf).

"The first weeks of study, he would always devote to the construction of a revision timetable. Weeks of patient effort would be spent planning, designing and creating a revision schedule, which, when finished, were minor works of art.

Every hour of every day was subdivided into different study periods, each labelled in his lovely, tiny copperplate hand; then painted over in watercolours, a different colour for each subject, the colours gradually becoming bolder and more urgent shades as the exam time approached. The effect was as if a myriad of tiny rainbows had splintered and sprinkled across the poster-sized sheet of cream wove card.

The only problem was this: because the timetables often took seven or eight weeks, and sometimes more, to complete, by the time Rimmer had finished them, the exam was almost on him. He'd then have to cram three months of astronavigation revision into a single week. Gripped by an almost deranging panic, he'd then decide to sacrifice the first two days of that final week to the making of another timetable. This time for someone who had to pack three months of revision into five days."

Do not attempt to create the perfect map. Have a bias towards action because the landscape will change and you will discover more through action. You learn by playing the game.

Listen to your ecosystems

There are many different forms of ecosystems and ways to exploit them. You can build powerful sensing engines (e.g. the ILC model) for future change, sources of cooperation with others, defensive and offensive alliances. But ecosystems need management; they need tending as a gardener tends a garden — sometimes you allow them to grow wild, sometimes you harvest, sometimes you help direct or constrain them. These are particular skills that you can develop, but most important is the principle — listen to them.

A bias towards the new

Whatever you do will evolve. So have a bias towards the new, be curious and take appropriate risks. Be willing to experiment.

Be the owner

Take responsibility for your environment, your actions within it and how you play the game. You could outsource this to a third party in the way a chess player could outsource their gameplay to another, but you won't learn and it is still you that loses.

Strategy is iterative, not linear

Understand that strategy is iterative. You need to adapt in fast cycles according to the changing environment. The best you can hope for is a direction, a constant process of learning and improvement of your gameplay along the way.

Do better with less

Have a bias towards continual improvement.

Set exceptional standards

Don't settle for as good as or slightly better than competitors. Always strive for the very best that can be achieved.

Strategy is complex

There will be uncertainty, emerging patterns and surprises along the way. That's the very nature of competition due to the involvement of other actors. Embrace this, don't fall for the temptation that you can plan the future. What matters is not the plan but the preparation and your ability to adapt.

Commit to the direction, be adaptive along the path

Once you've set a direction, commit to it. There will often be hurdles and obstacles but don't just simply abandon a direction because a single step is challenging. Try to find paths around the obstacles. If you're building a system and a common component is not as expected then that can often prove a market opportunity.

Move fast

The speed at which you move around the cycle is important. There is little point implementing FIRE-like principles in developing a system if it takes you a year to make a decision to act. An imperfect plan executed today is better than a perfect plan executed tomorrow.

There is no core

Everything is transient; whatever you think is core to your company won't be at some point in the future. The only things that are truly static are dead.

Exploit the landscape

Use the landscape to your advantage; there are often powerful force multipliers. You might decide not to take advantage of a competitor or a change in the market, but that should be a conscious choice.

Think big

Whilst the actions you take, the way that you organise and the focus on detail requires you to think small when it comes to inspiring others, providing direction and moral imperative then think big.

Your purpose is not to defend the narrow pass of Thermopylae but instead to defeat the Persian army and save the Greek states.

Be humble

Listen to others, be selfless, have fortitude and be humble. Inspire others by who you are and what you do. There are many ways to manipulate the landscape, e.g. with marketing by persuading others that what is a commodity is somehow different or that a product is unique to them. But these manipulations come with a cost, not just externally but internally. We can start to believe our own hype, our own infallibility and our "right" to the market. Avoid this arrogance at all costs.

As with climatic patterns, the more you play the game then the more forms of doctrine you'll discover. It's important to learn these continuously, so get used to using maps as a retrospective. Look for what has changed and always ask why? Of course, knowing about doctrine is not enough — you'll want to apply it. Don't pick and choose, apply them all. When it comes to applying doctrine then there are three basic cases:-

- the map solves doctrine for you (e.g. having a common language)
- you can use many maps to apply doctrine (e.g. use of multiple maps of different lines of business to reduce duplication and bias)
- you can apply doctrine directly to a map (e.g. cell based structures, cultural forms such as pioneer — settler — town planner), as shown in Figure 159

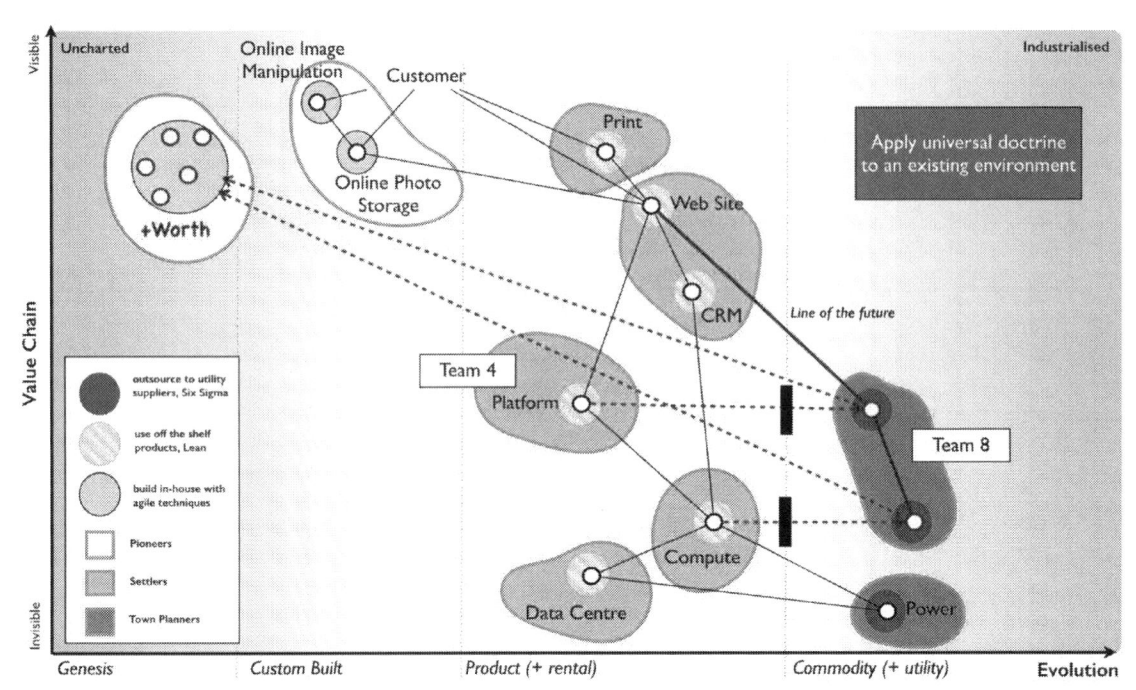

Figure 159: Apply doctrine

Step 5 — Learn and use gameplay

The other class of choice is context-specific. You will learn there exists many approaches that you can deploy in order to influence the map. These approaches depend upon the map and the position of pieces within it, i.e. they are not universal and you have to learn when and where to use them. To get you started, some basic forms of gameplay (often called stratagems) are:-

Gameplay

Open approaches

Whether source or data or practice, the act of making something open reduces barriers to adoption, encourages collaboration and accelerates the evolution of the component.

IPR

Intellectual property rights (IPR) can be used to slow evolution by limiting competition, even to the point of ring-fencing a component, making it difficult for others to evolve it further.

Fear, uncertainty and doubt

Often used to slow evolution by exploiting inertia to change within customers and forcing new entrants to divert energy away from the components and into countering the accusations.

Exploiting constraint

An existing constraint can be exploited to fragment a single player by increasing demand beyond their ability to supply (e.g. by creating a price war).

Sweat and Dump

A mechanism of disposing of legacy liability onto a third party by exploiting their own inertia to change.

Pig in a poke

A mechanism of dressing up a liability as some form of future business before divesting to a third party.

Two-factor markets

A mechanism of bringing providers and consumers together and exploiting network effects and aggregated data.

Sensing Engines (ILC)

A mechanism of being the first mover to industrialise a component, allowing others (the ecosystem) to build new industries upon it and then using consumption data to determine future candidates for industrialisation.

As with climatic patterns and doctrine, then the more you play the game, the more context-specific patterns you will discover. With your understanding of the landscape, an ability to anticipate change based upon climatic patterns and a knowledge of context-specific play that you can use to manipulate the map should enable you to determine where you could attack and how you can use gameplay to increase your odds of success. At the very least, you should be able to create a common understanding of where you're going and why you're taking certain approaches within the company — see Figure 160.

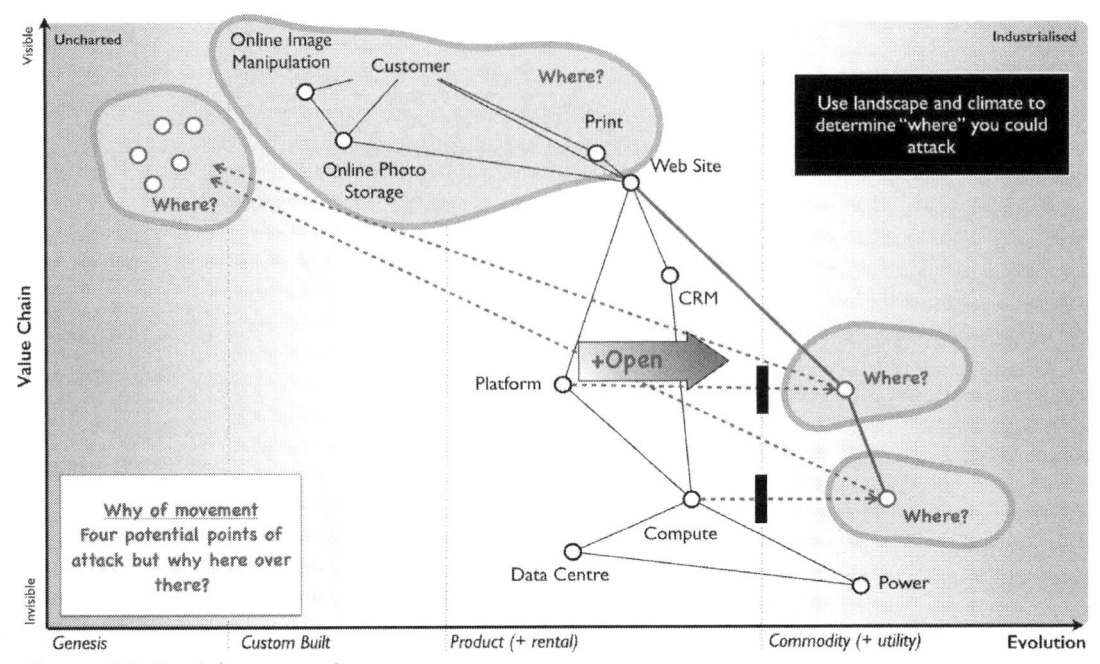

Figure 160: Applying gameplay

You then decide to act. You loop around the cycle and repeat this whole exercise. Don't hesitate with action, make your plans and roll the dice. It's worth remembering that one of your actions may be to change direction of the company itself, to alter your very purpose. You might start off as a paper mill but you might become a telecommunications company. Get used to it, there is no "core" to a company beyond short-term immediate focus.

A few things to remember

On biology

Terms like evolution, coevolution, adaptation, Red Queen, competition, adaptive renewal systems, cell based structures, ecosystem, flow and awareness might make you think that I'm talking about some form of biological system. That's because I am. A business is a living thing, not some physical machine. The more classical view of the machine has advantages in management thinking as it implies it's simple and can be managed just by pulling the right levers or adding the right algorithm. This works fine if you're in competition with others who think the same way, but don't assume everyone does.

Biological systems are highly resilient to change in total. Individual members or species might be taken out by some disease or some catastrophic event, but the system of life itself adapts and evolves through mutations in the entire population or exaptation (re-use of components for another purpose). A classical machine has a far more limited scope of resilience, no matter how well-designed or scenarios considered, and it does not evolve with its environment in the same manner. C. S. Holling distinguished between these two types of resilience as engineering versus ecological. Whereas engineering resilience is primarily about the efficiency of function, ecological resilience is focused on the existence of function.

A **fragile** system is one with low engineering and ecological resilience. It has very limited constraints of physical operation and it cannot adapt or cope with change well. It breaks easily and ceases to function.

A **robust** system is one with high engineering but low ecological resilience. It has a broader range of physical constraints that it can cope with but again, it cannot adapt to unexpected events. Many classical systems are designed to maintain the efficiency of function, given a set of broad constraints or defined changes, e.g. loss of a single engine in an aircraft.

A **fluid** system is one with low engineering resilience but high ecological resilience. Though elements of the system can be considered fragile (operating within limited constraints or occupying a niche), the system itself adapts rapidly to changing circumstances, i.e. the efficiency of function might decline rapidly due to a change but the function continues to exist. Many biological ecosystems can be considered fluid and the process of change is known as evolution, e.g. adaptation of a species to some new predator or environmental catastrophe.

A **resilient** system is one with high engineering and ecological resilience. Not only is the system capable of coping with a wide variety of physical extremes, the entire system rapidly adapts to a changing environment in order to exist. Nature in its entirety can be considered resilient and it has become so through the process of evolution. Nature consists of many biological ecosystems occupying niches and any change in physical conditions enables one biological ecosystem to invade the space of another. The efficiency and survival of life is preserved, bar the most catastrophic of shocks.

This last point is critical. It is evolution through competition and a changing environment that has made nature itself resilient. Evolution is driven by competition, and far from the gradual and peaceful concept that abounds in literature, it involves the entire annihilation of species and individual biological ecosystems in a violent orgy of death throughout history. Species have evolved mechanisms to survive this orgy of death. Your body builds muscle because of constant exercise, but burns that same muscle during starvation — it's all part of our body's energy management that has evolved to cope with change. Even death itself is a necessity to evolution and self-replication with constrained resources.

However, a consequence of this orgy has been diversity, and whether it is diversity between or within species, this is a critical element of ecological resilience. Lack of diversity is often a major weakness of classical engineering systems through systemic failure. If you want to create a system that is capable of adapting to constant change, is resilient to the unknown and has the best shot at longevity as a whole then nature is a past master at this. Learn from life itself.

On maps

Maps are about awareness. You should always remember:-

1. The map is constantly changing. These are living documents. With practice, it should take a few hours to map a business from scratch and these have to adapt as you discover more. This is relatively simple if they become embedded as a means of communication.
2. Maps are a means of learning about the environment and communicating this. It's an iterative process and it will take you years to become good at it. The really important lesson about maps is not how accurate or perfect they are but how you use them to continuously learn. Maps are not the "truth" but a guide that an entire army can collaborate and communicate around.
3. All models are wrong, some are merely useful. Someone will produce a more useful method of mapping, a better list of doctrine, a more insightful set of patterns. As there is no such thing as the "right" map, then feel free to alter the map in a way that makes it more useful to you.
4. If you're feeling that this is a lot to take in, well it is. Strategy is not a simple topic, despite our attempts to dress it up as such.

You are now ready. Well, you might have been ready long ago but I wanted to give myself the best chance, so it's more that I am now ready. Forward friends, and let us now play the game with a scenario in the next chapter.

Chapter 12 - The scenario

You are a member of the executive board of a huge conglomerate focused on facilities management. You're attending a meeting of a wholly owned subsidiary company with their executives. You're on a fact-finding mission, trying to determine what the future of this subsidiary is.

There has been some recent positive noise about the subsidiary from analysts and also some interest by third parties in potential acquisition. This company offers a single product, which is a software system that monitors a data centre's consumption of power in order to determine whether it is being used effectively. The product is known as Phoenix.

The Company

The CEO introduces the company and their vision to provide customers with the best tool in the market for reducing power consumption and improving environmental performance. The CEO talks about their mission to "help reduce IT's impact on the planet" and there is noticeably a great sense of pride and self-belief within the group. The CEO reiterates their core values in a presentation. The values are described as being instrumental to the company's success and they include responsibility, integrity, transparency, compassion, empathy, adaptiveness and decisiveness. The CEO then provides some background information, more for your benefit than anyone else's.

What is Phoenix?

The system involves a proprietary software package that performs analytics across data gathered from a sensor that is installed within a customer's data centre. The sensor is a highly expensive piece of kit that is manufactured by third parties. The sensor monitors the electricity input, the temperature and airflow within the building.

The analytics software is based upon a decade of best practice experience for the use of these sensors. The algorithms contained within the software package are considered to be the essential core IP of the subsidiary, and they differentiate this product from everything else on the market. These algorithms are a carefully guarded secret. The software package also consumes a set of environmental data (which is provided by the company), which contains performance information on common hardware.

Operation of Phoenix

The setup on a client site requires:-

- installation of the sensor
- setting up a highly redundant server, which contains the software package
- installing agents on each machine in the data centre to provide performance information to the analytics tool over the network
- describing the initial layout of the data centre to the analytics tool
- allowing the system to run for several days to collect data

The system contains a learning AI, which, over time, develops recommendations for improving the efficiency of power use, from air conditioning, air flow, positioning of equipment, type of equipment and modes of operation. It has been shown to consistently reduce 10% of energy consumption within client sites with constant active monitoring. The process of setting up a new client involves a two-day installation of equipment and software on premise. The service is charged for on an initial hardware and setup cost, followed by a two-year renewable software licence. You note that the group is clearly proud of its accomplishments, the technological marvel they have created and their ability to deliver against their vision. Next up to speak is the head of marketing.

Marketing & Business Development

The name Phoenix inspires the ideas of regrowth, of nature and of power, and this is heavily used in branding and marketing materials. The company is the largest vendor of such energy efficiency systems in Europe, providing a complete service from on-premise software package to sensor install. Your systems currently account for 43% of the 2016 market, which is estimated at £301 million p.a., according to the latest analyst figures. The head of marketing discusses several successful online campaigns, its strong brand in the European industry, and a recently run customer survey that has found a good to high level of satisfaction in over 90% of the client base.

Whilst the subsidiary has some competitors in Europe, most of these are offering highly custom-built solutions that are extremely expensive. The head of marketing also points to data showing the current European market is only a fraction of the £3 billion p.a. applicable market and opportunities exist in growing market share, growing the current market and also expansion overseas. In terms of growing market share, an aggressive sales and marketing plan has been developed to increase MaSh from 43% to 65% by 2021. Phoenix is considered to be the leading European technology in the space, according to latest analyst reports.

In terms of international expansion, there are incentives for encouraging growth in markets such as Brazil, in which currently no company is providing a well-developed product solution. The head of strategy agrees and interjects by stating, "We consider this to be a highly attractive future emerging market and one the company plans to exploit." You notice the head of sales nodding in agreement.

The US market is larger and considered to be more mature. Over the last seven years, there has been a software as a service offering in the US, which uses the same sensor technology but with the main software package provided through a public cloud and sold on a utility basis rather than a licence fee, i.e. the client is only charged for when it is active and running. This has been considered successful and now commands nearly 40% of the US market. However, the US company involved has also been operating in Europe over the last five years. The competitor represented less than 3% of the European market in 2015, but their CEO has claimed in the press that they are growing rapidly and almost doubling in size each year, with £15M in revenue in 2015. Though the competitor has not announced its final figures for 2016, it's estimated by some reports to be around £25M. The head of sales adds that this is not a truly digital business as it still requires install of the sensor (either by the client or through a consultancy) and connection of the sensor to the public service. They state, "The US competitor might have a cloud based solution but they lack our relationships."

The CIO comments that the US solution provides some features that Phoenix does not have. including cross company reporting, industry analytics and a public API. There are also a number of other companies building products on top of this competitor's public API, and their CEO describes a "fairly active development community is growing around this". The Chief Digital Officer (who also runs the product group) adds that we will be building a cloud service. You sense a bit of tension here. You're aware that the organisation was recently restructured with a younger and more dynamic CDO brought into the company. The CIO (the last remaining member of the original team who founded the company) has found herself more sidelined to internal IT and data management.

The CDO comments that there have also been recent social media stories about the US competitor "eating up" the business models of some of those product companies that have built on their API by adding similar capability into their own system. The head of sales suggests that the competitor is struggling to find its way and is being forced to resort to such cannibalistic action. He adds that "We rarely come across the US company in competitive tenders, and in any case, there are security concerns cited by some clients due to their cloud approach."

Sales

The head of sales takes over the presentation and starts to run through the growth of the company. It's obvious that there's a lot of coordination between marketing, sales and digital, and this team seems to be working well together. In 2016, the company had a record year, with £123 million in revenue and over 6,277 customers, including 690 new customers, 600 pre-threshold (installed and running but within the first two years before renewal begins), and 4,987 on two-year renewal. The digital group has been helping in providing mobile tools, communication and other capabilities for the sales team, along with marketing tools for more targeted advertising. The expected growth in clients is provided in Figure 161.

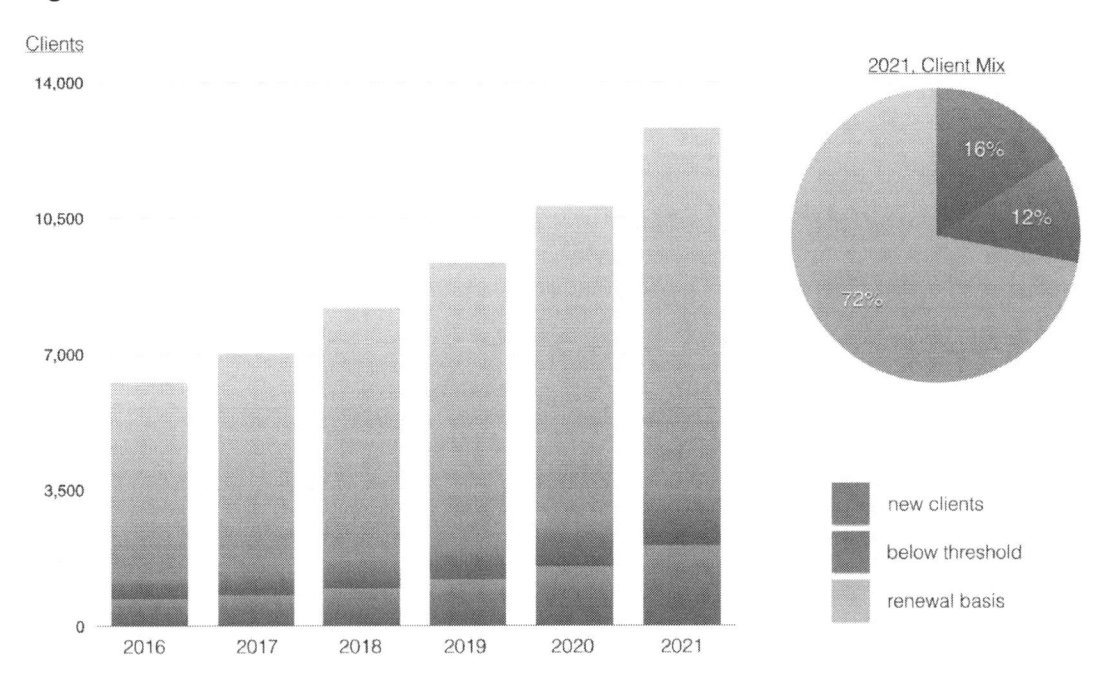

Figure 161: Growth in clients

The attrition rate has been high in recent years at 9%, but the sales team believes this is due to a lack of new features and a high cost of software licence renewal. To combat this, the digital and product team is being expanded, with a focus on new features, and the renewal price will be frozen for the next two years (leading to a drop in price in real terms), with possible further reductions due to an efficiency drive. It is believed that this combination should enable the company to reduce the attrition rate to 5% or less.

Digital & Product Development

Over the last year, the digital team has worked on improving both the social media reach, the website and the tools used in the company. The focus is now on product improvements and the development of a cloud service.

Cloud Service

This will be one of the most significant investments taken in the history of the company, starting in 2018 and intended for launch near the end of 2020 with £45 million invested. The service will be provided on a licence basis in order not to create conflict with the existing model and is considered to be a counter for any future threat from the US competitor, as well as necessity for a modern technology company. It is expected that by 2023 (three years after launch), the cloud service will contribute almost £50M p.a. and account for over 10% of the company's revenue (see Figure 162).

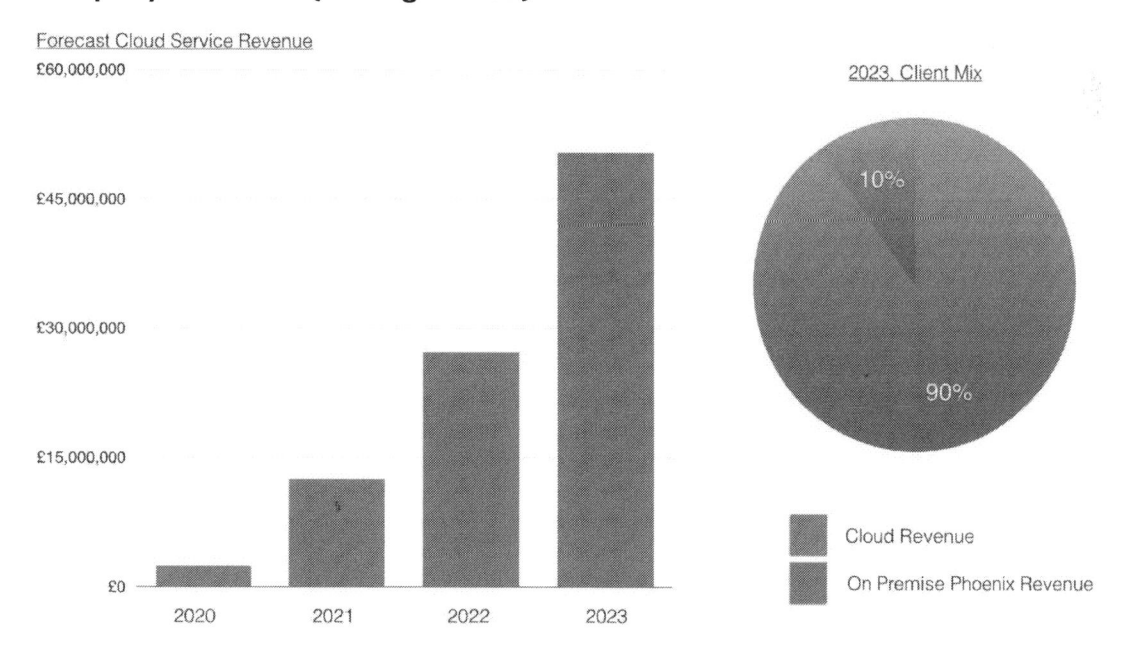

Figure 162: Cloud Service revenue

The Phoenix cloud service will provide cross company reporting and advanced analytics. These capabilities will also be included in the on-premise service and the company will promote this hybrid model of public or private alternatives. The public service will run on a major cloud provider, using emerging DevOps practices. The core algorithms and logic of Phoenix will be maintained but adapted to this new world. The business model was then explored, including a business model canvas (Figure 163) outlining the new service.

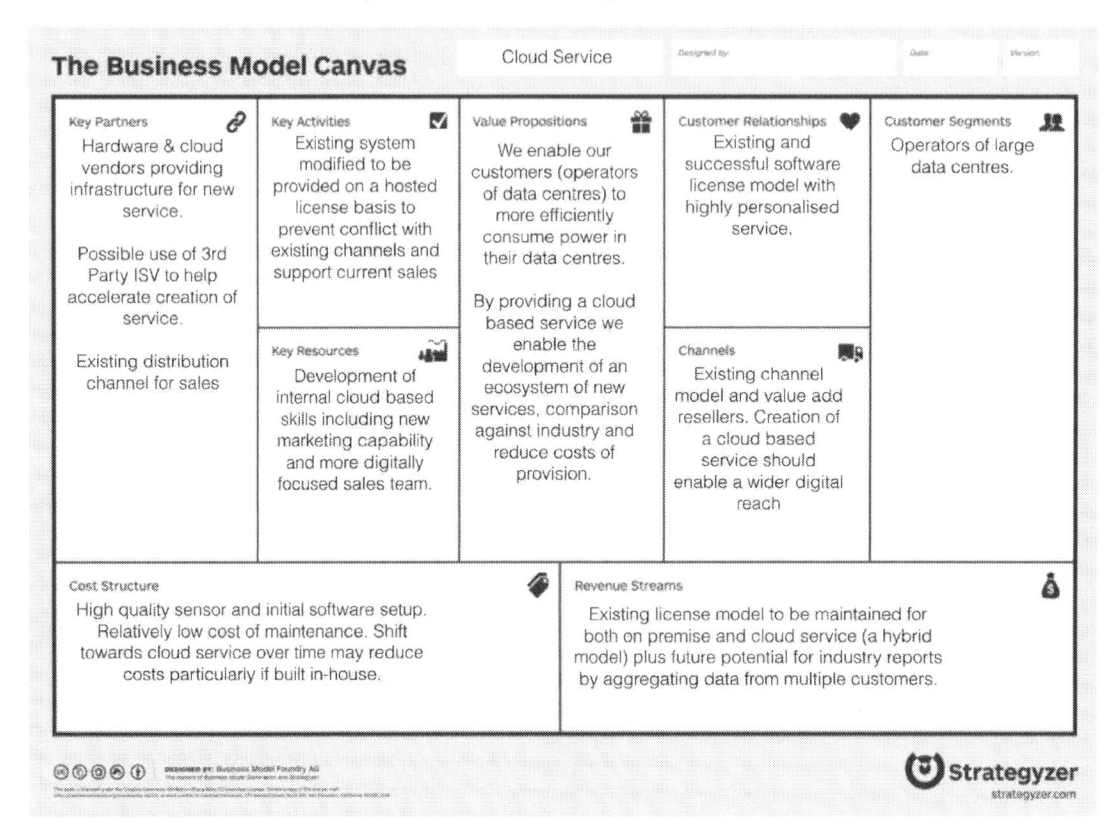

The Business Model Canvas — Cloud Service				
Key Partners Hardware & cloud vendors providing infrastructure for new service. Possible use of 3rd Party ISV to help accelerate creation of service. Existing distribution channel for sales	**Key Activities** Existing system modified to be provided on a hosted license basis to prevent conflict with existing channels and support current sales **Key Resources** Development of internal cloud based skills including new marketing capability and more digitally focused sales team.	**Value Propositions** We enable our customers (operators of data centres) to more efficiently consume power in their data centres. By providing a cloud based service we enable the development of an ecosystem of new services, comparison against industry and reduce costs of provision.	**Customer Relationships** Existing and successful software license model with highly personalised service. **Channels** Existing channel model and value add resellers. Creation of a cloud based service should enable a wider digital reach	**Customer Segments** Operators of large data centres.
Cost Structure High quality sensor and initial software setup. Relatively low cost of maintenance. Shift towards cloud service over time may reduce costs particularly if built in-house.		**Revenue Streams** Existing license model to be maintained for both on premise and cloud service (a hybrid model) plus future potential for industry reports by aggregating data from multiple customers.		

Figure 163: Business Model Canvas. Business Model Canvas framework from Strategyzer

Technology changes

Despite the benefit to clients in terms of energy savings through efficiency that Phoenix creates, there exists some concern over the high cost of the system in the market, as was noted in the customer survey. There are two potential routes for reducing the cost – the sensor technology and data costs.

Sensor technology

The sensor technology accounts for 73% of the installation charge of £67K. There is a range of new, more commodity-like sensors that has been launched in China by an extremely large manufacturer. These are far simpler, vastly cheaper (about 1/100th of the price of the existing sensors) and highly standardised. However, they are also extremely basic and lack the sensitivity and capability of the sensor that Phoenix uses. The CDO points out that the product team has attempted replacing the expensive sensor with one of these cheaper versions but the performance and analysis was severely degraded, making the system almost unworkable. The CIO interrupts and says that "a potential solution could be to use lots of the cheaper sensors".

The CDO points out that such an approach has been discussed several times before and would require a complete rewrite of Phoenix and an entirely new set of algorithms and techniques to be developed, requiring a new R&D program. The head of operations who manages installations also chimes in that it would require a complete overhaul to process and an extensive upgrade path for over 6,000 existing installations. The CEO also adds that it would undermine the intellectual property developed in Phoenix. This is finally capped off with the heads of marketing and sales both adding that this would create a marketing nightmare at a time of building both a new business in Brazil and a cloud service. You sense that there is frustration with the group and the CIO on this topic, which has apparently been raised many times before.

However, the operations, CDO and sales head all agree that despite these cheaper sensors being not good enough for the job that the client expects, they nevertheless think it's worth keeping an eye on the market. They are aware of the concept of disruptive innovation and how these cheaper sensors could develop. The CDO now turns to another opportunity.

Data set

One of the costs to the company is in the environmental data provided in Phoenix. This data requires extensive testing and modelling of various bits of kit commonly used within data centres. Whilst this is done in-house by the IT department, there is now a data set available on the market, which offers this. It is considered by the product team to be good enough and vastly cheaper than the solution from the in-house IT team. The CDO estimates that by buying in the outside data set then the company could reduce the costs of Phoenix by 3% – 4% and we should move forward with this idea. The sales and marketing heads agree that the company should not only focus on improving our existing software package but reduce costs where possible. The CIO agrees with this assessment, despite the obvious implications for IT.

Strategy

The head of strategy now discusses the future direction for the company. In a recent meeting, a number of directions were discussed with the entire executive team. These focused on the strengths of the company, the weaknesses in the existing product line, the potential opportunities in emerging markets and future threats, such as the US player. Though the discussions have been "challenging", the team developed a key number of actions that were considered to be urgent for the company. These were distilled into a new vision document called "Growth and sustainability for Phoenix". These options were then investigated with the wider company management team through a collaborative effort, to create a priority list (see Figure 164), which was then agreed with the CEO to provide a final direction.

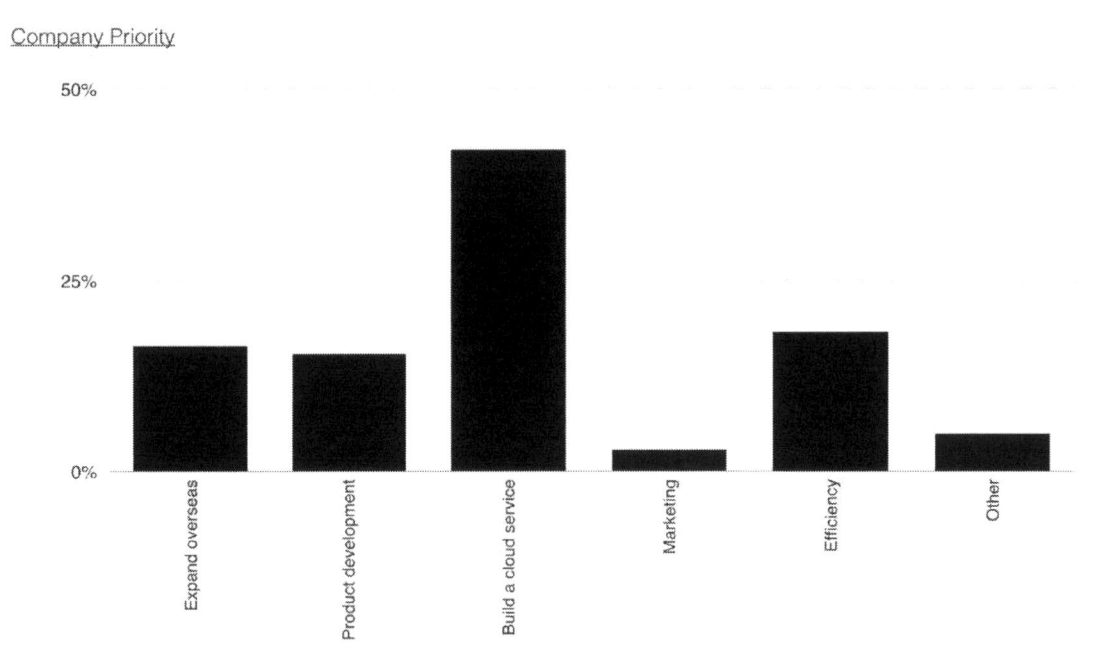

Figure 164: Management priority order

The focus and the priorities of the company are:-

1. Creation of a digital **"cloud** based" service for provision of the software.
2. Investigating the use of the data conversion product that is available in order to improve **efficiencies** and reduce cost.
3. **Expansion** of existing product into overseas markets such as Brazil.
4. Increasing the **development** effort on our existing product line, including more advanced reporting and other innovative features.

5. Undertake a significant **marketing** campaign to promote our solution in the existing market.

Finance

The CFO provides an overview of the company performance, including a basic P&L for the company with estimates for future years (Figure 165) that costs the program of changes highlighted by the strategy.

Year	FY 2016	est 2017	est 2018	est 2019	est 2020	est 2021
Total install base	6,277	7,020	8,200	9,350	10,800	12,800
Revenue (£M)	£123.2	£139.1	£163.2	£201.7	£238.3	£292.3
Re-occuring S/W License (£M)	£59.8	£66.4	£77.2	£94.8	£108.9	£126.6
New S/W License (£M)	£16.6	£19.0	£22.9	£31.4	£41.0	£56.5
Total S/W revenue	£76.4	£85.4	£100.0	£126.3	£149.9	£183.1
Installation / Consultancy (£M)	£46.7	£53.6	£63.2	£75.5	£88.3	£109.2
Cost of Goods Sold (£M)	£38.5	£44.1	£51.8	£61.5	£71.2	£86.9
Gross Profit (£M)	£84.6	£95.0	£111.4	£140.3	£167.1	£205.4
Gross Margin (%)	69%	68%	68%	70%	70%	70%
SG&A (£M)	£52.5	£62.0	£83.4	£86.8	£99.1	£112.0
Sales	£9.9	£12.5	£14.7	£16.1	£20.3	£23.4
Marketing	£8.6	£11.1	£18.0	£18.2	£23.8	£26.3
Operations	£7.3	£8.0	£9.2	£10.2	£11.6	£13.5
Digital & Product Development	£7.4	£11.1	£24.5	£26.4	£27.8	£32.2
IT	£10.9	£9.3	£6.0	£5.2	£5.1	£5.0
Admin	£6.2	£7.4	£8.1	£7.1	£6.7	£7.3
Finance	£2.2	£2.5	£3.1	£3.6	£3.8	£4.4
EBITDA (£M)	£32.1	£33.0	£28.0	£53.4	£68.0	£93.4
EBITDA (%)	26%	24%	17%	26%	29%	32%

Figure 165: P&L

The CFO highlights the following:-

- The company is profitable with a revenue in excess of £120M p.a., a 10% YoY (year on year) growth and an EBITDA of 26%. The company has a healthy cash flow and reserves.
- There has been a recent re-organisation in 2016, with digital combining with product development (previously under the CIO) but now run under the CDO. There has been investment in this space, particularly in new technology areas within the company such as the use of social media and cloud based tools. There has also been an investment in features within Phoenix and a recruitment drive for talent.

- It is expected that the digital group will expand significantly over the next two years with the development of the cloud service, which is anticipated for launch near the end of 2020. Though the company is experiencing growth, the investment will have a material effect on EBITDA during 2017 and 2018. There will also be a major marketing campaign around the cloud service, starting in 2020.
- The IT function now runs internal systems and data management. It is expected that efficiency savings can be made in core legacy systems and that shift towards an external data set will reduce IT costs significantly in 2018. This will be offset by some increase due to the cost of setting up operations in Brazil.
- The launch of the Brazil setup is planned for 2018. This will include a significant marketing drive, some additional admin (HR), finance and IT costs, along with increased sales costs.
- By 2021, it is expected that the launch of Brazil, the cloud service along with the efficiency drive in IT, will have significantly impacted revenue growth and improved EBITDA. The company by 2021 will have transformed to a more sales, marketing and digital led organisation.

The CEO concludes the meeting and privately apologises afterwards for the reaction of the CIO. He explains "It has been difficult because of the changes. However, this organisation is no longer a startup and some people just have not found adjusting to this new world that easy." You ask what he plans for the CIO and he comments with a wry smile, "Well, Sarah did express some interest in setting up the Brazil operation but I think she knows that sometimes, you just have to move on."

Task

You have a call in forty-five minutes with the executive board. That's how long you have to make your choices. The clock is ticking. So find a stopwatch and start it.

Your first task is to determine whether the company is heading in the right direction. You should determine whether you agree with the priority order given in Figure 166. If not, write down what your priority order would be. If you decide to invoke "other" then scribble down what that other is.

Priority Order	Company	You
Creation of a digital "cloud based" service for provision of the software	1	
Investigating the use of the data conversion product that is available in order to improve efficiencies in operation	2	
Expansion of existing product into overseas markets such as Brazil	3	
Increasing the development effort on our existing product line including more advanced reporting and other innovative features.	4	
Undertake a significant marketing campaign to promote our solution in the existing market.	5	
Other		

Figure 166: Priority order

Once you've decided your priority order then your next task is to determine what you're going to say to the executive board.

A note to the reader

Do try the exercise and spend that forty-five minutes on it. The temptation is always to skip to the next chapter and find the "answer" — if there is such a thing. However, that misses the whole point. This scenario is about you learning to play the game and to do so, you need to put yourself in an uncomfortable position of getting things maybe wrong or maybe right. Try not to guess; try and work out why you feel this is the right or maybe the wrong thing to do. If you get flummoxed then give yourself a bit more time, maybe an hour and half at max, but force yourself to make the choice.

You're playing with the future of a subsidiary and all the lives that it affects. There are people whose dreams and livelihoods will change by what you say and what you choose, along with a fortune to be won or squandered. You need to feel that pressure, the discomfort of not having long to decide and imperfect information to decide upon. You also need a way to communicate your findings to the rest of the executive board. This challenge isn't supposed to be easy or comfortable.

If you're feeling lost or out of your depth, remember, we started this journey with "Being lost". Every executive feels this, whether they care to admit it or not. You're being plunged into the water because eventually, you have to play the game and there's only so much you can do with reading. Don't get disheartened, this is all part of learning.

Chapter 13 - Something wicked this way comes

It may be unlucky for some but I'm going to start this Chapter 13 by announcing that I'm not going to give you an answer to the scenario — yet. Instead, I'm going to give you some analysis, just in case you're needing a bit of help. If you're some wizard that has already worked through the scenario, determined the right strategy and have a solution, then that's fine, you can skip unlucky 13 and head straight into the next chapter. This is more for the rest of us mere mortals, who like me, have found themselves totally lost when faced with problems such as the scenario. I'm not going to use any additional information other than that already provided — in other words, there's no mystery character inserted in the last paragraph that committed the crime — see all those loathsome detective novels that make you go "where did that come from?"

I'm also going to explain this analysis in quite some detail. I apologise in advance if this is tedious but I've spent a lifetime reading mathematics texts that go — "it is therefore obvious that" — only to continuously discover that it's not obvious to me. I am going to start by creating a map of the environment and use it with some of those basic climatic patterns. I'm also going to add in a bit about market position — that'll become clear as we go through. Remember, maps are just a communication tool and so feel free to annotate and adapt them as you need.

From this basic map, we're going to examine the state of the company and its proposed strategy. We're finally going to use time-turner magic (for all you Harry Potter fans out there) to wind the clock back in time and give you a chance to choose your order again and decide once more what you want to say to the executive board.

A map of the scenario

To start with, we need to create a basic map. The company unfortunately doesn't talk a great deal about user needs, but we can infer that the user need is either about saving money or being green (possibly even a legal requirement). This need requires some form of efficiency analysis, which is provided by the company as a product — Phoenix. We also know the market, whilst reasonably sized (£301 million), is seen to be far smaller than the applicable market (£3 billion), and so the market of clients is not yet fully mature. Hence, to begin with, I'm just going to add the client which needs efficiency analysis to our map and position the pieces roughly where I think they should be (see Figure 167).

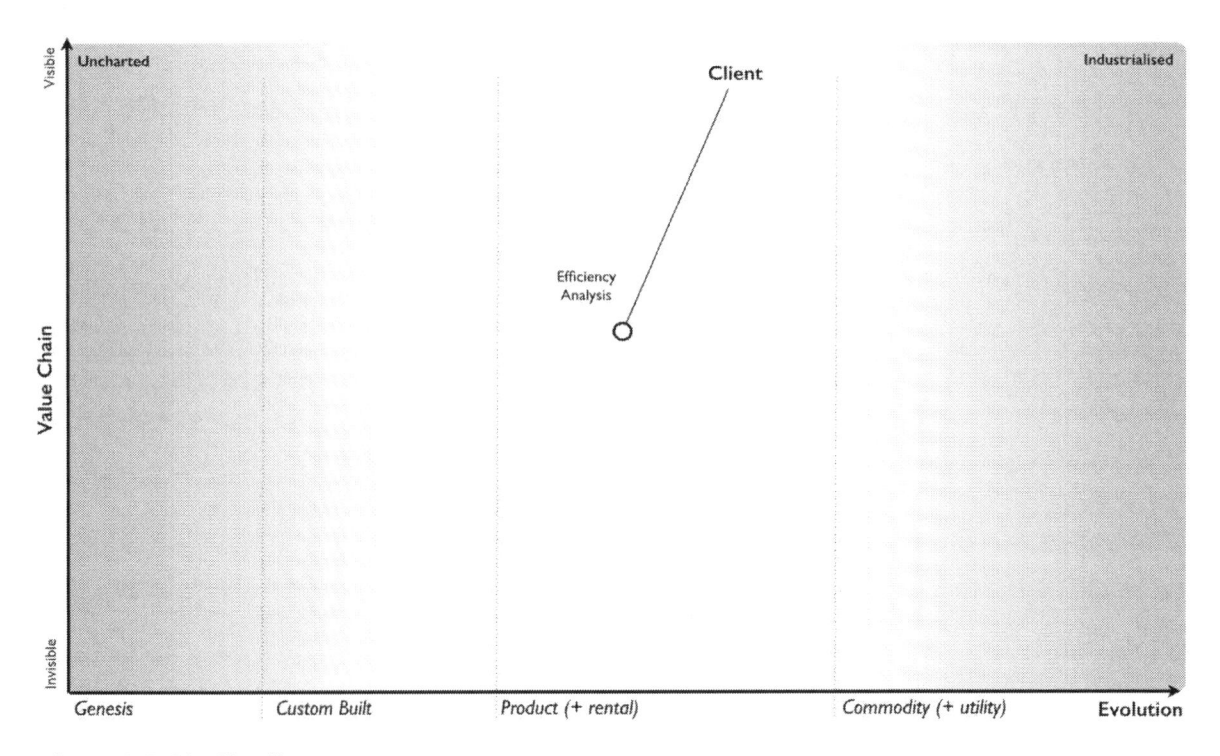

Figure 167: Starting the map

I also know that Phoenix requires some form of sensor and this sensor seems to be a highly expensive product. The clue that this isn't some form of resource constraint is that a more commodity version is provided in China. I also know that the sensor (or at least the system using the sensor) requires some form of custom-built data set, which our own in-house IT team creates. I'm not quite sure how this operates but for the time being, I'll attach this as a need for the sensor.

Finally, I'm aware that Phoenix has some form of system logic, based upon best practice use of the sensors. I know that changing the sensor to multiple commodity sensors would "require a complete rewrite of Phoenix" (the CDO told us this). So, I can now extend my map with these components (Figure 168). It's not perfect, no map ever is. I've marked on the sensor logic as a practice (i.e. it seems to be connected with how we use sensors) and the environmental data as data.

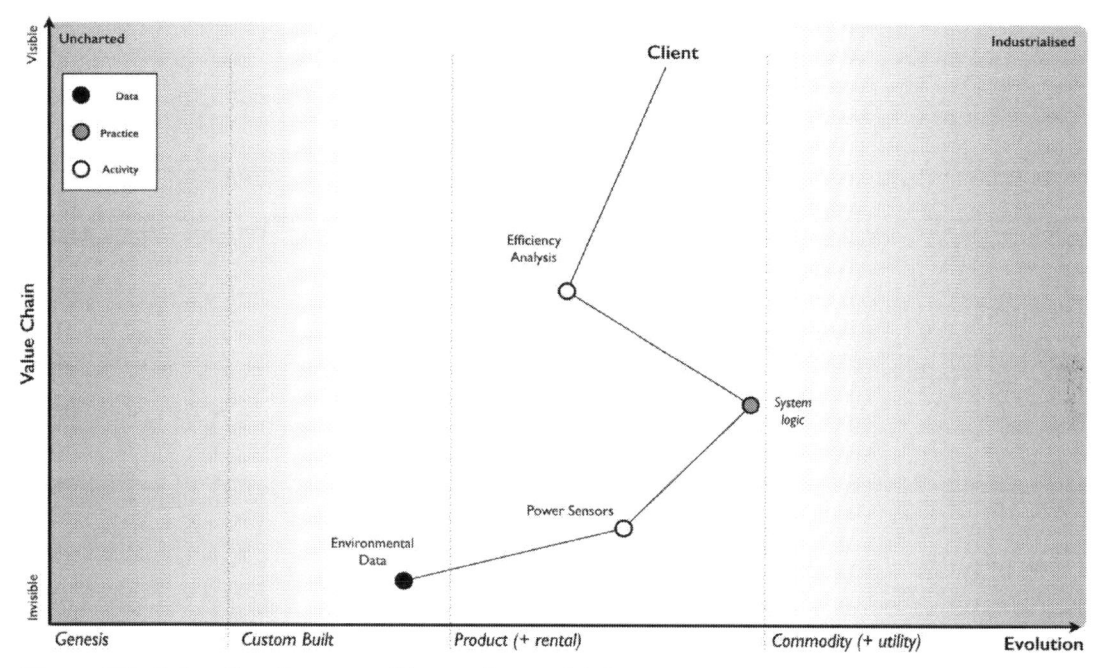

Figure 168: Extending the map with practice and data

The head of marketing also told us that the US was a more mature market and Brazil was less developed in the area of such efficiency analysis software. I'll assume that the markets are competitive (i.e. there is supply and demand competition), particularly since we're talking about setting up a business in Brazil. It's a bit of a gamble but I'll assume that the head of marketing has done at least a small modicum of homework. We can now mark on these markets, with lines (red dotted) to describe how they are changing – see Figure 169.

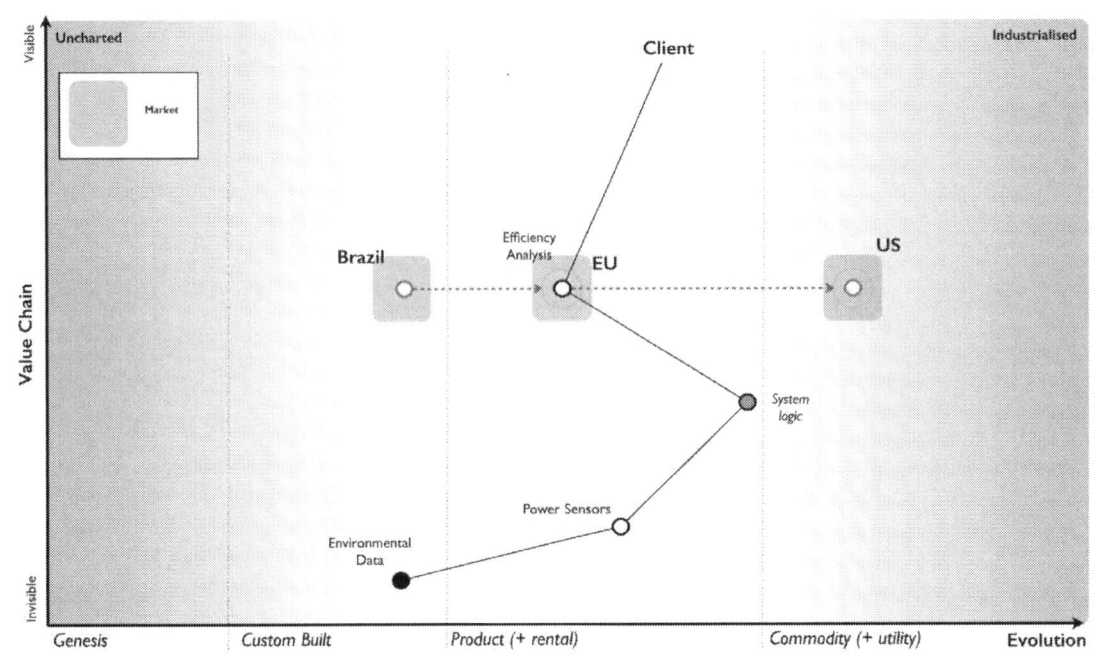

Figure 169: Adding markets

We also know that a range of "more commodity-like sensors" have been launched in China and that there is now a "data set available on the market", which I'll assume is some form of product or rental arrangement. Obviously, there's a couple of assumptions here, but these could be clarified with a few questions. I've marked on these changes to the map in Figure 170.

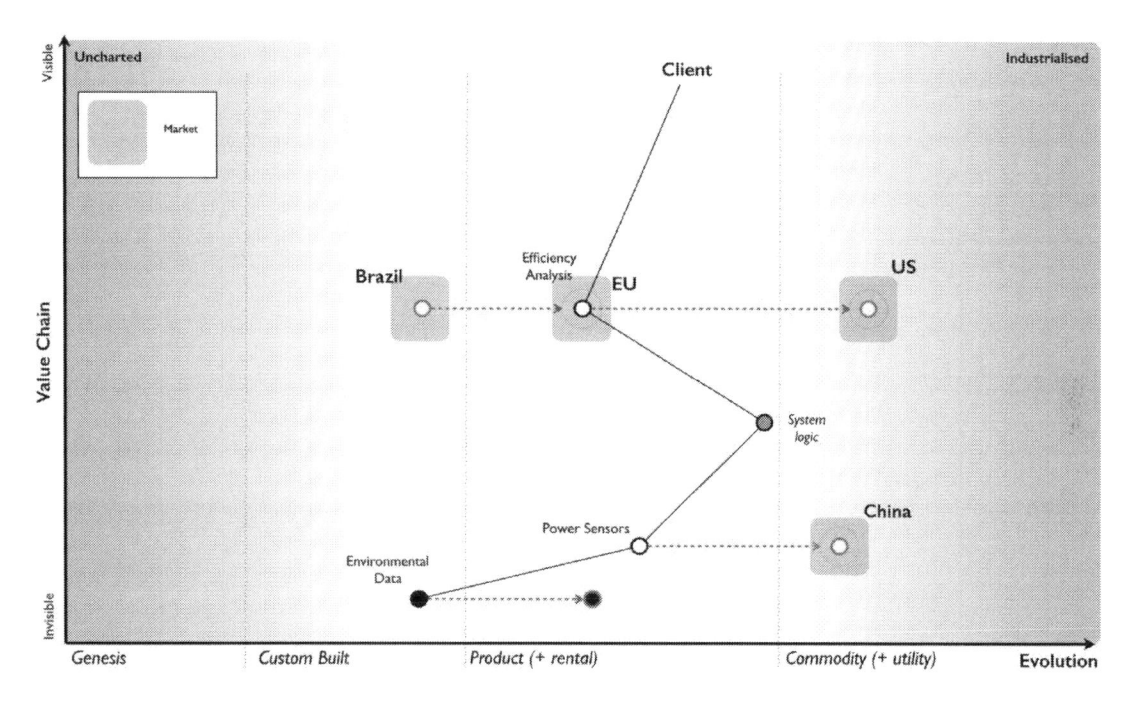

Figure 170: Adding China and the data set

Now, whilst it might not be a perfect map, it does provide us some form of overview on the environment, and certainly something we can use to challenge the assumptions I've made. There is however a bit more to add.

We can infer from the comments on the US competitor, the company's plans for Phoenix's own cloud solution to represent a mere 10% of revenue by 2023, their pride at the "technological marvel they have created", and the statement of "security concerns cited by some clients due to their cloud approach" that this group will have some inertia to the cloud change. We also know more explicitly that with the commodity sensors being described as "not good enough for the the job" and an alternative path of using "lots of the cheaper sensors" being widely dismissed, despite the cost of the sensors, the price differential and customer concerns over cost, we will find resistance to change here as well. We should add this inertia to our map (Figure 171).

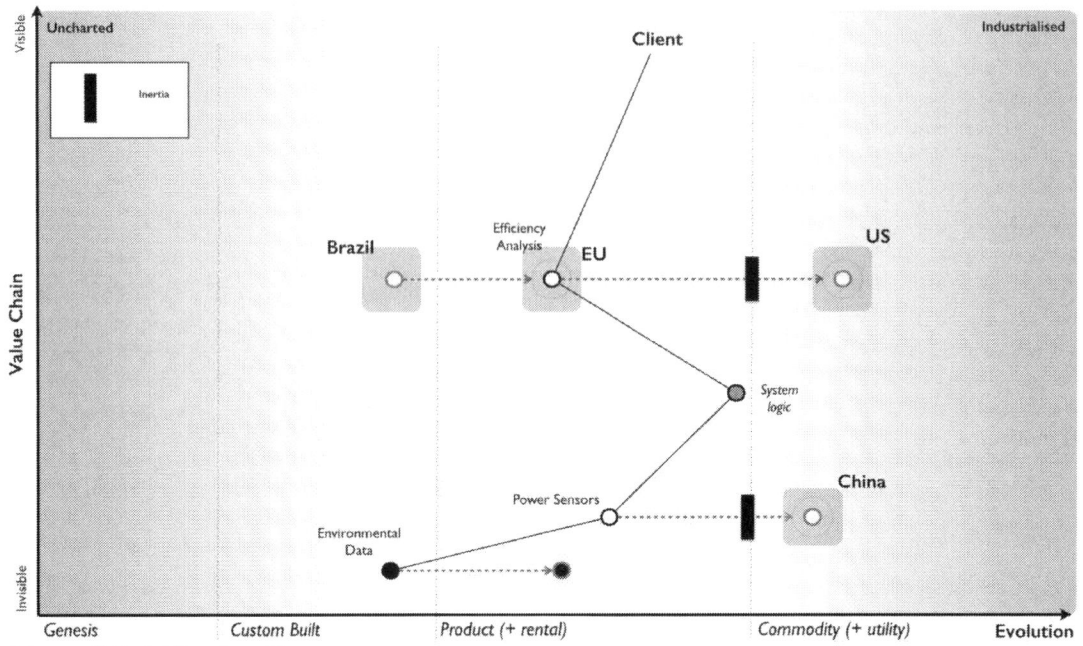

Figure 171: Adding inertia

In our market, we have a US player that is also operating in the more mature US market. They are already providing features we do not (we will assume this meets some user need that we might possibly not be aware of), they have companies building novel components and potentially products on top of their API, and the system they are offering is more of a utility.

It's still based however on the expensive sensors and we can assume they have developed their own system logic, which is equivalent to ours. I've added this into Figure 172.

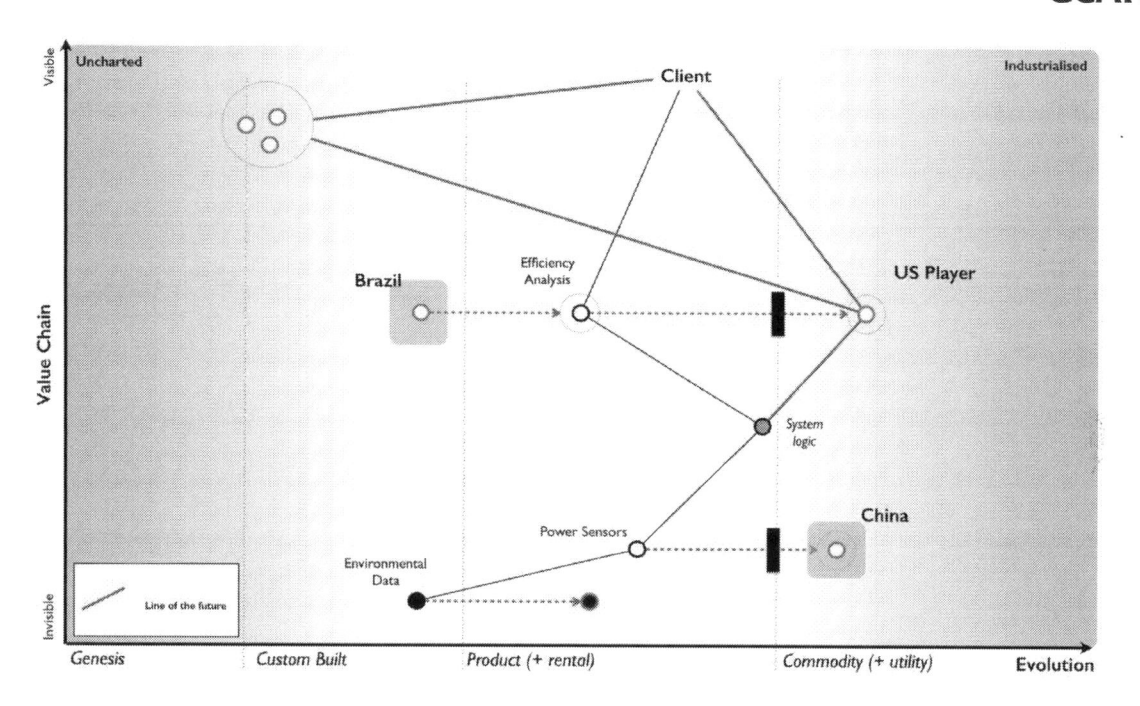

Figure 172: The US player

The shift towards more utility versions requires four factors – concept, technology, suitability and attitude (see Chapter 9 – charting the future). In this case, concept, suitability and technology clearly exist as we have a US competitor providing the service. In terms of attitude then it's a question of whether your clients are dissatisfied with the current method of provision. It's not the 90% of customers rating Phoenix as good to high levels of satisfaction that concern me, it's the 10% who didn't. Specifically, the concern of a "high cost of the system in the market, as was noted in the customer survey". I'm going to assume therefore that we are firmly on the path towards utility as the factors seem to be there and a player is already making that move.

The US player claims to be "doubling in size each year", and the anticipated revenue growth from £15M to £25M is somewhat supportive of this, especially if we consider the potential for economies of scale and price cuts. Alas, we have no information to confirm that consideration. We should note that they have a "fairly active development community" growing around their API and have been accused of "eating up the business models of some of those product companies". Contrary to this being a desperate act of cannibalisation, it is more likely part of an ILC like gameplay (as described in Chapter 5 – the play and a decision to act).

This is exceedingly dangerous as the larger that ecosystem grows then the more innovative, more efficient and more customer focused the competitor becomes.

They are already ahead of us in both utility forms, provision of an API and core features. Let us add this bit of gloom and doom to our map.

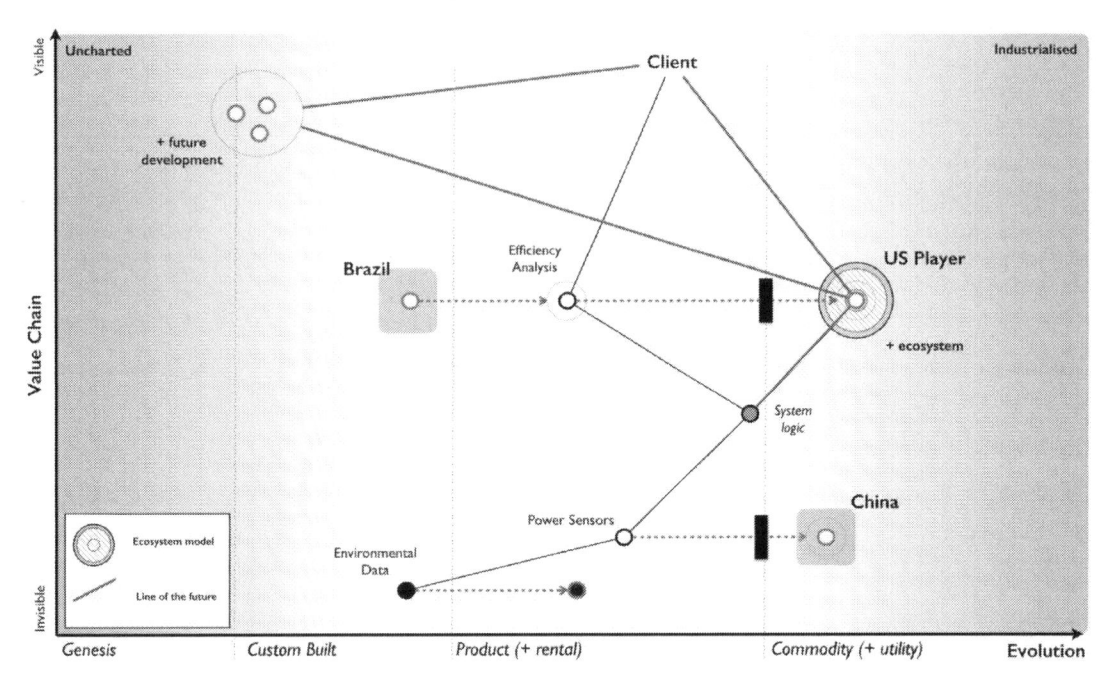

Figure 173: Ecosystem moves of the US player

In the "P&L" provided by the CFO, we have revenue forecasts all the way to 2021 — a very wishful bit of thinking. We know the shift from product to utility tends to demonstrate a punctuated equilibrium, and so it's not unreasonable to assume the growth rate of the US player will continue. This is usually one of those hard things to accept because we get comfortable with the illusion of a perceived slow change from one product to another product (see Chapter 10 — I wasn't expecting that). It can take 20 to 30 years, sometimes more, for the product industry to develop, and then 10 to 15 years for it all to be dismantled. For Phoenix, this war has been going on regardless of whether the company is aware or not.

Added on top of that an ILC model, then this growth rate is likely to be reinforced because the US player will extend further ahead of Phoenix. Hence, we can add our predicted revenue and extrapolate the US revenue onto the same graph — see Figure 174.

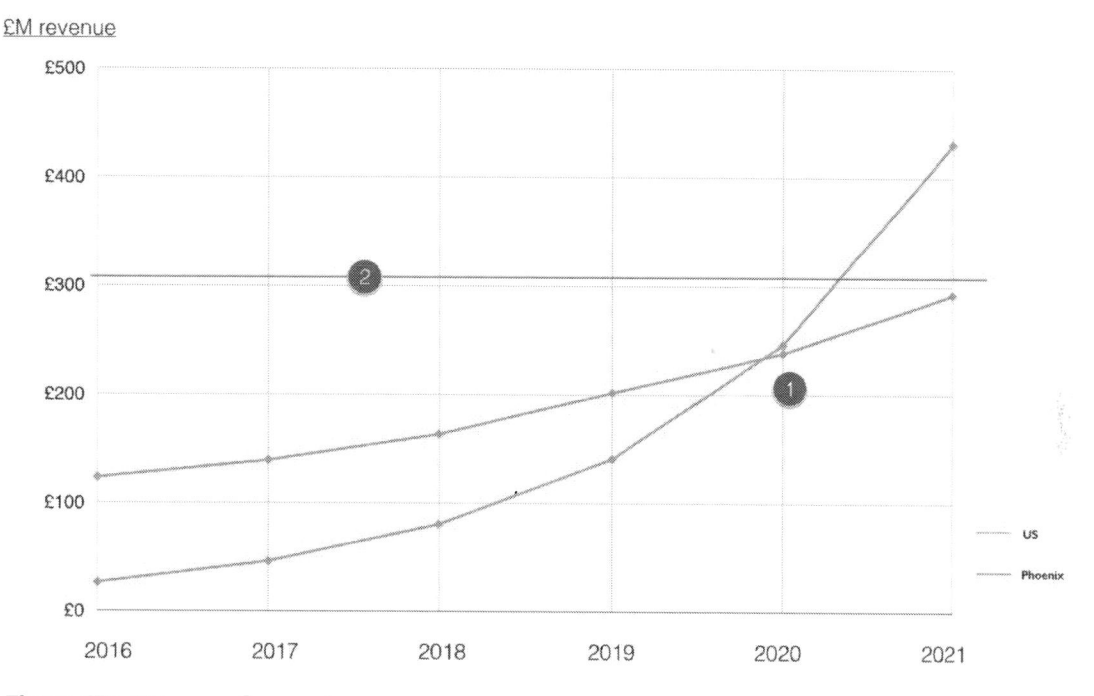

Figure 174: Revenue forecasts

There are a couple of comments worth noting. First (Point 1) is that by 2020 or thereabouts, the US player will be about the same size of revenue as Phoenix. The problem is the US player will be an entirely cloud based service with a large ecosystem that they are using to sense future changes. Our Phoenix cloud service would have just launched and we will be a startup; a minnow after spending

£45 million in a future market that is dominated by this US giant. Even by 2023, our cloud revenue is only expected to be 10% of our overall revenue. This is calamitous.

To compound this, the current market is only just north of £300M (Point 2) and by 2020, then the combined revenues of Phoenix and the US player will vastly exceed this. Even given growth of the current market, we can assume we're going to be head to head in a battle with the US player. One of us is not going to get what we're hoping for. Unfortunately, we will be playing the part of David with our trusty sling versus a Goliath who has turned up with an entire army of brothers armed with general purpose machine guns. This is not going to be pretty for us. Alas, it gets worse.

In Chapter 9 – charting the future – we discussed the concept of coevolution of practice with activity. Looking at our map, we can apply the same pattern to sensors. The commodity sensors available in China are likely to trigger an entire new set of practices. Our CIO hinted at this with the statement, "a potential solution could be to use lots of the cheaper sensors", which our CDO dismissed with the normal inertia of one wedded to a past practice — "require a complete rewrite of Phoenix". Whether we like it or not, a new emerging practice is coming and our existing system logic needs the rewrite (see Figure 175).

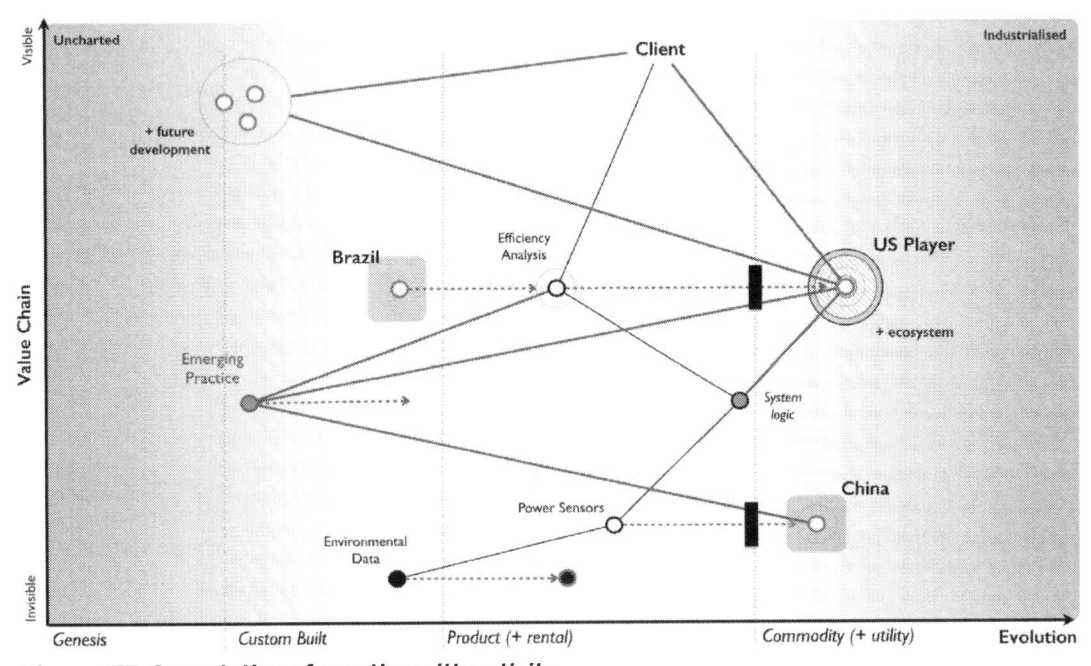

Figure 175: Coevolution of practice with activity

What this means is not only do we have a future battle with a Goliath but the entire system logic of Phoenix and our code base that is built upon years of good to best practice with these highly expensive sensors is about to become legacy. I've summarised this all in the map below (Figure 176), dropping the line between the co-evolved practice and our product, as that is fairly redundant. Of course, someone is bound to suggest we do that at some point in the future, however, I'd rather focus on where the future is going, i.e. utility rather than futility. We will use this map to examine the company strategy.

Now, you might argue with the position of pieces on the map or components that have been missed or assumptions that have been made, but that's the entire point of a map. To expose all of this in a visual form that we can then challenge.

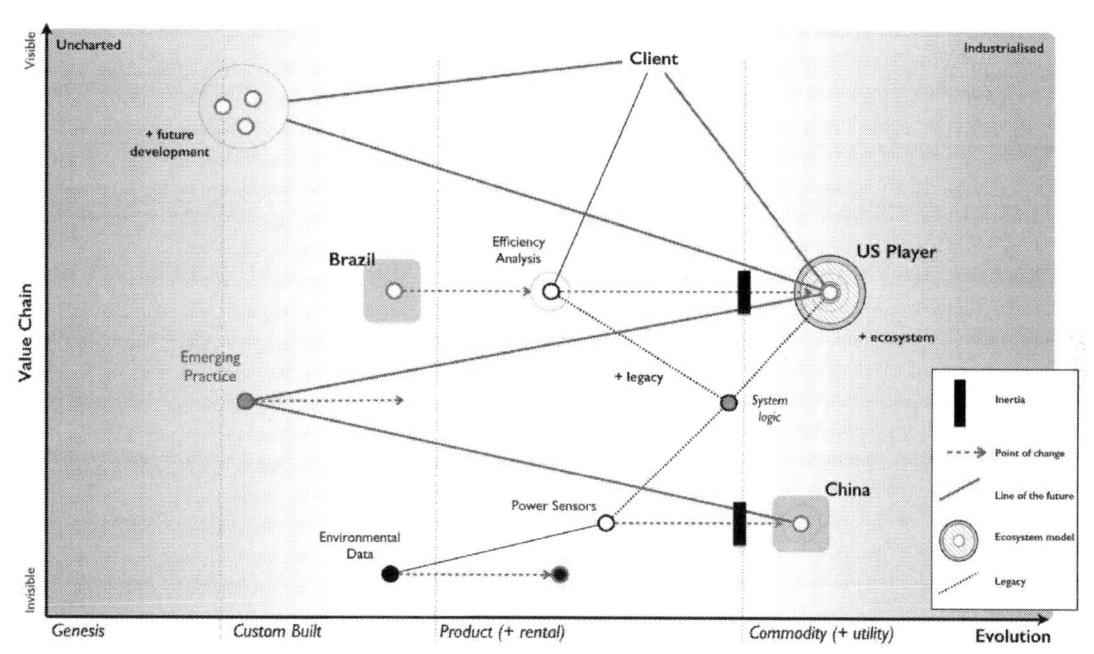

Figure 176: The map

Examining the strategy

With our map in hand, let us now look at the strategy of the company. I've marked on each point which relates to the strategy in Figure 177 and we will go through each in turn.

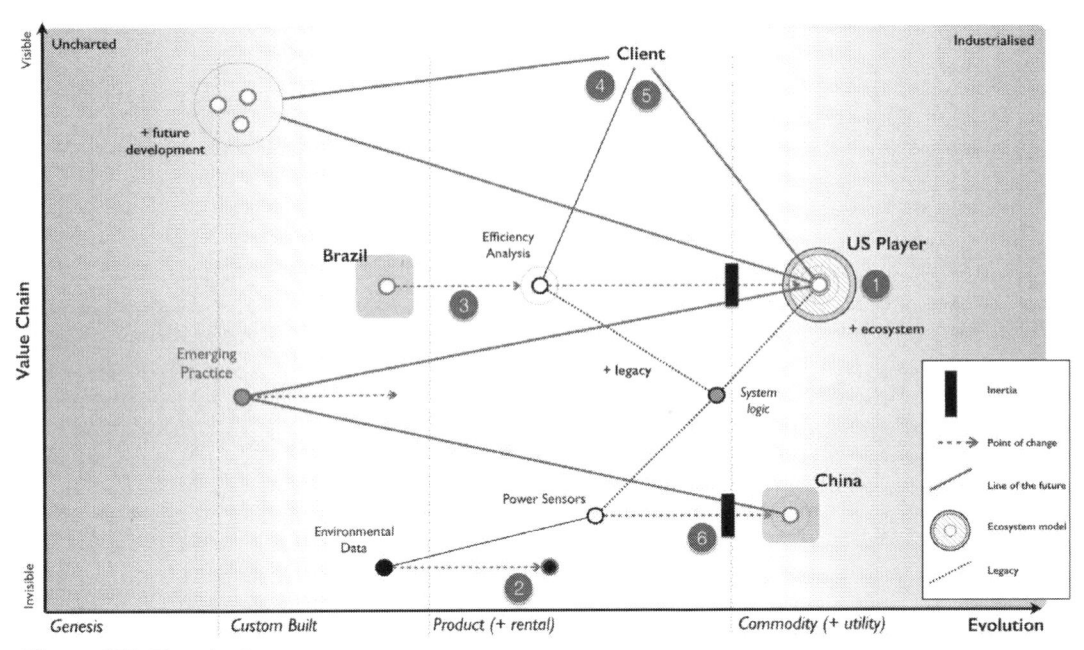

Figure 177: The strategy

Point 1: Creation of a digital "cloud based" service for provision of the software. By the time our cloud service hits the market in 2020, we're likely to be a minnow against a giant with a well-developed ecosystem model. If they're running an ILC model, which seems possible, then they will be out-innovating us, more efficient, more customer-focused and larger. They will be far ahead of us and our cloud effort doesn't even mention building an API or running any form of ecosystem game. To cap it all off, we're even bringing an old licensing model with us and a system logic that is likely to become legacy and replaced by co-evolved practice. In terms of getting it wrong, this is a fabulous way of wasting £45 million.

Point 2: Investigating the use of the data conversion product that is available in order to improve efficiencies and reduce cost. A fairly sensible proposal on cost efficiency but not one that should be high up the priority list in such a battle.

Point 3: Expansion of existing product into overseas markets such as Brazil. It might create some short-term gain but this is also a dangerous path. Our business model in a more mature market is going to be chewed up, but rather than face this, we're going to take our model and attempt to re-apply it to a less mature or emerging market. All that will happen is our competitor will chew up both markets and we are simply spending money laying the groundwork for them to attack the emerging market. It would probably be more favourable to our shareholders to give half the money to the competitor for marketing in Brazil and return half the money to the shareholders than to build up future liability. This isn't as bad as the cloud effort but this will increase inertia to change due to the belief that the short-term gain translates to our past model still being successful.

Point 4: Increasing the development effort on our existing product line, including more advanced reporting and other innovative features. There is always value in focusing on user needs, but in this case, we're not addressing the problem of our competitor but patching over it in the very short term. Unfortunately for us, if the competitor is using an ILC model then we are in competition with the entire ecosystem that has built upon the competitor's API. If for example that includes 200 software companies then our poor product development team is going up against the might of 200 software teams. This situation only gets worse as the ecosystem grows. This is a path of spending money and still losing by ever-increasing margins.

Point 5: Undertake a significant marketing campaign to promote our solution in the existing market. It doesn't fix any of the problems but at least it might give us a short-term revenue boost.

Point 6: Keep an eye on the sensors from China. Though not explicitly stated or highlighted as a strategy, it's worth calling out that the approach is to keep a watchful eye on the sensors. Given the fairly predictable impact these will have, this is less than encouraging.

If you want to mess up strategy then the CEO has done a glorious job. Fortunately, there's also some opportunities to be considered. Firstly, the market in Brazil is an opportunity, but re-using our old business model might not be the wisest idea.

Secondly, there was an interest in acquisition of this company. Just because you know it's a future train wreck, this doesn't mean others do (remember, most don't map). As someone who has done a bit of work in M&A then coming face to face with a company hurtling towards a cliff edge whilst there is "positive noise about the subsidiary from analysts and also some interest by third parties in potential acquisition" is surprisingly common and lucrative. You are a board member for the conglomerate and should look to maximise the opportunity.

Thirdly, the system logic is heading towards legacy and we will have our own DevOps moment with an emerging practice. Fortunately, we're not the only ones facing this as the US company has the same problem. Maybe they're not as smart as we think? Maybe they're working on a solution? We don't know, but this is a potential weakness.

Lastly, there's a final opportunity in the data set. Yes, a product is now available but that doesn't mean we can't try and out-commoditise this and turn data into some form of utility with an open data play (Point 1, Figure 178).

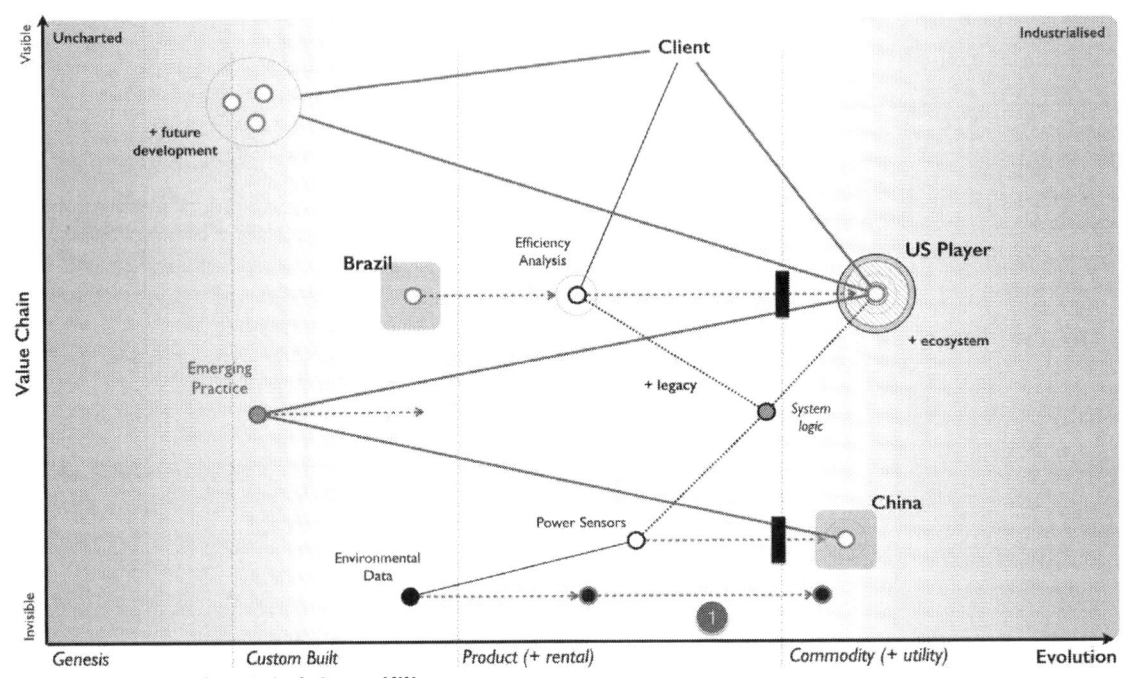

Figure 178: Turning data into a utility

The strategy outlined by the subsidiary needs some serious work on it. However, before jumping the gun, let us take a look at the company again. The strategy might be bad but the question is whether the company is recoverable in the time frame.

Examining doctrine

When I want to get a sense of company and its ability to adapt, to cope with the unexpected, to learn and to be resilient to competition itself, then I start looking at the universal principles it applies. I'm not looking for resilience to known scenarios but our ability to adapt to the unknown and to cope with the flow of evolution. In this case, the CEO talks about the values of the company, which include "responsibility, integrity, transparency, compassion, empathy, adaptiveness and decisiveness".

These values seem all perfectly reasonable, however, there are two things to consider. Firstly, companies are often very good at saying one thing and then doing something else. Secondly, executives and consultants are often very good at coming up with simple "truths" that have no data behind them. I can only judge this in terms of what I have evidence for, hence the Wardley Doctrine in Chapter 11 — a smorgasbord of the slightly useful.

For example, let us take empathy. It seems like it should matter, but does it? Is it a universal principle? What evidence do I have that it works in all cases and isn't context-specific? Maybe empathy matters more in a care home than on a factory line? I don't know and so I can't judge on this. However, there's lots of things I was told in the scenario that I can comment on. I've highlighted the areas of doctrine in Figure 179 using a light grey (for that warm, fuzzy feeling), dark grey (for concern) and grey (potential for setting off alarm bells) motif.

	Be transparent (a bias towards open)	Focus on high situational awareness (understand what is being considered)	Use a common language (necessary for collaboration)	Challenge assumptions (speak up and question)
Communication	Know your users (e.g customers, shareholders, regulators, staff)	Focus on user needs	Think fast, inexpensive, restrained and elegant (FIRE, formerly FIST)	Remove bias and duplication
Development	Use appropriate methods (e.g. agile vs lean vs six sigma)	Focus on the outcome not a contract (e.g. worth based development)	Be pragmatic (it doesn't matter if the cat is black or white as long as it catches mice)	Use standards where appropriate
	Use appropriate tools (e.g. mapping, financial models)			
	Manage inertia (e.g. existing practice, political capital, previous investment)	Optimise flow (remove bottlenecks)	Think small (as in know the details)	Effectiveness over efficiency
Operation	Do better with less (continual improvement)	Set exceptional standards (great is just not good enough)	Manage failure	
	Provide purpose, mastery & autonomy	Think small (as in teams)	Distribute power and decision making	Think aptitude and attitude
Structure	Design for constant evolution	There is no one culture (e.g. pioneers, settlers and town planners)	Seek the best	
Learning	Use a systematic mechanism of learning (a bias towards data)	A bias towards action (learn by playing the game)	A bias towards the new (be curious, take appropriate risks)	Listen to your ecosystems (acts as future sensing engines)
	Be the owner (take responsibility)	Move fast (an imperfect plan executed today is better than a perfect plan executed tomorrow)	Think big (inspire others, provide direction)	Strategy is iterative not linear (fast reactive cycles)
Leading	Strategy is complex (there will be uncertainty)	Commit to the direction, be adaptive along the path (crossing the river by feeling the stones)	There is no core (everything is transient)	Be humble (listen, be selfless, have fortitude)
	Exploit the landscape			

Figure 179: Doctrine

Amber warning

My areas of concern are:-

Design for constant evolution

When someone talks about how the "organisation was recently restructured" then this is a signal to me that the organisation didn't cope with constant evolution. They may have reformed to a structure that now does but I see no evidence one way or the other.

Think small (as in teams)

Given the above, the discussion on how the "digital group will expand significantly over the next two years" raises an eyebrow. I'd want to know more. Are we talking about a hefty department or some cell based way of operating (e.g. Two Pizza)?

A bias towards the new (be curious, take appropriate risks)

The discussion about the sensors and how "it's worth keeping an eye on the market" raises another eyebrow. I'd expect to see more directed action towards this change. I'm somewhat comforted by the use of the data set.

Listen to your ecosystems (acts as future sensing engines)

When your customers are concerned about the "high cost of the system in the market, as was noted in the customer survey", then a response of "renewal price will be frozen for the next two years" is not encouraging.

Strategy is iterative, not linear (fast reactive cycles)

There is nothing iterative about the strategy proposed. This might just be a reflection of the way it is presented, but it's worth a question.

Strategy is complex (there will be uncertainty)

There is no concept of uncertainty presented. It's more a set of action statements and a plan that goes far into the future.

Be humble (listen, be selfless, have fortitude)

From "being instrumental to the company's success" to the quote, "some people just have not found adjusting to this new world that easy", to the observation that the company is "clearly proud of its accomplishments, the technological marvel they have created and their ability to deliver against their vision", then there's a touch of entitlement and maybe a bit of arrogance to them.

Red Alert!

My areas of concern pale into insignificance compared to the areas that might have me running out the door screaming, setting the klaxon off. These include:-

Focus on high situational awareness (understand what is being considered)

I see no evidence of this, and a simple mapping of the environment has raised concerns that are not even discussed. I'd want to see clear evidence that the company actually understands its environment.

Use a common language (necessary for collaboration)

I see an abundance of different graphics but no consistent mechanism of discussion, other than verbal stories often laced with terminology. I'd want to understand how we actually communicate.

Challenge assumptions (speak up and question)

An extremely valid challenge over sensors was given by the CIO but dismissed, and even described as being "discussed several times before". The palpable sense of "frustration with the group and the CIO on this topic" indicates a team that is not listening. The answers given to the challenge are all symbols of inertia — pre-existing practice, assets etc. I'd be digging here.

Focus on user needs

The lack of description of user needs is significant. Statements like, "The attrition rate has been high in recent years at 9% but the sales team believes this is due to a lack of new features and a high cost of software licence renewal" are all very well and good, but I'm not interested in what the sales team thinks; I'd want to know what the user needs and wants.

Think fast, inexpensive, restrained and elegant (FIRE, formerly FIST)

A £45 million investment on a cloud effort over two years is not what I'd be expecting from a company following FIRE principles. This may be a simple consequence of summarisation to an executive level, but I'd want to see evidence that we're not embarking on building some Death Star.

Manage inertia (e.g. existing practice, political capital, previous investment)

Whilst inertia appears to be clear, the only challenge to it (e.g. sensors) is knocked back. In fact, the CEO got in on the act talking about intellectual property. I'd want to ask a few more questions here.

Use a systematic mechanism of learning (a bias towards data)

I see no evidence of this and of past lessons being applied. There's no concept of climatic patterns or learning. I'd want to explore this more.

Exploit the landscape

I see no evidence of understanding, let alone exploiting the landscape. It might exist in mental models and some form of intrinsic common understanding, but I'm not overwhelmed by this.

By the pricking of my thumbs

In my analysis, the strategy is barking up the wrong tree and I have significant concerns over the company itself. I would not be confident that this company is either heading in the right direction or capable of adapting to the uncertain future. The only person I have some confidence in is the CIO that the company is so desperately trying to get rid off. But that's me. Your analysis may be different. You may have seen something I have not. So let us take this unlucky Chapter 13, invoke some dark magic and do the time warp again.

The Task

You have a call in forty-five minutes with the executive board. That's how long you have to make your choices. The clock is ticking. So find a stopwatch and start it.

Your first task is to determine whether the company is heading in the right direction. You should determine whether you agree with the priority order given in Figure 180. If not, write down what your priority order would be. If you decide to invoke "other" then scribble down what that other is.

Priority Order	Company	You
Creation of a digital "cloud based" service for provision of the software	1	
Investigating the use of the data conversion product that is available in order to improve efficiencies in operation	2	
Expansion of existing product into overseas markets such as Brazil	3	
Increasing the development effort on our existing product line including more advanced reporting and other innovative features.	4	
Undertake a significant marketing campaign to promote our solution in the existing market.	5	
Other		

Figure 180: Priority order

Once you've decided your priority order then your next task is to determine what you're going to say to the executive board.

A note to the reader

Do try the exercise and spend that forty-five minutes on it. If you get flummoxed then give yourself a bit more, but set a time limit — no more than an hour and half. Force yourself to make a choice.

Though I've provided some analysis, there's still a lot to think about. What is right for the company? What is right for the conglomerate that you're a board member of? What options are open to you? How do you message this to both the company and the board? If you're struggling then realise that's good. This is a learning exercise and you don't learn unless you challenge yourself and embrace difficult problems.

In the next chapter, I'll give you my solution. Now, this doesn't mean that my solution is the right one. There could be a myriad of better ways of dealing with this case. Maybe you've found one? Maybe you have a different analysis? All I can tell you is how I would solve it, and through the medium of maps, explain my reasoning and my choices. Being a map, you're free to challenge any and all assumptions I've made. In fact, that's the point of a map, and I welcome the challenge because it gives me the opportunity to learn.

Chapter 14 - To thine own self be true

The hardest thing about mapping is coming to terms with a simple fact that there is no right answer. Mapping enables you to observe the environment, the constant flow of evolution and moves of other players, but it won't tell you what to do. There are alas no simple steps for you to follow to success. There are no plans that guarantee to bring you a fortune. I face this obstacle regularly when companies ask "How will mapping benefit me?" to which the answer that "it depends upon what you observe and then what you do" is seldom welcome. They often want the concrete, the definite and a world of levers you can pull or buttons you can press. I long to say, "By turning this mapping dial, you will save 12% of costs" or "Press the mapping button to increase your rates of successful innovation by 34%", but it just isn't true. The benefits are context-specific and they depend upon you.

The journey of mapping is one of abandoning the simple mechanistic world and embracing an iterative path of learning. Yes, there are patterns we can learn. Yes, there are universal principles we can apply. Yes, there exists context-specific gameplay. Despite this and in spite of our ability to observe the environment, it is still awash with uncertainty. The uncharted is uncertain, the timing of various patterns are uncertain, and the actions of others are uncertain. Even the future value of something is inversely proportional to the certainty we have over it. The more uncertain, the more risky and also the more potential value. Evolution itself, the very heart of these Wardley Maps, can't be measured over time, and instead, we have to measure over certainty. This use of uncertainty is an intrinsic part of learning to map, but as any map shows, not everything is uncertain and even the uncertain can be exploited.

Fortunately, nature has provided us the ability to cope with this, to be resilient and to learn from a constantly changing world. This ability is known as cognitive reasoning, or in layman's terms, the application of thought. We can use the patterns and our understanding of the landscape to try and create a more favourable result. Sometimes we will get this right, but more importantly, sometimes we will get this wrong. Every failed attempt is an opportunity to learn, assuming we use a systematic method of learning. Every mistake learned can be taught to others, assuming we use a common method of communication. There is a lot of future value in error. By learning these patterns, it helps us constrain the bewildering number of possible moves to the adjacent probable. Hence, we learn that the industrialisation of artificial intelligence to commodity components and utility services will enable a rapid growth of new things built on top of it. We just can't say what those new things will be but we can prepare for this change.

Sometimes, the lessons learned from mapping are nothing more than "Ere be dragons". This is true of the uncharted space, which contains highly risky and uncertain sources of future value that require us to experiment, discover and gamble. Other times, the lessons are more concrete, such as the shift from product to utility will result in coevolution of practice. Embracing this spectrum, from the uncertain to the certain, from the unknown to the known, from the uncharted to the industrialised, is for many the most uncomfortable bit of the journey.

So to the exercise at hand. I will explain with maps my reasoning as to the choices that I would make in this scenario. My reasoning is not the "right" answer but instead, it is simply "my" answer. It may be the case that you read this and say, "I wish I'd thought of that", or maybe you have a better answer, in which case, I'd be delighted to learn from you. Challenge, communication, learning and embracing uncertainty are the very core of mapping.

My play

Back in 2008, when I was faced with the situation that our scenario is very vaguely derived from, it had taken me about 45 minutes to scribble out a map with a pen on paper and work through to an "answer". In case you need a map for the scenario, I provided their chosen strategy (Figure 181) and a map, on which I've outlined the strategy (Figure 182).

Priority Order	Company	You
Creation of a digital "cloud based" service for provision of the software	1	
Investigating the use of the data conversion product that is available in order to improve efficiencies in operation	2	
Expansion of existing product into overseas markets such as Brazil	3	
Increasing the development effort on our existing product line including more advanced reporting and other innovative features.	4	
Undertake a significant marketing campaign to promote our solution in the existing market.	5	
Other		

Figure 181: The Phoenix strategy

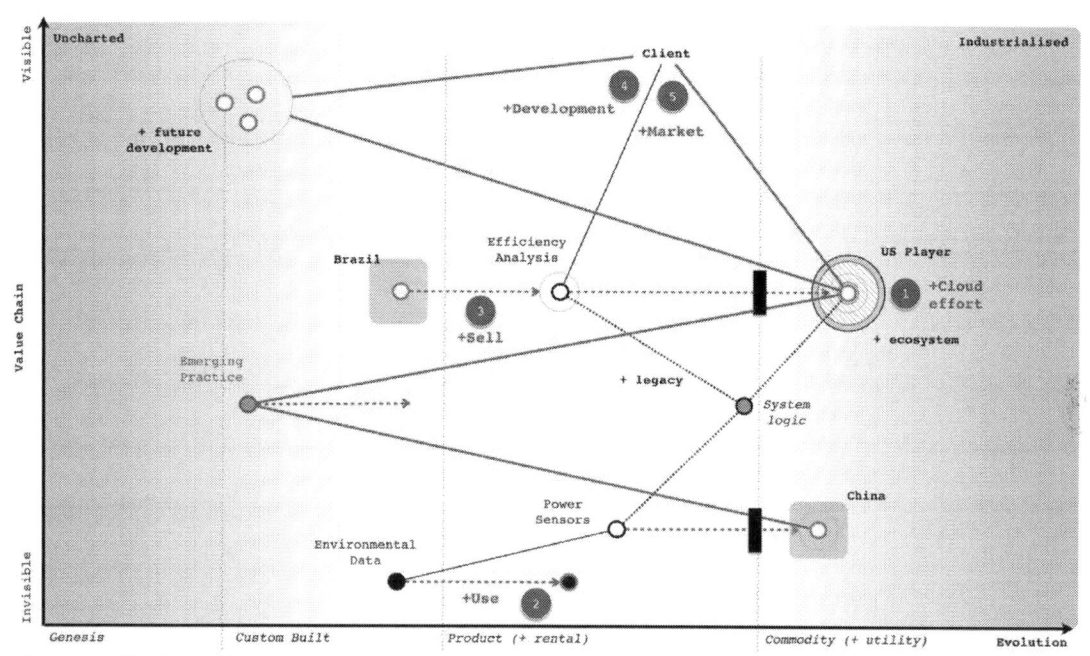

Figure 182: Map with strategy

As discussed in Chapter 13 – something wicked this way comes – then I view that the strategy is about as poor as you can get. To cap it all off, the company itself has serious flaws in its makeup and composition. The CEO, supported by a group of well-trained executives, is boldly charging the army over a cliff whilst trying to get rid of the one person who might possibly save them – the former CIO.

To work through this problem to final a possible answer then we need to first distinguish where we could attack. Even on a simple map like this, there's lots of points we could focus on. It's much the same with a game of chess; there's usually a huge number of potential moves you could make. The trick is sorting out which ones are of interest, and that takes experience and practice of the game. In Figure 183, I've listed the obvious wheres on our map, ignoring the more wishful thinking such as "buy up the Chinese sensor manufacturer".

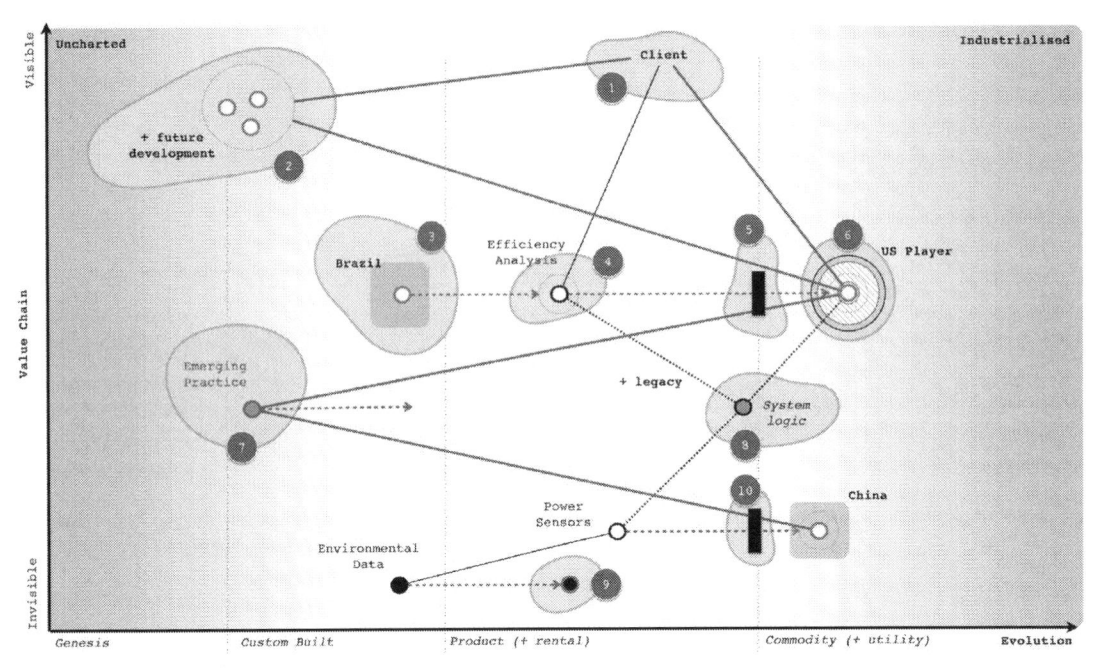

Figure 183: The wheres

1. focus on marketing towards our users
2. develop new and uncertain capabilities
3. exploit the Brazil market
4. sell the company
5. exploit inertia in customers to the change
6. build a cloud service
7. build something with the new emerging practice
8. dispose of the legacy
9. industrialise the data space
10. exploit inertia in the industry around the China sensors

In such a map, there are always many paths. One path describes how the company thought of its future and the strategic choices it was making. It's quite clear that the company could not see the threat of the sensors and coevolution of practice or how dangerous the US company was, or even how it had inertia to change. In all likelihood, such a company wouldn't even understand how things evolve. In their mind, they might have an unwritten map, but it'll look more like Figure 184. To this company, their strategy makes sense because they don't understand how the landscape is changing. The commodity sensors are just a disconnected component that they believe they have choice over, or the cloud is just an optional choice. They have none of the anticipation that is brought on by an understanding of climatic patterns.

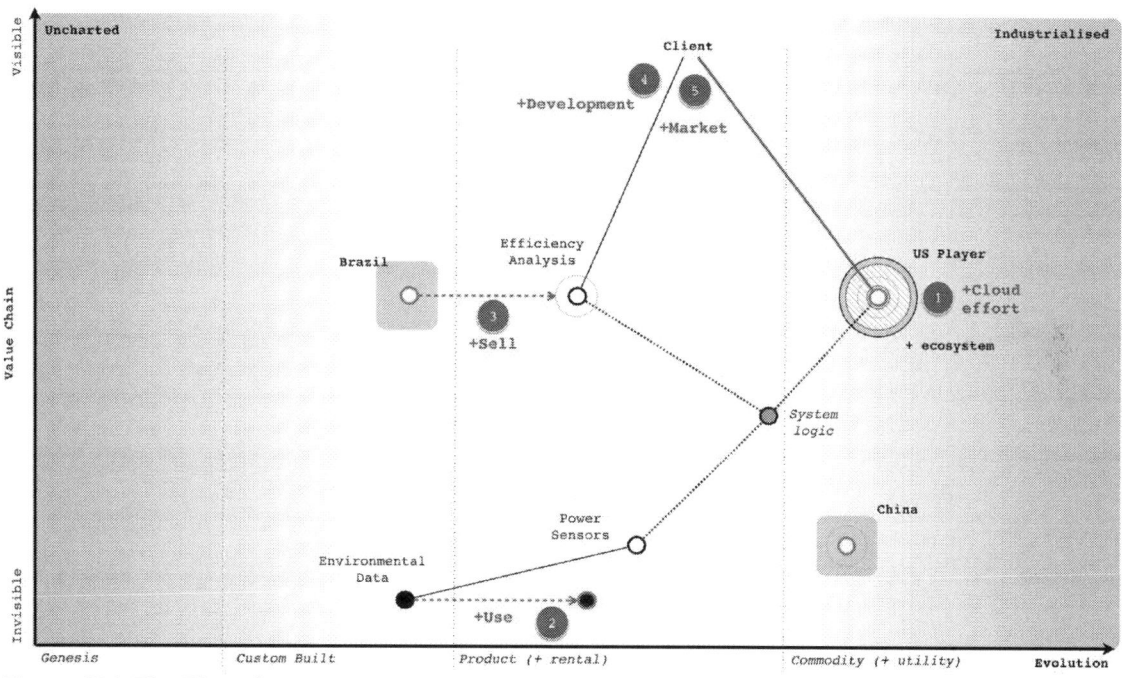

Figure 184: The Phoenix map

That said, they were motivated. It's a judgement call here as to whether an organisation can be altered in a time frame that enables you to exploit an environment. In this case, given the principles (i.e. doctrine) exhibited then I'd say not. There isn't enough time to alter the company and go head to head with the US competitor; this is a battle better withdrawn from for now.

However, I have several secret weapons. First, the US competitor is using the same expensive sensor and they probably have their own internal inertia to change, given their success in the US, which means their code base will become legacy. Secondly, just because I can anticipate the future situation then that doesn't mean the market can. From the analyst reports and interest in acquisition, we know that Phoenix is seen as a bit of a star in the market. Lastly, we also have that CIO, who shows some promise, some insight, despite the company's attempt to get rid of her.

Applying a bit of thought to the map, another path now becomes available, or in this case, two paths, as it's a combination of simultaneous plays. I've marked these in orange and grey on the map in Figure 185.

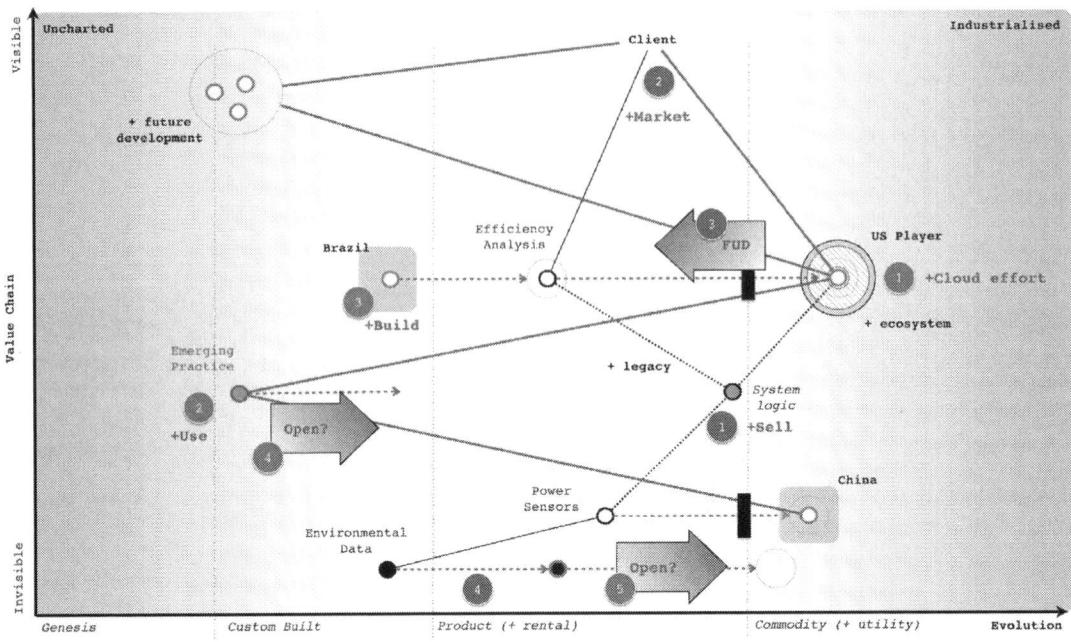

Figure 185: My play

The grey play — Pig in a Poke

I'm going to sell this company (**grey Point 1**). I'm going to want to maximise my return, which means I'll put effort into marketing (**Point 2**) and promoting Phoenix as the future in this market, reinforcing those analyst messages. I'm also going to encourage the marketing team to heavily play on concerns over any cloud effort (**Point 3**). Hence a bit of fear, uncertainty and doubt (FUD) is useful.

I'm not going to give up on our cloud effort; I'm just going to recommend the cloud project is cut down to less than a million and run as a prototype / experiment. I'll also pull back on the expansion into Brazil. I want to make sure the company costs are kept down and the company is seen as attractive as possible. I'd also agree that we need to use the data product in the market and look to downsize the team in IT responsible for that. In fact, I have another purpose for them. Whilst my fellow board members would be aware of this play, I wouldn't explain it in this way to the executives of the subsidiary. They'd probably disagree; they have oodles of inertia and I don't want to dampen their enthusiasm. To them, I'd explain one story, which is:-

"I agree on the marketing push in our existing market and focusing on our product development. I share your concerns over the security issues of cloud and the competitor being forced to eat their own ecosystem. I wouldn't like for us to be in that position. I'd like us to scale back on our cloud project for the time being and run a few small-scale experiments. I do like the idea of entering the Brazil market but right now, I think we need to concentrate on the European market. I wouldn't want us to lose ground to the US player because we're focused elsewhere. However, I completely agree with the efficiency drive and removing the in-house capability regarding the dataset. I also agree that we should watch the Chinese sensors but our focus needs to be on building up profitability within Europe and making Phoenix soar."

I'd also have a quiet chat with the CEO about the problem CIO and offer to move her to another group in the conglomerate in order that the CEO can focus on the task at hand. I'd suggest we have another project that could possibly do with some of those un-needed IT people as well.

My real goal here is pig in a poke. I want to maximise the capital returned through the disposal of the subsidiary. Before you state that no-one in the market would buy Phoenix then print out the scenario (Chapter 12) and try it out on a group of executives. To make your life easier, I've provided a link to a PDF of the scenario. If those executives don't know how to map, they'll probably choose the cloud, Brazil and efficiency efforts around data. If you talk to them about whether they think Phoenix has potential then most will say yes. These are the people you'd want to be selling Phoenix to.

The orange play — the Future

Whilst the grey play is all about making significant capital through a disposal of Phoenix, the orange play in the map above is all about building the future.

I do want to build that cloud service (**orange Point 1**) but I want the technology based upon the emerging practice that will develop around the commodity sensors (**Point 2**). I'm going to create a secret project, a separate subsidiary to do this, and I'm likely to put the CIO I've just nabbed in charge. I also want to consider looking at driving these emerging practices to become more standard through an open approach (**Point 3**).

I won't be building the service in Europe but in Brazil (**Point 4**). Firstly, this is an untapped market, but secondly, I want to keep out of the fight between Phoenix and the US player in Europe. Once the new service is established in Brazil and after my disposal of the Phoenix subsidiary, then I'm going to look at expanding from Brazil into Europe and the US by exploiting the weakness of those competitors (i.e. their legacy code base, based upon expensive sensors). For good measure, I'm going to look for another ILC type ecosystem play around data (**Point 5**) by using an open data approach.

I'm going to be spending some time on this new subsidiary, making sure it's set up right and we don't get a repeat of Phoenix. I'd be looking for cell based structure, use of attitudes, FIRE, willingness to challenge, and all that good stuff outlined in doctrine. To begin with, I need four basic teams (see Figure 186), which I'm going to have to flesh out pretty quickly, but I'd be hoping that the CIO will help me nab a few of the right people from the data group that Phoenix wants to remove.

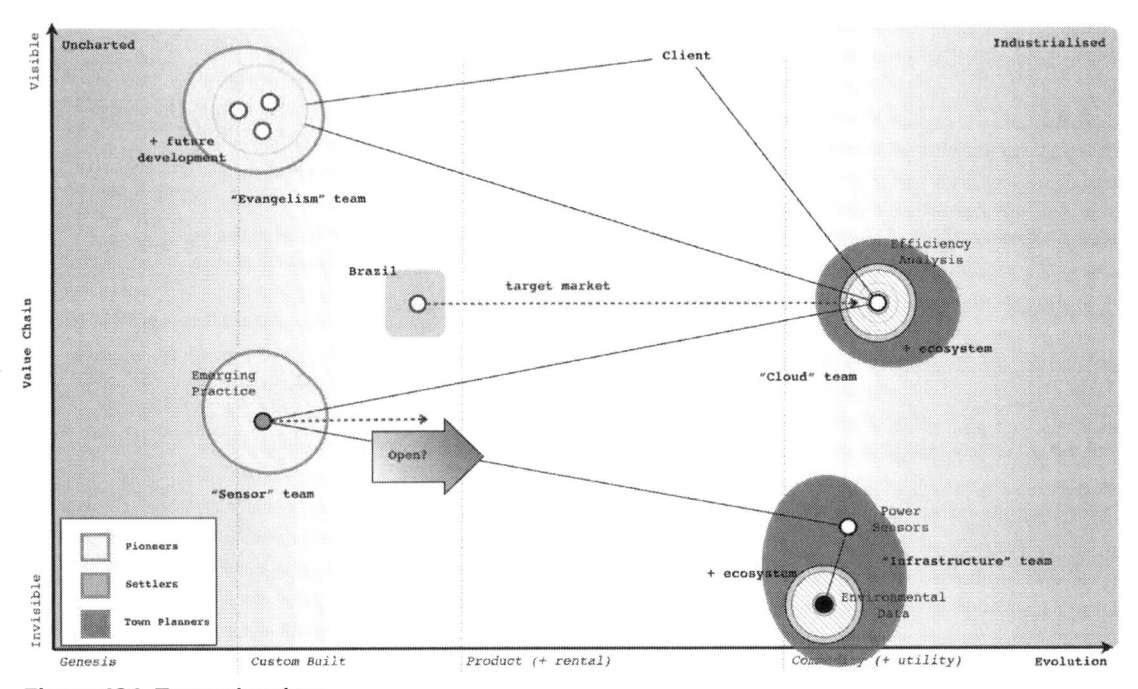

Figure 186: Team structure

This is how I would play the game in order to maximise the benefit for the conglomerate. The return from the disposal will vastly exceed any investment needed. I could probably use it to fund a dozen new startups whilst returning a generous reward to the conglomerate. However, this play took me 45 minutes. I'm sure with a bit of effort then a better play can be found. Maybe you have it? I am willing to learn.

Feeling guilty and the executives

The above play feels a bit "sneaky". Remember, your focus is on what is of benefit to the conglomerate and you never know, Phoenix could have a glorious future. In cases like this, you need to put away concerns over the subsidiary and be true to yourself. Give them a chance to explore their own future in the comfort of someone else's purse. Don't lie to people; even the words I've put down for the

CEO contain no lies. I've just omitted my own concerns, which he wouldn't share anyway. If I thought those executives might then maybe I would take a different path. Remember, the above play could be wrong, you may be selling the golden goose, which is why you'd need the rest of your executive board to challenge it.

Also, it's not "sneaky" to sell off something that you believe will head over the cliff to another. They may be able to see something you can't and you're not responsible for them — caveat emptor. It's also not "sneaky" to emphasise Phoenix as the future. Those analysts have been making positive noise in the scenario and maybe they're right?

I said above that many executives would go for the cloud, Brazil and efficiency options and wouldn't look to sell Phoenix. They would see Phoenix as having potential. How do I know this? Well, I've run the scenario with over 200 executives from different companies and I've tested their response before they could map and after. The result is shown in Figure 187.

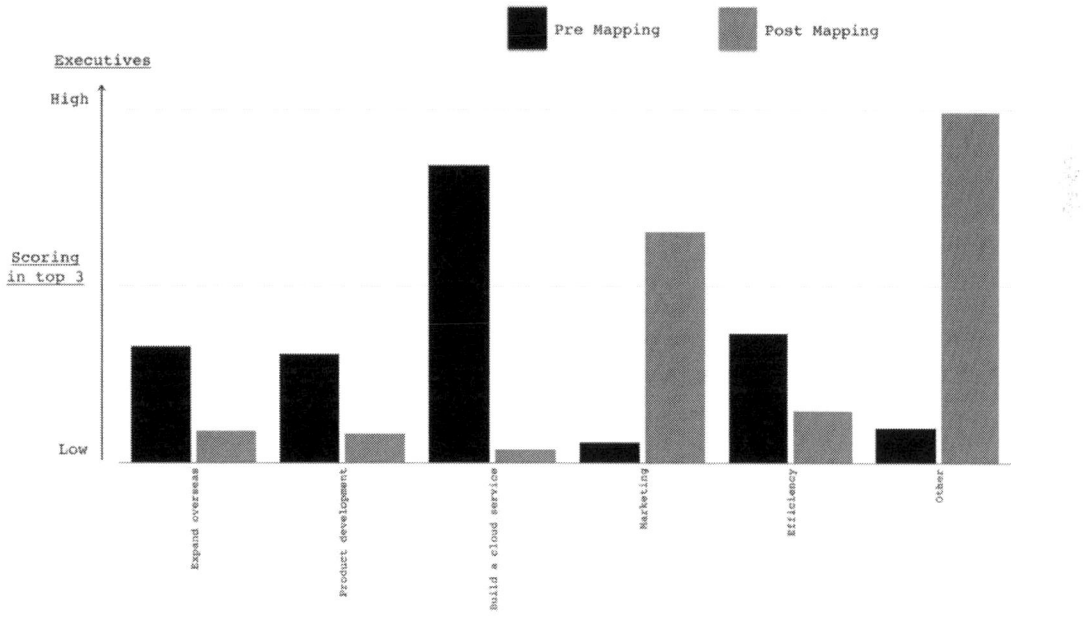

Figure 187: Response to the scenario

Before they could map, the response was always towards building the cloud service. After learning to map, the response shifted to selling the company ("other"). The interesting thing to note is the scenario has many common tools used in business — a P&L to an overview of the market — but the addition of mapping changed the response significantly. The real question to ask is how many past decisions made on those common tools would have been different had they used maps?

Chapter 15 - On the practice of scenario planning

One difficulty that people face with the Phoenix scenario outlined in the previous chapters is the question of role. It's not unusual to look at the scenario and its corresponding plays such as "pig in a poke" and ask what happens to the people. A common retort is "leadership is all about people and the leader should sacrifice themselves for their people". It's a noble idea.

As difficult as it is, you have to remember that in the scenario, you are an executive of the conglomerate and your focus is on maximising its advantage. The game is somewhat different if you're the CEO of the subsidiary. That which brings maximum advantage for one perspective is not necessarily that which brings the maximum benefit for another. There are often many competing interests and many maxima in a single landscape. Whilst the game itself is rarely zero sum (i.e. if I win then you lose or vice versa), as both competitors can often benefit through collaboration; your focus should be on maximising your advantage. The pursuit of such will result in conflict, whether it's with your competitors or the conflict between the shareholders' desire for profit versus the consumers' desire for lower product cost. There is always some other trade-off if you look hard enough.

When you examine a map, you need to go beyond just the landscape, the why of movement (i.e. this choice over that), the why of purpose (to be this or that), and to consider your role and that of others. There are many actors in a map and they have different perspectives. Even the consumer's view of the landscape can be different from that of the producer. Mapping simply shows you a landscape; you have to apply thought, you have to balance conflicts, and you have to strive for your maximum advantage. But isn't this cold-hearted? Aren't you treating people, and that means real lives, as dots on a canvas? Yes, it can be dispassionate. But remember, you also have to lead, and that requires trust from others. There is a cost associated with brutal corporate action through loss of trust. Which brings us to another trade-off, as you have to balance present action versus future. Become known as being too Machiavellian, too brutal and your reward will be that too few will follow you. Seeking the path with least conflict, to win the war without fighting, and to demonstrate how all can benefit is the pinnacle of the craft of war.

Balancing these conflicts, focusing on your role, removing your own bias and understanding the different maxima that exist is one of the hardest challenges that I know for leadership. Without maps, it's almost impossible to make sense of this in an unseen landscape. Hence, we just fall back to gut feel and notions of "it seems the right thing to do". The practices of mapping are the trivial entry point into this world as they simply expose it rather than solve. The complexity of playing the game is vastly more than just seeing the board, knowing the rules and a few opening plays. I often suspect this is why we relish story-telling, magic frameworks such as 2x2s, and secrets of success in management. We paper over a complex world with simple to understand "truths", regardless of how incorrect they are, because it makes management easier and gives us a sense of control.

To tease out the concept of role, I'm going to use a generalised scenario that has two variants – one that covers product to product substitution and the other that covers product to utility. I'll use a single map to describe both, and I'm going to focus on the pattern of change from product to utility rather than user needs. You should be familiar enough with mapping by now that such shortcuts are permissible.

The "generalised" scenario

You are the founder / CEO of a company that produces a product. You've developed a successful business. You are proud of what you have accomplished and the team you have built. In one variant, your product (Point A1) is being substituted by another product (A1 to A2), e.g. BlackBerry versus Android. In the other variant, your product is being substituted by a utility (A1 to A3), e.g. traditional hosting versus cloud computing. I've drawn these variants on a single map in Figure 188.

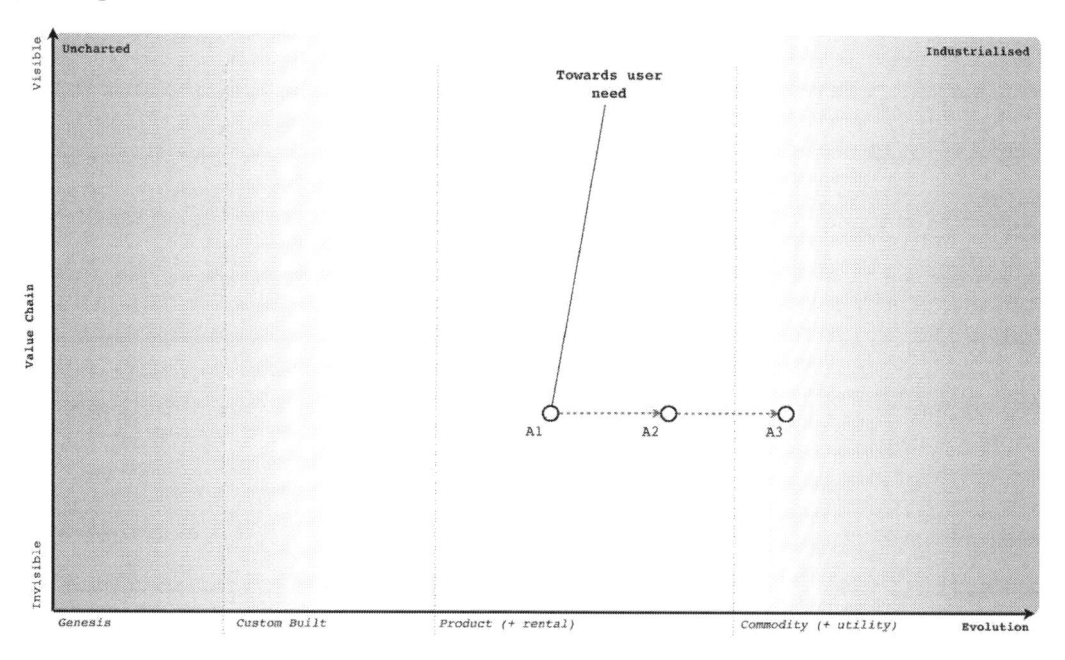

Figure 188: A changing space

In any business relationship, there are more than just products involved. There is the practice of how the product is used, data about the product, data consumed by the product, and even knowledge about the construction of the product. I've marked examples of this onto Figure 189 for our product. How do I know I've put the dots in the right place? I don't. Maps can be tools for explaining general concepts, and in this case, I will just assume that the practice around how to use our product is well-developed, along with the data that underpins it.

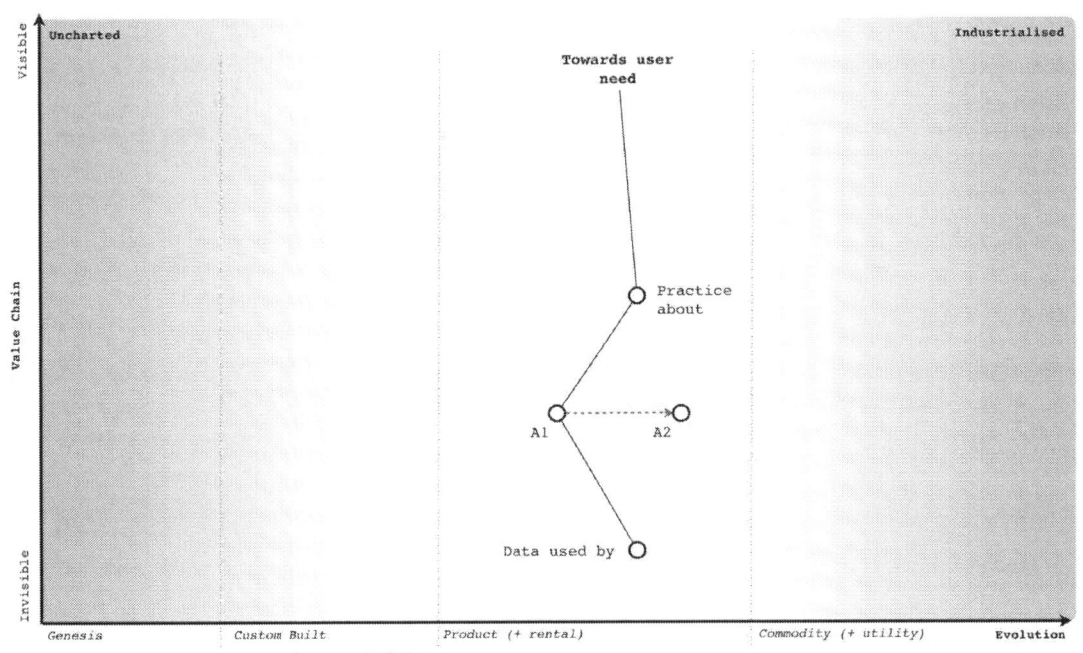

Figure 189: Adding practice and data

Now, let us consider the first variant where our product is undergoing substitution from A1 to A2. We are RIM; our flagship BlackBerry product is under assault from a range of new Android phones that have appeared on the market. With such substitutions then the existing data, practice and knowledge of the market tends to be maintained, i.e. an Android phone might substitute the BlackBerry but the practice of using smartphones, the data around the market, and even knowledge about construction and use will tend to incrementally improve rather than be substituted itself. I've marked this change onto Figure 190.

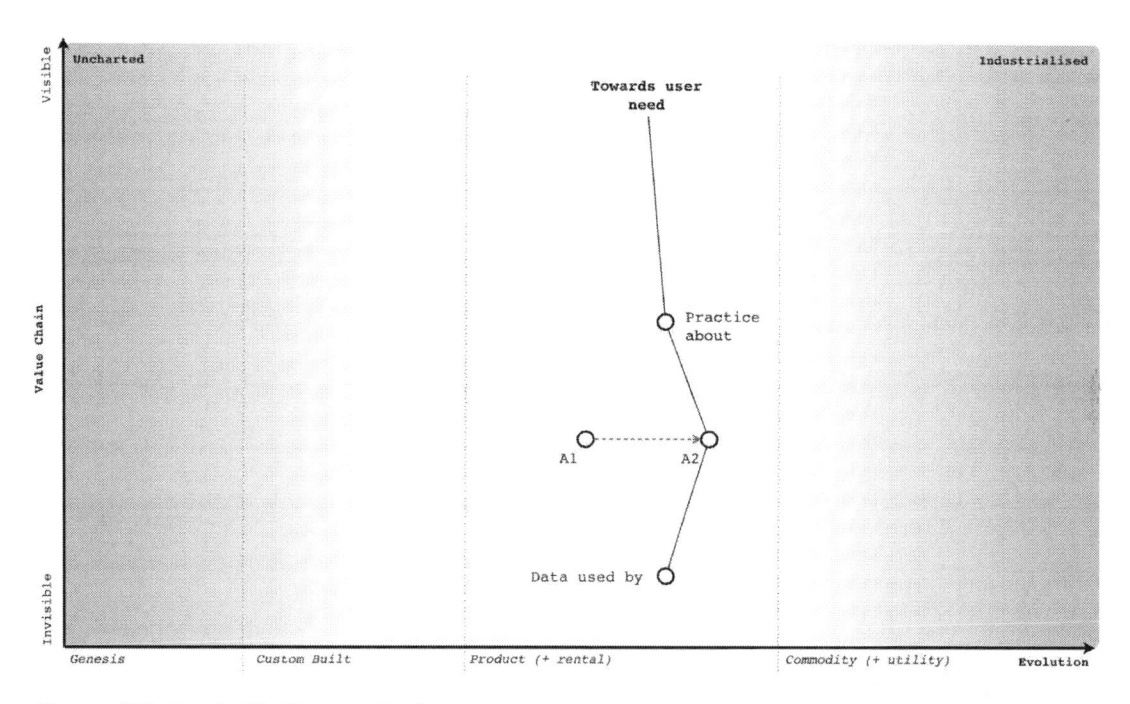

Figure 190: A substituting product

Unsurprisingly, we are going to have inertia to this change. A significant source of this will be our own past success, often represented by our own sales data, our own marketing collateral and our own reward systems. These systems will encourage us to believe that the change won't happen, and with good reason. Such product to product substitutions are highly unpredictable. Whilst it is easy to look back in hindsight and describe the success of the iPhone, there was no guarantee that the iPhone would succeed in disrupting the existing market. In fact, the guru of disruption Clayton Christensen stated that the iPhone would fail.

But, let us assume we've often experienced such substitutions and we suspect this is happening now to our product. We might have inertia but we understand its source and how to overcome it. For consumers of our product, there will also be some inertia to the change, but as long as the practice remains equivalent then this is often mild. Changing a type of phone used within a company (i.e. from BlackBerry to Android) is a far easier problem than introducing the concept of a mobile phone for the first time. The latter requires a fundamental shift in any established practices of communication; the former is simply a refinement. I've marked the main source of inertia onto our map in Figure 191.

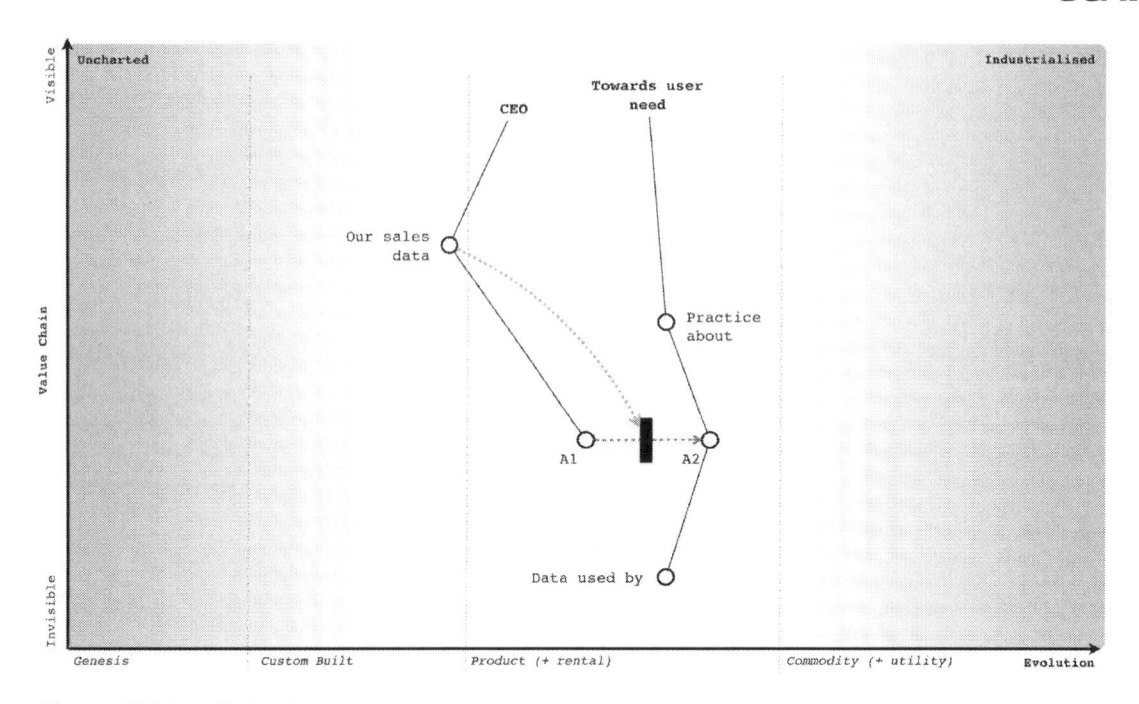

Figure 191: Inertia to change

As the CEO of a company facing a potential substitution then my understanding of this change provides me with options. The most common of which is known as Charles Handy's 2nd Curve, or in other words, the exploitation of an existing position in order to create a future position. This second curve works because substitution doesn't happen overnight. We don't wake up one morning and discover that the entire world has changed. There is still value to be extracted from the "legacy" position before any crisis point is reached. I can use this time and any revenue created from the legacy to invest in and leapfrog our competitors by building a better or adjacent product that exploits the change in the market. I could even employ a more radical shift or some combination of any of the above with concepts of differentiation.

Since the practice around the activity is unlikely to change then I also have the skills, experience, knowledge, brand (another form of capital), process and data within my company to play this game. I might not however have the culture, and there is still any internal inertia to overcome, so it's not a trivial problem. As a founder CEO, my tendency will often be towards the fight. Words such as "I've built this company, I want to succeed and I want to create a glorious future for my people" are not uncommon. In this context then I can create a vision that builds upon our past practice and experience. I can sell a purpose of creating a new future and explain why we need to make this change. There's never any guarantee to success but as long as I've seen the change and react quickly enough then I can often overcome it. This does require a strong will, fast action and a willingness to gamble because product substitutions are unpredictable and you can't plan for this uncertain change in advance. I've given an idealised example of this in Figure 192 using the concept of leapfrogging a competitor.

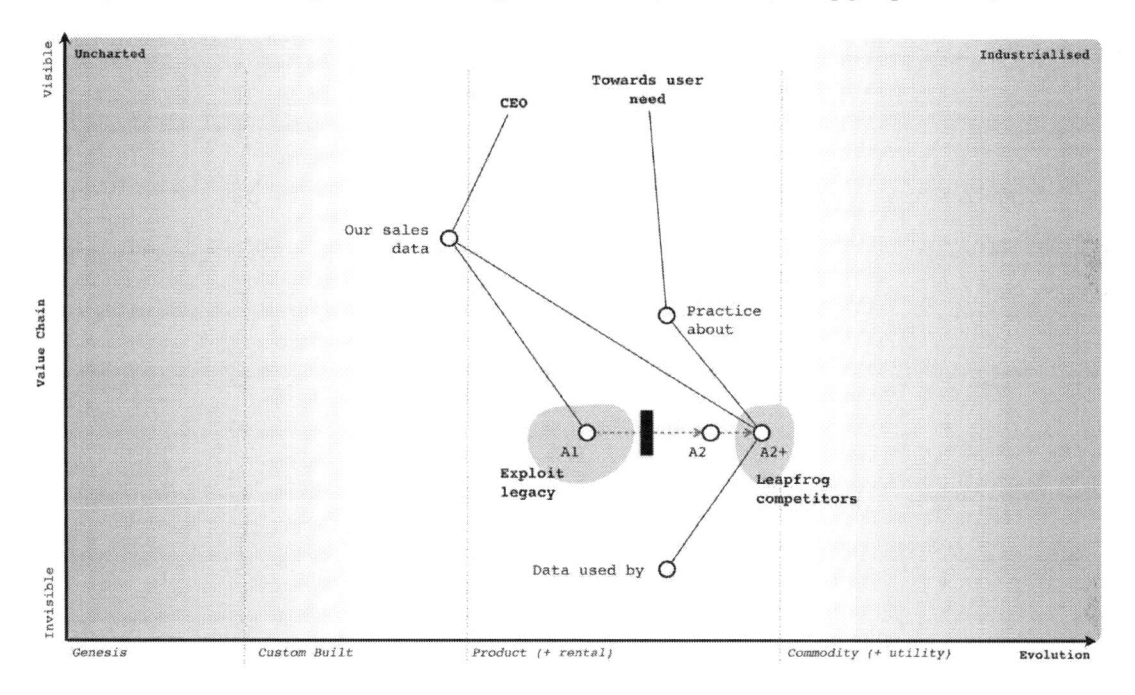

Figure 192: Leapfrogging a competitor

Let us now change our role into that of a hedge fund manager. In this case, I'm left with a bit of a quandary. We've seen the appearance of a product that might substitute the company's but there is no guarantee that it will. This means that I don't know which company to invest in for the future — it's a gamble. Also, if the CEO of the company being substituted is switched on then they might play a comeback with a second curve and a new product. Apple is one of those companies that has successfully played a second curve several times, bringing us new products, from the iPod to the iPhone to the iPad. A lot depends upon my confidence with the CEO and whether they have done this before. My tendency would be to hedge my bets here and closely monitor.

Here, we have two distinct roles, that of CEO (and the options you might play) and that of the hedge fund manager. However, the desire of the founder CEO to create a future for their company can be easily aligned with the desires of the hedge fund manager. There might be tension but there's no real conflict between the roles. Whether the two views are aligned is often more a question of confidence and whether the right culture exists.

Play it again

Let us now play this scenario again and consider the second variant and the substitution of the company's product by a utility (e.g. A1 to A3). Along with inertia, there are a number of complications caused by common economic patterns. The first complication is caused by co-evolution of practice. As with more recent examples (e.g. cloud computing and the rise of DevOps) then the changing characteristics of the activity as it evolves from product to utility will result in co- evolved practices. This will also apply to any data and knowledge of the space. I've marked this change in Figure 193, focusing on practice.

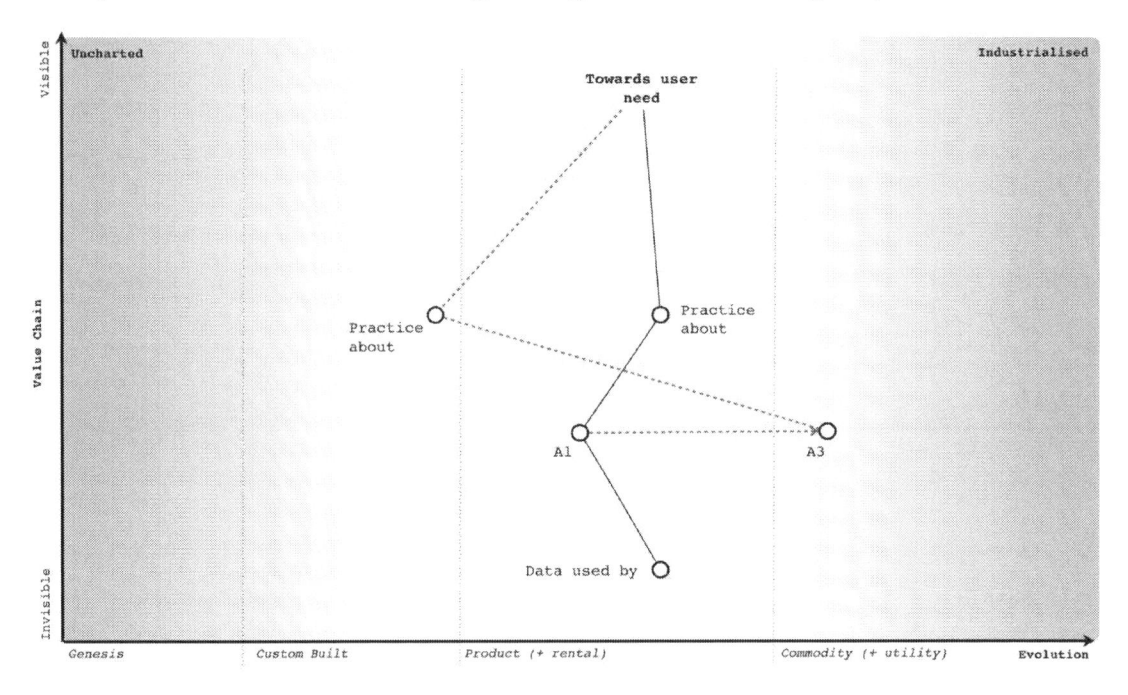

Figure 193: Coevolution of practice

It's not enough to simply react to the change of activity; we have to understand that the entire practice and associated components will also change. The second complication is that changes from product to utility tends to exhibit a punctuated equilibrium (a rapid period of change), so we have to deal with not only legacy in product but legacy in skill-sets and cope with this in double quick time.

The third complication is the "legacy" practices, data and knowledge will significantly reinforce inertia to the change at a time when change is rapid. This doesn't help me to adapt nor give me much time to exploit the legacy, but alas, it's far worse than that. My ability to perceive the crisis point will be diminished by the statements of confidence in the current way, despite the simple fact that in this case, the shift from product to utility is anticipatable in advance. As the CEO, you will be told from all directions why this change won't happen. Your sales team will tell you this, your own engineers are likely to say this, and even your customers. Despite the inevitability of the change, you are given every reason to believe that it won't happen. The same happened in cloud and it has happened many times before.

In a short period of time, we will have a change of activity, a change of practice, and three major sources of inertia to contend with. Our past sales data, the change of practice itself (which will be resisted by our own people), and the impact of a change of practice on our customers (they will also tend to resist) will try to dull our senses and demand we stay put. I've marked these sources of inertia onto Figure 194.

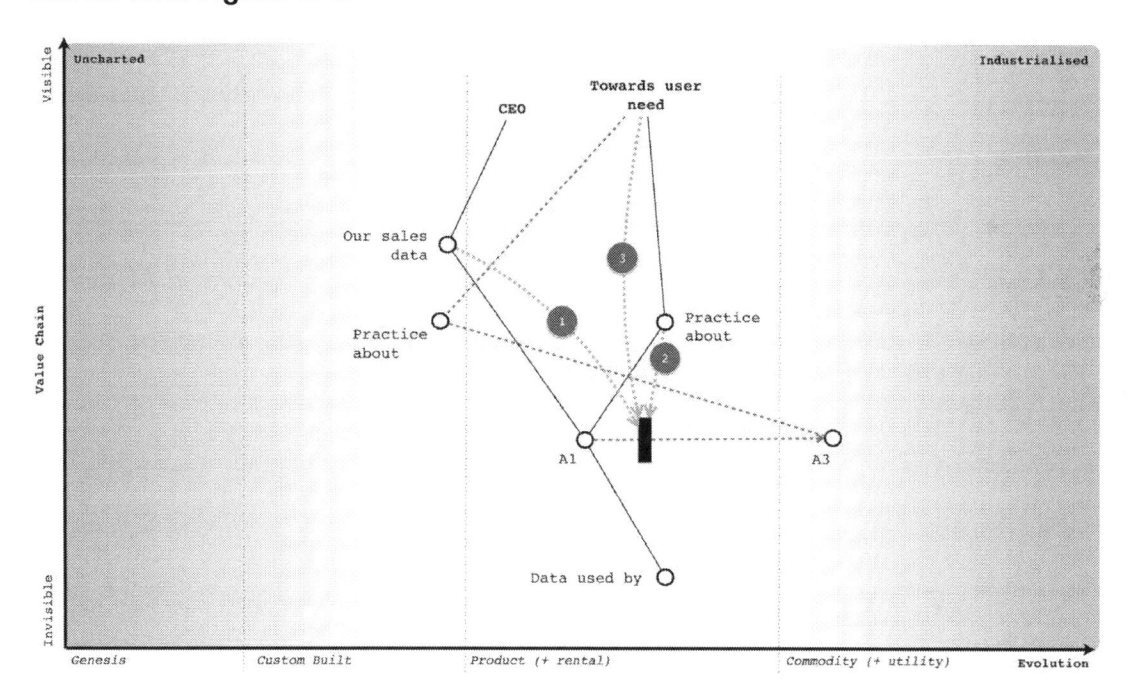

Figure 194: Three points of inertia

But, it's even worse than this. Not only do you have to overcome multiple sources of inertia but the fourth complication is your choice of direction is far more limited in scope. Beyond niche specialisation, there is no product option in a utility world. You can try to substitute the competitor's utility with your own but this is a very difficult game, especially if you don't have the skill-sets and the capability to do this. If you're dominated by legacy practice, data and knowledge then it is highly unlikely that you will have that capability. Any alternative path you wish to introduce will need to be far more radical. You might think that companies can play a second curve in this position and build a future whilst exploiting the past, but the mechanics are so different, the practices so alien and situational awareness often so poor that the crisis point is usually upon them when most are still debating if there even might be a future crisis point. To compound this, they have none of what they need — none of the practice, none of the data and none of the knowledge.

However, let us assume that you're a canny CEO and you know these problems. Your desire is still to build that glorious future. You want to play the second curve game and understand there is limited opportunity in the utility space as you're late to the party. Instead, you're going to create a radical new future. You'll have to completely reinvent a "successful" company with not only a new set of uncertain activities but also a new set of uncertain practices. This is about as radical as it gets. It's an enormous gamble, even as a startup, but you'll be trying to do this with an existing company with a legacy business that not only wants to fight you every step of the way but few will understand why you are embarking on this route. Talk about the Augean stables; this is not going to be an easy or pleasant task.

This doesn't mean it cannot be done, but the level of situational awareness and gameplay required are off the charts. There's a long history of CEOs trying to implement radical and poorly understood changes being ousted by boards. I've seen numerous successful examples of the second curve played out in product to product substitution, but by the same measure, I've seen as many second curve failures played out in a product to a utility world. All the past giants of computing infrastructure that tried to play a second curve game against the new cloud entrants have failed, with the possible exception of Microsoft. But then, Microsoft wasn't a hardware company under direct assault, and it had more space to play the game in.

Of course, it doesn't have to be this way. This form of change, the substitution from product to utility, can be anticipated well in advance, and there is no reason that a company should find itself in that position. Naturally, almost all companies fail to anticipate it because they lack any form of situational awareness or mechanism of systemic learning. Most don't understand basic economic patterns and hence, fail to anticipate and prepare for them. Whether this is fortunate or unfortunate is a question of your perspective.

However, let us assume that your company faces this dreadful position of being substituted by a utility, but you are Queen Boudica, the warrior leader, the stuff that legends are made of, and you won't give up the fight. Well, it's not only your company, your staff and your customers who are going to fight you in your pursuit of a better future — it's also the financial markets. To explain why, let us once again switch to the role of the hedge fund manager.

The Hedge Fund Manager

To begin, let us focus for a moment on cloud computing. It represents a timely expression of this form of product to utility substitution, with a rapid period of change and co-evolved practices that were all highly anticipatable. At the same time this is occurring, there is also a significant legacy of activities and practice. So, ask yourself the question of where do you invest? The immediate response tends to be — "in the cloud space" — because that's now seen as the future. But this wasn't the case in 2008. There was still lots of uncertainty in the market due to poor situational awareness, despite the change being highly anticipatable. Let us assume that you are that rare beast, a hedge fund manager with a good helping of situational awareness. You don't tend to be caught unawares by highly anticipated changes. You're not the sort of person who lets go of the glass of wine and complains in surprise that it fell to the ground rather than levitated through the magic of thought leadership. You know that there are precise and meaningful patterns in life, and incantations of "ecosystem, innovation, platform, abracadabra" don't actually work.

In this case, you will understand that for you then longer-term capital gains will be made by investing in that future focused space, i.e. those utility providers. However, you're a canny sort and know this is only part of the story. There is also the potential for shorter-term benefits as companies provide services to those with legacy activities and practice. As the hedge fund manager, you should be aware that the legacy will eventually diminish, but there exists money now. Any short-term benefit depends upon those companies operating in the legacy space focusing on returning capital to shareholders.

To maximise my advantage, I'd be looking to invest in the long-term capital gains from those developing the future industry, but at the same time, reap short-term benefits (in terms of dividends) from those extracting value from legacy. However, I'm assuming that the CEOs playing in the legacy space know their role. The ideal situation is a CEO that is sweating legacy business models to return value to shareholders, often combined with acquisition of equivalent business (again for synergies, i.e. more sweating). As a hedge fund then I'm after a "rent extraction" machine — "up those licence fees, squeeze those costs, return that capital" is the motto! Of course, eventually, those companies will run out of runway, i.e. there's no-one else left in the legacy space to acquire or there's no more cost-cutting to be done and the business model will continue to decline. From a hedge fund perspective, this is also fine because you're also already invested in the future. Shortly before the cracks start to appear in the legacy space then I'd be moving capital out and starting to short. Trebles all round.

This play of "sweating" an existing business is very different from the second curve. There are many variations of the play, from sweat and dump (i.e. disposal of the legacy) to sweat and acquire (i.e. buying up similar assets to gain greater opportunity for cost cutting and efficiency). They sound brutal but they have a number of discrete benefits. For the hedge fund, it means high short-term dividends. For the executive, it maintains and can even grow share price for a time. This sort of play can often sustain a legacy space for a decade or more. However, it's important to understand your role. If you're an executive in such a space then your role is to sweat and return dividends. You have to maximise this local opportunity until it is overwhelmed by the debt of the past. But, as a founder CEO of a company in that legacy position, then you are likely to ask "what's the plan for the future?"

Tricky. The honest answer is probably none. I'll come to that "probably" in a moment. Your role is to sweat, return capital and disappear over the horizon — well, that's the investment view. Let us just say that most founders don't react well to this. However, as the CEO, you need to realise that you've not only got your sales team, employees (with the exception of a few rebels) and customers fighting against your attempts to make a future, but if you're really unlucky then you've probably also got savvy hedge fund managers trying to dissuade you of the notion. Your future is one of rent extraction and the cliff — hardly the glorious image that most hope to create.

As the CEO, you can try and push back against the hedge fund but they will tend to fight you. As the fund manager then I would have already invested in those new entrants that are building the more certain future with their utility services. Anything you spend is capital that you should be returning to me, not gambling on some uncertainty. I'm investing in you to maximise the local conditions and it's returning dividends that is keeping your share price and your rewards up. Get this wrong and you'll find that the financial markets can themselves be a significant source of inertia to changing direction. From a point of view of the market, this is actually fairly optimal. The legacy is removed whilst the future flourishes. Your role in such a position is one of legacy removal and the market will not reward you for not playing that role.

In the first variant (product to product substitution) then as the CEO, you're playing a second curve because it's the right context-specific play. You're trying to build a new future, given a possible substitution of your core product set and an impending future crisis point. You can often achieve this because you have the skills (i.e. capability), process and data to support such efforts. In the second variant (product to utility substitution) then as the CEO, you should be playing some form of "sweating" game because it's the right context-specific play. You're not trying to build a future, not trying to run a second curve, but trying to extract as much value as possible before the system collapses. The nature of what you do, your role in the game, changes with context.

"What if I want to build a future?", "I refuse to go quietly!", "What about the people?" are often phrases I hear, especially with founders when we discuss this. Well, you can't tell employees that the company has no future and so you probably need to play a bit of theatre and paint a picture of one.

"That's dishonest! I want to build an actual future!" are often common replies.

Well, there is an upside to playing the game. "Probably none" doesn't mean none and there is a path, though it's not an easy one. The odds of you achieving a future position without exceptional situational awareness and a culture to match are not great, but they are something. Leadership is neither easy nor is it necessarily comfortable. The first advantage of playing along with the role is that you're buying time. This gives your employees more of a future (which I'm sure they would thank you for), and so as unpalatable as it is (the waves of cost-cutting) then consider it a more graceful withdrawal for the company from the market. With skill, this can easily last a decade or more. However, we can go one step further and create a future, assuming we don't make the grand mistake.

The grand mistake

This is known as the spiral of death and it is one of the most commonly repeated mistakes in business. It's also a company killer. Let us assume that the shift from product to utility (what I describe as the "war") is upon us and we're in the position of "rent extraction" from a legacy. Capital is already flowing from our industry into new industries, whether more evolved utilities or higher order systems that have been created on top of this. We're watching this marvellous new world forming but we are on the sidelines. The good news is that we're maintaining our position for now through some form of sweating play. You're going through the fairly difficult time of constantly cutting costs in order to restore profitability and return dividends, even though revenue is declining. You may be acquiring and performing more of the same. It's a tough spot, especially when you look at spectacular growth elsewhere. Your problem is that the revenue will continue to erode due to evolution in the value chain. You need to somehow respond by adapting and possibly moving up the value chain, despite the resistance and any inertia created by your legacy customers, your sales data and often your own people. But the financial markets are demanding more and you know you're going to have to cut deeper. It's a bit miserable but there is a path to the future.

The grand mistake is that we tend to cut away exactly the things we need to create that future. In any lay-offs, for example, it is very easy to use metrics based upon performance in the "past" world and therefore remove those seen as less successful in that previous era. That doesn't sound too bad but the result is that you end up with a higher density of people successful in the past models (which are now in decline due to evolution) and hence, you'll tend to reinforce your cultural inertia to change. Whoops.

Unfortunately, we also tend to remove the radicals, the troublemakers and the pioneers. Again, that doesn't sound too bad because we've got to become more "efficient". Unfortunately, those often annoying people are also the ones most likely to stick a soldering iron into a pot of ink, create inkjet printers and save the company. Whoops again. To compound this even more, we often cut far deeper than we need to because we reward those with past success in order to retain them. In our effort to keep the past going, we've cut away those very things that might give us a future. Our revenue then declines further and the spiral continues.

Much of this spiral of death played out in RIM as it attempted to cut costs, return to profitability, reinvent the past, and it found itself lacking in the capability it needed to create a future. In the most ironic examples, you often hear companies that have undergone aggressive cost-cutting talk about their need for talent (often as "the war for talent") in order to create a future and how they want to transform, e.g. "be more like Netflix". The irony is, if they actually asked Netflix where they got their talent from, they will often point back at the very same companies with the line "we got it from you".

I have sat in that room listening to an executive talking about building a future team like this or that "Silicon Valley" group, whilst knowing that the very same team that the executive proclaims as the future was made redundant by the company eighteen months previously. In the worst cases, the very team that was carelessly disposed of cannot now be literally afforded. In one case, I was even asked how much it would cost to rebuild Fotango. With the original team? Today, given that many are millionaires and some run unicorns? An eye-watering sum.

So let us assume that as a canny CEO, you're not only playing the game to buy time but you're being careful not to invoke the spiral of death by reinforcing your own inertia and removing the radicals that might save you. What are you playing for? The lucky break.

Phew, that was close

The "sweating" game buys you one thing — time — but don't waste it. As much as investment companies might want you to return capital, you need to resist this to some extent. A bit of experimentation added with time can sometimes find you the radical route into a brave new world, often in an unrelated area. Take IBM today, after 19 consecutive quarters of declining revenue and no let up to the woe then you'd probably conclude that they are in a tough spot. They're betting on Watson (and other initiatives), but at the same time, other larger players — Amazon, Google, Microsoft — are circling in that space. It's tough, it can't be easy, and lots of job cuts have already happened. But cutting costs buys IBM time; it gives it more chance to keep rolling the dice for that lucky break, assuming that they're not cutting away the radicals, the pioneers and the very people who might save them.

What might that lucky break be? Who knows? The uncharted space is uncertain, which is why you have to experiment. Maybe they'll turn Watson internally and create the first artificial intelligence CEO — that would probably terrify the strategy consultancy industry. Maybe their future is being acquired and getting squeezed in some grander game to buy time. Oracle? Who knows? The actions of other actors are difficult to determine. All you can hope to do is play for time.

If you get your lucky break, you will of course be able to claim that you played the second curve as you build a glorious new future. I'd ask you not to forget that you got lucky, but chances are that survivorship bias will overwhelm you and you'll craft some epic tale to rationalise it all. There's nothing wrong with being lucky, but for whatever reason, it doesn't normally fit the CEO narrative. The desire for magic secrets is fairly compelling, and whilst more likely to be honest, the story of success through "pure blind luck" doesn't fit the bill. That said, using a "sweating" play to buy time in order to maximise your chances to find a lucky path out of trouble is a perfectly reasonable rearguard action. Your goal however is the experimentation and to pray to the fates. Hence the importance of not going around removing the very capabilities that you need to come up with that lucky break. You have to be very careful with where you cut. It's hardly the more forward thinking, purposeful and deliberate play of a second curve or preparing for the inevitable industrialisation of a space in advance, but it gives you a chance.

The scenario above concerns substitution; one variant is product to product, one is product to utility. The way you play the game, your role in the game and how you'll be treated by others are very different. Obviously, I've simplified the "generalised" scenario because most companies have a diversified set of offerings, so the actual play depends upon your context. It's also why position and movement are critical, i.e. finding yourself in a position of having an entire legacy product set being substituted by a utility is entirely preventable as it can be anticipated. Equally, you should be playing the second curve game when you're riding high on the product wave and not when things are starting to go south.

Unfortunately, you can find yourself at the helm of a company where the decisions that should have been made long ago weren't and the position is woeful. Your range of options is often curtailed by past bad choices. One of the other saving graces is that situational awareness is not only poor in companies but it also turns out to be poor in investment houses. This might not solve your problem in the product to utility case by creating a future, but it can provide a route to selling a bigger story and creating a perception of one. This can buy you even more time as you try to work your way out of the problem.

Will the maps help me?

Maps unfortunately don't tell you what to do. They are a means of communication, collaboration and learning patterns. You have to apply thought and find the most probable path to survival and success, but there is always the lucky break and its nemesis, the Black Swan. That process of decision and the application of thought to a map is wrapped up in your understanding of the landscape, the climatic patterns impacting it, your understanding of gameplay, your role (as perceived by yourself and others) and ultimately, choice. There is always an analytical and emotional element to that choice, which is why it is so draining. The analytical side will tell you what is likely to happen, where not to invest and where you might invest. However, parts of the map are uncharted ("Ere be Dragons"), parts are uncertain (product to product substitution) and the gameplay of competitors is often unknown. Whilst we know that the industrialisation of one thing (such as electricity) opens up adjacent possibilities of novel higher order systems (e.g. radio, TV, refrigeration blankets), it is not possible to say which one of those will succeed. In the end, there is always an element of gut feel and leading the charge. This cannot be removed but neither should it dominate everything.

Leading the charge is also important because we have to act. It's movement that is the key to learning. Without movement, we do not discover, we do not explore, we do not learn, and in most cases, we simply die. Maps simply provide a systematic way of learning, of not repeating old mistakes, of applying patterns from one context to another and not blindly marching to your doom along a well-trodden path with signs saying "doom, doom, 'ere be doom". Of course, you might still decide that this is the best path for you. Maps don't tell you what to do, they help explain the landscape.

Common failures of sensible executives

With that in mind, I buried several common failures of sensible executives within the Phoenix scenario in the previous chapter. It's worth going through those now. Do remember that people aren't daft. Executives don't make these mistakes because of a lack of wit. The problem is blindness. If you cannot see the board, whether visually or through some mental model, then you cannot learn patterns and you are moving in the dark, stumbling from one step to another as though it's the first step you or anyone else has ever taken down that well-trodden path. It may be well signposted with "doom, doom, 'ere be doom" and a hundred other companies may have walked along that path and met "doom", but without a map, you're going to feel that it's an undiscovered path to future success. This is especially true if you're unfortunate enough to attend that one conference with a CEO talking about how they built a successful company by travelling down that path and it wasn't "blind luck". One person's survivorship bias can be a killer to others.

We often bemoan CEOs over their pay or lack of performance, and whilst in some cases, it is justified, many are caught in a world not of their making, trying to navigate without any understanding of the landscape, whilst bombarded by inertia and magic solutions. This is also why leadership requires fortitude. Being in a position of having to make the hard choices and the physical and mental exhaustion of playing the games is one of the reasons why I don't seek leadership positions. I've often found myself in that position out of necessity, but why anyone would seek to be in that position is beyond me. Anyway, assuming you're unlucky enough to find yourself in the role then a few common mistakes:-

Expand into an overseas market

When our existing market is undergoing a shift from product to more commodity (or utility) then there is often the temptation to avoid the problem by selling into a less developed market. This can buy some time but at the cost of increasing inertia to the change that's needed. You're actively avoiding the problem and the competitor will not only chow down on your existing market but the one you're busy helping to create for them.

We need to innovate more

The problem with trying to innovate your way out of a war (i.e. substitution from product to utility) is that the creation of the novel and new is highly uncertain by nature. It's a gamble. However, this is not what most people actually mean when they talk of innovation. What they're really saying is we need to "innovate" around our product, i.e. "We need to differentiate".

Well, in this case, it's far too easy for the competitor to play a tower and moat game by copying any successful innovation you create for a product. To explain tower and moat, let us switch roles for a moment and become the company that has launched a utility service into a market that is surrounded by products. You occupy the future position and know full well that your competitors will have inertia to the change. They will often react by not only spreading fear, uncertainty and doubt but by trying to differentiate their product offerings with some form of "innovation". What you do is copy and add these to your utility service. Your focus is to build up a tower of revenue (your utility service) surrounded by a huge moat, devoid of any differential value.

The competitors' efforts to innovate in a product world end up just enhancing this by helping you to copy and grow the moat. When the competitors finally wake up and make the plunge into our future market then they're likely to have been delayed because of efforts to differentiate their products with newfangled things (not a good move in a punctuated equilibrium, i.e. rapidly changing market) and they will actually have nothing different to offer. This is pretty much a disaster. So, now let us switch back to our role as product player. If our response to a utility provider entering into our market is "innovate", then as long as it's truly radical and entering a different market and assuming we're aware that this is a huge gamble, then it's a reasonable move. If it's "innovation" around a product then I hope you can see by now what's going to happen. Bad move. "Doom, doom, 'ere be doom."

Beyond the whole "tower and moat" play then attempts to differentiate a product in a game of utility substitution brings two other dangers. First, there is the existing consumers' inertia to change, which is often represented by a desire to maintain the existing model rather than to adapt. They will encourage you in this differentiation play and it becomes very easy to be seduced by it. The problem is that as their competitors adapt, the pressure on them mounts to adapt (the Red Queen), and though they tell you they want the past, they often end up buying the future. There's no point in complaining that "this is what the customers said they wanted", as it should be obvious by now that what a customer says they want and what they actually need are often not the same. This is also why mapping doesn't use an anchor of customer want but uses need instead.

The second problem depends upon whether your competitor is using some form of ecosystem model. If they're using an ILC (innovate — leverage — commoditise, see Chapter 5) model then their rate of apparent innovation, efficiency and customer focus will all increase with the size of their ecosystem. This means that as much as we try to out innovate, we can easily be overwhelmed by their ecosystem. For example, look at Amazon Web Services. When you consider AWS, don't think of it as going up against a company with a rapidly growing $12bn in revenue and thousands of developers; instead, you're taking on the entire AWS ecosystem. You should think of the ecosystem as Amazon's entire R&D effort and ask, do you really have what it takes?

We need to cut costs to return profitability

Whilst cost-cutting can be useful to prolong the past and buy time, be careful to avoid the spiral of death caused by self-reinforcing inertia. The past is going, you need to accept this. If you've been caught in such a legacy position then understand your role. Either you're heading for the cliff and aiming for a well-padded retirement or using this in the hope of a "lucky break"; hence, you're buying more time and encouraging experimentation.

We need to price cut

Price cuts are a perfectly useful form of gameplay but again, be careful. Unless you understand the competitor's value chain then you're unlikely to know if they have constraints that limit their own price reductions. It's very easy to get into a game of last

man standing with a competitor that has significantly more potential for price reductions than you do.

We need to focus on core

In a time when those core parts of your value chain are evolving to a more industrialised form, then this can often become simply reinforcement of inertia, combined with wishful thinking. Core is a transient concept and, as such, it changes.

All of the above can equally be useful, if applied in the right context. But what has this got to do with the practice of scenario planning? This entire chapter has been all about introducing you to the concept of variants, of different possible scenarios, of different roles, of different contexts and the interplay between them. With this in mind, let us plunge into another scenario.

The "LFP" Scenario

Who are you?

You are the CEO of a small software company with 100 employees. You have been approached by a global conglomerate that is interested in commissioning your company to build them a new service.

The service

The service should be designed to help sell large format printers (LFP), one of their main products. Each LFP sells for in excess of $2,000. The service must consist of:-

- a microsite for potential customers interested in finding out more about large format printers. The site should provide a link to an online testing application.
- an online testing application for potential customers to upload an image and have printed on the LFP of their choice. The visitors to the testing application can either be direct (i.e. through marketing) or indirect (i.e. via the microsite).
- a back-end system to distribute the printed image to the potential customer, including a brochure on the LFP used and a follow on sales call.
- each delivered print will be considered a lead.

Because of past bad experiences, the client has moved towards more value based contracts (known as worth based development). They would like you to invest in, build and operate the service, and they will pay you $40 for each customer lead delivered. You will retain ownership of any IP related to the service, though there is a clause for exclusive provision to the client for the length of term of the contract, which is one year.

Sales and Marketing

Sales and marketing feel this is a good project because of the brand name. They've examined the LFP market, which has a CAGR (compound annual growth rate) of 4.5% with over 310,000 units shipped. Currently, the client represents around 15% market share. Though it is considered to have the best LFP products in the space, it is also seen as losing ground due to weak marketing. Sales highlight that if successful then this project could be sold elsewhere. The potential market is significant and it provides a valuable in-road into the client for other projects.

Project Management

Your project management team is keen to try working on an outcome basis. They argue that this is a potential future model that might solve many of the client conflicts they've experienced in the past. Gaining experience in such a space seems worthwhile. They've looked at the client figures and developed a financial model with systems, development, marketing and finance.

Finance & Legal

Your CFO is cautious and points out that there are some significant downsides if things go wrong. For example, one possible outcome is that we end up with a net cash outflow of almost $800k before disposal of any assets. There is unfortunately a complication, which the CFO highlights. There are two competing proposals for building our solution. One is to build using in-house infrastructure (a build "in-house" variant); the other is to build using a public code execution environment that provides charging at the functional level based upon consumption of resource (a build "public" variant).

The net effect of this is the build "public" option has higher but more variable costs, whereas the build "in-house" variant has significant stepwise increases in investment once the service exceeds 100,000 users per month. These stepwise increases are due to additional development (requires a more distributed architecture), the infrastructure itself and hosting. Legal points out that once we sign up to the contract, we're responsible for providing and funding the service for one year and hence, if we get this wrong, we have to fund the investment regardless of whether we see a corresponding revenue increase. Given the uncertainties, the CFO has modelled both the "in-house" and "public" variants of the scenario with each examining four possible outcomes. The outcomes vary according to:-

- the number of **direct** visitors to the testing application
- the number of microsite visitors
- the rate of conversion of microsite visitors to use the testing application (**indirect** visitors)

The CFO is unconvinced by marketing's conversion rate from total visitors (i.e. both direct and indirect) of the testing application to leads. Given that we're being paid by the lead, the CFO views this as critical. The CFO agrees that marketing has put together a compelling case of how the service will be a roaring success, but highlights that no-one seems willing to provide a probability for each of the outcomes. There is a lot of uncertainty over which of the four will be more likely.

In terms of operational cost such as print and distribution, the CFO is more satisfied that we have a good handle on this. The CFO also notes that the in-house solution does return hardware assets that have value after depreciation is considered. These could be disposed of or repurposed but we have a somewhat less than perfect record here. The normal ROI (return on investment) the company expects to make on any project is around 40%.

The two variant models (in-house, public) of the scenario, each covering four possible outcomes, are provided in Figures 195 and 196. The figures are provided as a "best guess" estimate of the four outcomes. What the actual outcome will be is uncertain. In the "in-house" variant, some disposal figures have been provided for the in-house assets, assuming these are not repurposed.

In-house variant (one-year project, possible extension)	Outcome 1	Outcome 2	Outcome 3	Outcome 4
Price per lead	$40	$40	$40	$40
Direct visitors	7,000	7,000	14,000	14,000
Microsite visitors	50,000	400,000	400,000	800,000
Conversion rate	8%	8%	12%	12%
Indirect visitors	4,000	32,000	48,000	96,000
Total visitors per month	11,000	39,000	62,000	110,000
Conversion to lead	18%	18%	18%	18%
Number of leads	1,980	7,020	11,160	19,800
Revenue per month	$79,200	$280,800	$446,400	$792,000
cost of distribution	$2,970	$10,530	$16,740	$29,700
cost of print	$7,920	$28,080	$44,640	$79,200
cost of site maintenance	$9,000	$15,000	$15,000	$15,000
cost of site hosting	$12,000	$40,000	$40,000	$40,000
cost of marketing	$2,000	$60,000	$80,000	$160,000
Total cost per month	$33,890	$153,610	$196,380	$323,900
Net income per month	$45,310	$127,190	$250,020	$468,100
Annual net income	$543,720	$1,526,280	$3,000,240	$5,617,200
Early stage investment				
Development	$120,000	$320,000	$320,000	$320,000
Infrastructure, s/w licenses	$200,000	$2,100,000	$2,100,000	$2,100,000
Total Investment	$320,000	$2,420,000	$2,420,000	$2,420,000
Annual net cash flow	$223,720	-$893,720	$580,240	$3,197,200
ROI	69.9%	-36.9%	24.0%	132.1%
End year disposal of assets	$94,000	$980,000	$980,000	$980,000
Annual net cash flow (+ disposal)	$317,720	$86,280	$1,560,240	$4,177,200
ROI (+ disposal)	99.3%	3.6%	64.5%	172.7%

Figure 195: The "in-house" variant modelled on four outcomes

Public variant (one-year project, possible extension)	Outcome 1	Outcome 2	Outcome 3	Outcome 4
Price per lead	$40	$40	$40	$40
Direct visitors	7,000	7,000	14,000	14,000
Microsite visitors	50,000	400,000	400,000	800,000
Conversion rate	8%	8%	12%	12%
Indirect visitors	4,000	32,000	48,000	96,000
Total visitors per month	11,000	39,000	62,000	110,000
Conversion to lead	18%	18%	18%	18%
Number of leads	1,980	7,020	11,160	19,800
Revenue per month	$79,200	$280,800	$446,400	$792,000
cost of distribution	$2,970	$10,530	$16,740	$29,700
cost of print	$7,920	$28,080	$44,640	$79,200
cost of microsite	$5,000	$40,000	$40,000	$80,000
cost of testing application	$22,000	$78,000	$124,000	$220,000
cost of marketing	$2,000	$60,000	$80,000	$160,000
Total cost per month	$39,890	$216,610	$305,380	$568,900
Net income per month	$39,310	$64,190	$141,020	$223,100
Annual net income	$471,720	$770,280	$1,692,240	$2,677,200
Early stage investment				
Development cost	$320,000	$320,000	$320,000	$320,000
Total investment	$320,000	$320,000	$320,000	$320,000
Annual net cash flow	$151,720	$450,280	$1,372,240	$2,357,200
ROI	47.4%	140.7%	428.8%	736.6%

Figure 196: The "public" platform variant modelled on four outcomes

Engineering

Development has also provided a map of the space, which covers both the "in-house" and "public" variants. The difference is simply explained as a shift from a more product style of platform (requiring us to build, maintain and operate our own product stack) to a more utility environment. One significant change with this shift is function based billing, through which greater transparency, clarity and variability on IT expenditure can be achieved.

These environments are relatively new but development believes that building skills in this "serverless" space (the common term used in the market for public code execution platforms, despite the obvious existence of servers under the hood) is essential for future competitiveness. The map is provided in Figure 197, with Point 1 being the in-house solution and Point 2 being the public platform solution. The CFO has marked on various metrics used in the above models.

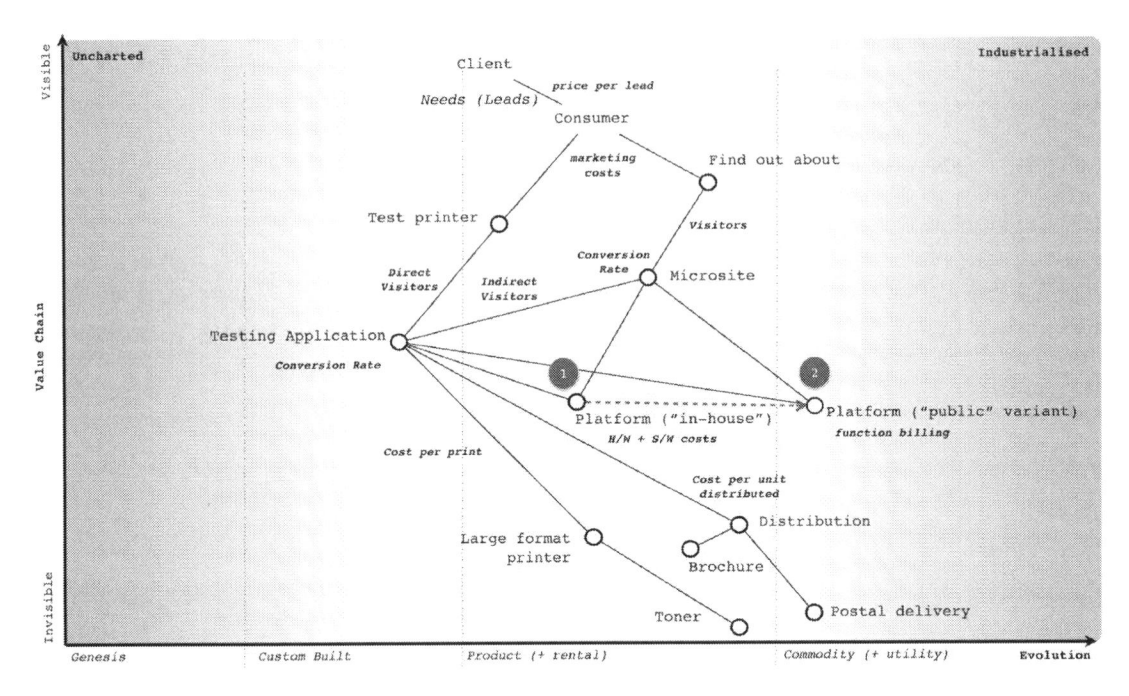

Figure 197: A map of the landscape

Systems and security both have concerns. Whilst security is concerned over the lack of experience in this space, it also recognises a necessity to develop appropriate skills. Systems highlights that it has ample skills in developing such environments and it can build the environment more effectively than a generalised public provider. There's a bit of derision about the "serverless" term. The head of systems also says that by embarking on a route of using an untested public service for such a visible and important project then we're sending a worrying message to the systems team.

The board

The board is uncomfortable with this project, preferring the more tested routes of contract negotiation that the company has established. However, though not comfortable, there is no objection to it.

Your choice

You have the map, the background and the financial models. You need to consider the landscape, the roles involved, your role and what's the best way to play this game. Once you've signed the contract then the company will be taking the risk and paying for an early stage investment. That early stage investment may significantly rise, depending upon which outcome starts to emerge.

Given everything you've been told, you now need to decide:-

- Do you sign the contract or not?
- If you do sign, which variant do you go for (in-house or public)?
- Are there any other changes that you would make?

Chapter 16 - Super Looper

The LFP example is based upon a real-world event. I say "based" because I usually take time to disguise the actual event to protect any guilty parties. In this case, the haphazard and stumbling CEO was… me. I'm very wary that my long experience with mapping means that I tend to gloss over parts through assumption. In much the same way, I spent six years assuming everyone already knew how to map, and it wasn't until 2011 that I started to realise they didn't. With that in mind, I'm going to go into excessive detail in the hope that I don't miss anything useful to you. To keep it relevant and not just a history lesson, I'm going to go through the steps of how you would tackle the LFP scenario as if it was happening today.

To begin

I always start with the strategy cycle. To me, it doesn't matter whether I'm looking at nation states, industry, corporates, systems or even individuals — the strategy cycle applies. For completeness, I have repeated this cycle in Figure 198.

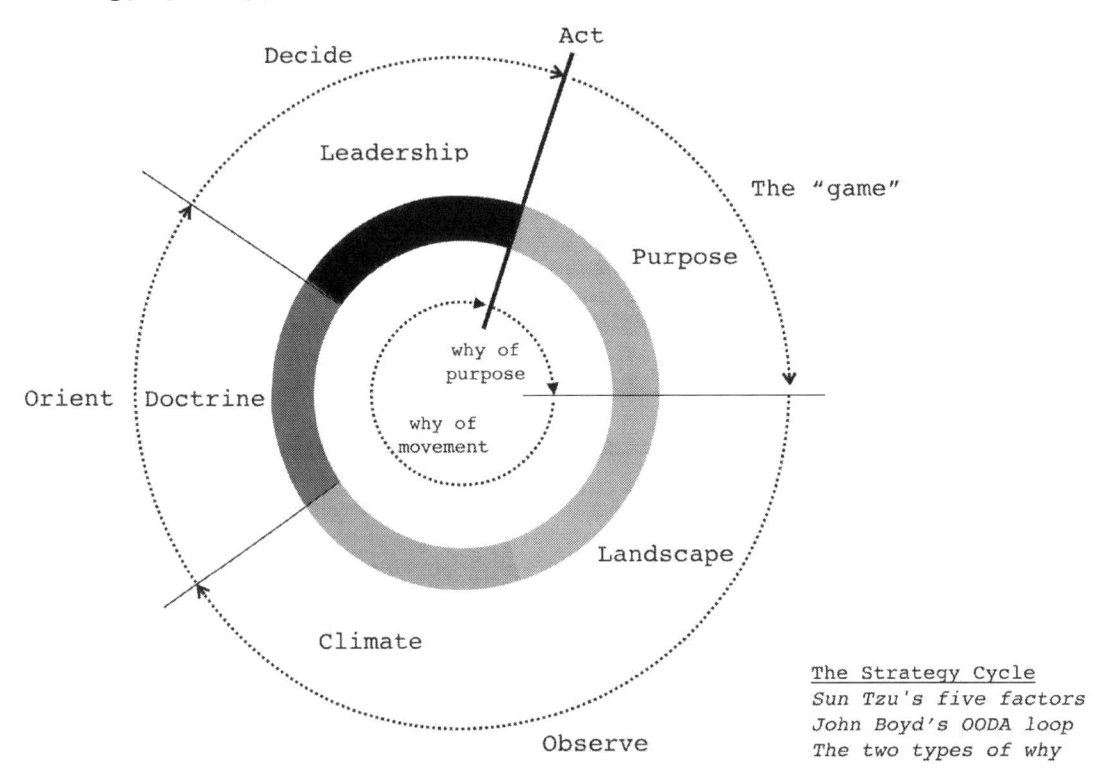

Figure 198: The strategy cycle

Our initial purpose for this LFP system is to help create leads for our client. That is what they need and it is also how we will be measured and paid. We don't have to agree to the proposal but if we choose to accept it then our focus must start here. Of course, we have our own needs — to survive, to make a profit, to have fun — which we could choose to map. In this case, I've chosen not to because this is a teaching aid and I want to keep it simple.

We know we also have a "why of movement" question in the scenario — do we build the entire system "in-house" or do we use elements of a "public" platform? Do we go here or there? Why? Before we can answer this, we need to understand the landscape a bit more. Fortunately, a map has been kindly provided by engineering, along with the more common financial models. I do love a good spreadsheet. I've spent years of my life immersed in cash flows, GAAP, chart of accounts, options analysis, business models and all manner of delightful things. However, a word to the wise — put these to the back of your mind for the moment. The financials can often be skewed by a bias to the present. So, as tempting as it is to dive straight into the financials, start with the landscape.

With the map provided, one immediate thing I'm going to note is that we have inertia against using the public platform space via both security and the systems group. I'm going to mark that onto the map in Figure 199 and cut out the superfluous "in-house", "public" terms, as it should be obvious by now.

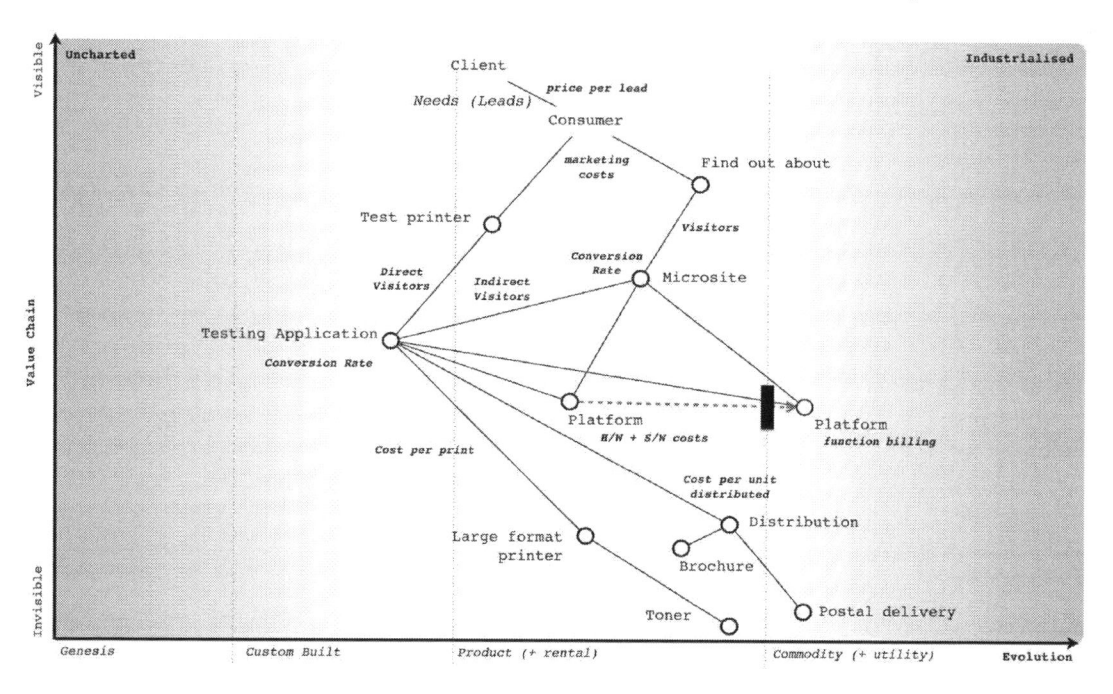

Figure 199: Adding inertia

Now let us focus on that platform change, the shift from product to a more industrialised form, which in this case means utility. As noted many times before, we have a common economic pattern of coevolution, i.e. as an act evolves, we often see a corresponding coevolution of practice. Let us concentrate here, remove all the other bits of the map and add in coevolution. I've done this in Figure 200.

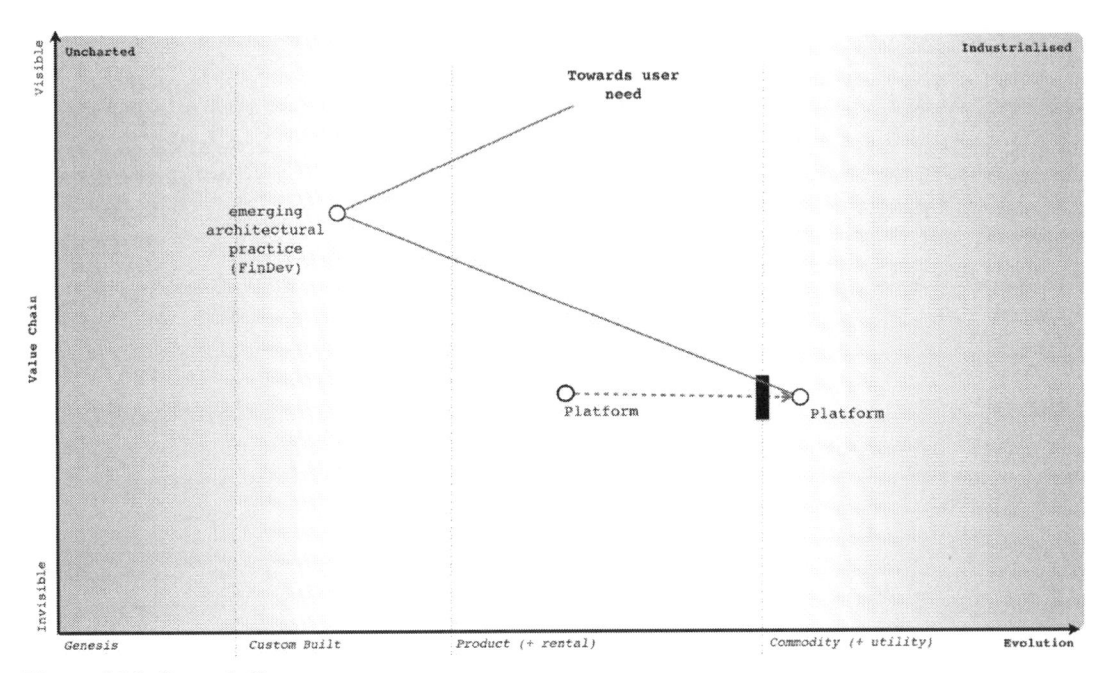

Figure 200: Coevolution

By applying that basic pattern to our map, we can anticipate that as the world shifts towards more utility platforms, some newfangled practice (a sort of DevOps 2.0) will emerge. We don't know what those practices will be as they will emerge in the uncharted space. But we do know they will emerge shortly after the formation of utility platforms and that we will have inertia to this change. We also know that such changes tend to be rapid (the punctuated equilibrium) and we can also go a bit further in our "prognostications" or, as I prefer to call them, cowardly custard pronouncement of self-evident trends.

The nodes on the maps represent stocks of capital. The lines represent flows of capital between stocks. With evolution from product to a more industrialised form then we normally expect to see flows of capital away from the past industry into the more industrialised providers and / or new higher order systems and / or new practices. I've marked these flows of capital and where to invest and what will become legacy onto Figure 201.

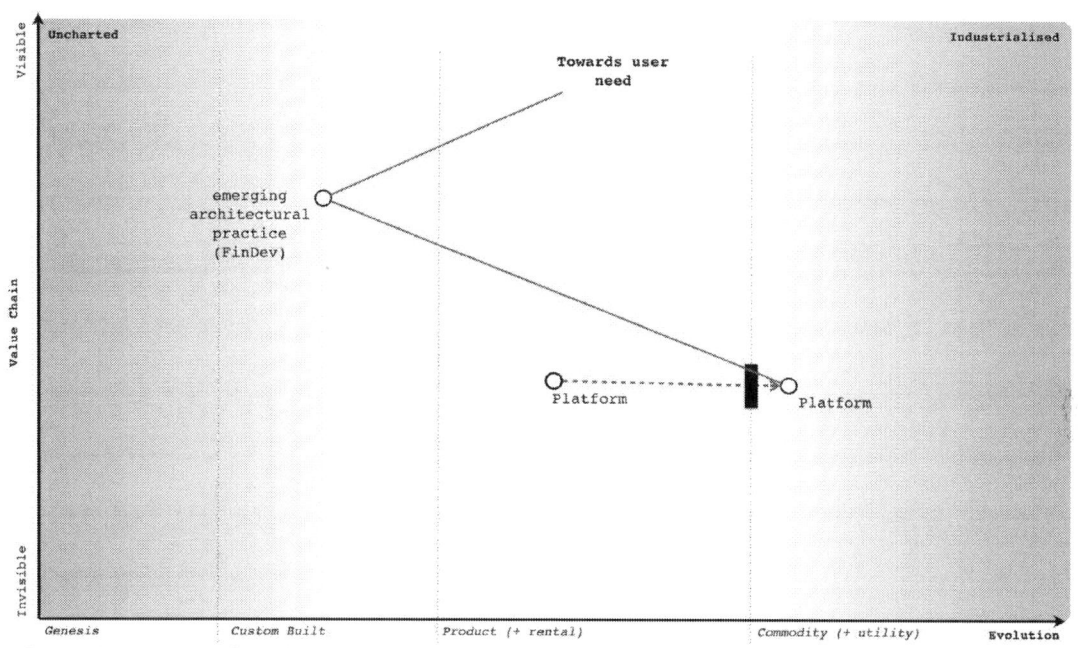

Figure 201: Flows of capital

We describe these industrialised components along with the new higher order systems that they enable as the "new industry". There will also be new practices (i.e. co-evolved) that will replace those past practices. The new higher order systems will themselves enable new needs (technically, they expand the adjacent possible, the realm of new things we can do) which means new customers. The past ways stuck behind inertia barriers, increasingly devoid of capital, will die off.

If this sounds familiar, then it should. This is what Joseph Schumpeter termed "Creative Destruction". The question is, when will this happen? For that, I turn to weak signals and examine those four conditions — does the concept of utility platform exist, is the technology there, is it suitable, and do we have the right attitude (see Figure 202)?

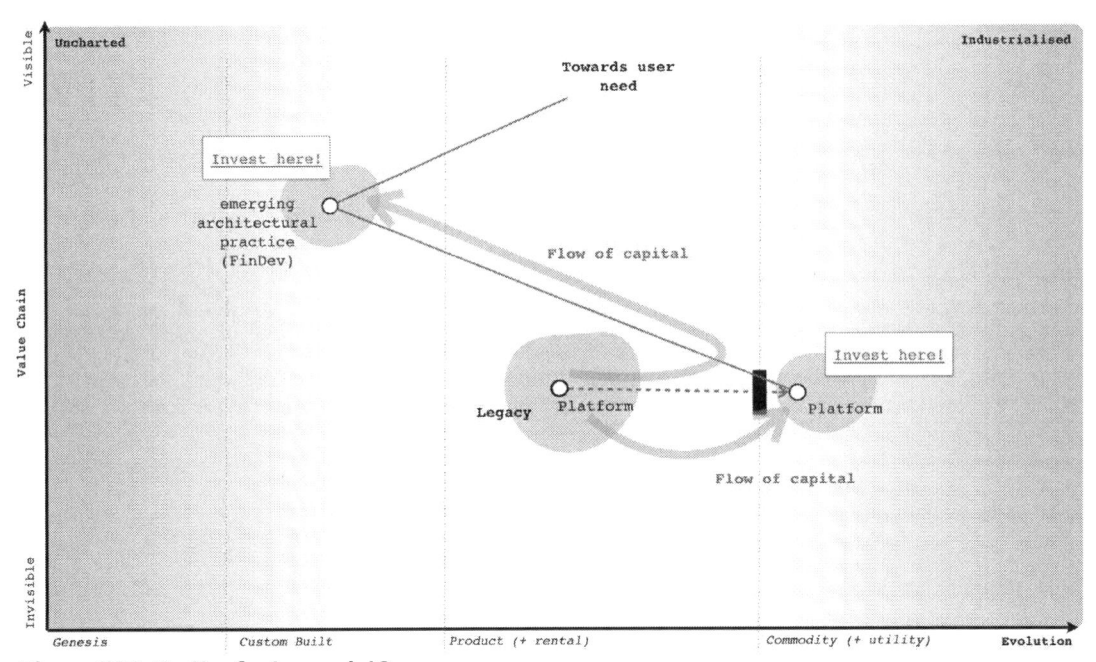

Figure 202: Do the factors exist?

In this case, someone is providing such a platform, hence the concept and technology exist. We have services like AWS Lambda. In the scenario, there's obviously some sort of dissatisfaction with the current models otherwise, the client wouldn't be looking for a new way of doing things. The attitude seems to be there; maybe this platform space will help? But is it really suitable? I tend to use weak signals to help determine that but you can also use the cheat sheet. When you examine an activity, it often has characteristics from more than one stage of evolution, e.g. it might be strongly product and a little bit commodity or vice versa. You can use this to help you refine your understanding of where something is by simply going through each characteristic and counting "is it more this or that?"

When discussing something about to evolve from one stage to another then I'm looking for more of the evolved characteristics. In this LFP case, I'm looking for whether platform has more "commodity" characteristics. I've published a more advanced cheat sheet in Figure 203, with each stage (I to IV), the terms used for different types of components (activities, practices, data and knowledge), plus the general characteristics.

Stage	I	II	III	IV
Activity	Genesis	Custom	Product (+rental)	Commodity (+utility)
Data	Unmodelled	Divergent	Convergent	Modelled
Practice	Novel	Emerging	Good	Best
Knowledge	Concept	Hypothesis	Theory	Universally Accepted
Characteristics				
Ubiquity	Rare	Slowly increasing	Rapidly increasing	Widespread in the applicable market / ecosystem
Certainty	Poorly understood / exploring the unknown	Rapid increases in learning / discovery becomes refining	Rapid increases in use / increasing fit for purpose	Commonly understood / an expected norm
Publication Types	Describe the wonder of the thing / the discovery of some marvel / a new land / an unknown frontier	Focused on build / construct / awareness and learning / many models of explanation / no accepted forms / a wild west.	Maintenance / operations / installation / comparison between competing forms / feature analysis e.g. merits of one model over another	Focused on use / increasingly an accepted, almost invisible component
General Properties				
Market	Undefined market	Forming market / an array of competing forms and different models of understanding	Growing market / consolidation to a few competing but more accepted forms.	Mature market / stabilised to an accepted form
Knowledge management	Uncertain	Learning on use / focused on testing prediction	Learning on operation / using prediction / verification	Known / accepted
Market (Ecosystem) Perception	Chaotic (non linear) / Domain of the "crazy"	Domain of "experts"	Increasing expectation of use / Domain of "professionals"	Ordered (appearance of being linear) / trivial / formula to be applied
User perception	Different / confusing / exciting / surprising / dangerous	Leading edge / emerging / uncertainty over results	Increasingly common / disappointed if not used or available / feeling left behind	Standard / expected / feeling of shock if not used
Perception in Industry	Future source of competitive advantage / unpredictable / unknown	Seen as a competitive advantage / a differential / looking for ROI and case examples	Advantage through implementation / features / this model is better than that	Cost of doing business / accepted / specific defined models
Focus of value	High future worth but immediate investment	Seeking ways to profit and a ROI / seeking confirmation of value	High profitability per unit / a valuable model / a feeling of understanding / focus on exploitation	High volume / reducing margin / important but invisible / an essential component of something more complex
Understanding	Poorly understood / unpredictable	Increasing understanding / development of measures	Learning education / constant refinement of needs / measures	Believed to be well defined / stable / measurable
Comparison	Constantly changing / a differential / unstable	Learning from others / testing the water / some evidential support	Competing models / feature difference / evidential support	Essential / any advantage is operational / accepted norm
Failure	High / tolerated / assumed to be wrong	Moderate / unsurprising if wrong but disappointed	Not tolerated / focus on constant improvement / assumed to be in the right direction / resistance to changing the model	Surprised by failure / focus on operational efficiency
Market action	Gambling / driven by gut	Exploring a "found" value	Market analysis / listening to customers	Metric driven / build what is needed
Efficiency	Reducing the cost of change (experimentation)	Reducing cost of waste (Learning)	Reducing cost of waste (Learning)	Reducing cost of deviation (Volume)
Decision Drivers	Heritage / culture	Analysis & synthesis	Analysis & synthesis	Previous experience

Figure 203: The Cheat Sheet

So, let us examine the platform space today in 2017. What we're focused on is a code execution environment, which in the product world is normally described as some form of platform stack (e.g. LAMP or .NET) or in the utility space, where we have the emergence of systems such as Lambda. It's important to focus on the "code execution environment" as unfortunately, platform is one of those hand wavy terms that gets used to mean any old tripe — see also ecosystem, innovation, disruption, and almost anything in management that is popular. Don't get me started on this one as I'm not a fan of the field I work in. I'm sure, along with strategy consultants talking about "earlobes for leadership" (HBR, November, 2011), I suspect it wouldn't take me long to find a cacophony (the collective noun for a group of strategy consultants) of them talking about how a "cup of tea is a innovative platform" or some other load of dingo's kidneys.

From the cheat sheet, comparing stage III (product) and IV (commodity), I'll score up how many commodity characteristics exist for platform:-

- Ubiquity? Is the platform space rapidly increasing OR widespread in the applicable market? I think it's fair to say that this is very widespread. It's not a case that you normally have to suggest to a developer that they consider using a platform to build something; they often have their favourite stack, whether it's LAMP or something else. We can give a tick for commodity here. [1/1]
- Certainty? Are we seeing a rapid increase in use (i.e. rapid diffusion in all companies) with platforms that are increasingly fit for purpose OR are they already commonly understood, just an expected norm? I think we can say that most developers would be surprised to walk into a company that was excited about its platform roll-out. They'd expect some sort of platform to exist. Strike two for commodity. [2/2]
- Publication types? Are trade journals dominated by articles covering maintenance, operations, installation and comparison between competing forms of platforms with feature analysis, e.g. merits of one model over another? OR are trade journals mainly focused on use, with platforms becoming increasingly an accepted, almost invisible thing? If we go back to 2004 then journals were dominated by discussion on this platform or that platform — LAMP vs .NET and the best way to install. Today, this is much less and most of the discussion is about use. Strike three for commodity. [3/3]
- Market? When we examine the platform market, are we talking about a growing market with consolidation to a few competing but more accepted norms? OR are we talking about a mature, stabilised market with an accepted form? From my perspective then the platform market seems mature and stable with an accepted form — .NET, Java, NodeJS, LAMP, etc. Commodity wins. [4/4]

- Knowledge management? Are we mainly learning about how to operate a platform, starting to develop and verify metrics for performance OR is this field established, well-known, understood and defined? In this case, platform probably wobbles on the side of product rather than commodity. Hence, product wins and it's now [4/5] for commodity.
- Market perception? Do we have increasing expectation of use of some form of platform and is the field considered to be a domain of "professionals" OR are platforms now considered trivial, almost linear in operation and a formula to be applied? Though we are getting there, product still wins and hence, it's now four to commodity out of six. [4/6]
- User perception? When it comes to platforms, are they increasingly common and a developer would be disappointed if it was not used or available? Would there be a sense of feeling left behind if your company was not using a platform OR are they standard, expected and there would be a feeling of shock if you went to a company that didn't use some form of standard platform (whether .Net, LAMP or other)? I think I can probably say that commodity wins this one. It would be shocking to find a company that didn't use some form of platform approach, and it's that "shock" that tells you this is in the commodity space. [5/7]
- Perception in industry? Advantage in platform is now mainly seen through implementation and features (i.e. this platform is better than that platform) OR platform is now considered a "cost of doing business"; it's accepted and there are specific defined models. It would be difficult to imagine a software house today that didn't view a platform as a "cost of doing business", so whilst there's some wobble, I'd argue that commodity edges this. [6/8]
- Focus of value? Are platforms considered to be areas of high profitability per unit and a valuable model? Do we feel that we increasingly understand platforms and vendors are focused on exploiting them? OR are platforms more in the high-volume space, considered "known", often mass produced with reducing margin? Are platforms essentially an important but increasingly invisible component of something more complex? In this case, especially with provision of utility-like services, then commodity wins again. [7/9]
- Understanding? In the platform space, are we focused on education with a rapidly growing range of books and training combined with constant refinement of needs and measures? OR do we believe platforms and the concepts around them to be well-defined, almost stable, with established metrics and even respected certification programs? This is a tough one. I steer to the side of commodity but can easily see a case for it being still in product. [8/10]

- Comparison? Do we have competing models for platforms with feature difference? Are authors publishing some form of evidence based support for comparison, i.e. why this platform is better than that because of this feature and why you should use them over not using them? OR are platforms just considered essential, an accepted norm and any advantage is discussed in terms of operations — this is cheaper or faster than that? This is a tough one, but in this case, I'd edge towards product. We're not quite at the pure operational comparison. Product wins. [8/11]
- Failure modes? When it comes to a platform, is failure not tolerated? By this, I don't mean there is no failure — a distributed environment based upon principles of design for failure copes with failure all the time. But do we have an expectation that the entire platform system won't fail? Are we focused on constant improvement? Do we assume that the use of such a platform is the right model and there exists some resistance to changing it? OR have we gone beyond this? Are we now genuinely surprised if the platform itself fails? Is our focus on operational efficiency and not stopping the fires? Whilst there will be many companies with the homegrown platform effort and inevitable out of control fires, as an industry, we've moved into the commodity space. [9/12]
- Market action? Is the platform space entrenched in market analysis and listening to customers? What shade of blue do you want that wheel to be? OR has it become more metric driven and building what is needed? Commodity wins here, just. [10/13]
- Efficiency? When it comes to platforms, are we focused on reducing the cost of waste and learning what a platform is, OR are we focused on mass production, volume operations and elimination of deviation? Again, especially since utility services such as Amazon Lambda now exist, then I'd argue that commodity edges this. [11/14]
- Decision drivers? When making a choice over what platform to use, do we undertake a significant analysis and synthesis stage, gathering information from vendors and analysts on its suitability, OR do we just pick the platform based upon previous experience? Tough one, but again, I view that commodity just edges this in the market overall, though some companies love their requests for tender. [12/15]

Overall, we can safely say that the platform space is firmly in stage IV (commodity + utility) in 2017. It's also fair to say that platform isn't quite yet the industrialised commodity that electricity is, and there's a bit further to go.

Hence, what do I know from my map and the basic patterns so far? Platform is moving into stage IV (an industrialised component) with provision of utility services. This will happen rapidly (a punctuated equilibrium), with such a shift (known as the "war") normally taking 10–15 years. There will be a coevolution of practice associated with this. Many companies will have inertia. Capital will flow into the more industrialised platform space and those higher order systems built upon it — there is going to be lots of future opportunity here. Capital will also flow out of those spaces stuck behind inertia barriers — not exactly where you want to be. Or is it?

At this point, we need to think about our purpose. My goals as a "retiring" CEO might be very different from the "upstart warrior" CEO. Let us assume I'm more Queen Boudica than Victor Meldrew and I want to fight for a bold future for my "people", rather than just giving up on the battle and exploiting where we are for my comfortable "retirement". My cultural heritage is therefore more inclined to investing in the new space rather than just exploiting the legacy. This assumes I have a choice in the matter and fortunately, in 2017, I'm not yet in a position where I'm forced to exploit the legacy as the change is only just starting in earnest. I'm a little late but not that late. Whoot!

But, hang on, aren't I deciding here? I haven't gone through doctrine yet and I'm already talking about how to play the game and where to attack. The strategy cycle is a cycle that you will loop around many times in coming to your decision. Each time you loop around, new information and biases form that will change your purpose, your view of the landscape and ultimately, your choice. This is all normal. It's not a rigid linear path. It's a guide. At this point, let us peek at those financial models.

Getting messy with numbers

The first thing to note is that numbers are not reality. Just because it's written in a spreadsheet, doesn't mean it is going to happen any more than a Gantt chart tells you what the future really holds. In this case, the CFO has had the good sense to examine a range of outcomes for two variants (the build "in-house" and the use a "public" platform) and then complain about the lack of probability provided. I like this CFO.

Let us assume that after some badgering, we have managed to tease out some probability figures for the outcomes from marketing and sales — outcome 1 (10%), outcome 2 (10%), outcome 3 (15%) and outcome 4 (65%). I happen to agree with the CFO that sales and marketing may well have bias here. Later in this chapter, I'll explain mechanism for how you might more accurately determine those probabilities. Obviously, our choice of building "in-house" or using a "public" platform doesn't impact those probabilities. They are independent. In Figure 204, I've added probability onto the financial models for each of the variants.

In-House variant	Outcome 1	Outcome 2	Outcome 3	Outcome 4	Total
Probability	10%	10%	15%	65%	100%
Total Investment	$320,000	$2,420,000	$2,420,000	$2,420,000	
Total Return	$317,720	$86,280	$1,560,240	$4,177,220	
Opportunity loss	$128,000	$968,000	$968,000	$968,000	
Net Benefit / Loss	$189,720	-$881,720	$592,240	$3,209,220	
Expected return	$18,972	-$88,172	$88,836	$2,085,993	$2,105,629

Public variant	Outcome 1	Outcome 2	Outcome 3	Outcome 4	Total
Probability	10%	10%	15%	65%	100%
Total Investment	$320,000	$320,000	$320,000	$320,000	
Total Return	$151,720	$450,280	$1,372,240	$2,357,200	
Opportunity loss	$128,000	$128,000	$128,000	$128,000	
Net Benefit / Loss	$23,720	$322,280	$1,244,240	$2,229,200	
Expected return	$2,372	$32,228	$186,636	$1,448,980	$1,670,216

Figure 204: Options analysis

Let us go through the terms:-

- Probability: the likelihood of this outcome occurring according to sales and marketing.
- Total investment: the total amount of capital we're putting into this effort.
- Total return: the amount of capital being returned (after repayment of investment). This is the annual net cash flow, including any disposals.
- Opportunity loss: the return I would have expected had I spent the capital on other projects. In the LFP scenario, our standard return on investment (ROI) is 40%.
- Net Benefit / Loss: how did this investment do compared to my standard expected return, i.e. total return — opportunity loss?
- Expected return: the net benefit / loss * the probability of this occurring.

By summing the expected returns for each outcome, we can determine the value of each variant. The best expected return comes from building "in-house". But wait, didn't we say this building in-house was the future legacy? Well, as I did point out, most financial models have a bias to the present and hence, they discount the future. The problem is that by following this path, we're building up the legacy practice (and related inertia) and not positioning ourselves to build a future market. We might maximise our short-term position but we end up in a dreadful long-term one.

Can we somehow financially account for inertia and future position? Yes. The essential question between the variants is the following — are we prepared to gamble $435k of expected return to explore and potentially secure a more lucrative but undefined future position? To analyse this is very complex. So, what do we do? Well, at this point, we depart paths. I will build monstrous complexities for navigation and do things to spreadsheets that shouldn't be done. You can SWOT it.

SWOT? But isn't SWOT the curse of simplistic management? Yes, but it also has its uses, particularly if we understand the landscape. The problem with SWOT isn't that it is useless but instead, we apply it to landscapes we don't understand.

We have two variants — build in-house and public platform. The strength of build in-house is we're familiar with this approach within our teams and it provides the greater expected return. Its weakness is we build up our legacy position, which comes with the threat of increased inertia and future inability to change. On the other hand, using a public platform play has different characteristics. Its strength is that we build up experience in the future space, and though it has a less expected return, it provides an opportunity to develop skills and explore new opportunity. The weakness is we're unfamiliar with this and the threat is that if it fails, we lose face with the customer but also potentially political capital with the board. The path you decide really depends upon who you are. The "retiring" CEO will tend to plummet for in-house and the short-term expected return, whilst the "warrior" CEO is more likely to go for the public platform and a long-term future.

At this point, questions such as "But what if those probabilities are wrong?" and "What if the options I'm looking at aren't right?" should be racing through your mind. So, let us tackle that bit.

Getting probability probably sort of right

As with most things in life, there exists huge amounts of uncertainty over which outcome will occur. This is only exceeded by a willingness of people to tell you that they would have chosen a different outcome if in fact you pick the wrong one. Fortunately, you can exploit this. First up is to use the Marquis De Condorcet's work and get everyone familiar with the business to assign probabilities and take the average of the lot. A more refined version is to use an information market.

Information markets are fairly simple concepts that are fiendishly difficult in practice because of unintended consequences. A basic example of one is as follows. Let us assume we want to know from the company whether a project called "X" will fail to deliver or succeed. We create a bond (called project X), which will pay a certain principal (e.g. $200) if the project is successful at a specified date, but will return $0 if it is not. We give everyone in the company one bond and $200 as a bonus. We then let them trade the bond in our own internal market.

Along with the nice "thank you" for a $200 gift (which has its own secondary benefits), the bond itself may be worth up to $200 or might be nothing at all. So, people will tend to trade it with others. If I expect the bond is 90% likely to fail then I'll be over the moon to sell it to someone else for $40 (the strike price) and a bit gutted if it subsequently succeeds as they cash in an additional $160 bounty ($200 the bond's principal – the $40 strike price). The price on the internal market will reflect the likelihood or not of the bond, i.e. the question asked. The use of such information markets is well over a decade old, but there can be lots of political complications in practice, particularly if you get an individual starting to make a small fortune on this. There's nothing wrong with that; they're somehow providing you accurate information on the future but it can cause "difficulties".

I mention information markets more to point out that there are lots of ways of skinning Schrodinger's cat and finding probability. I'm certain there must be a good few books out there on this topic, so I'll leave that to the reader to go explore. The question on probability is always how much is that information worth to you? The cheapest way is to guess yourself, the slightly more expensive way is to aggregate other people's guesses, and the far more expensive (but also far more accurate) tends to be the use of an information market. But let us assume our probabilities are "right", despite my reservations and those of the CFO. This doesn't mean one outcome will happen, it's just a probability. We must still roll the dice.

Hence, what we know so far is that we have this opportunity to build an LFP system, there are two variants (in-house, public platform), and whilst the in-house variant gives a greater expected short-term return, the platform play prepares us for the future and the coevolution of practice that will happen. Let us get back to our strategy loop and start looking at doctrine, especially the issue of "managing inertia".

Managing inertia

We have the map, we can anticipate certain change, and we can already see there is inertia. The question now becomes, what sort of inertia do we have? Back in 2008, I used to categorise inertia into four basic types with numerous subtypes.

I've tidied this up since then. The basic forms of inertia are provided in Figure 205, including tactics to counter and counter points.

Category	Type	Tactic to counter	Counter points and messaging
Disruption of Past Norms	Change of business relationship (loss of social capital)	Vendor Management	Right for its time / Past has evolved / Point to other departments / Lead the charge
	Loss of existing financial or physical capital	Future Planning	Asset write down / Look to sweat and dump or dispose / Point to savings vs increasing running costs of legacy
	Loss of political capital	Modernisation	Emphasis on future agility & efficiency / Make the business aware / Building for the future
	Threat to barriers to entry	Unavoidable Change	Already happening in the market
Transition to the New	Investment in knowledge capital	Training	Cost of acquiring external skills will be high / motivation of staff
	Cost of acquiring new skillsets	Organisational development	Develop capabilities in-house / use hack days / use conferences / create centres of gravity
	Investment in new business relationships	Vendor Management	Developing relationships with the right suppliers / understanding the market
	Changes to governance, management and practices	Awareness of Co-evolution	Practices have to adapt as activities evolve / Point to other past practices
Agency of the New	Suitability	Weak Signals & prior identification	Examine ubiquity vs certainty
	Lack of second sourcing options	Supply Chain Management	Use and development of standards, open source options, limit feature use to reduce lock-in, use of abstraction layers
	Lack of pricing competition	Market Analysis	Single or multiple vendors, examine switching costs, use of brokers
	Loss of strategic control	Strategic Planning	Examine buyer / supplier relationship, understand the market is commoditising and is now a volume operations game
Business Model	Declining unit value	Awareness of Evolution	Avoid death spiral, Look at alternative opportunities e.g. ecosystem use
	Data for Past Success counteracts	Portfolio Management	Risk Mitigation, look at disposal / spin-off
	Resistance from rewards and culture	Human Resources	Higher rewards for adaptation, Education, Promote situational awareness
	External financial markets reinforce existing models	Analyst Relationships	Spinning a future story

Figure 205: Inertia

All forms of inertia relate to some loss of capital, whether physical, social, financial or political. We know that two groups (security and systems) are exhibiting inertia, however, such visible signs are usually not the problem as we're aware of it and hence, it can be managed. The danger is always the group that haven't quite made themselves clear.

In the case of security, the inertia is probably related to two types. First, we have uncertainty over the use of a platform play and any co-evolved practices that might emerge. This will require "Investment in knowledge capital". We can overcome this with either training or providing time and resources to develop the necessary skills. We can certainly provide an argument that if we fail to do this then the future cost of acquiring these skills will be higher and we will also miss out on shorter-term motivation for staff. The second type of inertia is "Changes to governance, management and practices". Coevolution is always difficult for people to get to grips with as it means that their existing and perfectly valid best practice for a product world becomes no longer relevant. We can only overcome this by explaining coevolution usually by pointing to past examples. Both types of inertia are relatively simple to manage.

Slightly trickier are the systems groups. Along with the two types of inertia mentioned above, we're likely to have two additional types, especially since the group builds and controls the underlying infrastructure behind any homegrown platform efforts. These additional types are "loss of political capital" and "change of business relationship (loss of social capital)".

The "loss of political capital" includes fear over becoming irrelevant in the future, loss of status and loss of past empires. Don't underestimate or dismiss this as it's very uncomfortable for those who face it. You counter by giving people a path to the future and relevance in it. Start by acknowledging what has been achieved and move onto modernisation. You need to emphasise the importance of future agility, efficiency, importance to the business and how we must build for the future. You also must include them in this future. At this stage, with utility platforms just in the early stages of industrialisation then such action is relatively trivial. The co-evolved practices haven't been developed and so there's plenty of time for training, re-skilling and the re-application of essential system concepts, from configuration management to versioning in a more utility platform world. In all likelihood, the biggest danger is that by helping your systems team develop into this world at this stage, they'll become super valuable in the not so distant future. It is however, far better to have a small army of super valuable people that everyone else is trying to poach than to be left with a bunch of legacy skills and trying to desperately poach from others.

The co-evolved practice will be different from the past but someone has to develop that capability, no-one yet has those skills, and why shouldn't it be your systems team? Unfortunately, what normally often happens is that companies don't anticipate obvious changes and leave it late. This creates an added complication, which I'll discuss in a moment.

The "change of business relationship (loss of social capital)" is the second additional type of inertia you must contend with. Within a company, there's often a pre-existing relationship with vendors who might be supplying products or services. This relationship creates inertia to change, i.e. we have our familiar and favourite vendor. In normal circumstances, you can deal with this inertia through normal vendor management approaches. You can emphasise that the time is right for a change, that the past has evolved and we need to re-evaluate the vendor's offering. However, there's the complication mentioned above.

If you've left it late then the vendor of a product may well be spreading huge amounts of fear, uncertainty and doubt over the more utility form to your own team. They will probably have tried to convince your own team (e.g. in this case, our systems team) that they have no future in this "future world". If they're canny, they would have encouraged articles in related trade press spreading the same message. This is all designed to get your own people buying the vendor's product rather than adopting to the new world. If you haven't had that conversation about the future and painted that path, this can make it much harder for you to overcome any "loss of political capital".

You can try and say, "Don't worry but we will invest in retraining" but this is also where any past Machiavellian efforts or brutal corporate action will bite you in the bottom. If there exists doubt in your trustworthiness then they won't follow but will resist. Whatever you do, as annoying as it is to be confronted by this, remember one thing. They are behaving perfectly rationally. You are the wally who left it late to deal with a highly anticipatable change and therefore caused the mess. If you want someone to blame, buy a mirror.

Unfortunately, we all make mistakes. This is also why you must always consider not only our action today but the future consequences of such action. Having that trust can bail you out of your own facepalm. However, we're not in that position with the LFP scenario yet. We shall assume we have a team who can have an open and honest conversation. We can anticipate where the future is heading with the map and we're going to share this. We're going to have that discussion and invest time and money in bringing our systems and security teams into this new world with new skills and new capabilities. We leave no-one behind and we certainly don't turn up five years late to the battle in a blind panic.

Alas, we might still have a problem. There's potentially another source of inertia and it's a powerful one. The board. We know they have a concern but aren't going to raise an objection… yet. Now, that can either be just a general question on the change or could be hiding something else. We need to explore that. It could be as simple as "Data for past success counteracts", i.e. they're used to us operating in one way and we've not been down this path. It could be concerns over "Loss of existing financial or physical capital" because we've invested in data centres. It could be a question of political capital or that one board member has looked at the model and wants to focus on short-term expected return rather than building a future.

Whatever the cause, you need to find it and to fix it. That's one of your many jobs as the CEO. There are also many other forms of inertia, and so for completeness, though not necessarily relevant in the LFP scenario, we will quickly run through the other types of inertia:-

- "Threat to barriers to entry", the fear that a change will enable new competitors. Whilst that fear may be justified, it is often an unavoidable change that is already happening in the market and outside of your control. You cannot ignore it.
- "Cost of acquiring new skill-sets" is one of the more bizarre sources of inertia because not only do you not have a choice but the cost of acquiring skills will often increase over time. This is a common consequence of a punctuated equilibrium where huge numbers of companies that are very late to the party simultaneously declare this change as the future and promptly cause a shortage of skills. There are many ways to counter this and mitigate the cost — assuming this is done in a timely fashion — from developing in-house, use of conferences to creating centres of gravity to attract talent.
- "Suitability", one reasonably common form of inertia, comes in the form of questions over whether it's ready, e.g. ready for production, is the market ready for this, are customers ready? The best way to counter is through weak signals and examination of the components (e.g. using the cheat sheet).
- "Lack of second sourcing options" is often a valid concern but can be used to disguise other forms of inertia. Back in 2008, it was not uncommon to hear a company say without irony something of the form — "We're an Oracle shop. We've thought about using public cloud but were worried about the potential for getting locked in with Amazon. We want to see more choice". If you can overcome the irrational side of the debate and any tendency to point out the ridiculous flaw in the argument, then this is all about supply chain management, trade-offs and use of standards where appropriate. There are a wide range of techniques to mitigate it.

- "Lack of pricing competition" is another reasonable concern, which really points to how well-functioning the market is. Do we have single or multiple vendors? What are the switching costs?
- "Loss of strategic control" is usually wrapped up with fears of letting go, and in the cloud space, led to the idea of "server huggers". However, there are some valid aspects to the concern around buyer versus supplier power relationship. Most of this can be overcome with strategic planning and examination of different scenarios, i.e. what should we do if the supplier rapidly increases price? etc.
- "Declining unit value" is usually a business concern related to a desire to maintain the past. The only way to counter is through awareness of evolution and how markets aren't static. You need to look at alternative opportunities — think Charles Handy's 2nd curve and try to avoid the spiral of death.
- "Data for past success counteracts", an extremely common form of inertia, particularly if the company has been successful. Most companies build up a significant stock of data that informs them how successful the past was. This will often be used to argue that the future will be more of the same. You need to take a leaf out of portfolio management and realise that your portfolio will change over time. Options analysis and risk management approaches can be useful here to avoid having all your eggs in one "past" basket.
- "Resistance from rewards and culture" — hugely problematic for most companies and easily exploitable by competitors. Performance bonuses linked to selling an existing product set can be a significant source of inertia and weakness. You can manage this through HR by using higher rewards for adaptation, education, longer-term thinking and promoting greater situational awareness.
- "External financial markets reinforce existing models" — another common but tricky form of inertia to deal with. As discussed in the previous chapter, it's important to understand your context and the role being played by others such as fund managers. There are certain techniques that can be deployed here to overcome market inertia, including spinning a future story.

Where are we?

We have a map of the landscape, we've applied basic economic patterns to anticipate change, we can see opportunity in co-evolved practice and obstacles in inertia to the change, we have financial models and understand how we can trade off higher short-term expected returns for building a future position.

Though we have inertia, we also have an idea of the types and how to deal with it. Our awareness of the situation is expanding. This is good. This is how it should be.

In the above, I specifically state "anticipate change" because we cannot predict evolution over time (see Chapter 7, section "the trouble with maps"). We must use characteristics or weak signals or information markets to give us a probability of when the change will happen or even if it's occurring today. Mapping is all about probability rather than time; the uncharted space is uncertain and the industrialised space is more known. To predict over time would mean we could say "in 453 days, this [activity or practice or business model] will change from A to B". As far as I'm concerned, that is straying into the realm of charlatans, crystal ball fanatics and soothsayers.

I often hear people counter with vague notions of time, e.g. "at some point in the future". That is not predicting over time as time requires a "when". I cannot, nor have I ever been able to, predict evolution over time. Of course, I'm fully aware that I have my own inertia caused by my own past success with mapping and that the subject itself will evolve (see Chapter 7, section "a map of mapping"). Someone else may well find a way to map over time. I will no doubt dismiss it and be proved wrong. I do hope I have the wit to use my own tool on myself at that time. "When" will this happen? As I said, I can't predict over time and the weak signals aren't even strong enough for me to guess.

In terms of the strategy cycle, we've observed the environment and moved on to orientating around it with doctrine such as "manage inertia". However, let us explore the cycle a bit further.

Getting primitive

In this section, I'm going to look at how we organise around the LFP scenario and put down a few markers for strategic play that we might consider. Once I have a general outline, I'll often loop around this several times with others to refine, to create alternative scenarios, to alter course, before finally deciding upon a choice of action. When it comes to organisation then I not only use a self-contained cell based structure (i.e. small teams) with the right aptitudes (finance, engineering, marketing) but also for the last decade, I've been using attitude (pioneers, settlers and town planners).

I note recently that Kent Beck has been discussing a model called 3X — eXplore, eXpand and eXploit. This is excellent as there's nothing like independent discovery to give a bit more substance to a topic. Pioneers eXplore, settlers eXpand our understanding and town planners eXploit by industrialising with each group operating and maintaining its own space. This all deserves a good hat tip to Robert Cringely and his marvellous book, "Accidental Empires". Anyway, back to our map. Since we've previously built our own systems then I'll assume we know how to do this and it would be superfluous to cover the build in-house variant. Instead, I will focus on the platform change and how to organise around this. In Figure 206, I've outlined the two obvious cells that we need to consider when using the public platform.

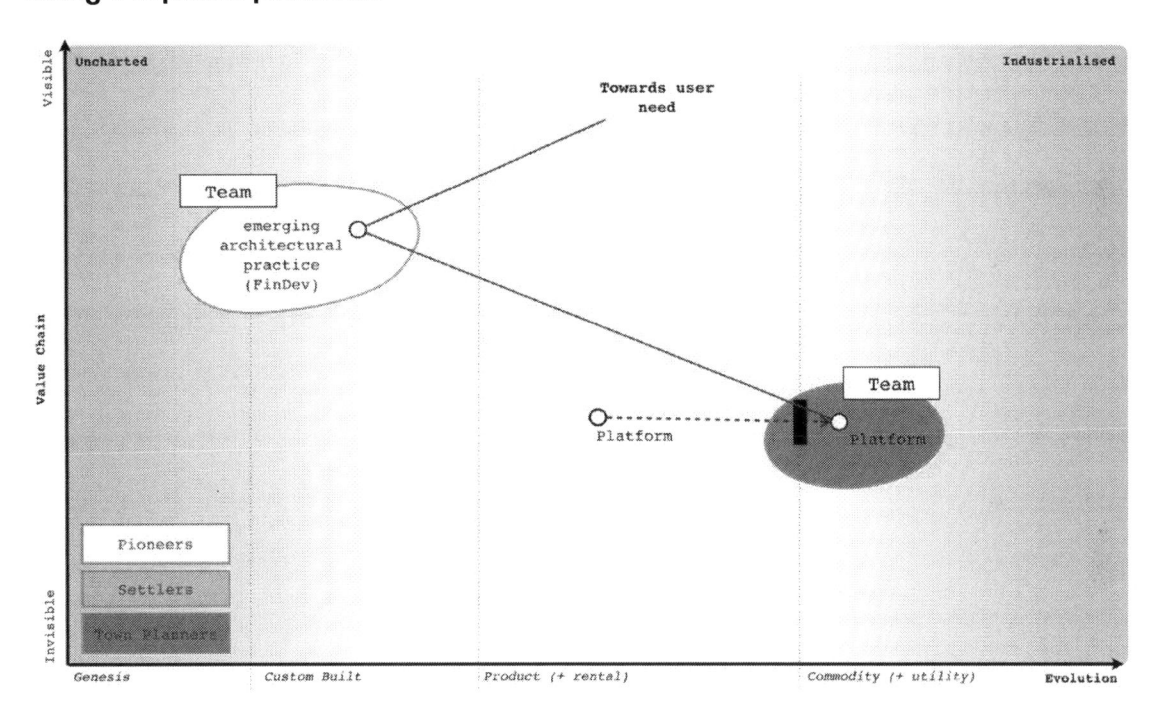

Figure 206: The structure

One cell refers to town planning around the platform. Obviously, someone else is providing the platform as a utility service to us but we still need to make sure that we create a highly industrialised process around monitoring the platform, access control and how much we're getting billed. This is not something new and chances are that the provider will be offering tools to make it easy. However, there are a new set of practices that will develop around the financial cost of a function, re-use of functions, the type of events and how we monitor the code itself. This is not so much related to the platform itself but how we use it. In much the same way, the practices that changed industry were not so much about whether we paid the right electricity bill but how we used it to do other things. What those new practices will be is uncertain. I can guess, based upon experience of running a code execution platform (i.e. serverless environment) with Zimki in 2005. But it's no more than a guess.

We can also at this point start adding some primitive gameplay. For example, we could — if we have decided to play a legacy game and not build for the future market — spread fear, uncertainty and doubt over the utility platform. Alternatively, we might play an open play around the co-evolved practices to help them evolve more quickly. We might do this to create a name for ourselves in this

space, to build a "centre of gravity" around the skill-sets needed in anticipation that this will become a lucrative market for us. I've outlined these two very simple plays in Figure 207.

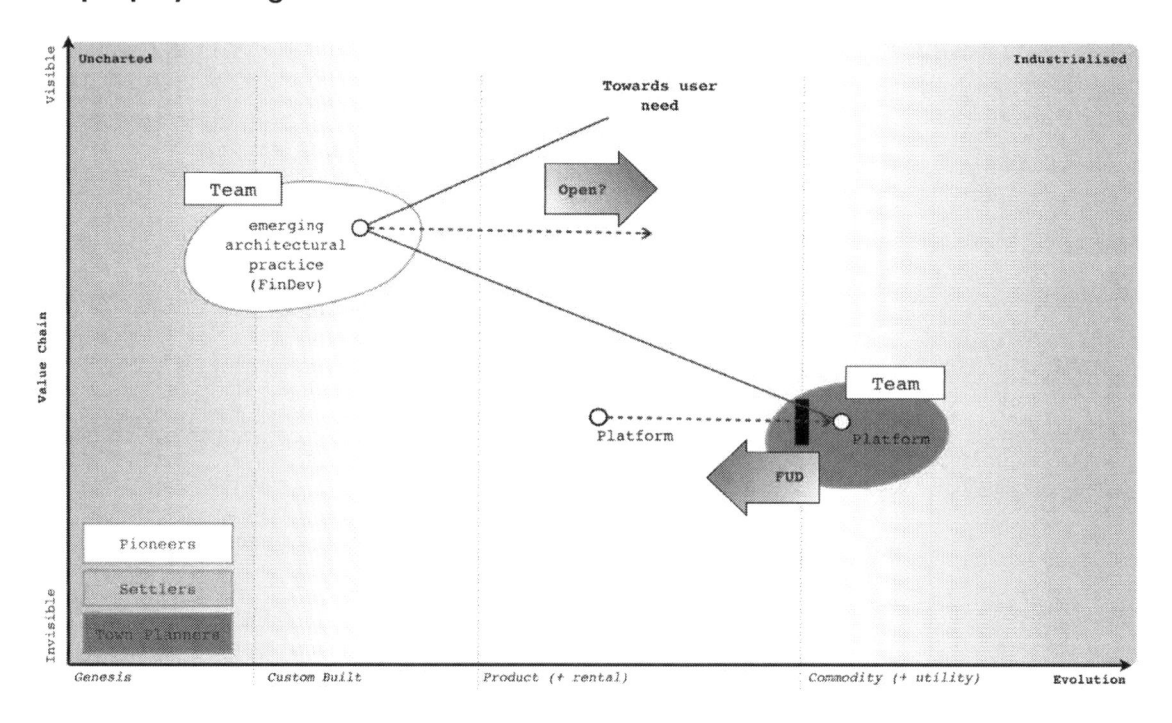

Figure 207: Two basic plays

So, complying with my natural bias, I'm going to focus on creating a future position and market rather than exploiting a legacy position and waiting for the future to catch up and do horrible things to me. I can do this because I haven't yet left it too late to make that choice. I'm going to try and own those future co-evolved practices, build a centre of gravity and use open source to achieve this. I'll accept the lower expected return in exchange for a stronger future position and not building up my legacy. I'll add my structure and gameplay around the platform space onto my LFP map — see Figure 208.

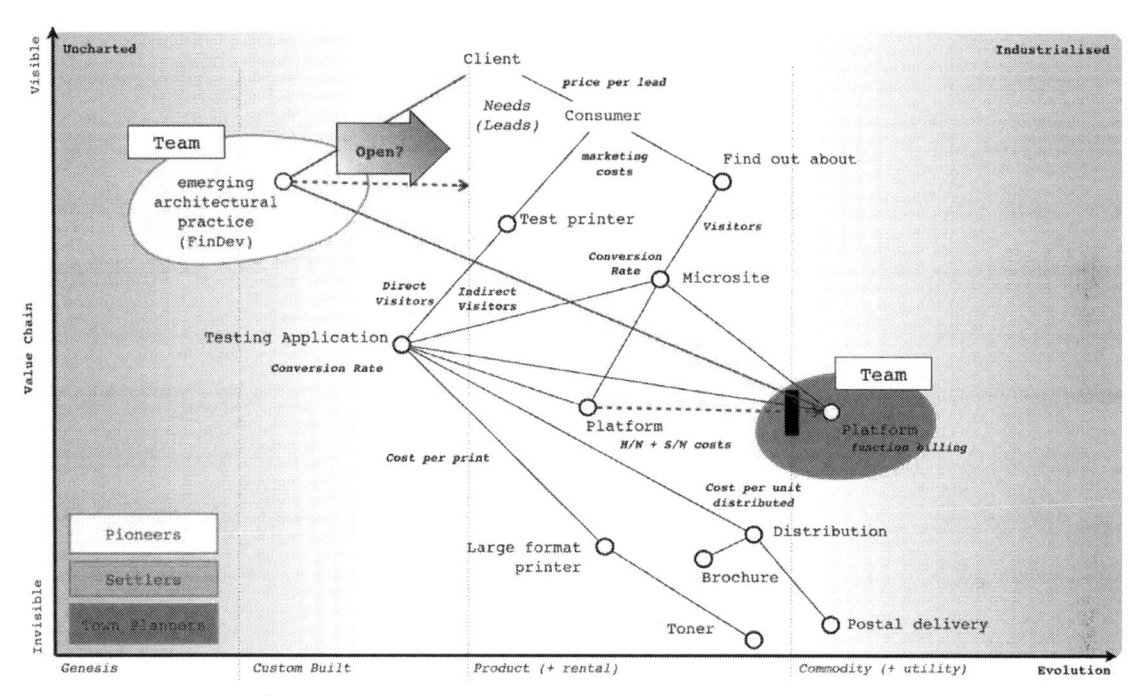

Figure 208: Future orientated LFP map

The first thing to note is that the map is a bit messy and things seem to be in the wrong position, i.e. somehow, my emerging architectural practice is above my microsite in terms of user needs, despite the client not mentioning anything about this changing world. This is fine. All maps are imperfect representations, and with a bit of fiddling around and moving pieces, then I can create something that appears to represent the situation more clearly — see Figure 209.

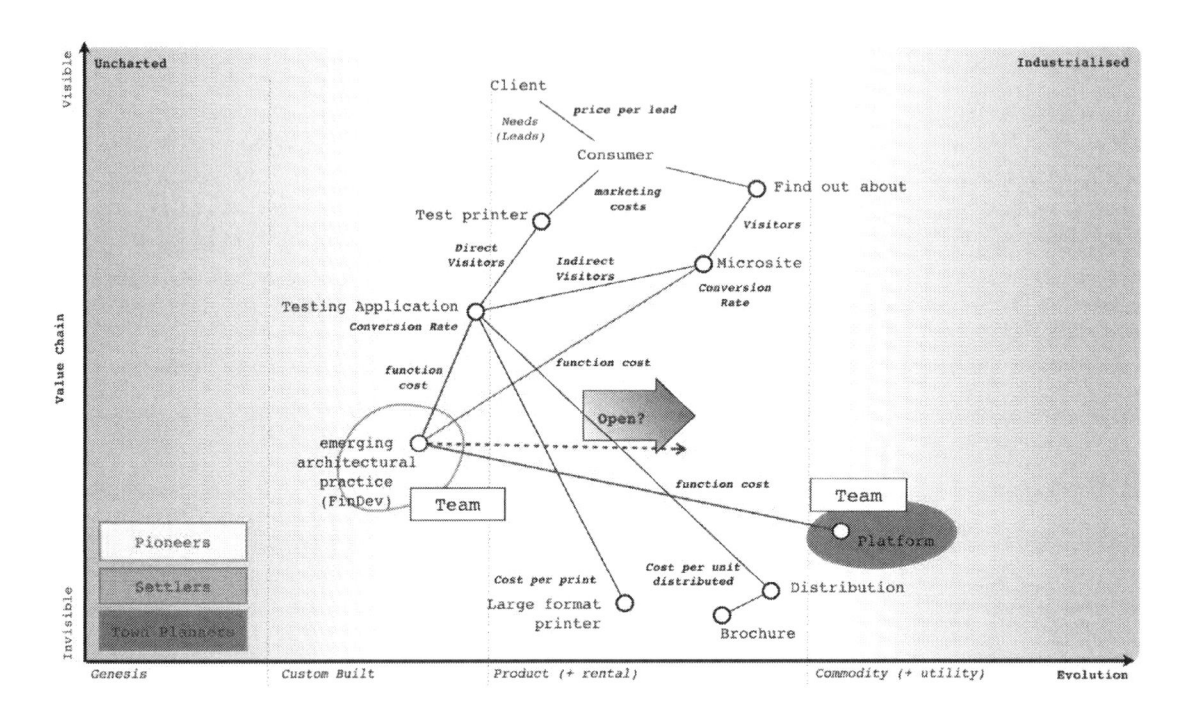

Figure 209: A clearer map

This fiddling around with maps is all part of exploring a space. It allows us to challenge assumptions with others, to collaborate across multiple aptitudes (finance, engineering etc.) and even attitudes (pioneers, settlers etc.), to apply past lessons learned and come up with a common understanding. We can now flesh out the space a bit more, and being mindful of our current capabilities (that's assuming you know how many pioneers, settlers and town planners you have — most don't), create the structure we're going to use — Figure 210.

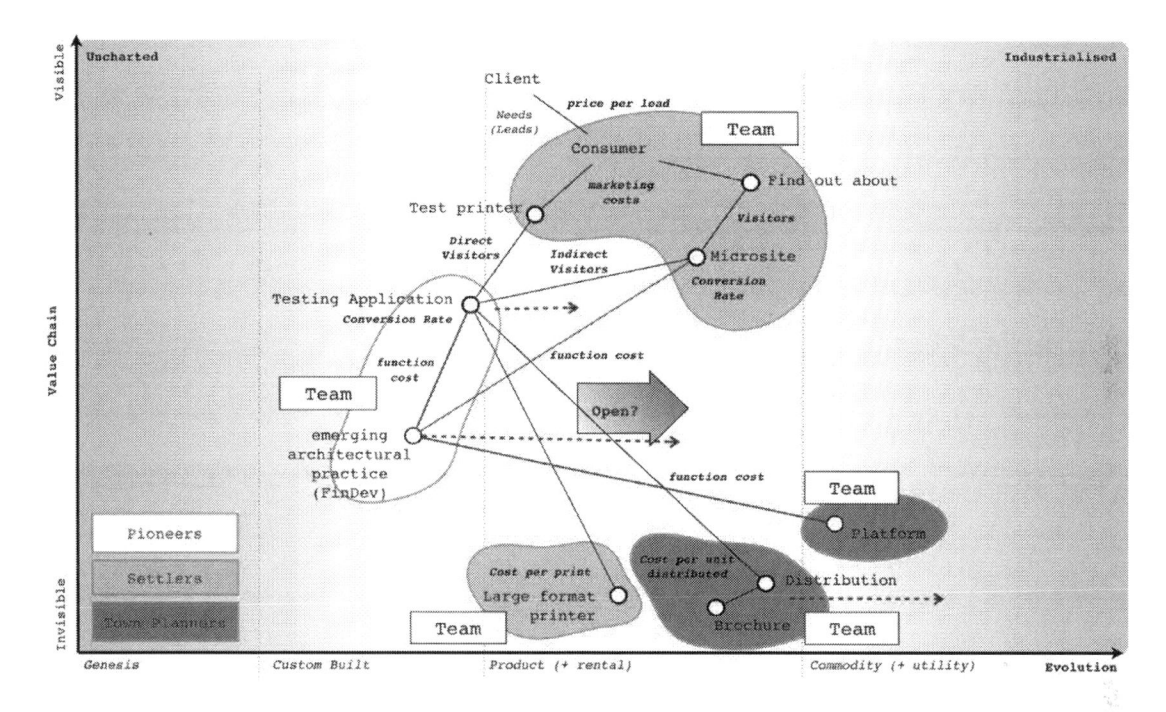

Figure 210: The structure

Looping around and common problems

We now understand the landscape, the trade-off between short-term expected return and future position, the structure needed, the main sources of inertia and some basics on the gameplay. Our situational awareness is constantly improving. The next thing we do is loop around the strategy cycle again and refine it. But isn't that time consuming? Yes.

With experience, for a business that has a map, then a single loop (what we're covering in this chapter) could take anywhere up to 30 minutes. Add a couple of loops, discussions between people and you could have easily blown an hour or two before you commit to the choice. Add to that the additional hour or so it might take to create that first map and the financial models and yes, you could be looking at half a day. That is of course an incredibly long time to go from concept to decision to act.

To be honest, I can't think of many examples where it has taken anywhere near that long. There are a few M&A activities (covering hundreds of millions) where I have taken a day or so, but that is the exception and only occurs in fields that I'm not familiar with. Being locked in a room or given people to interview and ask the question "Should we buy this company?" often involves extracting information from others. Most of the time was spent developing an understanding of the landscape because very little existed. However, we should acknowledge that mapping does take some time and I don't know how to make it faster. It's one of the obvious weaknesses of mapping versus gut feel, which can just be instant.

Another problem is complexity. First, mapping exposes the complexity of what exists. In the example of Themistocles SWOT (Chapter 1, the importance of maps in military history), it's usually obvious to everyone that you should use a map not a SWOT to run a battle. We understand this because we're familiar and comfortable with geographical maps. However, there is a downside, which is that a map is inherently more complex than a 2x2 such as a SWOT, and this makes management more challenging and requires more thought. But what if you're not familiar with maps?

Let us consider how Vikings used stories for navigation. Put yourself in the role of a Viking navigator, having spent 20 years learning epic tales and being trusted with steering the boat. Imagine someone says to you that you don't need a story but you could use a map. The first time someone shows you a map, all you will see is a diagram with dots on it. You will have difficulty in understanding how such a thing can replace your twenty years of learning epic tales. You'll tend to react negatively because of experience, i.e. you know the stories work. You'll have a natural human bias to that which is comfortable and previously experienced. The map will be unfamiliar, even alien, and its complexity will overwhelm you. It will take many points of exposure and realisation that a map would have been better than a story before most will put in the effort and thought necessary to use it.

Go back to the Themistocles SWOT. Imagine if battles had been run with SWOTs and someone came up and said, "I've got a map thing that might help." The reaction would be overwhelmingly negative to begin with because it's unfamiliar (not a SWOT) and complex. It can also threaten those who have spent 20 years learning how to "Battle with SWOTs" or "Navigate with stories" because at its heart, it is basically saying that they've been meme copying all this time without understanding the landscape. Into this mix, you can throw in the issue that exposing the complexity also exposes assumptions made and opens decisions to more challenge — another thing people don't tend to like. You've got quite a mountain to climb with mapping. Which is probably why those with a military experience (and some familiarity with situational awareness) have an easier path to mapping. The worst cases are normally those who have no military background, 20 years or so of "strategy" experience and an MBA.

However, let us assume you persevere, you create a map, you loop around the strategy cycle and over time (and hour or two, possibly more), through the application of thought, then a context- specific path becomes clear. What now? I tend to double-check it as a final step. I find that using a business model canvas is brilliant for this as by that stage, you should have everything you need to fill it in. Let us assume that you decide to build the LFP system using the public platform. What now? Well, let us roll the dice and see what happens.

Opportunities multiply as they are seized

You've decided to build the LFP system, using it as a springboard to develop a future position around the co-evolved practice that will emerge in the platform space. You've overcome your internal inertia through discussion, formed the teams and explained this to the board. You'll sacrifice some short-term expected return for a future position with an eye to repackaging the solution and selling it to others, along whilst developing a new practice in the co-evolved space. You roll the dice and it comes up… outcome 2. Oh, damn.

The LFP system isn't going quite as well as we might hope. Fortunately for us, we didn't build in the in-house variant, otherwise we'd be losing money right now and our discussions with the board might be getting more testy. The problem with our options analysis is that we didn't price in any variability and risk appetite. The in-house variant was riskier because it not only had the highest expected return but the lowest — there was a widespread. In this case, outcome 2 is a net loss. We can chalk that up as a future learning lesson (or in my case, past painful lesson). However, let us compare what happens with outcome 2 in both variants. Let us say that despite things not going so well, both marketing and engineering have dived in and come up with proposals. There are two options on the table. So, which, if any, do we choose?

- Engineering say they could improve code efficiency by 75% for $350K
- Marketing say they could add 400K extra microsite visitors for $150K each month

Let us go through each variant. In Figure 211, I've added the financial impact for the proposals on the in-house variant.

In-house variant	Outcome 2	Development Proposal	Marketing Proposal	Dev + Mkt
Price per lead	$40	$40	$40	$40
Direct visitors	7,000	7,000	7,000	7,000
Microsite visitors	400,000	400,000	800,000	800,000
Conversion rate	8%	8%	8%	8%
Indirect visitors	32,000	32,000	64,000	64,000
Total visitors per month	39,000	39,000	71,000	71,000
Conversion to lead	18%	18%	18%	18%
Number of leads	7,020	7,020	12,780	12,780
Revenue per month	$280,800	$280,800	$511,200	$511,200
cost of distribution	$10,530	$10,530	$19,170	$19,170
cost of print	$28,080	$28,080	$51,120	$51,120
cost of site maintenance	$15,000	$15,000	$15,000	$15,000
cost of site hosting	$40,000	$40,000	$40,000	$40,000
cost of marketing	$60,000	$60,000	$210,000	$210,000
Total cost per month	$153,610	$153,610	$335,290	$335,290
Net income per month	$127,190	$127,190	$175,910	$175,910
Annual net income	$1,526,280	$1,526,280	$2,110,920	$2,110,920
Early stage investment				
Development	$320,000	$670,000	$320,000	$670,000
infrastructure, s/w licenses	$2,100,000	$2,100,000	$2,100,000	$2,100,000
Total Investment	$2,420,000	$2,770,000	$2,420,000	$2,770,000
Annual net cash flow	-$893,720	-$1,243,720	-$309,080	-$659,080
ROI	-36.9%	-44.9%	-12.8%	-23.8%
End year disposal of assets	$980,000	$980,000	$980,000	$980,000
Annual net cash flow (+ disposal)	$86,280	-$263,720	$670,920	$320,920
ROI (+ disposal)	3.6%	-9.5%	27.7%	11.6%

Figure 211: Financial impact on in-house variant

Since outcome 2 is happening, we will use this as the base case and add the impacts from the proposals. The first thing to notice is that the development proposal doesn't make the case better but instead, it makes the finances worse. Why? Because the cost is already sunk, and spending money on refactoring doesn't improve the financial case as there is nothing to be recovered through code efficiency. The only possible saving grace would be through releasing some hardware to get a quicker sale of it and less depreciated value. That's in the realm of wishful thinking in most cases. Sadly, it's often difficult to justify spending more money on a refactoring effort in such circumstances. The marketing proposal however gives us some uplift. At least it recovers some of the pain. Our final expected return is still below our normal of 40% but we're saving a bit of face. The combination of both development and marketing gives us the benefits of marketing combined with the loss of development. It's far better to just do the marketing proposal.

Ok, so let us repeat this exercise but now look at the public platform variant, which is the one we actually chose. I've created the model in Figure 212.

Public platform variant	Outcome 2	Development Proposal	Marketing Proposal	Dev + Mkt
Price per lead	$40	$40	$40	$40
Direct visitors	7,000	7,000	7,000	7,000
Microsite visitors	400,000	400,000	800,000	800,000
Conversion rate	8%	8%	8%	8%
Indirect visitors	32,000	32,000	64,000	64,000
Total visitors per month	39,000	39,000	71,000	71,000
Conversion to lead	18%	18%	18%	18%
Number of leads	7,020	7,020	12,780	12,780
Revenue per month	$280,800	$280,800	$511,200	$511,200
Cost of distribution	$10,530	$10,530	$19,170	$19,170
Cost of print	$28,080	$28,080	$51,120	$51,120
Cost of microsite	$40,000	$10,000	$80,000	$20,000
Cost of testing application	$78,000	$19,500	$142,000	$35,500
Marketing	$60,000	$60,000	$210,000	$210,000
Total cost per month	$216,610	$128,110	$502,290	$335,790
Net income per month	$64,190	$152,690	$8,910	$175,410
Annual net income	$770,280	$1,832,280	$106,920	$2,104,920
Early stage investment				
Development		$320,000	$670,000	$320,000	$670,000
Total Investment		$320,000	$670,000	$320,000	$670,000
Annual net cash flow		$450,280	$1,162,280	-$213,080	$1,434,920
ROI		140.7%	173.5%	-66.6%	214.2%

Figure 212: Financial impact on public platform variant

The first thing to note is that we're in much better shape with outcome 2 because we didn't have that initial sunk cost of investment. But then something odd happens. If you look at the development option, by spending money on refactoring then we make a much better return. In fact, it's a huge return! Hang on, how's that possible? Well simply put, we're paying for consumption of the utility platform (such as AWS Lambda), based upon our actual use. If you make the code more efficient then you pay less. There is suddenly a financial reason for refactoring code. There are many other benefits with such platforms, from consuming services to code re-use, but the changes to the way we write, refactor and monitor code are significant. This is what coevolution is all about and in this case, it's the collision between development and finance.

The second thing to note is that marketing is a net loss. How is that possible when in the in-house variant, it's positive? On a consumption basis, the cost to acquire and cost of operation for each new user significantly exceeds the additional revenue they create, and so it's a loss at this acquisition price. The marketing proposal doesn't make sense in the public platform variant because there's direct linkage of actual cost against revenue. But in the in-house variant, then most of the costs of operation have already been spent in the initial upfront investment. It's a sunk cost. In which case, given we've already spent most of the money and we're actually comparing the acquisition cost versus the additional revenue, the marketing proposal makes sense in the in-house variant, precisely because you've already blown most of the cost.

But hang on, the third option of both marketing and development looks better than all of them. How can that be? In this case, the reduced cost of each user on the service (because of refactoring, i.e. the development effort) means that the total cost per new user (i.e. marketing acquisition plus operational) is now less than the additional revenue they create. The sum of the whole is greater than the sum of the individual parts. Hence, the last option gives us the best choice and that's where we invest. The shift towards utility platforms and billing at the functional level fundamentally changes your entire investment approach in projects. From no more nonsense about additional IT users having a marginal cost of zero (i.e. we've sunk a lot of cost and can't actually allocate them) to refactoring suddenly becoming a financial consideration. The true costs (not just of acquiring but operating) of marketing are hence exposed.

We're already starting to experience some of those co-evolved practices and this looks like a big change. This is why I created that first platform back in 2005, but as you'll come to learn, these opportunities jump at you when you embrace the future. But, why didn't I continue and rebuild the platform after the parent company decided it wanted to go elsewhere? Well, I spent a bit of time working on printed electronics and then met an astronaut, but that's the next chapter.

Something to remember

The one thing I want you to remember from this discussion is that spreadsheets are wonderful but they're not a substitution for situational awareness. Loop through the cycle, understand your landscape, anticipate change, manage inertia, structure around it and then apply tools, choices and biases to help you decide where to act. Maps however aren't a substitution for thought, they're an enabler of it. By now, you should be thinking about how you can use maps to communicate across finance, engineering, operations, purchasing and strategy, from anticipation of change to organisational structure. As you'll discover soon enough, this is only the beginning.

Oh, and in terms of the original questions, then my answer would be:-

- Do you sign the contract or not?

    Sign it

- If you do sign, which variant do you go for (in-house or public)?

    Public platform, variant 2

- Are there any other changes that you would make?

    I would use this as an opportunity to explore a future business

So, did I tell you the story about how I met a real-life spaceman? That's next.

Chapter 17 - To infinity and beyond

I was working on the use of printed electronics with paper (think of digital interactivity within a normal book) when I got that phone call from a friend about "this spaceman who really wants to meet you". I was curious, so I went along to meet someone called Mark at Canonical. I didn't know what to expect. The first few minutes were certainly interesting.

Shuttleworth: "I'm Mark. I've been told you're a good UX designer."

Me: "I don't know anything about design."

… silence.

It was an awkward pause. Then Mark, realising the next hour was probably a waste of his time, asked me to tell him something I did know about. I talked about evolution, the changes in the industry, and before long, we were into graphs, maps and cloud computing. The time flew by. We kept talking. I was introduced to others, and in what seemed like lightning speed, I was working at Canonical. I had one job, to bring Ubuntu into the cloud. I called my friend, asked him what had happened. Steve just responded, "I knew you'd get along." Life is full of pleasant troublemakers like Steve.

The first day I arrived for work, I was all excited and had the usual confused look of a rabbit staring at headlamps. My boss, who also happened to be another Steve, did the usual rounds of introductions. That was an interesting moment. Whilst I delighted in the warmth of the people I met, the first five responses to my role of bringing Ubuntu into the cloud were negative — "it's a fad", "why are we doing that?" etc. I knew I was going to have to build a cabal pretty quickly and create some momentum. However, my first official task was to look at the virtualisation strategy that had been written. It was one of those "oh, what have I done?" moments. Fortunately, it didn't take long to find others with common interests — Rick Clark, Soren Hansen, Nick Barcet and many others. Steve George (my boss) was also one of the most supportive people I've worked for, a good friend, and then there was Mark. Without Mark, none of this would have happened.

The problem to begin with was that Canonical was focused on the server and desktop market. It was up against huge giants such as RedHat and Microsoft. It was making valiant, almost heroic efforts, but Canonical was small. Many wanted to focus on the server OS, to generate revenue from support licences, and to a few then the Cloud was a distraction. The problem was one of focus and what I needed to do was change the mindset. To explain this issue and why it mattered, I'm going to cover a number of concepts, from the Three Horizons to Porter, before returning back to Canonical.

The Three Horizons

The three horizons was a model put forward in the Alchemy of Growth, 1999. It discussed three views that any corporation had to take.

Horizon 1: the core business that provides the greatest profits and cash flows that need to be extended and defended.

Horizon 2: are the emerging opportunities and businesses that will drive medium-term growth. These may include new ventures that you are investing in that are expected to generate substantial future profits.

Horizon 3: These are ventures that should ensure the company's long-term future. They can include research projects or pilot programs, or even investment in startups.

When I joined Canonical, horizon one was the core support revenue. Horizon two included new concepts such as online storage, the app store and extending onto more devices. Horizon three was... well, I'm quite convinced a few would have thought that my work on cloud would be in this category. Whilst this model of three horizons is a reasonable way of examining a company, I personally find it inadequate. I often find that some confuse it with the pioneer — settler — town planner model of organisation (Chapter 4) by associating town planners with horizon one and pioneers with horizon three. To explain the weakness with the model, I'm going to use the map of mapping that I introduced earlier in Chapter 7. To save you scrambling back through past chapters, I've provided that map here in Figure 213.

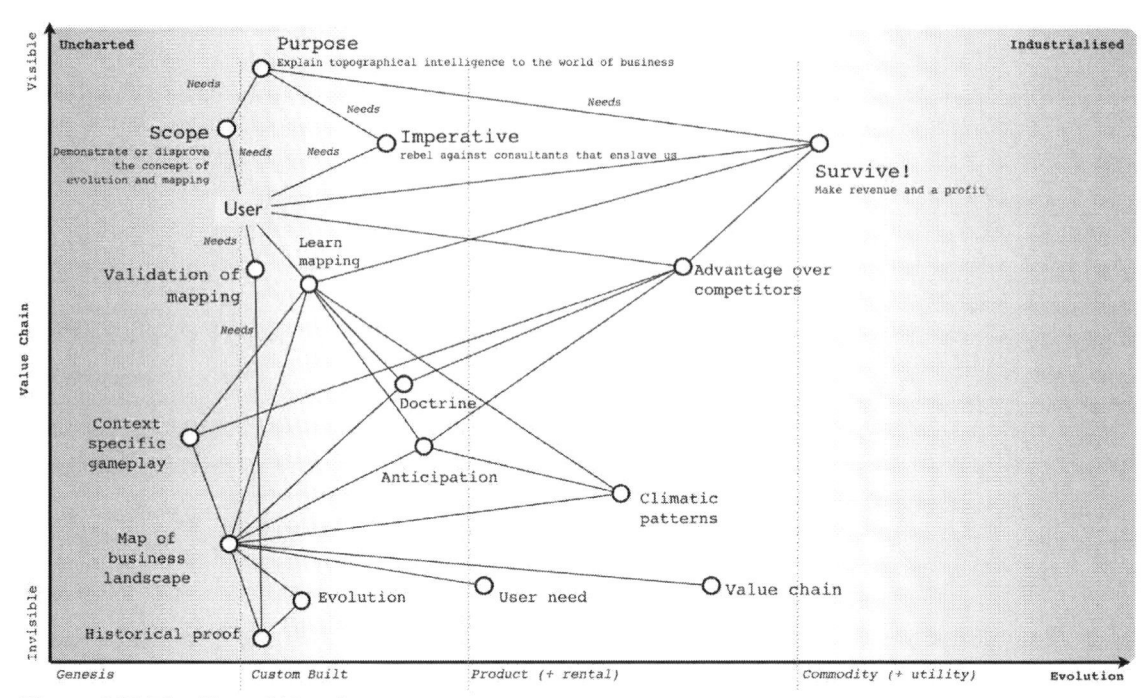

Figure 213: The Map of Mapping

Let us now assume that we decide to use the map of mapping to build a new business. I'm going to take a part of the above map and concentrate around the provision of forecasting (i.e. anticipation of known changes) to others. I could have quite easily built a comfortable life around the weak signals that I had developed for forecasting change by creating a small boutique consultancy providing market and technological forecasts. The premise behind such a business is provided in Figure 214. My purpose with such a business would have been to simply survive (i.e. make money); the user would be after an advantage over competitors and would likely measure this by the return on capital invested in a space. The business itself would provide anticipation services based upon known climatic (economic) patterns that use maps of the industry.

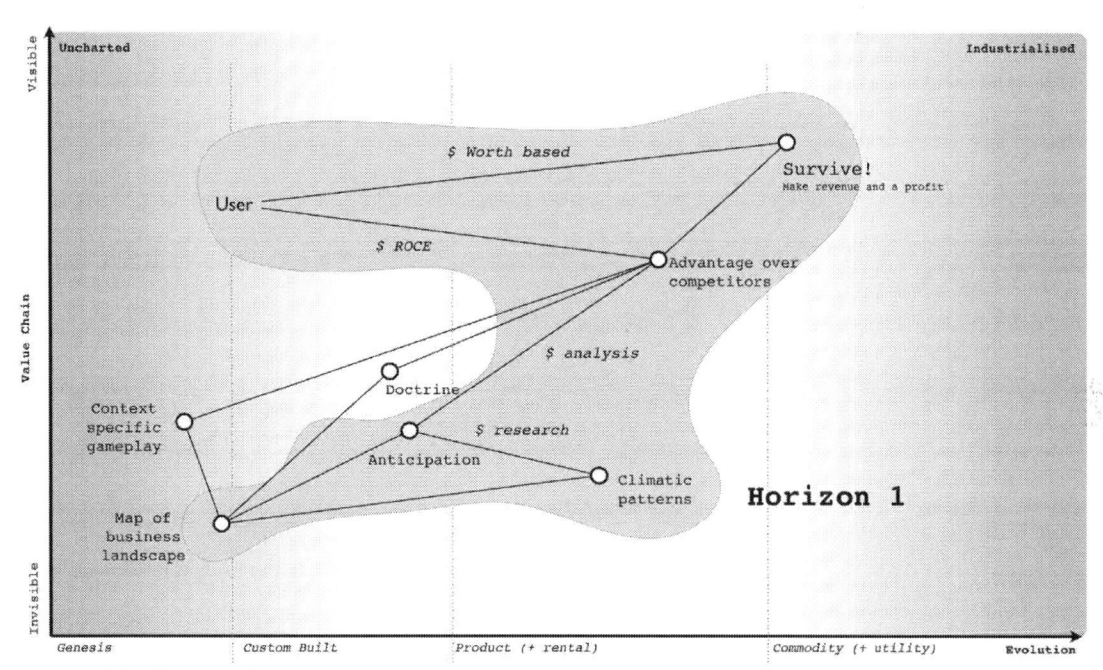

Figure 214: Forecasting Service

Horizon one would be that boutique consultancy business. I'd have been protecting (i.e. not making creative commons) the twenty odd common economic patterns that I know about that impact the environment. I'd probably use a worth based mechanism (or outcome based, as it is called today) for charging. I could also extend this map to cover in more detail the social capital components of trust and the activities needed to either perform the analysis or run the company. Remember, you can map all forms of capital, whether data, practice, activity, knowledge or social. Let us hypothesise that I had decided to build this company and by hook or by crook, turned it into a small success. What would my horizon two be?

In this case, the diffusion of knowledge and evolution caused by supply and demand competition would drive many of those components to a more industrialised space. At some point, I'd have to prepare myself for my boutique consultancy entering a world where products did the same thing. I would know in advance that we'd have inertia to that; any shift from one stage of evolution to another (e.g. custom to product) causes inertia through past success. It's one of those climatic patterns. I've mapped this change in Figure 215.

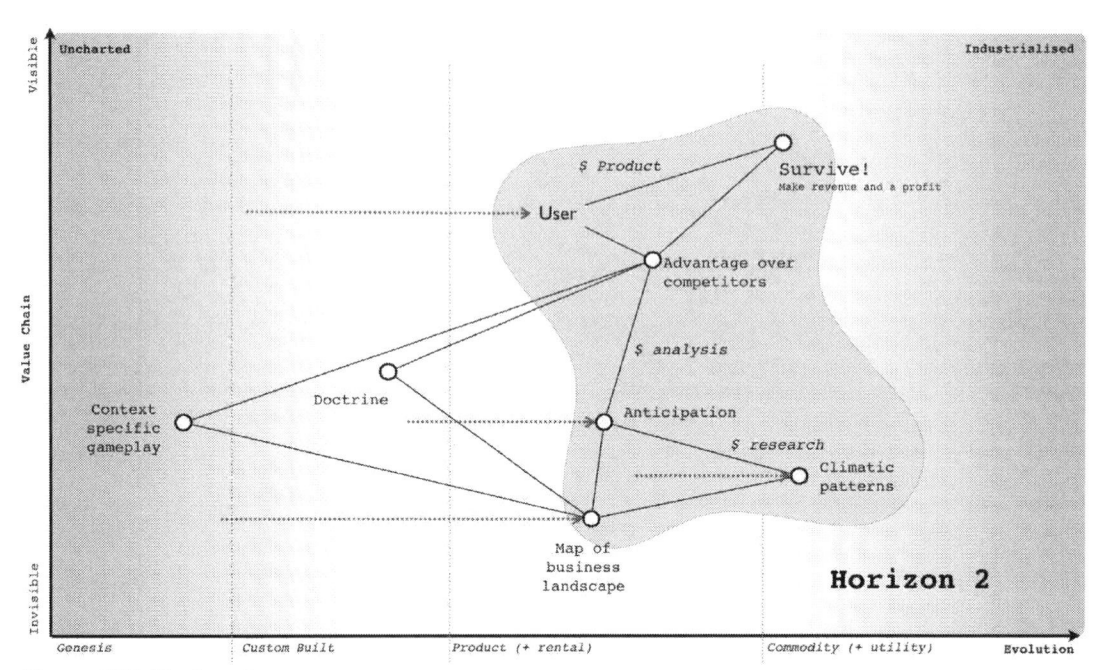

Figure 215: Horizon two

But, with foresight — and I'd hope that I'd be using mapping on myself — then it would be relatively trivial to anticipate and overcome the inertia. How about horizon three? In this case, we get a divergence. I could for example focus on further industrialisation to a more utility service exposed through some form of API — Anticipation as a Service or AaaS for short. Of course, such as change along with mirth over the acronym would come with significant inertia created by any existing product based business model. Alternatively, I could expand into something new such as the use of doctrine for competitor analysis or the arms sale of context-specific gameplay, or even some novel, uncharted, higher order system that I haven't even considered. I've shown these divergent horizon threes in Figure 216.

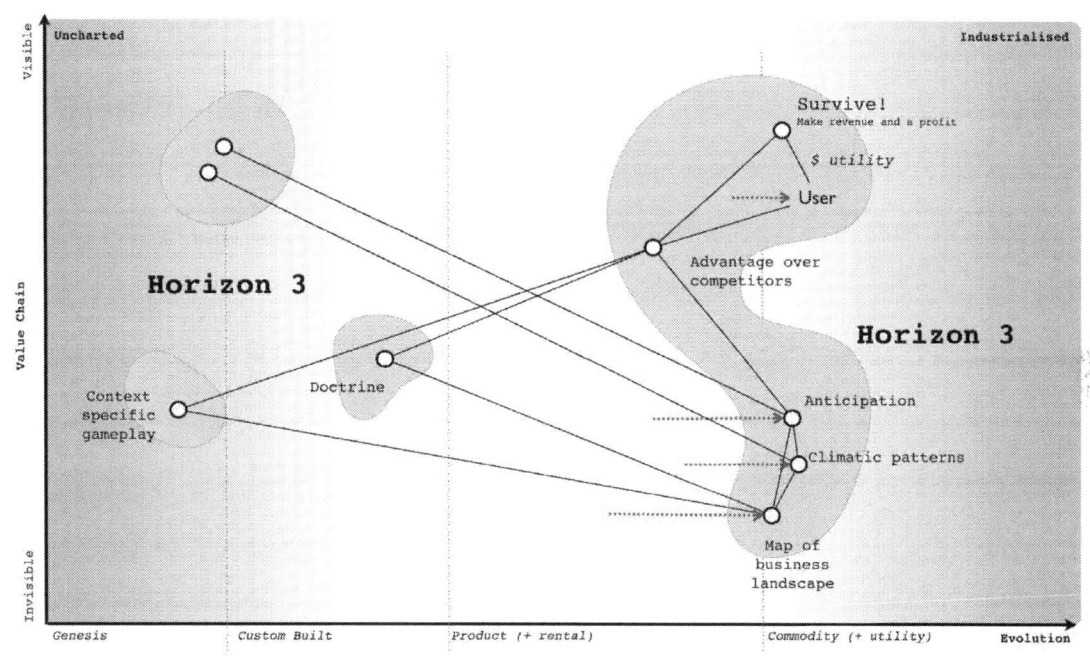

Figure 216: Horizon three

Now let us add the pioneer — settler — town planner model onto the horizon three map (see Figure 217). Remember, each team has different attitudes, which is what pioneer, settlers and town planners represent. Each team not only builds but operates and maintains their own work until such time that another team takes it away from them. The important thing to note is that horizon three consists of town planners or settlers or pioneers, or all of them, depending upon where I choose to focus.

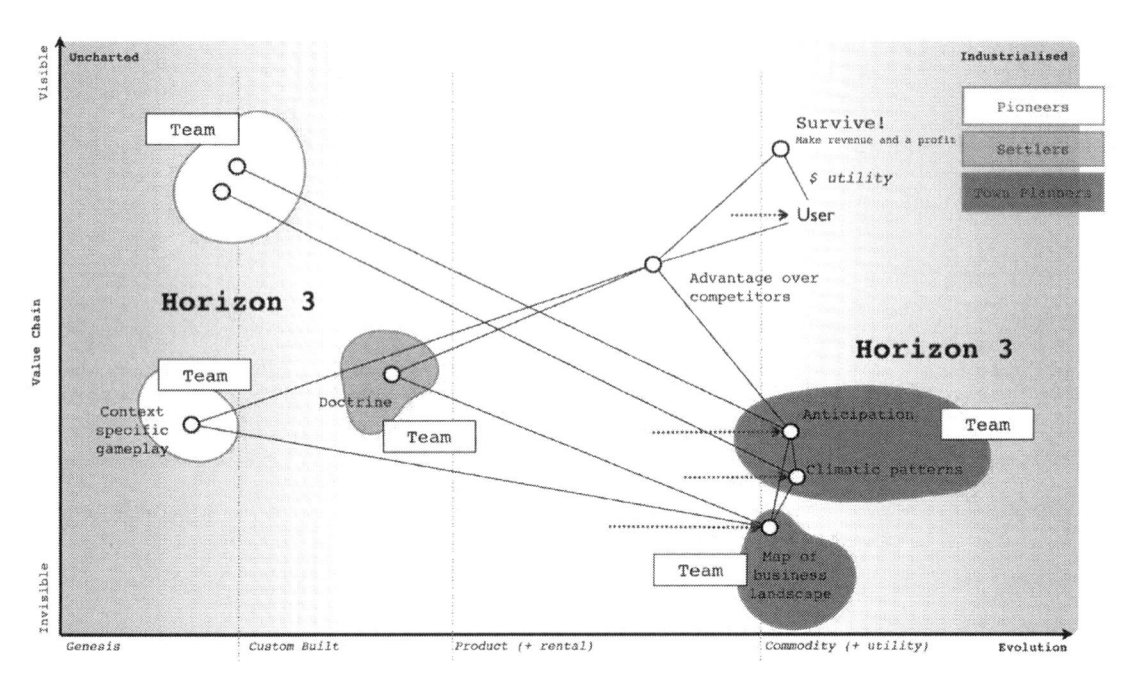

Figure 217: PST added to horizon three

The horizons are context-specific. You cannot simply overlay them onto a PST model or even the concept of evolution by saying "genesis is horizon three", as it depends upon where you are and the landscape surrounding you. For example, depending upon where the business is on the map then horizon three could be either genesis of a new act, or shifting a product to a commodity or even a new product. That of course assumes that by horizon three, you mean far future. If you stick with horizons as being broadly evolution based (i.e. genesis to product to commodity) then you can find that horizon three is sometimes your core business, sometimes your future and sometimes your far future. Horizons don't stack up well with evolution and it quickly becomes messy unless you accept a terminology of horizon one as current to horizon three as far future and allow them to exist on different parts of the map.

Another thing to note is that the horizons can often be broadly anticipatable. This is the thing I find inadequate with the horizon model because without a map and the learning of common economic (aka climatic) patterns then it becomes all too easy to miss the obvious. It is why I find the three horizons useful as a high-level concept but overall weak in practice on their own. It also fails to help me adequately deal with inertia or legacy.

The issue of legacy

In Chapter 9, we examined the climatic patterns of coevolution, i.e. practices can co-evolve with the evolution of an activity. There is usually some form of inertia to a changing activity, and this can be compounded by coevolution of practice. In Figure 218, I've taken the original diagram from chapter and added some inertia barriers for the shift from product to utility for both compute and also platform.

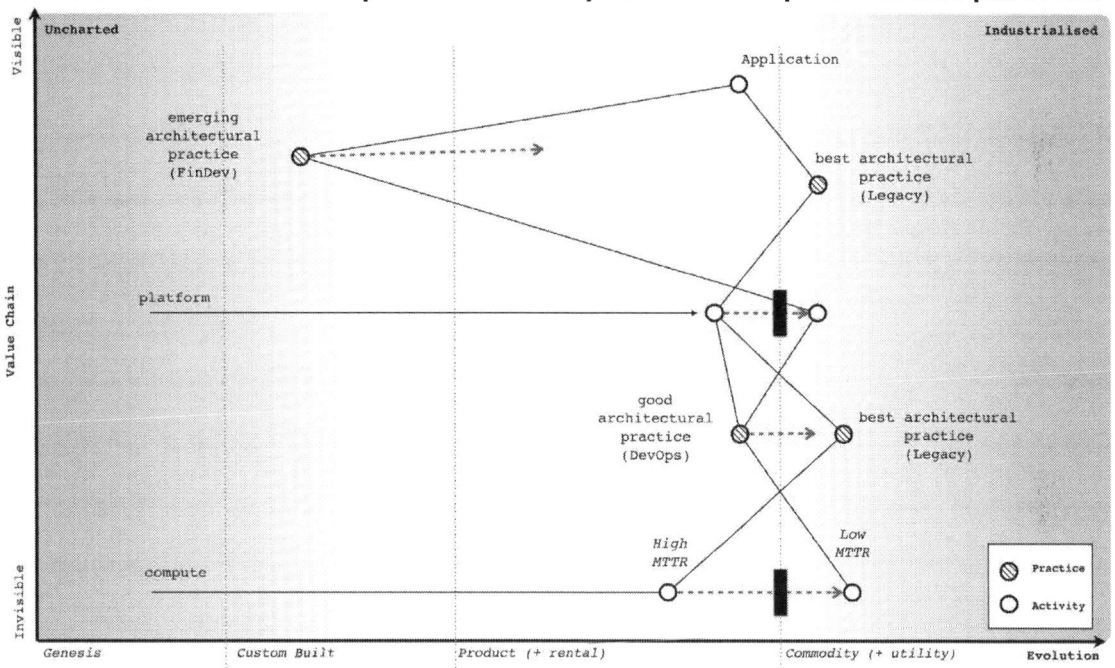

Figure 218: Change of Compute and Platform

As previously discussed, there are many forms that inertia can take. However, the question I want us to consider is what represents legacy in this map? The two obvious areas for legacy are those trapped behind inertia barriers, e.g. compute as a product and platform as a product (i.e. platform stacks). The next obvious includes those related practices, i.e. best architectural practice associated with compute as a product. What is not so obvious to begin with is the issue that as components evolve, enabling higher order systems to appear, then the lower order systems become less visible and for most of us, legacy. The departments that ran switchboards in most companies were once a highly important and often visible aspect of communication. For many companies, that activity has been consumed into either reception or call centres in much the same way that email has consumed the postal room. We still send letters to each other (more than ever before) but they are digital. In the map above, the role of the components underneath the platform layer are going to become less visible. Dealing with and managing infrastructure will become as legacy to most companies as the switchboard is today.

Hence, another area of legacy would be the practices and activities below the platform layer, which includes concepts such as DevOps. In 2017, such a statement tends to receive a strong negative reaction. Most react with the same forms of inertia as those who reacted against cloud in 2006. Many will claim that DevOps is more than infrastructure as it's about development and culture. Depending upon how far in the future you're reading this from, you'll probably be quite surprised by this and even more likely, you will have never heard of DevOps.

As with all such things, DevOps was a child and reaction against the prevailing methods of management. It co-opted concepts from earlier schools of thought (e.g. ITIL), including iterative approaches, use of components, configuration management, services approach, a focus on users and measurement, whilst simultaneously distancing itself from them. It added its own dogma and created a separate tribe. The same will happen in platform; a new school of thought will emerge that will copy and build upon DevOps but deny it has any relationship to it. DevOps will become "what my mum and dad does", as the rebellious child declares its independence and denies any inheritance from the former. Many of the genes of DevOps will be found in this new generation (though they will rarely admit it, painting DevOps as some form of strawman version of itself); some of the genes will become recessive and new genes will dominate.

I've marked these main areas of legacy onto our map in Figure 219. To do this, I've used the concepts of inertia and how industrialised components enable not only higher order systems but become less visible themselves. I've also added on a typical PST structure. As we can see, many of the legacy areas exist within the settlers and the town planning teams.

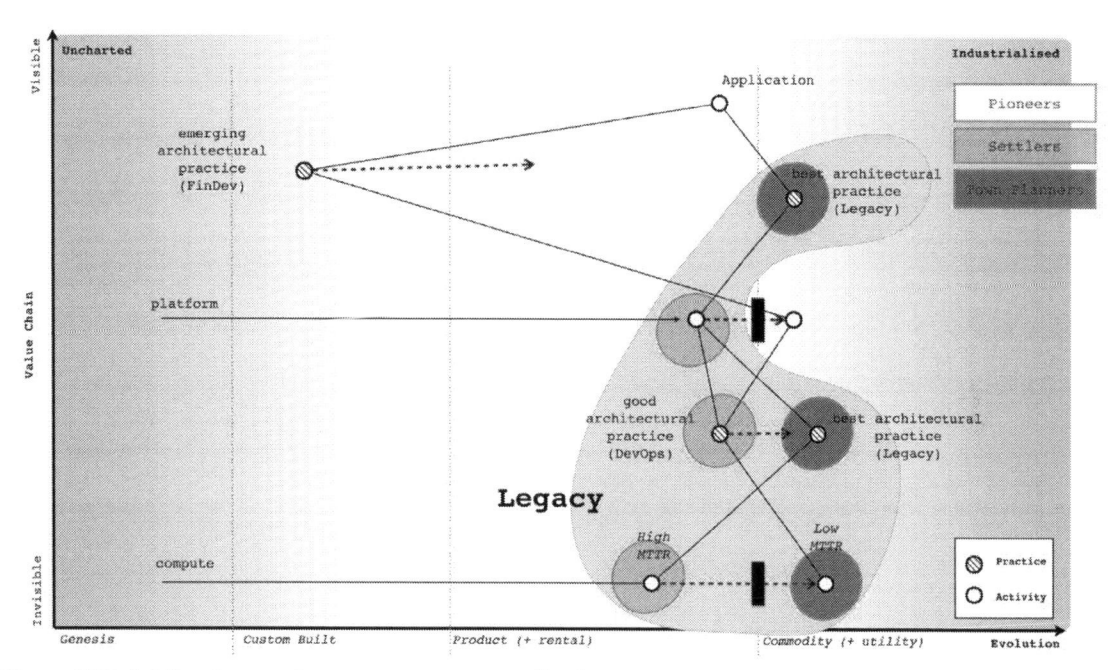

Figure 219: Adding legacy (a consumer perspective)

There is also a perspective to be considered here. I'm looking from the point of view of someone who consumes compute. If I'm a major provider, whether platform in the future or utility compute today, then much of this is definitely not legacy any more than power generation systems are to electricity providers. From the perspective of a major provider then legacy would look more like Figure 220, i.e. it will consist of activities (and related practices) that are stuck behind inertia barriers but not the impact of lower order systems becoming less visible. What becomes increasingly invisible to others (i.e. consumers) is still very visible to providers.

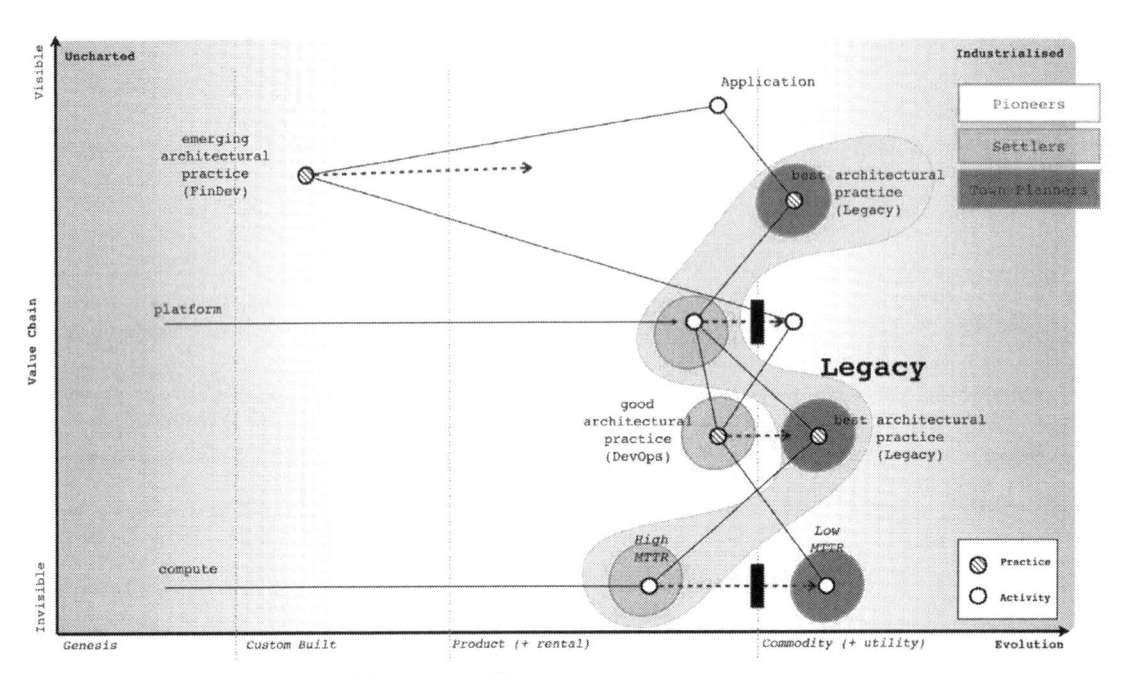

Figure 220: Legacy from a provider perspective

Despite the unfortunate tendency of people to associate the town planning groups with legacy, it should be clear from the above that this is not the case. Cloud computing has been all about industrialisation by town planners to utility services. The recent legacy has been past product models, a realm of settlers. If we take the consumer perspective from Figure 219, then the future is a mix of settlers building applications, pioneers discovering emerging practices that combine finance with development (whilst denying any inheritance from DevOps), and town planners busily creating the empires of scale around platform utility services. I've shown this future in Figure 221, and it's where companies should be investing in 2017.

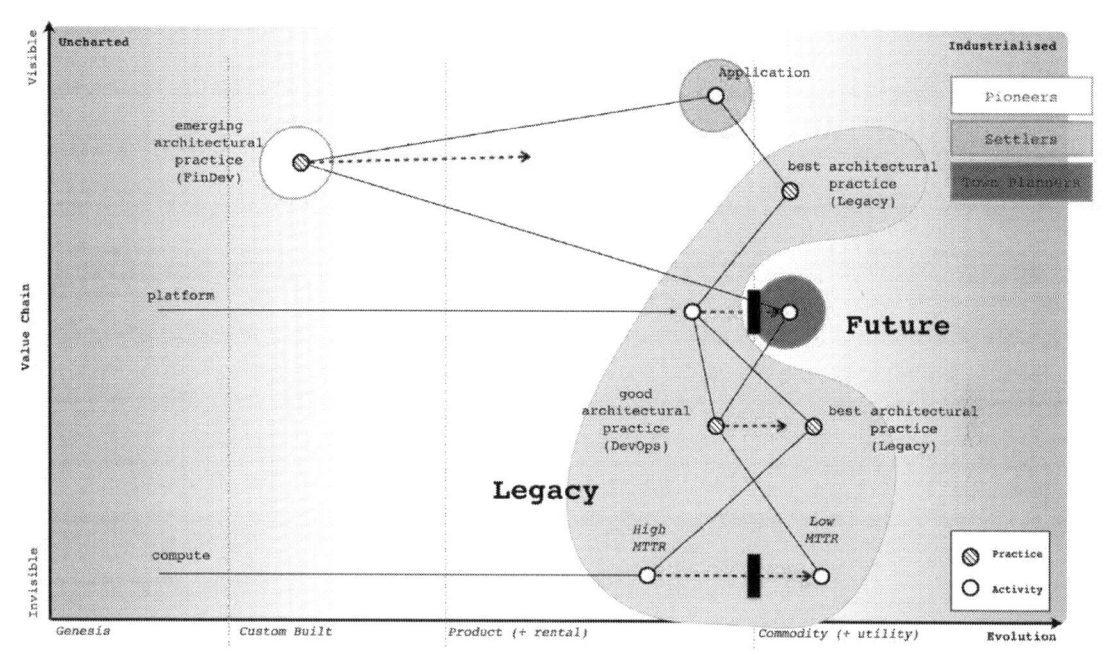

Figure 221: The future, from a consumer perspective

It's important to note that legacy can be anywhere. It can be caused by a custom-built activity that has failed to evolve or a product based business in a utility world. Legacy is simply a consequence of a failure to evolve, and it is not associated with one group such as pioneers, settlers or town planners but instead, all. When it comes to managing legacy then it's really important to understand those points of change and the impact of coevolution. This will become second nature to you but it's worth practicing. There's another perspective beyond the three horizons, beyond inertia and legacy, which we also need to discuss. It's the perspective of Porter's forces.

On Porter

For those unfamiliar with Porter's five forces, these are rivalry within the industry, threats of new entrants, threats of substitution, and the bargaining power of suppliers versus consumers. In this section, we're going to examine these five forces through the lens of the peace, war and wonder cycle (see Chapter 9).

In the time of wonder, it is a battle to become established. The field is not yet developed and there are no "new entrants" as there are no established figures to be "new entrants" against. Everything is new, uncertain and uncharted. It is the wild west, Ere be Dragons", and the home of split infinitives. The consumers hold the power and it is they who decide whether this industry will succeed or not, despite their initial inability to know whether they need it.

In the time of peace, there is a constant tug of war between supplier and consumer power over the products produced. The developing giants are normally well protected from new entrants in a game of relative competition. The exception is the occasional threat of substitution. It is this substitution by a different product that tends to be the dominant factor.

In the time of war, new entrants providing a more industrialised form of the act threaten the existing giants that are stuck behind inertia barriers. It becomes a fight for survival for these giants and they are often poorly equipped. It is not a case of a product becoming substituted by another product but instead, an entire industry being changed to more industrialised forms. It is often assumed that the shift towards utility provision means centralisation, but this is not the case.

Whilst the interaction of all consumers (demand competition) and all suppliers (supply competition) drives the process of evolution, the question of whether a specific activity or data set centralises or decentralises depends upon the actions of individual actors (suppliers and consumers) in this market. For example, it would have been relatively trivial for the hardware manufacturers to create Amazon clones and a price war in the IaaS space around 2008–2010 in order to fragment the market by increasing demand beyond the capability of Amazon to supply due to the constraint of building data centres. I had these exact conversations with Dell, IBM and HP throughout 2008 and 2009. I even told them that their own inertia would fight against this necessary change and they would deny the existence of the punctuated equilibrium until it was too late. The fact they didn't act and lost their own industry is entirely the fault of their own executives and also one of the major factors why we have seen centralisation in the IaaS space.

Centralisation depends upon the actions of specific actors (in this case, the inaction of hardware suppliers and hosting companies). In the future, this may in fact yo-yo from centralised to decentralised or find a balance between the two (as with electricity provision and self-generation). Such a change in the means of production is however unlikely to change the interfaces themselves, i.e. a shift from central to self-generation does not mean a change in voltage or frequency for domestic power provision. The future interfaces of computing have already been defined.

The point to remember with Porter's forces is the balance between these forces tends to change as any component evolves. It also isn't static within a stage of evolution — for example, the yo-yo between centralisation and decentralisation with a corresponding yo-yo between supplier and consumer bargaining power. However, as a general guide, I've provided in Figure 222 the most dominant forces you're likely to encounter.

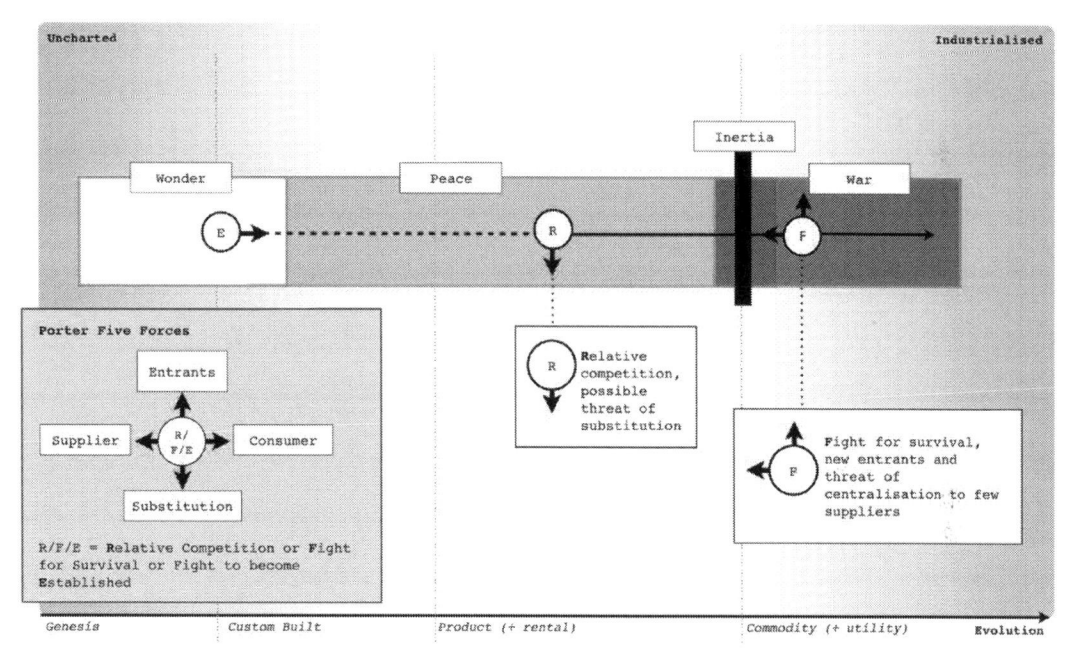

Figure 222: Porter's forces and evolution

Examining Canonical

With a basic understanding of horizons, Porter's forces and legacy, then we can now examine the business of Canonical. The horizon one (core business) was related to selling support on the server OS (operating system). However, compute was evolving to more utility provision. Hence, with the exception of large cloud providers then the server OS support was likely to become a legacy business. Instead, we needed to focus on horizon two and the commercial use of guest OS on top of these large, virtualised computing environments. We understood that companies would have inertia to these changes, and being a shift from product to commodity forms, it was likely to be a punctuated equilibrium (period of rapid change). We also understood that the biggest threats into this space would be new entrants, and given the state of strategic play in many companies then we were likely to see centralisation. I've drawn these concepts onto the map in Figure 223.

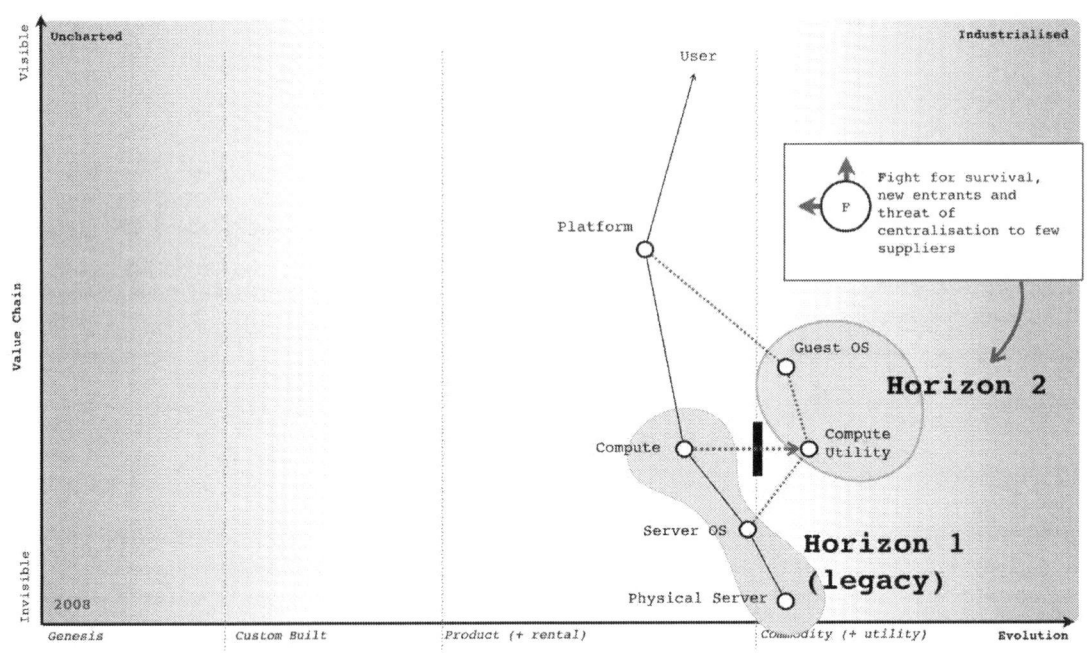

Figure 223: The changing market

We also understood that co-evolved practices would emerge, that we were unlikely to see significant savings in IT but instead, increased development activity and that a further horizon, the shift of platform from product to utility, was possible. I've marked up these horizons onto Figure 224.

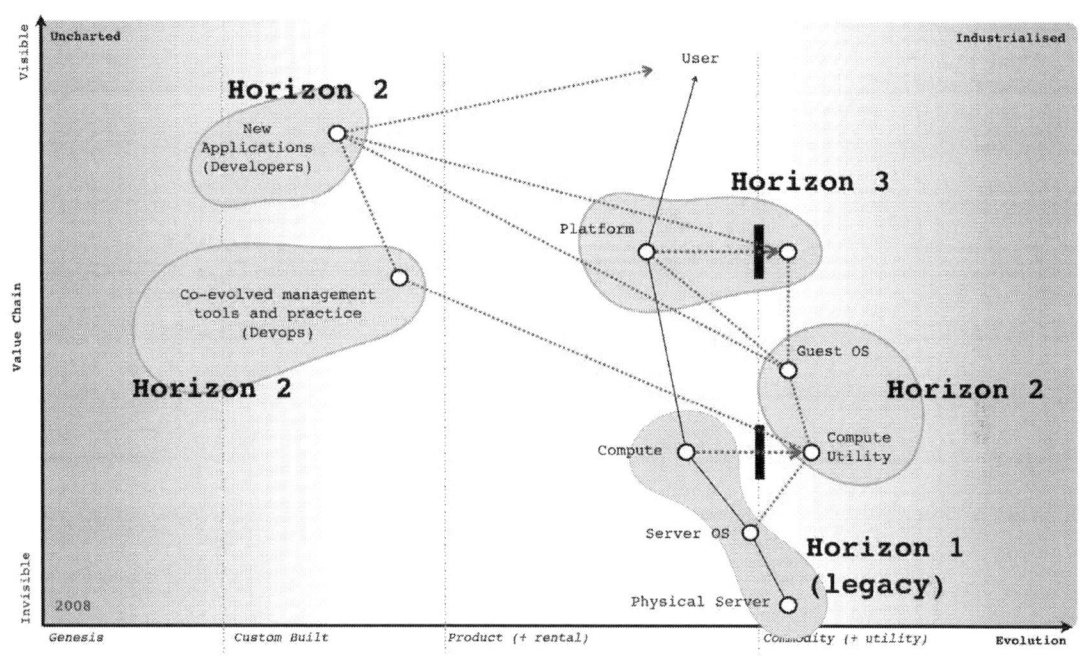

Figure 224: The horizons

In terms of play, we understood that moving fast and land grabbing the guest OS territory was essential. To help in this, we also needed to support those developing applications or building tooling around those co-evolved practices. If we found examples of platforms plays in this space, we also needed to be invested in this. We understood that many potential customers would have inertia, hence we'd have to provide some forms of transitional or private cloud offer, even if this did nothing more than get the conversation started.

We also knew our competitors had inertia. As soon as I discovered Red Hat salespeople were rewarded bonuses based upon satellite subscriptions (used for security updates) then I quickly set about promoting a message that security should be "free" in the cloud. There's nothing like threatening someone's bonus to get them to turn against a change. Our focus was clear within my cabal. Mark did an amazing job of turning this into the entire company focus. Rick and others set about putting in engineering effort to make it happen. Steve gave me all the firepower and cover I needed. For my part, I mainly focused on promoting Ubuntu's cloud message, being involved in the community, highlighting targets to bring on board and trying to stop people rebuilding or getting in the way of things that the community was doing.

An outline of the play is provided in Figure 225 and the result in Figure 226. Within eighteen months, Ubuntu went from a small part of the operating system to dominating the cloud guest OS. My part was a minor but instrumental role and I have to applaud the marvellous teams at Canonical and within the community for making it happen. A small company of three hundred took on the might of two giant hordes, but unlike the Spartans, this time we won. My proudest moment came from hearing a CIO talk about how "the future was all Red Hat and then suddenly, it was all Ubuntu". I played a small part in that.

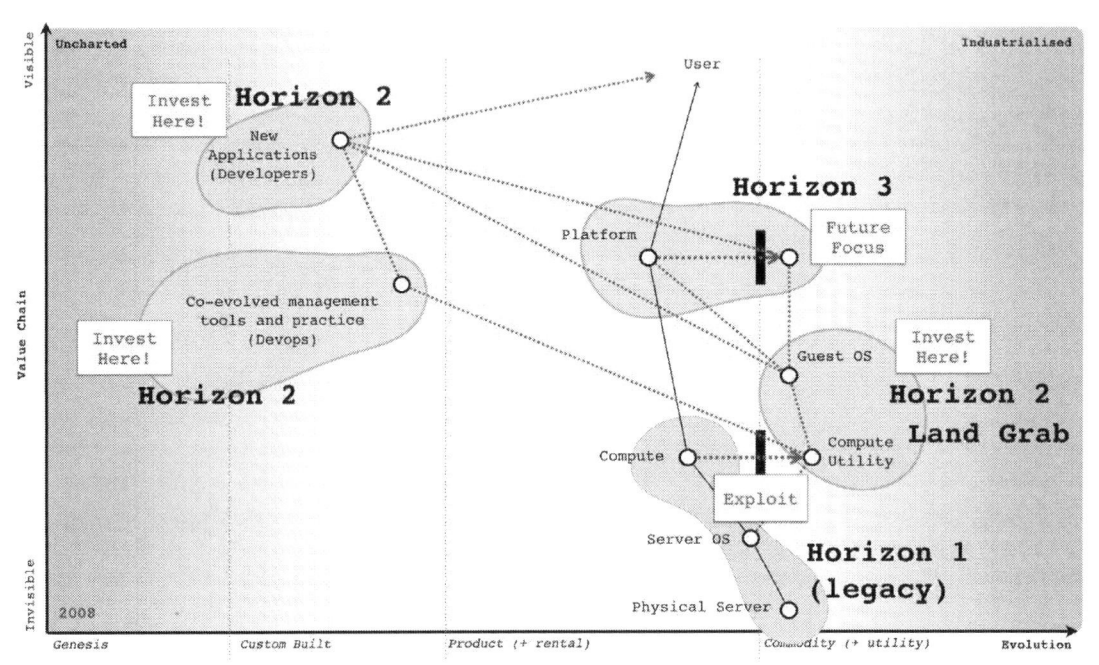

Figure 225: Our focus

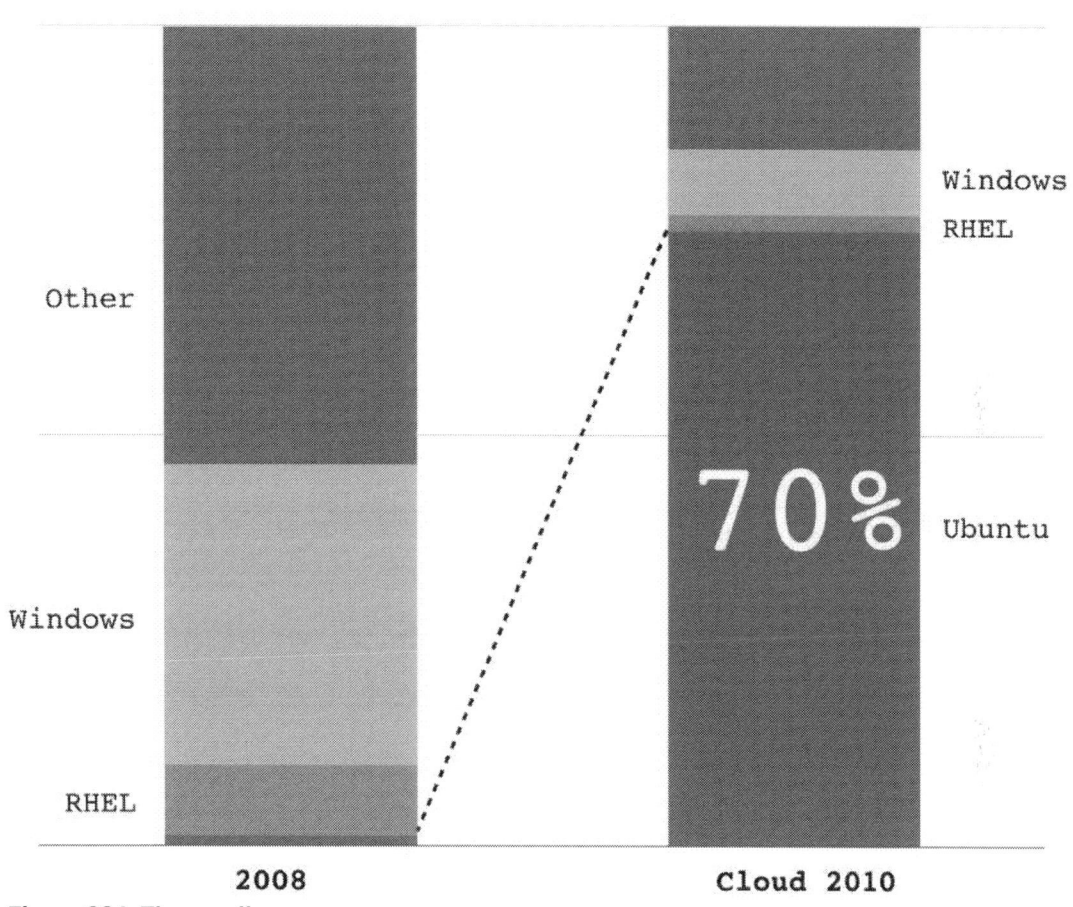

Figure 226: The results

I often hear people talk about how Canonical was lucky; well, there's always some element of luck but the moves were deliberate. Obviously, people can just say the timing was lucky but they'd be wrong on that as well. I had a helping hand with timing, thanks to Gartner. They probably don't even realise but I think it's worth explaining.

On the question of timing

I'm not a big fan of Gartner but Figure 227 is one of the most useful graphs they've ever produced. It's a hype cycle of emerging technologies created in 2008. It uses the earlier y-axis of visibility, which later on became expectations. How can the axis change whilst the graph remains the same? Ah, that's the beauty of it, but first, a bit more background.

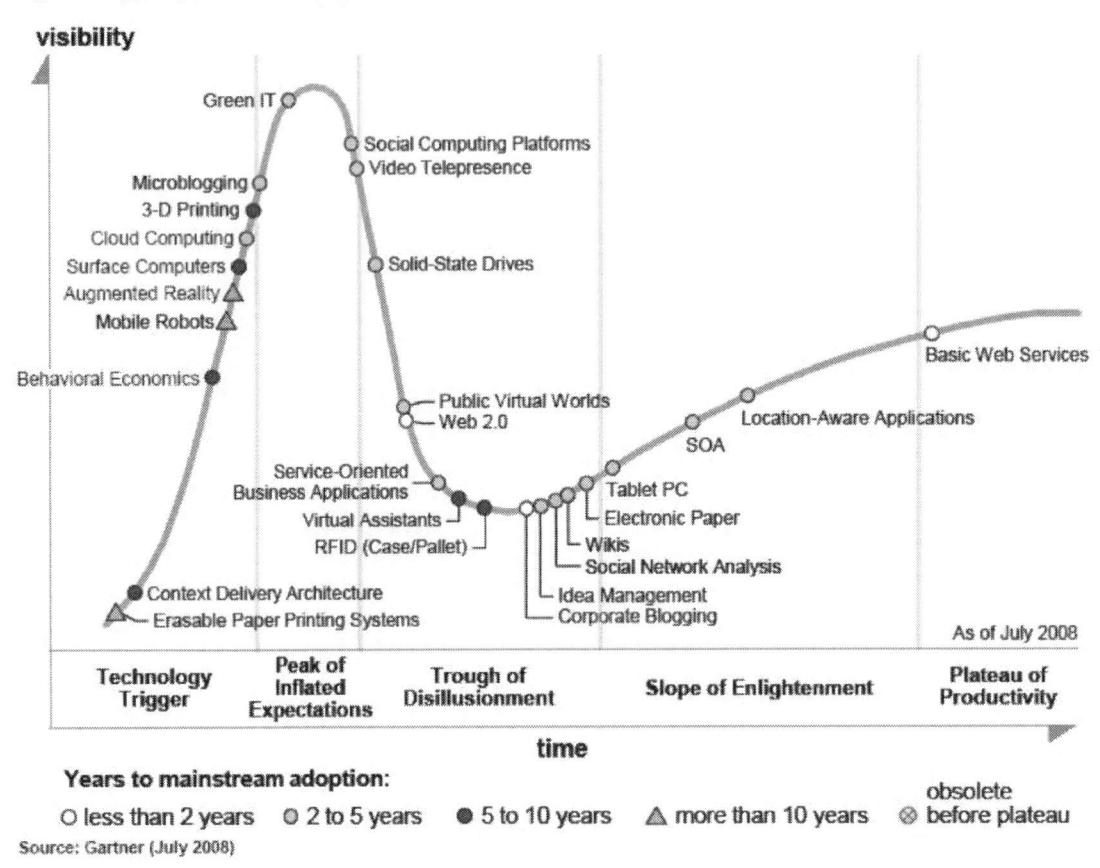

Figure 1. Hype Cycle for Emerging Technologies, 2008

Figure 227: Gartner emerging technologies, 2008

During my time in the wilderness prior to Canonical, I had been looking at various ways of measuring impacts from evolution. One of the issues I had come up against was the evolution of any single act creates two waves of opportunity. One of these waves is focused on differential value (i.e. it's something you have but I don't), and the second wave is around operational value (i.e. we both provide this but you do so more efficiently). Both the waves appear to have a learning element and then a sharp decline as the change diffuses and evolves further. I've provided examples of these waves in Figure 228.

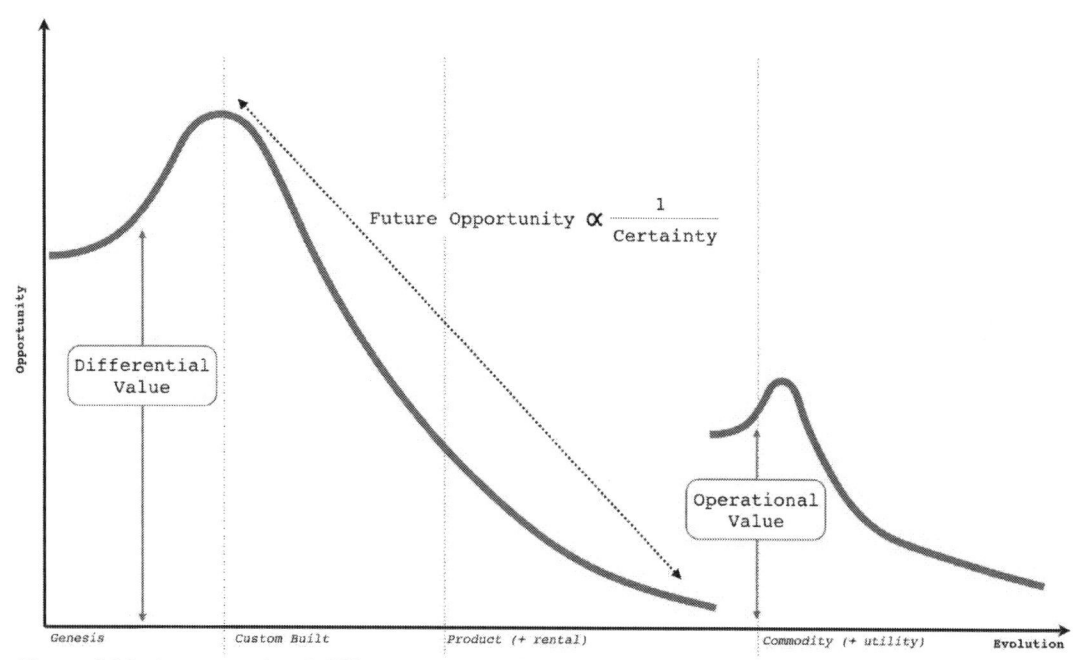

Figure 228: An example of different waves of value

Of course, opportunity is only part of the equation. There are volume effects and the cost involved, particularly in development of something novel. There's also risk as the uncharted space is by its very nature is uncertain. However, I developed a generalised benefit curve, which for differential value is shown in Figure 229. An almost identical benefit curve appears to exist for operational value, but that occurs much later in evolution and is related to the co-evolved practices that emerge.

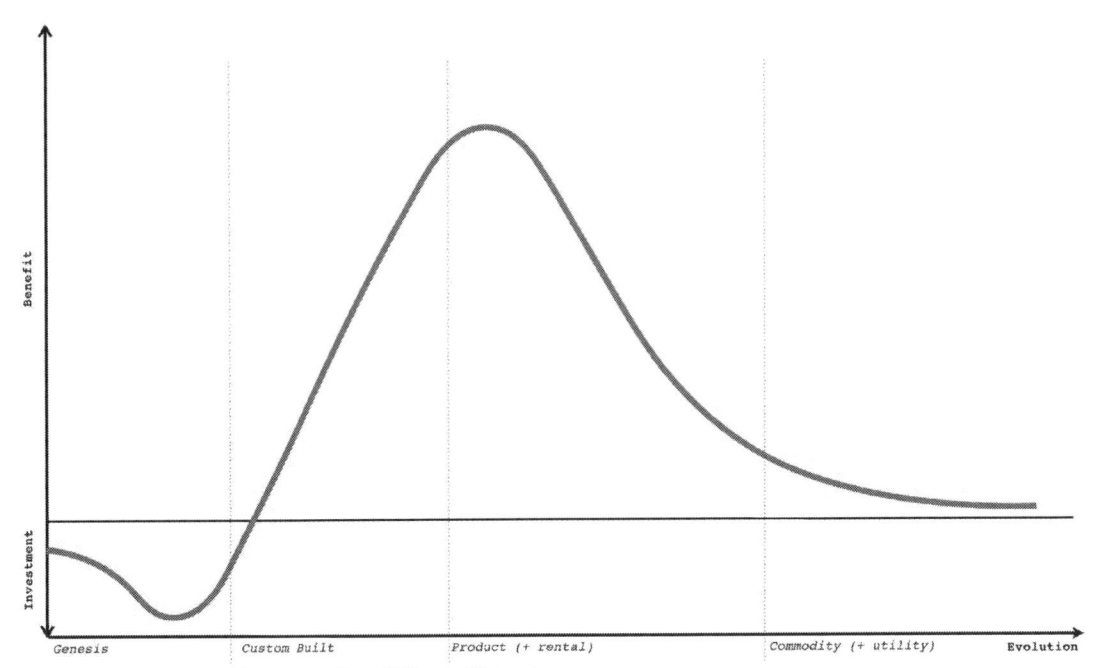

Figure 229: A benefit curve for differential value

From the benefit curve, the early stages of genesis are all about investment. As it evolves, the cost of production reduces and we start to realise some of the benefit. We're still in the custom-build stage; others are starting to copy but in general, the cost of production is reducing fast enough to overcome any differential loss due to copying. Alas, at some point, the cost of production is low enough and the activity defined enough that someone produces a product. On the upside, the cost to implement is plummeting, but alas, the differential value is declining faster as more companies actually implement. The models I developed all had variations of this shape. I'm not comfortable enough with the data, so think of it more as a mental model and a possible curiosity.

Whilst exploring this space, I then became fascinated by timing issues. Let us pretend we've recently read a whitepaper on some marvellous new activity. That activity is described as having some benefit but it also involves cost. By the time I get around to implementing the activity then it will probably have evolved. It might provide a different benefit to what I was expecting, i.e. it costs less because it's a product, but there's little differential value as everyone else is also doing this. I've superimposed the evolution of an act onto the benefit curve in Figure 230 to highlight this point.

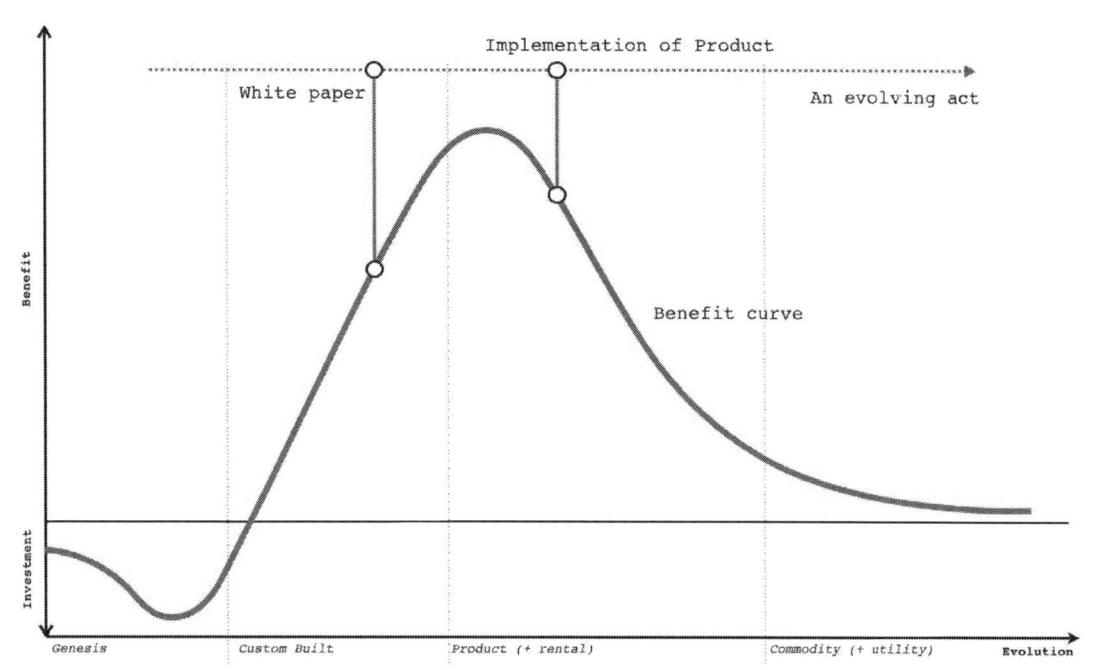

Figure 230: Changing benefit with evolution and implementation

I then modelled this delta between what I was expecting to get and what I got over time. The model I used made lots of horrible assumptions, it's uncomfortably close to voodoo and is about as solid as a tower of jelly. At some point in the future, I might go and revisit this, but I don't normally mention this little side journey. However, there was one remarkable thing about the delta expectation curve over time — it resembles a Gartner hype cycle (see Figure 231).

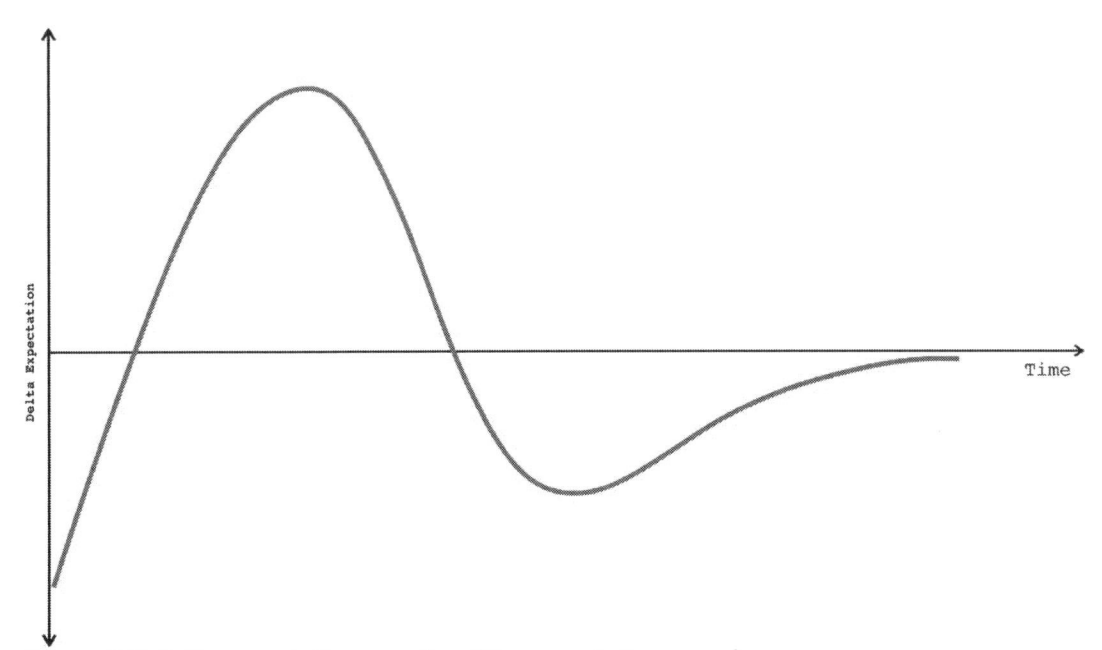

Figure 231: Delta expectation over time (the expectation curve)

We have the same peak of inflated expectation and the same trough of delusion. My first reaction was horror.

The evolution curve on which mapping is built uses ubiquity versus certainty. If I can model from Gartner's hype cycle to evolution then I can take the points on a hype cycle and measure precisely where something is on the certainty axis of evolution. For things that are uncertain then this should be impossible as the ability to precisely measure something that is uncertain is the stuff of magic folk. My first reaction was Gartner's hype cycle proved evolution was wrong. I was a bit perplexed at that point, especially since I had found mapping so useful. Fortunately, I met with a friend who pointed to a great big hole in my argument. I was assuming that Gartner's hype cycle was based upon the measurement of some physical property. If it wasn't, if it was just aggregated opinion (of consultants, analysts or industry), then there's no measurement of the uncertain as it's just opinion. It's an opinion of where something is, not a measurement of where it actually is. As I subsequently found out, the hype cycle is subjective opinion.

Along with being quietly relieved that I hadn't yet disproved what I was finding useful, it also opened up a new opportunity. I have two benefit curves — one for differential value and one for operational value. They both shared a common expectation versus time pattern. If I look at an evolving component then where it appears in the early stages on the expectation curve for differential value can be the same place it appears on the expectation curve for operational value when it's more evolved — see Figure 232

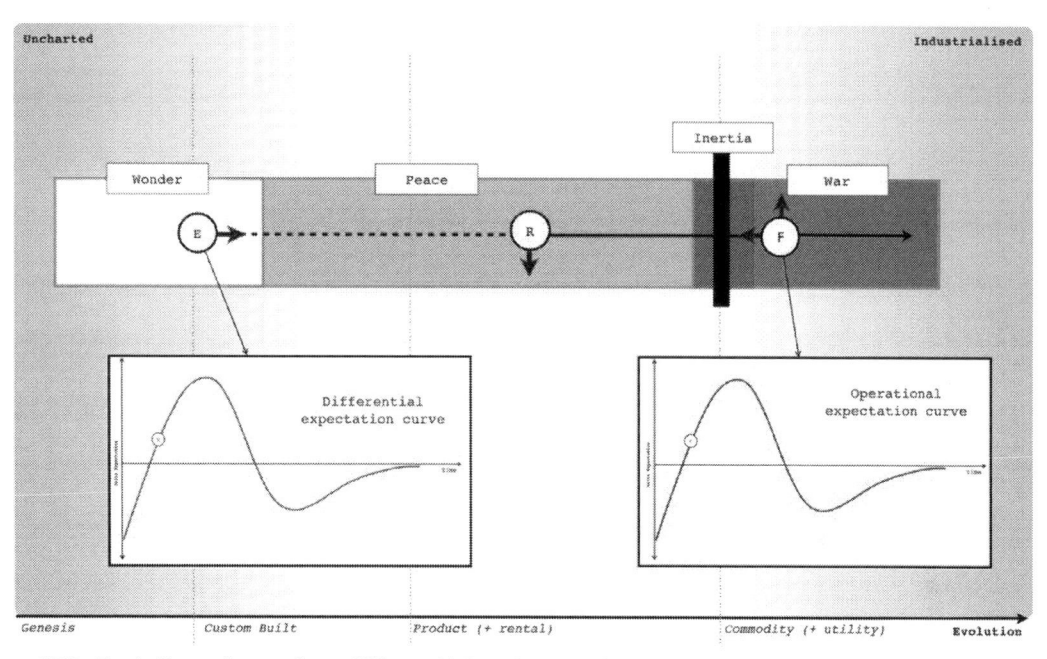

Figure 232: Evolution of an act on differential and operational expectation curves

I also had a weak signal using publication types that could identify when things are likely to start to industrialise and enter a war (see Chapter 9). I've reprinted the last analysis on this that I undertook in 2014 in Figure 233. What I'd like you to notice is that the shift from product to utility for computing infrastructure was well into a war in 2014. Whereas the war for 3D printing and the use of commoditised 3D printers is some way off.

Points of Change	2014	2015-2020	2020-2025	2025-2030	2030-2035	2035-2040	2040-2045	2045-2050
	Now	Near			Far			
IaaS	War							
PaaS	War							
SaaS	War							
Big Data		War						
Robotics			War					
Currency (blockchain)			War					
Sensor as a Service			War					
IoT				War				
Immersive				War				
3D printing				War				
Social Change				War				
GMO				War				
Genetic Engineering				War				
Intelligent Agents					War			
Printed Electronics					War			
Hybrid Printing						War		
Bio Manufacturing						War		
Epigenetics						War		
Materials						War		

Figure 233: When is the war likely?

In 2008, I already knew (from my weak signals) that we were entering the war phase for computing infrastructure, whereas 3D printing had a long time to go before it started to industrialise. I also suspected that both a relatively novel activity (e.g. 3D printing) and an industrialising activity (cloud) could appear at the same place on two different expectation curves — one for differential value and one for operational value (Figure 232 above). So, let us look at that Gartner hype cycle again and highlight two components — cloud computing and 3D printing.

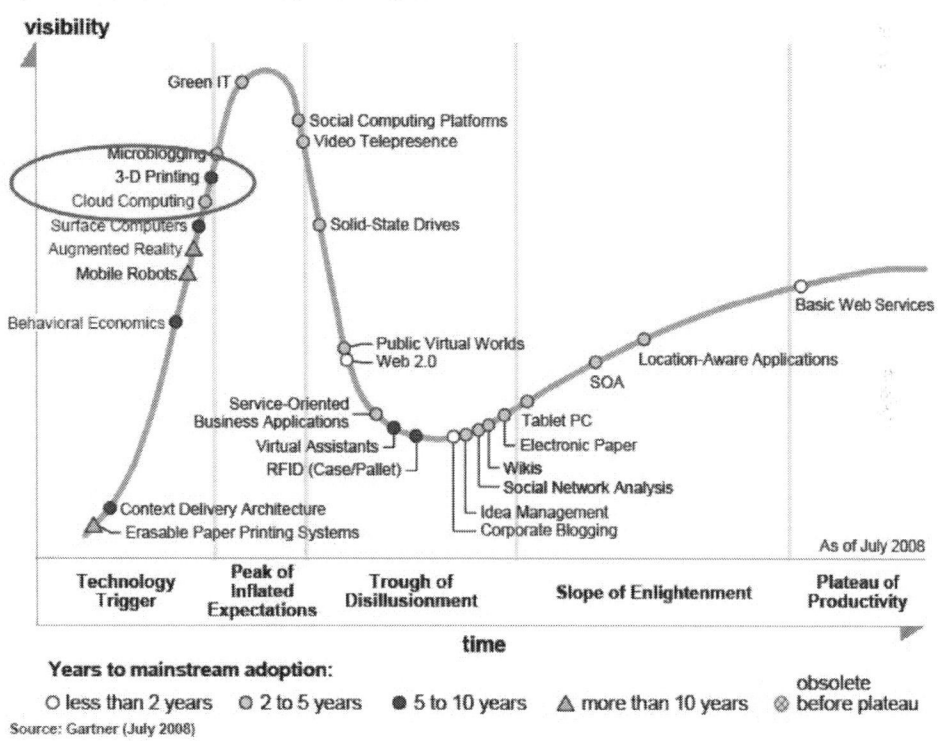

Figure 234: Cloud computing and 3D printing

They both appeared at roughly the same place. This told me something that I've subsequently found quite useful. The Gartner hype cycle doesn't distinguish between differential and operational value as both are on the same curve. So, why does that matter? Well, in the case of cloud computing, which was the industrialisation of computing and all about operational value, then you'd want to be going "all in" during 2008. Being in the early stage of this expectation curve just reinforces the point that people are learning about a change that you absolutely want to be a first mover to. The last thing you'd want to do is wait until it reaches the plateau of productivity, by which time the war would be well and truly over. If you're a vendor, this would be curtains. Gartner even calls out that this is moving fast with its time to mainstream adoption for cloud (light blue circle).

However, in the case of 3D printing then you do want to wait or be a fast follower. It has a long, long way to go before it industrialises, and you've got an entire product stage it has to evolve through. In fact, 3D printing will reach the plateau of productivity and see relatively widespread adoption as a product long before it industrialises. At some future time (2025–2030), as it starts to industrialise, then it'll probably reappear in the technology trigger usually under a slightly different meme. When it comes to 3D printing then you could wait a bit and get involved in the product space or wait much longer until the "war" is upon that industry, at which point you'd need to go "all in".

Two points — cloud computing and 3D printing — on almost exactly the same position of the hype cycle required radically different approaches to investment and strategy. One was "all in", the other was "wait and see". Being of aggregated opinion, I do find the hype cycle quite useful, as long as I separate out what stage of evolution something is in first. I often talk to CIOs who tell me they invest when something is in the stage of enlightenment. That's a fairly reasonable way of losing every major technological war in business.

For me in 2008, this hype cycle helped reinforce the message that we had to go all in; it was a land grab for this territory. I also took comfort that many of my competitors probably read exactly the same hype cycle and thought they had time. Let us emphasise that point — I was going "all in" when competitors thought they had time; it's a help yourself to the future buffet with no-one saying you can't have 7th helpings because everyone else got the date wrong. Thank you Gartner, you probably have no idea how much you've helped me. Better luck next time IBM, HP, Dell, Red Hat… assuming they survive what is to come.

Anyway, the gameplay above was 2008 to early 2010. In mid 2010, after capturing pretty much the entire market (a space that has massively grown since, with Ubuntu still the "top dog" in 2016), I then headed back into research. My work was done. Naturally, I left Mark and others with a variety of plays to use, along with a specific focus on the platform space. I don't necessarily agree with all the steps they've made but I respect their choices and they play a good game. I suppose, that's the real point — they are playing the game, not me, but in some small way, I helped them to improve. Before we dive into the strategy space, we should take a peek at another part of my journey into Government. Hence, let us boldly go into the next chapter.

Chapter 18 - Better for Less

All change please

In early 2009, I met Liam Maxwell. That name might not mean much to you unless you work in Government, but he has been an influential figure in government technology throughout the world, a strong advocate of mapping, and a good friend since that first encounter. We met when I was speaking at some random conference in London on evolution and technology. By happenstance, Liam was in the audience. We got chatting and discovered we had common interests and ways of thinking about technology. I was soon invited to the "Triple Helix" group, which consisted of a motley crew of interesting people — Jerry Fishenden, Mark Thompson and others. They wanted to try and help fix problems they saw in Government IT. It was a non-partisan group, i.e. many of us came from different political backgrounds.

For myself, I felt completely out of my depth. This was "big IT", as in huge projects with hundreds of millions spent on massive scale systems that I had usually only heard about because of some failure hitting the mainstream press. There were also big personalities. I met Francis Maude (he was in the opposition Cabinet at the time), which mainly consisted of me trying not to mumble "you're Francis Maude", given I was a bit awestruck. What on earth was I, a state school kid who had lived on a council estate, doing in the Houses of Parliament talking to people I'd seen on TV?

I was also introduced to various departments who kindly offered to give me an hour or so explaining how "big IT" happened. What I saw shook me, but then I hadn't really seen "big IT" in the commercial world, having mainly built companies or worked for moderate-sized groups. The first, and most obvious thing, I noted was the lack of engineering skills, despite the scale of these engineering projects. I would be introduced to engineer after engineer that in effect turned out to be a glorified project manager. The answer to everything seemed to be "outsource it", a mantra that had been encouraged by hordes of management consultants. I tried to explain how this would inevitably lead to cost overruns because some components would be novel but usually got an answer blaming poor specification. It seemed that no matter how many times a project failed, the answer was "better specification" or "better outsourcing". This was dogma run wild. I became increasingly aware that these groups were not only dependent upon the vendors but many lacked the skills necessary to challenge the quotations given.

There was no concept of maps and no effective mechanism of communication, learning or sharing. Everything was isolated. Duplication was rife. Before anyone goes on about how bad Government is, let me be clear that this pales into insignificance compared to the inefficiencies and ineffectiveness of the private sector. I might have seen the same system rebuilt a hundred times in Government, but in the commercial world, I've seen 350 separate teams of people rebuilding the same IT project in one organisation at the same time. Anything that the Government gets wrong, the private sector excels at showing how much more wrong is possible.

Anyway, Government was still a shock. There were some weak measures of cost control but barely any concept of price per user or transaction or user needs or anything that I had started to take for granted. There was one project that Liam asked me to guess the price on. I responded around £300k after looking through the details. It was north of £50m. I had real trouble wrapping my head around such figures, but then I've seen a billion dollars spent on no-hope, obviously doomed to fail from the beginning efforts in the private sector. I'd always assumed there was some greater wisdom that I wasn't aware of. It was becoming clear that this wasn't the case. In Government, however, this tended to make me annoyed. I don't mind survival of the least incompetent in the private sector because eventually, someone will come along and do a better job. In Government, there is no someone and getting things right is critical. I have family that live in social housing who would be horrified at the waste.

In between plotting Ubuntu's dominance of cloud, I started to spend my spare time working with this group on writing the "Better for Less" paper. It had rapidly become clear that not only did Government spend huge sums on individual projects but that those projects had deplorable rates of success. "Only 30% of Government IT projects succeed, says CIO," shouts the May 2007 edition of Computer Weekly. How was it possible for projects to spend such inflated sums and fail so frequently?

The more I looked, the more I uncovered. This wasn't a problem of civil servants and a lack of passion to do the right thing but instead, a cultural issue, a desire to not be seen to fail, which inevitably ended up in failure. The skills had been outsourced to the point that outsourcing was the only option, with few left that could effectively mount a challenge. There was a severe lack of transparency. Getting the IT spend in Government to the nearest billion was nigh on impossible. The words "How can you not know this?" seemed to constantly trip from my tongue. Shocked had become flabbergasted.

Of course, the reasons why we were building things often seemed even more ludicrous. Most of the systems were being designed badly to fit legislation and policy that they had barely considered their own operational impact. Any concepts of what users (i.e. citizens) might want from this was far removed. Interaction with citizens felt more of an inconvenience to achieving the policy. You should remember that I had spent five years running online services for millions of users. This policy-driven approach to building IT was the antithesis of everything I had done.

To compound it all, the silo approach or departmentalism of projects had meant that groups didn't even talk with each other. Whitehall had somehow developed an approach of creating and maintaining expensive, often duplicated IT resources that often failed but also didn't interact with each other in effective ways. In 2003, I was used to web services providing discrete component services that were consumed by many other services. In 2005, I was used to mapping out environments with clear understanding of user needs, components involved and the potential for sharing. In 2010, whilst sitting in one of these department meetings, flabbergast became horror. I was looking at approaches that I hadn't seen since the mid '90s and discussing policy issues with people that lacked the skill to make rational choices. Where skill did exist, the Government had bizarre stratifications of hierarchy, which often meant that the people who could make the right choices were far removed from the people making the choices. "Big IT" just seemed to be a euphemism for snafu, and it was only "big" in terms of cost, lack of solid management information and failure rates. When it came to the number of users served and performance, it was decidedly "average", verging on "small".

With Fotango, we had dealt with millions of users from our warehouse base in the technology desert (at that time) of Old Street. We used an open plan environment, which brings its own problems; we used hack days, scrum meetings and town halls to counter communication difficulties. Despite our best efforts, our use of small teams and our small size, it was inevitable that the layers of hierarchy and politics would impact communication. However, the scale of our communication issues was trivial compared to entrenched structures, politics and communication failures within these departments. The scale of the problems was "big", even if the IT wasn't.

The "Triple Helix" group needed to start somewhere, so we started with a basic set of principles.

Doctrine: Think big

We need to get out of the mindset of thinking about specific systems and tackle the whole problem. We needed to break away from these isolated individual systems. We needed to change the default delivery mechanism for public services towards online services using automated processes for most citizens. We needed an approach that focused relentlessly on delivery to the citizen and their needs. This was going to be the "big" idea.

Doctrine: Do better with less

Such an approach had to be transparent and measured in terms of cost. It had to provide challenge for what was currently being built. From this, we developed the idea of a scrutiny board, which later became spend control under OCTO. It wasn't enough to simply reduce spending; our focus was on dramatically reducing waste whilst improving public services. We couldn't do this without measurement.

We understood that this would not be a big bang approach but an iterative process — a constant cycle of doing better with less. To this end, we proposed the use of open data with a focus on the Government becoming more transparent. We also added the use of open source, including the practices associated with it and the use of open standards to drive competitive markets.

Doctrine: Move fast

We understood that there would be inertia to the changes we were proposing and that existing culture and structures could well rise to combat us. We put in place an initial concept of workstreams that targeted different areas. The idea was that if we ever put this in place then we'd have 100 days or so to make the changes before resistance overwhelmed us. If it wasn't up and running in that time then we would have missed our window.

Doctrine: Commit to the direction, be adaptive along the path

To enable the change, we needed a clear and effective message from authority, combined with a commitment to change. However, in the past, this has been notoriously difficult as only one minister in the Cabinet Office (Tom Watson MP) prior to 2010 had any real commitment to understanding technology. However, with a change of Government, there might be an opportunity with a new ministerial team.

To support all of this, we proposed a structure based upon the innovate — leverage — commoditise model. The structure included innovation funds operating at local levels, a scrutiny board encouraging challenge along with a common technology service providing industrialised components. The structure was based upon concepts of open; it was data driven with emphasis on not just defining but measuring success. It was iterative and adaptive, using constant feedback from the frontline and citizens alike. To support this, we would have to develop in-house capabilities in engineering, including more agile-like approaches. We would also need to build a curriculum for confidence and understanding of the issues of IT for mid ranking to senior officials and ministers.

We would need to take a more modular approach to creating systems that encouraged re-use. We would need to be prepared to adapt the model itself as we discovered more.

Doctrine: Be pragmatic

We accepted that not everything would fit into the structure or workstreams that we had described. A majority would and it was the cost reduction and improvement in those cases that would generate the most savings. However, it was important to acknowledge that a one size fits all approach would not work and will be vulnerable to inertia. Pragmatism to achieve the change was more important than ideology. We also had to maintain the existing IT estate whilst acknowledging that the future will require a fundamentally different approach based upon agile, open and effective local delivery. We would have to not only audit but sweat the existing assets until they could be replaced.

Doctrine: A bias towards the new

We focused on an outside-in approach to innovation, where change was driven and encouraged at the local level through seed funds rather than Government trying to force its own concept of change through "big IT". The role of central Government was reduced to providing engineering expertise, an intelligent customer function to challenge what was done, industrialised component services, encouragement of change and showing what good looked like.

Doctrine: Listen to your ecosystems (acts as future sensing engines)

We viewed the existing centralised approach as problematic because it was often remote from the real needs of either public service employees, intermediaries or citizens alike. We envisaged a new engineering group that would work in the field and spot and then nurture opportunities for change at the frontline, working closely with service delivery providers.

Though the bulk of the work of the "Triple Helix" group was completed sometime beforehand, Liam published the resultant paper "Better for Less" in September 2010. Whilst the paper is certainly not as widely known as Martha Lane Fox's letter on "revolution, not evolution", it had some small impact. The ideas and concepts within the paper were circulated within Government and provided some support to structures that were later created, whether spend control or the development of in-house engineering capability in Government Digital Services or the development of training programs. I occasionally meet civil servants who have read the paper or used its concepts. I can feel comfort in knowing that the work was not in vain but helped tip the needle. But I also discovered that I had made a terrible mistake in the paper. That mistake was assumption.

A little too much of what you wanted

With the transformation starting within Government IT, Liam had taken the role as CTO of HMG. I would occasionally pop in and discuss the changes, even meeting up with departments to review projects with part of spend control. I was often brutal, challenging the cost, the lack of customer focus and the endless attempts to specify that which was uncertain. It was during one of these discussions that I mapped out the space and used the map to show a particularly galling cost overspend and how a vendor was trying to lock us in with ever-increasing upgrade costs. Using the map, I pointed out to Liam how we could break this vendor's stranglehold. He nodded and then said something very unexpected — "What's that?"

What happened in the next five minutes was an eye-opening revelation to me. I had known Liam for some time — we had worked together on the "Better for Less" paper and discussed the issues of evolution — but somehow, in all of this, I had never explained to him what my maps were. Whilst Liam could see the potential of maps, I was befuddled. How did he not know what these were?

I started talking with other CEOs, CIOs and CTOs and rapidly discovered that nobody knew what maps were. Even more shocking, despite my assumption that everyone else had their own way of mapping, it turned out that no-one did. It finally dawned on me that the incredibly wise senior executive in the Hotel Arts who had asked, "Does this strategy make sense?" wasn't testing me — he didn't have a clue. But this question had sent me spiralling off on this journey (see Chapter 1). It seemed it wasn't just me who had been faking it as a CEO.

It was in 2013 that this revelation truly hit home. I was working for the Leading Edge Forum (a private research organisation) with access to the great and good of many industries and many governments. I had undertaken a very informal survey of around 600 companies and concluded that only four of those companies had anything remotely equivalent to a map. In each of these cases, they were using mental models. The entire world was playing a game of chess without ever looking at the board. Suddenly, my success at taking over the entire cloud space with Ubuntu despite the wealth and size of competitors made sense. Their inability to counter my moves was simply due to blindness. The executives may have been paid million-dollar salaries but they were playing snap in a game of chess.

Part of the problem with the "Better for Less" paper was that I had assumed that everyone had some form of maps. Without these, it would be next to impossible to remove duplication and bias, to introduce challenge into the system and to apply the right methods. I had talked about spend control becoming the institutional seat of learning for Government, but this wasn't going to happen if nobody had maps to compare. I cannot underestimate how important that simple statement from Liam was. Without it, I could have carried on assuming everyone knew how to map for many more years. I owe Liam a great debt of thanks.

An Opportunity

In late 2013, I wrote a paper for the Cabinet Office called "Governance of Technology Change". I used this paper to try to combat what I saw as a "tyranny of agile" and to introduce the ideas of continuous learning through maps. I already had a handful of examples where maps had proved useful in Government, such their use in the development of IT systems within HS2 (High Speed Rail) by James Findlay. These examples were few and far between. The problem within Government was a past tendency to one size fits all. Outsourcing was now being overtaken with a new and inappropriate one size fits all called agile. Without maps, it's easy to fall into one size fits all trap. To show you what I mean, let us take a map for an IT system in HS2 and overlay the different methods, techniques and types of attitudes you would use — see Figure 235.

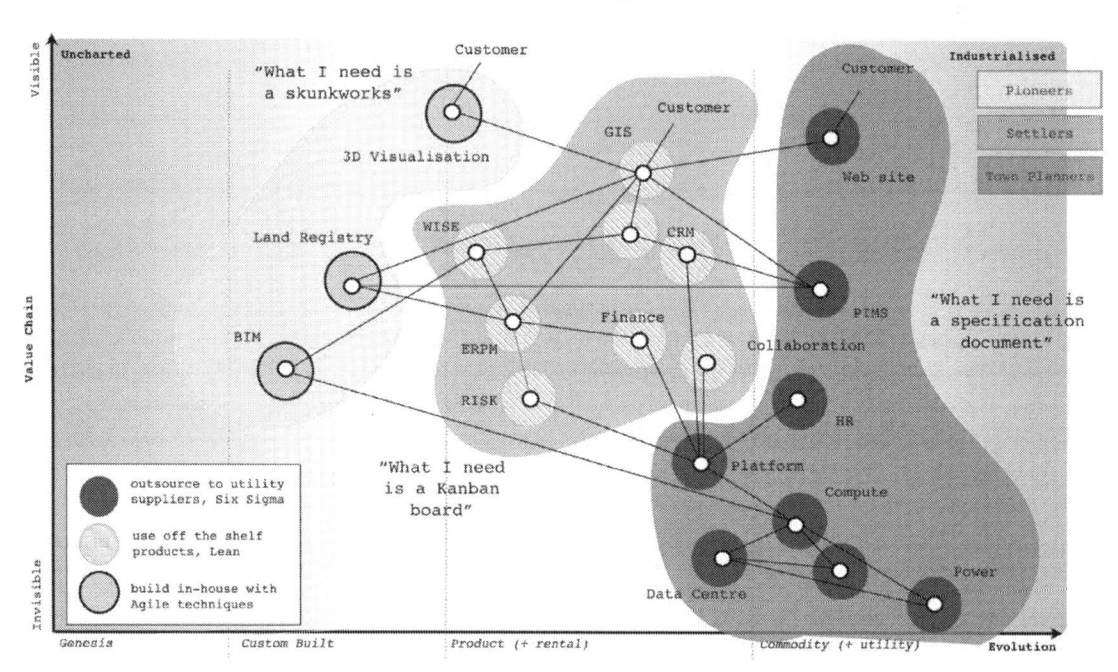

Figure 235: High Speed Rail Map with overlaid techniques

By now, it should be obvious to you how we need to use a changing landscape of multiple methods at the same time to manage a complex system such as this. However, imagine if you had no map. The temptation and ease at which a one size fits all can be used or replaced by another should be obvious. How would you counter an argument for using an agile technique to build an HR system, given the success of agile in building a land registry system? They're the same, right? This is what happens when context is lost. It is how you end up trying to outsource everything or agile everything.

Be warned, this path won't win you many friends. I've been in conferences where I've got into raging arguments with people trying to explain to me that agile works everywhere. This is often followed by other conferences and raging arguments with people trying to explain that Six Sigma works everywhere. In both cases, they'll often explain failure as "not doing it in the right way" or "using the wrong bits", and never that there exists a limit or context to the method. It's no different with the "better specification" problem. The failure is always blamed on something else and not that specification, agile or Six Sigma shouldn't have been used for those parts.

During my years of using mapping, the "use of appropriate methods" was just one of a long list of context-specific gameplays, climatic (economic) patterns and doctrine (universally useful principles) that I had discovered through my use of maps. I turned to my list of doctrine to help write the "Governance of Technology Change" paper and to correct some of my failures in the original "Better for Less". I used these principles to propose a new form of governance structure that built upon the work that was already done. The key elements of doctrine used were:-

Doctrine: Focus on high situational awareness (understand what is being considered)

A major failing of "Better for Less" was the lack of emphasis on maps. I had to increase situational awareness beyond simple mental models and structures such as ILC. To achieve this, we needed to develop maps within Government, which requires an anchor (user need), an understanding of position (the value chain and components involved), and an understanding of movement (evolution). To begin with, the proposed governance system would clearly reflect user needs in all its decision-making processes. The users included not only departmental users but also the wider public who will interact with any services provided. It was essential, therefore, that those users' needs were determined at the outset, represented in the creation of any proposal and any expected outcomes of any proposal are set against those needs. But this was not enough. We also needed the value chain that provided those user needs and how evolved the components were. Maps therefore became a critical part of the governance structure.

Doctrine: Be transparent (a bias towards open)

The governance system had to be entirely transparent. For example, proposals must be published openly in one place and in one format through a shared and public pipeline. This must allow for examination of proposals, both internally and externally, of Government to encourage interaction of departments and public members to any proposal.

Doctrine: Use a common language (necessary for collaboration)

The governance system had to provide a mechanism for coordination and engagement across groups, including departments and spend control. This requires a mechanism of shared learning — for example, discovery and dissemination of examples of good practice. To achieve this, we must have a common language. Maps were that language.

Doctrine: Use appropriate methods (e.g. agile vs lean vs Six Sigma)

Governance had to accept that there are currently no single methods of management that are suitable for all environments. The use of multiple methods and techniques based upon context had to become a norm.

Doctrine: Distribute power and decision-making

Departments and groups should be able organise themselves as appropriate to meet central policy. Hence, the governance procedure should refrain from directly imposing project methodologies and structure on departments and groups and allow for autonomous decision-making. Improvements to ways of operating could be achieved through challenging via maps, i.e. if one department thought that everything should be outsourced, we could use their own maps to help them challenge their own thinking.

Doctrine: Think fast, inexpensive, restrained and elegant (FIRE)

Governance should encourage an approach of fast, inexpensive, simple and tiny, rather than creation of slow, expensive, complex and large systems to achieve value for money. Any reasonably large technology proposal should be broken down into smaller components, with any in-house development achieved through small teams. The breaking down of large systems would also help demonstrate that multiple methods were usually needed, along with encouraging re-use. However, we would have to be prepared for inertia and counter arguments such as the "complexity of managing interfaces". The interfaces existed, regardless of whether we tried to ignore them or not.

Doctrine: Use a systematic mechanism of learning (a bias towards data)

The governance system must provide a mechanism of consistent measurement against outcomes and for continuous improvement of measurements. This is covered in Chapter 6 and it is a primary role for any spend control group.

The paper was written and delivered in 2013. Unfortunately, I suspect in this instance, it has gathered dust. The problem with the paper was familiarity. Many of the concepts it contained are unfamiliar to most and that requires effort and commitment to overcome. That commitment wasn't there, the tyranny of agile continued and the inevitable counter reaction ensued. There was and is a lot of good stuff that has been achieved by Government in IT since 2010. The people who have worked and do work there have done this nation proud. However, more could have been achieved. In my darkest and more egotistical moments, I suspect that had I not assumed everyone knew how to map then I might have been able to move that needle a bit more by introducing these concepts more prominently in the "Better for Less" paper. But alas, this is not my only failure.

Assumptions and bias

Assumption is a very dangerous activity and one that has constantly caught me out. In the past, I had assumed that everyone knew how to map, but the real question is why did I think this? The answer in this case is a bias known as the false consensus bias. I tend to assume that if I know something then everyone else must know it as well. It's the reason why it took me six years to discover that others weren't mapping. It was also behind my assumptions in the "Better for Less" paper.

When it comes to bias with maps then there are two main types you need to consider. The first is evolutionary bias and our tendency to treat something in the wrong way, e.g. to custom-build that which is a commodity. By comparing multiple maps then you can help reduce this effect. The second broad and powerful group of biases are cognitive biases. Maps can help here but only through the action of allowing others to challenge your map. The most common and dangerous types of cognitive biases I have faced (and my description of these as "most common and dangerous" is another bias) are:-

Confirmation bias

A tendency to accept or interpret information in a manner that confirms existing preconceptions. For example, a group latching onto information that supports their use of some process being different from industry and hence, justifying the way they've built it.

Loss aversion bias

The value of losing an object exceeds the value of acquiring it, e.g. the sunk cost effect. Examples heard include "had we not invested this money, we wouldn't use this asset to do this". Often a significant root cause of inertia.

Outcome bias

A tendency to look at the actual outcome and not the process by which the choice was made. Commonly appears in meme copying other companies when little to no situational awareness exists, e.g. "we should be like Amazon".

Hindsight bias

A tendency to see past events as being more predictable than they were. An example would be describing the evolution of compute from mainframe to client / server to cloud as some form of ordained path. The problem is that the "apparent" path taken at a high level depends upon how evolved the underlying components were (e.g. storage, processing, network). If processing and storage were vastly more expensive than network, then we would tend toward centralisation. Whereas, if network was more expensive then we would tend towards decentralisation.

Cascade bias

A belief that gains more plausibility through its repetition in public circles, e.g. many of the false myths of cloud such as Amazon's "selling of spare capacity".

Instrumentation bias

The issue of familiarity and a reliance on known tools or approaches to the exclusion of other methods. Summarised by the line, "If all you have is a hammer, everything looks like a nail."

Disposition bias

A desire not to lose value, i.e. selling of assets that have accumulated value but resist selling assets that have declined in the hope that they will recover. This is another common source of inertia through the belief that an existing line of business or asset acquired that is performing poorly will recover.

Dunning–Kruger effect

Tendency for the inexperienced to overestimate their skill and the experienced to underestimate.

Courtesy bias

A tendency for individuals to avoid giving their true opinion to avoid causing offence to others, e.g. to not forcibly challenge why we are doing something, especially when it is considered a "pet project" of another.

Ambiguity bias

A tendency to avoid uncertainty where possible and/or to attempt to define uncertainty, e.g. to specify the unknown.

Survivorship bias

Only examining the data that achieves some end state rather than that which doesn't. At the heart of mapping is a survivorship bias. The evolution curve (described in Chapter 7) that is used as the basis of the x-axis of a map was built from data for components that had survived to become a commodity. It shows a path of "If a component evolves to a commodity then it will traverse through these stages." But what about the components that didn't survive? Unfortunately, I was not able to distinguish another pattern to explain them, other than to say they followed the path of evolution and died in one of the stages. Most visibly (because we can get access to data), components die in the custom-built stage and I can only assume (because it's nigh on impossible to get data) that the most common stage of death is genesis where there exists the highest degree of uncertainty. Of course, assumption is a dangerous thing.

Applying doctrine

So far in this chapter, I've covered various aspects of doctrine and the issues of bias and assumption. There is a reason to my madness. One of the most common questions I'm asked is which bits of doctrine should we apply first? The answer to this is, I don't know.

Based upon my experience, I do believe (and that may be bias) that there is an order to doctrine. For example, before you can apply a pioneer — settler — town planner structure (i.e. design for constant evolution) then you need to first implement other forms of doctrine. A rough order is:-

1. Start by understanding your user needs (i.e. focus on user needs).
2. Improve your understanding of the detail by describing the value chain needed to support your user needs (i.e. know the details).
3. Increase your situational awareness by creating a map of the environment. This is achieved by taking your value chain and adding in evolution to visualise how things change (i.e. focus on situational awareness).
4. Use your map to apply appropriate methods, to constrain the system into small contracts and to remove bias and duplication.
5. Convert the small contracts into a cell-based structure with autonomous teams (i.e. think small teams).
6. Apply appropriate attitudes to the teams, such as pioneer, settler and town planner, and introduce a system of theft to enable a system that copes with constant change (i.e. think aptitude and attitude).

Though we can deduce an order for some of the principles within doctrine, beyond broad strokes then I don't know what bits of doctrine matter more, i.e. is transparency more important than setting exceptional standards?

Alas, it will probably take me many decades to sort through this and obviously, due to coevolution effects then new practices and new forms of organisation will appear during that time. Hence, doctrine is itself changing over time. This is one of those painting the Forth bridge situations, which by the time I've finally sorted out an order, it has changed. However, I can take a guess on the order of importance based upon experience. I've split doctrine into a set of discrete phases that you should consider, but at the same time, I want you to remember that I will be suffering from my own biases. So, take it with a big pinch of salt and don't feel concerned about deviating from this. It is only a guide. My phases of doctrine are provided in Figure 236.

Category	Wardley's Doctrine (universally useful patterns that a user can apply)			
Communication	Be transparent *(a bias towards open)*	Focus on high situational awareness *(understand what is being considered)*	Use a common language *(necessary for collaboration)*	Challenge assumptions *(speak up and question)*
Development	Know your users *(e.g. customers, shareholders, regulators, staff)*	Focus on user needs	Think fast, inexpensive, restrained and elegant *(FIRE, formerly FIST)*	Remove bias and duplication
	Use appropriate methods *(e.g. agile vs lean vs six sigma)*	Focus on the outcome not a contract *(e.g. worth based development)*	Be pragmatic *(it doesn't matter if the cat is black or white as long as it catches mice)*	Use standards where appropriate
	Use appropriate tools *(e.g. mapping, financial models)*			
Operation	Manage inertia *(e.g. existing practice, political capital, previous investment)*	Optimise flow *(remove bottlenecks)*		Effectiveness over efficiency
	Do better with less *(continual improvement)*	Set exceptional standards *(great is just not good enough)*	Think small *(as in know the details)*	
Structure	Provide purpose, mastery & autonomy	Think small *(as in teams)*	Manage failure	
			Distribute power and decision making	Think aptitude and attitude
	Design for constant evolution	There is no one culture *(e.g. pioneers, settlers and town planners)*	Seek the best	
Learning	Use a systematic mechanism of learning *(a bias towards data)*	A bias towards action *(learn by playing the game)*	A bias towards the new *(be curious, take appropriate risks)*	Listen to your ecosystems *(acts as future sensing engines)*
Leading	Be the owner *(take responsibility)*	Move fast *(an imperfect plan executed today is better than a perfect plan executed tomorrow)*	Think big *(inspire others, provide direction)*	Strategy is iterative not linear *(fast reactive cycles)*
	Strategy is complex *(there will be uncertainty)*	Commit to the direction, be adaptive along the path *(crossing the river by feeling the stones)*	There is no core *(everything is transient)*	Be humble *(listen, be selfless, have fortitude)*
	Exploit the landscape			

Phase I
Phase II
Phase III
Phase IV

Figure 236: Phases of Doctrine

The phases are:-

Phase I – Stop self-harm

The focus in this first phase is simply awareness and removal of duplication. What I'm aiming for is not to radically change the environment but to stop further damage being caused. Hence, the emphasis is on understanding your user needs, improving situational awareness, removing duplication, challenging assumptions, getting to understand the details of what is done and introducing a systematic mechanism of learning — such as the use of maps with a group such as spend control.

Phase II – Becoming more context aware

Whilst phase I is about stopping the rot, phase II builds upon this by helping us to start considering and using the context. Hence, the emphasis is on using appropriate tools and methods, thinking about FIRE, managing inertia, having a bias towards action, moving quickly, being transparent about what we do, distributing power and understanding that strategy is an iterative process.

Phase III – Better for less

I name this section "Better for Less" because in hindsight (and yes, this is likely to be a bias), there were some fundamental lessons I missed (due to my own false-consensus bias) in the original paper. Those lessons are now mostly covered in phases I & II. In this phase, we're focusing on constant improvement, which means optimising flows in the system, seeking the best, a bias towards the new, thinking big, inspiring others, committing to the path, accepting uncertainty, taking responsibility and providing purpose, master and autonomy. This is the phase that is most about change and moving in a better direction, whereas the previous phases are about housekeeping.

Phase IV – Continuously evolving

The final phase is focused on creating an environment that copes with constant shocks and changes. This is the point where strategic play comes to the fore and where we design with pioneers, settlers and town planners. The emphasis is on constant evolution, use of multiple cultures, listening to outside ecosystems, understanding that everything is transient and exploiting the landscape.

Are the phases right? Almost certainly not, and they are probably missing a significant amount of undiscovered doctrine. However, they are the best guess I can provide you with. There are two other parts of doctrine that I've glossed over. Both are worth highlighting. One is managing failure, the other is being humble.

On the question of failure

When it comes to managing failure then life is a master. To categorise failure, I tend to use C. S. Holling's concepts of engineering versus ecosystem resilience — see Figure 237.

	Diversity is low	Diversity is high
High Engineering resilience (maintaining efficiency of function)	**ROBUST** — Broader range of physical constraints but cannot adapt to unexpected events. Many classical systems are designed to maintain the efficiency of function given a set of broad constraints or defined changes e.g. loss of a single engine in an aircraft. Can suffer from systemic failure.	**RESILIENT** — Capable of coping with a wide variety of physical extremes with the entire system rapidly adapting to a changing environment in order to exist. Nature in its entirety can be considered resilient consisting of many biological ecosystems occupying niches. Any change in physical conditions enables one biological ecosystem to invade the space of another. The efficiency and survival of life is preserved bar the most catastrophic of shocks.
Low	**FRAGILE** — Limited constraint of physical operation. Cannot adapt or cope with change. Breaks easily and ceases to function.	**FLUID** — Though elements of the system can be considered fragile (operating within limited constraints or occupying a niche), the system itself adapts rapidly to changing circumstances i.e. the efficiency of function might decline rapidly due to a change but the function continues to exist. Many biological ecosystems can be considered fluid and the process of change is known as evolution e.g. adaptation of a species to some new predator or environmental catastrophe.

Ecological resilience (maintaining existence of function) — Low to High

based on CS Holling, 1996, Engineering versus Ecological resilience

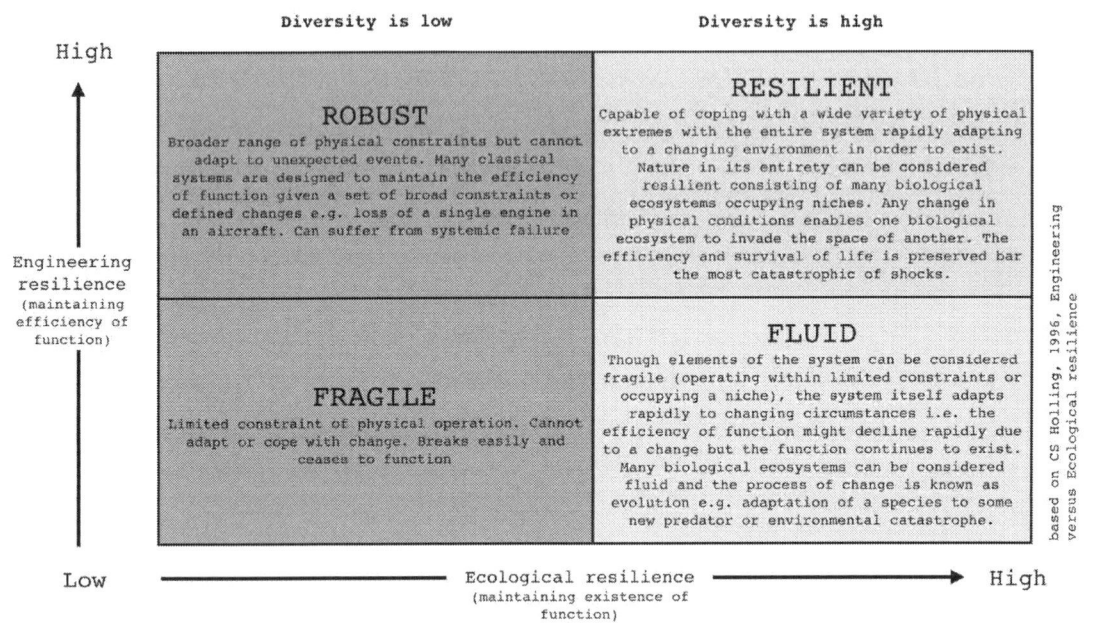

Figure 237: Types of Failure

Engineering resilience is focused on maintaining the efficiency of a function. Ecological resilience is focused on maintaining the existence of the function. In terms of sustainability then the goal of any organisation should be to become resilient. This requires a structure that can adapt to constant evolution, along with many supporting ecosystems. Unfortunately, most larger organisations tend to be in the robust category, constantly designing processes to cope with known failure modes and trying to maintain the efficiency of any capital function when shock occurs, i.e. constantly trying to maintain profitability and return to shareholders. Whilst efficient, the lack of diversity in terms of culture and thought means these organisations tend to be ill prepared for environments that rapidly change outside of its "comfort zone".

Doctrine: Be Humble

If we're going to discuss bias and failure in the technology world then there's probably no better example than OpenStack. It's also one that I'm familiar with. When I was at Canonical, one of my cabal who helped push the agenda for Ubuntu in the cloud was Rick Clark. He is a gifted engineering manager and quickly picked up on the concepts of mapping. He is also a good friend. It was a year or so later that Rick was working for Rackspace. Rick and I had long discussed an open play against Amazon in the cloud, how to create an ecosystem of public providers that matched the Amazon APIs and force a price war to increase demand beyond Amazon's ability to supply, hence fragmenting the market. I was delighted to get that call from Rick in early 2010 about his plans in this space and by March 2010, I agreed to put him centre and front stage of the cloud computing summit at OSCON. What was launched was OpenStack.

My enthusiasm and delight however didn't last long. At the launch party that evening, I was introduced to various executives and during that discussion, it became clear that some of the executive team had added their own thought processes to Rick's play. They had hatched an idea that was so daft that the entire venture was under threat. That idea, which would undermine the whole ecosystem approach, was to differentiate on stuff that didn't matter — the APIs. I warned that this would lead to a lack of focus, a collective prisoner dilemma of companies differentiating, a failure to counter the ecosystem benefit that Amazon had, and a host of other problems, but they were adamant. By use of their own API, they would take away all the advantages of Amazon and dominate the market. Eventually, as one executive told me, Amazon would have to adopt their API to survive. The place was dripping in arrogance and self-confidence.

I tried to support as much as I could but nevertheless, I had quite a few public spats on this API idea. In the end, by 2012, I had concluded that OpenStack, rather than being the great hope for a competitive market, was a "dead duck", forced to fighting VMware in what will ultimately be a dying and crowded space, whilst Amazon (and other players) took away the future. I admire the level of marketing, effort and excitement that OpenStack has created and certainly, there are niches for it to create a profitable existence (e.g. in the network equipment space), but despite the belief that it would challenge Amazon, it has lost. The confidence of OpenStack was ultimately its failure. The hubris, the failure to be pragmatic, its decision not to exploit the ecosystems that already existed, and its own self-belief has not served it well. It was a cascade failure of significant proportions, with people believing that OpenStack would win just because others in their circles were saying so in public. Many would argue today that OpenStack is not a failure and the goals of supporting a competitive market of public providers were not its aim, nor was it planning to take on Amazon. That is simply revisionist history and an attempt to make the present more palatable.

Yes, OpenStack has made a few people a lot of money, but it's a minnow in the cloud space. Certain analysts do predict that the entire OpenStack market will reach $5 billion in 2020. Even if we accept this figure at face value, and this is for an entire market, AWS revenue hit $12 billion in 2016. The future revenue for an entire market in 2020 is less than half the revenue for a single provider in 2016 and growing at a slower rate? You'd have to stretch the definition to breaking point to call this a success, hence I suspect the importance of a bit of revision. Nevertheless, the battle is a long game and there is a route back to the public arena through China, where many better players exist.

You need to apply thought

One of the problems of mapping is that people expect it to give them an answer. Maps aren't a 2x2 where your goal is to get into some corner to win the magic prize. All maps do are help you understand the environment, challenge what you're doing, encourage learning and the application of a bit of thought. There can exist all sorts of feedback loops for the unwary. For example, let us consider healthcare.

A question of healthcare

You have a government that has needs, including a need for people to vote for it, assuming it's a democracy. Those voters also have needs, one of which is to survive. In the case of medical conditions, this requires treatment, of which there is a pipeline of treatments. From once novel treatments such as antibiotics, which have become highly industrialised, to more novel treatments today such as CRISPR. Over time, all these novel approaches evolve to become industrialised and other novel approaches emerge. Hence, a pipeline. Obviously, such treatment has a cost, hence we assume there is a budget for healthcare along with treatment centres. Now, let us assume that the government has decided to provide universal healthcare. Since this won't be cost free then we will require some taxes. We can quickly map this up — see Figure 238.

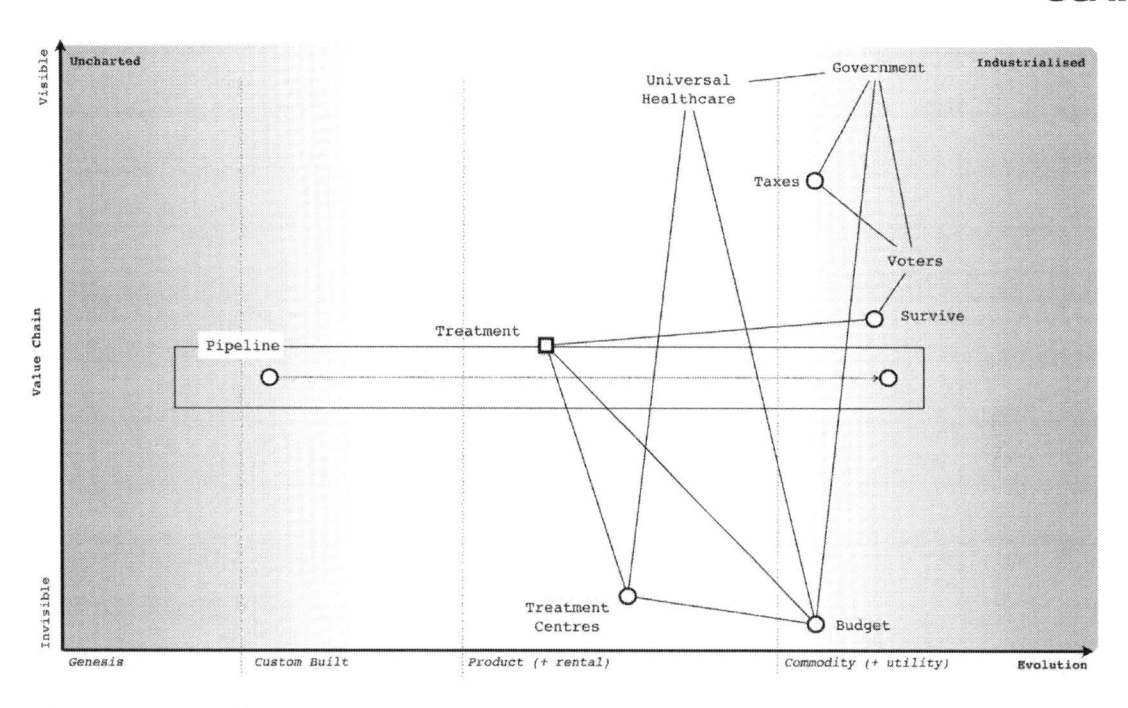

Figure 238: Map of universal healthcare

As maps go, this is incredibly simplistic, missing a whole raft of stuff, and could be significantly improved. But, I'm using this for an example and so it'll do for now. Let us look at that map. We can certainly start to add financial figures for flow and we can start to question why treatment centres are not highly industrialised. Surely, they're the same? However, let us add something else. We shall consider preventative care.

The government has decided to introduce a preventative care program that voters are required or encouraged to attend. Obviously, there's a budget impact (i.e. the spending on preventative care), but the good news is that through the use of preventative care, we can reduce the overall volume of treatment (i.e. some diseases are preventable), thereby reducing cost and meeting the needs of patients to survive longer. Everyone is happy! Except, there's a problem. Whilst the aim of reducing cost, providing a better service to more people and enabling people to live longer is a noble goal, the problem is that our people live longer! Unfortunately, what we subsequently discover is longer-lived people incur increased treatment costs due to the types of disease they die from or the need for some form of support. There is a feedback loop between preventative care and treatment. I've marked this up in Figure 239.

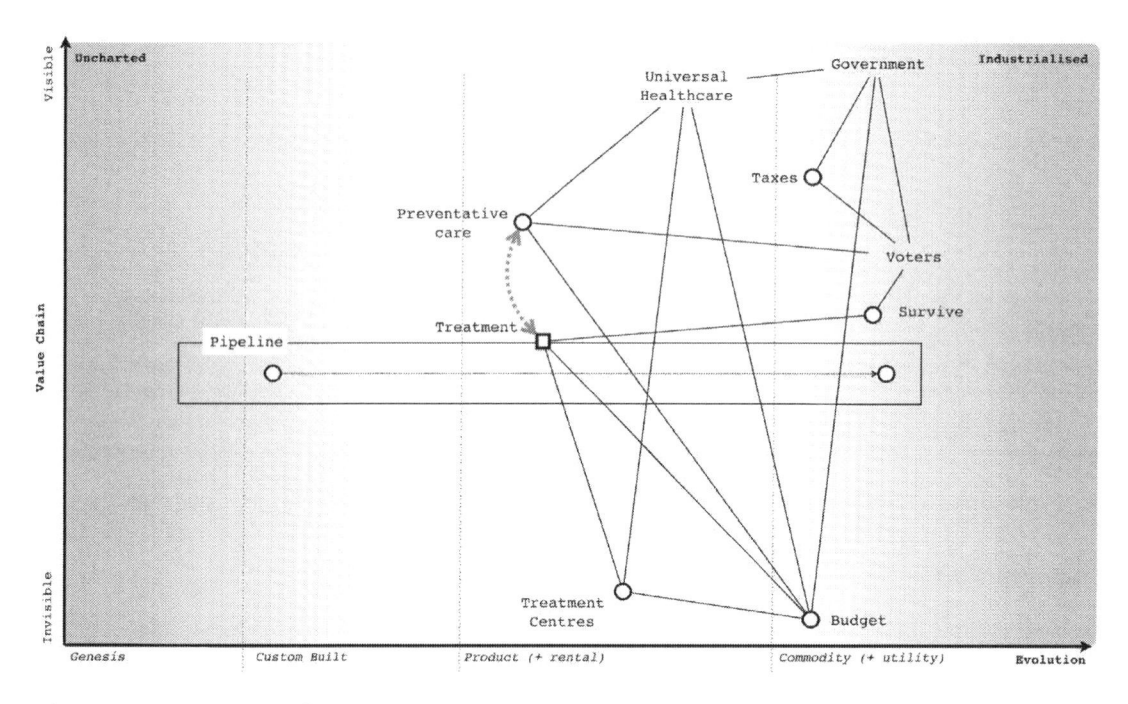

Figure 239: Healthcare feedback

The problem we now face is a growing older population (due to the preventative healthcare we introduced) that requires increased treatment costs. What at one point seemed to be a benefit (preventative healthcare) has turned into a burden. What shall we do? Assuming we're not some sort of dictatorship — we did need people to vote for us — and so the Viking ceremony of Ättestupa is out of the question, we need to somehow reduce the treatment costs. The best way of doing this is to accelerate the pipeline, i.e. we want treatments to industrialise more quickly. To achieve this, we need more competition, which could either be through reducing barriers to entry, setting up funds to encourage new entrants, or using open approaches to allow treatments to more rapidly spread in the market. Let us suppose we do this; we set up a medical fund to encourage industrialisation — see Figure 240.

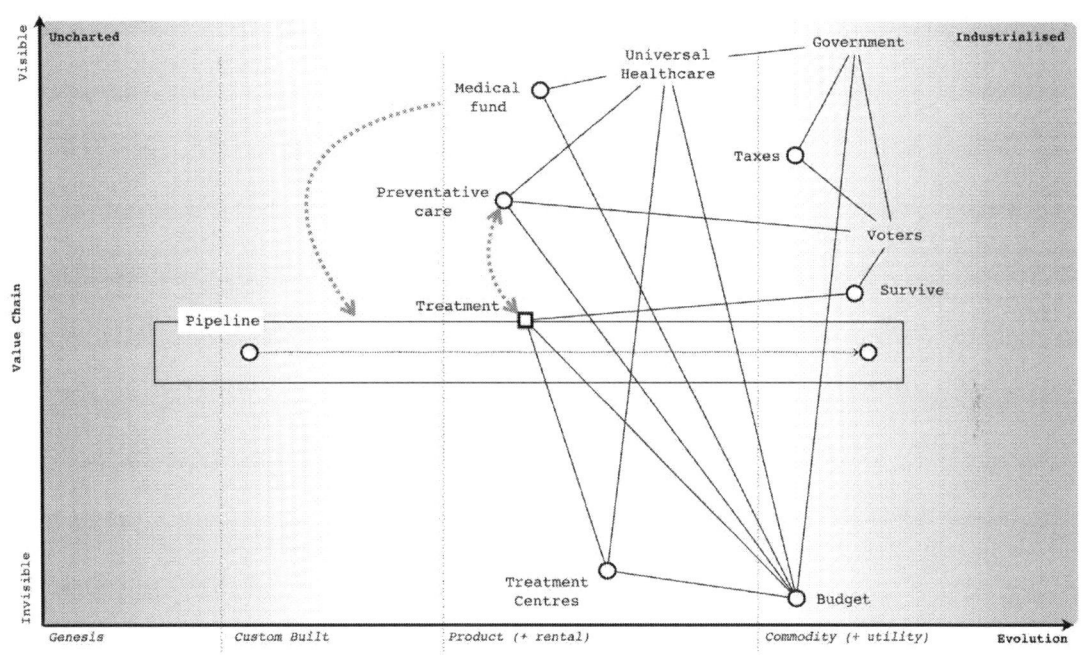

Figure 240: Medical fund

So, people are living longer but we're countering any increased cost due to our approach of industrialisation in the field of medicine. Everyone is happy, right? Wrong. You have companies who are providing treatments in that space and they probably have inertia to this change. Your attempts to industrialise their products faster mean more investment and loss of profits. Of course, we could map them, use it to help understand their needs and refine the game a bit more. However, the point I want to raise is this. There are no simple answers with maps. There are often feedback loops and hidden surprises. You need to adapt as things are discovered. However, despite all of this, you can still use maps to anticipate and prepare for change. I know nothing about healthcare but even I know (from a map) that *if you're going to invest in preventative care then you're going to need to invest in medical funds to encourage new entrants into the market.*

I italicised the above because unfortunately, this is where a lack of being humble and the Dunning-Kruger effect can have terrible consequences. It is easy to be seduced into an idea that you understand a space and that your plan will work. Someone with experience of medicine might look at my statement on preventative care and medical funds and rightly rip it to shreds because I have no expertise in the space, I do not know what I'm talking about. But I can create a convincing story with a map unless someone challenges me. Hence, always remember that all maps are imperfect and they are nothing more than an aid to learning and communication. They are not "right".

A question of planning — OODA and the PDCA

The idea that we should plan around a forecast and the importance of accuracy in the forecast is rooted in Western philosophy. The act of planning is useful in helping us understand the space; there are many predictable patterns we can also apply but there is a lot of uncertainty and unknowns, including individual actors' actions. Hence, when it comes to planning, we should consider many scenarios and a broad range of possibilities. As Deng Xiaoping stated, managing the economy is like crossing the river by feeling the stones. We have a purpose and direction but adapt along the path. This is at the heart of the strategy cycle — Observe the environment, Orient around it, Decide your path and Act — and it is known as OODA.

At this point, someone normally mentions Deming's PDCA cycle — plan, do, check and act. To understand the difference, we need to consider the OODA loop a little more. The full OODA loop by John Boyd is provided in Figure 241

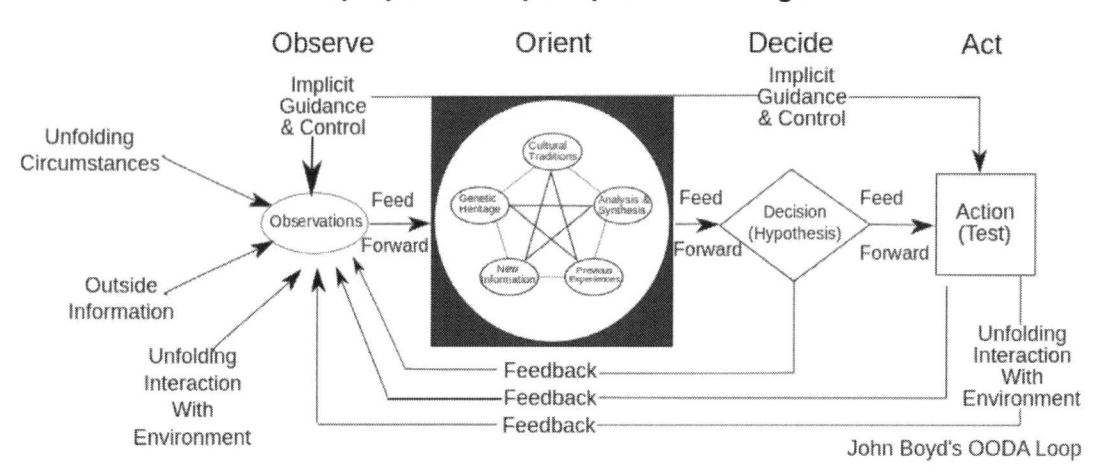

Figure 241: OODA

There are several components that I'd like to draw your attention to in the orient part of the loop. Our ability to orient (or orientate, which is an alternative English version of the word) depends upon our previous experience, cultural heritage and genetic disposition to the events in question. In terms of an organisation, its genetic disposition is akin to the doctrine and practices it has.

Now, if an event is unknown and we're in the uncharted space of the map then there is nothing we can really plan for. Our only option is to try something and see what happens. This is the world of JDI or just do it. It is a leap into the unknown and an approach of do and then check what happened is required. However, as we understand more about the space, our previous experience and practices grow in this area. So, whilst our first pass through the OODA loop means we just do and check, further loops allow us to start to plan, then do, check the result and act to update our practices. This is PDCA. As our experience, practices and even measurements grow then our decision process itself refines. We can concretely define the event, we can provide expected measurements, we can analyse against this and look to improve what is being done and then control the improvements to make sure they're sustainable. This is DMAIC. The OODA loop can result in very different behaviours, from just trying something out to DMAIC, depending up how much experience and heritage exist with what is being managed, i.e. how evolved it is and how familiar and certain we are with it. I've summarised this in Figure 242.

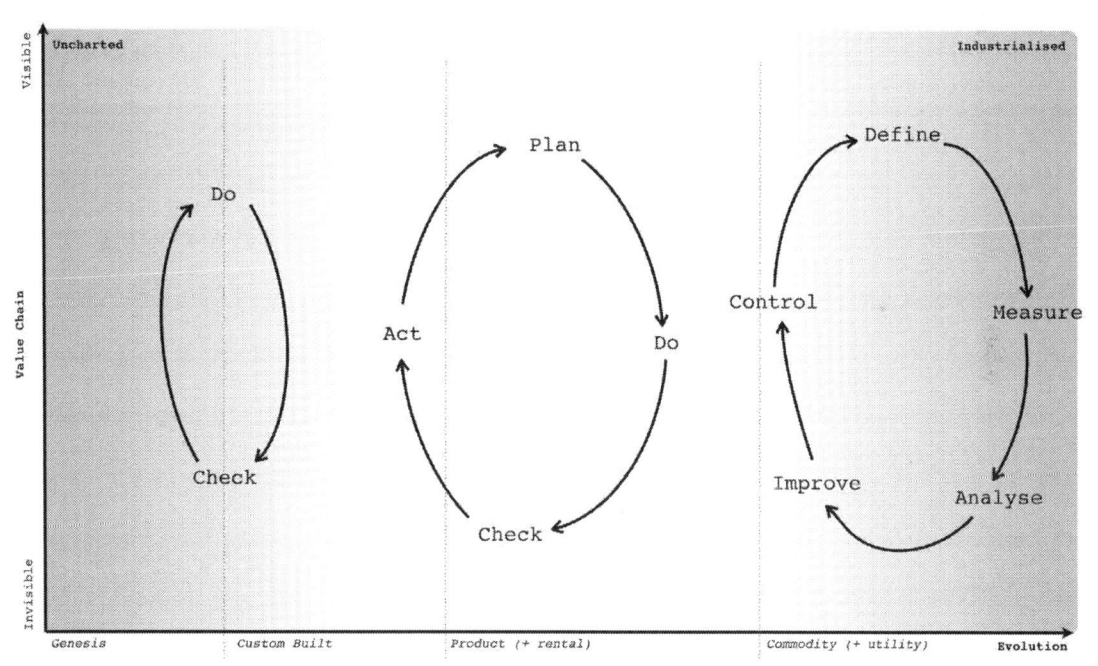

Figure 242: JDI to PDCA to DMAIC

A question of privilege

Whilst all plans must adapt, that doesn't mean we can't scenario plan and prepare for possible outcomes. Let us take another example; in this case, the self-driving car. In Figure 241, I've described the automotive industry in mapping form. We start with the basic user need of getting from A to B. We then extend into route management (i.e. doing so quickly), comfort and affordability. We also include status — a car isn't just about moving from A to B; it's also about looking good whilst doing so. From this, we extend into a pipeline of cars with some more commodity-- like, especially in terms of features. I call out a couple of discrete parts, from entertainment to infotainment systems, and we continue down the value chain itself. You might disagree with the components and their position but that's the purpose of a map, to allow this form of challenge.

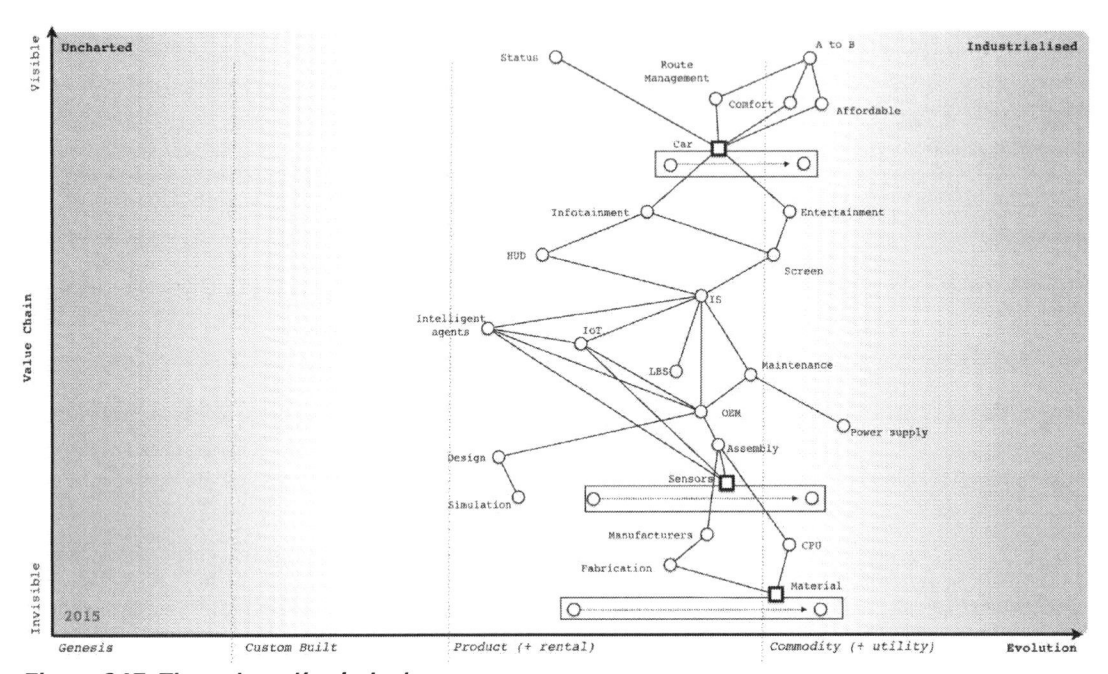

Figure 243: The automotive industry

However, that is a map for today, or more specifically, for 2015, when it was written. What we can now do is roll the map forward into the future. What emerges is a picture of self-driving cars (i.e. intelligent agents in all cars), an immersive experience (the Heads Up and Screen have been combined), and the vehicle itself becoming more commodity-like, even potentially more utility-like.

Hence, you can think of a world in 2025 where increasingly, we don't own cars but pay for them on a utility basis. The cars are self-driving and increasingly immersive. The car that drives me to a meeting might have been the car that drove you to the theatre last night. However, using this map, we can also see some other connections that we might not have considered before — see Figure 244.

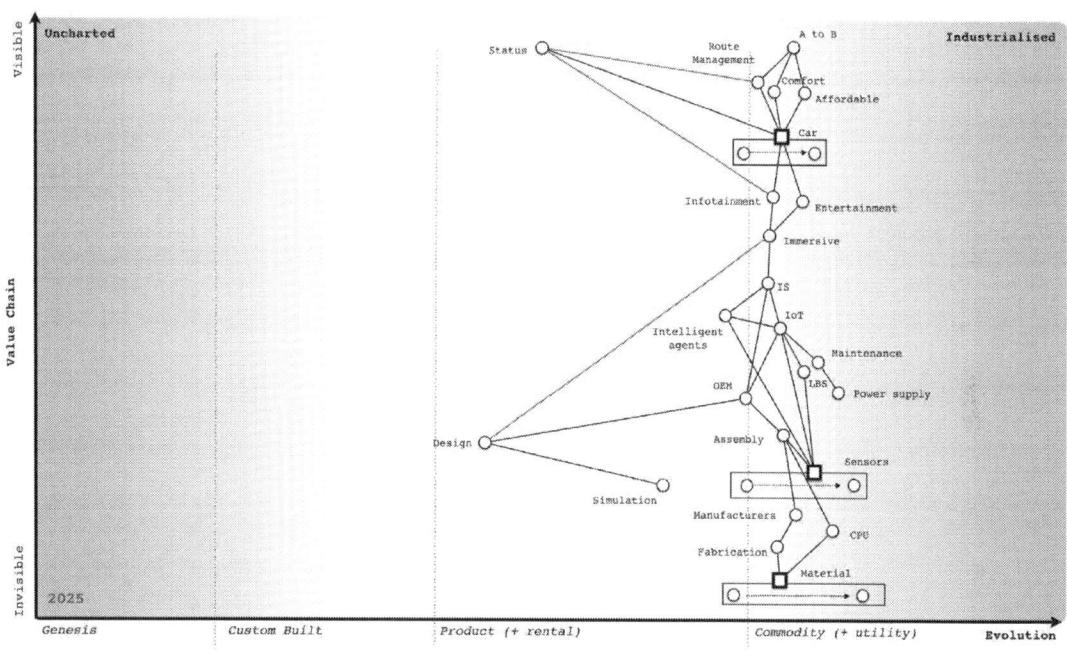

Figure 244: The automotive industry, 2025

First is the rising importance of design in creating the immersive experience (shown as the red connection line). Second is the issue of status and that immersive experience. If the cars are the same, we still have that need of status to be met. One way to achieve this is to have digital subscription levels, e.g. platinum, silver and bronze, and to subtly alter the experience in both immersion and the look of the car, depending upon who is currently occupying. A standard bronze member might get adverts, whilst a platinum member would be provided to more exclusive content. But that doesn't really push the concept of status. The third addition is a link (in red) between status and route management. If a platinum member needs a car then they should be higher priority. But more than this, if you need to go from A to B, whilst you're driving (or more accurately, being driven), then lower-class members can pull over into the slower lane. With human drivers, that isn't going to happen, but with self-driving vehicles then such privilege can be automated. Of course, there'd be reactions against this, but any canny player can start with the argument of providing faster routes to emergency vehicles first (e.g. fire, ambulance), and once that has been established, introduce more commercial priority. Later, this can be further reinforced by geo-fencing privilege to a point that vehicles won't drive into geographies unless you're of the right membership level.

Obviously, this has all sorts of knock-on social effects and such reinforcement of privilege and the harm it could cause needs to be considered. Governments should scenario plan far into the future. However, the point of maps is not just to help discuss the obvious stuff, e.g. the loss of licensing revenue to the DVLA, the impacts to traffic signalling, the future banning of human drivers (who are in effect, priced off the road due to insurance) or the impacts to car parks. The point of maps is to help us find that which we could prepare for. Of course, we can take this a step further. We've previously discussed the use of doctrine to compare organisations and the use of the peace, war and wonder cycles to identify points of change. In this case, we can take the automotive industry map rolled forward to 2025, add our weak signals for those points of war and try to determine what will rapidly be changing in the industry at that time. We can then look at the players in that market, try to identify opportunities to exploit, or even look at nation state gameplay.

In the case of the automotive industry, I've marked the points of war that will be occurring (or would have just occurred) by 2025 and then added on the gameplay of China in that space. This is provided in Figure 245. What it shows is that China is undergoing significant strategic investment in key parts of the value chain prior to these points of industrialisation. It is also building a strong constraint-based form of gameplay around raw materials by acquiring significant assets in this space. If you overlay the Chinese companies in the market and then run a similar exercise for the US, what emerges is quite surprising. Whilst many have assumed that this future will be dominated by US and Silicon Valley companies, it looks increasingly likely that the future of the self-driving car belongs to China.

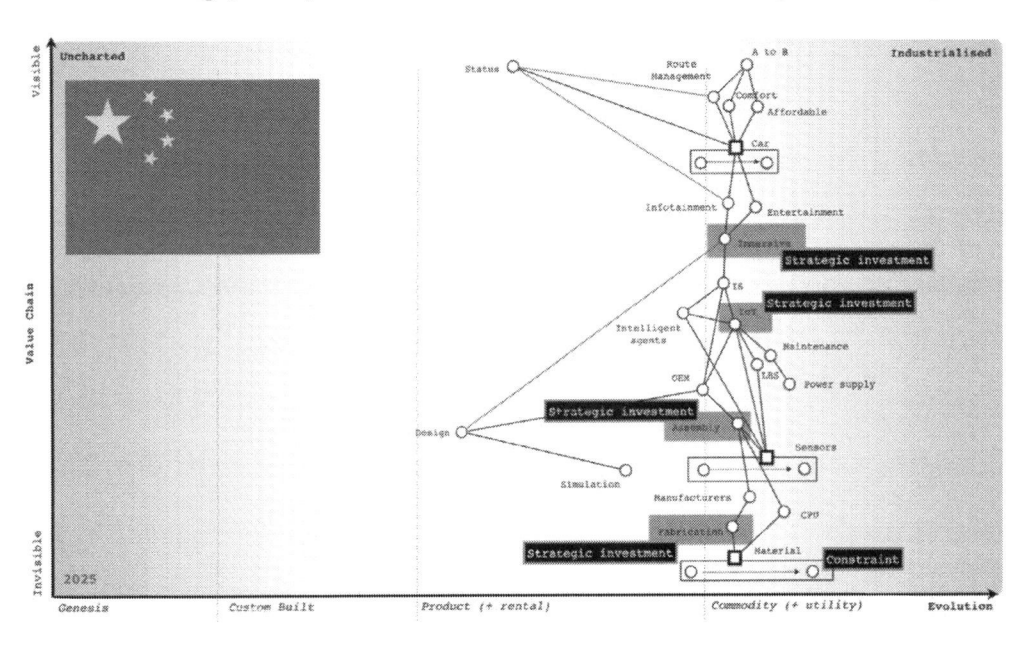

Figure 245: Automotive, points of war and gameplay

An exercise for the reader

We've covered quite a bit in this chapter, from fleshing out various concepts around doctrine to the issue of bias to the question of failure and feedback loops to scenario planning. Some of these concepts we have touched upon before in previous chapters, but then learning mapping is like the strategy cycle itself — an iterative process. Of course, practice matters.

First, I'd like you to look at your organisation and go through Figure 236. Work out which bits of doctrine you use and which bits you're poor at or don't exist at all. Using the phases as a guide, come up with a plan of action for improving doctrine.

Second, I'd like you to take one line of business and use a map to push it ten years into the future. Think about what might happen, what feedback loops might appear and what opportunities you could exploit.

Lastly, since you've already compared yourself against doctrine, I'd like you to look at competitors for the line of business that you mapped into the future and examine their doctrine. Don't limit yourself to existing competitors but think about who could exploit the changing environment and look at them. I want you to think about any bias you might have that will convince you they won't be a threat. Also, if they did make a move then how resilient is your organisation to change? Do you have a diversity of culture, practice and thought that would enable you to adapt?

Chapter 19 - On playing chess

In this chapter, I'm going to introduce some basic concepts that we will use and expand upon when exploring the issue of strategy itself. These concepts include stepping stones, use of policy, nature of capital and finding a balance.

Stepping stones

Manipulating the environment to your advantage is the essence of strategy. In the case of Fotango, we understood our competitive environment and that we were losing the battle in the online photo service business. We were losing this external battle because we had to focus internally on our parent company's needs, and that absorbed what little resources we had for investment. Alternative services such as Flickr were rapidly dominating the space. Any differential we had with the service was in image manipulation, but being a relatively novel act and uncertain, we had no way of foretelling its future. We certainly were unable to predict the rise of Instagram and what would happen next — this was 2005. We were also aware that our existing business with the parent company would eventually be caught up in their outsourcing efforts. In other words, I was losing the external battle and would eventually lose the internal one.

The strategy game starts with being honest with yourself. You're not going to improve if you believe that everything is perfect, despite the evidence. If you accept this then even failure provides an opportunity to learn. Strategy is all about observing the landscape, understanding how it is changing and using what resources you have to maximise your chances of success. Obviously, you need to define what success is and that's where your purpose comes in. It's the yardstick by which you currently measure yourself. However, as this is a cycle, your very actions may also change your purpose, and so don't get stuck on it. Ludicorp was once a failing online video game company that shut down its Game Neverending in 2004 and became a massively successful online photo service known as Flickr. It's worth noting that after Flickr, the founder, Stewart Butterfield, then went on to create another online video game company — Tiny Speck. Its game, known as Glitch, was shut down in 2012. As with Ludicorp, the founder had once again singularly failed to deliver on the promise of a huge online video game, but in the process of doing this for a second time, he had also created Slack, which is now a massively successful company valued in the billions. If Stewart had "stuck to his purpose" or "focused on the core of online video games" then we probably wouldn't have Flickr or Slack and we'd all be poorer for it.

Back to Fotango, I knew we had to act. We needed to free up resources and find a new path. I knew that such action would have to create a new purpose for the organisation in order for us to have a future. I didn't know how much time I really had, how much political clout I could use to hold back the wolves, nor even what it was we were going to do. Somehow, we needed to find a way to flourish as the unwritten purpose of every organisation and of every organism is always to survive. Using our maps, we determined that creating a utility platform or infrastructure play was the best option as there were established product markets; these markets were suitable for utility provision and incumbents would have inertia to change. Both approaches would not only enable us to build a new business but free up capital through more efficient use of resources in our existing business. However, infrastructure itself was capital intensive, and despite our profitability, we had imposed constraints, from capital expenditure to being both profitable and cash flow positive each and every month.

However, I gambled that if we believed the market was about to change then others would see the same. Some new entrant such as Google would play the infrastructure game. If they launched such a play, we could then exploit this by building our platform on top, rather than just consuming our own infrastructure. The timing was going to be critical here. We could make enough savings from our existing business through the provision of our own utility infrastructure environment to initiate our own public platform play. To grow the new business quickly, we would need someone else to make that big infrastructure play or else constrain our own platform growth to a manageable level. I had talked to the rest of the board, highlighted this future trillion-dollar market opportunity and bought enough slack (or rope, depending upon your point of view) to do it anyway.

The PaaS play (what you would call serverless today) also suited our capabilities because we had the skills required to build a low cost, large-scale distributed architecture. This would also act as a barrier to entry for others. The nagging question was who would trust this online photo service for their coding platform? By open sourcing the PaaS technology itself (Zimki), we planned to overcome many of the adoption fears and rapidly drive towards creating a standard. If we were lucky then others would set up as Zimki providers (offering their own PaaS play). This suited us because our ultimate goal was not to be a PaaS provider but to build the exchange, brokerage and assurance industries on top of this. We had used maps to extend far beyond the obvious and speculate at what was coming next. The PaaS play was simply our beach-head. Our strategy was developed from our map and our understanding of it. We would use both the landscape and our capabilities to our advantage to the best of our understanding.

We launched, and shortly after, Amazon (not Google) launched an infrastructure service known as EC2. We didn't care who it was as we were over the moon. We positioned our platform to build upon Amazon's infrastructure, we rapidly grew, and then we were shut down (in 2007). The parent company's outsourcing plan overtook my own. They did not believe in this space, this purpose. The future to them was not cloud and I had miscalculated. I had enough political capital to get started but nowhere near enough to stop the outsourcing change. I tried the usual routes of management buy-out, even VC funding, but the asking price was either too high, the VC too focused elsewhere or just too sceptical. You have to remember that this was between 2006 and early 2007. Investors wanted to hear web 2.0, collective intelligence and user-driven network effects. Terms like "compute utility" and "coding platform" were just not "something we'd invest in". There were exceptions, such as BungeeLabs, but as one investor told me, "Wrong approach, wrong technology and wrong place. No-one has ever heard of a successful tech firm from Old Street, London." It was a cutting point but fair enough; we were operating in a barren land with the barest whiff of tech companies and good souls. This was a long way from the heartland of Silicon Valley, though of course, Old Street these days is known as Silicon Roundabout.

The crunch then came, and I had choice. Dismantle the service and the team, take a cushy number within the parent company or resign. I decided to take the hit. Cloud became that billion-dollar industry and serverless will grow far beyond that, realising that trillion-dollar dream. If you're reading this and that hasn't happened yet then you still might not agree. Just wait. This story has its uses. When we consider mapping, there are multiple methods to use them to create an advantage or an opportunity. For example:-

Method 1) You can use a map to see how components that are evolving can be combined to create new activities or to support your own efforts. If what you're doing is focusing on building something new in the uncharted area of the map then you should note that whatever you do will be risky — it's the adjacent unexplored, an unknown area. In Figure 246, I've given an example in the mobile phone space where each higher order system combined underlying components with more industrialised technology. The map assumes a timeframe of the early to mid 2000s — obviously these components have evolved since then. The play of combining industrialised components to expand into the adjacent unexplored with some new higher order activity is a high-risk stepping stone. You don't know what you'll find nor where it could lead next. It might be the next best thing since sliced bread but the past is littered with failed concepts. The problem with Figure 246 is that we always look back from the perspective of today and highlight the path by which success was achieved. There were other ideas, such as phones integrated with projectors, printers, firearms, umbrellas, clothing, and even into a tooth, which have all been, gone and are quickly forgotten.

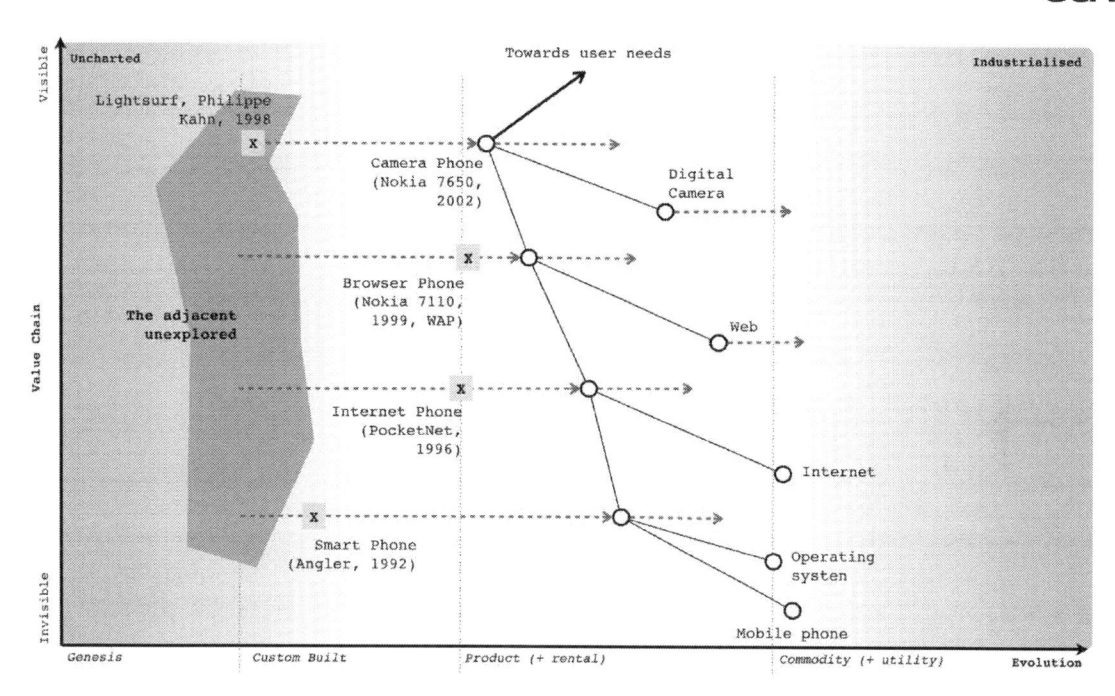

Figure 246: Combination plays

In our case, we used our maps to anticipate future developments, including exchanges, assurance reporting, application marketplace, billing facilities and a brokerage service.

Method 2) Beyond removal of duplication and bias, you can also use a map to find efficiencies and constraints by examining links within the value chain. For example, take something as trivial as a desktop rollout. You might find that you're forced to treat the operating system as more of a product than a commodity because some essential business application is tightly coupled to the operating system. By understanding and breaking this link, such as forcing the application into a browser, you can often treat a wide number of other components as a commodity. From our position, we understood that building data centres would be a constraint to building an IaaS play and that infrastructure was a constraint to building a PaaS. This also created opportunities, i.e. if one player launched in IaaS and became dominant then competitors could launch equivalent services and use a price war to force up demand beyond the ability of the first mover to supply (this assumes that competitors had their wits about them). Given that we had the underlying infrastructure technology known as Borg to do this, we could exploit such an opportunity.

Method 3) Another way is to take advantage of both evolution and inertia itself, e.g. by driving any component to a more evolved state, such as from product to commodity. These are potential goldmines, hence I tend to look at those components that are described as being in the product stage but are close to becoming a commodity. I look for those four factors (concept, suitability, technology and attitude) to exist in the market. I even double-check by asking people. The problem here is that people who work in that space often have inertia to this idea and will tell you endless reasons why it won't work and this or that thing can't become a commodity. You want that inertia to exist because then all your competitors will have that inertia and equally dismiss the change, but you also wanted to get to the truth of the matter. The question becomes, how do I find out whether it's really suitable for a shift to commodity when almost everyone in the field will tell me it isn't because of inertia? To find out if something is viable, I cheat. I find a group of people familiar with the field and ask them to imagine that we have already built such a service. I then ask them to write down exactly what it looks like and what it would need. The modern way of doing this is to get them to write the press release. If they can do this clearly, precisely and without recourse to hand waving, then we've got something widespread and ubiquitous enough to be suitable for an industrialised play.

Whichever method you use, aim to make this a stepping stone to a further play. For example, in the case of Zimki, then:-

- creating a utility service in the platform space and exposing it through APIs was a stepping stone towards running an ILC (ecosystem) like game.
- open sourcing Zimki was simply a stepping stone to achieving an exchange with many providers.
- the play to open source Borg (our underlying infrastructure system) was a counter play against any one competitor becoming dominant in the IaaS space.

This idea of future possibilities through stepping stones is an important concept within strategy. If we look at the first method again (i.e. banking on recombination efforts in the uncharted space) then this is often a bad position to find yourself in. More often than not, it leads to a dead end — the phone firearm or the phone tooth. I tend to refer to these high-risk approaches as "gambling" rather than "opportunities", because opportunities should expand your future possibilities and not reduce them. If you're going to gamble then the only way to consistently make this work is to be lucky. Try instead not to gamble as much as focus on expanding future possibilities. Just because you could do something, doesn't mean you should do it. Strategy is as much about saying what you won't do as it is about what you will do. This is summed up in the highly mischievous phrase, "opportunities expand as they are seized", which is often misinterpreted as "grab everything", which is precisely not what you should be doing. This is also why Fotango pivoted from a declining online photo service to a platform play, as it expanded our possibilities. See also Stewart Butterfield, who seems to have become a master of such pivots. This doesn't however guarantee success as these are opportunities and not certainties.

Policy or technology?

Throughout this book, I've heavily relied upon examples from the technology industry. The reason for this is that information technology has been undergoing profound change in the last decade. If it had been the legal industry that had been impacting so many value chains (though there are past examples of industrialisation, with will-writing and current trends for general purpose contracts through AI) then this book would have mainly focused on the legal industry. Despite this technology industry focus, most of my work tends to deal with nation or industry level competition and touches upon areas of policy. The concepts of strategy, mapping and finding opportunities apply equally well in this space. Remember, your map is not just activities but includes practice, data, knowledge and all forms of capital (including social).

Scenario — first pass

Since Brexit is very much the talk of the town, I'm going to focus on one specific area, namely that of standards. However, I'm not going to start with a UK-centric view but instead, let us pretend that you're a regulator in some mythical country. Your role is covering the pharmaceutical industry, e.g. you're working for the Office of Compliance within an administrative body (i.e. equivalent to the Food & Drug Administration, USA). Your purpose is to shield patients from poor quality, unsafe, and ineffective drugs through compliance strategies and risk-based enforcement actions. To this end, you use strategic and risk-based decisions that are guided by law and science to foster global collaboration, promote voluntary compliance and take decisive and swift actions to protect patients. It's exciting and noble-sounding stuff! Well, it should be as I lifted those words from the FDA website. But why do you exist? You exist because bad medicines kill people and those people tend to be voters. Any government knows that being in charge and doing nothing when people are dying doesn't tend to win elections in a democracy. There are no positives about bad medicines and there's no way to spin this.

When something goes wrong then you need to investigate and take action (often legal enforcement). In light of this, you tend to do audits of facilities and enforce compliance to standards that you also develop. But there's a problem. The pharmaceutical industry is a global and complicated supply chain. The drugs in your local chemist shop probably were delivered through a series of warehouses and transportation systems (facilities) with plenty of opportunities for things to go wrong. Before this, it was manufactured (in another facility) with the active / inactive components being chemicals, which themselves were delivered through a series of warehouses, import / export, transportation systems and manufacturers. Even the raw material to make the chemicals can come through another set of facilities, which can include refiners and miners. The supply chain can be very long, very complicated and provides many points where disaster can be introduced. It's also global, and when you cross international borders then you have no guarantee that the standards that you apply are also the standards that are in practice applied elsewhere. Which is why you, as a regulator, probably push for global standards and close cooperation with other agencies. You work with other nations to develop supply chain toolkits, covering good manufacturing practice, transportation practice, and product security to track and trace.

Let us assume that you have brought in legislation that demands that pharmaceutical companies must know their supply chain, i.e. we want the origin, history and interactions of every component that went into the drug. Let us also assume that some companies don't see the benefit of exposing their supply chain but instead, see cost beyond a one up, one down approach, i.e. they know the boundary of their suppliers — we bought this from them — and who they supplied their products to. From a regulatory viewpoint, whether pharma, automotive, consumer goods or any other, then this is not enough, especially when the supply chain crosses an international boundary. We could attempt to introduce legislation that they must know about the entire supply chain but this will invoke potentially huge lobbying bodies against us. At this point, someone normally shouts a technological solution such as "use blockchain" to create a chain of custody. Beyond the issue of implementation, the idea of a public blockchain is normally faced with criticism that being public, it would expose the sales of the company to competitors. Often, there is a push to modify the idea and make it private. Such a private chain would in itself create a new hurdle for new entrants trying to get into an industry, and whilst barriers to entry might be welcomed by some companies to reduce competition, the purpose of regulators didn't include "protect incumbents from competition". It's a thorny issue. How to protect the public but allow for competition?

Part of the problem noted above is the inertia to having a publicly visible global supply chain, whether using blockchain or not. It is amusing that if you ask executives within the industry whether they know what their competitors are selling, they will often answer "Yes". There is an entire industry of marketing, competitor analysis and surveillance companies that everyone feeds in order to gain competitive intelligence on what others are doing. In fact, so complicated is the internal supply chain of gigantic manufacturers that, when combined with discounts, promotions, variability in production, fraud, returns and even error within their own internal systems, sometimes, companies can only approximate what they've sold. One executive even told me that they knew what their competitors were selling better than they knew what they were selling themselves, hence they had also started to use a marketing analysis company on their own company. An argument for radical transparency is to simply recognise this (i.e. be honest) and eliminate the cost of such competitive intelligence by making the blockchain open. However, this also threatens to expose the inefficiencies, waste and practices within the supply chain, which is probably where the real inertia exists. The problem with exposing waste is that it doesn't tend to go down well with either customers or shareholders. Let us assume that this is the scenario in our case. The first thing I want you to do is to take 30 minutes and come up with ideas of how you will solve all of this.

Scenario — second pass

So, how do you as a regulator manage this? Well, let us start with a map. I provided the map in Figure 247 and will give a brief explanation underneath.

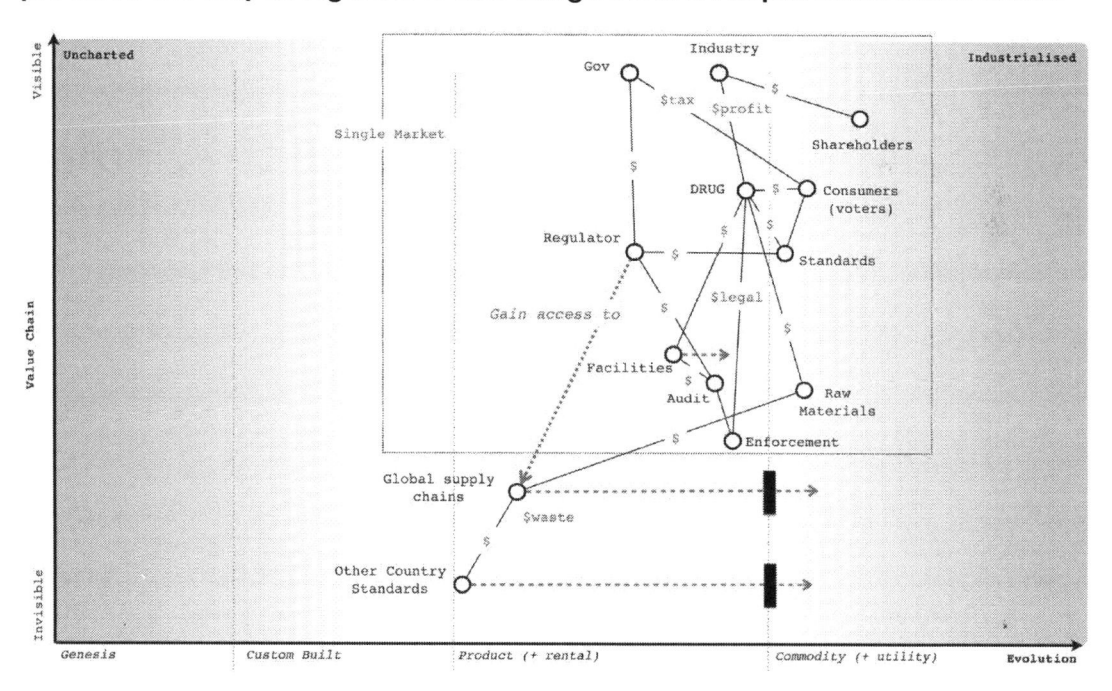

Figure 247: Regulator's map

From the map, we start with the industry itself. It has a need for investors (i.e. shareholders), which involves a bidirectional flow of capital, e.g. investment from the shareholders and return on investment to the shareholders. I've simply marked this as a "$" to represent a financial flow in both directions. Remember, each node (circle) is some form of stock of capital (whether physical, practice, information or otherwise) and each line is a flow of capital. In order to pay for the return on investment (whether dividends or share buybacks), the industry needs to do something that makes a profit. This involves making the DRUG, which in this case I've described as a quite well-evolved product. Obviously, in practice, there is a pipeline of drugs (from the novel and new to the more commodity), but this map will suffice for our purposes.

To make a profit on the drug then there are costs in making it and hopefully, revenue from selling it. Our drug therefore needs consumers. Hence, we have a bidirectional flow of capital with consumers, i.e. the physical drug is exchanged for monetary $. Now, those consumers also want the drug not to kill them and hence, they need standards that ensure (as much as it is possible) that the drug is safe. Those standards add to the cost of the drug, i.e. certification to a standard doesn't come for free. Let us assume that if our industry could get away without standards, they probably would, as such costs reduce profits, which the industry needs in order to pay the return to shareholders. Fortunately for those consumers, someone else needs them. That someone is the Government, and what it needs are voters. These voters just happen to be also consumers. Hence, in order to gain its voters, the Government has a need for regulators, who in turn create and police the standards that satisfy the needs of the consumers. Naturally, standards without enforcement is worthless and hence, the regulators use audits, which in turn use legal enforcement against the drug itself. This gives the industry two costs. The first cost is that of implementing the standard, which is usually a bidirectional capital flow of investment in standards for a certification that the drug meets the standard. The second cost is the cost of legal enforcement, i.e. a failure to meet the standard, which can take many forms, from court cases to product recall to enforced action.

But how are those audits conducted? In general, it is against the facilities involved, whether this is the distribution point (i.e. the chemist shop), the warehouse, the transportation system or the manufacturer. Product can be taken from any of these points and tested or the facility inspected. Obviously, that involves a cost, which in part is hopefully recovered from the standards process or at worst, from taxes from the voters. You can simply follow the lines on the map (which represent capital flow) to determine possible ways of balancing this out. How you balance that out is a matter of policy.

At this point, the map starts to become a little bit more complicated. For this map, I have considered all of the flows so far to be inside a border, i.e. we manufacture and distribute within a single market (the dotted blue line border in our map). This could be a single nation or a multilateral FTA (free trade agreement) or a common market with agreed standards. Now let us look at the raw materials (another source of cost for the drug) and bring in the idea of import and export from outside of this market. This is going to bring into play a bewildering array of import and export arrangements, warehouses, manufacturers, transportation systems and an entire global supply chain. As per the scenario, we have a one up, one down form of understanding within the industry and hence, the global supply chain in all its details is poorly understood. Also, as per the scenario, there is significant waste in these global supply chains. In general, from experience, I have yet to find one where there isn't. Another problem is that outside of the common market then standards will tend to be specific to other countries. These might be more evolved than within the market, but I'm going to assume for this exercise that they are less evolved, less developed, hence the manner in which I've drawn standards on the map.

Our regulator has all the power it needs to enforce legislation on facilities within its market, but it wishes to gain access to information related to the global supply chain. It wants to make these supply chains both more clearly defined and transparent. It also wants to bring standards in the outside market up to its own level and ideally, increase cooperation with other countries. However, both efforts will face inertia, i.e. resistance to change and extensive lobbying, if we attempt to do this through legislation. The inertia over global supply chains will normally be disguised as competitive reasons (fear of exposing information to competitors) but it is usually related to cost and fear of exposing the waste that exists. The second case of inertia includes resistance from other nations and their regulators to any imposition of standards by another party. Sovereignty is a big deal for lots of people. So, considering your ideas from the first pass at this scenario, take another 30 minutes and come up with what you would do, and try to avoid "use a blockchain". Think of non-technical opportunities, i.e. policy.

Scenario — my answer

One of the beauties of maps is that I can describe a space and what I intend to do about it, allowing others to challenge me. Now, I'm no regulator but I can propose a solution. It might be a dreadful solution, there might be far better ways of doing this, the map could be more accurate, but that's the point. Maps are fundamentally about communication. It's also important to note that every choice you make (if you have a map) can be reviewed in the future and learnt from. Mapping itself isn't about giving you an answer; it's about helping you think about a space and learn from what you did. You won't get good at mapping or strategic play if you don't either act or put the effort into understanding a space before you act and review it later. It's a bit like playing a guitar — there's only so much you can read from books; eventually, you have to pick up the instrument and use it. This is when you really start learning.

Hence, I'll give you my answer, which took about 30 minutes, but on the provision that we all understand that many of you will have a better answer. If you shared those maps with me then I might learn (something I'd appreciate). Let us start with a map on which I've marked my play (see Figure 248) and I'll go through my reasoning after.

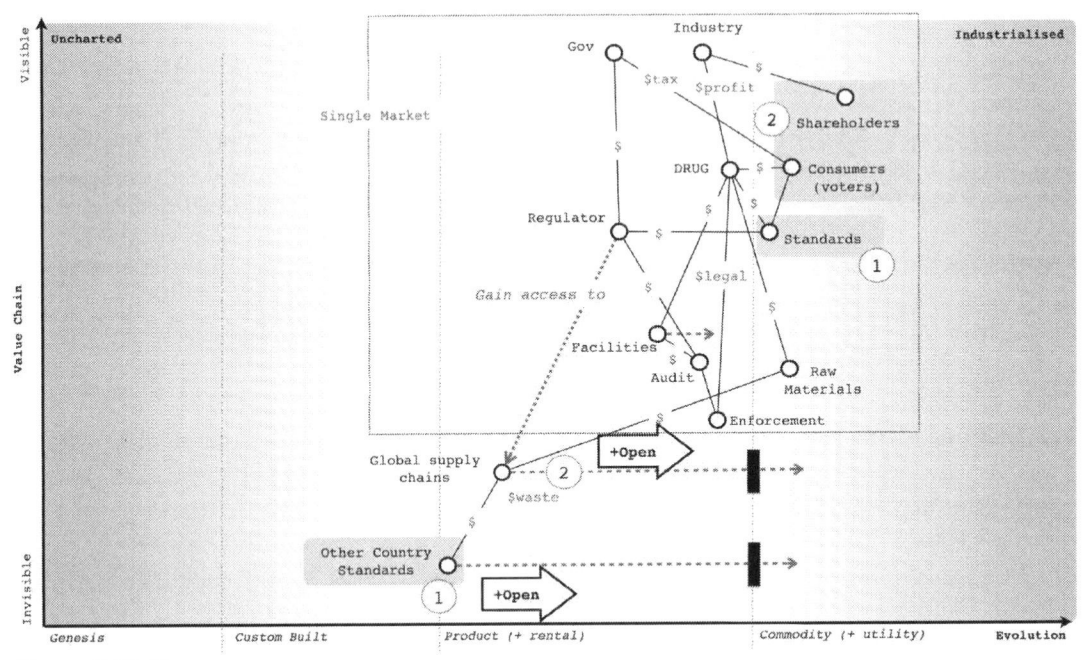

Figure 248: My answer

I have two parts to my answer. The first (marked as number one in red circles) is to open up the data, practice and systems that I use to build and manage standards to other countries. The reason for this is that I want to drive standards to a globally accepted norm and make it as easy as possible for other nations to learn from our experience and reduce cost. In return for such a generous gesture, I'm aiming to "buy" both ease of use and interaction when dealing with other country agencies, including good cooperation through a hefty element of goodwill. By opening it all up, I'm also carefully avoiding trying to impose any standard but instead, encourage adoption. I might have invested in building those systems (i.e. invested financial capital in activities, practices and data) as a government, but I'm trading that capital for data and social capital from others.

The second part of my play (the red number two) is to name and shame. I would aim to deliberately undertake a campaign of highlighting waste in global supply chains and the poor understanding that companies have over their actual supply chain. This will involve us working with other countries to understand the supply chain, hence another purpose to step one. I'm going to direct this campaign towards shareholders and customers in order to create pressure for change, despite the inertia that executives within the company might have. I don't care how the industry solves the problem (they can use blockchain if they wish) but I'd intend to use policy to drive for a more open approach on global supply chains. The two parts are needed because having a global supply being transparent is useful but not as useful if the standards involved throughout the chain are similar or at least the details can be accessed. Now, you might fundamentally disagree with this approach and that's fine. It might surprise you to discover that I'm not a regulator and have little to no idea about the current state of the pharmaceutical industry. Hence the mythical company. But disagreeing is part of the purpose of a map. It exists to enable precisely these sorts of discussions by exposing the assumptions. However, it's also important to note that action and strategy doesn't have to involve specific technology (e.g. blockchain) but can instead be driven through policy. There is a tendency in today's world to immediately jump for a technological solution when other routes are available, e.g. frictionless trade doesn't necessarily require magic smart borders.

The nature of capital and purchasing it

A map of a competitive environment is simply a map of capital (i.e. stocks of physical, knowledge, data, social, financial and information assets) and flows between them. What a map also adds is the concept that those capital stocks have a position in a chain of needs and they are not static, they are moving (i.e. evolving) themselves. From the original evolution graph then evolution is itself related to the ubiquity and certainty of the thing. The value of any thing is also related to certainty, i.e. some things we're more certain about and can precisely define a value because the market is defined, whilst other things we're unsure of. This uncertainty is often embedded in a concept known as potential value, i.e. when we say "this has potential value", we mean "this has an uncertain amount of future value" compared to the current market. Roughly speaking (and based upon an idea proposed by Krzysztof Daniel), then:-

$$\text{Evolution}(x) \propto \frac{\text{Current Value}(x)}{\text{Current Value}(x) + \text{Potential Value}(x)}$$

$$\text{Certainty of Value}(x) \propto \frac{\text{Current Value}(x)}{\text{Current Value}(x) + \text{Potential Value}(x)}$$

If Potential Value (x) >> Current Value (x) then

$$\text{Certainty of Value}(x) \propto \frac{1}{\text{Potential Value}(x)}$$

$$\text{Potential Value}(x) \propto \frac{1}{\text{Certainty of Value}(x)}$$

What this is saying is that novel and new things that have a high potential value have inherently a lot of uncertainty around them. Hence all the risk in the uncharted space as we just don't know what is going to happen, despite our belief in some huge future potential value. As the market develops and more actors become involved because that market becomes more defined, then the uncertainty declines because of competition. But, so does the potential value, as the current market is becoming more defined, divided and industrialised. In other words, by investing in some activity (e.g. computing in the early days) then by simply doing nothing at all, the value of that investment will change as the industry evolves through competition.

I said roughly for two reasons. Firstly, potential value itself implies uncertainty and hence, the "equation" above breaks down to uncertainty is inversely proportional to certainty, i.e. the less certain of something we are then the more uncertain we become. It's the self-referencing flaw of Darwin's evolutionary theory and survival of the fittest. We define the "fittest" by those who survive. Hence, evolutionary theory breaks down to survival of the survivors. This obvious circular reference doesn't mean it isn't useful. The second issue is the actual relationship between value and evolution isn't simple. The value of an investment in an activity and its related practices and other forms of capital, which we spend financial capital on to acquire (e.g. by training), doesn't just decline with evolution. There are step changes as it crosses the boundary between different evolution stages. For example, a massive investment in computing as a product (e.g. servers, practices related to this and other components such as data centres) changes as compute shifts from product to utility. What was once a positive investment can quickly become a technical debt and a source of inertia. The act of computing might be becoming more defined, ubiquitous and certain but our past investment in assets can quickly turn into a liability.

In practice, the early adopters of one stage of evolution (e.g. buying compute as a product such as servers) can quickly find themselves as the laggards to the next stage of evolution (e.g. cloud) because of their past investment and choices. The same change appears to also happen up and down the value chain. For example, with serverless (a shift of platform from product to utility) then often, the first movers into the world of cloud (i.e. utility infrastructure) and DevOps (i.e. co-evolved practice) exhibit the characteristics of laggards to the serverless world, whilst some companies that many would describe as laggards to cloud are the early adopters of serverless.

These changes in the value of a stock are problematic because in accountancy and financial reports, we rarely reflect the concept of evolution. At best, we use the idea of depreciation of some form of static stock but fail to grasp that the stock itself isn't static. The balance sheet of a company might look healthy but can hide a huge capital investment that has not only been depreciated but is now undergoing a potential change in the stage of evolution, e.g. data centres, servers and related practices that will quickly become a huge financial burden requiring massive investment, retraining and re-architecting.

The idea that suddenly an asset can become a liability due to a change of evolutionary stage in the industry is not one that fits well with double entry book-keeping. In other words, Assets = Equity + Liability doesn't work quite so well when Assets become Liabilities due to outside forces. It's not that these things can't be accounted for; it's simply that we generally don't. This is one of the dangers of looking at a company's finances. We can often make statements on the market evolving and impacting revenue but less frequently consider the debt that a change in evolution can cause. This also is not something that should surprise us. Unless there are genuine constraints then with enough competitive pressure, all the technical/operational obstacles to evolution (the four factors of technology, suitability, attitude and concept) will be overcome and such changes will happen. It's never a question of if but when.

However, it's not just accounting methods that tend to be inadequate when it comes to evolution. As we've discussed at length, it's also development methods and even purchasing techniques. In Figure 249 below, I've provided a map of a system, which, starting from user needs, is disaggregated into components through a chain of needs. This has in turn been broken into small contracts with appropriate methods applied. However, the method of purchasing is also context-specific. In the uncharted space, where items have high potential value combined with lots of uncertainty, then a venture capital or time and material type approach is needed for investment. As the same act evolves and we start to develop an understanding of it with introduction of concepts like MVP (minimal viable product) then a more outcome-based approach can be used. We're still trying to mitigate risk but this time, we have a target and a rough goal of what we're aiming for. As a product evolves, we can switch to a more commercial, off the shelf (COTS) type arrangement. Finally, as it becomes defined, we have a known market and are focused on a more unit or utility-based pricing around defined standards and expectations.

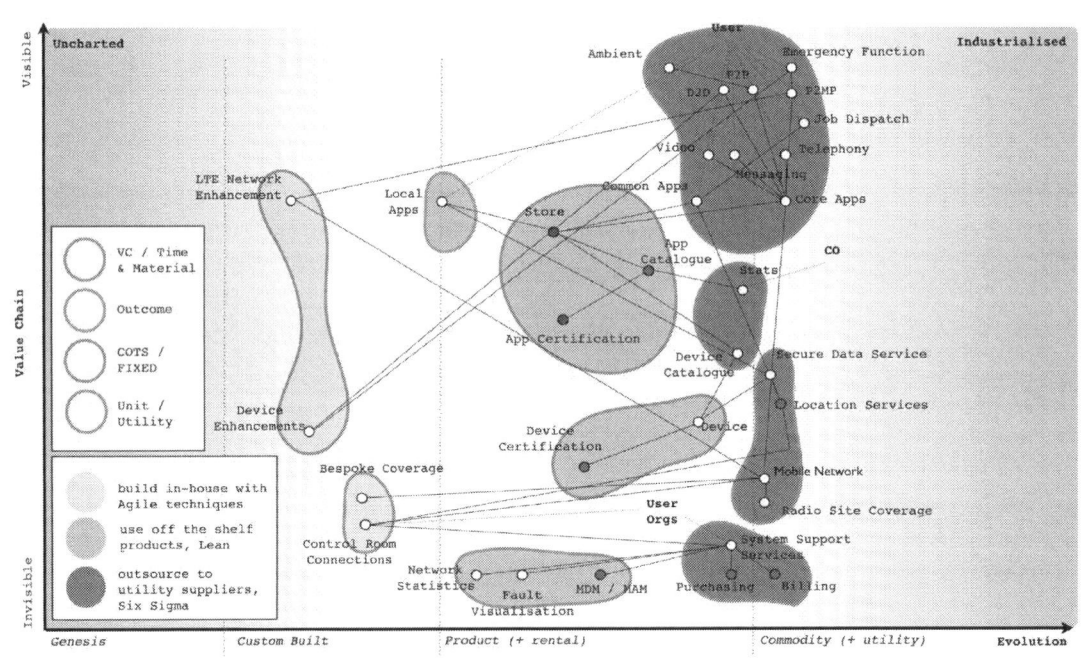

Figure 249: Capital and Purchasing

The point of this is that not only does capital evolve (whether activities, practices, data or otherwise) but so does the means by which we should purchase it. In any organisation, you need at least four different purchasing frameworks across the company. In any large, complicated system, there isn't such a thing as a one size fits all purchasing method and you'll need to use multiple of these frameworks. Unless, of course, you like things such as explaining massive change control cost overruns and trying to blame others. Maybe that floats your boat because it's simple and at least the vendor provides nice conferences. Oh, and if you want to fry your noodle, the implications of the above is that there isn't actually one way of accounting for things. That field also happens to be context-specific, i.e. the way you account for things in the uncharted space (the genesis of the things) is different from how you account for commodities in the industrialised space. However, getting into discussions on different accounting methods — innovation accounting, the use of options, how we combine them — and attempting to upset the entire world of financial reporting is something that we'll have to leave until much later on. Having written the global chart of accounts for one enormous multinational, I have a lot of sympathy for accountants.

Finding a balance

Whether it's finding opportunities (i.e. stepping stones that expand your future possibilities), using policy to change the game rather than just technology, or whether it's the flows of capital within a system and how we account for or purchase it — these are all elements that we use in gameplay. There is also the issue of balance within the system, i.e. inertia is both a good thing in terms of keeping you from industrialising an industry too early but a disaster if you haven't effectively managed it when an industry is industrialising. In the same manner, an investment in some form of capital asset can rapidly become a liability as the space evolves. As you develop, you'll learn to keep all of this in balance.

The maps themselves can help guide you but you'll need to scenario plan around them. There are rarely simple answers. In the next chapters, we're going to start going through a long list of specific patterns of play before we come back and break down an entire industry. To prepare you, I've listed the general forms of gameplay in Figure 250. I've organised the table by broad category, i.e. user perception, accelerators, de-accelerators, dealing with toxicity, market impacts, defensive, attacking, ecosystem, competitor, positional and poison. Each of the following chapters will deal with a single category (eleven chapters in total), using maps and, where possible, examples to demonstrate the play. By now, you're probably ready and dangerous enough to start playing chess with companies, or at least start learning how to do so.

Category	Wardley's Gameplay (context specific patterns that user can apply)		
User Perception	Education	Creating artificial needs	Confusion of choice
	Brand and marketing	Fear, uncertainty and doubt	Artificial competition	Lobbying / counterplay
Accelerators	Market enablement	Open approaches	Exploiting network effects	Co-operation
	Industrial policy			
De-accelerators	Exploiting constraint	IPR	Creating constraints	
Dealing with toxicity	Pig in a poke	Disposal of liability	Sweat and dump	Refactoring
Market	Differentiation	Pricing policy	Buyer / supplier power	Harvesting
	Standards game	Last man standing	Signal distortion	Trading
Defensive	Threat acquisition	Raising barriers to entry	Procrastination	Defensive regulation
	Limitation of competition	Managing inertia		
Attacking	Directed investment	Experimentation	Centre of gravity	Undermining barriers to entry
	Fool's mate	Press release process	Playing both sides	
Ecosystem	Alliances	Co-creation	Sensing Engines (ILC)	Tower and moat
	Two factor markets	Co-opting and intercession	Embrace and extend	Channel conflicts & disintermediation
Competitor	Ambush	Fragmentation play	Reinforcing competitor inertia	Sapping
	Misdirection	Restriction of movement	Talent raid	Circling and Probing
Positional	Land grab	First mover	Fast follower	Weak signal / horizon
Poison	Licensing play	Insertion	Designed to fail	

Figure 250: Gameplays

Printed in Great Britain
by Amazon